GUIDE TO AMERICAN CINEMA, 1965–1995

Reference Guides to the World's Cinema

Guide to the Cinema of Spain
Marvin D'Lugo

GUIDE TO AMERICAN CINEMA, 1965–1995

Daniel Curran

Reference Guides to the World's Cinema
Pierre L. Horn, Series Adviser

GREENWOOD PRESS
Westport, Connecticut • London

Library of Congress Cataloging-in-Publication Data

Curran, Daniel.
    Guide to American cinema, 1965–1995 / Daniel Curran.
        p. cm.—(Reference guides to the world's cinema, ISSN
1090–8234)
    Includes bibliographical references and index.
    ISBN 0–313–29666–9 (alk. paper)
    1. Motion pictures—United States—History. I. Title.
II. Series.
PN1993.5.U6C87   1998
791.43'0973—dc21   96–53269

British Library Cataloguing in Publication Data is available.

Library of Congress Catalog Card Number: 96–53269
ISBN: 0–313–29666–9
ISSN: 1090–8234

First published in 1998

Greenwood Press, 88 Post Road West, Westport, CT 06881
An imprint of Greenwood Publishing Group, Inc.

Printed in the United States of America

The paper used in this book complies with the
Permanent Paper Standard issued by the National
Information Standards Organization (Z39.48–1984).

10 9 8 7 6 5 4 3 2 1

for my parents, Jerry and Cathy

CONTENTS

SERIES FOREWORD

For the first time, on December 28, 1895, at the Grand Café in Paris, France, the inventors of the *Cinématographe*, Auguste and Louis Lumière, showed a series of eleven two-minute silent shorts to a public of thirty-five people each paying the high entry fee of one gold Franc. From that moment, a new era had begun, for the Lumière brothers were not only successful in their commercial venture, but they also unknowingly created a new visual medium quickly to become, throughout the world, the half-popular entertainment, half-sophisticated art of the cinema. Eventually, the contribution of each member of the profession, especially that of the director and performers, took on enormous importance. A century later, the situation remains very much the same.

The purpose of Greenwood's *Reference Guides to the World's Cinema* is to give a representative idea of what each country or region has to offer to the evolution, development, and richness of film. At the same time, because each volume seeks to present a balance between the interests of the general public and those of students and scholars of the medium, the choices are by necessity selective (although as comprehensive as possible) and often reflect the author's own idiosyncracies.

André Malraux, the French novelist and essayist, wrote about the cinema and filmmakers: "The desire to build up a world apart and self-contained, existing in its own right . . . represents humanization in the deepest, certainly the most enigmatic, sense of the word." On the other hand, then, every *Guide* explores this observation by offering discussions, written in a jargon-free style, of the motion-picture art and its practitioners, and on the other provides much-needed information, seldom available in English, including filmographies, awards and honors, and ad hoc bibliographies.

Pierre L. Horn
Wright State University

INTRODUCTION

Having spent a couple of years amid a swirl of films from 1965 to 1995, I began to think that this thirty-year stretch of filmmaking—a little less than one-third the total span of the motion picture industry—has the look of a transition period. It features some of the greatest films ever made and nearly all of the biggest moneymakers, yet it feels nestled in between the demise of the Hollywood studio system and the technological advances that the future holds. It is perhaps no accident that the period begins with MGM's *The Sound of Music*, one of the last great epics that the studio system produced, and ends with *Toy Story*, Pixar's revolutionary computer-animated hit; it's a long way from Sam Goldwyn and Louis B. Mayer to Steve Jobs. During these thirty years many of the names that helped create American film history have passed on—directors Frank Capra, Charlie Chaplin, Allan Dwan, John Ford, Alfred Hitchcock, Howard Hawks, Buster Keaton, and Orson Welles and actors Fred Astaire, James Cagney, Marlene Dietrich, Henry Fonda, Greta Garbo, Cary Grant, Gene Kelly, Boris Karloff, Groucho Marx, Edward G. Robinson, Ginger Rogers, Barbara Stanwyck, and John Wayne. We have seen Hollywood transform. The past has given way to the television generation of directors, then the film school generation, the independent filmmaker, and the minority directors and actors. This is not our father's (or mother's) Hollywood; it is, in fact, a closer representation of our America. It is a Hollywood in which a film can cost under $100,000 or over $100 million and still reach a wide audience. There is a nostalgia for the motion picture history of movie palaces and double features, but a great percentage of today's movie audience has no such recollection. Since 1965, we have seen the advent of color television, UHF, the camcorder, the video rental business, cable television, laser discs, pay-per-view, interactive storytelling, virtual reality games, IMAX, the Internet, and quick-time movie clips on our home computers.

As the millennium races to a close, the film industry seems headed for a new dawn. The era of filmmaking from 1965 to 1995 is merely the bridge we have crossed to get there.

THE FILMS AND PEOPLE

This is not an attempt to list the greatest films of the period nor the greatest actors and directors but an attempt to give a representation of the times. While, of course, the usual suspects are lined up within these pages, so too are a few new additions. I've tried to remember character actors (whose faces are as integral to our love of the movies as those whose names are more recognizable), genre pictures, and independents. Too often, supporting players like Jack Warden or directors like Larry Cohen or films like *The Honeymoon Killers*, *El Norte*, and *Swoon* are unjustly neglected. Likewise, an attempt has been made to not overrepresent certain directors such as Steven Spielberg, Martin Scorsese, and Francis Ford Coppola, whose every film, arguably, is worthy of inclusion for either its greatness or the magnitude of its failure. The difficulty in a book with these parameters is the definition of an ''American film'' or an ''American filmmaker.'' Was Hitchcock an American filmmaker? Probably not. Was he an integral part of Hollywood? Irrefutably. Since the limits of publishing suggest that a line has to be drawn somewhere, I've decided to draw it in close proximity of our borders. Films that are not essentially American are not included; in other words, I've left out British films released by a Hollywood studio (e.g., Universal's *Brazil*). Likewise, actors whose careers are not essentially based in America are omitted (e.g., Michael Caine), while I've included those with a creative output that is nearly exclusively American (e.g., England's Julie Andrews and Czechoslovakia's Milos Forman). Finally, there exist those actors and directors whose career precedes 1965; John Wayne and Marlon Brando have been included, while others whose careers are more identified with the pre-1965 period (even if just barely) have been omitted. My apologies to Robert Aldrich, Blake Edwards, Burt Lancaster, Billy Wilder, Shelley Winters, and others. As for the considerable contribution of writers, producers, and studio heads, their omission here is entirely based on scope—no one can deny producer Joel Silver's influence on the action film or Joe Eszterhas' on the business of American screenwriting. I have attempted to address this in the appendixes.

THE ENTRIES

Each biographical entry consists of such information as birth date, birth name if considerably altered, a look at the career, and filmographies that consist of all motion picture credits and notable network or cable television work. Since television, especially the cable channels HBO and Showtime, has become an increasingly viable and lucrative creative medium for filmmakers, it seems counterproductive to list only theatrical films. Additional honors, quotes, and bibliographies are peppered throughout. Honors include Academy Awards and nominations; Los Angeles and New York Critics Awards; Directors Guild (DGA) and Writers Guild (WGA) Awards; Cannes, Berlin, and Venice Festivals; and Emmys, Tonys, and Grammys where relevant. Quotes have been selected in some pieces to provide an opposing viewpoint or just some additional insight, while bibliographies are limited to books. I'm generally opposed to filmographies that are so filled with codes that they are unreadable; I have, however, used the following abbreviations in the filmographies—tvm (television movie), tvms (television miniseries), ctvm (cable television movie), mv (music video) and ep (executive producer). Short films are also included, and they are defined as any film running under sixty minutes. Finally, as to gender, I have opted to refer to all performers as actors; I personally take some offense to the sexist use of the word ''actress'' as a word, which exists mostly for the sake of awards shows.

CRITERIA FOR INCLUSION

With few exceptions, it's all purely subjective. Some films and filmmakers are obvious inclusions, others are significant in some respect, while others still have been overlooked and/or reevaluated. As time wore on, and space became valuable, I realized that there were so many more films I could have written about. Alas, space is the enemy. Because I believe (as Hegel does) that history is a reflection of the historian, this book is necessarily a reflection of the author. The span of this book roughly coincides with the years that I've been alive— these films are as much a part of my generation and me as Vietnam, ''The Brady Bunch,'' Watergate, the Sex Pistols, Ronald Reagan, the shuttle disaster, and Michael Jordan. The best insight, then, into this book and me is the following list of some of my favorite films of the period and why, in random order— *Badlands* and *Days of Heaven* for the combination of poetry and American myth; *Three Days of the Condor* for its ability to show the distrust of government and the idealism of the people; *Schindler's List* for Spielberg's gift of putting a human face on history; Don Siegel for his position as a maverick filmmaker who chose to examine ethics and morality in American culture; Clint Eastwood, who defined, for better or worse, what it means to be a man, and Gena Rowlands, for what it means to be a woman; *The Big Red One* for making me understand, more than any other war film, the heroism of our veterans; John Cassavetes for celebrating the actor and revealing human emotions; *Night of the Living Dead* because of the cathartic nature of its gruesome violence, which exposed me to thoughts and images I never dared dream as a young boy; *Cutter's Way* and *Diner* for their comments on loyalty and friendship; *Five Easy Pieces* because of Billy Green Bush's laugh, *Manhattan* because of Mariel Hemingway's laugh, and *Terms of Endearment* because of Debra Winger's laugh; *McCabe and Mrs. Miller* for the snow; *The Exorcist* because of Mike Oldfield's chilling score and *The Moderns* because of the warmth of its score; and *Hoop Dreams* for its indomitable human spirit . . . and all the other ones I've forgotten.

A very special thanks to the people who helped to make this book a reality—first and most passionately, my wife, Jennifer Leigh Howe, who was with me every step of the way, clacking away at the keyboard and tirelessly giving feedback, and who is also the person I love most to sit beside in a dark theater; Dr. Judd Chesler, my friend and movie mentor, who not only suggested I write this book but helped me to see films in a different light; Brian Brock, Tibby Rothman, and Christine Tope for their words of support; James J. Mulay for digging up those elusive details; and Jay Robert Nash for getting me started down this road with *The Motion Picture Guide*.

GUIDE TO AMERICAN CINEMA, 1965–1995

A

AIELLO, DANNY. Born June 20, 1933, in New York; actor. Receiving his training on the New York stage, he entered film at the relatively late age of forty as a character actor and has built a career playing strong-willed, Italian-American characters. His first two films were *Bang the Drum Slowly* and *The Godfather, Part II*, though he did not achieve real attention until his role in *Once Upon a Time in America* as Police Chief Aiello, the boorish, proud papa whose newborn son is switched in the hospital nursery. Other memorable parts include Mia Farrow's loutish husband in *The Purple Rose of Cairo*; Johnny Cammareri, who charmed audiences by dropping to his knees to propose marriage to Cher in *Moonstruck*; Sal the pizzeria owner, his Oscar-nominated role in *Do the Right Thing*; and the cross-dressing fashion aficionado in *Ready to Wear*.

Filmography: Bang the Drum Slowly (1973); The Godfather, Part II (1974); The Front (1976); Fingers (1977); Bloodbrothers (1978); Defiance (1980); Hide in Plain Sight (1980); Chu Chu and the Philly Flash (1981); Fort Apache, the Bronx (1981); Amityville II: The Possession (1982); A Question of Honor (1982, tvm); Blood Feud (1983, tvms); Deathmask (1983); Old Enough (1984); Once Upon a Time in America (1984); "Lady Blue" (1985–1986, tvs); Key Exchange (1985); The Protector (1985); The Purple Rose of Cairo (1985); The Stuff (1985); Man on Fire (1987); Moonstruck (1987); The Pickup Artist (1987); Radio Days (1987); The January Man (1988); White Hot (1988); Do the Right Thing (1988); "Papa Don't Preach" (1988, mv); Harlem Nights (1989); Russicum (1989); The Closer (1990); Jacob's Ladder (1990); Shock Troop (1990); Once Around (1991); Hudson Hawk (1991); 29th Street (1991); Mistress (1992); Ruby (1992); Me and the Kid (1993); The Pickle (1993); The Cemetery Club (1993); Save the Rabbits (1994); The Professional (1994); Ready to Wear (Prêt-à-Porter) (1994); Two Much (1995).

Honors: Academy Award nomination for Best Supporting Actor (*Do the Right Thing*); Los Angeles Film Critics Award for Best Supporting Actor (*Do the Right Thing*); Los Angeles Drama Critics Award ("Hurlyburly" 1988); Emmy for Outstanding Individual Achievement in a Children's Program ("Family of Strangers").

AIRPORT (1970), drama. Directed and written by George Seaton (from the novel by Arthur Hailey); produced by Ross Hunter; photographed by Ernest Laszlo; edited by Stuart Gilmore; music by Alfred Newman; released by Universal; 137 minutes. *Cast*: Burt Lancaster, Dean Martin, Jean Seberg, Jacqueline Bisset, George Kennedy, Helen Hayes, Van Heflin, Maureen Stapleton, Barry Nelson, Dana Wynter, Barbara Hale, Lloyd Nolan.

The link between the melodramas of the 1950s and 1960s (many of which bore producer Ross Hunter's signature) and the coming decade's mania for disaster films, *Airport* is essentially a commercial, star-studded drama that lacks the gimmickry of the subsequent entries in the series. With only the last half hour fitting the genre requirements for a disaster film (a bomb blows a hole in the plane), the majority of the film is a Hollywoodized treatment of male–female relationships: airport head Mel Bakersfield (Lancaster) is falling in love with fellow worker Tanya (Seberg) while facing divorce from his wife (Wynter), who is tired of sharing him with his job; married pilot Vernon Demerest (Martin) is falling in love with the stewardess (Bisset), whom he has gotten pregnant; and distraught bomber D. O. Guerrero (Heflin) is trying to make amends to his estranged wife, Inez (Stapleton), by taking out a generous life insurance policy on his soon-to-be-ended life. Limits are stretched by setting this all during the worst blizzard in years (blanketing Chicago's fictional Lincoln Airport in a downy white) *and* stalling a jet at the end of the only open runway *and* leveling threats to shut down the airport immediately because of an ongoing investigation of deafening noise levels. The suspense comes from the race to move the plane from the runway before the damaged plane lands. While certainly not a Paddy Chayefsky condemnation of malevolent institutions, there is a running thesis that all of the airport's problems can be traced to corporate mismanagement and shrinking government appropriations; an elderly lady (Hayes) habitually stows aboard, deceitful passengers try to sneak valuables through customs, bombers wander onto planes with briefcases filled with dynamite, and ground crews are woefully understaffed and ill equipped. It's all gloss and glitz on the surface, but at least there's some meat to the otherwise sappy script. That's more than can be said for the next three films in the series—all of which feature George Kennedy's Joe Patroni, whose role as the no-nonsense, cigar-chomping, working-class hero of the ground crew is one of the high points of this picture.

Sequels: *Airport 1975* (1974, Jack Smight); *Airport 77* (1977, Jerry Jameson); and *The Concorde—Airport '79* (1979, David Lowell Rich).

Awards: Academy Award for Best Supporting Actress (Hayes); Academy Award nominations for Best Picture, Adapted Screenplay, Cinematography, Art Direction, Sound, Editing, Score, Costume Design.

ALDA, ALAN. Born January 28, 1936, in New York City; actor, director, screenwriter. Father is actor Robert Alda. Still best known as Captain Benjamin Franklin "Hawkeye" Pierce of television's "M*A*S*H," Alda has carved out a niche for himself in film as the archetypically earnest and acerbic middle-class American. In 1978, after his rise in popularity on the small screen, he starred in a pair of Broadway adaptations—Neil Simon's *California Suite* and Bernard Slade's *Same Time, Next Year*—and the following year tried his hand at screenwriting with *The Seduction of Joe Tynan*. He has since focused his talents on directing, writing, and starring in his films. His feature film directorial debut came in 1981 with *The Four Seasons*, a likable Simon-like comedy about relationships and friendships that, like his subsequent efforts, suffers from a broad sitcom style that betrays his television beginnings. Curiously, his best performances of the last twenty years have come not in his own films but in Woody Allen's *Crimes and Misdemeanors* as a self-important television director and in the HBO production *And the Band Played On* as AIDS researcher Dr. Robert Gallo.

Filmography as actor: Gone Are the Days (1963); Paper Lion (1968); The Extraordinary Seaman (1969); Jenny (1969); The Mephisto Waltz (1970); The Moonshine War (1970); To Kill a Clown (1972); Playmates (1972, tvm); Truman Capote's "The Glass House" (1972, tvm); Isn't It Shocking? (1973, tvm); Kill Me If You Can (1977, tvm); California Suite (1978); Same Time, Next Year (1978); The Seduction of Joe Tynan (1979), also screenplay; Crimes and Misdemeanors (1989); Whispers in the Dark (1992); Manhattan Murder Mystery (1993); And the Band Played On (1993, ctvm); White Mile (1994, ctvm); Canadian Bacon (1995).

Filmography as director, writer, and actor: "M*A*S*H" (1972–1983, tvs); The Four Seasons (1981); Sweet Liberty (1986); A New Life (1988); Betsy's Wedding (1990).

Additional credits: "Marlo Thomas and Friends Free to Be . . . You and Me" (1974, variety special) actor, director; "6 Rms Riv Vu" (1974, special), actor, codirector; "We'll Get By" (1974–1975, tvs) writer, creator, ep; Susan and Sam (1977, tv) writer, producer; "The Four Seasons" (1984, tvs) actor, writer, ep.

Honors: New York Film Critics Circle Award for Best Supporting Actor (*Crimes and Misdemeanors*); Emmys for Best Actor ("M*A*S*H" 1973, 1981), Director ("M*A*S*H" 1976), and Writing ("M*A*S*H" 1978); DGA Award ("M*A*S*H" 1976).

ALEXANDER, JANE. Born Jane Quigley October 28, 1939, in Boston; actor, producer. Although much more active in television than in motion pictures, her compelling film work through the 1970s garnered her four Academy Award nominations. She made her Broadway debut in 1968 in "The Great White Hope," later reprising that role in the film adaptation and earning the first of her Academy Award nominations. Her versatility is evident in her résumé— Broadway performances (her 1992–1993 role in Wendy Wassersteins's "The Sisters Rosensweig" being her most recent), some twenty television movies and miniseries (bringing to life such strong women as Eleanor Roosevelt, Calamity

Jane, and Georgia O'Keeffe), producer of the 1993 PBS documentary series "Dancing," and her position as the chair of the National Endowment for the Arts beginning in 1993.

Filmography: The Great White Hope (1970); The Gunfight (1971); The New Centurions (1972); All the President's Men (1976); Eleanor and Franklin (1976, tvm); Eleanor and Franklin: The White House Years (1977, tvm); The Betsy (1978); Kramer vs. Kramer (1979); Brubaker (1980); Playing for Time (1981, tvm); Night Crossing (1981); Testament (1983); Calamity Jane (1984, tvm) also producer; City Heat (1984); Malice in Wonderland (1985, tvm); Sweet Country (1986); Square Dance (1987) also ep; Building Bombs (1989, documentary) narrator; A Marriage: Georgia O'Keeffe and Alfred Stieglitz (1991, tv) also ep; The Star Maker (1995).

Honors: Academy Award nominations for Best Actress (*The Great White Hope, Testament*) and Supporting Actress (*All the President's Men, Kramer vs. Kramer*); Emmy for Best Supporting Actress (*Playing for Time*); Tony Award for Best Supporting Actress (*The Great White Hope 1969*).

ALICE DOESN'T LIVE HERE ANYMORE (1974), drama. Directed by Martin Scorsese; screenplay by Robert Getchell; produced by David Susskind and Audrey Maas; photographed by Kent Wakeford; edited by Marcia Lucas; music by Richard Salle; released by Warner Bros.; 112 minutes. *Cast*: Ellen Burstyn, Kris Kristofferson, Billy Green Bush, Diane Ladd, Harvey Keitel, Alfred Lutter, Lelia Goldoni, Vic Tayback, Jodie Foster, Valerie Curtin.

Along with Jill Clayburgh's Erica in *An Unmarried Woman*, Ellen Burstyn's Alice is the most important feminist character to emerge from Hollywood films of the 1970s—a woman asserting herself, however embryonically, as an individual voice. What is most surprising is that it comes from Martin Scorsese, a director far better known for his brutal, alienated male characters. Given the opportunity to start life anew after the death of her constrictive husband, Alice packs her belongings and her son Tommy (Lutter) into the station wagon and heads off for Monterey, California, in the pursuit of her long-forgotten dream to be a singer. En route she becomes involved with men both brutal (Keitel) and honorable (Kristofferson). An exceptional film that has been overlooked in the usual assessment of the Scorsese canon, though the involvement of Burstyn cannot be overlooked; she is the one who shepherded the project through Warners and hired Scorsese for his first studio picture. The popular television sitcom "Alice" followed and starred Linda Lavin. "For me *Alice* was like a New Yorker's view of the West" (Scorsese, in Mary Pat Kelly's *Martin Scorsese: A Journey*).

Awards: Academy Award for Best Actress; Academy Award nominations for Supporting Actress (Ladd) and Screenplay.

ALIENS (1986), sci-fi. Directed and written by James Cameron; produced by Gale Anne Hurd; photographed by Adrian Biddle; edited by Ray Lovejoy; music by James Horner; special effects by Stan Winston; released by 20th Century

Fox; 135 minutes. *Cast*: Sigourney Weaver, Carrie Henn, Michael Biehn, Paul Reiser, Lance Henriksen, Bill Paxton.

This second and most thematically complete entry in the "Alien" trilogy is a feminist sci-fi adventure that fills the screen with knockout action sequences while refreshingly subverting the entire tired action genre by casting a woman as the macho-cum-maternal heroine. Awakening after drifting through space for fifty-seven years (having propulsed the alien creature from the life pod at the end of *Alien*), Ripley (Weaver) returns to the alien's home planet for another battle. This time the creature, a repulsive *vagina dentate*, has destroyed a colony of humans of which a nearly feral young girl Newt (Henn) is the only survivor. It all leads up to a final battle as the motherly Ripley tries to save Newt from the clutches of the egg-laying Alien Queen. As he did with Linda Hamilton's Sarah Connor in *The Terminator*, director James Cameron has again given us one of the most fiercely independent woman characters in film history. While detractors could misread Cameron's message as saying that a woman must be manly to be heroic, the film is more complex than that—although Ripley has proven herself a physical, mental, and emotional equal to men, she must still fight to overcome their learned gender-based biases. More significantly, the film raises issues of innate versus learned roles of motherhood and nurturing as Ripley (who is haunted by pregnancy nightmares) is forced into a maternal role with Newt.

Other Films in Series: Sigourney Weaver appeared as Ripley in the first *Alien* (1979), directed by Ridley Scott; and in *Alien*³ (1992), directed by David Fincher.

Awards: Academy Awards for Best Sound Effects, Visual Effects, Editing; Academy Award nominations for Best Actress, Score, Editing, Art Direction, Sound.

ALL THAT JAZZ (1979), musical/drama. Directed, cowritten, and choreographed by Bob Fosse; screenplay with, and produced by, Robert Alan Arthur; photographed by Giuseppe Rotunno; edited by Alan Heim; music by Ralph Burns; 123 minutes. *Cast*: Roy Scheider, Jessica Lange, Ann Reinking, Leland Palmer, Cliff Gorman, Ben Vereen, Keith Gordon, John Lithgow.

A hallucinatory musical that, while not as unified or dynamic as *Cabaret*, remains notable as one of the most soul-baring autobiographic statements in film. Scheider stars as Fosse's alter ego Joe Gideon, a driven, self-centered, womanizing choreographer who is putting together elements of a new show. In contrast to his creative life is his spiritual and physical death—he is a man whose passion for the purity and perfection of movement causes him to lose sight of the woman who loves him (Reinking) and the young dancer daughter who adores him. As he grows physically exhausted and decrepit, he comes face-to-face with his own mortality in the form of a radiant angel (Lange). As expected, the dance numbers are blistering, though the finale's Ben Vereen-hosted television spectacle seems hopelessly dated. The real revelation here is Scheider—after a career of gritty roles in *The French Connection*, *Jaws*, and *The*

Sorcerer, he makes an eerie transformation into a nimble, walking-on-clouds Fosse.

Awards: Academy Awards for Art Direction, Score, Editing, Costume Design; Academy Award nominations for Best Picture, Actor, Director, Screenplay, Cinematography; Cannes Film Festival Palme d'Or (shared).

ALL THE PRESIDENT'S MEN (1976), political drama. Directed by Alan J. Pakula; screenplay by William Goldman (from the book by Bob Woodward and Carl Bernstein); produced by Walter Coblenz; photographed by Gordon Willis; edited by Robert L. Wolfe; music by David Shire; released by Warner Bros.; 138 minutes. *Cast*: Robert Redford, Dustin Hoffman, Jason Robards, Jack Warden, Martin Balsam, Hal Holbrook, Jane Alexander, Meredith Baxter, Ned Beatty, F. Murray Abraham, Lindsay Crouse, Valerie Curtin.

Still shocking twenty years after the Watergate break-in and subsequent investigation, this adaptation of the Bob Woodward–Carl Bernstein book is a masterpiece of America's post-Vietnam disillusionment. Redford and Hoffman (as Woodward and Bernstein, respectively) are the cub *Washington Post* reporters whose story about a burglary at Democratic headquarters begins as routine but gradually implicates more and more figures in the Nixon White House. Flawless performances from the leads, as well as Robards as *Post* editor Ben Bradlee, Alexander as the skittish bookkeeper, and Holbrook as the key informant "Deep Throat." Simply one of the greatest movies of the era—not only an example of masterful film acting but also a thoughtful reflection on the times.

Awards: Academy Awards for Best Supporting Actor (Robards), Screenplay, Art Direction, Sound; Academy Award nominations for Best Picture, Director, Supporting Actress (Alexander), Editing; New York Film Critics Circle Awards for Best Film, Director, Supporting Actor; WGA Award.

ALLEN, WOODY. Born Allen Stewart Konigsberg December 1, 1935 in Brooklyn; director, screenwriter, actor, comedian. Formerly married to Louise Lasser and Mia Farrow. Starting as a stand-up comic and a "Tonight Show" gag writer, Allen not only has become the most recognizable comic persona since Chaplin, Keaton, and Lloyd but also has developed into the most prolific American filmmaker of his generation. With an emphasis on Jewish guilt, a preoccupation with death, and a fanatical love of jazz, Allen's films have spanned from the zaniness of *What's Up Tiger Lily?*, *Take the Money and Run*, *Bananas*, and *Sleeper*, to the strained seriousness of *Interiors*, *September*, and *Alice*. Still, *Annie Hall* is his masterpiece—a smart, personal, stylized, WASPy love story that earned him four Oscar nominations (he won for Director and Screenplay). The 1980s saw a continued path of experimentation marked by a lengthy personal and professional relationship with Mia Farrow, who would appear in all of his films from 1982's *A Midsummer Night's Sex Comedy* through 1992's *Husbands and Wives*. His post-Farrow films have a decidedly more emotional and free-spirited nature to them, perhaps marking yet another stage in Allen's evolution as a filmmaker. In addition to the thirteen pictures with Farrow, Allen has been responsible for some of the most memorable female performances in American film—Keaton in *Annie Hall*, Mariel Hemingway in *Manhattan*, Charlotte Rampling in *Stardust Memories*, Dianne Wiest in *Hannah and Her Sisters*, Gena Rowlands in *Another Woman*, and Juliette Lewis in *Husbands and Wives*. His frequent behind-the-camera collaborators include producers Jack Rollins, Charles Joffe, and Jean Doumanian; cinematographers Gordon Willis, Carlo Di Palma, and Tonino Della Colli; cowriter Marshall Brickman; production designers Santo Loquasto and Mel Bourne; editors Ralph Rosenblum and Susan E. Morse. He has most recently returned to the stage, writing one of the three one-act plays that constitute *Death Defying Acts*. He is the author of the books *Getting Even* (1971) and *Without Feathers* (1976). "Allen is building a canon of works which will probably look much richer as a whole, some time in the future, than some of the films may look now, subjected to the cavils of contemporary critics" (Gerald Mast, *The International Dictionary of Films and Filmmakers,* vol. 2).

Filmography: What's Up Tiger Lily? (1966), also actor; Don't Drink the Water (1969, tvm) from his play; Cupid's Shaft (1969, tv short); Pygmalion (1969, tv short), also writer, actor; The Woody Allen special (1969, tv variety special) also writer, actor; Take the Money and Run (1969), also actor; Bananas (1971) also actor; Everything You Always Wanted to Know about Sex* (*but were afraid to ask) (1972) also actor; Sleeper (1973) also actor; Love and Death (1975) also actor; Annie Hall (1977) also actor; Interiors (1978); Manhattan (1979) also actor; Stardust Memories (1980) also actor; A Midsummer Night's Sex Comedy (1982) also actor; Zelig (1983) also actor; Broadway Danny Rose (1984) also actor; The Purple Rose of Cairo (1985); Hannah and Her Sisters (1986) also actor; Radio Days (1987) also actor; September (1987); Another Woman (1988); Crimes and Misdemeanors (1989) also actor; New York Stories, "Oedipus Wrecks" episode (1989) also actor; Alice (1990); Shadows and Fog (1991) also actor; Husbands and Wives (1992) also actor; Manhattan Murder Mystery (1993) also actor; Bullets over Broadway (1994) also cowriter; Don't Drink the Water (1994, tvm) also actor; Mighty Aphrodite (1995) also actor.

Filmography as Actor and Writer: What's New Pussycat? (1965); Casino Royale (1967); Play It Again Sam (1972).

Filmography as Actor Only: The Front (1976); The Tempest (1982); King Lear (1987); Scenes from a Mall (1991).

Honors: Academy Awards for Best Director (*Annie Hall*) and Screenplay (*Annie Hall, Hannah and Her Sisters*); Academy Award nominations for Best Director (*Interiors, Broadway Danny Rose, Hannah and Her Sisters, Crimes and Misdemeanors, Bullets over Broadway*), Screenplay (*Interiors, Manhattan, Broadway Danny Rose, The Purple Rose of Cairo, Hannah and Her Sisters, Radio Days, Crimes and Misdemeanors, Husbands and Wives, Bullets over Broadway, Mighty Aphrodite*) and Actor (*Annie Hall*); Los Angeles Film Critics Award for Best Director (*Hannah and Her Sisters*); New York Film Critics Circle Awards for Best Picture (*Hannah and Her Sisters*) and Director (*Annie Hall, Hannah and Her Sisters*); DGA Award (*Annie Hall*); DGA Lifetime Achievement Award; WGA Award (*Radio Days*); Cannes Film Festival Fipresci Prize

(*The Purple Rose of Cairo*); Venice Film Festival Award for Lifetime Achievement (1995).

Selected bibliography

Blake, Richard. *Woody Allen: Profane and Sacred*. Metuchen, NJ: Scarecrow Press, 1995.

Curry, Renee R. *Perspectives on Woody Allen*. Boston: G. K. Hall, 1996.

Girgus, Sam B. *The Films of Woody Allen*. London: Cambridge University Press, 1993.

Jacobs, Diane. . . . *But We Need the Eggs: The Magic of Woody Allen*. New York: St. Martin's Press, 1982.

Lax, Eric. *On Being Funny: Woody Allen and Comedy*. New York: Charter House, 1975.

————. *Woody Allen: A Biography*. New York: Knopf, 1991.

ALTMAN, ROBERT. Born February 20, 1925, in Kansas City, Missouri; director, screenwriter, producer. The most daring and critically acclaimed Hollywood director of the period, Altman has been a creative force from his earliest film successes (*That Cold Day in the Park* and *Brewster McCloud*) to his cameo-rich metropolitan epics of the 1990s (*The Player*, *Short Cuts*, *Ready to Wear* (*Prêt-à-Porter*), and the 1996 release *Kansas City*). His genius comes in his ability to allow his audience to experience the film alongside the characters— as a viewer, one always has the sense that the film is existing around you, not just in front of you. Because of his technical experimentation (multiple sound tracks, which are an aural equivalent to cubism; frequent use of the wide-screen format) and multilayered narratives, it feels as if you've been dropped into the middle of a country music festival (*Nashville*), a war (*M*A*S*H*), a Hollywood movie studio (*The Player*), a wedding (*A Wedding*), a political campaign (*Tanner '88*), or the seaside comic book town of Sweethaven (*Popeye*). Working with a stock company that includes Rene Auberjonois, Keith Carradine, Geraldine Chaplin, Sandy Dennis, Paul Dooley, Shelley Duvall, Robert Fortier, Michael Murphy, Bert Remsen, John Schuck, Lily Tomlin, and recent additions Jennifer Jason Leigh and Tim Robbins, Altman has established himself as a superb director of actors, eliciting rare and daring performances from stars Warren Beatty, Carol Burnett, Cher, Julie Christie, Mia Farrow, Elliott Gould, Paul Newman, Sissy Spacek, Donald Sutherland, and Robin Williams. Exploring cultural iconography (James Dean, Buffalo Bill, Popeye, politicians, and the movie, music, and fashion industries) and exploding genre conventions (the western, the war film, and detective fiction), Altman is a risk taker whose worst films (*O. C. and Stiggs*, *Beyond Therapy*) even manage to retain a modicum of interest. In addition to his motion picture work, he has worked extensively since the 1980s in theater, television (*The Caine Mutiny Court Martial* and the cable series "Tanner '88"), and opera ("McTeague"). His television work of the 1950s and 1960s includes episodes of "Alfred Hitchcock Presents," "Bonanza," "Maverick," "Route 66," and "Combat." "The Altman of the 80s was often a very different director from the Altman of the 70s: arguably less inventive, but far more exacting, less of a virtuoso, more of a polished craftsman'' (Michael Wilmington, *Los Angeles Times*, November 11, 1990). "Robert Altman is an artist and a gambler'' (Alan Rudolph, *Film Comment*, March–April 1994).

Filmography: "The Whirlybirds'' (1957–1958, tvs); The Delinquents (1957); The James Dean Story (1957); "Roaring Twenties'' (1960–1961, tvs); "Bonanza'' (1960–1961, tvs); Nightmare in Chicago (1964) also producer; Countdown (1968); That Cold Day in the Park (1969); Brewster McCloud (1970); M*A*S*H (1970); McCabe and Mrs. Miller (1971); Images (1972); The Long Goodbye (1973); California Split (1974); Thieves like Us (1974); Nashville (1975); Buffalo Bill and the Indians, or Sitting Bull's History Lesson (1976); Three Women (1977); A Wedding (1978); A Perfect Couple (1979); Quintet (1979); Health (1980); Popeye (1980); Come Back to the 5 and Dime, Jimmy Dean, Jimmy Dean (1982); Streamers (1983); Secret Honor (1984); Fool for Love (1985); The Laundromat (1985, ctvm); The Dumb Waiter (1987, tvm); The Room (1987, tvm); "Les Boreades'' episode of Aria (1987); Beyond Therapy (1987); O. C. and Stiggs (1987); The Caine Mutiny Court Martial (1988, tvm) also producer; Tanner '88 (1988, ctvm); Vincent and Theo (1990); The Player (1992); Black and Blue (1993, television music performance special); The Real McTeague: A Synthesis of Forms (1993, opera special); Short Cuts (1993); Ready to Wear (Prêt-à-Porter) (1994).

Additional credits: The Bodyguard (1948) story credit; Events (1970) actor; Welcome to L.A. (1976) producer; The Late Show (1977) producer; Remember My Name (1978) producer; Rich Kids (1979) producer; Endless Love (1981) actor; Lily in Love/Jatszani Kell (1985) producer; The Moderns (1988) producer; Mrs. Parker and the Vicious Circle (1994) producer.

Honors: Academy Award nominations for Best Director (*M*A*S*H, Nashville, The Player, Short Cuts*); Cannes Film Festival Palme d'Or (*M*A*S*H*) and Director (*The Player*); New York Film Critics Circle Awards for Best Picture (*Nashville*) and Director (*Nashville, The Player*); Independent Spirit Awards for Best Director and Screenplay (*Short Cuts*); DGA D. W. Griffith Lifetime Achievement Award (1994); Berlin Film Festival Golden Bear (*Buffalo Bill and the Indians, or Sitting Bull's History Lesson*); Emmy Award for Best Director ("Tanner '88'').

Selected bibliography

Karp, Alan. *The Films of Robert Altman.* Metuchen, NJ: Scarecrow Press, 1981.

Kass, Judith M. *Robert Altman: American Innovator.* New York: Popular Library, 1978.

Keyssar, Helen. *Robert Altman's America.* New York: Oxford University Press, 1991.

Kolker, Robert Phillip. *A Cinema of Loneliness: Penn, Kubrick, Coppola, Scorsese, Altman.* New York: Oxford University Press, 1980.

McGilligan, Patrick. *Robert Altman: Jumping Off the Cliff.* New York: St. Martin's Press, 1989.

O'Brien, Daniel. *Robert Altman: Hollywood Survivor.* New York: Continuum, 1995.

Plecki, Gerard. *Robert Altman.* Boston: Twayne, 1985.

AMERICAN GRAFFITI (1973), comedy. Directed and cowritten by George Lucas; screenplay with Gloria Huyck and Gloria Katz; produced by Francis Ford Coppola and Gary Kurtz; photographed by Ron Everslage and Jan D'Alquen; edited by Verna Fields and Marcia Lucas; released by Universal; 110 minutes. *Cast*: Richard Dreyfuss, Ronny Howard, Paul LeMat, Charles Martin Smith,

Cindy Williams, Candy Clark, Mackenzie Phillips, Wolfman Jack, Harrison Ford, Bo Hopkins, Joe Spano, Suzanne Somers, Kathy Quinlan, Debralee Scott, Del Close.

Set during one 1962 evening in California, this optimistic and nostalgic comedy successfully counters the cynicism of the times as four teens—Curt (Dreyfuss), Steve (Howard), Terry/Toad (Smith), and Laurie (Williams)—face the realization that they are growing up. Lucas' ability to capture the period feel and to convey teenage frustration makes this a classic American film. Great hot rods, Mel's Diner (still a California landmark), Wolfman Jack spinning the evocative sound track, and a memorable supporting cast—LeMat as the "older" hotrodder with the 1932 Deuce Coupe; Phillips as the young girl who cruises with him; Ford as the drag racer with the 1955 Chevy; Clark as the older girl who befriends Toad; and, of course, Somers as the enigmatic blond in the T-Bird. The film cost $750,000 and grossed $55 million, sparking a mania for anything 1950s, while the popularity of both Ron Howard and Cindy Williams led to the subsequent television sitcoms "Happy Days" and "Laverne and Shirley." "*American Grafitti* set the guidelines for almost all the big box office youth films that followed" (Elayne Rapping, *Cineaste* 16, nos. 1–2, 1987–1988).

Sequels: Lucas executive produced *More American Graffiti* (1979, B.W.L. Norton), featuring much of the original cast with the exception of Dreyfuss.

Awards: Academy Award nominations for Best Picture, Director, Supporting Actress, Screenplay, Editing; New York Film Critics Circle Award for Best Screenplay; included in the Library of Congress' National Film Registry (1995).

ANDERS, ALLISON. Born 1955 in Ashland, Kentucky; director. A high school dropout and former welfare mother who later enrolled in the University of California–Los Angeles film school, Anders has a simple, unobtrusive vision that has catapulted her to the forefront of the American independent filmmaking scene, a position that has not been acknowledged by commercial success. With her films *Gas Food Lodging* and *Mi Vida Loca*, she has told stories of women searching for hope in a world where almost none is possible. Both films, while stylistically expressive, paint the worlds of their female characters with a near-documentary palette that enlivens the trailer park of *Gas Food Lodging* and the Echo Park barrio of *Mi Vida Loca*. A rare, solo voice in American film that has, as yet, fallen on only trained ears.

Filmography: Border Radio (1988) codirector and cowriter with Kurt Voss; Gas Food Lodging (1992); Mi Vida Loca/My Crazy Life (1994); Rebel Highway (1994, ctvm); Four Rooms (1995).

Honors: New York Film Critics Circle Award for Best New Director (*Gas Food Lodging*); MacArthur Foundation "genius grant" (1995).

ANDREWS, JULIE. Born Julia Elizabeth Wells October 1, 1935, in Walton-on-Thames, England; actor, singer. Dynamic Broadway sensation who starred on stage in *The Boyfriend* (1954), *My Fair Lady* (1956–1960), and *Camelot* (1960) and then proceeded to lose all three roles when the productions were adapted to the screen. Her break in film came with 1964's *Mary Poppins*, earning her an Academy Award for Best Actress (ironically beating Audrey Hepburn, who essayed the Eliza Doolittle role in the film *My Fair Lady*). Although unmistakably British, she has appeared almost exclusively in American Hollywood productions and is a much more integral part of this country's film industry than of her homeland. As Mary Poppins and then as the blissful Maria in *The Sound of Music*, she charmed a generation of filmgoers who responded favorably to her air of goodness and optimism. She is not, however, limited to wholesome fare—Alfred Hitchcock cast her in his Cold War espionage thriller *Torn Curtain*, and Andrew's second husband and longtime collaborator Blake Edwards played against expectations by letting her go topless in *S.O.B.* and then casting her as the cross-dressing star of *Victor/Victoria*. In addition to Edwards, she has collaborated twice with directors Robert Wise (*The Sound of Music, Star!*) and George Roy Hill (*Hawaii, Thoroughly Modern Millie*). In 1995 she returned to Broadway after a thirty-five-year absence in the Edwards-directed Broadway hit *Victor/Victoria*. "She can sing about such things as 'raindrops on roses and whiskers on kittens' and make you want to sing along instead of throw up" (Danny Peary, *Alternate Oscars*).

Filmography: The Rose of Baghdad (1949); The Americanization of Emily (1964); Mary Poppins (1964); The Sound of Music (1965); Hawaii (1966); Torn Curtain (1966); Thoroughly Modern Millie (1967); Star! (1968); Darling Lili (1970); The Tamarind Seed (1974); 10 (1979); Little Miss Marker (1980); S.O.B. (1981); Victor/Victoria (1982); The Man Who Loved Women (1983); Duet for One (1986); That's Life! (1986); Our Sons (1991, tvm); A Fine Romance (1992); "Julie" (1992, tvs).

Honors: Academy Award for Best Actress (*Mary Poppins*); Academy Award nominations for Best Actress (*The Sound of Music, Victor/Victoria*); Emmy for Outstanding Musical Variety Series ("The Julie Andrews Hour" 1972), Tony nomination (*Victor/Victoria* 1995, declined).

ANNIE HALL (1977), comedy/romance. Directed and cowritten by Woody Allen; screenplay with Marshall Brickman; produced by Jack Rollins and Charles H. Joffe; photographed by Gordon Willis; edited by Ralph Rosenblum; released by United Artists; 93 minutes. *Cast*: Diane Keaton, Woody Allen, Tony Roberts, Carol Kane, Paul Simon, Colleen Dewhurst, Janet Margolin, Shelley Duvall, Christopher Walken, Marshall McLuhan, Dick Cavett, John Glover, Jeff Goldblum, Shelley Hack, Beverly D'Angelo, Gary Muledeer, Sigourney Weaver.

The film where it all comes together for Woody Allen—the Groucho Marxist witticisms, the Chaplinesque pathos, the Freudian analysis, and the Bergmanesque reflections of the past. It's the story of television writer Alvy Singer (Allen, in a role that easily parallels real life), who meets an emotionally fraught eccentric named Annie Hall (Keaton, whose real last name is Hall), and in the simplest of plotlines, they meet, fall in love, and fall out of love, and Alvy reminisces about her. However, it's not *what* happens but *how* it happens; Allen manages to uncover the universal truths about falling in and out of love as if they have been articulated for the very first time. Often feeling like a filmed confession (Allen directly addresses the camera), Alvy gropes at childhood recollections, questions his own existence, and struggles to understand his love for Annie. Among the most memorable moments are Alvy and Annie's awkward meeting at the tennis club; the conversation in which their real thoughts appear in subtitles; the dinner with Grammy Hall; the lobster-cooking fiasco; Tony Robert's UV-ray repellent suit; the convenient appearance of Marshall McLuhan in the theater lobby; and Keaton's rendition of "Seems like Old Times." Diane Keaton won a much-deserved Oscar for her portrayal of Annie Hall, a character who, with her breakthrough fashion sense and her penchant for the phrase "la-dee-dah," is one of the most original in film history. "It is everything we never wanted to know about Woody's sex life and were afraid he'd tell us anyway" (John Simon, *New York*, May 2, 1977).

Awards: Academy Awards for Best Picture, Director, Actress, Screenplay; Academy Award nomination for Best Actor; New York Film Critics Circle Awards for Best Picture, Director, Actress, Screenplay; DGA Award; included in the Library of Congress' National Film Registry (1992).

APOCALYPSE NOW (1979), war. Directed, produced, and cowritten by Francis Ford Coppola; screenplay with John Milius; photographed by Vittorio Storaro; edited by Richard Marks; music by Carmine Coppola and Francis Ford Coppola; song "This Is the End" by the Doors; released by United Artists; 139 mins. *Cast*: Marlon Brando, Robert Duvall, Martin Sheen, Dennis Hopper, Frederic Forrest, Albert Hall, Sam Bottoms, Larry Fishburne, G. D. Spradlin, Harrison Ford, Scott Glenn, Bill Graham, Colleen Camp.

The last of the three major Vietnam films to be released in 1978–1979 (along with *Coming Home* and *The Deer Hunter*), Francis Ford Coppola's antiwar-fever dream is the most confounding and expressionistic of the bunch. More concerned with visually representing an idea of war than actually presenting the war itself, this Conradian trip down the Mekong River is the tale of man's search for his true nature. Martin Sheen, in a chilling performance, stars as Willard, a U.S. Army captain who has been ordered to travel deep into the jungles to assassinate Colonel Kurtz (Brando), a renegade Green Beret who is now living among the natives as their leader. On this symbolic journey back through time into the blackness of man's soul, Willard has one surrealistic encounter after another—the demented Kilgore (Duvall) and his Wagnerian helicopter base; a United Service Organizations (USO) site with grinding showgirls; grotesque heads impaled on poles. Paralleling Willard's perilous journey was the production itself—it went grossly over budget (from $13 million to $30 million) and over schedule (238 days), with a typhoon that destroyed the massive Dean Tavoularis set and a heart attack that sidelined Sheen for seven weeks. The result, for all of its flaws, is a megalomaniacal artistic achievement that, by its sheer audacity alone, cannot be ignored. The parts are perhaps greater than the sum, but *what* parts—Kilgore's declaration, "I love the smell of napalm in the morning"; the "Ride of the Valkyries" helicopter sequence; Willard's breakdown in the Saigon Hotel; the invisible spear attack on the gunboat; and the chiaroscuristic lighting from Vittorio Storaro during Brando's hypnotic mumblings. The story of the film's troubled production is told in Eleanor Coppola's book *Notes* and George Hickenlooper and Fax Bahr's 1991 documentary *Hearts of Darkness: A Filmmaker's Apocalypse*, which incorporates some incredible location footage shot by Eleanor Coppola. "Francis' film is a real step towards film as literature" (Eleanor Coppola, *Notes*). "*Apocalypse Now* is but this decade's most extraordinary folly" (Frank Rich, *Time*, August 27, 1979).

Awards: Academy Awards for Cinematography, Sound; Academy Award nominations for Best Picture, Director, Supporting Actor (Duvall), Adapted Screenplay, Art Direction, Editing; Cannes Film Festival Palme d'Or and Fipresci Prize.

ARQUETTE, ROSANNA. Born August 10, 1959, in Chicago; actor. Eldest sister of actors Patricia, Alexis, and David. Quirky and energetic actor who found her first moderate success in television starring opposite Bette Davis in the miniseries *The Dark Secret of Harvest Home* and as Shirley Jones' daughter in the series "Shirley." Her first starring role on the big screen came in John Sayles' *Baby, It's You*, but a trio of 1985 films put her in the spotlight—*After Hours*, *Desperately Seeking Susan*, and *Silverado*. Unfortunately, her choices since then, with the exception of a rich performance in Martin Scorsese's episode of *New York Stories*, have proven to be either unwise or unseen. A much-publicized romance with rock performer Peter Gabriel and a relocation to Europe (where she starred in the overseas megahit *The Big Blue*) filled up much of the late 1980s and early 1990s before she returned in full force with a memorable supporting role as a drug addict in 1994's *Pulp Fiction*. "Something of a more voluptuous cross between Nastassia Kinski and Audrey Hepburn" (*Variety*, March 9, 1983).

Filmography: Having Babies II (1977, tvm); Mom and Dad Can't Hear Me (1978, tvm); The Dark Secret of Harvest Home (1978, tv miniseries); More American Graffiti (1979); Shirley (1979–1980, series); G.O.R.P. (1980); A Long Way Home (1981); S.O.B. (1981); The Wall (1982, tvm); Johnny Belinda (1982); Baby, It's You (1983); Off the Wall (1983); One Cooks, the Other Doesn't (1983, tvm); The Parade (1984, tvm); After Hours (1985); The Aviator (1985); Desperately Seeking Susan (1985); Silverado (1985); 8 Million Ways to Die (1986); Nobody's Fool (1986); "A Family Tree," episode of Trying Times (1987, tvm); Amazon Women on the Moon (1987); Promised a Miracle (1988, tvm); The Big Blue (1988); Black Rainbow (1989); "Life Lessons" episode, New York Stories (1989); Separation (1990, tvm); Sweet Revenge (1990, tvm); Son of the Morning Star (1990, miniseries); Wendy Cracked a Walnut (1990); Flight of the Intruder (1991); The Linguini Incident (1991); In the Deep Woods (1992, tvm); Fathers and Sons (1992); Nowhere to Run (1993); La Cite de la Peur: Une Comedie Familiale (1993); The Wrong Man (1993, tvm); Nowhere to Hide (1994, tvm); Pulp Fiction (1994); Search and Destroy (1995).

ASHBY, HAL. Born 1929 in Ogden, Utah; died December 27, 1988, in Malibu, California; director, editor. Hitchhiking from Utah to Los Angeles at age seventeen and bouncing from job to job before landing as a multilith operator at Republic Studios, Ashby worked his way up the ranks from apprentice editor to editor. His fruitful editorial association with director Norman Jewison led to Jewison's producing Ashby's directorial debut, *The Landlord*. Throughout the 1970s, he delivered one superb film after another—each possessing a breezy, freewheeling style in which the personal concerns of the characters are reflective of the social concerns of the day. The freedom he allows his actors is evident in the many excellent performances that fill his works, specifically Randy Quaid in *The Last Detail*, Lee Grant in *Shampoo*, David Carradine (as Woody Guthrie) in *Bound for Glory*, Jon Voight in *Coming Home*, and Peter Sellers in *Being There*. Sadly, nothing he directed from 1980 until the end of his life showed even a hint of his considerable talent.

Filmography: The Landlord (1970); Harold and Maude (1971); The Last Detail (1973); Shampoo (1975); Bound for Glory (1976); Coming Home (1977); Being There (1979); Second-Hand Hearts (1980); Let's Spend the Night Together (1982, concert film); Lookin' to Get Out (1982); The Slugger's Wife (1985); 8 Million Ways to Die (1986).

Additional credits: The Cincinnati Kid (1965) editor; The Loved One (1965) editor; The Russians Are Coming, the Russians Are Coming (1966) editor; In the Heat of the Night (1967) editor; The Thomas Crown Affair (1968) supervising editor; Gaily, Gaily (1969) associate producer.

Honors: Academy Award for Best Editing (*In the Heat of the Night*); Academy Award nominations for Best Director (*Coming Home*) and Editing (*The Russians Are Coming, the Russians Are Coming*).

AYKROYD, DAN. Born July 1, 1952, in Ottawa, Canada; actor, comedian. Married to actor Donna Dixon. Starting his career with Toronto's Second City comedy troupe, he found fame as a member of the original cast of Saturday Night Live, creating such memorable characters as Beldar Conehead and pitchman E. Buzz Miller and satirizing Presidents Nixon and Carter. Together with John Belushi, he created the comic team of Jake and Elwood Blues, and they rode the energetic duet to fame in *The Blues Brothers* from a script that Aykroyd cowrote. His stock rose even higher when he starred in the box office smash *Ghostbusters*, another project he cowrote. His one foray into directing, *Nothing but Trouble*, proved nothing but routine. Shifting away from sight-gags and one-liners, he played it straight in *Driving Miss Daisy*, earning an Oscar nomination for his excellent performance as Miss Daisy's son Boolie.

Filmography: Love at First Sight (1977) also screenplay; 1941 (1979); Mr. Mike's Mondo Video (1979); The Blues Brothers (1980) also screenplay; Neighbors (1981); Doctor Detroit (1982); Nothing Lasts Forever (1982); Trading Places (1983); Twilight Zone—the Movie (1983); Ghostbusters (1984) also screenplay; Indiana Jones and the Temple of Doom (1984); Into the Night (1985); Spies like Us (1985) also screenplay; One More Saturday Night (1986) ep; Dragnet (1987) also screenplay; Caddyshack II

(1988); The Couch Trip (1988); The Great Outdoors (1988); My Stepmother Is an Alien (1988); Driving Miss Daisy (1989); Ghostbusters II (1989) also screenplay; Loose Cannons (1989); Masters of Menace (1991); Nothing but Trouble (1991) also screenplay, director; My Girl (1991); "Yellow," episode of "Tales from the Crypt" (1991, ctvm); This Is My Life (1992); Sneakers (1992); Chaplin (1992); Coneheads (1993); My Girl 2 (1994); Exit to Eden (1994); North (1994); Rainbow (1995, released 1996); Tommy Boy (1995); Casper (1995); Canadian Bacon (1995).

Honors: Academy Award nomination for Best Supporting Actor (*Driving Miss Daisy*); Emmy Award for Best Writing ("Saturday Night Live" 1976).

B

BACON, KEVIN. Born July 8, 1958 in Philadelphia; actor, director. Married to actress Kyra Sedgewick. Gifted, fresh-faced actor who has an ability to play both light comedy and hard-edged drama to equal effect. He appeared on the television soap operas ''The Guiding Light'' and ''Search for Tomorrow'' and in some minor film roles (including *National Lampoon's Animal House* and *Friday the 13th*) before gaining notice as Fenwick in *Diner*. In this role as the alcoholic black sheep of an upper-class family Bacon shows his versatility at playing smart comedy (his disgust at the quiz show contestants; his drunk scene in the Christmas manger) and dark drama (his plea for money from his haughty brother). While *Diner* made critics take notice, *Footloose* brought him his first commercial success. The last few years have marked a shift toward harsher, darker characters, with especially effective performances as the military lawyer in *A Few Good Men*, the psychopath in *River Wild*, and Alcatraz inmate Henri Young in *Murder in the First*.

Filmography: National Lampoon's Animal House (1978); Starting Over (1979); The Gift (1979, tvm); Friday the 13th (1980); Hero at Large (1980); Forty Deuce (1981); Only When I Laugh (1981); Diner (1982); Enormous Changes at the Last Minute (1983); The Demon Murder Case (1983, tvm); Mr. Roberts (1983, tvm); Footloose (1984); Quicksilver (1986); Planes, Trains and Automobiles (1987); White Water Summer (1987); End of the Line (1988); She's Having a Baby (1988); Criminal Law (1988); Lemon Sky (1988, tvm); The Big Picture (1989); Flatliners (1990); Tremors (1990); He Said, She Said (1991); Queens Logic (1991); Pyrates (1991); JFK (1991); A Few Good Men (1992); The Air up There (1994); The River Wild (1994); Murder in the First (1994); Apollo 13 (1995); Balto (1995) voice.

BADLANDS (1974), crime drama. Directed, written, and produced by Terrence Malick; photographed by Tak Fujimoto, Bryan Probyn, and Steve Larner; edited by Robert Estrin; music by George Tipton; released by Warner Bros.; 95 minutes. *Cast*: Martin Sheen, Sissy Spacek, Warren Oates, Ramon Bieri.

This debut feature from former American Film Institute student Terrence Malick is (along with *Days of Heaven*) one of his two sensational studies of Americana. Inspired by real-life figures Charles Starkweather and Carole Fugate, *Badlands* is the story of garbageman/James Dean wannabe Kit (Sheen) and naive teenager Holly (Spacek), who become lovers and set off across South Dakota on a killing spree. Directed by Malick with a rare combination of humanity and technical proficiency, the film is more of a study of midwestern stasis than a precursor to Hollywood's fascination with mass murderers. Unlike Arthur Penn with the eponymous gangsters of *Bonnie and Clyde* or Oliver Stone with Mickey and Mallory of *Natural Born Killers*, Malick addresses the mythology that surrounds Kit and Holly without ever fueling it. Much of the brilliance of the film comes from Malick's ability to sense the growing ennui of the youth culture and the dawning punk rock movement; Kit and Holly are closer, in many ways, to the emotionally stunted punk lovers Sid Vicious and Nancy Spungeon than to Starkweather and Fugate. Sheen and Spacek both deliver flawless performances in everything from their dialect to the way they wear their clothes (Spacek in her girlish white short-shorts and Sheen in his T-shirt, jeans, and boots). Warren Oates as Spacek's father is equally superb, especially in the moment when his face registers that Kit is about to kill him—''Suppose I shot you? How'd that be?'' The haunting score includes Carl Orff's percussive ''Musica Poetica'' and the Mickey and Sylvia pop tune ''Love Is Strange.'' ''It is as though James Dean's legacy of rebellion had drifted off into esthetic, cinematic heaven, leaving his coopted alter ego to plague us'' (Elayne Rapping, *Cineaste* 16, nos. 1–2, 1987–1988).

Awards: Included in the Library of Congress' National Film Registry (1993).

BAKSHI, RALPH. Born October 26, 1938, in Haifa, Palestine; director of animation and live action. Beginning as a cel painter for the CBS Terrytoon unit and eventually working his way to director of the cartoon shows ''Casper and Friends'' and ''Spiderman,'' Bakshi was named head of the Paramount cartoon department in 1966, just a year before it was shut down. Influenced by the work of Robert Crumb, he tapped into a new audience when his X-rated animated features *Fritz the Cat* and *Heavy Traffic* proved that animation wasn't just for kids anymore. His next two studio films, *Coonskin* and *Hey, Good Lookin'*, explored racial and social issues but were themselves targeted as racist, causing Paramount to cancel plans to release the former, while Warner Brothers shelved the latter until 1982. Unfortunately, his shift to a rotoscoping style of animation (in which live action is traced onto animation cels) and an indulgence in sword-and-sorcerer fantasy has failed to duplicate his earlier success. Only with his intelligent, mature, racy, and likewise controversial Saturday morning cartoon series ''Mighty Mouse: The New Adventures'' did he recapture the attention of critics. While his heavily promoted live action/animation film *Cool World* could boast rising star Brad Pitt, it too tanked at the box office.

Filmography: Fritz the Cat (1972) also screenplay; Heavy Traffic (1973) also screenplay; Coonskin (1975) also screenplay; Hey, Good Lookin' (1975, released 1982) also producer, screenplay; Wizards (1977) also producer, screenplay; The Lord of the Rings (1978); American Pop (1981) also producer; Cannonball Run II (1983) animation sequences only; Fire and Ice (1983) also producer; The Rolling Stones' "Harlem Shuffle" (1986, mv); Tattertown (1988, ctv short); "Mighty Mouse: The New Adventures" (1987–1989, tvs); "Hound Town" (1989, tvs); This Ain't Bebop (1989, short); The Butter Battle Book (1989, ctv special); also producer; Cool World (1992); The Cool and the Crazy (1994, ctvm) also screenplay.

BALDWIN, ALEC. Born Alexander Rae Baldwin III April 3, 1958, in Amityville, New York; actor. Married to Kim Basinger; brother of actors Stephen, Daniel, and William. Stage-trained at the Lee Strasberg Institute, he is one of only a handful of actors who glide comfortably between the stage and both comic and dramatic film roles. Cutting his teeth in television on soap operas and movies-of-the-week before catching the public's eye on "Knot's Landing," Baldwin made his mark on the big screen as the straitlaced suburban husband in *Beetlejuice*. His stock as a Hollywood dramatic lead rose as the heroic Jack Ryan in Tom Clancy's *The Hunt for Red October* and as the ruthless insurance sales motivator in the adaptation of David Mamet's *Glengarry Glen Ross*. His work on stage includes a bravura turn in Caryl Churchill's Broadway satire *Serious Money* and the off-Broadway smash *Prelude to a Kiss*, reprising the latter role in the unsuccessful film of the same name.

Filmography: "The Doctors" (1980–1982, tvs); "Cutter to Houston" (1983, tvs); "Knot's Landing" (1984, tvs); Sweet Revenge (1984, tvm); Love on the Run (1985, tvm); Dress Grey (1986, tvms); Forever, Lulu (1986); Alamo: 13 Days to Glory (1987, tvm); Beetlejuice (1988); Married to the Mob (1988); She's Having a Baby (1988); Talk Radio (1988); Working Girl (1988); Great Balls of Fire (1989); Alice (1990); The Hunt for Red October (1990); Miami Blues (1990); The Marrying Man (1991); Glengarry Glen Ross (1992); Prelude to a Kiss (1992); Malice (1993); The Getaway (1994); The Shadow (1994); A Streetcar Named Desire (1995, tvm); Heaven's Prisoner (1995); Two Bits (1995) narrator.

BANCROFT, ANNE. Born Anna Maria Louisa Italiano September 17, 1931, in Bronx, New York; actor, screenwriter, director. Married to Mel Brooks. Hugely talented actress of screen, stage, and television who seems equally comfortable in all venues. Under contract to 20th Century Fox early in her career, she later returned to the stage in the acclaimed 1958 Broadway production of *Two for the Seesaw*. Her achievements on the stage hit a new high when she was cast as Annie Sullivan in *The Miracle Worker*, a role she would reprise in the 1962 Arthur Penn film. She then carved out a place in film history with her cool and detached performance in *The Graduate* as the married seductress Mrs. Robinson, immortalized in song by Simon and Garfunkel. Having previously directed a television project and an unreleased feature, Bancroft made her feature film directorial debut with the interesting, but unspectacular, comic drama *Fatso*. Married since 1964 to comic genius Mel Brooks, she's appeared under his direction in a handful of comedies and has also starred in two dramatic films he has produced, *84 Charing Cross Road* and *The Elephant Man*. Some of her finest, though not necessarily most acclaimed, work has come in recent years with the Paddy Chayefsky-penned PBS television drama *The Mother* and the underrated, multigenerational American drama *How to Make an American Quilt*.

Filmography of key pre-1965 films: Nightfall (1956); The Miracle Worker (1962); The Pumpkin Eater (1964).

Filmography: The Slender Thread (1965); 7 Women (1996); The Graduate (1967); Young Winston (1972); The Prisoner of Second Avenue (1974); The Hindenburg (1975); Silent Movie (1976); Lipstick (1976); The Turning Point (1977); Fatso (1980); Elephant Man (1980); To Be or Not to Be (1983); Garbo Talks (1984); Agnes of God (1985); 84 Charing Cross Road (1986); 'Night Mother (1986); Torch Song Trilogy (1988); Bert Rigby, You're a Fool (1989); Love Potion No. 9 (1991); Honeymoon in Vegas (1992); Point of No Return (1993); Mr. Jones (1993); Malice (1993); The Mother (1994, tv); How to Make an American Quilt (1995); Home for the Holidays (1995); Dracula: Dead and Loving It (1995).

Filmography as writer, director: Annie: The Woman in the Life of a Man (1970, tv); Fatso (1980).

Honors: Academy Award for Best Actress (*The Miracle Worker*); Academy Award nominations for Best Actress (*The Pumpkin Eater*, *The Graduate*, *The Turning Point*, *Agnes of God*); Cannes Film Festival Best Actress Award (*The Pumpkin Eater*); Berlin Film Festival Award for Best Actress (*84 Charing Cross Road*); Tony Awards (*Two for the Seesaw*, 1958; *The Miracle Worker*, 1960); Emmy Award (*Annie: The Woman in the Life of a Man*); inductee in the Theatre Hall of Fame (1992).

BARKIN, ELLEN. Born April 16, 1954, in Bronx, New York; actor. Formerly married to Gabriel Byrne. Sexy, asymmetrically attractive leading lady who trained at the High School for the Performing Arts and the Actors Studio before landing a minor role on the television soap ''Search for Tomorrow.'' Her feature film debut was in Barry Levinson's *Diner* as Beth, the unhappy wife of Shrevie, who finds it too complicated to reorganize her husband's records and not only doesn't care what's on the b-side of ''Good Golly Miss Molly'' (it's ''Hey, Hey, Hey, Hey'') but can't understand why *he* cares. That same year she co-starred with Susan Sarandon in the off-Broadway production of *Extremities*. She made the transition to leading lady starring opposite Dennis Quaid with a smoldering performance in Jim McBride's *The Big Easy* and continued the trend opposite Al Pacino in *Sea of Love*. Of her more recent films, the Hollywood pictures *Man Trouble*, *Bad Company*, and *Wild Bill* have fared considerably less well than her riskier independent pictures *Mac*, *This Boy's Life*, and *Into the West*, the latter costarring former husband, Gabriel Byrne.

Filmography: We're Fighting Back (1981, tvm); Diner (1982); Tender Mercies (1982);

Daniel (1983); Eddie and the Cruisers (1983); Enormous Changes at the Last Minute (1983); The Adventures of Buckaroo Bonzai: Across the 8th Dimension (1984); Terrible Joe Morgan (1984, tvm); Harry and Son (1984); Terminal Choice (1985); The Big Easy (1986); Desert Bloom (1986); Down by Law (1986); Made in Heaven (1987); Siesta (1987); Clinton and Nadine (1988, ctvm); Johnny Handsome (1989); Sea of Love (1989); Switch (1991); Mac (1992); Man Trouble (1992); This Boy's Life (1993); Into the West (1993); Bad Company (1995); Wild Bill (1995).

BARRYMORE, DREW. Born February 22, 1975, in Los Angeles; actor. As part of a thespian lineage of near-mythic proportions, the six-year-old Barrymore became a symbol of the sweet suburban child as Gertie in *E.T. The Extra-Terrestrial* only to slide into a period of substance abuse and rehabilitation while still a young teen. Amazingly, she has managed a comeback, which has pushed her into the forefront of young Hollywood actors with such charismatic performances as Holly in *Boys on the Side*. While she has primarily become famous for her various escapades—her troubled teen years; her subsequent 1989 autobiography/confessional *Little Girl Lost*; her celebrated romances and a very brief marriage; her array of tattoos; her *Playboy* session; and her "flash" to David Letterman—she has begun to show the signs of a promising acting career. "What can you say about an actress who survived the simultaneous onset of a mid-life crisis and puberty?" (J. Hoberman, *Village Voice*, February 2, 1993).

Filmography: Altered States (1980); Bogie (1980, tvm); E.T. The Extra-Terrestrial (1982); Firestarter (1984); Irreconcilable Differences (1984); Stephen King's Cat's Eye (1985); The Adventures of Con Sawyer and Hucklemary Finn (1985, tv); The Screaming Woman (1986, ctv short); Babes in Toyland (1986, tvm); Conspiracy of Love (1987, tvm); 15 and Getting Straight (1989, tvm); Far from Home (1989); See You in the Morning (1989); Motorama (1991); Poison Ivy (1992); The Sketch Artist (1992, ctvm); Guncrazy (1992, ctvm); "2000 Malibu Road" (1992, tvs); The Amy Fisher Story (1993, tvm); Doppelganger/Doppelganger: The Evil Within (1993, ctvm); No Place to Hide (1993); Wayne's World 2 (1993); Bad Girls (1994); Inside the Goldmine (1994); Boys on the Side (1995); Batman Forever (1995); Mad Love (1995).

Selected bibliography

Barrymore, Drew, and Todd Gold. *Little Girl Lost*. New York: Pocket Books, 1989.

BASINGER, KIM. Born December 8, 1953, in Athens, Georgia; actor. Married to actor Alec Baldwin. Stunning, blond leading lady with a true talent for physical comedy who is often underused in less-than-demanding roles. With an early appearance on the television series "Charlie's Angels," a starring role in the movie-of-the-week *Katie: Portrait of a Centerfold*, and a 1982 pictorial in *Playboy* magazine, she layed the groundwork for the sexual provocation of Adrian Lyne's stylish but ridiculous *9 1/2 Weeks* and again steamed up the screen as Vicki Vale in *Batman*. While she has shown her range with Robert Altman's *Fool for Love* and Robert Benton's *Nadine*, she has, for the most part, appeared in forgettable light comedies. In 1994 she starred with husband, Alec Baldwin, in the remake of Sam Peckinpah's *The Getaway*, a commercial flop that raised questions about both stars' abilities to carry a film to box office heights. Later that year she reteamed with Altman in *Ready to Wear (Prêt-à-Porter)* in a superb performance as the fashion reporter who weaves the scattered plot together. From 1992 to 1995 she was involved in a long-running court battle involving her decision to not appear in the film *Boxing Helena*.

Filmography: "Dog and Cat" (1977, tvs); Katie: Portrait of a Centerfold (1978, tvm); "From Here to Eternity" (1980, tvs); Hard Country (1981); Mother Lode (1982); The Man Who Loved Women (1983); Never Say Never Again (1983); The Natural (1984); Fool for Love (1985); 9 1/2 Weeks (1986); No Mercy (1986); Blind Date (1987); Nadine (1987); My Stepmother Is an Alien (1988); Batman (1989); The Marrying Man (1991); Final Analysis (1992); Cool World (1992); Wayne's World 2 (1993); The Real McCoy (1993); The Getaway (1994); Ready to Wear (Prêt-à-Porter) (1994); Tom Petty's "Mary Jane's Last Dance" (1995, music video).

BATES, KATHY. Born June 28, 1948, in Memphis, Tennessee; actor. A superbly gifted performer with a nearly unparalleled rage and intensity who has shone on stage and the silver screen. Making her off-Broadway debut in 1983's *Vanities* and starring the same year as the suicidal daughter in the Broadway production of *'Night Mother*, she went on to win the Obie for her work in 1985's *Frankie and Johnny in the Claire de Lune* (a role played years later by the more conventionally beautiful Michelle Pfeiffer in the film adaptation). After some accomplished supporting work, she carved out her place in American film lore with her chilling, Oscar-winning performance as the psychotic, sledgehammer-wielding Annie Wilkes in *Misery* and again made an impression the following year as Evelyn Crouch in *Fried Green Tomatoes*. After a supporting role in the television miniseries "Stephen King's The Stand," Bates again turned to the novelist's work and starred in the unjustly overlooked *Dolores Claiborne* as a bitter, but devoted, mother who is charged with murdering both her abusive husband and her demanding employer.

Filmography: Taking Off (1971); Straight Time (1978); Come Back to the 5 and Dime, Jimmy Dean, Jimmy Dean (1982); Two of a Kind (1983); The Morning After (1986); Summer Heat (1987); Arthur 2 on the Rocks (1988); My Best Friend Is a Vampire (1988); Roe vs. Wade (1989, tvm); No Place like Home (1989, tvm); High Stakes (1989); Signs of Life (1989); Dick Tracy (1990); White Palace (1990); Men Don't Leave (1990); Misery (1990); At Play in the Fields of the Lord (1991); Fried Green Tomatoes (1991); The Road to Mecca (1991); Prelude to a Kiss (1992); Shadows and Fog (1992); Used People (1992); Hostages (1993, ctvm); Stephen King's The Stand (1994, tvms); A Home of Our Own (1994); Curse of the Starving Class (1994, ctvm); North (1994); Dolores Claiborne (1995); Angus (1995); The West Side Waltz (1995, tvm).

Honors: Academy Award for Best Actress (*Misery*).

BEATTY, NED. Born July 6, 1937, in Louisville, Kentucky; actor. Portly supporting actor who moved from Broadway into film with an unforgettable performance in *Deliverance*, sending shock waves through audiences that watched as he was brutalized by mountain men and forced to "squeal like a pig." A role in John Huston's *The Life and Times of Judge Roy Bean* followed, leading to a succession of quality films in the 1970s and culminating with an Oscar nomination for his work as enraged television chairman Arthur Jensen in *Network*. Since then his career has been peppered with hugely commercial pictures (Spielberg's *1941* and as Gene Hackman's lackey Otis in *Superman* and *Superman II*), interesting independent films (*The Ballad of Gregorio Cortez* and the excellent Irish film *Hear My Song*), and entirely forgettable time-wasters.

Filmography: Deliverance (1972); The Life and Times of Judge Roy Bean (1972); The Last American Hero (1973); The Thief Who Came to Dinner (1973); White Lightning (1973); W. W. and the Dixie Dancekings (1974); The Execution of Private Slovik (1974, tvm); Nashville (1975); All the President's Men (1976); The Big Bus (1976); Mikey and Nicky (1976); Network (1976); Silver Streak (1976); Exorcist II: The Heretic (1977); Gray Lady Down (1977); Shenanigans/The Great Bank Hoax (1977); Alambrista! (1978); Superman (1978); 1941 (1979); Promises in the Dark (1979); The American Success Company (1979); Wise Blood (1979); Friendly Fire (1979, tvm); Hopscotch (1980); Superman II (1980); The Incredible Shrinking Woman (1981); The Toy (1982); The Ballad of Gregorio Cortez (1983); Stroker Ace (1983); Touched (1983); Restless Natives (1985); Robert Kennedy and His Times (1985, tvm); Back to School (1986); The Big Easy (1986); The Fourth Protocol (1987); Rolling Vengeance (1987); The Trouble with Spies (1987); After the Rain (1988); Midnight Crossing (1988); Physical Evidence (1988); Purple People Eater (1988); Shadows in the Storm (1988); Switching Channels (1988); The Unholy (1988); Ministry of Vengeance (1989); Time Trackers (1989); Twist of Fate/Black Water (1989); Blind Vision (1990); Big Bad John (1990); Captain America (1990); Chattahoochee (1990); A Cry in the Wild (1990); Repossessed (1990); Angel Square (1991); Going Under (1991); Hear My Song (1991); Prelude to a Kiss (1992); Illusions (1992); Rudy (1993); Ed and His Dead Mother (1993); "Homicide: Life on the Streets" (1993–1995, tvs); Radioland Murders (1994); The Legend of O. B. Taggart (1995); Just Cause (1995).

Honor: Academy Award nomination for Best Supporting Actor (*Network*).

BEATTY, WARREN. Born Warren Beaty March 30, 1937, in Richmond, Virginia; actor, director, producer, screenwriter. Married to Annette Bening; sister is Shirley MacLaine. One of the last of Hollywood's classic movie stars, Beatty is also a truly gifted writer and director whose talents are frequently overshadowed by his celebrity. With a background that includes theatrical training from Northwestern University and Stella Adler and a three-episode stint on television's "The Many Loves of Dobie Gillis," Beatty broke onto the scene as a sexually charismatic star with his performance opposite Natalie Wood in Elia Kazan's *Splendor in the Grass*. He then established himself with serious critics in his two pictures with director Arthur Penn—the moody, existential study of paranoia, *Mickey One*, and their masterpiece *Bonnie and Clyde*, on which Beatty also served as producer. Like the outsider Clyde Barrow, his best characters are those who live on the outer edge of society—the western antihero in Robert Altman's *McCabe and Mrs. Miller*, the loner journalist in *The Parallax View*, and the libidinal hairdresser in *Shampoo*. The next twelve years saw only two films from Beatty, both of which he also wrote, produced, and directed—the splendidly romantic *Heaven Can Wait* (in collaboration with Buck Henry) and the lush *Reds*, the story of journalist John Reed—both of which earned him an armload of Oscars. Since then, however, his films have lacked the spark of his previous work—his notoriously unsuccessful *Ishtar*, while not nearly as bad as reported, is still a minor effort; his third outing as writer-director-producer, *Dick Tracy*, is a beautiful, but lightweight, entertainment; both *Bugsy* and *Love Affair* are classy, but ultimately tired, productions. "Bright as they come, intrepid, and with that thing all women secretly respect: complete confidence in his sexual powers" (Elia Kazan, *A Life*).

Filmography of key pre-1965 films: Splendor in the Grass (1961); Lilith (1964).

Filmography since 1965: Mickey One (1965); Kaleidoscope (1966); Promise Her Anything (1966); Bonnie and Clyde (1967); The Only Game in Town (1970); $ (1971); McCabe and Mrs. Miller (1971); The Parallax View (1974); The Fortune (1975); Shampoo (1975); Heaven Can Wait (1978) also codirector with Buck Henry, producer, writer; Reds (1981) also producer, writer; Ishtar (1987); The Pick-Up Artist (1987) ep; Dick Tracy (1990) also producer, director; Truth or Dare (1991, documentary); Bugsy (1991) also producer; Love Affair (1994).

Honors: Academy Award for Best Director (*Reds*); Academy Award nominations for Best Picture (*Bonnie and Clyde, Heaven Can Wait, Reds*), Director (*Heaven Can Wait*), Actor (*Heaven Can Wait, Reds, Bugsy*), and Screenplay (*Shampoo, Heaven Can Wait, Reds*); DGA Award (*Reds*); Los Angeles Film Critics Award for Best Picture (*Bugsy*).

Selected bibliography

Quirk, Lawrence J. *The Films of Warren Beatty*. New York: Citadel Press, 1979.
Spada, James. *Shirley and Warren*. New York: Macmillan, 1985.
Thomson, David. *Warren Beatty and Desert Eyes: A Life and a Story*. New York: Doubleday, 1987.

BEAUTY AND THE BEAST (1991), animation. Directed by Gary Trousdale and Kirk Wise; screenplay by Linda Woolverton; produced by Don Hahn; edited by John Carnochan; music by Alan Menken, songs by Menken and Howard Ashman; released by the Walt Disney Company/Buena Vista; 84 minutes. *Voices*: Paige O'Hara, Robby Benson, Rex Everhart, Richard White, Jesse Corti, Angela Lansbury, Jerry Orbach, David Ogden Stiers, Jo Anne Worley.

The poetry and romance of the 1757 fairy tale by Marie Leprince de Beaumont will endure for all time, enchanting generation after generation with its simplicity and truthfulness. It was magical in the hands of Jean Cocteau in his visually astounding 1946 French film *La Belle et La Bete*, and it is just as magical in this brilliantly animated picture from the Disney collective. By combining elements of the original fairy tale with the Disney legacy of cel animation, the future of computer animation, and the American tradition of the musical, the makers of this *Beauty and the Beast* have concocted an invigorating romantic potion. The simple story tells of freewilled young Belle (O'Hara) and spoiled prince-turned-Beast (Benson), who, despite their initial revulsion, see the beauty in one another and fall in love. With characters that are more dimensional than in most films, this celebration of love and life is easily as relevant for adults as for children. The Alan Menken music and Howard Ashman lyrics provide for some of the most inspired songs in the American musical in many years. Both a comment on the state of popular film and the perfection of the Disney factory, *Beauty and the Beast* is, amazingly, the first Disney animated film to be nominated for a Best Picture Oscar.

Awards: Academy Awards for Best Score, Best Song ("Beauty and the Beast"); Academy Award nominations for Best Picture, Songs ("Belle" and "Be Our Guest"), Sound; Los Angeles Film Critics Award for Best Animated Feature.

BEING THERE (1979), comedy/political satire. Directed by Hal Ashby; screenplay by Jerzy Kozinski (from his novel); produced by Andrew Braunsberg; photographed by Caleb Deschanel; edited by Don Zimmerman; music by John Mandel; released by United Artists; 130 minutes. *Cast*: Peter Sellers, Shirley MacLaine, Melvyn Douglas, Jack Warden, Richard Dysart, Richard Basehart.

If only for the image of Peter Sellers' Keatonesque stone face, *Being There* is a film worth seeing. Fortunately, Ashby's insular vision of a moron who ascends to greatness has other points in its favor; it's a gentle satire that, underneath its airy surface, brutally slices at American politics and the influence of the media. Chauncey "Chance" Gardiner (Sellers) is a simpleton who, after a lifetime as a gardener, is left to fend for himself when his master dies. With a knowledge of the world that is limited to only what he's seen on television, Chance wanders the streets of Washington, D.C., until he is taken in by Eve (MacLaine), the youngish wife of dying millionaire kingmaker Ben Rand (Douglas). Although Chance's intelligence is limited to gardening, everyone, including the president of the United States (Warden), is taken by Chance's simple, sage-like witticisms until he is elevated to the status of national hero. Seller's final major film before his death in 1980 and Ashby's last important film, *Being There* is a thoroughly charming tale that gets you smiling, then knocks you off guard with its wicked cynicism. The final image of Chance walking on water after being named as a possible presidential candidate by Ben's power brokers drives home Ashby's point—Americans are so numb to the sensate experience of actually being that they can no longer differentiate between idiot and savior.

Awards: Academy Award for Best Supporting Actor (Douglas), Academy Award nomination for Best Actor (Sellers); New York Film Critics Circle Award for Best Supporting Actor (Douglas).

BELUSHI, JOHN. Born January 24, 1949, in Chicago; died March 5, 1982, in Los Angeles; actor, comedian. Brother is Jim Belushi (*Salvador*, *Red Heat*, *K-9*). Brilliant comic performer whose crude animal qualities were made palatable by an underlying sensitivity. Beginning at Chicago's Second City before becoming one of the legendary original cast members of NBC's "Saturday Night Live," he was catapulted to a comic plateau previously occupied by the likes of Lenny Bruce and Richard Pryor. He unleashed his wildness on-screen in *National Lampoon's Animal House* as the maniacal Bluto Blutarsky, who raised the food fight to an art form. Spinning off the Jake and Elroy Blues characters from "Saturday Night Live," Belushi and frequent collaborator Dan Aykroyd appeared in the musical comedy romp *The Blues Brothers* and, in turn, carved out a recording and touring career as well. Belushi then surprised detractors by turning in a relatively restrained dramatic performance as a newspaper columnist stuck in the Rockies in *Continental Divide*. Unfortunately, the promise he showed as an actor was never to be fully realized. His fast-lane lifestyle caught up with him at age thirty-three after a drug overdose in Los Angeles' Chateau Marmont hotel. His life was given the treatment by journalist Bob Woodward in the book *Wired*, which itself was adapted into a movie of the same name in 1989.

Filmography: La Honte de la Jungle/Jungle Burger (1975) voice only; Goin' South (1978); National Lampoon's Animal House (1978); Old Boyfriends (1978); 1941 (1979); The Blues Brothers (1980); Continental Divide (1981); Neighbors (1981).

Selected bibliography

Woodward, Bob. *Wired*. New York: Pocketbooks, 1984.

BENJAMIN, RICHARD. Born May 22, 1938, in New York City; actor, director. Married to actress Paula Prentiss. Boyish actor who made a name for himself in the Broadway production of Neil Simon's *Star-Spangled Girl* (1966) and on the television series "He and She" (1967–1968, with co-star Prentiss) before appearing on film in Philip Roth's *Goodbye, Columbus*. A series of similarly tepid, sensitive roles followed, including another Roth character in *Portnoy's Complaint*. He made a wise career shift to directing in 1982 with the enjoyable Peter O'Toole vehicle *My Favorite Year*. His subsequent films, however, have become increasingly less engaging.

Filmography as actor: Goodbye, Columbus (1969); Catch-22 (1970); Dairy of a Mad Housewife (1970); The Marriage of a Young Stockbroker (1971); The Steagle (1971); Portnoy's Complaint (1972); The Last of Sheila (1973); Westworld (1973); The Sunshine Boys (1975); House Calls (1978); Witches' Brew (1978); Love at First Bite (1979); Scavenger Hunt (1979); The Last Married Couple in America (1980); First Family (1980); How to Beat the High Cost of Living (1980); Saturday the 14th (1981).

Filmography as director: My Favorite Year (1982); City Heat (1984); Racing with the Moon (1984); The Money Pit (1986); Little Nikita (1988); My Stepmother Is an Alien (1988); Downtown (1990); Mermaids (1990); Made in America (1993); Milk Money (1994).

BENTON, ROBERT. Born September 29, 1932, in Waxahachie, Texas; director, screenwriter. Onetime contributing editor and art director of *Esquire* magazine who began his career as a screenwriter with a fruitful collaboration with David

Newman. Though they first teamed in 1966 to write a Broadway play (*It's a Bird . . . It's a Plane . . . It's Superman* and later the off-Broadway hit *Oh, Calcutta!*), their screenplay for *Bonnie and Clyde* pushed them into the spotlight. Oddly underrated, despite his mantelful of awards, his style and tone are of the humanist school of Jean Renoir, Roberto Rossellini, and François Truffaut, and his best films (*Kramer vs. Kramer* and *Nobody's Fool*) address the subject of the American family with an acute sense of perception. While the well-crafted *Nadine* and *Billy Bathgate* have not been examples of his best work, his *Nobody's Fool* is an unqualified masterpiece of subtle humanism and a remarkable showcase of film acting.

Filmography: Bonnie and Clyde (1967) screenplay; There Was a Crooked Man (1970) screenplay; Bad Company (1972); Oh! Calcutta! (1972) screenplay; What's Up, Doc? (1972) screenplay; The Late Show (1977); Superman (1978) screenplay; Kramer vs. Kramer (1979); Still of the Night (1982); Places in the Heart (1984); Nadine (1987); The House on Carroll Street (1988) ep; Billy Bathgate (1991); Nobody's Fool (1994).

Honors: Academy Awards for Best Director (*Kramer vs. Kramer*) and Screenplay (*Kramer vs. Kramer*, *Places in the Heart*); Academy Award nominations for Best Director (*Places in the Heart*) and Screenplay (*Bonnie and Clyde*; *The Late Show*, *Nobody's Fool*); DGA Award (*Kramer vs. Kramer*); Los Angeles Film Critics Awards for Best Director (*Kramer vs. Kramer*) and Screenplay (*Kramer vs. Kramer*); Berlin Film Festival Award for Best Director (*Places in the Heart*).

BIG RED ONE, THE (1980), war. Directed and written by Samuel Fuller; photographed by Adam Greenberg; edited by Morton Tubor; music by Dana Koproff; released by United Artists; 113 minutes. *Cast*: Lee Marvin, Mark Hamill, Robert Carradine, Bobby DiCicco, Kelly Ward, Stephane Audran.

Platoon overlaid a blatant Good versus Evil battle onto its story of young soldiers, *Apocalypse Now* is more allegory than war film, *The Deer Hunter* and *Coming Home* deal with the psychological aftereffects of battle, *Patton* is a gung-ho biopic that revels in the grandeur of battle, and *Full Metal Jacket* is a black comedy about dehumanization in the military, but this brilliant World War II film from Sam Fuller surpasses them all in relaying the impact of battle. It is an account of his days with the First Infantry Division (as the "One" was officially known)—a three-year stretch from 1942 to 1945 during which time Fuller received the Bronze Star, the Silver Star, and a Purple Heart. The film follows one unit, led by a steely, but human, sergeant (Marvin), as they traverse North Africa, Sicily, Belgium, and Czechoslovakia. Structured episodically, the film features a number of powerful scenes, not the least of which are the capture of the big gun in Sicily (after which the elderly Italian women make the Americans a lavish dinner); the assault on the Germans who have holed up in a lunatic asylum (a scene that ends with an inmate's wildly firing a machine gun and exclaiming, "I am one of you . . . I am sane"); and the liberation of the concentration camp in Czechoslovakia, during which Hamill snaps and methodically fires dozens of rounds into a German soldier who has hidden in an oven. A film of profound beauty and intelligence, it raises questions that are at the very core of existence—questions about life, death, killing, friendship, and heroism. Lee Marvin is as good as he's ever been, and Mark Hamill is a complete surprise in a considerably less heroic role than his Luke Skywalker. "A film made as if the Second World War had ended ten minutes ago" (David Thomson, *A Biographical Dictionary of Films*).

BIRD (1988), biopic/drama. Directed and produced by Clint Eastwood; written by Joel Oliansky; photographed by Jack N. Green; edited by Joel Cox; music by Lennie Niehaus; released by Warner Bros.; 161 minutes. *Cast*: Forest Whitaker, Diane Venora, Michael Zelniker, Samuel E. Wright, Keith David, Sam Robards.

From the first explosive moment, when we see Forest Whitaker as Charlie "Bird" Parker jamming on "Lester Leaps In," it's clear that this is a perfectly cast movie. Under Eastwood's quietly daring direction and with the support of Jack N. Green's morose cinematography, the brilliant Whitaker has flawlessly re-created the mood of Parker's life and music. A revolutionary saxophone player who did for jazz what Stravinsky did for classical music, the volatile Parker led a dark, self-destructive life in which he struggled with drink, heroin, and racism. By the end of his short life (he died at thirty-four, a victim of heart attack, pneumonia, and cirrhosis), he had changed the face of music and influenced every jazz player who would follow. The film rides the emotional highs and lows of the relationship between Bird and his wife, Chan (played so lovingly by the underused Venora), but the most painful moment is Bird's drunken and remorseful succession of telegrams to Chan after learning of the death of their daughter, Pree. Standing alongside Bertrand Tavernier's Dexter Gordon vehicle *Round Midnight* as the best motion picture about jazz, it is also one of the best attempts at examining the creative process. "The film has a musical movement, casting at will back and forth through time in order to piece together the harmonies as well as the self-destructiveness of Parker's life" (Richard Combs, *Sight and Sound*, Winter 1988/1989).

Awards: New York Film Critics Circle Award for Best Supporting Actress; Cannes Film Festival Awards for Best Actor and Grand Prix de la Commission Superieure Technique.

BLACK, KAREN. Born Karen Blanche Ziegler July 1, 1942, in Park Ridge, Illinois; actor. Formerly married to screenwriter L. M. Kit Carson. Female lead whose film career began in Francis Coppola's *You're a Big Boy Now* in 1967 after she was spotted in a 1965 Broadway production of *The Chiller*. She then went on to a handful of superlative American films of the 1970s, most notably, *Easy Rider*, *Nashville*, and Hitchcock's final effort, *Family Plot*. But she is perhaps best remembered as Rayette Dispesto, the fluff-headed, but sweet, waitress who is hopelessly devoted to her unfeeling boyfriend (Jack Nicholson) in *Five Easy Pieces*. With the exception of Altman's *Come Back to the 5 and*

Dime, Jimmy Dean, Jimmy Dean and Henry Jaglom's *Can She Bake a Cherry Pie?* she has appeared in few films of note in the last two decades. In 1986, she costarred with her son Hunter Carson (by L. M. Kit Carson) in *Invaders from Mars*, Tobe Hooper's sci-fi remake of the 1953 favorite.

Filmography: You're a Big Boy Now (1966); Easy Rider (1969); Hard Contract (1969); Five Easy Pieces (1970); Born to Win (1971); Cisco Pike (1971); Drive, He Said (1971); A Gunfight (1971); Portnoy's Complaint (1972); Rhinoceros (1972); The Outfit (1973); The Pyx (1973); The Great Gatsby (1974); Law and Disorder (1974); Airport 1975 (1974); Nashville (1975); Day of the Locust (1975); Burnt Offerings (1976); Crime and Passion (1976); Family Plot (1976); In Praise of Older Women (1977); Capricorn One (1978); Killer Fish (1979); The Last Word (1979); Separate Ways (1979); The Squeeze (1980); Chanel Solitaire (1981); The Grass Is Singing (1981); Miss Right (1981); Come Back to the 5 and Dime, Jimmy Dean, Jimmy Dean (1982); Can She Bake a Cherry Pie? (1983); Martin's Day (1983); Growing Pains (1984); The Blue Man (1985); Savage Dawn (1985); Cut and Run (1986); Flight of the Spruce Goose (1986); Invaders from Mars (1986); Hostage (1987); It's Alive III: Island of the Alive (1987); Dixie Lanes (1988); The Invisible Kid (1988); Homer and Eddie (1989); Out of the Dark (1989); The Children (1990); Mirror, Mirror (1990); Night Angel (1990); Overexposed (1990); Twisted Justice (1990); Zapped Again (1990); The Killers Edge (1991); Haunting Fear (1991); Club Fed (1991); Quiet Fire (1991); Evil Spirits (1991); Rubin and Ed (1991); Auntie Lee's Meat Pies (1991); The Player (1992); Hitz (1992); Children of the Night (1992); Caged Fear (1992); The Double O Kid (1993); The Roller Blade Seven (1993); Final Judgment (1993); Bound and Gagged: A Love Story (1993); The Trust (1993); The Wacky Adventures of Dr. Boris and Nurse Shirley (1994).

Honors: Academy Award nomination for Best Supporting Actress *(Five Easy Pieces)*; New York Film Critics Circle Award for Best Supporting Actress *(Five Easy Pieces)*.

BLADE RUNNER (1982), sci-fi/film noir. Directed by Ridley Scott; written by Hampton Fancher and David [Webb] Peoples (from the novel by Philip K. Dick); produced by Michael Deeley; photographed by Jordan Cronenweth; edited by Terry Rawlings; music by Vangelis; released by Warner Bros.; 114 minutes (1992 director's cut, 116 minutes). *Cast*: Harrison Ford, Rutger Hauer, Sean Young, Edward James Olmos, M. Emmet Walsh, Daryl Hannah, William Sanderson, Brion James, Joe Turkel, Joanna Cassidy, James Hong.

A cinematic tour de force that ranks with the cornerstones of futuristic megalopolis visions—*Metropolis* (1926) and *Things to Come* (1936)—but solely on a visual level. It's Los Angeles, in the year 2019, and the combined talents of Ridley Scott, cinematographer Jordan Cronenweth, and production designer Lawrence G. Paull have created a world that is a mad mix of ancient Mayan architecture, rainy urban Saigon, smoggy Los Angeles, neon Times Square, and 1920s art deco. Traversing this seedy landscape is the morose and detached Deckard (Ford), a "blade runner" whose job is to "retire" (read: kill) errant androids who've escaped their work camps and traveled to Earth. In this case, four punkish and very deadly androids—led by white-haired *uber*-Replicant Roy Baty (Hauer)—are stalking their inventor, Tyrell (Turkel), in order to get a new lease on their four-year life span. Based on Philip K. Dick's novel *Do Androids Dream of Electric Sheep?*, the film's muddled narrative raises questions about what it means to be human but curiously leaves the viewer coldly disconnected to any of the characters. Darryl Hannah is a wonder as Pris, whose acrobatic assault on Deckard provides the film's one true moment of life. The poorly written, though informative and oddly endearing, film noir voice-over was excised, as was the upbeat ending in the "Director's Cut"—an increasingly frequent endeavor that has as much to do with laser disc marketing as it does with aesthetic intentions. "To enjoy *Blade Runner*, you need only disregard, as far as possible, the actors and dialogue" (Stanley Kauffman, *The New Republic*, July 19, 26, 1982).

Awards: Academy Award nominations for Art Direction, Best Visual Effects; included in the Library of Congress' National Film Registry (1993).

BLANK, LES. Born November 27, 1935; director. One of the most important recorders of regional American culture, documentarian Blank is best known for *Burden of Dreams*, a feature-length look at the obsessive vision of director Werner Herzog during the making of *Fitzcarraldo*. Drawn to such celebratory times as Mardi Gras (*Always for Pleasure*) and polka dancing (*In Heaven There Is No Beer?*), Blank makes offbeat short films that are about fun and gratification; a quick glance at his film titles spells out Blank's interests—the blues, dance, pleasure, hot pepper, garlic, beer, creole cooking, yum, yum, yum!—and he perfectly captures the essence of these interests in his films. His *Chulas Fronteras* has been included in the Library of Congress' National Film Registry.

Filmography: Dizzy Gillespie (1965); The Blues Accordin' to Lightnin' Hopkins (1968); God Respects Us When We Work but Loves Us When We Dance (1968); Spend It All (1971); A Well Spent Life (1971); Dry Wood (1973); Hot Pepper (1973); Chulas Fronteras (1976); Always for Pleasure (1978); Del Mero Corazon (1979); Poto and Cabengo (1979); Chicken Real (1980); Garlic Is as Good as Ten Mothers (1980); Werner Herzog Eats His Shoes (1980); Burden of Dreams (1982); In Heaven There Is No Beer? (1983); Sprout Wings and Fly (1983); Turumba (1983); In the Land of Owl Turds (1987); J'ai Ete au Bal (1989); Yum, Yum, Yum! A Taste of Cajun and Creole Cooking (1990).

Honor: American Film Institute Maya Deren Award for Lifetime Achievement (1990).

BLAZING SADDLES (1974), comedy/western. Directed and cowritten by Mel Brooks; screenplay with Andrew Bergman, Richard Pryor, Norman Steinberg, Alan Uger; produced by Michael Hertzberg; photographed by Joseph Biroc; edited by John C. Howard and Danford Greene; music by John Morris; song "Blazing Saddles" by Morris and Brooks, sung by Frankie Laine; released by Warner Bros.; 93 minutes. *Cast*: Cleavon Little, Gene Wilder, Slim Pickens, David Huddleston, Liam Dunn, Alex Karras, John Hillerman, George Furth, Mel Brooks, Harvey Korman, Madeline Kahn, Dom DeLuise, Richard Collier, Count Basie.

A massive audience-pleaser that is of debatable worth as a comedy, *Blazing*

Saddles is a picture that wallows in infantile humor, racist and homosexual epithets, and moderately witty absurdities. The inane plot begins as evil developer Hedley Lamarr (Korman) tries, with the help of the lascivious Governor Le Petomane (Brooks), to swindle a desert town out of its land by appointing a black sheriff and throwing the town into a state of chaos. Although the racist locals are ready to kill Sheriff Bart (Little), he is befriended by the quick-drawing gunslinger Jim (Wilder), and together they plot to save the town. The huge commercial success of the film—it grossed $45 million upon its release—probably says more about the times than about the film itself. Former Detroit Lion football player Alex Karras is memorable as Mongo, the horse-slugging maniac; Little makes the best of his two-dimensional sheriff; and Kahn is amusing in a rather predictable parody of Marlene Dietrich. Overall, however, the film smacks of a vaudeville routine gone sour.

Awards: Academy Award nominations for Best Supporting Actress (Kahn), Editing, Song; WGA Award.

BLOOD SIMPLE (1984), crime/thriller. Directed and cowritten by Joel Coen; produced and cowritten by Ethan Coen; photographed by Barry Sonnenfeld; edited by Roderick Jaynes, Don Wiegmann, and Peggy Connolly; music by Carter Burwell; released by Circle Films; 97 minutes. *Cast*: John Getz, Frances McDormand, Dan Hedaya, M. Emmet Walsh, Samm-Art Williams.

The remarkably assured debut feature from the Coen brothers, which is so packed with film noir influences that it feels as if it must have been based on some undiscovered James M. Cain novel. With the same seething passions as *The Postman Always Rings Twice* and *Double Indemnity*, the intrigue revolves around the double-crossing of Visser (Walsh), a vile private eye who is contracted by bar owner Marty (Hedaya) to kill his adulterous wife, Abby (McDormand), and her lover, Ray (Getz). When Visser instead empties his gun into Marty, a chain reaction of unpredicted twists occurs. Replete with playful and stylish camera work by Barry Sonnenfeld, brilliantly understated performances (especially the naturalistic McDormand), and an intricately woven plot, *Blood Simple* set the stage for the Coens' subsequent successes.

BLOW OUT (1981), thriller. Directed and written by Brian De Palma; produced by George Litto; photographed by Vilmos Zsigmond; edited by Paul Hirsch; music by Pino Donaggio; released by Filmways; 108 minutes. *Cast*: John Travolta, Nancy Allen, John Lithgow, Dennis Franz, Peter Boyden.

After a succession of obvious Hitchcockian derivations, De Palma stands his influences on ear with this genre-transcending mix of politics, horror, and thriller that grabs pieces of the tragedy at Chappaquiddick, the cover-up of Watergate, the high-tech surveillance gadgetry of *The Conversation*, and the deconstruction of Antonioni's like-titled, visual parallel *Blow-Up*. John Travolta (in a performance that proves that his 1990s resurgence is no fluke) stars as Jack Terry, a sound engineer who records effects for trashy horror and porno films. One evening, Jack captures the sounds of a car swerving off a bridge and into the water. Inside the submerged car a popular presidential candidate has drowned, but Jack is able to save his prostitute companion Sally (Allen). Although everyone believes the candidate's death to be accidental, Jack's audiotape (combined with a film taken by Franz's Manny Karp) proves that the tire blowout was actually caused by a gunshot. By wiring Sally, Jack attempts to prove his theory, but things go terribly wrong. The final sequence in which Sally's blood-curdling death scream is used as a sound effect in a cheap horror movie while a tormented Jack tries to block out the guilt is a brilliant De Palma moment that twists reality and film into an impossible knot.

BLUE VELVET (1986), thriller. Directed and written by David Lynch; produced by Fred Caruso; photographed by Frederick Elmes; edited by Duwayne Dunham; music by Angelo Badalamenti; released by the De Laurentiis Entertainment Group (DEG); 120 minutes. *Cast*: Dennis Hopper, Kyle MacLachlan, Laura Dern, Dean Stockwell, Brad Dourif, Isabella Rossellini, Hope Lange.

A masterpiece of twisted Americana that probes deep under the blue skies, red roses, green grass, and white picket fences of cheery Lumberton, North Carolina, and settles underneath in its bug-infested soil. Jeffrey Beaumont (MacLachlan) and Sandy (Dern) are the archetypical good-kids-in-love who, via a victimized lounge singer (Rossellini), get sucked into a mysterious sadomasochistic underworld reigned over by the inherently evil Frank Booth (Hopper). A surrealistic mélange of taboo images fills the screen in this lush, modernized reworking of the small town evil that Hitchcock uncovered in his *Shadow of a Doubt*. Exquisitely photographed by Frederick Elmes and featuring a dreamy orchestral score by Angelo Badalamenti. "One of the most original films in years, Blue Velvet has not only split critical and public opinion down the center it has, in the process, become a strange cultural phenomenon" (*The Motion Picture Guide*).

Honors: Academy Award nomination for Best Director; Los Angeles Film Critics Awards for Best Director and Supporting Actor.

BODY HEAT (1981), film noir. Directed and written by Lawrence Kasdan; produced by Fred T. Gallo; photographed by Richard H. Kline; edited by Carl Littleton; music by John Barry; released by Warner Bros.; 113 minutes. *Cast*: William Hurt, Kathleen Turner, Richard Crenna, Ted Danson, J. A. Preston, Mickey Rourke.

With blazing fires lighting the Florida night and glistening bodies intertwined on the bedsheets, one can almost feel the heat coming from the screen in this debut feature from Lawrence Kasdan. Matty Walker (Turner) is a classic femme fatale, a sultry vision in a tempting white dress whose body temperature runs a couple of degrees high. Immediately lured into her web is Ned Racine (Hurt), a local, not-so-smart lawyer who follows his libido right to her front door. Together they carry out the murder of Matty's husband, and only then does Ned realize that he's no match for this black widow. Kasdan, having already proven his mettle as a master of genre pieces with his screenplays for *The Empire Strikes Back* and *Raiders of the Lost Ark*, here turns to the film noir stylings of *Double Indemnity* and *The Postman Always Rings Twice* for this tale of lust, murder, and double crosses. Although the story is familiar, and the characters genre archetypes, he gives it all a decidedly modern spin by freeing the characters from the constraints of their clothes—the naked flesh drips sweat, hands grope and squeeze body parts, legs part, and lovers moan. The "sex" scenes between Fred MacMurray and Barbara Stanwyck never looked like this; nor were they meant to. The 1940s and 1950s films noir carefully and inventively danced around the main issue—sex; in *Body Heat*, we finally see the sexual passion that was hinted at for so long.

BOGDANOVICH, PETER. Born July 30, 1939, in Kingston, New York; director. Married to actor L. B. Straten; formerly married to producer and production designer Polly Platt. Having studied with Stella Adler at age fifteen prior to directing summer theater and a few off-Broadway productions (notably Clifford Odets' *The Big Knife* in 1959–1960), Bogdanovich found work authoring monographs for the Museum of Modern Art film series in the early 1960s before following the French model of film critics turned directors. After cutting his teeth on a couple of Roger Corman pictures in the mid-1960s, he was given an opportunity to write and direct *Targets*—one of the most ingenious comments about the influence of movies on the criminal mind. However, his next picture, *The Last Picture Show*, put him at the forefront of Hollywood's auteur-driven filmmakers of the early 1970s. Praised in *Newsweek* as "the greatest American film since *Citizen Kane*," the dusty, elegiac tale of love and adolescence in a small Texas town not only captured the look and feel of classic Hollywood cinema but also featured early performances by Jeff Bridges, Timothy Bottoms, and Cybill Shepherd. Two more hit pictures followed—*What's Up, Doc?*, his first foray into screwball comedy, and *Paper Moon*, the beautiful depression-era story of a father and daughter. His career spiraled downward with the release of his next three pictures—*Daisy Miller*, *At Long Last Love*, and *Nickelodeon*. Since then Bogdanovich has made a number of little-seen and underappreciated pictures with only his 1985 Cher-starrer *Mask* finding an audience. *Saint Jack* is a gutsy look at a prostitution ring in Singapore; *They All Laughed* and *Illegally Yours* are both respectable additions to the screwball comedy genre; and *The Last Picture Show* sequel, *Texasville*, is an interesting commentary on midlife that expectedly falls short of its predecessor. *The Thing Called Love*, however, is one of his best films since the early 1970s—a four-character relationship piece set against the backdrop of Nashville's country music scene. Unfortunately, despite the star power of River Phoenix (whose death hampered the film's release) and the rising stock of Sandra Bullock and Samantha Mathis, the film received only a regional release and was quickly relegated to video store shelves. Often overshadowing his work, Bogdanovich's high-profile public life has included an eight-year romance with Cybill Shepherd; a friendship with *Playboy*'s Hugh Hefner; an engagement to former *Playboy* centerfold and *They All Laughed* star Dorothy Stratten, who was later brutally murdered; a subsequent book by Bogdanovich titled *The Killing of the Unicorn*, which dealt with the murder; and his eventual marriage to Dorothy's half sister L. B. Stratten. Bogdanovich has written *The Cinema of Orson Welles*, *The Cinema of Howard Hawks*, *The Cinema of Alfred Hitchcock*, *Fritz Lang in America*, *John Ford*, *Allan Dwan: The Last Pioneer*, and a collection of essays titled *Pieces of Time*. ''Despite his devotion to such humanists as Renoir and McCarey, the director's true mentor—in style, spirit and masterly direction of actors—is that ultimate technician, William Wyler'' (Richard Corliss, *Cinema: A Critical Dictionary*).

Filmography: Targets (1968) also producer, screenplay, editor, actor; Directed by John Ford (1971) also screenplay; The Last Picture Show (1971) also screenplay; What's Up, Doc? (1972) also producer and story; Paper Moon (1973) also producer; Daisy Miller (1974) also producer; At Long Last Love (1975); Nickelodeon (1976) also screenplay; Saint Jack (1979) also screenplay, actor; They All Laughed (1981); Mask (1985); Illegally Yours (1988) also producer; Texasville (1990) also producer; Noises Off (1992) also producer; The Thing Called Love (1994).

Additional Credits: Voyage to the Planet of Prehistoric Women (1965) additional direction, uncredited; The Wild Angels (1966) 2d unit director, coeditor, coscreenplay (all uncredited), actor; The Trip (1967) actor; Lion's Love (1969) actor; The Other Side of the Wind (1970, unreleased) actor; F for Fake (1973) voice; Diaries, Notes and Sketches—Volume 1 Reels 1–6: Lost Lost Lost (1975) actor; Opening Night (1978) actor; The City Girl (1983) ep.

Honors: Academy Award nominations for Best Director and Screenplay (*The Last Picture Show*); New York Film Critics Circle Award for Best Screenplay (*The Last Picture Show*); Venice Film Festival Critics Circle Prize (*Saint Jack*).

Selected bibliography

Sherman, Eric, and Martin Rubin. *The Director's Event*. New York: Signet, 1972.
Yule, Andrew. *Picture Shows: The Life and Films of Peter Bogdanovich*. New York: Limelight, 1992.

BONNIE AND CLYDE (1967), crime/gangster. Directed by Arthur Penn; screenplay by Robert Benton and David Newman; photographed by Burnett Guffey; edited by Dede Allen; music by Charles Strouse, song ''Foggy Mountain Breakdown'' by Flatt and Scruggs; released by Warner Bros.; 111 minutes. *Cast*: Warren Beatty, Faye Dunaway, Michael J. Pollard, Gene Hackman, Estelle Parsons, Denver Pyle, Dub Taylor, Evans Evans, Gene Wilder.

The most controversial American film of the late 1960s, Arthur Penn's glorification of Bonnie Parker and Clyde Barrow is, in retrospect, neither a masterpiece (as its defenders claim) nor claptrap (as its now-silenced critics once shouted). Under Penn's inspired direction of Robert Benton and David Newman's script, the film is a nostalgic, rollicking ride with gleefully charismatic performances, knee-slapping Flatt and Scruggs banjo music, and playful car chases in Keystonian fast motion. From the sexually charged opening scene as the naked Bonnie inquires of Clyde, "Hey boyyy-oyyy! What you doin' with my mama's car?" to Clyde's assertive "We rob banks," to the final bloody ambush, *Bonnie and Clyde* is a delirious piece of entertainment inspired by the playful cinema of the French New Wave's François Truffaut and Jean-Luc Godard (both of whom were offered the script before Penn). Now, nearly thirty years later, the film, as engaging as it is, feels like a misguided attempt to glamorize the lives of two brutal killers (the unattractive Bonnie and the homosexual Clyde) by casting ravishing movie stars Faye Dunaway and Warren Beatty. While Penn's film once belonged to the counterculture of the 1960s (it parallels the superior *Easy Rider* in its antiestablishment values), it seems curiously out of step with that generation's call for truth and integrity. It now feels closer to the Hollywood of the 1930s with its blatant disregard for truth, its focus on glamour, and its Hays code "Crime Doesn't Pay" ending. "There is *evil* in the *tone* of the writing, acting and direction of this film, the calculated effect of which is to incite in the young the delusion that armed robbery and murder are mere 'happenings'" (Page Cook, *Films in Review*, October 1967). "*Bonnie and Clyde* opened the bloodgates, and our cinema has barely stopped bleeding since" (Robert Phillip Kolker, *A Cinema of Loneliness*).

Awards: Academy Awards for Supporting Actress (Parsons), Cinematography; Academy Award nominations for Picture, Director, Actor, Actress, Supporting Actor (Hackman, Pollard), Screenplay, Costumes; New York Film Critics Circle Award for Screenplay; WGA Award; included in the Library of Congress' National Film Registry (1992).

BOYLE, PETER. Born October 18, 1933, in Philadelphia; actor. Bearish, muscular, balding actor and former Christian Brothers monk who often dons a knit cap to play various working-class thugs, blackmailers, and bone-crunchers. As working-class bigot Joe Curran in *Joe* he tapped into the right-wing, antihippie rage prevalent of the times to create a brutal, profanity-spewing antihero. Additional roles as the campaign manager in *The Candidate* and as the bartender in *The Friends of Eddie Coyle* helped establish him as a charismatic, rough-edged performer—an image that was greatly altered when Mel Brooks cast him as the Monster in *Young Frankenstein*. Drawing on his Second City comedy training, Boyle perfectly combined a keen comic timing and a genuine softness with the necessary sense of menace associated with the role. Unfortunately, after appearing as a cabbie in *Taxi Driver* and as Senator Joe McCarthy in the television production of *Tail Gunner Joe*, his career took a downward turn. He appeared in one turkey after another, occasionally surfacing in such honorable failures as Wim Wenders' *Hammett* or Alex Cox's *Walker*. Signs of a resurgence have begun to show in the 1990s with *The Shadow* and *While You Were Sleeping* and a recurring role on "NYPD Blue" as an Alcoholics Anonymous counselor.

Filmography: The Virgin President (1968); Medium Cool (1969); Diary of a Mad

Housewife (1970); Joe (1970); T. R. Baskin (1971); The Candidate (1972); Crazy Joe (1973); The Friends of Eddie Coyle (1973); Ghost in the Noonday Sun (1973); Kid Blue (1973); Slither (1973); Steelyard Blues (1973); Young Frankenstein (1974); Swashbuckler (1976); Taxi Driver (1976); Tail Gunner Joe (1977, tvm); The Brink's Job (1978); F.I.S.T. (1978); Beyond the Poseidon Adventure (1979); Hardcore (1979); From Here to Eternity (1979, tvms and series); In God We Trust (1980); Where the Buffalo Roam (1980); Outland (1981); Hammett (1982); Yellowbeard (1983); Johnny Dangerously (1984); Turk 182 (1985); Joe Bash (1986, tvs); The In Crowd (1987); Surrender (1987); Walker (1987); Conspiracy: The Trial of the Chicago Seven (1987, ctvm); Funny (1988); Red Heat (1988); The Dream Team (1988); Guts and Glory: The Rise and Fall of Oliver North (1989, tvm); Speed Zone (1989); Men of Respect (1990); Solar Crisis (1990); Shadow of the Wolf: Kickboxer II (1991); The Santa Clause (1994); Killer (1994); The Shadow (1994); "NYPD Blue" (1994–1995, tvs); While You Were Sleeping (1995).

Honor: Emmy Award for Best Guest Actor ("The X-Files" 1995).

BOYZ N THE HOOD (1991), drama. Directed and written by John Singleton; produced by Steve Nicolaides; photographed by Charles Mills; edited by Bruce Cannon; music by Stanley Clarke; released by Columbia Pictures; 107 minutes. *Cast*: Lawrence Fishburne, Ice Cube, Cuba Gooding, Jr., Nia Long, Morris Chestnut, Tyra Ferrell, Angela Bassett.

A refreshingly simple and pure piece of filmmaking that, unlike so many contemporary pictures from young directors, values story and acting over the smoke screen of bravura camera work and editing. Set in the Crenshaw district of South Central Los Angeles, the film contrasts the hope-filled future of high school senior Tre Styles (Gooding, Jr.) with the portentous hopelessness of his best friend, aspiring football star Ricky Baker (Chestnut), and Ricky's older, ex-con brother Doughboy (Ice Cube). The key difference between Tre and the Baker brothers is the influence of a father; Ricky and Doughboy have no male authority figure in their lives, while Tre has the guidance of his ethical and loving father Furious Styles (Fishburne). Confidently directed by the twenty-three-year-old John Singleton (his debut), the film is a remarkable comment on the plague of black-on-black violence that ends with the optimistic "Increase the Peace" message. His Oscar nomination for Best Direction made him the youngest person ever to receive that honor. "Singleton brings out the insane combustibility in ordinary encounters—the jostling among teenagers that ends with guns blazing" (David Denby, *New York*, July 22, 1991).

Awards: Academy Award nominations for Best Director, Screenplay; New York Film Critics Circle Award for Best New Director; Los Angeles Film Critics New Generation Award.

BRANDO, MARLON. Born April 3, 1924, in Omaha, Nebraska; actor, director. The actor who changed film acting with his provocative and expressionistic Method style, shattering the stage-bound technique of all who preceded him and influencing all who followed. By the mid-1960s, however, Brando, uncomfortable with his phenomenal success, had purposely turned his image against itself and, as a result, lost most of his audience. As the suffering, horse-loving wanderer in *The Appaloosa*, the pummeled sheriff in *The Chase*, and the whip-snapping, latent homosexual southerner in John Huston's *Reflections in a Golden Eye*, Brando settled into a position he had only flirted with in such films as *The Teahouse of the August Moon*—that of an artistic explorer who was more concerned with pushing himself than catering to audience expectations. While gambles such as Charles Chaplin's *A Countess from Hong Kong* failed, Gillo Pontecorvo's allegorical Marxist adventure *Burn!* paid off artistically if not commercially. By 1972, Brando had all but been erased from the Hollywood slate, only to reemerge in two of his finest roles—the omnipotent Don Vito Corleone of *The Godfather* and the despairing widower Paul of *Last Tango in Paris*, both of which earned him the sort of raves that recalled Stanley Kowalski and Terry Malloy. Every gesture, from the Don's jowl scratching to the dying Paul's removal of the gum from his mouth is imbued with, and modulated by, a genius level of awareness that has no match in American film. A force of nature as unpredictable and powerful as the weather, the physically expanding Brando then set off on a career that is equal parts madness, whimsy, and passion, winding out the 1980s with just three more film roles—the giddy gunfighter in *The Missouri Breaks*; the $3 million cameo as Jor-El, father of *Superman*; and the magnetic mumblings of Colonel Kurtz in *Apocalypse Now*. After a rare television appearance as an American neo-Nazi in *Roots: The Next Generations* and a playful role as a Milk-Dud popping tycoon in *The Formula*, he announced one of his frequent retirements only to return in Euzhan Palcy's antiapartheid film *A Dry White Season*. After the monotonous excess of *Christopher Columbus: The Discovery*, Brando turned to a pair of intelligent comedies in which he costarred with two popular young actors—opposite Matthew Broderick in *The Freshman*, as Carmine Sabatini, a fictional character on whom Don Vito Corleone was based (a self-reflexive twist on movie reality), and opposite Johnny Depp in *Don Juan DeMarco*, as a jaded psychotherapist who rediscovers romance through a supposedly crazy patient. His enigmatic autobiography *Songs My Mother Taught Me* was published in 1994. "It was as if *The Godfather* and *Last Tango in Paris* exhausted him. . . . His final disguise is as a fat man too lazy to learn his lines, pasting them on the camera, on his fellow performers' foreheads for the closeup" (Richard Schickel, *Film Comment*, February 1985).

Filmography of key pre-1965 films: The Men (1950); A Streetcar Named Desire (1951); Viva Zapata! (1952); Julius Caesar (1952); The Wild One (1953); On the Waterfront (1954); Guys and Dolls (1955); Sayonara (1957); The Fugitive Kind (1960); One-Eyed Jacks (1961) also director; Mutiny on the Bounty (1962).

Filmography since 1965: The Appaloosa/Southwest to Sonora (1966); The Chase (1966); A Countess from Hong Kong (1967); Reflections in a Golden Eye (1967); Candy (1968); The Night of the Following Day (1968); Burn!/Quemada! (1969); The Nightcomers (1971); The Godfather (1972); Last Tango in Paris (1972); The Missouri Breaks (1976); Superman (1978); Apocalypse Now (1979); Roots: The Next Generations (1979, tvms); The Formula (1980); A Dry White Season (1989); Christopher Columbus: The Discovery (1992); The Freshman (1990); Don Juan DeMarco (1995).

Honors: Academy Awards for Best Actor (*On the Waterfront, The Godfather*); Academy Award nominations for Best Actor (*A Streetcar Named Desire, Viva Zapata!, Julius Caesar, Sayonara, Last Tango in Paris*) and Supporting Actor (*A Dry White Season*); Cannes Film Festival Awards for Best Actor (*Viva Zapata!, On the Waterfront*); New York Film Critics Circle Awards for Best Actor (*On the Waterfront, Last Tango in Paris*); Emmy for Best Supporting Actor (*Roots: The Next Generations*).

Selected bibliography

Brando, Marlon, and Robert Lindsey. *Songs My Mother Taught Me*. New York: Random House, 1994.

Grobel, Lawrence. *Conversations with Brando*. New York: Hyperion, 1991.

Manso, Peter. *Brando: The Biography*. New York: Hyperion, 1994.

Schickel, Richard. *Brando: A Life in Our Times*. New York: Macmillan, 1991.

BRIDGES, JEFF. Born December 4, 1949, in Los Angeles; actor. Father is Lloyd Bridges; brother is Beau Bridges. Distinctly American leading man with an effortless, somewhat cocky manner who is arguably one of the most under-appreciated actors of his day. Like his brother, he appeared frequently with his father on television's "Sea Hunt" (1957–1961) before coming into his own in *The Last Picture Show* as Duane Jackson, the small-town football hero in love with the sultry Jacy Farrow. In the twenty-five years that have followed, Bridges has had a remarkably solid career playing emotional cripples, drifters, failures, and dreamers in such pictures as Robert Benton's *Bad Company*, John Huston's *Fat City*, William Richtert's *Winter Kills*, Michael Cimino's *Thunderbolt and Lightfoot*, Bob Rafelson's *Stay Hungry*, Ivan Passer's *Cutter's Way*, and Martin Bell's *American Heart* (an impressive physical transformation with his long hair and full mustache). Despite a few real duds (*King Kong, Blown Away*), he has been a consistently impressive performer who never fails to bring a sense of passion to his characters. Among the best of his more recent characters are the obsessed auto designer Preston Tucker in Francis Ford Coppola's *Tucker: The Man and His Dream*, piano man Jack Baker in Steve Kloves' *The Fabulous Baker Boys*, the spiritually renewed plane crash survivor in Peter Weir's *Fearless*, and the guilt-ridden radio host in Terry Gilliam's *The Fisher King*. "He's the most American—and loosest—of all the young actors, unencumbered by stage diction and the stiff, emasculated poses of most juveniles" (Pauline Kael, *New Yorker*, October 1, 1973). "Jeff Bridges is as close as the modern era has come to Robert Mitchum" (David Thomson, *A Biographical Dictionary of Film*).

Filmography: The Company She Keeps (1950); Halls of Anger (1970); The Last Picture Show (1971); Bad Company (1972); Fat City (1972); The Iceman Cometh (1973); The Last American Hero (1973); Lolly-Madonna XXX (1973); Rancho Deluxe (1974); Thunderbolt and Lightfoot (1974); Hearts of the West (1975); Stay Hungry (1975); King Kong (1976); Somebody Killed Her Husband (1978); American Success Company (1979);

Winter Kills (1979); Heaven's Gate (1980); Cutter's Way (1981); Kiss Me Goodbye (1982); The Last Unicorn (1982); Tron (1982); Against All Odds (1983); Starman (1984); Jagged Edge (1985); 8 Million Ways to Die (1986); The Morning After (1986); Nadine (1987); Tucker: The Man and His Dream (1988); The Fabulous Baker Boys (1989); See You in the Morning (1989); Texasville (1990); The Fisher King (1991); Fearless (1993) American Heart (1992) also producer; The Vanishing (1993); Blown Away (1994); Wild Bill (1995).

Honors: Academy Award nominations for Best Actor (*Starman*) and Best Supporting Actor (*The Last Picture Show*, *Thunderbolt and Lightfoot*); Independent Spirit Award for Best Actor (*American Heart*).

BROADCAST NEWS (1987), romantic comedy. Directed, written, and coproduced by James L. Brooks; produced with Penney Finkelman Cox; photographed by Michael Ballhaus; edited by Richard Marks; music by Bill Conti; released by 20th Century Fox; 131 minutes. *Cast*: William Hurt, Holly Hunter, Albert Brooks, Robert Prosky, Lois Chiles, Joan Cusack, Jack Nicholson.

This touching and sarcastic study of three television newsroom personalities features the superb writing and direction of James L. Brooks (who tackled the same milieu in television's "The Mary Tyler Moore Show") and the flawless performances of Hurt, Hunter, and Brooks. Hurt is Tom Grunick, a handsome, but shallow, news anchor who doesn't understand much of what he reports. Hunter is Jane Craig, a producer and consummate professional (no family, no social life). Brooks is her best friend, the hilarious Aaron Altman, a cynical veteran correspondent who dreams of anchoring. The pivotal scene is when Tom sheds a tear during a piece on date rape—Aaron is appalled at the phony sensitivity, Jane is moved, and we later learn that Tom's tear is fake. "A wholly entertaining film that boasts three of the finest performances to grace the screen in 1987" (*The 1988 Motion Picture Annual*).

Honors: Academy Award nominations for Best Picture, Actor (Hurt); Actress (Hunter); Supporting Actor (Brooks); Screenplay; Cinematography; Editing; Los Angeles Film Critics Award for Best Actress; New York Film Critics Circle Awards for Best Picture, Director, Actress, Actor (Nicholson), Screenplay; 38th Berlin International Film Festival Award for Best Actress.

BRODERICK, MATTHEW. Born March 21, 1962, in New York City; actor. Son of actor James Broderick. Talented, boyish young actor who is probably still best known as the computer whiz in the high-tech thriller *WarGames* and the star of John Hughes' self-reflexive teen adventure *Ferris Bueller's Day Off*. Better known for comedy and light drama, he turned in a remarkable dramatic performance as Robert Gould Shaw in the Civil War drama *Glory* and again as Charles MacArthur in *Mrs. Parker and the Vicious Circle*. While he has yet to achieve a level of box office success in movies that define one as a star, he has received his due accolades on stage with his 1995 Tony for the Broadway production of *How to Succeed in Business Without Really Trying*.

Filmography: Max Dugan Returns (1982); WarGames (1983); 1918 (1985); Ladyhawke (1985); Ferris Bueller's Day Off (1986); On Valentine's Day (1986); Project X (1987); Biloxi Blues (1988); Torch Song Trilogy (1988); Family Business (1989); Glory (1989); The Freshman (1990); Out on a Limb (1992); The Night We Never Met (1993); A Life in the Theatre (1994, ctvm); The Road to Wellville (1994); The Lion King (1994) voice; (1994); Arabian Nights (1995) voice.

Honors: Tony Awards (*Brighton Beach Memoirs* 1983, *How to Succeed in Business Without Really Trying* 1995).

BRONSON, CHARLES. Born Charles Buchinsky November 3, 1921, in Ehrenfield, Pennsylvania; actor. Married to actor Jill Ireland until her death in 1990. Craggy-faced, narrow-eyed leading man who played the cold-blooded killer in numerous action pictures in the 1950s and 1960s (most notably *Machine Gun Kelly*, *The Magnificent Seven*, *The Great Escape*, and *The Dirty Dozen*) before gaining international attention as the enigmatic and almost wordless Harmonica in *Once Upon a Time in the West*. His career was soon overshadowed by the arrival of Clint Eastwood, whose similar strong and silent persona brought him superstardom under the direction of Don Siegel. While Bronson did appear in a number of entertaining, if exceedingly violent, actioners (many directed by Michael Winner), his star never shone as bright as Eastwood's. He did, however, occasionally surprise with *Mr. Majestyk*, *Hard Times*, *Breakheart Pass*, and *Death Wish*. The latter features his vigilante character Paul Kersey, which preceded Stallone's John Rambo by many years.

Filmography of key pre-1965 films: Pat and Mike (1952); Apache (1954); Vera Cruz (1954); Run of the Arrow (1957); Machine Gun Kelly (1958); The Magnificent Seven (1960); The Great Escape (1963).

Filmography since 1965: Battle of the Bulge (1965); The Sandpiper (1965); This Property Is Condemned (1966); The Dirty Dozen (1967); Guns for San Sebastian (1968); Villa Rides (1968); Once Upon a Time in the West (1968); Rider on the Rain (1970); Twinky (1970); Violent City (1970); Cold Sweat (1971); Someone behind the Door (1971); Red Sun (1971); Chato's Land (1972); The Mechanic (1972); The Valachi Papers (1972); The Stone Killer (1973); Valdez il Mezzosangue (1973); Death Wish (1974); Mr. Majestyk (1974); Breakheart Pass (1975); Breakout (1975); Hard Times (1975); From Noon till Three (1976); St. Ives (1976); Telefon (1977); The White Buffalo (1977); Love and Bullets (1979); Borderline (1980); Cabablanco (1980); Death Hunt (1981); Death Wish II (1981); 10 to Midnight (1983); The Evil That Men Do (1984); Death Wish 3 (1985); Murphy's Law (1986); Assassination (1987); Death Wish 4: The Crackdown (1987); Messenger of Death (1988); Kinjite: Forbidden Subjects (1989); The Indian Runner (1991); Donatto and Daughter (1993); Death Wish V: The Face of Death (1993).

Selected bibliography

Downing, David. *Charles Bronson*. New York: St. Martin's Press, 1983.
Vermilye, Jerry. *The Films of Charles Bronson*. New York: Citadel, 1980.

BROOKS, ALBERT. Born Albert Einstein July 22, 1947, in Los Angeles; actor, director, screenwriter, comedian. Brother Bob is television stunt comic Super Dave Osborne; father, Harry Einstein, was late comic Parkyakarkus. Biting satirist who had established himself as a television performer (''The Steve Allen Show'') and stand-up comic (with the albums ''Comedy Minus One'') before his memorable film debut in *Taxi Driver* as the campaign worker who becomes stressed when his order of political buttons reads ''We *Are* the People'' instead of ''*We* Are the People.'' He later earned an Oscar nomination for his hilarious turn as the cynical, aspiring network news anchor Aaron Altman in *Broadcast News*. His four films as director have, just in their titles alone, been barbed observations of American life, specifically, family (*Real Life*, a parody of the PBS series ''An American Family''), love (*Modern Romance*), yuppie ideals (*Lost in America*), and death (*Defending Your Life*). While Woody Allen has been busy perennially turning out neurotic adult comedies, Albert Brooks has steadily proven to be the director with the keener obervation of middle-class angst.

Filmography as director: Real Life (1978); Modern Romance (1981); Lost in America (1985); Defending Your Life (1991).

Filmography as actor: Taxi Driver (1976); Private Benjamin (1980); Twilight Zone—The Movie (1983); Unfaithfully Yours (1983); Broadcast News (1987); I'll Do Anything (1994); The Scout (1994) also screenplay.

Honor: Academy Award nomination for Best Supporting Actor (*Broadcast News*).

BROOKS, JAMES L. Born May 9, 1940, in North Bergen, New Jersey; director, screenwriter, producer. Establishing himself as a creative force in television with such landmark shows as ''Room 222,'' ''The Mary Tyler Moore Show,'' and ''Taxi'' and years later with ''The Simpsons,'' he has shown repeatedly his remarkable ability to mirror the attitudes, hopes, and concerns of real people. He focused this acute perception on the big screen with two of the most popular and acclaimed movies of the 1980s—his emotionally wrenching adaptation of Larry McMurtry's novel *Terms of Endearment* (earning him writing, producing, and directing Oscars), and the smart television-themed comedy *Broadcast News* (earning a pair of Oscar nominations). Over the next few years, he focused his producing skills on films for Penny Marshall (*Big*), Cameron Crowe (*Say Anything*), and Danny DeVito (*The War of the Roses*) before hopping back in the director's chair with his commercially and critically disregarded comedy (and aborted musical) *I'll Do Anything*.

Filmography as director, writer, producer: Terms of Endearment (1983); Broadcast News (1987); I'll Do Anything (1994).

Additional credits: ''Room 222'' (1969–1974, tvs); ''The Mary Tyler Moore Show'' (1970–1977, tvs); ''Rhoda'' (1974–1978, tvs); ''Taxi'' (1978–1983, tvs); Real Life (1978) actor; Starting Over (1979) producer, writer; Modern Romance (1981) actor; ''The Tracey Ullman Show'' (1987–1990, tvs); Big (1988) producer; Say Anything (1989) ep;

The War of the Roses (1989) producer; "The Simpsons" (1990– , tvs); "The Critic" (1994– , tvs).

Honors: Academy Awards for Best Picture, Director, and Screenplay (*Terms of Endearment*); Academy Award nominations for Best Picture and Screenplay (*Broadcast News*); DGA Award (*Terms of Endearment*); Los Angeles Film Critics Award for Best Director (*Terms of Endearment*); New York Film Critics Circle Awards for Best Picture, Director, and Screenplay (*Broadcast News*); Emmy Awards for Best Comedy Series ("The Mary Tyler Moore Show" 1974, 1975, "Taxi" 1978, 1979, 1980, and "The Tracey Ullman Show" 1988), Best Writing ("The Mary Tyler Moore Show" 1970, 1976 and "The Tracey Ullman Show" 1989) and Best Animated Program ("The Simpsons" 1989, 1990, 1994).

BROOKS, MEL. Born Melvin Kaminsky June 28, 1926, in New York City; producer, director, screenwriter, actor. Married to Anne Bancroft. A broad, brash, and often hilarious comic best known for his genre spoofs. His ethnic brand of comedy was honed in television (as writer of "Your Show of Shows" and creator of "Get Smart") and found a wide audience in theatrical features. The zaniness began with his first film, *The Producers*, and peaked with the back-to-back success in 1974 of *Blazing Saddles* and *Young Frankenstein*, two of the most successful comedies of their time. As audience tastes move away from his infantile, vaudeville style of humor and his penchant for genre spoofs, nothing he has directed in the last two decades has even approached his previous successes. His company Brooksfilms, however, has produced a string of challenging dramatic films that include works by David Lynch (*The Elephant Man*) and David Cronenberg (*The Fly*). His audio collaboration with Carl Reiner on "The 2000-Year-Old Man" remains a comic classic and has been turned into an animated production.

Filmography: The Critic (1963) animated short as writer, narrator; The Producers (1967) also screenplay; The Twelve Chairs (1970) also screenplay, actor; Blazing Saddles (1974) also screenplay, actor; Young Frankenstein (1975) also screenplay; Silent Movie (1976) also screenplay, actor; High Anxiety (1977) also producer, screenplay, actor; History of the World Part I (1981) also actor, producer, screenplay; Spaceballs (1987) also actor, producer, screenplay; Life Stinks (1991) also actor, producer, screenplay; Robin Hood: Men in Tights (1993) also producer.
Additional credits: "Get Smart" (1965, tvs) cocreator; Putney Swope (1969) actor; Shinbone Alley (1971) from book; The Muppet Movie (1979) actor; The Elephant Man (1980) producer; Frances (1982) producer; To Be or Not to Be (1983) producer, actor; Sunset People (1984) actor; The Doctor and the Devils (1985) ep; 84 Charing Cross Road (1986) ep; The Fly (1986) ep; Solarbabies (1986) ep; Look Who's Talking Too (1990) actor; The Vagrant (1991) ep.

Honors: Academy Awards for Best Short Subject (*The Critic*), Screenplay (*The Producers*); Academy Award nominations for Best Screenplay (*Blazing Saddles*; *Young Frankenstein*); WGA Award (*The Producers*); Emmy Award for Best Writing ("The Sid Caesar, Imogene Coca, Carl Reiner, and Howard Morris Special" 1966).

BULLITT (1968), action/drama. Directed by Peter Yates; written by Alan R. Trustman and Harry Kleiner (from the novel by Robert L. Pike); produced by Philip D'Antoni; photographed by William Fraker; edited by Frank P. Keller; music by Lalo Schifrin; released by Warner Bros.; 113 minutes. *Cast*: Steve McQueen, Robert Vaughn, Jacqueline Bisset, Don Gordon, Robert Duvall, Simon Oakland, Norman Fell.

If for no other reason, the hyperkinetic car chase through the streets of San Francisco alone makes this Peter Yates-directed action film one of the most important films of the late 1960s. Not only did it influence William Friedkin's choreography of the breathtaking chase sequence in *The French Connection* (also from *Bullitt* producer Philip D'Antoni), but it became a mold for countless similar chases on film and television. The story, a modern-day film noir, follows Frank Bullitt (McQueen), a police detective who is assigned to protect a mobster for forty-eight hours until his Monday morning deposition. When the mobster is murdered, Bullitt has no choice but to keep the news from his superiors while trying to locate the killers. The story itself progresses rather slowly (especially the romance between McQueen and Bissett), but this only makes the chase sequence even more dynamic by contrast. Filled with screeching tires, fishtailing cars, scraping metal, it's shot after shot of high-octane filmmaking in which the danger is immediate and felt at every turn—a danger that most imitators have failed to replicate. "Probably the best car chase of the sound-film era" (William Friedkin, *Directors in Action*).

Award: Academy Award for Editing.

BULLOCK, SANDRA. Born July 26, 1964, in Arlington, Virgina; actor. Infectiously adorable leading lady who, in high school, was aptly voted "Most Likely to Brighten Your Day" and who, with her wit, beauty, energy, and sense of comic timing, has been rightly compared to Carol Lombard. She gained notice in 1993 as the delightful, wisecracking, futuristic police officer opposite Sylvester Stallone in *Demolition Man* and again in two less widely seen films of that year—Peter Bogdanovich's *A Thing Called Love* (as the dingy, musically inept Linda Sue Linden) and *Wrestling Ernest Hemingway*. However, the blood-pumping action film *Speed* turned her into a superstar. Her role as the surrogate bus driver enabled her to play the All-American girl-next-door who surprises even herself when she finds an inner strength that transforms her into an action hero. Later that year she continued to brighten the days of movie audiences with the romantic comedy *While You Were Sleeping* and even managed to turn the otherwise forgettable thriller *The Net* into a minor hit.

Filmography: Bionic Showdown: The Six Million Dollar Man and the Bionic Woman (1989, tvm); Religion Inc./A Fool and His Money (1990); Who Shot Patakango? (1989); The Preppie Murder (1989, tvm); "Working Girl" (1990, tvs); Love Potion No. 9 (1992); When the Party's Over (1992); Me and the Mob (1992); The Vanishing (1993); The Thing Called Love (1993); Demolition Man (1993); Wrestling Ernest Hemingway (1993); Speed (1994); While You Were Sleeping (1995); The Net (1995).

BURSTYN, ELLEN. Born Edna Rae Gillooly December 7, 1932, in Detroit, Michigan; actor. After undergoing a variety of name changes, she found success on Broadway as Ellen McRae in 1957's "Fair Game" and continued performing under that name until the 1970 Paul Mazursky film *Alex in Wonderland*. In the following year, in *The Last Picture Show* as Lois Farrow (mother of Cybill Shepherd's Jacey), Burstyn became one of that cast of unknowns to rise to stardom. From 1971 to 1974, Burstyn worked in succession with some of the hottest maverick directors in Hollywood—Peter Bogdanovich, Bob Rafelson, William Friedkin, Martin Scorsese, and Paul Mazursky again—in a series of complex, well-written roles. Her performance as Alice Hyatt for Martin Scorsese (in a film that she packaged and moved through the Hollywood system) is the high point of this period, emerging as one of the most important feminist characters of the 1970s. Alain Resnais' remarkable narrative experiment *Providence* offered Burstyn an opportunity to show off her considerable skills in an especially tricky and acrobatic performance. Best Actress nominations followed in 1978 and 1980, but in the following decade the quality roles were no longer coming her way, and her film appearances became less frequent. From 1982 to 1985 she served as the first female president of Actor's Equity, and from 1982 to 1985 was cohead of the Actor's Studio. Of her handful of Hollywood roles in the 1990s, her brilliance in the ensemble picture *How to Make an American Quilt* cannot go without mention.

Filmography: The Big Brain (1963, tv); For Those Who Think Young (1964); Goodbye, Charlie (1964); Pit Stop (1969); Alex in Wonderland (1970); Tropic of Cancer (1970); The Last Picture Show (1971); The King of Marvin Gardens (1972); The Exorcist (1973); Alice Doesn't Live Here Anymore (1974); Harry and Tonto (1974); Providence (1977); A Dream of Passion (1978); Same Time, Next Year (1978); Resurrection (1980); Silence of the North (1981); The People vs. Jean Harris (1981, tvm); The Ambassador (1984); In Our Hands (1984); Twice in a Lifetime (1985); Surviving (1985, tvm); Act of Vengeance (1986, ctvm); "The Ellen Burstyn Show" (1987, tvs); Dear America (1987); Pack of Lies (1987, tvm); Hanna's War (1988); Grand Isle (1991); Dying Young (1991); The Cemetery Club (1993); Getting Out (1994, tvm); When a Man Loves a Woman (1994); Roommates (1995); The Baby-Sitters Club (1995); How to Make an American Quilt (1995).

Honors: Academy Award for Best Actress (*Alice Doesn't Live Here Anymore*); Academy Award nominations for Best Actress (*The Exorcist, Same Time, Next Year, Resurrection*) and Supporting Actress (*The Last Picture Show*); New York Film Critics Circle Award for Best Supporting Actress (*The Last Picture Show*); Tony Award (*Same Time, Next Year* 1975).

BURTON, TIM. Born August 25, 1958, in Burbank, California; director, producer. Oddball visionary who has created a gallery of freaks, monsters, and misfits—all of which have been sketched with extreme love and admiration, thereby separating him from other less genuine, but more self-consciously hip, filmmakers. Beginning as an animation student at Cal Arts, Burton received a scholarship in his second year to intern in the Walt Disney animation program, where he worked on *The Black Cauldron* (though nothing of his work was used in the film). Influenced as a child by classic (and not so classic) sci-fi and horror films and as a young adult by the spirit of punk rock, Burton's alienated-in-suburbia characters are the focus of even his early short films—*Vincent* (narrated by boyhood idol Vincent Price) is the six-minute tale of a troubled young boy, while the thirty-minute *Frankenweenie* (deemed unreleasable by the then-creatively stagnant Disney Studios, which produced it) is a variation on the Mary Shelley tale that parallels a young boy and his dead dachshund with the famed scientist and his regenerated monster. He broke out as a commercial filmmaker with the delightful and inventive *Pee-Wee's Big Adventure*, which features Pee-Wee Herman as a childlike innocent on a spiritual quest for his missing bicycle. His morbid humor was in full force with *Beetlejuice*, a surprise hit that featured Winona Ryder in a wardrobe of black and Michael Keaton in a high-energy performance as a wisecracking deceased spirit. For his next film, *Batman*, Burton reteamed with a completely transformed Keaton, bringing a nightmarish adult perspective to the nocturnal caped crusader of the comic book. The result, a visually expressive, but narratively muddled, megahit, led to the more macabre sequels *Batman Returns* and *Batman Forever*, the latter of which had Burton producing while handing over the directing chore to Joel Schumacher. Burton's two best films are also his most personal and sentimental—*Edward Scissorhands* and *Ed Wood*—both Eds played by Burton's perfect nonconformist alter ego Johnny Depp. The former is a beautifully romantic fairy tale about a pure-hearted young outcast with shears for hands, while the latter is a poignant black-and-white biography of an obsessed Hollywood director and his friendship with Bela Lugosi. Although Burton is credited only as producer and creator of the wondrous 1994 stop-motion animated puppet film *The Nightmare before Christmas* (directed by Henry Selick), his signature is all over the reedy outcast character of Jack Skellington.

Filmography: Vincent (1982); Frankenweenie (1984, released 1992); "Aladdin and His Wonderful Lamp" episode of Shelley Duvall's Faerie Tale Theatre (1984, ctv); Pee-Wee's Big Adventure (1985); Beetlejuice (1988); Batman (1989); Edward Scissorhands (1990); Batman Returns (1992); Ed Wood (1994).

Additional credits: Singles (1992) actor; Tim Burton's The Nightmare before Christmas (1993) creator, producer; "Family Dog" (1993, tvs) ep; Cabin Boy (1994) producer; Batman Forever (1995) producer; James and the Giant Peach (1996) producer.

BUSCEMI, STEVE. Born December 13, 1957, in Brooklyn, New York; actor, director. Distinctively a New Yorker, this wiry, wild-eyed, frenetic performer (and former New York firefighter) has appeared in numerous independent films, usually cast as a likable pawn. Although he first attracted attention as the lead in the low-budget AIDS-related film *Parting Glances*, he is generally best known for his memorable minor roles in *Mystery Train* (as Charlie); *New York Stories* (as the subway performance artist in "Life Lessons"); and in the films

of the Coen Brothers, specifically as "Chet!," the overly enthusiastic hotel bell-
man in *Barton Fink*. Greater recognition came with more substantial roles as
the aspiring filmmaker in *In the Soup* and as the fast-talking Mr. Pink in *Reservoir Dogs*. In addition to his acting work, Buscemi has also directed for the
stage and, in 1995, directed the feature *Tree's Lounge*, which was released in
1996.

Filmography: The Way It Is, or Eurydice in the Avenues (1984); No Picnic (1986);
Parting Glances (1986); Sleepwalk (1986); Force of Circumstance (1987); Heart (1987);
Kiss Daddy Good Night (1987); Call Me (1988); Coffee and Cigarettes (Memphis) (1988,
short); Heart of Midnight (1988); Vibes (1988); Bloodhounds of Broadway (1989); Borders (1989); Mystery Train (1989); "Life Lessons" episode of New York Stories (1989);
Slaves of New York (1989); Lonesome Dove (1989, tvms); King of New York (1990);
Miller's Crossing (1990); Tales from the Darkside: The Movie (1990); The Grifters
(1990); Barton Fink (1991); Billy Bathgate (1991); Trusting Beatrice (1991); Zandalee
(1991); Crisscross (1992); Reservoir Dogs (1992); In the Soup (1992); Painted Heart
(1992); Me and the Mob (1992); Rising Sun (1993); Twenty Bucks (1993); Ed and His
Dead Mother (1993); What Happened to Pete? (1993, short) director; The Last Outlaw
(1993, ctvm); "Forever Ambergis" episode of Tales from the Crypt (1993, ctv); Airheads
(1994); Floundering (1994); The Hudsucker Proxy (1994); Pulp Fiction (1994); Someone
to Love (1994); Scene Six, Take One (1994, short); Living in Oblivion (1995); Desperado
(1995); Things to Do in Denver When You're Dead (1995).

Honor: Independent Spirit Award for Best Actor (*Reservoir Dogs*).

BUSEY, GARY. Born June 29, 1944, in Goose Creek, Texas; actor. Talented,
country-bred actor and former drummer under the name Teddy Jack Eddy
(1963–1970) who has often appeared as a rabble-rousing, no-nonsense heavy,
though the role that has brought him the most attention, ironically, has been as
Buddy Holly in *The Buddy Holly Story*. His early supporting work is memorable
in *Thunderbolt and Lightfoot* and *Straight Time*, while his later work has consisted of tough-guy roles in such box office hits as *Lethal Weapon*, *Predator 2*,
Under Seige, and *The Firm*. His offscreen antics have often landed him in the
spotlight, with a near-fatal motorcycle accident in 1988 and a near-fatal drug
overdose in 1995.

Filmography: Angels Hard as They Come (1971); Dirty Little Billy (1972); Hex (1972);
The Last American Hero (1973); Lolly-Madonna XXX (1973); Thunderbolt and Lightfoot (1974); "The Texas Wheelers" (1974–1975, tvs); The Execution of Private Slovik
(1974, tvm); You and Me (1975); The Gumball Rally (1976); A Star Is Born (1976);
Big Wednesday (1978); The Buddy Holly Story (1978); Straight Time (1978); Foolin'
Around (1979); Carny (1980); Barbarosa (1982); D.C. Cab (1983); Bear (1984); Insig-
nificance (1985); Silver Bullet (1985); The Hitchhiker (1985, ctvm); Eye of the Tiger
(1986); Half a Lifetime (1986, ctvm); Let's Get Harry (1987); Lethal Weapon (1987);
Act of Piracy (1988); Bulletproof (1988); Hider in the House (1989); Predator 2 (1990);
My Heroes Have Always Been Cowboys (1991); Point Break (1991); Wild Texas Wind
(1991, tvm); The Player (1992); Canvas (1992); Under Seige (1992); Chrome Soldiers
(1992, ctvm); Rookie of the Year (1993); South Beach (1993); The Firm (1993); "Since

I Don't Have You'' episode of ''Fallen Angels'' (1994, ctvm); Drop Zone (1994); Chasers (1994); Surviving the Game (1994); Oasis Cafe (1995, short); Man with a Gun (1995, ctvm); Warriors (1995).

Honor: Academy Award nomination for Best Actor (*The Buddy Holly Story*).

BUTCH CASSIDY AND THE SUNDANCE KID (1969), western. Directed by George Roy Hill; written by William Goldman; produced by Paul Monash and John Foreman; photographed by Conrad Hall; edited by John C. Howard, Richard C. Meyer; music by Burt Bacharach; released by 20th Century Fox; 112 minutes. *Cast*: Paul Newman, Robert Redford, Katharine Ross, Strother Martin, Jeff Corey, Cloris Leachman.

The year 1969 saw the release of two of the most important and most dissimilar westerns in American film history—George Roy Hill's *Butch Cassidy and the Sundance Kid* and Sam Peckinpah's *The Wild Bunch*—two films that represent entirely antithetic discourses on the myth of heroism in the Old West. Where Peckinpah's heroes are violent killers whom we grow to admire as men, Butch and Sundance begin as charming and childlike rogues who, no matter what their crimes, repeatedly win us over with their charm. Essentially truthful in its characterizations, the film tells the story of a pair of bank robbers who travel through the West and into Bolivia, where the ''bandits Yanqui'' meet their end—a moment of western lore captured in a safe, bloodless freeze-frame. With its entertaining tone and its bath of golden nostalgia, it is no surprise that the film became the top-grossing western of all time. As Butch, Newman added yet another legendary role to his long career while, as Sundance, Redford proved himself to be one of the most bankable stars in Hollywood. Katharine Ross as Sundance's girlfriend, Etta Place, followed up her role in *The Graduate* with a performance strong enough to keep up with her two charismatic costars. Her bicycle-riding scene with Newman to the Burt Bacharach–Hal David tune ''Raindrops Keep Falling on My Head'' is one of the most joyful scenes you'll ever see.

Awards: Academy Awards for Best Original Screenplay, Cinematography, Score, Song; Academy Award nominations for Best Picture, Director, Sound; WGA Award.

C

CAAN, JAMES. Born March 26, 1939, in Queens, New York; actor. Superb actor who always has a storm of violence churning beneath his calm and casual facade. With stage training from Sanford Meisner, Caan was given the opportunity to display his sense of danger as a vicious young thug in *Lady in a Cage*, his first billed feature role. After a pair of films for Howard Hawks, Caan began his fruitful collaboration with Francis Ford Coppola in a remarkably vulnerable role as the mentally impaired ex-football player in *The Rain People* before achieving cinematic immortality as the volatile Sonny Corleone in the first two *Godfather* films. The 1970s proved kind to Caan, with gutsy, gritty performances in *Cinderella Liberty*, *The Gambler*, *The Killer Elite*, and the underrated *Rollerball*. The next decade started out promisingly with Caan's sole directing achievement *Hide in Plain Sight* and his emotionally complex lead role in *Thief*, but an acting hiatus followed as he battled his increasingly destructive drug dependency. He returned with a vengeance in 1987 with Coppola's *Gardens of Stone*. His subsequent films have been hit-or-miss, ranging from the commercial successes *Misery* and *Honeymoon in Vegas* to the risky, but less warmly greeted, *For the Boys* and *Flesh and Bone*.

Filmography: Irma La Douce (1963) uncredited; Lady in a Cage (1964); The Glory Guys (1965); Red Line 7000 (1965); El Dorado (1967); Games (1967); Submarine X-1 (1967); Countdown (1968); Journey to Shiloh (1968); The Rain People (1969); Rabbit, Run (1970); Brian's Song (1971, tvm); T. R. Baskin (1971); The Godfather (1972); Cinderella Liberty (1973); Slither (1973); Freebie and the Bean (1974); The Gambler (1974); The Godfather, Part II (1974); Funny Lady (1975); The Killer Elite (1975); Rollerball (1975); Harry and Walter Go to New York (1976); Another Man, Another Chance (1977); A Bridge Too Far (1977); Comes a Horseman (1978); Little Moon and Jud McGraw (1978); Chapter Two (1979); Hide in Plain Sight (1980) also director; Thief

(1981); Les Une et les Autres (1981); Kiss Me Goodbye (1982); Gardens of Stone (1987); Alien Nation (1988); Dick Tracy (1990); Misery (1990); For the Boys (1991); The Dark Backward (1991); Honeymoon in Vegas (1992); Flesh and Bone (1993); The Program (1993); A Boy Called Hate (1995); Things To Do In Denver When You're Dead (1995).

Honor: Academy Award nomination for Best Supporting Actor (*The Godfather*).

CABARET (1972), musical. Directed by Bob Fosse; written by Jay Presson Allen; produced by Cy Feuer; photographed by Geoffrey Unsworth; edited by David Bretherton; music by John Burns, songs by John Kander and Fred Ebb; released by Allied Artists; 124 minutes. *Cast:* Liza Minnelli, Joel Grey, Michael York, Helmut Griem, Fritz Wepper, Marissa Berenson.

A revolutionary film musical that thrust the genre past mere entertainment and made possible the rise (however short-lived) of the musical as social commentary. The progenitor of *Jesus Christ Superstar, Tommy, Hair, Pennies from Heaven*, and *Absolute Beginners*, this virtuosic directorial effort from Bob Fosse is set in Berlin during the days between the Weimar's end and Nazism's dawn. Refraining from the scenes of characters breaking into song midsentence, *Cabaret* is instead split between cabaret tunes at the Kit-Kat Club and the Berlin street scenes, which are mirrored in the lyrics. On stage we get bawdy routines starring the devilish master of ceremonies (Grey) and his fleshy showgirls; while outside, in a very decadent Berlin, Kit-Kat star Sally Bowles (Minnelli) enjoys the good life with her bisexual, Oxford-educated lover Brian (York) and their mutual conquest, Baron Maximilian von Huene (Griam). As the stage show progresses, so too does the real-life influence of Hitler and his jackboots until the Kit-Kat audience is polluted with swastika-adorned thugs. Based on Christopher Isherwood's 1939 collection of short stories, John van Druten's 1951 play *I am a Camera*, and the popular 1966 musical, *Cabaret* is Hollywood at its best—a startlingly original vision that features exquisite production design and cinematography, splendidly risqué choreography, and show-stopping, give-it-all-you-got performances from Minnelli and Grey. Their exuberant and naughty routine during ''Money'' is one of the film's most exciting moments, while one of its most chilling is the beer garden scene—a perfect specimen of Aryan youth warbles a beautiful version of ''Tomorrow Belongs to Me'' as his countrymen, one by one, rise up and sing along. ''After Cabaret [*sic*] it should be a while before performers once again climb hills singing or a chorus breaks into song on a hayride'' (Pauline Kael, *The New Yorker*, February 19, 1972).

Honors: Academy Awards for Best Actress (Minnelli), Supporting Actor (Grey), Director, Cinematography, Art Direction, Editing, Music Adaptation, Sound; Academy Award nominations for Picture, Screenplay; included in the Library of Congress' National Film Registry (1995).

CAGE, NICOLAS. Born Nicolas Coppola January 7, 1964, in Long Beach, California; actor. Married to Patricia Arquette; nephew of Francis Ford Coppola. Heavy-lidded actor who seems just as comfortable in smart comedies such as

Peggy Sue Got Married, Moonstruck, Raising Arizona, and *It Could Happen to You* as he does in edgier, dramatic roles as *Rumblefish, Birdy,* and *Wild at Heart.* After creating an off-kilter, regular-guy, comic persona that occasionally bordered on Rain Man territory, he spun that image on edge with his razor-sharp portrayal of Sailor Ripley in David Lynch's *Wild at Heart;* he would continue to play rubes, but there would now be a sense of danger lurking beneath their skin. He reached a new level of intensity in 1995 with two of his most assured roles to date—the bulked-up psychotic Little Junior of *Kiss of Death* and the self-destructive alcoholic of *Leaving Las Vegas,* the latter earning him his finest critical notices since the emotionally complex *Birdy.*

Filmography: Fast Times at Ridgemont High (1982) billed as Nicolas Coppola; Rumblefish (1983); Valley Girl (1984); Birdy (1984); The Cotton Club (1984); Racing with the Moon (1984); The Boy in Blue (1986); Peggy Sue Got Married (1986); Moonstruck (1987); Raising Arizona (1987); Vampire's Kiss (1988); Never on Tuesday (1989); Tempo di Uccidere (1989); Fire Birds (1990); Wild at Heart (1990); Zandalee (1991); Honeymoon in Vegas (1992); Red Rock West (1993); Amos and Andrew (1993); Deadfall (1993); Guarding Tess (1994); Trapped in Paradise (1994); It Could Happen To You (1994); Kiss of Death (1995); Leaving Las Vegas (1995).

Honors: Academy Award for Best Actor (*Leaving Las Vegas*); Cannes Film Festival Jury Prize (*Birdy*); New York Film Critics Circle Award for Best Actor (*Leaving Las Vegas*); Los Angeles Film Critics Award for Best Actor (*Leaving Las Vegas*).

CAMERON, JAMES. Born August 16, 1954, in Kapuskasing, Ontario, Canada; director, screenwriter, producer. Formerly married to producer/screenwriter Gale Anne Hurd and director Kathryn Bigelow. Inspired to become a filmmaker after seeing *Star Wars,* he has since become the one true heir to that George Lucas style of filmmaking—mythic, big-budget, effects-driven entertainment. With humble beginnings on a number of no-budget Roger Corman pictures, he catapulted himself into the sci-fi forefront with *The Terminator,* simultaneously transforming Arnold Schwarzenegger into a megastar. He then helped reinvent Sylvester Stallone's career by scripting *Rambo: First Blood Part II.* His subsequent three pictures took epic sci-fi pictures to the next level, filling the void that was created after Lucas' departure from the creative end of filmmaking. A perfectionist, Cameron pushed the technology to the envelope with his underwater filming techniques in *The Abyss* and then again with his experimentation in computer imaging in *Terminator 2: Judgment Day.* He has found less success, however, in his Lightstorm Entertainment producing efforts for Kathryn Bigelow (*Point Break* and *Strange Days*) and in his one non-sci-fi project, the Schwarzenegger action movie *True Lies.* His special effects company, Digital Domain, has, along with Lucas' ILM, changed the face of Hollywood filmmaking effects.

Filmography: Piranha II: Flying Killers (1981); The Terminator (1984) also screenplay; Aliens (1986) also screenplay; The Abyss (1989) also screenplay; Terminator 2: Judgment Day (1991) also screenplay, producer; True Lies (1994) also screenplay, producer.

Additional credits: Battle beyond the Stars (1980) art director; Happy Birthday, Gemini

(1980) set dresser assistant; Galaxy of Terror (1981) production designer and 2d unit director; Rambo: First Blood Part II (1985) screenplay; Point Break (1991) ep; Strange Days (1995) screenplay, producer.

CANDIDATE, THE (1972), political drama. Directed by Michael Ritchie; screenplay by Jeremy Larner; produced by Walter Coblenz; photographed by Victor J. Kemper and John Korty; edited by Richard Harris and Robert Estrin; music by John Rubenstein; released by Warner Bros.; 109 minutes. *Cast*: Robert Redford, Peter Boyle, Don Porter, Melvyn Douglas, Allen Garfield, Quinn Redaker, Michael Lerner, Karen Carlson, Natalie Wood.

An understated look at life on the campaign trail that is not only one of the most realistic portrayals of American politics, but also one of the most disheartening. Redford stars as Bill McKay, a liberal Californian whose father is the former governor of the state. Although McKay holds no political aspirations, he is drafted by strategist Lucas (Boyle) into a sure-lose campaign against incumbent senator Crocker Jarmon, an arm-pumping, baby-hugging politician. Promised that he can say and do whatever he pleases, McKay manages to win the election, only to realize that he, even the most idealistic of grassroots campaigners, is a political empty shell with nothing new to say. Starting on the campaign trail with hope and idealism, McKay becomes a media creation designed with one purpose only—to be a party candidate and survive the race; anything more, like actually winning and effecting change, is immaterial. Redford is a perfect casting choice, without whom the movie would fall flat; more than any other actor of his generation, he perfectly embodies the charismatic appeal that is the essense of both the movie star and the politician.

Award: Academy Award nomination for Best Screenplay.

CANDY, JOHN. Born October 31, 1950, in Toronto; died March 4, 1994, in Mexico; actor, comedian. Large and lovable comic actor who began his career in 1972 as part of Chicago's Second City comedy group. Four years later, along with Eugene Levy, Rick Moranis, and Harold Ramis, Candy returned to his native Toronto and began "Second City TV," the now-legendary late-night cult comedy series. His movie career received the needed impetus from Steven Spielberg, who cast him in his *1941*, but his most visible association is with John Hughes, for whom he starred in seven movies. Although his movie career effectively spans only fifteen years, he's appeared in some of the most popular comedies of the 1980s and 1990s, most notably, *Stripes, National Lampoon's Vacation, Splash, Little Shop of Horrors, Armed and Dangerous, The Great Outdoors, Uncle Buck, Home Alone,* and *Cool Runnings*. Like his seriocomic contemporaries Steve Martin and Bill Murray, he began to show a flair for drama in his more recent work, especially *JFK* and *Only the Lonely*.

Filmography: Class of '44 (1973); It Seemed like a Good Idea at the Time (1975); Find the Lady (1976); Tunnelvision (1976); The Clown Murders (1976); "Second City TV" (1977–1984, tvs) also writer; The Silent Partner (1978); 1941 (1979); Lost and Found

(1979); The Blues Brothers (1980); The Courage of Kavik, the Wolf Dog (1980, tvm); Double Negative/Deadly Companion (1980); Heavy Metal (1981) voice; Stripes (1981); Going Berserk (1983); National Lampoon's Vacation (1983); Splash (1984); Sesame Street Presents: Follow That Bird (1985); Brewster's Millions (1985); Summer Rental (1985); Volunteers (1985); The Last Polka (1985, ctv special) also ep; Armed and Dangerous (1986); The Canadian Conspiracy (1986); Little Shop of Horrors (1986); Planes, Trains and Automobiles (1987); Spaceballs (1987); The Great Outdoors (1988); Hot to Trot (1988) voice; Speed Zone (1989); Uncle Buck (1989); "Camp Candy" (1989–1993, tvs) host, voice; Who's Harry Crumb? (1989) also ep; Home Alone (1990); The Rescuers Down Under (1990) voice; Masters of Menace (1991); Delirious (1991); Nothing but Trouble (1991); Only the Lonely (1991); JFK (1991); Career Opportunities (1991); Once Upon a Crime (1992); Cool Runnings (1993); Hostage for a Day (1985, tvm) also producer, director; Wagons East (1994); Canadian Bacon (1995).

Honor: Emmys for Outstanding Writing ("Second City TV" 1982, 1983).

CARNAL KNOWLEDGE (1971), drama. Directed and produced by Mike Nichols; written by Jules Feiffer; photographed by Giuseppe Rotunno; edited by Sam O'Steen; released by Avco Embassy; 97 minutes. *Cast:* Jack Nicholson, Art Garfunkel, Candice Bergen, Ann-Margret, Rita Moreno, Carol Kane, Cynthia O'Neal.

Underappreciated upon its release, this is one of the most candid explorations of male–female sexual relationships. College buddies Jonathan (Nicholson) and Sandy (Garfunkel) are both virgins on the prowl for their first girl; Jonathan is arrogant and sexually manipulative, while Sandy is gentle and compassionate. They both fall for Cindy (Bergen), a literate and effervescent woman who is attracted to Sandy's warmth and Jonathan's animalism. She sleeps with both of them, but neither she nor Jonathan tells Sandy. As the years wear on, Sandy and Jonathan remain friends, but they are not equipped emotionally to deal with the realities of their empty lives. Sandy is now married to Cindy and having an affair on the side, while Jonathan has "shacked up" with the increasingly troubled Bobbie (Ann-Margret). At the height of their sexual desperation they revert back to their boyish selves and agree to swap partners, but it has near-disastrous results. Still they remain friends; Sandy finds an idealistic younger woman (Kane) who makes him feel pure, while Jonathan sinks into narcissistic despair with a prostitute (Moreno) who "excites" him by reciting scripted lines about his own sexual power. A masterpiece of bitterness and self-delusion from Nichols and Feiffer that is energized by uniformly excellent performances, a bold structure, and a daring visual style.

Award: Academy Award nomination for Best Supporting Actress (Ann-Margret).

CARPENTER, JOHN. Born January 16, 1948, in Carthage, New York; director, screenwriter, composer. America's premiere B-movie director since his debut in the mid-1970s, John Carpenter has followed the tradition of Howard Hawks as a genre director, though he has yet to reach Hawks' level of critical success or social relevancy. His *Assault on Precinct 13* recalls Hawk's classic western *Rio Bravo*, while *The Fog* recalls the unseen menace of Val Lewton's horror classics, but the comparisons exist only on a stylistic level without the sociopolitical implications of the previous masters. With a background at the University of Southern California film school, he began promisingly enough with an Oscar-winning short film (*The Resurrection of Bronco Billy*) and a well-received $60,000 sci-fi send-up called *Dark Star*. Just four years later, he directed one of the most important and commercially successful horror films of the decade—the spectacularly chilling *Halloween*, a smash hit that tapped into the fears of America's teenagers and marked the first in a long line of ''promiscuous teenager'' movies. His subsequent work has ranged from moderate success (*Escape from New York*, *Christine*), to noble failure (*They Live*), to the artfully haunting (*Prince of Darkness* with its Cocteau influence, *In the Mouth of Madness*, and *Starman*). In addition to writing and directing, he composes the music for most of his films. ''If I had three wishes, one of them would be 'Send me back to the 40s and the studio system and let me direct movies' '' (Carpenter quoted in David Thomson's *A Biographical Dictionary of Film*).

Filmography as director: Revenge of the Colossal Beasts, Gorgo versus Godzilla, Terror from Space, Sorcerer from Outer Space, Warrior and the Demon, Gorgon the Space Monster (1956–1962, shorts); The Resurrection of Bronco Billy (1970, short); Dark Star (1974); Assault on Precinct 13 (1976); Someone's Watching Me! (1978; tvm) also screenplay; Halloween (1978); Elvis (1979, tvm); The Fog (1980) also actor; Escape from New York (1981); The Thing (1982); Christine (1983); Starman (1984); Big Trouble in Little China (1986); Prince of Darkness (1987); They Live (1988); Memoirs of an Invisible Man (1992); ''The Gas Station'' and ''Hair'' episodes of John Carpenter Presents Body Bags (1993, ctvm) also ep; In the Mouth of Madness (1995); Village of the Damned (1995).

Additional credits: Zuma Beach (1978, tvm) screenplay; Halloween II (1981) producer, screenplay; Halloween III: The Season of the Witch (1982) producer; The Philadelphia Experiment (1984) ep; Black Moon Rising (1986) screenplay; The Boy Who Could Fly (1986); Eyes of Laura Mars (1978) screenplay; Better Later than Never (1979, tvm) screenplay; The House on Carroll Street (1988) actor; El Diablo (1990, ctvm) ep, screenplay; Blood River (1991, tvm) screenplay.

Honors: Academy Award for Best Short Subject (*The Resurrection of Bronco Billy*); Los Angeles Film Critics New Generation Award (1979).

CARRADINE, KEITH. Born August 8, 1949, in San Mateo, California; actor. Son of actor John Carradine; brother of Robert Carradine; half brother of David Carradine; and father of Martha Plimpton. A charismatic, if unlikely, leading man whose long association as an ensemble member in the films of Robert Altman and Altman protégé Alan Rudolph has established him as one of the most consistently excellent (and likewise underrated) actors in American film. From his first film for Altman (*McCabe and Mrs. Miller*) to his most recent film for Rudolph (*Mrs. Parker and the Vicious Circle*) he has proven himself an almost archetypical American—a reputation that has only been enforced by his acclaim as a stage performer in the Broadway production of *The Will Rogers Follies*. Still, his greatest accolades have come not as an actor but as a singer/songwriter with the graceful "I'm Easy" from Altman's *Nashville*. His Broadway debut came in 1969–1970 as Claude in *Hair*, and his television premiere came a short while later in a 1971 episode of "Bonanza." He has appeared in some twenty television films, as well as a 1972 episode "Kung Fu," starring his half brother David.

Filmography: A Gunfight (1971); McCabe and Mrs. Miller (1971); Hex (1972); Antonie et Sebatien (1973); The Emperor of the North Pole (1973); Idaho Transfer (1973); Thieves like Us (1974); Lumiere (1975); Nashville (1975); You and Me (1975); Welcome to L.A. (1976); The Duelists (1977); Old Boyfriends (1978); Pretty Baby (1978); Sgt. Pepper's Lonely Hearts Club Band (1978); An Almost Perfect Affair (1979); The Long Riders (1980); Southern Comfort (1981); Choose Me (1984); Maria's Lovers (1985); Trouble in Mind (1985); Half a Lifetime (1986, ctvm); The Inquiry/L'Inchiesta (1987); Murder Ordained (1987, tvms); Backfire (1987); The Moderns (1988); Street of No Return (1989); Cold Feet (1989); The Forgotten (1989, ctvm) also ep; The Bachelor/Mio Caro Dotter Graesler (1990); Daddy's Dyin . . . Who's Got the Will? (1990); The Ballad of the Sad Cafe (1991); Crisscross (1992); Andre (1994); Mrs. Parker and the Vicious Circle (1994); The Tie That Binds (1995); Wild Bill (1995); "Last Chance" (1995, tvs).

Honors: Academy Award for Best Song (*Nashville*); Tony nomination (*The Will Rogers Follies* 1991).

CARREY, JIM. Born January 17, 1962, in Toronto, Ontario, Canada; actor. Owing a debt to the wild, physical antics of Jerry Lewis, Carrey has positioned himself as the most commercially succcessful comic actor of his generation. Dropping out of high school at sixteen, he appeared in the forty-eight-minute Canadian television film *Rubberface* before relocating to Los Angeles at nineteen. After a mercifully short-lived stint in the NBC sitcom "The Duck Factory," he slogged through some comic roles and a pair of Buddy Van Horn-directed Clint Eastwood projects (*The Dead Pool, Pink Cadillac*) before hitting the next level of success in the Fox television comedy variety show "In Living Color." There he perfected the brand of physical comedy that has propelled him into the realm of superstar. He attracted attention when his salary reached the $20 million per picture mark—a well-deserved paycheck in consideration of the fact that his movies consistently earn that money back on their opening weekend. While he may be accused of appealing to the lowest common denominator of American film audiences, he must be given accolades for his metamorphic physical comedy. Of his *Dumb and Dumber* role, Richard Schickel wrote that "Carrey is both symbol and satirist of our apparently irresistible dumbing down" (*Time*, January 9, 1995).

Filmography: Rubberface (1981, short tvm); "The Duck Factory" (1984, tvs); Finders Keepers (1984); Once Bitten (1985); Peggy Sue Got Married (1986); The Dead Pool (1988); Earth Girls Are Easy (1989); Pink Cadillac (1989); "In Living Color" (1990–

1994, tvs); High Strung (1991); The Itsy Bitsy Spider (1992, short) voice; Ace Ventura: Pet Detective (1994); The Mask (1994); Dumb and Dumber (1994); Ace Ventura: When Nature Calls (1995); Batman Forever (1995).

CARRIE (1976), horror. Directed by Brian De Palma; screenplay by Lawrence D. Cohen (from the novel by Stephen King); produced by Paul Monash; photographed by Mario Tosi; edited by Paul Hirsch; music by Pino Donaggio; released by United Artists; 97 minutes. *Cast*: Sissy Spacek, Piper Laurie, Amy Irving, William Katt, John Travolta, Nancy Allen, Betty Buckley, P. J. Soles.

An essay on teenage rage and alienation, themes that serve as perfect raw material for a horror film. Elevated by Sissy Spacek's haunting portrayal of a high school girl with untapped telekinetic powers, the film is not only one of Brian De Palma's best efforts but also the finest adaptation of a Stephen King horror tale. Withdrawn both from her fellow students and from her religious fanatic mother (superbly played by Piper Laurie), the confused and sexually repressed Carrie is finally pushed over the edge at a school dance when she becomes the victim of a cruel joke (she's crowned prom queen) and is drenched by a bucket of pig's blood. In the ultimate teenage revenge fantasy, she summons her supernatural powers to kill her classmates, destroy the school, and unleash her fury on her domineering mother. The image of the smiling Carrie being showered with blood is one of the classic moments in the horror genre, as is the ''gotchya'' scare of the hand reaching up through the grave.

Awards: Academy Award nominations for Best Actress (Spacek) and Supporting Actress (Laurie).

CASSAVETES, JOHN. Born December 9, 1929, in New York City; died February 3, 1989, in Los Angeles; director, screenwriter, actor. Married until his death to actor Gena Rowlands; son Nick is an actor and director; daughter Zoe is also an actor. Despite the fact that he lived and worked in the hub of the American film industry, this maverick director is most strongly identified as the antithesis of everything Hollywood. His films value character over plot, performance over technical proficiency, and honesty over artificiality and, as a result, have alienated audiences who shrink at such raw emotion. At the same time, however, he found favor with both critics who had grown tired of the status quo and independent filmmakers who continue to find inspiration in his anti-Hollywood form and content. After nearly a decade of acting in television and film (Martin Ritt's interracial drama *Edge of the City* stands out), Cassavetes directed his first feature, the independently produced *Shadows*, an exciting, improvisational work that swelled with the vibrancy of real-life characters, neon-lit night scenes, and the socially relevant issue of racism. The critical success of the film brought Cassavetes to the attention of Hollywood, where he was hired to direct the studio films *Too Late Blues* and *A Child Is Waiting*—plot-heavy, socially conscious projects that failed to showcase his true talents, though the latter contains a marvelously stark performance from Judy Garland. He returned to the raw style that best suited him in *Faces*, a brutally truthful look at the wants and needs of a married couple that featured two of Cassavetes' future group of stock players, Gena Rowlands, and Seymour Cassel. Throughout the remainder of his career, he continued to work with a "family" that included actual relatives—Rowlands, her mother, Lady Rowlands, his children, his art director cousin Phedon Papamichael—and close friends Cassel, Peter Falk, and Ben Gazzara. While much has been made of his improvisational filmmaking techniques (he often said only the emotions were improvised), what is most powerful about his films is the prevailing sense of family; the real love between these people is apparent, and that love lends to our appreciation of the films. Of his greatest films (*Faces*, *Husbands*, *A Woman Under the Influence*, *Opening Night*), none were especially successful commercially (*Opening Night* barely saw a release), and only Columbia's *Gloria* and Cannon Films/MGM/UA's *Love Streams* received full studio support. His final film, the smart *Double Indemnity* takeoff *Big Trouble*, is a Cassavetes film in name only that bares little relationship to his other pictures; he accepted the job as a favor to star Peter Falk when cowriter Andrew Bergman was removed as director. To supplement his rather expensive habit of self-financing motion pictures, Cassavetes, like Orson Welles before him, often took acting jobs to help pay the bills. While most of the films would have benefited if he were behind the camera as well, Robert Aldrich's *The Dirty Dozen*, Roman Polanski's *Rosemary's Baby* (unforgettable as the duplicitous husband), and Elaine May's *Mikey and Nicky* are the exceptions. Two documentaries have been made about Cassavetes—*"I'm Almost Not Crazy . . .": John Cassavetes: The Man and His Work* (1983) and *John Cassavetes* (1990), part of the PBS American Masters series. " 'Actor,' in Cassavetes' terms, might be extended to include the entire film crew, since he reputedly leaves the camera operator as free to discover how best to shoot a scene as he leaves the actors to discover what it means" (Richard Combs, *Cinema: A Critical Dictionary*). "For all their hectoring anti-intellectualism, his movies are frequently object lessons in how we might behave more decently and caringly toward one another" (Jonathan Rosenbaum, *Chicago Reader*, September 20, 1991).

Filmography as writer and director: Shadows (1960); Too Late Blues (1961) also producer; A Child Is Waiting (1962) director only; Faces (1968); Husbands (1970); Minnie and Moskowitz (1971); A Woman Under the Influence (1974); The Killing of a Chinese Bookie (1976); Opening Night (1977); Gloria (1980) also producer; Love Streams (1984); Big Trouble (1986) director only.

Filmography of key pre-1965 films as actor: Edge of the City (1957); "Johnny Staccato" (1959–60, tvs) also director of some episodes; The Killers (1964).

Filmography as actor since 1965: Devil's Angels (1967); The Dirty Dozen (1967); Roma Come Chicago (1968); Rosemary's Baby (1968); If It's Tuesday, This Must Be Belgium (1969); Machine Gun McCain/Gli Intoccabili (1969); Capone (1975); Mikey and Nicky (1976); Two-Minute Warning (1976); Brass Target (1978); The Fury (1978); Flesh and Blood (1979, tvms); Whose Life Is It Anyway? (1981); The Haircut (1981/aired in 1988, ctv short); The Incubus (1982); The Tempest (1982); Marvin and Tige (1983).

Honors: Academy Award nominations for Supporting Actor (*The Dirty Dozen*), Screenplay (*Faces*) and Director (*A Woman Under the Influence*); Venice Film Festival Critics Awards (*Shadows, Faces*), and the Golden Lion for Best Picture (*Gloria*); Berlin Film Festival Golden Bear for Best Picture (*Love Streams*); Los Angeles Film Critics Career Achievement Award (1986).

Selected Bibliography

Carney, Ray. *The Films of John Cassavetes: Pragmatism, Modernism and the Movies.* London: Cambridge University Press, 1994.

CASSEL, SEYMOUR. Born January 22, 1932, in Detroit; actor. An energetic supporting player whose wild-eyed looks, full head of blond hair, heavy mustache, and ever-present cigar have become his trademark. Trained at the Actors Studio, he soon became associated with John Cassavetes, serving as associate producer on *Shadows* and appearing in most of the director's films. In 1968, he received an Oscar nomination for his performance as the impassioned hippie in *Faces*, and three years later he costarred with Gena Rowlands in Cassavetes' idiosyncratic and touching love story *Minnie and Moskowitz*. After a long drought in the late 1970s and early 1980s, he reemerged in a string of quality Hollywood films (*Tin Men, Colors, Dick Tracy, Honeymoon in Vegas*, and *Indecent Proposal*) but has also kept true to the independent spirit of his roots, appearing most memorably in Alexandre Rockwell's *In the Soup*.

Filmography of key pre-1965 films: Murder, Inc. (1960); Shadows (1960) associate producer; Too Late Blues (1961); The Killers (1964).

Filmography since 1965: Coogan's Bluff (1968); Faces (1968); The Sweet Ride (1968); The Revolutionary (1970); Minnie and Moskowitz (1971); Nightside (1973, tvm); Black Oak Conspiracy (1976); Death Game (1976); The Killing of a Chinese Bookie (1976); The Last Tycoon (1976); Opening Night (1977); Scott Joplin (1977); Valentino (1977); Convoy (1978); California Dreaming (1979); Ravagers (1979); Sunburn (1979); The Mountain Men (1980); Angel on My Shoulder (1980, tvm); King of the Mountain (1981); Blood Feud (1983, tvms); I Want to Live (1983, tvm); Love Streams (1984); Eye of the Tiger (1986); Beverly Hills Madam (1986, tvm); Survival Game (1987); Tin Men (1987); Track 29 (1987); Colors (1988); Johnny Be Good (1988); Plain Clothes (1988); Wicked Stepmother (1989); Tennessee Williams' Sweet Bird of Youth (1989, tvm); Cold Dog Soup (1990); Dick Tracy (1990); White Fang (1991); Mobsters (1991); Diary of a Hitman (1991); Face of a Stranger (1991, tvm); Dead in the Water (1991, ctvm); Cold Heaven (1992); Adventures in Spying (1992); Honeymoon in Vegas (1992); Chain of Desire (1992); In the Soup (1992); Boiling Point (1993); Trouble Bound (1993); When Pigs Fly (1993); Love Is like That (1993); American Standoff (1993, short); Indecent Proposal (1993); Handgun (1994); Tollbooth (1994); It Could Happen to You (1994); Chasers (1994); Imaginary Crimes (1994); There Goes My Baby (1994); Someone to Love (1994); Partners (1994, ctv short); "Under Suspicion" (1994–1995, tvs); Dark Side of Genius (1995); Things to Do in Denver When You're Dead (1995); Four Rooms (1995).

Honors: Academy Award nomination for Supporting Actor (*Faces*); New York Film Critics Circle Awards for Best Actor (*Minnie and Moskowitz*) and Best Supporting Actor (*Faces*).

CAT BALLOU (1965), comedy/western. Directed by Elliot Silverstein; screenplay by Frank Pierson and Walter Newman (from the novel by Roy Chanslor); produced by Harold Hecht; photographed by Jack Marta; edited by Charles Nelson; music by Frank DeVol, song "The Ballad of Cat Ballou" by Mack David and Jerry Livingston, performed by Nat King Cole and Stubby Kaye; released by Columbia; 97 minutes. *Cast*: Lee Marvin, Jane Fonda, Michael Callan, Dwayne Hickman, Tom Nardini, Nat King Cole, Stubby Kaye, John Marley, Jay C. Flippen.

Blazing Saddles may be the most successful western spoof on record, but *Cat Ballou* is the first and the funniest. Boldly and cleverly toying with the mythology of the genre, this energetic romp mocks the iconography of the gunslinger, the Native American, the schoolmarm, and the preacher by completely defying expectation and twisting these archetypes into unusually modern figures. Fonda stars as the title character, Catherine "Cat" Ballou, a seemingly proper young lady who returns from an eastern school to learn that her father (Marley) is being forced off his land by a group of greedy land developers. When nasty and noseless hired gun Tim Strawn (Marvin) kills her father, Cat (who is secretly a fan of Old West stories and legends) hires her own gunslinger, the once-notorious Kid Shelleen (also Marvin). Instead of a steely protector, however, Shelleen is a bumbling drunk who, despite his inability to keep his pants up and his habit of falling out of his saddle, is still a crack shot . . . as long as he guzzles a bit of whiskey first. Keeping the picture clipping along at a fast pace are Nat King Cole and Stubby Kaye, who wander through the frame to shape the legend of Cat Ballou via song. A significant role for Lee Marvin, which marked a transition from villainous character actor to his second career as offbeat older leading man.

Awards: Academy Award for Best Actor; Academy Award nominations for Best Screenplay, Editing, Song, Score; Berlin Film Festival Award for Best Actor.

CAZALE, JOHN. Born 1936 in Boston; died March 12, 1978, in New York; actor. An intense, marvelously talented actor who made only five film appearances in his career—in five of the greatest films of the 1970s. His Fredo Corleone, the weak-willed lackey of *The Godfather* and its sequel, provides the necessary counterpoint to Pacino's Michael. He is equally brilliant in Coppola's *The Conversation* and Michael Cimino's *The Deer Hunter*, but it's starring opposite Al Pacino as the despondent simpleton Sal in *Dog Day Afternoon* that he will probably be best remembered. His career was unfortunately cut short after cancer took his life in 1978.

Filmography: The Godfather (1972); The Conversation (1974); The Godfather, Part II (1974); Dog Day Afternoon (1975); The Deer Hunter (1978).

CHASE, CHEVY. Born Cornelius Crane Chase October 8, 1944, in New York City; actor, comedian. A popular and often very funny comic who began his career off-Broadway and eventually found stardom as one of the not-ready-for-prime-time-players on NBC's "Saturday Night Live" (SNL). Contributing to his success were his slapstick President Ford pratfalls and his deadpan delivery as the "Weekend Update" news anchor. Soon after leaving SNL, he starred opposite Goldie Hawn in a pair of enjoyable, if featherweight, romantic comedies (*Foul Play, Seems like Old Times*), but his subsequent films (*Fletch, Caddyshack, National Lampoon's Vacation*, and their many sequels) have become increasingly repetitive and grating. His return to television in 1993 with an irreverent talk show was a resounding misfire that lasted scarcely one month.

Filmography: "The Great American Dream Machine" (1971–1972, tvs); The Groove Tube (1974); "Saturday Night Live" (1975–1977, tvs) also writer; Tunnelvision (1976); Foul Play (1978); Caddyshack (1980); Oh Heavenly Dog (1980); Seems like Old Times (1980); Modern Problems (1981); Under the Rainbow (1981); Deal of the Century (1983); National Lampoon's Vacation (1983); Fletch (1985); National Lampoon's European Vacation (1985); Sesame Street Presents: Follow That Bird (1985); Spies like Us (1985); Three Amigos! (1986); Caddyshack II (1988); The Couch Trip (1988); Funny Farm (1988) also producer; Fletch Lives (1989); National Lampoon's Christmas Vacation (1989); L.A. Story (1991); Nothing But Trouble (1991); Memoirs of an Invisible Man (1992); Hero and a Half (1992); Last Action Hero (1993); "The Chevy Chase Show" (1993, tvs) also writer, producer; Cops and Robbersons (1994); Man of the House (1995).

Honors: Emmy Awards for Best Writing ("Saturday Night Live" 1975 and 1976, "The Paul Simon Special" 1977) and Best Actor ("Saturday Night Live" 1975 and 1976).

CHEECH AND CHONG. Richard (Cheech) Marin: Born July 13, 1946, in Los Angeles; actor, director, screenwriter. Thomas Chong: Born May 24, 1938, in Edmonton, Alberta, Canada; actor, director, screenwriter; daughter Rae Dawn Chong is an actor. Popular, counterculture comedy duo formed in 1970 whose record albums extolling the virtues of marijuana led to a career in motion pictures. The hippie "parents" to such 1990s MTV idiot offspring as Beavis and Butthead, Cheech and Chong found massive popularity with their debut feature *Cheech and Chong's Up in Smoke*. With their pot-smoking humor becoming less and less relevant in the "Just Say No" years, the duo separated in 1985. Marin's subsequent solo effort, *Born in East L.A.*, spawned a hit single that spoofed Bruce Springsteen's "Born in the U.S.A."

Cheech and Chong filmography: Cheech and Chong's Up in Smoke (1978) also screenplay; Cheech and Chong's Next Movie (1980) also screenplay, directed by Chong; Cheech and Chong's Nice Dreams (1981) also screenplay, directed by Chong; Things Are Tough All Over (1982) also screenplay; Cheech and Chong's Still Smokin' (1983) also screenplay, directed by Chong; Yellowbeard (1983) actors; Cheech and Chong's

The Corsican Brothers (1984) also screenplay, directed by Chong; After Hours (1984) actors.

Cheech Marin filmography as actor: Born in East L.A. (1987) also screenplay, director; Oliver and Company (1988); Ghostbusters II (1989); Rude Awakening (1989); Troop Beverly Hills (1989); The Shrimp on the Barbie (1990); The Lion King (1994) voice; A Million to Juan (1994).

Tommy Chong filmography as actor: National Lampoon's Senior Trip (1995).

CHER. Born Cherilyn Sarkisian May 20, 1946, in El Centro, California; actor, singer. Formerly married to singer Sonny Bono and singer Gregg Allman. Pop superstar of the late 1960s and early 1970s whose singing career with then-husband Sonny Bono resulted in a string of hit singles ("I Got You Babe" was a top-10 hit in 1965) and the television series "The Sonny and Cher Comedy Hour." Although she appeared in some inconsequential films in the 1960s, her acting career really took hold with her Oscar-nominated role as Meryl Streep's lesbian pal Dolly in *Silkwood*, followed four years later by her Oscar-winning role as Loretta Castorini in *Moonstruck*. From the late 1980s on, however, her acting has taken a back seat to her resurgence as a singer.

Filmography: Wild on the Beach (1965); Good Times (1967); Chastity (1969); "The Sonny and Cher Comedy Hour" (1971–1974, tvs); Come Back to the 5 and Dime, Jimmy Dean, Jimmy Dean (1982); Silkwood (1983); Mask (1985); Moonstruck (1987); Suspect (1987); The Witches of Eastwick (1987); Mermaids (1990); The Player (1992); Ready to Wear (Prêt-à-Porter) (1994).

Honors: Academy Award for Best Actress (*Moonstruck*); Academy Award nomination for Best Supporting Actress (*Silkwood*); Cannes Film Festival Award for Best Actress (*Mask*).

Selected bibliography

Quirk, Lawrence J. *Totally Uninhibited: The Life and Wild Times of Cher*. New York: William Morrow, 1991.

CHINATOWN (1974), crime drama. Directed by Roman Polanski; screenplay by Robert Towne; produced by Robert Evans; edited by Sam O'Steen; music by Jerry Goldsmith; released by Paramount; 131 minutes. *Cast*: Jack Nicholson, Faye Dunaway, John Huston, Perry Lopez, John Hillerman, Darrell Zwerling, Diane Ladd, Roy Jensen, Roman Polanski, Burt Young.

One of the greatest examples of film noir in American cinema, this masterful evocation of 1930s Los Angeles features a tour de force performance from Jack Nicholson as a Chandleresque private eye who gets entangled in an enigma much more complex than he can imagine. Initially hired to shadow a philandering husband, J. J. Gittes (Nicholson) soon finds himself unraveling a mystery involving the beautiful Evelyn Mulwray (Dunaway), with whom he is falling in love, her corrupt and powerful father, Noah Cross (Huston), and an illegal land deal to supply water to Los Angeles. Although he thinks he's pretty smart, Gittes is no match for the diabolical Cross and is downright naive in comparison to

Mulwray, whose daughter/sister is the product of an incest. The sharply written script from Robert Towne, Polanski's stylish direction, and Nicholson's acting brilliance combine to create a rare commercial film that is both psychologically complex and thematically mature; a film that is equal parts commerce and art. From the most minute details (Gittes' remark on the slight imperfection in Evelyn's iris), to the explosive confrontations (Evelyn's dark and hysterical "My sister, my daughter . . ." admission of incest) *Chinatown* is the art of Hollywood filmmaking at its very best.

Sequel: Nicholson directed and starred in *Two Jakes* (1990), from a script by Robert Towne.

Awards: Academy Award for Best Screenplay; Academy Award nominations for Best Picture, Actor, Actress, Director, Cinematography, Art Direction, Sound, Score, Editing, Costume Design; New York Film Critics Circle Award for Best Actor; included in the Library of Congress' National Film Registry (1991).

CHOOSE ME (1984), drama/romance. Directed and written by Alan Rudolph; produced by Carolyn Pfeiffer and David Blocker; photographed by Jan Kiesser; edited by Mia Goldman; song "Choose Me (You're My Choice Tonight)" by Luther Vandross and Marcus Miller, sung by Teddy Pendergrass; released by Island Alive; 114 minutes. *Cast*: Keith Carradine, Lesley Ann Warren, Genevieve Bujold, Patrick Bauchau, Rae Dawn Chong, John Larroquette.

The third part of a loose trilogy of moody, circular tales of love and chance (*Welcome to L.A.*, *Remember My Name*), this passionately artificial comedic drama is Alan Rudolph's first completely realized effort. From the bluesy strains of the Teddy Pendergrass title song, the film is an intoxication—the sensual neon reds, the free-flowing scotch and Smirnoff, the pooled light from corner street lamps, the whispered voices of a radio talk show, and the constant state of sexual craving. Lacking a traditional narrative, the film is advanced by the needs of its characters—at the center of whom is popular radio romance adviser Dr. Nancy Love (Bujold). Although she's ill equipped to understand her own repressed ability to love, she has no problem diagnosing the miserable, loveless masses. When a mysterious stranger (Carradine) drifts into town, he reawakens the sleeping loins of Dr. Love and also works his magic on her roommate Eve (Warren) and aspiring poet Pearl (Chong). A unique director in American film, Rudolph is a pure romantic who creates an artificial world in order to better understand the genuine desires of his characters.

CIMINO, MICHAEL. Born February 1941 in New York; director, screenwriter. Momentarily brilliant American film director who was inconsequential before his earth-shattering Vietnam film *The Deer Hunter* and has proven to be inconsequential afterward. Still, if he were relegated to directing bad sitcoms for the remainder of his career, nothing could take away from the absolute greatness of *The Deer Hunter*. His follow-up film, *Heaven's Gate*, helped sink United Artists but is neither masterpiece nor bomb; instead, it is a visually majestic picture that is crippled by its confusing narrative (no doubt a result of the merciless editing) and weak characters. Had he directed only these pictures and disappeared (à la Terrence Malick), he would be a mythic figure in American film. Instead, he went on to three substandard potboilers that have practically reduced him to a mere curiosity. "Cimino is the most intelligent mythmaker since the young Norman Mailer" (Stephen Schiff, *Boston Phoenix*, February 13, 1979).

Filmography: Thunderbolt and Lightfoot (1974) also screenplay; The Deer Hunter (1978) also producer, story; Heaven's Gate (1980) also screenplay; Year of the Dragon (1985) also screenplay; The Sicilian (1987) also producer; Desperate Hours (1990) also producer.

Filmography as writer: Silent Running (1971); Magnum Force (1973).

Honors: Academy Award for Best Director (*The Deer Hunter*); DGA Award (*The Deer Hunter*); Los Angeles Film Critics Award for Best Director (*The Deer Hunter*).

Selected bibliography

Bach, Steven. *Final Cut*. New York: William Morrow, 1985.
Bliss, Michael. *Martin Scorsese and Michael Cimino*. Metuchen, NJ: Scarecrow Press, 1985.

CLAYBURGH, JILL. Born April 30, 1944, in New York City; actor. Married to playwright David Rabe. Schooled in drama at Sarah Lawrence College, this plainly attractive leading lady came to prominence in the mid-1970s via Broadway, where she appeared in *The Rothschilds* (1970) and *Pippin* (1972). Onscreen she has frequently played such psychologically complex women as the abandoned wife and mother in *An Unmarried Woman*, the incestuously tempted mother in *La Luna*, the independent businesswoman in *Starting Over*, the Valium addict in *I'm Dancing As Fast As I Can*, and the American lawyer in Israel in *Hannah K*. While most of her recent films have gone unseen, her performances in *Shy People* and *How to Make an American Quilt* are reminders of what a mature, self-assured actor Clayburgh can be.

Filmography: "Search for Tomorrow" (1967–1970, tvs); The Wedding Party (1969); The Telephone Book (1971); Portnoy's Complaint (1972); The Thief Who Came to Dinner (1973); The Terminal Man (1974); Hustling (1975, tvm); Gable and Lombard (1976); Silver Streak (1976); Semi-Tough (1977); An Unmarried Woman (1978); La Luna (1979); Starting Over (1979); It's My Turn (1980); First Monday in October (1981); I'm Dancing As Fast As I Can (1982); Hannah K (1983); In Our Hands (1984); Where Are the Children? (1986); Shy People (1987); Beyond the Ocean (1990); Reason for Living: The Jill Ireland Story (1991, tvm); Whispers in the Dark (1992); Day of Atonement (1992); Rich in Love (1992); For the Love of Nancy (1994, tvm); Naked in New York (1995); How to Make an American Quilt (1995).

Honors: Academy Award nominations for Best Actress (*An Unmarried Woman, Starting Over*); Cannes Film Festival Award for Best Actress (*An Unmarried Woman*).

CLOSE, GLENN. Born March 19, 1947, in Greenwich, Connecticut; actor, producer. A terrifically strong and confident leading lady, she has proven her versatility with success in motion pictures, television, and on stage. After being spotted in the Broadway musical *Barnum* by director George Roy Hill, she was memorably cast in her debut film role as Jenny Fields, mother of Garp and inspiration for the radical "Ellen Jamesian" feminist movement. Beginning with *Jagged Edge* (as a female defense lawyer) and continuing with *Fatal Attraction* (as the frizzy-haired, knife-wielding Alex), *Dangerous Liaisons* (as the Marquise de Merteuil), and *Reversal of Fortune* (as Sunny Von Bulow), she has delivered a succession of perfectly mannered performances for the big screen that established her as one of the most talented stars in Hollywood. Although her film work in the 1990s has been disappointing, she has satisfied her fans with tremendous television work in the "Hallmark Hall of Fame" drama *Sarah, Plain and Tall* and *Serving in Silence: The Margarethe Cammermeyer Story*, the story of a navy colonel discharged from the military for admitting her lesbianism. Her stage work has also been highly praised, especially her version of fading movie star Norma Desmond in Andrew Lloyd Webber's smash musical *Sunset Boulevard*.

Filmography: The World According to Garp (1982); The Big Chill (1983); The Stone Boy (1983); Greystoke: The Legend of Tarzan, Lord of the Apes (1984) voice only; The Natural (1984); Something about Amelia (1984, tvm); Jagged Edge (1985); Maxie (1985); Fatal Attraction (1987); Dangerous Liaisons (1988); Light Years (1988); Immediate Family (1989); Hamlet (1990); Reversal of Fortune (1990); Meeting Venus (1990); Sarah, Plain and Tall (1991, tvm) also ep; Skylark (1993, tvm); The House of the Spirits (1994); The Paper (1994); Serving in Silence: The Margarethe Cammermeyer Story (1995, tvm).

Honors: Academy Award nominations for Best Actress (*Fatal Attraction, Dangerous Liaisons*); Academy Award nominations for Best Supporting Actress (*The World According to Garp, The Big Chill, The Natural*); Los Angeles Film Critics Award for Best Supporting Actress (*The World According to Garp*); Emmy Award for Best Actress (*Serving in Silence: The Margarethe Cammermeyer Story*); Emmy Award nominations for Best Actress (*Something About Amelia, Sarah, Plain and Tall*); Tony Awards for Best Actress (*The Real Thing* 1984, *Death and the Maiden* 1993, *Sunset Boulevard* 1995).

CLOSE ENCOUNTERS OF THE THIRD KIND (1977), sci-fi. Directed and written by Steven Spielberg; produced by Julia Phillips and Michael Phillips; photographed by Vilmos Zsigmond; edited by Michael Kahn; music by John Williams; released by Columbia; 135 minutes (a "Special Edition," released in 1980, runs 132 minutes). *Cast*: Richard Dreyfuss, Francois Truffaut, Teri Garr, Melinda Dillon, Cary Guffey, Bob Balaban, Lance Hendrickson, Carl Weathers.

A unique, mature sci-fi film more concerned with characters than aliens or unidentified flying objects (UFOs), this is essentially Spielberg's essay on faith and dreams. Electric company lineman Roy Neary (Dreyfuss) is one of a select handful of chosen people who are "contacted" by a benevolent alien force during a close encounter of the third kind (the first kind is a mere sighting; the second kind is physical evidence). His family fails to comprehend his maddening obsession with UFOs or his goofy habit of forming dirt or mashed potatoes into an unexplained mountainous shape, but two others who have had similar encounters—an Indiana farm woman Jillian (Dillon) and her young son (Guffey)—share the same obsession. Together they travel—or, rather, are drawn—to Devil's Tower in Wyoming (the odd shape they've been envisioning), where they and a team of scientists led by Frenchman Claude Lacombe (Truffaut) make contact with an awe-inspiring, brightly lit mother ship the size of a small city. Unlike other films of the genre, the interest here is in the sense of wonderment that the characters experience. It is an innocent, when-you-wish-upon-a-star dream come true for anyone who has ever looked to the skies and hoped for some sign from above. Spielberg displays his usual mastery, while Dreyfuss possesses the necessary quality of boyishness that makes his character so likable. The contact theme from John Williams is probably the most memorable five-note sequence in movie history, especially the call-and-response between the scientists and the mother ship's booming bass notes. "A kind of inquisitive awe for the unknown that transcends the paranoia and melodrama so widespread in science fiction" (David Thomson, *A Biographical Dictionary of Film*).

Awards: Academy Award for Best Cinematography; Academy Award nominations for Best Director, Supporting Actress (Dillon), Art Direction, Sound, Score, Editing, Visual Effects.

COBURN, JAMES. Born August 31, 1928, in Laurel, Nebraska; actor. Handsome, wide-grinned actor who has made a career of playing tough guys and government agents but gained fame in the mid-1960s with the spy spoofs *Our Man Flint*, *In like Flint*, and *The President's Analyst*. While he does display an unlikely flair for comedy, he seems more suited to action and war films. His finest work has come with director Sam Peckinpah (*Major Dundee*; as the aging outlaw-turned-sheriff Pat Garrett in *Pat Garrett and Billy the Kid*; and *Cross of Iron*), though his gloriously hammy villain in *The Last of Sheila* and his hard-as-nails, bare-knuckle fighter in *Hard Times* are deserving of praise. "James Coburn is a modern rarity: an actor who projects lazy, humorous sexuality" (David Thomson, *A Biographical Dictionary of Film*).

Filmography of key pre-1965 films: The Magnificent Seven (1960); Hell Is For Heroes (1962); Charade (1963); The Great Escape (1963).

Filmography since 1965: A High Wind in Jamaica (1965); The Loved One (1965); Major Dundee (1965); Dead Heat on a Merry-Go-Round (1966); Our Man Flint (1966); What Did You Do in the War, Daddy? (1966); In like Flint (1967); The President's Analyst (1967) also producer; Waterhole Number 3 (1967) also producer; Candy (1968); Duffy (1968); Hard Contract (1969); Last of the Mobile Hot-Shots (1969); The Carey Treatment (1972); Duck, You Sucker (1972); The Honkers (1972); Harry in Your Pocket (1973); The Last of Sheila (1973); Pat Garrett and Billy the Kid (1973); The Internecine Project (1974); A Reason to Live, a Reason to Die (1974); Bite the Bullet (1975); Hard Times/The Streetfighter (1975); Battle of Midway (1976); The Last Hard Men (1976); Sky Riders (1976); Cross of Iron (1977); White Rock (1977, documentary) narrator; The

Silent Flute/Circle of Iron (1978) story only; Firepower (1979); Goldengirl (1979); The Muppet Movie (1979); The Baltimore Bullet (1980); Loving Couples (1980); Mr. Patman (1980); High Risk (1981); Looker (1981); Martin's Day (1983); The Leonski Incident (1985); The Lion's Roar (1985); Death of a Soldier (1986); Walking after Midnight (1988); Call from Space (1989); Tag Till Himlen (1989); Young Guns II (1990); Hudson Hawk (1991); Maverick (1994); The Avenging Angel (1995).

COEN, JOEL, AND ETHAN COEN. Joel Coen: Born November 29, 1954, in St. Louis Park, Minnesota; director, screenwriter. Ethan Coen: Born September 21, 1957, in St. Louis Park, Minnesota; producer, screenwriter. Unique among American filmmakers, the Coen brothers exist somewhere between commercial cinema and the art film; their films boast labyrinthine structures, comic book flourishes of camera movement and composition, crackling dialogue, and a fresh sense of invention but also offer name actors and studio backing. With just five films to their credit, three have been for 20th Century Fox and one for Warner Brothers, and these feature such top acting talents as Gabriel Byrne, Nicolas Cage, John Goodman, Albert Finney, Holly Hunter, Jennifer Jason Leigh, Paul Newman, Tim Robbins, and John Turturro. The brothers are among the most stylistic filmmakers working anywhere in the world, drawing comparison to the precisely controlled style of Peter Greenaway, Raul Ruiz, and Jeunet-Caro. Yet their films see only modest results at the box office. Hollywood frequently dilutes the vision of the independent filmmaker, but the Coens have used the studio system to their advantage; they are cine-literate visionaries whose art assuages the guilt of commerce-minded studio executives. They demanded immediate attention with their independently financed debut feature *Blood Simple*, an impassioned study in film noir double-crossing. They then proceeded to set a predictable pattern of unpredictability by following with a broad comedy (*Raising Arizona*), an elegant gangster drama (*Miller's Crossing*), an introspective black comedy about Hollywood and the creative process (*Barton Fink*), and a Capra-esque fantasy (*The Hudsucker Proxy*). As dissimilar as these films initially appear, each is devoted to the struggles of the common man: the small town Texans who become entangled in a murder plot, the desert trailer dwellers who just want a baby, the immigrant gangsters destroyed by a breakdown of ethics, the intellectual screenwriter terrorized by the working-class neighbor whom he only pretends to understand, and the hula-hooping rube who becomes chief executive officer (CEO). Ironically, however, these films are targeted not to a mass audience but to the art house few; the cinema of the Coen brothers may be the cinema of the common man, but their style belongs to the cinephile.

Filmography: Blood Simple (1984); Crimewave (1985) screenplay; Raising Arizona (1987); Miller's Crossing (1990); Barton Fink (1991); The Hudsucker Proxy (1994).

Filmography (Joel Coen only): Fear No Evil (1981) editor; The Evil Dead (1983) editor; Spies like Us (1985) actor.

Honor: Cannes Film Festival Palme d'Or (*Barton Fink*).

COHEN, LARRY. Born April 20, 1936, in New York City; director, screen-writer, producer. Neglected, intelligent, and subversive B-movie director whose offbeat social commentaries push the boundaries of genre expectations. After a great deal of television writing for such 1960s shows as the courtroom dramas "The Defender" and "Arrest and Trial," the western "Branded," the spy drama "Blue Light," and the sci-fi series "The Invaders" (the latter three of which he also created), Cohen made the switch to motion pictures, where he tackled yet another genre with the "blaxploitation" films *Black Caesar* and *Hell Up in Harlem*. It is with the horror film, however, that Cohen has made his mark—first with his remarkable *It's Alive*, a gruesome story of a young couple who give birth to a monster child (a result of a negligent pharmaceutical com-pany), then with *God Told Me To*, a twisted combination of film noir, sci-fi, and horror film that culminates in a confrontation with Jesus Christ in a dingy New York City basement, and finally with *Q*, a surprisingly effective thriller about a giant killer bird (Quetzalcoatl) that has nested atop the Chrysler Build-ing. However, his overall greatest achievement may be *The Private Files of J. Edgar Hoover*, a tell-all curiosity that takes an unflinching look at the fascist techniques of Federal Bureau of Investigation (FBI) chief J. Edgar Hoover and the skeletons in the closet of both John and Bobby Kennedy. Despite his obvious low-budget limitations, Cohen's sociopolitical insights are so refreshing that one can easily overlook the technical weaknesses of the films. Often featuring the droll and earnest Michael Moriarity, his films are frequently injected with a subtle sense of humor, especially *The Stuff*, a wicked satire on consumerism, marketing, and junk food.

Filmography as writer, director: In Broad Daylight (1971, tvm); Bone/Dial Rat for Terror/Beverly Hills Nightmare (1972) also producer; Black Caesar (1972) also producer; Hell Up in Harlem (1973) also producer; It's Alive (1974) also producer; God Told Me To/Demon (1976) also producer; The Private Files of J. Edgar Hoover (1977) also pro-ducer; It Lives Again (1978) also producer; Full Moon High (1981) also producer; Q/The Winged Serpent (1982) also producer; Perfect Strangers (1983) also producer; Special Effects (1985); The Stuff (1985) also ep; Deadly Illusion (1987); It's Alive III: Island of the Alive (1987) also ep; A Return to Salem's Lot (1987) also ep; Wicked Stepmother (1989) also ep; The Ambulance (1990).

Filmography as writer: I Deal in Danger (1966); Return of the Seven (1966); Daddy's Gone A-Hunting (1969); El Condor (1970); The American Success Company (1979); I, the Jury (1981); Scandalous (1984) story only; Best Seller (1987); Maniac Cop (1988) also producer; Maniac Cop 2 (1990) also producer; Guilty as Sin (1993); Body Snatchers (1994) story only.

Filmography as actor: Spies like Us (1985).

COLUMBUS, CHRIS. Born 1959 in Spangler, Pennsylvania; director, producer, screenwriter. A screenwriting protégé of Steven Spielberg (*Gremlins, The Goon-ies, Young Sherlock Holmes*) and directing protégé of John Hughes (*Home Alone, Home Alone 2: Lost in New York*, and *Only the Lonely*), Chris Columbus finally shed those skins with the box office comedy smash *Mrs. Doubtfire*, a Robin Williams vehicle that twists *Tootsie* into high farce. Like his mentors in the school of suburban family films, Columbus uncovers the broad comedy that is inherent in the battles that are waged between spouses, siblings, and offspring who live under one roof. Via his cleverly tagged company 1492 Productions, he works in an unabashedly commercial realm and has emerged as one of Hollywood's most mainstream talents; while not as imaginative as former mentor Spielberg, he clearly shows more restraint and innocence than the cynical Hughes. His direction of the Hughes-penned *Home Alone* turned that picture into the then second highest grossing film of all time.

Filmography: Adventures in Babysitting (1987); Heartbreak Hotel (1988) also screenplay; Home Alone (1990); Only the Lonely (1991) also screenplay; Mrs. Doubtfire (1993); Nine Months (1995) also screenplay, producer.

Filmography as writer: Gremlins (1984); Reckless (1984); The Goonies (1985); Young Sherlock Holmes (1985); Gremlins 2: The New Batch (1990) from characters.

COMING HOME (1978), war drama. Directed by Hal Ashby; screenplay by Waldo Salt and Robert C. Jones (from story by Nancy Dowd); produced by Jerome Hellman; photographed by Haskell Wexler; edited by Don Zimmerman; released by United Artists; 126 minutes. *Cast:* Jane Fonda, Jon Voight, Bruce Dern, Robert Ginty, Penelope Milford, Robert Carradine.

Of its peers *The Deer Hunter* and *Apocalypse Now*, *Coming Home* is the one that deals solely with the effects of the war at home, and it does so with such humanity that it should not be overshadowed by the stylistic force of its counterparts. It tells the story of three people who are each indelibly marked by the horrors of war—Sally Hyde (Fonda), the model military wife; Captain Bob Hyde (Dern), the true patriot on his way to Vietnam; and Luke Martin (Voight), the paraplegic Vietnam vet. Stripping away the expressionistic camera style of Cimino's and Coppola's films, Ashby went with a character-driven, semidocumentary style (thanks to Haskell Wexler's superb photography) that stresses the emotional and physical changes of the three protagonists. The ending, with its triptych cross-cutting, is one of former editor Hal Ashby's finer moments.

Honors: Academy Awards for Best Actress, Actor (Voight), and Screenplay; Academy Award nominations for Best Picture, Director, Editing; Cannes Film Festival Award for Best Actor (Voight).

CONVERSATION, THE (1974), drama. Directed, written, and produced by Francis Ford Coppola; photographed by Bill Butler; edited by Walter Murch; music by David Shire; released by Paramount; 113 minutes. *Cast:* Gene Hackman, John Cazale, Allen Garfield, Frederick Forrest, Cindy Williams, Teri Garr, Michael Higgins, Harrison Ford, Robert Duvall.

Like *The Rain People* five years earlier, this is an internal film from Francis Ford Coppola that, nestled in between the achievements of *The Godfather* and

The Godfather, Part II, may seem like a comparatively minor achievement but is nothing short of a masterpiece. Harry Caul (Hackman) is a high-tech surveillance expert who obsessively keeps his own life a carefully guarded secret. His girlfriend Amy (Garr) can't penetrate his outer shell, nor can his assistants Stan (Cazale) and Paul (Higgins). As he becomes increasingly enmeshed in the surveillance of two intended victims in a murder plot (Williams and Forrest), he is shocked to learn that they in fact are the killers, not the victims. Then, believing his apartment has been bugged by unnamed and unseen enemies, he retreats deep into a state of numbing paranoia, despite the fact that he has nothing to hide, because he has no life of his own; Harry's just a high-tech vampire who sucks the life from whomever he is tracking. The complex and precisely textured sound work and editing were done by Walter Murch, who has a long history of collaboration with Coppola and George Lucas.

Awards: Academy Award nomination for Best Picture, Screenplay, Sound; Cannes Film Festival Palme d'Or; included in the Library of Congress' National Film Registry (1995).

COOL HAND LUKE (1967), prison drama. Directed by Stuart Rosenberg; screenplay by Donn Pearce and Frank R. Pierson (from the novel by Pearce); produced by Gordon Carroll; photographed by Conrad Hall; edited by Sam O'Steen; music by Lalo Schifrin; released by Warner Bros.; 126 minutes. *Cast:* Paul Newman, George Kennedy, J. D. Cannon, Lou Antonio, Robert Drivas, Strother Martin, Jo Van Fleet, Clifton James, Dennis Hopper, Wayne Rogers, [Harry] Dean Stanton, Anthony Zerbe, Joe Don Baker.

Newman is the iron-willed Luke, a convict on a southern chain gang who is doing time for drunkenly busting some parking meters. After earning the respect of convict boss Dragline (Kennedy), first in a brutal fistfight, then in a poker game, Luke becomes a target of the camp's captain (Martin), a man determined to break the fiercely independent Luke before he becomes too influential over his fellow prisoners. Expertly directed by Stuart Rosenberg, a former television director whose career failed to live up to the promise of this film. Newman (earning his fourth Oscar nomination) is as good as he's ever been, especially in the famous egg-eating scene as he downs fifty hard-boiled eggs as part of a bet. Also memorable is his pained warbling about his "plastic Jesus, sitting on the dashboard of my car" and, of course, Martin's unforgettable utterance: "What we got here is a failure to communicate."

Awards: Academy Award for Supporting Actor (Kennedy); Academy Award nominations for Actor, Adapted Screenplay, Score.

COPPOLA, FRANCIS FORD. Born April 7, 1939, in Detroit; director, screenwriter, producer. Brother of actor Talia Shire; father of actor Sofia Coppola; son of composer Carmine Coppola; uncle of Nicolas Cage. Like the Vietnam conflict, which was central to *Apocalypse Now*, Francis Ford Coppola is a frustrating contradiction. Unequivocally the greatest American filmmaker of the 1970s and arguably the most important of all American artists of the decade, he has sadly become the most disappointing of his contemporaries, if only because of his promise. Like Orson Welles before him, the expectation of genius has been overshadowed by years of artistic mediocrity and commercial compromise. With every new film, one still fully expects Coppola to dazzle us with the epic grandeur of *The Godfather* and *The Godfather Part II*, the psychological depth of *The Rain People* or *The Conversation*, or the stylistic gluttony of *Apocalypse Now*. Yet, instead, we get the familiar nostalgia of *Peggy Sue Got Married*, the oppressive art direction and characterless drama of *The Cotton Club* and *Dracula*, the insufferable self-indulgence of the "Life with Zoe" episode of *New York Stories*, or the desperate plea to recapture past glory in *The Godfather, Part III*. The first major Hollywood figure of the film school generation, he was hired out of the University of California–Los Angeles in 1961 to write a subsequently discarded draft of *Reflections in a Golden Eye* while also honing his directing skills with a handful of disowned nudie films. He attracted attention as a director with his second feature, the Roger Corman-produced *Dementia 13*, an effectively creepy horror film set in an Irish castle. Having the distinction of being the only director to go from ax-wielding Corman quickie to Fred Astaire musical, Coppola was completely out of his element directing and choreographing the legendary hoofer in the surprisingly good Warner Brothers adaptation of 1947's long-running stage hit *Finian's Rainbow*. Coppola followed with the low-budget effort *The Rain People*, a stunning psychological tale about a distraught, pregnant woman and the nearly retarded ex-quarterback she befriends, a work that has been unjustly overlooked in light of his later successes. Winning an Oscar for the screenplay of *Patton* (cowritten with Edmund North), Coppola was shot into a different orbit that produced, in quick succession, *The Godfather*, *The Conversation*, and *The Godfather, Part II*, firmly establishing him as an American master. Filling his "spare" time as producer of George Lucas' *THX 1138* and *American Graffiti* and screenwriter of *The Great Gatsby*, Coppola embarked upon his most massive undertaking, the catastrophe-plagued *Apocalypse Now*, a Vietnam fever dream that came close to killing star Martin Sheen and nearly destroyed Coppola financially. The picture, an artistic conundrum, went on to win the Palme d'Or at the Cannes Film Festival. The coming decade, however, saw the director become preoccupied with modern digital technology, much of which has since become an industry standard. Fulfilling a lifelong dream of running a movie studio, he expanded his American Zoetrope into just such a venture with his whimsical musical romance *One from the Heart*, a charming, if overblown, love story set against the backdrop of a studio-bound Las Vegas. The film, however, was a commercial disaster and sent American Zoetrope into bankruptcy. Although prolific through the 1980s, Coppola's films were less than magnificent—the two S. E. Hinton adaptations, *The Outsiders* and *Rumblefish*, featured excellent casts of soon-to-be-famous unknowns and expressionistic visuals but failed to find its elusive audience; the jazz-era film *The Cotton Club* lacked the epic quality it strove for; the Michael Jackson extravaganza *Captain Eo* was a celebrity exercise; and *Peggy Sue Got Married*, while occasionally hitting psychological truths, still felt like the weaker sibling of the much slicker *Back to the Future*. For a too-brief moment, Coppola again appeared to be back in the game with *Gardens of Stone*, a commercial and critical flop that told the intense story of a man in conflict over his love for the military and his hatred of the war in Vietnam, and *Tucker: The Man and His Dream*, an exhilarating document of a visionary (not unlike Coppola himself) who fights the auto industry in order to realize his dream of a new automobile. The transformation was only temporary, however; Coppola followed with the weakest episode of the *New York Stories* trilogy, the unworthy third installment of the *Godfather* saga, and the anemic *Dracula*. On the basis of his previous accomplishments one still expects greatness from Coppola, though he continues (with 1996's fantasy *Jack* and the John Grisham project *The Rainmaker*) to choose lucrative Hollywood studio projects over the personal style of filmmaking for which he is better suited. In addition to his achievements as a filmmaker, he made a brief foray into the publishing world with the 1970s purchase of San Francisco's *City Magazine* and has also become a highly regarded vintner with his Napa Valley winery. "The godfather of all film school-trained moviemakers" (Rob Edelman, *The International Dictionary of Films and Filmmakers*).

Filmography: Tonight for Sure (1962) also screenplay, producer; Dementia 13/The Haunted and the Hunted (1963); Battle beyond the Sun/Nebo Zovyot (1963) "direction" of American version; You're a Big Boy Now (1966); Finian's Rainbow (1968); The Rain People (1969); The Godfather (1972); The Conversation (1974); The Godfather, Part II (1974); Apocalypse Now (1979); One from the Heart (1982); The Outsiders (1983); Rumblefish (1983); The Cotton Club (1984); Captain Eo (1986); Peggy Sue Got Married (1986); Gardens of Stone (1987); Tucker: A Man and His Dream (1988); New York Stories, "Life with Zoe" episode (1989); The Godfather, Part III (1990); Dracula/Bram Stoker's Dracula (1993).

Additional credits: The Tower of London (1962) dialogue director; The Terror (1963) associate producer; Is Paris Burning?/Paris Brule-t-il? (1966) screenplay; This Property Is Condemned (1966) screenplay; Patton (1970) screenplay; THX 1138 (1971) ep; American Graffiti (1973) producer; The Great Gatsby (1974) screenplay; The Black Stallion (1979) ep; The Escape Artist (1982) ep; Hammett (1982) ep; Koyaanisqatsi (1983) presenter; The Black Stallion Returns (1983) ep; Mishima: A Life in Four Chapters (1985) ep; Lionheart (1987/released in 1990) ep; Tough Guys Don't Dance (1987) ep; Powaqqatsi (1988) producer; The Wind (1992) producer; The Secret Garden (1993) producer; Mary Shelley's Frankenstein (1994) producer; My Family/Mi Familia (1995) ep; Don Juan De Marco (1995) producer; Haunted (1995) ep.

Honors: Academy Awards for Best Picture and Director (*The Godfather, Part II*) and Screenplay (*Patton, The Godfather, The Godfather, Part II*); Academy Award nominations for Best Picture (*American Graffiti, The Conversation, Apocalypse Now*), Director (*The Godfather*) and Screenplay (*The Conversation*); DGA Awards (*The Godfather, The Godfather, Part II*); Cannes Film Festival Awards, Palme d'Or (*The Conversation, Apocalypse Now*) and the Fipresci Prize (*Apocalypse Now*).

Selected bibliography

Coppola, Eleanor. *Notes*. New York: Simon and Schuster, 1979.
Gelmis, Joseph. Interview in *The Film Director as Superstar*. New York: Doubleday, 1970.
Johnson, Robert K. *Francis Ford Coppola*. Boston: Twayne, 1977.
Kolker, Robert Phillip. *A Cinema of Loneliness: Penn, Kubrick, Coppola, Scorsese, Altman*. New York: Oxford University Press, 1980.
Zucker, Joel S. *Francis Ford Coppola: A Guide to References and Resources*. Boston: G. K. Hall, 1984.

CORMAN, ROGER. Born April 5, 1926, in Los Angeles; director, producer, distributor. If one person were to be chosen as the major force in American film from the 1960s through the 1990s, it might be Roger Corman, the ultimate independent filmmaker and catalyst in the careers of such Hollywood figures as Francis Ford Coppola, Martin Scorsese, Peter Bogdanovich, Jonathan Demme, Ron Howard, John Milius, Robert Towne, Alan Arkush, Penelope Spheeris, James Cameron, Carl Franklin, Robert De Niro, Jack Nicholson, Dennis Hopper, and former 20th Century Fox president Lawrence Gordon. Making his films at a breakneck pace (sometimes as quick as three days) and on nonexistent budgets, he has turned out over 200 movies, which have flooded international, cable, and video markets. Beyond the ridiculous movies with rubber sea monsters and the like are some hidden gems—*The Wild Angels*, *The Trip*, *Machine Gun Kelly*, *The St. Valentine's Day Massacre*, *Targets*, and the classic Edgar Allan Poe adaptations *The Pit and the Pendulum*, *Tales of Terror*, *The Raven*, *The Tomb of Ligeia*, and *The Masque of Red Death*. He formed New World Pictures in 1970 (ending his long association with American International Pictures), distributing his exploitation fare and such foreign classics as Truffaut's *Small Change*, Bergman's *Cries and Whispers*, and Fellini's *Amarcord*. In 1983, he founded the prolific Concorde/New Horizons, which continues the tradition of making inexpensive movies and serving as a training ground for upcoming filmmakers. "Roger Corman's Hollywood career seems to start where a director like Allan Dwan's leaves off, in low-budget exploitation movies realized with efficiency but minimal enthusiasm or expertise" (Tony Rayns, *Cinema: A Critical Dictionary*).

Filmography of key pre-1965 film as director and producer: Not of This Earth (1957); Machine Gun Kelly (1958); Cry Baby Killer (1958) producer only; A Bucket of Blood (1959); House of Usher (1960); The Last Woman on Earth (1960); Little Shop of Horrors (1961); The Pit and the Pendulum (1961); The Premature Burial (1961); Tales of Terror (1962); Tower of London (1962) director only; The Raven (1963); The Terror (1963); Dementia 13 (1963) producer only; The Masque of the Red Death (1964).

Filmography since 1965 as director and producer: The Tomb of Ligeia (1965); The Wild Angels (1966); The St. Valentine's Day Massacre (1967); The Trip (1967); Das Ausschweifende Leben des Marquis de Sade (1969) director only; How to Make It (1969) also actor; Bloody Mama (1970); Gas-s-s-s! (1970); Von Richtofen and Brown (1971) director only; Roger Corman's Frankenstein Unbound (1990) also screenplay.

Filmography since 1965 as producer or executive producer: The Dunwich Horror (1970); The Student Nurses (1970); Boxcar Bertha (1972); The Unholy Rollers (1972); I Escaped from Devil's Island (1973); Big Bad Mama (1974); Cockfighter (1974); Capone (1975); Death Race 2000 (1975); Lumiere (1975); Eat My Dust (1976); Fighting Mad (1976); Jackson County Jail (1976); Moving Violation (1976); Grand Theft Auto (1977); I Never Promised You a Rose Garden (1977); Thunder and Lightning (1977); Avalanche (1978); Deathsport (1978); Fast Charlie—The Moonbeam Rider (1978); Outside Chance (1978, tvm); Piranha (1978); Rock and Roll High School (1979); Saint Jack (1979); Battle beyond the Stars (1980); The Georgia Peaches (1980, tvm); Galaxy of Terror (1981); Smokey Bites the Dust (1981); The Territory (1981); Forbidden World (1982); Love Letters (1983); Space Raiders (1983); Suburbia (1983); The Warrior and the Sorceress (1983); Deathstalker (1984); Streetwalkin' (1985); Amazons (1987); Hour of the Assassin (1987); Munchies (1987); Slumber Party Massacre II (1987); Stripped to Kill (1987); Sweet Revenge (1987); Big Bad Mama II (1988); Daddy's Boys (1988); Dangerous Love (1988); The Drifter (1988); Nightfall (1988); Not of This Earth (1988); Watchers (1988); Andy Colby's Incredibly Awesome Adventure (1989); Bloodfist (1989); Crime Zone (1989); Dance of the Damned (1989); Heroes Stand Alone (1989); Last Stand at Lang Mei (1989); The Lawless Land (1989); Lords of the Deep (1989); The Masque of the Red Death (1989); Stripped to Kill II (1989); The Terror Within (1989); Time Trackers (1989); Two to Tango (1989); Wizards of the Lost Kingdom II (1989); Back to Back (1990); Bloodfist II (1990); A Cry in the Wild (1990); Full Fathom Five (1990); The Haunting of Morella (1990); Overexposed (1990); Primary Target (1990); Silk 2 (1990); Streets (1990); Transylvania Twist (1990); Watchers II (1990); Welcome to Oblivion (1990); Futurekick (1991); Hollywood Boulevard II (1991); Rock 'n' Roll High School Forever (1991); The Terror Within II (1991); The Assassination Game (1992); The Berlin Conspiracy (1992); Blackbelt (1992); Bloodfist III: Forced to Fight (1992); Bloodfist IV: Die Trying (1992); Body Chemistry: Voice of a Stranger (1992); Body Waves (1992); Dance with Death (1992); Deathstalker IV: Match of Titans (1992); Eye of the Eagle 3 (1992); Field of Fire (1992); Final Embrace (1992); Final Judgment (1992); Homicidal Impulse (1992); Immortal Sins (1992); In the Heat of Passion (1992); Munchie (1992); Play Murder for Me (1992); Quake! (1992); Raiders of the Sun (1992); Sorority House Massacre 2 (1992); Ultraviolet (1992); Carnosaur (1993); Dracula Rising (1993); Dragonfire (1993); 800 Leagues Down the Amazon (1993); Firehawk (1993); Little Miss Millions (1993); Live by the Fifth (1993); Stepmonster (1993); To Sleep with a Vampire (1993); Cheyenne Warrior (1994); In the Heat of Passion II (1994); Reflections in the Dark (1994); Unborn II (1994); The Alien Within (1995, ctvm); Attack of the 60 Ft. Centerfold (1995); Black Scorpion (1995, ctvm); Bloodfist VII: Manhunt (1995); Bram Stoker's Burial of the Rats (1995, ctvm); A Bucket of Blood (1995, ctvm); Carnosaur II (1995); The Crazysitter (1995); Dillinger and Capone (1995); Captain Nuke and the Bomber Boys (1995); Hellfire (1995, ctvm); Midnight Tease (1995); Not like Us (1995, ctvm); Not of This Earth (1995, ctvm); One Night Stand (1995); Piranha (1995, ctvm); Sawbones (1995, ctvm); The Spy Within (1995); Stranglehold (1995); Suspect Device (1995, ctvm); Terminal Virus (1995, ctvm); Virtual Seduction (1995, ctvm); Wasp Woman (1995, ctvm); Watchers III (1995).

Filmography as writer: Highway Dragnet (1954) story.

Filmography as actor: The Godfather, Part II (1974); Cannonball (1976); The Howling

(1980); The State of Things (1982); Swing Shift (1984); The Silence of the Lambs (1991); ''Eye'' episode of ''John Carpenter Presents Body Bags'' (1993, ctvm).

Honor: Los Angeles Film Critics Career Achievement Award (1996).

Selected bibliography

Corman, Roger, and Jim Jerome. *How I Made a Hundred Movies in Hollywood and Never Lost a Dime.* New York: Random House, 1990.

McGee, Mark Thomas. *Roger Corman: The Best of the Cheap Acts.* Jefferson, NC: McFarland, 1988.

Naha, Ed. *Roger Corman: Brillance on a Budget.* New York: Arco Press, 1982.

COSTNER, KEVIN. Born January 18, 1955, in Los Angeles; actor, producer, director. Affable and charming leading man whose strong, silent, and boyish demeanor has made him immensely popular. Once a stage manager at Los Angeles' Raleigh Studios, his career beginnings have become legendary—cast in Lawrence Kasdan's *The Big Chill* (1983) in the pivotal role of the dead friend, he was subsequently edited out, only to have Kasdan later cast him in *Silverado,* the first of their many collaborations. He's achieved popular success by playing idealistic, incorruptible characters in *The Untouchables, Field of Dreams,* and *The Bodyguard* and considerable critical success with his auteur turn as actor/director/producer in *Dances with Wolves.* Although he has given quietly powerful performances in *JFK* (as New Orleans D.A. Jim Garrison) and *A Perfect World,* his star has dimmed with a succession of commercially insignificant films (*Robin Hood: Prince of Thieves, Wyatt Earp, The War, Waterworld*) and a stretch of bad press in the same tabloids that previously venerated him. He formed Tig Productions in 1988 to develop his own projects and in 1995 purchased the rights to the Pulitzer-winning play *The Kentucky Cycle,* which he plans to direct, produce, and star in for HBO.

Filmography: Shadows Run Black (1981); Night Shift (1982); Stacy's Knights (1983); The Gunrunner (1983); Table for Five (1983); Testament (1983); American Flyers (1985); Fandango (1985); Silverado (1985); Sizzle Beach, U.S.A. (1986); No Way Out (1987); The Untouchables (1987); Bull Durham (1988); Chasing Dreams (1989); Field of Dreams (1989); Dances with Wolves (1990); Revenge (1990); Robin Hood: Prince of Thieves (1991); The Bodyguard (1992); JFK (1993); A Perfect World (1993); Wyatt Earp (1994); The War (1994); Rapa Nui (1994) producer; Waterworld (1995).

Honors: Academy Awards for Best Picture and Director (*Dances with Wolves*); DGA Award (*Dances with Wolves*); Berlin Film Festival Award for Outstanding Single Achievement (*Dances with Wolves*).

Selected bibliography

Keith, Todd. *Kevin Costner: The Unauthorized Biography.* London: Ikonprint Books, 1991.

CRAVEN, WES. Born August 2, 1949; director, screenwriter. Having contributed three of the most influential films of the horror genre, it is almost irrelevant that the rest of Craven's sizable body of work has failed to achieve equal success. His first two pictures—the low-budget revenge shocker *Last House on the Left* (with its tag line of "It's only a movie") and the more polished *The Hills Have Eyes*—both used the conventions of the genre to comment on the dark side of the American family within an intelligent sociopolitical context. After a period of television work, he burst back onto the scene with his box office hit *A Nightmare on Elm Street*. That film's Freddy Krueger with his floppy hat, red and green striped sweater, and metal glove with knife fingers has since become a horror figure as recognizable as Frankenstein or Dracula and considerably more witty. Of the rest of his films, many have slipped into parody, though he has garnered some critical attention with the voodoo-themed *The Serpent and the Rainbow* (a veiled comment on Haiti's Baby Doc political regime) and *People under the Stairs* (a misfire that can be read as a critique of urban blight). More recently, *Wes Craven's New Nightmare*, a subversive, self-reflexive addition to the Freddy Kreuger canon, lacked the audience-pleasing punch of its predecessors, while his attempt to combine horror and comedy in a Hollywood picture failed on all levels in the Eddie Murphy vehicle *Vampire in Brooklyn*.

Filmography: Last House on the Left (1973); The Hills Have Eyes (1977); Stranger in Our House (1978, tvm); Deadly Blessing (1981); Swamp Thing (1982); Invitation to Hell (1984, tvm); A Nightmare on Elm Street (1984); Chiller (1985, tvm); The Hills Have Eyes Part II (1985); Deadly Friend (1986); Casebusters (1986, tvm); numerous "Twilight Zone" episodes (1987–1988, tvs); The Serpent and the Rainbow (1988); Shocker (1989); Night Visions (1990, tvm) also writer, ep; People under the Stairs (1991); Wes Craven's New Nightmare (1994); Vampire in Brooklyn (1995).

Additional credits: Together (1971) assistant producer; You've Got to Walk It Like You Talk It or You'll Lose That Beat (1971) editor; It Happened in Hollywood (1972) editor; Flowers in the Attic (1987) screenplay only; A Nightmare on Elm Street Part III: Dream Warriors (1987) screenplay, ep; "The People Next Door" (1989, tvs) ep, story; Bloodfist II (1990) adviser; "Nightmare Cafe" (1992, tvs) ep, writer; "The Gas Station" episode of "John Carpenter Presents Body Bags" (1993, ctvm) actor; "Laurel Canyon" (1993, tv) producer; Wes Craven Presents Mind Ripper: Live in Horror, Die in Fear (1995, ctvm) ep.

CRUISE, TOM. Born Thomas Cruise Mapother IV July 3, 1962, in Syracuse, New York; actor. Married to Nicole Kidman; formerly married to actor Mimi Rogers. One of the most popular stars of his generation, he has steered his career from teen heartthrob to a daring, highly respected actor who has costarred with the likes of Paul Newman, Jack Nicholson, Dustin Hoffman, and Gene Hackman. Winning the hearts of many an adoring fan in the megahit *Top Gun* and displaying his true raw talent in *Rain Man*, his performance as Vietnam vet Ron Kovic in Oliver Stone's *Born on the Fourth of July* won him true respect as an actor. Though his two subsequent films, *Days of Thunder* and *Far and Away*, both flopped with audiences, he firmly reestablished his place with *A Few Good Men*, *The Firm*, and *Interview with the Vampire*. His role in the latter, as the bisexual vampire Lestat made famous in Anne Rice's novels, has proven to be his greatest risk to date. Amid charges of miscasting from the outspoken Rice, Cruise surprised fans and detractors alike with an intelligent and gutsy performance. "Cruise is one of the first young actors who seems unaffected by the impact of Brando or Clift, and much more inspired by the example of a Gable or a Grant" (David Thomson, *A Biographical Dictionary of Film*).

Filmography: Endless Love (1981); Taps (1981); All the Right Moves (1983); Losin' It (1983); The Outsiders (1983); Risky Business (1983); Legend (1985); The Color of Money (1986); Top Gun (1986); Cocktail (1988); Rain Man (1988); Born on the Fourth of July (1989); Days of Thunder (1990) also story; Far and Away (1991); A Few Good Men (1992); The Firm (1993); "The Frightening Frammis" episode of "Fallen Angels" (1994, ctv) director; Interview with the Vampire (1994) also producer.

Honor: Academy Award nomination for Best Actor (*Born on the Fourth of July*).

Selected bibliography

Sanello, Frank. *Cruise: The Unauthorized Biography*. Dallas, TX: Taylor, 1995.

CRYSTAL, BILLY. Born March 14, 1947, in Long Beach, New York; actor, screenwriter, director, comedian. A stand-up comic who broke ground in "Soap" as television's first openly gay character, Crystal made the transition to movies in Joan Rivers' *Rabbit Test*. His pleasing combination of comic timing and dramatic honesty was perfect for the blockbuster romantic comedy *When Harry Met Sally . . .* , his best-loved and most rewarding film to date. His directorial debut, *Mr. Saturday Night*, in which he also starred as an aging comedian, was an insightful, though ultimately flawed, work. In addition to his big-screen work, special note must be made of his refreshing run as the host of the Academy Awards telecast.

Filmography: "Soap" (1977–1981, tvs); Rabbit Test (1978); Animalympics (1979); This Is Spinal Tap (1984); "Saturday Night Live" (1984–1985, tvs); Running Scared (1986); The Princess Bride (1987); Throw Momma from the Train (1987); Memories of Me (1988); also screenplay, producer; When Harry Met Sally . . . (1989); City Slickers (1991) also ep; Mr. Saturday Night (1992) also director; City Slickers II: The Legend of Curly's Gold (1994) also screenplay; Forget Paris (1995) also screenplay, director, producer.

Selected bibliography

Crystal, Billy, and Dick Schaap. *Absolutely Mahvelous*. NY: Putnam 1986.

CULKIN, MACAULAY. Born August 26, 1980, in New York City; actor. Brother Kieran is also an actor; aunt is Bonnie Bedelia. After gaining some notoriety for his cute interplay with John Candy in *Uncle Buck*, the preteen Culkin hit the big time with his hands-to-the-cheeks expression of exasperation in *Home Alone*. Almost overnight he became a comic sensation, though the box office tallies on his non-*Home Alone* films reflect that his popularity has taken a speedy dive downward. Some significantly bad press and Hollywood's oft-publicized dislike of his father/manager Kit Culkin have only diminished his commercial worth.

Filmography: Rocket Gibraltar (1988); Uncle Buck (1989); Home Alone (1990); Home Alone 2: Lost in New York (1992); George Balanchine's The Nutcracker (1993); The Good Son (1993); Getting Even with Dad (1994); The Pagemaster (1994); Richie Rich (1994).

CURTIS, JAMIE LEE. Born November 22, 1958, in Los Angeles; actor. Married to actor/screenwriter/director Christopher Guest; daughter of Tony Curtis and Janet Leigh. Strong and convincing lead actor who has been effective in both comic and dramatic roles. Her first film, John Carpenter's *Halloween*, led to a succession of horror films and mediocre commercial films, while her 1987 role in French director Diane Kury's *A Man in Love* displayed a dramatic range that had only been hinted at previously. She later followed with a couple of strong, practically macho performances—*Blue Steel* and *True Lies*, each giving her some violent boy-toys to play with—though her strongest and most highly praised role is her comic turn opposite John Cleese in *A Fish Called Wanda*. She is also the author of the children's book *When I Was Little: A Four-Year-Old's Memoir of Her Youth*.

Filmography: Halloween (1978); The Fog (1980); Prom Night (1980); Terror Train (1980); Death of a Centerfold (1981, tvm); Halloween II (1981); Road Games (1981); Love Letters (1983); Trading Places (1983); The Adventures of Buckaroo Bonzai: Across the 8th Dimension (1984); Grandview, U.S.A. (1984); Perfect (1985); Amazing Grace and Chuck (1987); A Man in Love (1987); Dominick and Eugene (1988); A Fish Called Wanda (1988); Blue Steel (1989); Queens Logic (1991); Mother's Boys (1994); My Girl 2 (1994); True Lies (1994); The Heidi Chronicles (1995, ctvm); House Arrest (1995).

CUSACK, JOHN. Born June 28, 1966, in Evanston, Illinois; actor. Brother of actors Joan, Ann, Susie, and Bill. An accomplished and intelligent actor who has managed to rise above the fun, but generally insipid, roles of his early career. Starting with Rob Reiner's surprisingly charming *The Sure Thing*, Cusack began to show signs of his extensive theater training with the Piven Theater Workshop. As Chicago White Sox third baseman Buck Weaver in John Sayles' *Eight Men Out* he proved he could step out of the teen pack and deliver something even more resonant. His last real teen role, *Say Anything*, is remembered most for the cathartic moment when Lloyd Dobler, Cusack's love-struck character, holds his boom box high over his head as Peter Gabriel's ''In Your Eyes'' serenades his lover. With his next role, as the slick con man of Stephen Frears' *The Grifters*, he established himself as a suave, very together leading man. Other roles of interest include his excellent work for Woody Allen in *Shadows and Fog* and *Bullets over Broadway* and his portrayal of real-life Philadelphian Joey Coyle in the otherwise unsatisfying *Money for Nothing*. His theater work includes the formation of the New Criminals company (for which he directed the critically acclaimed 1990 play *Methuselem*) and involvement in Tim Robbin's the Actors Gang. The year 1995 saw the development of the feature film *Grosse Point Blank*, a black comedy cowritten and coproduced by Cusack through his film company New Crime Productions.

Filmography: Class (1983); Grandview, U.S.A. (1983); Sixteen Candles (1984); Better Off Dead (1985); The Journey of Natty Gann (1985); The Sure Thing (1985); One Crazy Summer (1986); Stand By Me (1986); Broadcast News (1987); Hot Pursuit (1987); Eight Men Out (1988); Tapeheads (1988); Fat Man and Little Boy (1989); Say Anything (1989); The Grifters (1990); True Colors (1991); Shadows and Fog (1992); Bob Roberts (1992); Roadside Prophets (1992); The Player (1992); Map of the Human Heart (1993); Money for Nothing (1993); The Road to Wellville (1994); Bullets over Broadway (1994); Floundering (1994).

CUTTER'S WAY (1981), drama. Directed by Ivan Passer; screenplay by Jeffrey Alan Fiskin (from the novel by Newton Thornburg); photographed by Jordan Cronenweth; edited by Caroline Ferriol; music by Jack Nitzsche; released by United Artists; 105 minutes. *Cast*: Jeff Bridges, John Heard, Lisa Eichhorn, Ann Dusenberry, Stephen Elliott, Arthur Rosenberg, Patricia Donahue, Geraldine Baron.

   One of the major oversights in American film has been lack of success and recognition for this beautiful and honest tale of the collapse of the American Dream. Lamenting the lack of heroism in the world and loudly raging against its corruption and power, Vietnam vet and multiple amputee Alex Cutter (Heard) concocts a plan to nail a powerful oil tycoon who may have murdered a prostitute. The only witness to the crime is Alex's best friend, Richard Bone (Bridges), an all-American playboy who skates through life without any convictions. Objecting to their plan (which involves delivering an extortion letter as bait) is Alex's alcoholic wife, Mo (Eichhorn), a beautiful, but jaded, woman who admires her husband's integrity but needs the friendship and (eventually) love of Rich. Directed with great sensitivity and poetry by Czech-born Ivan Passer, the film features excellent performances from Bridges as the emotional cripple, an almost unrecognizable Heard as the physical cripple, and the radiant Eichhorn, who is simply perfect as the woman who needs them both.

D

DAFOE, WILLEM. Born July 22, 1955, in Appleton, Wisconsin; actor. Striking actor with chiseled features and piercing eyes who began his career playing off-balance characters in *The Loveless*, *The Hunger*, and *To Live and Die in L.A.* before achieving star status and an Academy Award nomination as Sergeant Elias in *Platoon*. Since then he has taken on a number of challenging and intense roles that have proven him to be one of the most versatile actors in film, displaying both a chilling dark side (*Wild at Heart*, *Light Sleeper*) and a tender humanism (*Mississippi Burning*, *Tom and Viv*). While it may not be his best performance, his greatest role was undoubtedly that of Jesus Christ in Martin Scorsese's *The Last Temptation of Christ*. In addition to his film work, he is a member of New York's highly acclaimed theater company, the Wooster Group.

Filmography: The Loveless (1981); New York Nights (1982); The Hunger (1983); The Communists Are Comfortable (and Three Other Stories) (1984); Roadhouse 66 (1984); Streets of Fire (1984); To Live and Die in L.A. (1985); Platoon (1986); Dear America (1987); The Last Temptation of Christ (1988); Mississippi Burning (1988); Off Limits (1988); Born on the Fourth of July (1989); Triumph of the Spirit (1989); Cry-Baby (1990); Wild at Heart (1990); Flight of the Intruder (1991); The Doors (1991); Light Sleeper (1992); White Sands (1992); Body of Evidence (1993); Clear and Present Danger (1994); Tom and Viv (1994); The Night and the Moment (1994); Victory (1995).

Honor: Academy Award nomination for Best Supporting Actor (*Platoon*).

DANIELS, JEFF. Born February 19, 1955, in Georgia; actor. Leading man who excels at playing innocent, naive, bumbling characters. His most memorable early role was as Flap Horton of *Terms of Endearment*, a role that required him to remain likable despite being an adulterous husband and a failed father. He attracted further attention as the befuddled, pith-helmeted movie star who steps off the screen into real life in *The Purple Rose of Cairo* and as the recipient of seductress Melanie Griffith's sexual advances in *Something Wild*. After a stretch of misses, his stock as a popular actor skyrocketed in 1994, when he teamed up with megastar Jim Carrey in the successful *Dumb and Dumber*.

Filmography: Ragtime (1981); Terms of Endearment (1983); Marie (1985); The Purple Rose of Cairo (1985); Heartburn (1986); Something Wild (1986); Radio Days (1987); The House on Carroll Street (1988); Sweet Hearts Dance (1988); Checking Out (1988); Arachnophobia (1990); Love Hurts (1990); Welcome Home, Roxie Carmichael (1990); Gettysburg (1993); Speed (1994); Dumb and Dumber (1994).

DAVE (1993), comedy. Directed and coproduced by Ivan Reitman; screenplay by Gary Ross; produced with Lauren Shuler-Donner; photographed by Adam Greenberg; edited by Sheldon Kahn; music by James Newton Howard; released by Warner Bros.; 110 mins. *Cast*: Kevin Kline, Sigourney Weaver, Frank Langella, Kevin Dunn, Ving Rhames, Ben Kingsley, Charles Grodin, Bonnie Hunt, Arnold Schwarzenegger, Oliver Stone, Larry King, Jay Leno.

Coming just a year after William Jefferson Clinton won the presidential election on a message of hope (as in his Arkansas hometown) and impish Reform Party candidate Ross Perot electrified disfranchised American voters by forging a third party that employed plain-speaking, homespun rhetoric, screenwriter Gary Ross and Canadian-born director Ivan Reitman molded these sentiments into a smart, funny, and perceptive comedy in the populist tradition of Frank Capra. When a stroke reduces philandering president Bill Mitchell to a vegetative state, look-alike Dave Kovic (Kline) is pressured by White House insiders into doubling as the nation's leader. It's not long before Dave, seduced by the power, realizes he can actually effect change. He becomes a friendlier, funnier leader who connects with the populace better than the real Bill Mitchell and, in the process, rekindles "his" romance with First Lady Ellen (Weaver) while angering the duplicitous White House power monger Bob Alexander (Langella). Reitman, Ross, and Kline do a wonderful job of highlighting the widespread belief (that Perot helped propagate) that the common man is better equipped to run the country than the Washington insider. This is best articulated in Dave's successful attempt to balance the budget. As the fictional politicians make half-hearted overtures about crunching the numbers, Dave and his accountant pal Murray Blum (Grodin) are the ones who get the job done; it is proof of how easy the American presidency would be if the only special interests one needed to answer to were the American people themselves.

Award: Academy Award nomination for Best Screenplay.

DAVID HOLTZMAN'S DIARY (1968), fictional documentary. Directed, written, produced and edited by Jim McBride; photographed by Michael Wadleigh, Paul Glickman, and Paul Goldsmith (b&w); released by Paradigm Films; 74 minutes. *Cast*: L. M. Kit Carson, Eileen Dietz, Louise Levine, Lorenzo Mans.

One of the wittiest independent films of the 1960s, this debut feature from

Jim McBride (*Breathless, The Big Easy, Great Balls of Fire*) is a fictional film that satirically masquerades as a cinema verité documentary on the life of aspiring New York City filmmaker David Holtzman (Carson). He records his daily life in an effort to better understand himself and, in the process, loses his girlfriend and incurs the wrath of his artist friends. With his keen eye, McBride manages to create a fake documentary that could (and did) easily pass for the real thing, thereby reducing the entire cinema verité aesthetic to a storytelling device.

Award: Included in the Library of Congress' National Film Registry (1991).

DAVIS, GEENA. Born Virginia Davis January 21, 1957, in Wareham, Massachusetts; actor. Married to director Renny Harlin; formerly married to Jeff Goldblum. A gifted and attractive actor known for playing kooky characters who deep down have a certain strength and determination. Prancing around in her underwear in *Tootsie*, she caught the eye of not only Dustin Hoffman's Michael Dorsey but also the audience and critics. She showed her range in *The Fly*, starring opposite husband-to-be, Jeff Goldblum, and then earned an Academy Award as the oddball dog trainer Muriel Pritchett in *The Accidental Tourist*. After more bizarre roles in *Beetlejuice* and *Earth Girls Are Easy* (again with Goldblum), she turned in memorable performances in her two best films to date—as Thelma in *Thelma and Louise* and as Dottie in *A League of Their Own*. As Thelma, her transformation from oppressed wife to free-living outlaw made her one of the movies' greatest heroines—a woman liberated from the confines of a lousy marriage only to find that there's no place in society for someone like her. Perhaps the most singularly illustrative moment of Davis' star allure comes in *A League of Their Own* when, during tryouts for the women's baseball league, she snatches Rosie O'Donnell's fastball out of the air with her bare hand. Sadly, her recent efforts—*Angie, Speechless,* and *Cutthroat Island*—have been misguided commercial failures that have entirely failed to capture the Geena Davis persona. "She's got a dilemma on her hands," suggests *Thelma and Louise* screenwriter Callie Khouri. "How do you be a feminist spirit trapped in the body of a goddess?" (*Premiere*, February, 1994).

Filmography: Tootsie (1982); Fletch (1985); Transylvania 6–5000 (1985); The Fly (1986); The Accidental Tourist (1988); Beetlejuice (1988); Earth Girls Are Easy (1989); Quick Change (1990); Thelma and Louise (1991); A League of Their Own (1992); Angie (1994); Speechless (1994); Cutthroat Island (1995).

Honors: Academy Award for Best Supporting Actress (*The Accidental Tourist*); Academy Award nomination for Best Actress (*Thelma and Louise*).

DAVIS, OSSIE. Born December 18, 1917, in Cogdell, Georgia; actor, director, screenwriter. Married to actor Ruby Dee. After arriving in New York City and taking a series of low-paying jobs to support himself while writing, he discovered a love of the theater during his military career in World War II. After fifteen years of acting on Broadway, he wrote and appeared in the 1961 production of *Purlie Victorious*, two years later essaying that role (along with costar and wife, Ruby Dee) in the film *Gone Are the Days*. He made his motion picture directing debut with the ''blaxploitation'' crime comedy *Cotton Comes to Harlem*. With Ruby Dee, he formed Third World Cinema in an effort to bring more black and Hispanic filmmakers to the screen. His career found new life in the late 1980s through the work of director Spike Lee, who cast him in a number of excellent roles—Coach Odom in *School Daze*, Da Mayor in *Do the Right Thing*, and the Good Reverend Doctor, the father shattered by his son's drug dependency in *Jungle Fever*.

Filmography: No Way Out (1950); The Joe Louis Story (1953); The Cardinal (1963); Gone Are The Days (1963) screenplay, play; Shock Treatment (1964); The Hill (1965); A Man Called Adam (1965); The Scalphunters (1968); Sam Whiskey (1969); Slaves (1969); Cotton Comes to Harlem (1970) director, screenplay; Kongi's Harvest (1971) director; Black Girl (1972) director; Malcolm X (1972); Gordon's War (1973) director; Let's Do It Again (1975); Countdown at Kusini (1976) also director, screenplay; Hot Stuff (1979); The House of God (1979); Harry and Son (1984); Avenging Angel (1985); School Daze (1988); Do the Right Thing (1989); Route One/U.S.A. (1989); Joe versus the Volcano (1990); Jungle Fever (1991); Gladiator (1992); Malcom X (1992); Grumpy Old Men (1993); The Client (1994).

DAWN OF THE DEAD (1979), horror. Directed, written, and coedited by George A. Romero; produced by Richard Rubenstein; photographed by Michael Gornick; edited with Kenneth Davidow; music by Dario Argento; special effects, Tom Savini; released by United Film; 125 minutes. *Cast*: David Enge, Ken Foree, Scott Reiniger, Gaylen Ross, David Crawford, David Early.

A shocking orgy of blood, guts, and comic book violence that, amid all its exploding viscera, tackles themes of consumerism and greed while commenting on America's innate love of the shopping mall. The midpoint of Romero's classic ''Living Dead'' trilogy, which began with *Night of the Living Dead* and continued with *Day of the Dead*, this is a rowdy, action-packed picture that offers some truly terrifying moments. Unlike the previous film, however, this one balances its scares with a sick and twisted sense of humor guaranteed to disgust many a viewer. This ability to offend only heightens the film's reputation as one of the most insightful examinations of American life ever filmed; not since Billy Wilder's 1951 drama *The Big Carnival* has America looked so unrelentingly bleak. ''The zombies represent humanity in general and American consumers in particular by being the most logical and extreme example of greedy, selfish human behavior'' (*The Motion Picture Guide*).

DAYS OF HEAVEN (1978), drama. Directed and written by Terrence Malick; produced by Bert Schneider and Harold Schneider; photographed by Nestor Almendros, additional photography by Haskell Wexler; edited by Billy Weber; music by Ennio Morricone; released by Paramount; 95 minutes. *Cast*: Richard

Gere, Brooke Adams, Sam Shepard, Linda Manz, Robert Wilke, Jackie Shultis, Stuart Margolin, Richard Libertini.

Coming five years after *Badlands*, Terrence Malick's only other film to date is set during the post–Industrial Revolution as two lovers, Bill and Abbey (Gere and Adams), flee Chicago for America's heartland after Bill kills a steel mill foreman. Along with Abbey's young sister Linda (Manz, the film's narrator), they arrive in the Texas panhandle at harvest time and, posing as brother and sister, gradually unfold a plan in which Abbey marries the lonely, fatally ill landowner (Shepard). Bill's greed and duplicity backfire, however, when Abbey finds herself in love with her new husband, leading to a tragic fall for all involved. A mythical study of love's power that is set against the grandeur of America's Great Plains with two characters who underestimate the fatal consequences of corrupting their absolute love for one another. By altering the course of nature, they upset a delicate balance that erupts in what is one of the film's most biblical scenes—the cataclysmic fire that turns this panhandle paradise into ashes. Photographed by Nestor Almendros in wide screen and projected in 70mm, this is a visual feast that recalls the purity of silent film. ''A simple, timeless story with the enormous scope and resonance of myth through a clear vision unclouded by sentimentality and by a deft juxtaposition of image, music and character'' (*The Motion Picture Guide*).

Awards: Academy Award for Cinematography; Academy Award nominations for Score, Costumes; New York Film Critics Circle Award for Director; Cannes Film Festival Award for Best Director.

DE NIRO, ROBERT. Born August 17, 1943, in New York City; actor, director, producer. Formerly married to Diahnne Abbott. The most exciting actor of his generation, he has often been touted as the ''new Brando'' because of his Actors Studio training (under Lee Strasberg and Stella Adler) and his willingness to risk. Early on he appeared in several off-Broadway productions and three collaborations with Brian De Palma (*Greetings, The Wedding Party, Hi, Mom!*) before garnering effusive praise as ailing ballplayer John Hancock in *Bang the Drum Slowly*. As young Vito Corleone in *The Godfather, Part II* he earned his first Academy Award and was propelled into the pantheon of outstanding film actors. He has traveled from the darkest side of human nature (the satanic Louis Cypher in *Angel Heart*, Al Capone in *The Untouchables*, Max Cady in *Cape Fear*, the monster in *Mary Shelley's Frankenstein*), to the good-hearted ''schmuck'' (*Falling in Love, Stanley and Iris, We're No Angels, Mad Dog and Glory, Night and the City*). His richest roles, however, are those that fall in between—the morally splintered characters who live on the edge; he excels under the direction of such gifted visionaries as Francis Ford Coppola (*The Godfather, Part II*), Michael Cimino (*The Deer Hunter*), Bernardo Bertolucci (*1900*), Sergio Leone (*Once Upon a Time in America*), and his most frequent collaborator, Martin Scorsese. From his first moment as the mailbox-exploding punk Johnny Boy in *Mean Streets*, it is clear that De Niro commanded a monumental talent and screen presence. Their next four collaborations—*Taxi Driver*, *New York, New York*, *Raging Bull*, and *King of Comedy*—mark a union on par with the teams of John Ford and John Wayne or Josef von Sternberg and Marlene Dietrich. Together they have done their finest work, with cabbie Travis Bickle, sax man Jimmy Doyle, boxer Jake LaMotta, and comic Rupert Pupkin all functioning as alter egos for Scorsese and mirroring his themes of sin and redemption. However, their two subsequent collaborations (the cameo in *GoodFellas* and the unharnessed antics of *Cape Fear*) have failed to reach the level of their earlier work. More recently, De Niro, through his New York-based Tribeca Productions, has become involved in producing for film and television (''Homicide: Life on the Streets''). In 1993, he directed the provocative *A Bronx Tale*, in which he also starred.

Filmography: Greetings (1968); Sam's Song (1969); The Wedding Party (1969); Bloody Mama (1970); Hi, Mom! (1970); Born to Win (1971); The Gang That Couldn't Shoot Straight (1971); Bang the Drum Slowly (1973); Mean Streets (1973); The Godfather, Part II (1974); The Last Tycoon (1976); 1900 (1976); Taxi Driver (1976); New York, New York (1977); The Deer Hunter (1978); Raging Bull (1980); The Swap (1980); True Confessions (1981); The King of Comedy (1983); Falling in Love (1984); Once Upon a Time in America (1984); Brazil (1985); The Mission (1986); Angel Heart (1987); The Untouchables (1987); Dear America (1987); Midnight Run (1988); Jacknife (1989); We're No Angels (1989); Awakenings (1990); GoodFellas (1990); Stanley and Iris (1990); Guilty by Suspicion (1991); Cape Fear (1991); Night and the City (1992); Mistress (1992) also producer; Thunderheart (1992) producer; Mad Dog and Glory (1993); A Bronx Tale (1993) also director, producer; This Boy's Life (1993); Mary Shelley's Frankenstein (1994); Casino (1995); Heat (1995); Faithful (1995) ep.

Honors: Academy Awards for Best Actor (*Raging Bull*) and Supporting Actor (*The Godfather, Part II*); Academy Award nominations for Best Actor (*Taxi Driver, The Deer Hunter, Cape Fear*); New York Film Critics Circle Awards for Best Actor (*Mean Streets, Bang the Drum Slowly, Taxi Driver, Raging Bull, GoodFellas* and *Awakenings*); Los Angeles Film Critics Awards for Best Actor (*Taxi Driver, Raging Bull*); Venice Film Festival Career Award (1993).

Selected bibliography

Brode, Douglas. *The Films of Robert De Niro*. New York: Citadel, 1993.

DE PALMA, BRIAN. Born September 11, 1940, in Newark, New Jersey; director, screenwriter. Formerly married to actor Nancy Allen, who appeared in *Carrie, Home Movies, Dressed to Kill*, and *Blow Out*. Film director whose suffocating use of homage has overshadowed the fact that he is an outstanding technician with an almost unparalleled understanding of cinematic language. Along with contemporaries Francis Ford Coppola, Martin Scorsese, Steven Spielberg, and George Lucas, De Palma was one of the film school-trained directors who rose to great heights in the 1970s. His earliest works are edgy, satiric, low-budgeters, with his first real success being *Sisters*, an eerie psychological horror tale that set the stage for the themes that would be developed in his body of work—family conflict, sibling rivalries, incest, obsession, sadomasochism, voyeurism, punishment for displays of sexuality, and a prevailing sense of misogyny. His subsequent films are of varying quality, ranging from those best forgotten (*Wise Guys*), to the overly showy (*Scarface*, *The Untouchables*), to the indisputably Hitchcockian (*Obsession*, *Body Double*), to the exceptional (*Carrie*, *Blow Out*). In the adaptation of Stephen King's *Carrie* the supernatural (her telekinetic powers) mixes with the natural (a troubled young woman's awkward passage through puberty) in a perfect concoction of real-life horror. Filled with astounding performances, the film is a modern horror masterpiece. Equally impressive, but less well received, is *Blow Out*, the story of a motion picture soundman who embarks upon a futile effort to save a young woman who is caught in a massive political conspiracy. Since the popular success of *The Untouchables*, however, De Palma has delivered one commercial failure after the next, reaching a low point with *Bonfire of the Vanities*, the much anticipated and much maligned adaptation of Tom Wolfe's novel. He reversed his fortunes by teaming with Tom Cruise in 1995 on the production of the big-budget hardware movie *Mission: Impossible*, released in 1996 to critical indifference and commercial triumph. "If I could be the American Godard, that would be great" (De Palma, interview in 1969 in Joseph Gelmis' *The Film Director as Superstar*).

Filmography: Icarus (1960, short); 660214, The Story of an IBM Card (1961, short); Wotan's Wake (1962, short); Jennifer (1964, short); Mod (1964, short); The Wedding Party (1964/released in 1969) codirector, coeditor, coproducer, coscreenplay with Cynthia Munroe and Wilford Leach; Bridge That Gap (1965, short); Show Me a Strong Town and I'll Show You a Strong Bank (1966, short); The Responsive Eye (1966, documentary short); Greetings (1968) also screenplay, editor; Murder a la Mod (1968) also screenplay, editor; Dionysus in 69 (1970); Hi, Mom! (1970); Get to Know Your Rabbit (1972); Sisters (1973) also screenplay; Phantom of the Paradise (1974) also screenplay; Carrie (1976); Obsession (1976) also story; The Fury (1978); Home Movies (1979); Dressed to Kill (1980); Blow Out (1981); The First Time (1982) creative consultant; Scarface (1983); Body Double (1984); Bruce Springsteen's "Dancing in the Dark" (1984, mv); Wise Guys (1986); The Untouchables (1987); The Great O'Grady (1988, short) actor; Casualties of War (1989); Bonfire of the Vanities (1990); Raising Cain (1992); Carlito's Way (1993).

Selected bibliography

Bliss, Michael. *Brian De Palma*. Metuchen, NJ: Scarecrow Press, 1983.
Gelmis, Joseph. *The Film Director as Superstar*. New York: Doubleday, 1970.
Salamon, Julie. *Devil's Candy: The Bonfire of the Vanities Goes to Hollywood*. New York: Houghton Mifflin, 1991.

DEAD MAN WALKING (1995), drama. Directed, written (from the book by Sister Helen Prejean), and coproduced by Tim Robbins; produced with Jon Kilik and Rudd Simmons; photographed by Roger A. Deakins; edited by Lisa Zeno Churgin; music by David Robbins, songs by Bruce Springsteen, Eddie Vedder and Nusrat Fateh Ali Khan; released by Gramercy; 120 minutes. *Cast*: Susan Sarandon, Sean Penn, Robert Prosky, R. Lee Ermey, Raymond J. Barry, Scott Wilson.

Produced independently of Hollywood when no studio could find the guts to greenlight it, this true story of anti–death penalty crusader Sister Helen Prejean is an intelligent, politically complex picture that refuses to simplify the issue or the emotions. Sarandon plays Prejean, a liberal Catholic nun who is on a mission to bring convicted murderer Matthew Poncelet (Penn) closer to himself and to Christ before the state takes his life by lethal injection. To the credit of Robbins, nothing is easily resolved—the families of the savagely murdered teenage victims want revenge, and, when it finally comes, some still feel no satisfaction. Nor is Poncelet (a semifictional representation of a real figure) a sympathetic killer—he puts the make on Sister Prejean, spouts ignorant neo-Nazi slogans, and blames his troubles on everyone else. Still, it is clear where Robbins stands on the issue, and, as a result, he has made the most eloquent condemnation of a government's execution of its own citizens since Krzysztof Kieslowski's chilling 1988 Polish film *A Short Film about Killing*.

Awards: Academy Award for Best Actress; Academy Award nominations for Best Director, Actor, Song ("Dead Man Walking," Bruce Springsteen); Independent Spirit Award for Best Actor; Berlin Film Festival Silver Bear for Best Actor and Jury Prize.

DEATH WISH (1974), crime drama. Directed and coproduced by Michael Winner; screenplay by Wendell Mayes (from the novel by Brian Garfield); photographed by Arthur J. Ornitz; edited by Bernard Gribble; music by Herbie Hancock; released by Paramount; 93 minutes. *Cast*: Charles Bronson, Hope Lange, Vincent Gardenia, Steven Keats, William Redfield, Stuart Margolin, Jack Wallace, Christopher Guest.

A poor man's Harry Callahan, New York City architect Paul Kersey (Bronson) takes matters into his own hands when his wife is murdered, and his daughter brutally raped. Far from a quality piece of filmmaking, it is a disturbingly exhilarating tale of vigilantism that appeals, in a cheap, pornographic way, to certain primal instincts of revenge and retribution. Made during Charles Bronson's heyday, it is a response to the anxiety of urban living, which has influenced a slew of films ranging from *Taxi Driver*, to *Mad Max*, to *Falling Down*. Here, Paul Kersey is a good man who is driven by society to commit violence, though he does so with a heavy heart and a weak stomach (he vomits after bludgeoning one attacker). Unfortunately, as the sequels progressed, Bronson's character became less heroic and more fascistic—transforming from a legitimately enraged husband and father to a homicidal one-man judge, jury, and executioner.

Sequels: Bronson reprised his role in *Death Wish II* (1981, Winner); *Death Wish 3* (1985, Winner); and *Death Wish 4: The Crackdown* (1987, J. Lee Thompson).

DEER HUNTER, THE (1978), war drama. Directed and coproduced by Michael Cimino; screenplay by Deric Washburn (from a story by Washburn, Cimino,

Louis Garfinkle, and Quinn K. Redeker); produced with Barry Spikings, Michael Deeley, John Peverall; photographed by Vilmos Zsigmond; edited by Peter Zinner; music by Stanley Myers, main theme by John Williams; released by Universal; 183 minutes. *Cast*: Robert De Niro, John Cazale, John Savage, Christopher Walken, Meryl Streep, George Dzundza, Chuck Aspegren, Shirley Stoler, Rutanya Alda.

Michael Cimino's greatest achievement, this brutal examination of the nature of violence is one of the most penetrating commentaries on the American community ever made. At the core of the film are three Pennsylvania steelworkers—Michael (De Niro), Nick (Walken), and Steven (Savage)—who are just days away from leaving their small industrial town for Vietnam. Much of the beginning of the three-hour film is devoted to the bond between these men, their other friends (Cazale, Aspegren, Dzundza), and the women in their lives (mainly Streep) as seen in the sumptuous and richly detailed wedding scene of Steven and Angela (Alda). A sense of community is Cimino's primary interest in *The Deer Hunter* because that is the very foundation of America. While the horrors of war and the horrific Russian roulette scene are indelibly etched in the mind of every viewer, the real story takes place on the home front. Every single performance is riveting, especially Streep's naturalistic Linda, the woman who is involved with Nick but later falls in love with Michael. The film is packed with great scenes—the joyous pool-playing scene of the guys downing their Rolling Rocks and singing a spirited version of "I Love You Baby"; De Niro's postwar hunting confrontation with the deer; and the Russian roulette scene between Michael and Nick in Saigon. One of the most effective moments occurs in the bar after the hunt as Dzundza's classical piano playing calms the beer-swilling machismo of the guys and provides a bridge to the complete devastation of a Vietnamese village; it is, quite simply, one of the most beautiful sequences in film. "An utterly satisfying look at how traditional American heroism was consumed by the war it created—Vietnam" (Stephen Schiff, *Boston Phoenix*, February 13, 1979).

Honors: Academy Awards for Best Picture, Director, Supporting Actor (Walken), Editing, Sound; Academy Award nominations for Best Actor (De Niro), Actress (Streep), Screenplay, Cinematography; New York Film Critics Circle Awards for Best Picture, Supporting Actor (Walken); Los Angeles Film Critics Award for Best Director; DGA Award.

DELIVERANCE (1972), adventure/drama. Directed and produced by John Boorman; screenplay by James Dickey (from his novel); photographed by Vilmos Zsigmond; edited by Tom Priestly; music by Eric Weissberg, song "Duelling Banjos" by Weissberg and Steve Mandel; released by Warner Bros.; 109 minutes. *Cast*: Jon Voight, Burt Reynolds, Ned Beatty, Ronny Cox, Billy McKinney, Herbert "Cowboy" Coward.

A chilling, expertly directed tale of four "city boys" from Atlanta whose weekend canoeing excursion turns nightmarish when they underestimate the difference between them and the mountain men they encounter. The memorable opening sets the stage as the likable guitar-picking Drew (Cox) engages in a musical "duel" with a freakish, banjo-strumming boy. As the foot-stomping melody grows more intricate, Drew just stops playing, smiles, and admits "I'm lost." Everything that follows is explained in this moment—the city boys might think they fit in, but the backwoods life is something they'll never be able to handle. The Boorman themes of man and his quest and technology versus ecology are in full view here. As good as Cox, Voight, and Beatty are, Burt Reynolds gives the performance of his career.

Awards: Academy Award nominations for Best Picture, Director and Editing.

DEMME, JONATHAN. Born February 22, 1944, in Rockville Centre, New York; director. Nephew Ted is a director (*The Ref*). Eclectic, innovative director whose personal style has shifted from tongue-in-cheek exploitation, to quirky Americana, to urban hipness, to semiconventional storytelling. After film jobs as a publicist, reviewer, and sales rep in the 1960s, Demme moved to Los Angeles and joined the exploitation stable of Roger Corman's New World Pictures. Of his five Corman films (two as director, three as writer), the women-in-prison film *Caged Heat* is the best known, attracting a cult following that far exceeds its significance. More interesting are *Citizens Band* and *Melvin and Howard*, two charmingly offbeat films that take a nonjudgmental look at American values. After an unsatisfying Hollywood experience with *Swing Shift*, a potentially interesting, but diluted, World War II-era story of female factory workers, he followed with four very modern, very urban films—the performance films *Stop Making Sense* (with the Talking Heads) and *Swimming to Cambodia* (with monologist Spalding Gray) and the kitschy, music-heavy comedies *Something Wild* and *Married to the Mob*. He has taken a turn toward more conventional character-driven dramas with his two most recent projects—the complex and terrifying Oscar-winner *The Silence of the Lambs* and the disappointingly soft AIDS drama *Philadelphia*. In addition to his feature films, he has done television (the Columbo television movie *Murder in Aspic*, the Susan Sarandon–Christopher Walken PBS film *Who Am I This Time?*), documentaries (*Haiti Dreams of Democracy*, *Cousin Bobby*), and music videos for New Order, Fine Young Cannibals, the Neville Brothers, Neil Young ("The Complex Sessions"), and the MTV Sun City compilation. "Demme's America is not a blindly hopeful one. He recognizes the darkness behind the smiles, the hopelessness behind the bright slogans, the failure that comes with success, the claustrophobia within the vast landscape" (*The Motion Picture Guide*).

Filmography: Good Morning, Steve (1968, short); Caged Heat (1974); Crazy Mama (1975); Fighting Mad (1976) also screenplay; Citizens Band/Handle with Care (1977); Murder in Aspic (1978, tvm); Last Embrace (1979); Melvin and Howard (1980); Who Am I This Time? (1982, tvm); Swing Shift (1984); Stop Making Sense (1984); Sun City (1985, ctv documentary); The Perfect Kiss (1985, short); Something Wild (1986) also producer; Swimming to Cambodia (1987); "A Family Tree" episode of "Trying Times"

(1987, tvm); Haiti Dreams of Democracy (1988) also producer, screenplay; Married to the Mob (1988); The Silence of the Lambs (1991); Cousin Bobby (1992); Philadelphia (1993).

Additional credits: Eyewitness/Sudden Terror (1969) music coordinator; Angels Hard as They Come (1971) producer, screenplay; Black Mama, White Mama (1972) story; The Hot Box (1972) producer, screenplay; The Incredible Melting Man (1977) actor; Into the Night (1985) actor; Miami Blues (1990) producer; Household Saints (1993) ep; Devil in a Blue Dress (1994) ep.

Honors: Academy Award for Best Director (*The Silence of the Lambs*); New York Film Critics Circle Awards for Best Director (*Melvin and Howard*, *The Silence of the Lambs*); Berlin Film Festival for Best Director (*The Silence of the Lambs*).

Selected bibliography

Bliss, Michael, and Christina Banks. *What Goes Around Comes Around: The Films of Jonathan Demme.* Carbondale, IL: Southern Illinois University Press, 1994.

DEPP, JOHNNY. Born June 9, 1963, in Owensboro, Kentucky; actor. Charismatic young actor best known for his willingness to attach himself to risky projects directed by some of America's boldest directors. He became a teen idol with his role as undercover cop Tom Hanson on television's "21 Jump Street," and his career began to take shape with his role as the malformed misfit in *Edward Scissorhands.* Instead of bowing to the pressures of Hollywood's star system, he has continued to play in eclectic romantic movies that have cultivated his "outsider" persona—a "freak" with scissors for hands, a talentless, but driven, film director (Burton's *Ed Wood*), a Buster Keaton-esque mute (*Benny and Joon*), and a mythical lover (*Don Juan DeMarco*). In addition he has worked with "outsiders" John Waters (*Cry-Baby*) and Jim Jarmusch (*Dead Man*) and foreign filmmakers Emil Kusturica (*Arizona Dream*) and Lasse Hallstrom (*What's Eating Gilbert Grape*). In 1993, he opened the popular Hollywood nightspot the Viper Room. "Depp's face possesses a beauty usually reserved for apostles and saints and silent-movie stars" (Holly Millea, *Premiere*, February 1995).

Filmography: A Nightmare on Elm Street (1984); Private Resort (1985); Platoon (1986); "21 Jump Street" (1987–1990, tvs); Edward Scissorhands (1990); Cry-Baby (1990); Arizona Dream (1992/released 1995); Benny and Joon (1993); What's Eating Gilbert Grape (1993); Ed Wood (1994); Banter (1994, short) director; Don Juan DeMarco (1995); Dead Man (1995).

DERN, BRUCE. Born June 4, 1936, in Winnetka, Illinois; actor. Formerly married to actor Diane Ladd; daughter is Laura Dern; grandson of poet/playwright Archibald MacLeish. An actor who often plays conniving characters that border on the psychotic, he's twice appeared in films by Alfred Hitchcock (*Marnie* and *Family Plot* and an episode of "Alfred Hitchcock Presents"), which are partially responsible for his menacing typecasting. He established himself in the late 1960s and early 1970s, making a half-dozen pictures with Jack Nicholson—

excelling as the basketball coach in the Nicholson-directed *Drive, He Said* and starring opposite him as his deal-making brother in *The King of Marvin Gardens*. Still, his most unforgettable role is in *Silent Running* as the demented botanist Freeman Lowell, who pilots his space station greenhouse into the outer depths of the universe. He received an Academy Award nomination for *Coming Home* as the marine captain shattered by his wartime experiences in Vietnam.

Filmography: Wild River (1960); Hush . . . Hush, Sweet Charlotte (1964); Marnie (1964); The Wild Angels (1966); The St. Valentine's Day Massacre (1967); The Trip (1967); The War Wagon (1967); Waterhole Number 3 (1967); Hang 'Em High (1968); Psych-Out (1968); Will Penny (1968); Castle Keep (1969); Number One (1969); They Shoot Horses, Don't They? (1969); Bloody Mama (1970); Cycle Savages (1970); Rebel Rousers (1970); The Cowboys (1971); Brian's Song (1971, tvm); Drive, He Said (1971); The Incredible Two-Headed Transplant (1971); Silent Running (1971); The King of Marvin Gardens (1972); Thumb Tripping (1972); The Laughing Policeman (1973); The Great Gatsby (1974); Posse (1975); Smile (1975); Family Plot (1976); Folies Bourgeoises (1976); Won Ton Ton, the Dog Who Saved Hollywood (1976); Black Sunday (1977); Coming Home (1977); The Driver (1978); Middle Age Crazy (1980); Harry Tracy (1981); Tattoo (1981); That Championship Season (1982); On the Edge (1985); The Big Town (1987); 1969 (1988); World Gone Wild (1988); The Burbs (1989); After Dark, My Sweet (1990); Diggstown (1992); Amelia Earhart: The Final Flight (1994, ctvm); Wild Bill (1995); Mrs. Munck (1995).

Honors: Academy Award nomination for Best Supporting Actor (*Coming Home*); Berlin Film Festival Award for Best Actor (*That Championship Season*).

DEVITO, DANNY. Born November 17, 1944, in Asbury Park, New Jersey; actor, director. Married to actor Rhea Perlman (''Cheers''). Unique comic actor of indubitably condensed stature who had memorable roles early in his career (planning to blow up the Statue of Liberty in Martin Brest's New York University student film *Hot Dogs for Gaugin*, as Martini in *One Flew over the Cuckoo's Nest*, and as gang member Hog in *Goin' South*) before finding resounding success as the caustic Louie De Palmer in television's ''Taxi'' from 1978–1983. His return to the big screen brought increased fame when he appeared with Michael Douglas and Kathleen Turner in the popular adventure yarn *Romancing the Stone*, with the three of them reteaming in DeVito's second directorial outing, *The War of the Roses*. Most recently, he has alternated between comedy (twice costarring with Arnold Schwarzenegger in Ivan Reitman's *Twins* and *Junior*), drama (*Jack the Bear* and his own *Hoffa*), and producing through his Jersey Films (*Reality Bites*, *Pulp Fiction*). ''He has an uncanny ability to simultaneously repulse, amuse and move an audience—thanks, in part, to his not-so-secret weapon: shortness'' (Robert Seidenberg, *American Film*, September 1989).

Filmography: Dreams of Glass (1968); Hot Dogs for Gaugin (1970); La Mortadella/ Lady Liberty (1972); Hurry Up, or I'll Be 30 (1973); Scalawag (1973); The Sound Sleeper (1973, short) also writer, director, producer; Minestrone (1975, short) also writer, director, producer; One Flew over the Cuckoo's Nest (1975); The Van (1977); The

World's Greatest Lover (1977); Goin' South (1978); "Taxi" (1978–1983, tvs); Going Ape! (1981); Terms of Endearment (1983); Johnny Dangerously (1984); Romancing the Stone (1984); The Jewel of the Nile (1985); Head Office (1986); My Little Pony (1986); Wise Guys (1986); Ruthless People (1986); Throw Momma from the Train (1987) also director; Tin Men (1987); Twins (1988); The War of the Roses (1989) also director; Hoffa (1992) also director; Batman Returns (1992); Jack the Bear (1993); Renaissance Man (1994); Junior (1994).

Filmography as producer: Reality Bites (1994); Pulp Fiction (1994) ep; Get Shorty (1995); Feeling Minnesota (1995); Sunset Park (1995) ep.

Honor: Emmy Award ("Taxi" 1981).

DICAPRIO, LEONARDO. Born November 11, 1974, in Los Angeles; actor. The most exciting and feral teen actor in film since River Phoenix, he stunned the movie world with his portrayal of the retarded and mischievous young Arnie in *What's Eating Gilbert Grape*, starring opposite two other brilliant young actors, Johnny Depp and Juliette Lewis. Beginning his career with brief stints in the television series "Parenthood" and "Growing Pains," he found a home in film, starring in a handful of roles in which he's displayed a sense of mystery, beauty, sexiness, and antiheroism—as young Tobias Wolff in *This Boy's Life*, as 1970s basketball player/poet Jim Carroll in *The Basketball Diaries*, and as 1870s gun-runner/poet Arthur Rimbaud in *Total Eclipse*. He's barely graced the screen, but there is no doubt that he is a rarity; whether he will burn out à la Dean and Phoenix or sustain the force à la Dennis Hopper and Jack Nicholson is the only question that remains.

Filmography:: "Parenthood" (1990, tvs); "Growing Pains" (1991–1992, tvs); What's Eating Gilbert Grape (1993); This Boy's Life (1993); The Quick and the Dead (1995); Basketball Diaries (1995); Total Eclipse (1995).

Award: Los Angeles Film Critics New Generation Award (1993).

DIE HARD (1988), action. Directed by John McTiernan; screenplay by Jeb Stuart and Steven E. DeSouza (from the novel by Roderick Thorp); produced by Joel Silver and Lawrence Gordon; photographed by Jan De Bont; music by Michael Kamen; edited by Frank J. Urioste and John F. Link; released by 20th Century Fox; 131 minutes. *Cast*: Bruce Willis, Bonnie Bedelia, Alan Rickman, Reginald Veljohnson, William Atherton, Hart Bochner, Alexander Godunov.

Outstanding action film that has become the blueprint for countless subsequent Hollywood actioners. New York cop John McClane (Willis) is visiting his estranged wife (Bedelia) at her Christmas Eve office party in a Century City high-rise (in reality, 20th Century Fox's office tower). McClane hates Los Angeles, hates the Japanese company she works for (it prefers her to appear single), and hates the fact that she has reverted to using her maiden name. When a gang of German terrorists (led by Rickman in a chillingly calm performance) takes over the building, McClane goes to work to foil their plans. Of course, he eventually succeeds in doing so. Willis, the most talented actor in the action genre, creates an archetypal working-class hero—a wisecracking, resourceful, barefoot tough guy who is "bigger than life." Action megaproducer Joel Silver teamed with producer Lawrence Gordon, director John McTiernan (*Predator, The Last Action Hero*), and cameraman Jan De Bont (director of *Speed, Twister*) to create a magnificent action film replete with the requisite explosions, gun battles, and one-liners. The chief downside, however, is the substantial dose of misogyny, xenophobia, and flag waving that insidiously disguises itself as patriotism.

Sequels: Willis reprised his role in *Die Hard 2: Die Harder* (1990, Renny Harlin) and *Die Hard with a Vengeance* (1995, McTiernan).

DILLON, MATT. Born February 18, 1964, in New Rochelle, New York; actor. Brother Kevin is an actor. Photogenic antihero who began with a series of tough-but-sensitive street kid roles and has developed into an accomplished adult actor. He made an auspicious debut in *Over the Edge* as the rebellious and bored Richie, who turns a suburban community on its head when the adults refuse to listen to the frustrations of their kids. He continued to play variations on this theme, reaching the pinnacle with Rusty-James in Francis Ford Coppola's teen art film *Rumblefish*. Most of his subsequent work has been less successful— either the material hasn't worked or, as in the case of *The Saint of Fort Washington* or *Golden Gate*, the film has failed to find an audience despite his intelligent performance. In *Drugstore Cowboy* he realized his most mature acting as Bob, the sincere and slyly humorous drug addict who struggles to go straight.

Filmography: Over the Edge (1979); Little Darlings (1980); My Bodyguard (1980); Liar's Moon (1982); Tex (1982); The Outsiders (1983); Rumblefish (1983); The Flamingo Kid (1984); Rebel (1985); Target (1985); Native Son (1986); The Big Town (1987); Dear America (1987); Kansas (1988); Bloodhounds of Broadway (1989); Drugstore Cowboy (1989); A Kiss before Dying (1991); Singles (1991); Mr. Wonderful (1993); The Saint of Fort Washington (1993); Golden Gate (1994); Frankie Starlight (1995); To Die For (1995).

Honor: Independent Spirit Award for Best Actor (*Drugstore Cowboy*).

DINER (1982), comedy/drama. Written and directed by Barry Levinson; produced by Jerry Weintraub; photographed by Peter Sova; edited by Stu Linder; music by Bruce Brody; released by MGM/UA; 110 minutes. *Cast*: Steve Guttenberg, Daniel Stern, Mickey Rourke, Kevin Bacon, Timothy Daly, Ellen Barkin, Paul Reiser, Michael Tucker, Kathryn Dowling.

A semiautobiographical tale of growing up in late-1950s Baltimore that features great writing, great acting, and a truly magical combination of reality and nostalgia. Levinson, in his directing debut, tells the story of a group of twenty-something guys who hang out together at the local diner. The plot is minimal— Eddie (Guttenberg) is getting married and fears that the good times with his buddies are ending. It's the characters and the moments that Levinson has created that make this film so endearing—the exhaustive football quiz that Eddie's fiancée must pass in order for the wedding to occur *and* his demand that the bridal colors be those of the Baltimore Colts; Fenwick and his drunken harangue at the manger display ("kids did this"); the battle waged by Shrevie (Stern) against his wife Beth (Barkin) about her habitual inability to file his records in alphabetical order ("ask me what's on the flip side, go ahead, ask me"); Modell (Reiser) and his habit of indirectly asking for food ("Are you gonna eat those fries?"); and the poignant final freeze-frame of all the guys trying to catch the garter. It's a comedy that hits all the right marks, though ultimately it's a sad film about an entire generation of guys who can talk to their friends for hours on end but have absolutely nothing to say to the women they've married.

Award: Academy Award nomination for Best Screenplay.

DIRTY DOZEN, THE (1967), war drama. Directed by Robert Aldrich; screenplay by Lukas Heller and Nunnally Johnson (from the novel by E. M. Nathanson); produced by Kenneth Hyman; photographed by Edward Scaife; edited by Michael Luciano; music by Frank DeVol; released by MGM; 149 minutes. *Cast:* Lee Marvin, Ernest Borgnine, Charles Bronson, Jim Brown, John Cassavetes, Richard Jaeckel, George Kennedy, Trini Lopez, Ralph Meeker, Robert Ryan, Telly Savalas, Donald Sutherland, Clint Walker.

A testosterone-pumping war movie that is the best of Robert Aldrich's many all-male action pictures, each of which explores the nature of violence, machismo, teamwork, and individuality. Here Major Reisman (Marvin) assembles a team of pathological misfits, trains them, and sends them off on a suicide mission to a Nazi chateau. Following a pattern set by Hollywood World War II action dramas of the 1940s, Aldrich throws together a range of ethnic types and psychological profiles—there's the sadistic killer Archer Maggott (Savalas), the tough Pole Wladislaw (Bronson), the antiwhite black man Robert Jefferson (Brown), the demented southerner Vernon Pinkley (Sutherland), the Native American Samson Posey (Walker), and the grinning psycho Victor Franko (Cassavetes)—all of whom are molded to work together despite their hatred for one another. The result is a masterfully constructed piece (written by Nunnally Johnson and Lukas Heller) that, under Aldrich's crisp direction and leftist political ideas, becomes a harsh critique of a military that exists to turn human beings into ruthless killing machines and then celebrate them as heroes.

Awards: Academy Award for Best Sound Effects; Academy Award nominations for Best Supporting Actor (Cassavetes), Editing, Sound.

DIRTY HARRY (1971), action drama. Directed and produced by Don Siegel; screenplay by Harry Julian Fink, Rita M. Fink, Dean Riesner; photographed by Bruce Surtees; edited by Carl Pingitore; music by Lalo Schifrin; released by Warner Bros.; 102 minutes. *Cast*: Clint Eastwood, Reni Santoni, Harry Guardino, Andy Robinson, John Mitchum, John Vernon.

In his first of five incarnations as Dirty Harry Callahan, Clint Eastwood takes

his Sergio Leone "Man-with-No-Name" character one step further and transforms him into a fiercely independent, jaw-clenching San Francisco cop of few
words and many actions. When the Bay Area is terrorized by a psychopath,
Harry is assigned to the case. An outsider who lives beyond law and order and
follows his own path of justice, Harry Callahan is the classic rogue cop—a true
individual who cannot commit to the rules of the police force, anymore than he
can commit to a woman or a friend. Under Don Siegel's direction, *Dirty Harry*
is more than an action film—it is a complex examination of the American hero.
Although he acts outside the law, he demands the respect of both his police
department superiors and film audiences because of his unwavering resolve. The
incongruity is not lost on Siegel, who refuses to judge Harry Callahan and is
clearly aware of the fine line between rogue cop and psychopath; the film's
posters remind us that "Harry's the one with the badge." The final confrontation
is classic Dirty Harry; his .44 magnum trained on the wounded Scorpio (played
brilliantly by Andy Robinson), he mutters through clenched teeth: "I know what
you're thinking, punk. You're thinking, 'Did he fire six shots or only five?'
Now to tell you the truth I've forgotten myself in all this excitement. But being
this is a .44 Magnum, the most powerful handgun in the world, and will blow
your head clean off, you've got to ask yourself a question: 'Do I feel lucky?'
Well, do ya . . . punk?'' Then Harry fires one of the most cathartic bullets in
movie history. "A serviceable programmer for general action audiences, plus
extremists, sadists, revolutionaries, and law-and-order freaks" (*Variety*, December 22, 1971).

Sequels: Clint Eastwood reprised his Harry Callahan in *Magnum Force* (1973, Ted Post);
The Enforcer (1976, James Fargo); *Sudden Impact* (1983, Eastwood); *The Dead Pool*
(1988, Buddy Van Horn).

DO THE RIGHT THING (1989), drama. Directed, written, and coproduced by
Spike Lee; produced with Monty Ross; photographed by Ernest Dickerson; edited by Barry Alexander Brown; music by Bill Lee, song "Fight the Power"
by Public Enemy; released by Universal; 120 minutes. *Cast*: Danny Aiello,
Spike Lee, Ossie Davis, Ruby Dee, John Turturro, Richard Edson, Giancarlo
Esposito, Joie Lee, Rosie Perez, Bill Nunn, Robin Harris, John Savage, Guen-
veur Smith, Sam [Samuel L.] Jackson, Martin Lawrence, Frank Vincent.

Spike Lee's best film to date, it successfully combines his art and his politics
into a gripping, entertaining narrative. Set mostly in Sal's Famous Pizzeria in
New York's Bed-Stuy area on the hottest day of the summer, the story revolves
around the pizzeria's Italian owner (Aiello) and his black delivery man, Mookie
(Lee). Racial tensions are ignited when the politically astute Buggin' Out (Esposito) complains that there are no blacks on Sal's "Wall of Fame"—a photo
collection of famed Italians. The conflict turns violent, resulting in the police's
murdering a black man whom they've taken into custody. In the weeks before
its theatrical release, agitators tried to breed fear by promising riots in the streets;
no such disturbances occurred. "Spike Lee has made a film that works as idio-

syncratic art and powerful social commentary'' (Nelson George, *Five for Five*). ''It strikes you with the speed, color and style of graffiti: an urban in-your-face declaration'' (Marlaine Glicksman, *Film Comment*, July–August 1989).

Honors: Academy Award nominations for Supporting Actor (Aiello), Original Screenplay; Los Angeles Film Critics Awards for Best Picture, Director, Supporting Actor (Aiello), Score; New York Film Critics Circle Award for Cinematography.

DR. ZHIVAGO (1965), drama/romance. Directed by David Lean; written by Robert Bolt (from the novel by Boris Pasternak); produced by Carlo Ponti; photographed by Freddie Young; edited by Norman Savage; music by Maurice Jarre; released by MGM; 197 minutes. *Cast*: Julie Christie, Geraldine Chaplin, Omar Sharif, Tom Courtenay, Alec Guinness, Ralph Richardson, Rod Steiger, Rita Tushingham, Siobbhan McKenna, Klaus Kinski.

Teaming again with screenwriting partner Robert Bolt, David Lean has fashioned a picaresque vision from Boris Pasternak's Russian novel set during the early part of the twentieth century. It tells the story of the rise of Yuri Zhivago (Sharif) from young doctor to extraordinary novelist, his marriage to Tonya (Chaplin), and his passionate love for Lara (Christie). However, the real reason to see the film is to be absorbed by the lush romanticism of the stunning, perfectly composed, wide-screen vistas blanketed with snow and to hear the memorable strains of Maurice Jarre's score, both of which are more moving than the superficiality of the story and the characters. A phenomenal hit, the film grossed over $100 million—a major accomplishment for a three-hour-plus film at 1965 ticket prices. ''This may be faithful to Pasternak, but it makes for painfully slow going and inevitable tedium in a film'' (Bosley Crowther, *New York Times*, December 23, 1965).

Awards: Academy Awards for Best Screenplay, Cinematography, Art Direction, Score, Costumes; Academy Award nominations for Best Picture, Director, Supporting Actor (Courtenay), Sound, Editing.

DOG DAY AFTERNOON (1975), crime drama. Directed by Sidney Lumet; written by Frank Pierson; produced by Martin Bregman, Martin Elfand; photographed by Victor J. Kemper; edited by Dede Allen; released by Warner Bros.; 130 minutes. *Cast*: Al Pacino, John Cazale, Charles Durning, Chris Sarandon, Sully Boyer, Penny Allen, James Broderick, Carol Kane, Lance Henriksen.

An angry, energetic bank-heist film that follows the exploits of two inexperienced and frustrated men—the hyper Sonny (Pacino) and the dim-witted Sal (Cazale)—who decide to knock off the First Savings Bank of Brooklyn in broad daylight. The police and Federal Bureau of Investigation surround the building, thereby forcing Sonny and Sal to hold bank workers and patrons hostage. Much of what happens next revolves around Sonny's fervent attempts to negotiate their freedom and his desire to talk to his lover, Leon (Sarandon), whose need of money for a transsexual operation is the reason behind the robbery. This is one of the first films to explore the relationship between the criminal and the media, especially in the scene in which Sonny fuels the crowd and wins its support with his antiestablishment chant of "Attica, Attica!"

Awards: Academy Award for Best Original Screenplay; Academy Award nominations for Best Picture, Director, Actor, Supporting Actor (Sarandon) and Editing; WGA Award.

DONNER, RICHARD. Born Richard Donner Schwartzberg in 1939, in Bronx, New York; director, producer. Commercially ultrasuccessful director whose ability to create a smash Hollywood hit seems directly related to his lack of a distinct personal style or artistic vision. Both *The Omen* and *Superman* were huge hits in the 1970s, while his *Lethal Weapon* series (coproduced with Joel Silver), starring Mel Gibson and Danny Glover, has helped to redefine the "buddy film." His work as an executive producer has also been extremely fruitful, most notably with *Free Willy* and its sequel, coproduced by wife Lauren Shuler-Donner. The only film of his that shows as much heart as professionalism is the medieval romance *Ladyhawke*, which bears comparison with the classicism of Hollywood films of the 1930s and 1940s.

Filmography as director: X-15 (1961); Salt and Pepper (1968); Twinky (1970); The Omen (1976); Superman (1978); Inside Moves (1980); The Toy (1982); The Goonies (1985) also producer; Ladyhawke (1985) also producer; Lethal Weapon (1987) also producer; Scrooged (1988) also producer; Lethal Weapon 2 (1989) also producer; Lethal Weapon 3 (1992) also producer; Maverick (1994) also producer; Assassins (1995).

Filmography as executive producer: The Final Conflict (1981); The Lost Boys (1987); Delirious (1991); Free Willy (1993); Tales from the Crypt: Demon Knight (1994); Free Willy 2: The Adventure Home (1995).

DON'T LOOK BACK (1967), documentary. Directed, coproduced, and photographed by D. A. Pennebaker (b&w); produced with Richard Leacock, Albert Grossman, John Court; released by Leacock-Pennebaker Inc.; 96 minutes. *Cast:* Bob Dylan, Joan Baez, Donovan, Albert Grossman, Alan Price.

One of the earliest examples of Direct Cinema to achieve commercial success, this document of Bob Dylan's 1965 British tour capitalizes on the relationship between cinema and music. The film opens (after the Academy leader with its descending numbers) with an early music video for "Subterranean Homesick Blues" as a bored Dylan, standing on an empty city street, flips over a series of cards with key phrases from the song ("suckcess," "pawking metaws," "the vandals took all the handles"). This sets the film's playful tone as we proceed to see Dylan and his manager Albert Grossman (who doubled as the film's producer) as they start their tour—the backstage preparation, the deal making, the rabid fans, the hotel room jams with Donovan and Joan Baez, and the stage performances as a spotlit Dylan delivers his litany of hits. Throughout the film we see Dylan spar (in varying degrees of condescension) with defensive journalists who want to understand the Dylan phenomenon, though he never voices objections to Pennebaker's similarly inquisitive camera. The film crackles with life and today remains as fresh as it did upon its release, not at all diluted by the rock-and-roll documents it influenced (*Gimme Shelter, Woodstock, The Last Waltz*, Madonna's *Truth or Dare*, and the entirety of MTV). Songs include "The Times They Are a Changin'," "It's All Over Now, Baby Blue," "It's Alright Ma, I'm Only Bleeding," and "Don't Think Twice, It's Alright."

DOUGLAS, MICHAEL. Born September 25, 1944, in New Brunswick, New Jersey; actor, producer. A handsome leading man who is either blessed or cursed with more than a passing resemblance to father Kirk Douglas, Michael began his film career as an assistant director on his father's *Lonely Are the Brave*. He became a household name in the 1970s, costarring with Karl Malden in the television police drama "The Streets of San Francisco." In the meantime, however, he was busy establishing himself as a producer, netting a Best Picture Oscar with *One Flew over the Cuckoo's Nest*. His next outing as a producer was *The China Syndrome*, a timely nuclear disaster movie (it coincided with the Three Mile Island scare) in which he costarred with fellow producer Jane Fonda. He began to receive attention as a film actor with the innocuous, but charming, Indiana Jones-inspired knockoffs *Romancing the Stone* and *The Jewel of the Nile*, both of which costarred Kathleen Turner and Danny DeVito (they would team again for the enjoyable and inventive black comedy *The War of the Roses*). Douglas then hit superstardom as the adulterous husband in *Fatal Attraction*, the first of several roles in which he has played an Everyman victimized by either a woman or the oppressive American system. Tapping into the politically incorrect notion of white male rage that has pervaded the 1990s, Douglas has had box office success with *Basic Instinct* (cop victimized by a sexual predator), *Falling Down* (as D-FENS, American worker victimized by immigrants and minorities), and *Disclosure* (white-collar worker victimized by female boss). His 1995 release, *An American President*, was a colorless romantic comedy in which he starred as the president of the United States, a missed opportunity to play the ultimate victimized white male. "Michael Douglas has become the John Wayne of gender war movies, the Indiana Jones of the men's movement" (Bruce Newman, *New York Newsday*, December 4, 1994).

Filmography: Hail, Hero! (1969); Adam at 6 A.M. (1970); Summertree (1971); Napoleon and Samantha (1972); "The Streets of San Francisco" (1972–1975, tvs); Coma (1978); The China Syndrome (1979) also producer; Running (1979) also ep; It's My Turn (1980); The Star Chamber (1983); Romancing the Stone (1984) also producer; A Chorus Line (1985); The Jewel of the Nile (1985) also producer; Fatal Attraction (1987); Wall Street (1987); Black Rain (1989); The War of the Roses (1989); Basic Instinct (1992); Shining Through (1992); Falling Down (1993); Disclosure (1994); The American President (1995).

Filmography as producer only: One Flew over the Cuckoo's Nest (1975); Starman (1984) ep; "Starman" (1986, tvs); Flatliners (1990); Radio Flyer (1992); Made in America (1993).

Honors: Academy Awards for Best Picture (*One Flew over the Cuckoo's Nest*) and Actor (*Wall Street*).

DOWNEY, ROBERT, JR. Born April 4, 1965, in New York; actor. Father is director Robert Downey. Skilled young comic actor who displays a natural knack for physical comedy but can also effectively play characters with a dark side. He began his career at age five in the role of a puppy in his father's *Pound* and subsequently appeared in four more of his films (*Greaser's Palace, America, Rented Lips,* and *Too Much Sun*). After a number of minor roles and a stint as a cast member of television's "Saturday Night Live" (1985), he hit stride with two excellent performances—the unabashedly romantic Jack Jericho in *The Pick-Up Artist* and the decadent drug addict Julian Wells in *Less than Zero.* Of his more recent films, his lead role in *Chaplin* stands out as near perfection, though he has also excelled with his physically demanding performance in the otherwise unsuccessful *Heart and Souls* and as the crazed television personality Wayne Gale of *Natural Born Killers.* His personal life took a hit in 1995 when his long-standing drug habit became public after his multiple arrests and subsequent stint in rehab.

Filmography: Pound (1970); Greaser's Palace (1972); America (1982); Baby, It's You (1983); Firstborn (1984); Tuff Turf (1985); Weird Science (1985); Back to School (1986); Dear America (1987); Less than Zero (1987); The Pick-Up Artist (1987); 1969 (1988); Johnny Be Good (1988); Rented Lips (1988); Chances Are (1989); That's Adequate (1989); True Believer (1989); Air America (1990); Too Much Sun (1991); Chaplin (1992); Heart and Souls (1993); Short Cuts (1993); Natural Born Killers (1994); Only You (1994); Restoration (1995).

Honor: Academy Award nomination for Best Actor (*Chaplin*).

DREYFUSS, RICHARD. Born Richard Dreyfus October 29, 1947, in Brooklyn, New York; actor. Hailing from Brooklyn but raised in Los Angeles, where he attended Beverly Hills High, Dreyfuss is a leading man whose style is a pleasing mix of Jewish kid from Brooklyn and nonchalant Angeleno. He appeared in community theater in Los Angeles and the improvisational cabaret theater in San Francisco (with Rob Reiner) before landing his first bit part in *The Graduate* as one of Benjamin Braddock's nosy, disapproving neighbors at Berkeley. Other small roles in *American Graffiti* (as the brainy Curt) and *Dillinger* (as Baby Face Nelson) soon led to the lead in *The Apprenticeship of Duddy Kravitz.* He hit the jackpot as Steven Spielberg's alter ego in *Jaws* (as marine biologist Matt Hooper) and *Close Encounters of the Third Kind* (as the alien-obsessed Roy Neary)—roles that, combined with his Oscar-winning work in Neil Simon's *The Goodbye Girl,* brought him fame and established him as an actor who could deftly combine comic and dramatic intensity. He is especially solid in 1981's *Whose Life Is It Anyway?* as the quadriplegic former sculptor who battles hospital administrators and the courts to gain the right to end his life. After a much publicized battle with drugs and alcohol, he returned in top form as wire hanger-magnate Dave Whiteman in Paul Mazursky's *Down and Out in Beverly Hills.* Among the best of his recent work are his two turns as Holly Hunter's lover— the cocky fire-fighting pilot in *Always* and the arrogant salesman in *Once*

Around—and his moving portrayal of a music teacher in *Mr. Holland's Opus*. Dreyfuss has also frequently returned to the theater with roles as Cassius in *Julius Caesar* (1978), Iago in *Othello* (1979), and *Death and the Maiden* (1992).

Filmography: The Graduate (1967); Valley of the Dolls (1967); The Young Runaways (1968); Hello Down There (1969); American Graffiti (1973); Dillinger (1973); The Apprenticeship of Duddy Kravitz (1974); The Second Coming of Suzanne (1974); Inserts (1975); Jaws (1975); Close Encounters of the Third Kind (1977); The Goodbye Girl (1977); The Big Fix (1978) also producer; The Competition (1980); Whose Life Is It Anyway? (1981); The Buddy System (1984); Down and Out in Beverly Hills (1986); Stand by Me (1986); Nuts (1987); Stakeout (1987); Tin Men (1987); Moon over Parador (1988); Always (1989); Let It Ride (1989); Postcards from the Edge (1990); Rosencrantz and Gildenstern Are Dead (1990); Once Around (1991) also producer; What about Bob? (1991); Prisoner of Honor (1991, tvm) also producer; Lost in Yonkers (1993); Another Stakeout (1994); Silent Fall (1994); Mr. Holland's Opus (1995); The American President (1995).

Filmography as producer only: Quiz Show (1994) co-ep.

Honors: Academy Award for Best Actor (*The Goodbye Girl*); Academy Award nomination for Best Actor (*Mr. Holland's Opus*); Los Angeles Film Critics Award for Best Actor (*The Goodbye Girl*).

DUNAWAY, FAYE. Born January 14, 1941, in Bascom, Florida; actor. Formerly married to rock musician Peter Wolf. One of the biggest names in Hollywood during the 1970s, this radiant blond movie star made her debut in Otto Preminger's *Hurry Sundown* before securing her place in film history as Bonnie Parker in *Bonnie and Clyde*—her tawdry opening close-up as she applies her lipstick is one of Hollywood's classic moments. She starred as Milady in the box office hits *The Three Musketeers* and *The Four Musketeers*, but her magnificent performances as Evelyn Mulwray in *Chinatown* and as the icy Diana Christensen in *Network* solidified her status as one of the preeminent actors in movies. The 1980s, however, were less friendly, beginning with her acclaimed, but parodic, performance as Joan Crawford in *Mommie Dearest*. Not until 1987's *Barfly* did she return to form in a remarkably brave and raw outing as the filthy, drunken lover of author and poet Charles Bukowski. In 1994 she found herself at the center of a controversy over her removal by Andrew Lloyd Webber from his stage production of *Sunset Boulevard*.

Filmography: The Happening (1967); Bonnie and Clyde (1967); Hurry Sundown (1967); The Thomas Crown Affair (1968); A Place for Lovers (1969); The Arrangement (1969); The Extraordinary Seaman (1969); Little Big Man (1970); Puzzle of a Downfall Child (1970); Doc (1971); The Deadly Trap (1971); Oklahoma Crude (1973); The Three Musketeers (1973); Chinatown (1974); The Towering Inferno (1974); The Four Musketeers (1975); Three Days of the Condor (1975); Network (1976); Voyage of the Damned (1976); Eyes of Laura Mars (1978); Arthur Miller on Home Ground (1979); The Champ (1979); First Deadly Sin (1980); Mommie Dearest (1981); The Wicked Lady (1983); Supergirl (1984); Ordeal by Innocence (1985); Barfly (1987); Burning Secret (1988); Midnight Crossing (1988); The Gamble (1988); The Handmaid's Tale (1989);

Helmut Newton: Frames from the Edge (1989); Crystal or Ash, Fire or Wind, as Long as It's Love (1989); Wait until Spring, Bandini (1989); Cold Sassy Tree (1990, tvm) also producer; Arizona Dream (1992/released 1995); The Temp (1993); Don Juan DeMarco (1995).

Honors: Academy Award for Best Actress (*Network*); Academy Award nominations for Best Actress (*Bonnie and Clyde, Chinatown*).

Selected bibliography

Hunter, Allan. *Faye Dunaway*. New York: St. Martin's Press, 1986.

DUVALL, ROBERT. Born January 5, 1931, in San Diego, California; actor. A major acting force in American film, Duvall has displayed an aura of power and dignity ever since our very first glimpse of him as Boo Radley standing motionless behind Jem's bedroom door in *To Kill a Mockingbird*. After ten years of solid work (*The Chase, Bullitt, The Rain People, True Grit, M*A*S*H, THX 1138*), he reached another level in *The Godfather* and *The Godfather, Part II* as mob consigliere Tom Hagen, the soft-spoken, but powerful, Irishman behind the Corleone family. He has since split his career between playing intimidating men of power and influence (Lieutenant Colonel Kilgore in *Apocalypse Now*, Bull Meecham in *The Great Santini*) and vulnerable rural characters (*Tender Mercies, The Stone Boy, Rambling Rose, Wrestling Ernest Hemingway*). Especially impressive is his role as the retiring Los Angeles Police Department cop in *Colors*, with one of the most discomforting death scenes ever committed to film. His notable television work has included roles as Dwight D. Eisenhower (*Ike*) and Josef Stalin (*Stalin*) and a superb performance as the retired Texas ranger in *Lonesome Dove*. "The camera sees everything he does, which when he tries to describe it, seems like nothing at all. The behavior somehow becomes riveting" (Vincent Canby, *New York Times*, December 6, 1991).

Filmography: To Kill a Mockingbird (1962); Captain Newman, M.D. (1964); Nightmare in the Sun (1965); The Chase (1966); Bullitt (1968); Countdown (1968); The Detective (1968); The Rain People (1969); True Grit (1969); M*A*S*H (1970); The Revolutionary (1970); Lawman (1971); THX 1138 (1971); Tomorrow (1971); The Godfather (1972); The Great Northfield Minnesota Raid (1972); Joe Kidd (1972); Badge 373 (1973); Lady Ice (1973); The Outfit (1973); The Conversation (1974); The Godfather, Part II (1974); Breakout (1975); The Killer Elite (1975); The Eagle Has Landed (1976); Network (1976); The Seven-Per-Cent Solution (1976); The Greatest (1977); The Betsy (1978); Invasion of the Body Snatchers (1978); Ike/Ike: The War Years (1978, tvm); Apocalypse Now (1979); The Great Santini (1979); The Pursuit of D. B. Cooper (1981); True Confessions (1981); Tender Mercies (1982) also associate producer, songwriter; The Stone Boy (1983); The Terry Fox Story (1983, ctvm); The Natural (1984); 1918 (1985) song only; Belizaire the Cajun (1985); The Lightship (1985); Hotel Colonial (1986); Let's Get Harry (1987); Colors (1988); The Handmaid's Tale (1989); Lonesome Dove (1989, tvms); Days of Thunder (1990); A Show of Force (1990); Convicts (1991); Rambling Rose (1991); Stalin (1992, ctvm); Wrestling Ernest Hemingway (1993); Geronimo (1993); The Plague (1993); Falling Down (1993); The Paper (1994); Something to Talk About (1995); The Scarlet Letter (1995), The Stars Fell on Henrietta (1995).

Filmography as director: We're Not the Jet Set (1975, documentary); Angelo, My Love (1983) also producer, screenplay.

Honors: Academy Award for Best Actor (*Tender Mercies*); Academy Award nominations for Best Actor (*The Great Santini*) and Supporting Actor (*The Godfather, The Godfather, Part II*); New York Film Critics Circle Awards for Best Actor (*Tender Mercies*) and Supporting Actor (*The Godfather*); Los Angeles Film Critics Award for Best Actor (*Tender Mercies*).

DUVALL, SHELLEY. Born July 7, 1949, in Houston, Texas; actor, producer. An unknown twenty-year-old nonactor when Robert Altman cast her in *Brewster McCloud*, the plain, characteristically American-looking Duvall became one of his stock players and appeared in seven of his films from 1970 to 1980. She was perfectly cast by Altman in *Thieves like Us*, in the Keechie role first played by Cathy O'Donnell in Nicholas Ray's *They Live by Night*, and again later as a dead ringer for Olive Oyl in *Popeye*. Her starring role as Millie in Altman's *Three Women* is a tour de force that earned her the top prize at the Cannes Film Festival, though the picture barely received a release stateside. Her last great role was as Wendy Torrance, the confused and frightened wife in Stanley Kubrick's *The Shining*. In 1982 she formed Platypus Productions to produce children's films for video and cable television: ''Faerie Tale Theatre,'' ''Shelley Duvall's Tall Tales and Legends,'' ''Nightmare Classics,'' and ''Shelley Duvall's Bedtime Stories.''

Filmography: Brewster McCloud (1970); McCabe and Mrs. Miller (1971); Thieves like Us (1974); Nashville (1975); Buffalo Bill and the Indians, or Sitting Bull's History Lesson (1976); Annie Hall (1977); Three Women (1977); Popeye (1980); The Shining (1980); Time Bandits (1981); Frankenweenie (1984); Roxanne (1987); Suburban Commando (1991); The Underneath (1995).

Honors: Cannes Film Festival Award for Best Actress (*Three Women*); Los Angeles Film Critics Award for Best Actress (*Three Women*).

E

EARTHQUAKE (1974), disaster. Directed and produced by Mark Robson; screenplay by George Fox and Mario Puzo; photographed by Philip Lathrop; edited by Dorothy Spencer; music by John Williams; released by Universal; 122 minutes. *Cast*: Charlton Heston, Ava Gardner, George Kennedy, Lorne Greene, Genevieve Bujold, Richard Roundtree, Marjoe Gortner, Barry Sullivan, Lloyd Nolan, Victoria Principal, Walter Matthau, Monica Lewis, Pedro Armendariz, Jr., Donald Moffat.

One of the worst of the popular disaster films of the 1970s craze, *Earthquake* is nonetheless notable for its memorable use of ''Sensurround'' (the high-volume, low-frequency rumble that literally shook theater seats) and break-through matte work of visual effects artist Albert Whitlock. The plot is almost too predictable to merit remark—top-level engineer (Heston) is sick of his blowsy, suicidal wife (Gardner) and is having an affair with a widowed mother (Bujold) whose husband was killed on one of Heston's construction sites. Then the big one hits and reduces Los Angeles from sprawling metropolis to smoldering ruin. Like its counterparts, this one has a star-studded cast (including Walter Matthau in a minor role as a well-sodden drunk, billed jokingly as Walter Matuschanskayasky) and spectacular special effects, but it desperately lacks a script and a gratifying ending. It's from the bigger, harder, faster school of Hollywood filmmaking, which, in this case, can add louder to the list. The ''Sensurround'' was a costly gimmick popularized by Universal Pictures (and also used in 1976's *Midway*, 1977's *Rollercoaster*, and 1979's *Battlestar Galactica*), but more substantial is Whitlock's detailed matte work of the ravaged city; he helped revolutionize the art of visual effects, from the avian multitudes of *The Birds* (1963), to the enormous dust storms of *Bound for Glory* (1976), to the dirigible explosion in *The Hindenburg*. While in today's world of digital effects these may appear rudimentary, they are, in fact, the most believable aspect of *Earthquake*—definitely more believable than Ava Gardner as Lorne Greene's daughter!

Awards: Academy Award for Best Sound, a Special Achievement Award for Visual Effects, and a Technical Award for the Universal City Studios Sound Department for the "Sensurround" process; Academy Award nominations for Best Cinematography, Editing, Art Direction.

EASTWOOD, CLINT. Born May 31, 1930, in San Francisco; actor, director, producer. Former companion of actors Sondra Locke and Frances Fisher. As an actor, one of the biggest box office draws in the world, and as a director, one of the most critically praised of his time, Eastwood is a child of the depression who, like so many of his characters, lived in a transitory state for much of his early life. After bit parts in numerous Hollywood features (suffering the indignity of *Francis the Talking Mule*) and guest spots on the television westerns "Wagon Train" and "Maverick," he landed the role of the affable, clean-shaven cattleman Rowdy Yates on "Rawhide" (1959–1966). Hoping to break away from his conventional western character, Eastwood traveled to Italy for his trilogy of Sergio Leone pictures—*Fistful of Dollars, For a Few Dollars More*, and *The Good, The Bad, and the Ugly*. Defining and refining a new generation of western antihero, Eastwood's "Man with No Name" successfully expanded and subverted his television character; with his stubby cigar, serape, and flat-brimmed hat, this man of no name and few words is recognizable as a variation on the western archetype—the outcast, individualistic outlaw whose past and future are colored in equally hopeless shades of black. This figure would evolve into the rogue police detective via *Coogan's Bluff*, the first of Eastwood's five films with Don Siegel. As an Arizona lawman who travels to New York City to work a case, Eastwood's Coogan is the missing link between the Old West and the urban jungle, The Man with No Name and Detective Harry Callahan (*Dirty Harry, Magnum Force, The Enforcer, Sudden Impact*, and *The Dead Pool*). Having entrusted his persona to Leone and Siegel, Eastwood took the natural step of directing himself. Like John Ford and Sam Peckinpah before him, Eastwood would concern himself with the soul and morality of his outcasts by questioning their violent actions, their integrity, and their humanity. At the same time he shaped a generation's impression of what it meant to be a man. While the bulk of his greatest directing work has come in his westerns *Hang 'Em High, The Outlaw Josey Wales, Pale Rider* and his Oscar-winning effort *Unforgiven*, he has deftly traveled outside the genre with *Bronco Billy*, a wryly comic look at a Wild West star; *Bird*, the atmospheric biography of jazz great Charlie Parker; and *The Bridges of Madison County*, a rich and passionate love story. Of his recent performances in films other than his own, his portrayal as the emotionally tormented Secret Service agent in Wolfgang Peterson's *In the Line of Fire* reaches a level of honesty heretofore unseen in his acting, especially in the teary scene when he recounts the John F.

Kennedy assassination and how it would have been all right with him if he'd taken the fatal bullet instead. His Malpaso Productions, which began in 1968 with *Hang 'Em High*, is based in Carmel, California, where Eastwood is a restaurateur and former mayor.

Filmography of key pre-1965 films as actor: Francis in the Navy (1955); Lafayette Escadrille (1958); A Fistful of Dollars (1964).

Filmography as actor since 1965: For a Few Dollars More (1965); The Good, the Bad, and the Ugly (1966); Coogan's Bluff (1968); Hang 'Em High (1968); The Witches (1968); Where Eagles Dare (1968); Paint Your Wagon (1969); Kelly's Heroes (1970); Two Mules for Sister Sara (1970); The Beguiled (1971); Dirty Harry (1971); Joe Kidd (1972); Magnum Force (1973); Thunderbolt and Lightfoot (1974); The Enforcer (1976); Every Which Way but Loose (1978); Escape from Alcatraz (1979); Any Which Way You Can (1980) also song; City Heat (1984) also song; Tightrope (1984) also producer; The Dead Pool (1988) also producer; Pink Cadillac (1989); In the Line of Fire (1993); Don't Pave Main Street: Carmel's Heritage (1994) narrator.

Filmography as actor and director: Play Misty for Me (1971); Breezy (1973) director only; High Plains Drifter (1973); The Eiger Sanction (1975); The Outlaw Josey Wales (1975); The Gauntlet (1977); Bronco Billy (1980); Firefox (1982) also producer; Honky-tonk Man (1982) also producer; Sudden Impact (1983) also producer; Pale Rider (1985) also producer; Heartbreak Ridge (1986) also producer; Bird (1988) director and producer only; The Rookie (1990); White Hunter, Black Heart (1991) also producer; Unforgiven (1992) also producer; A Perfect World (1993); The Bridges of Madison County (1995) also producer.

Filmography as executive producer: Thelonius Monk: Straight, No Chaser (1988).

Honors: Academy Awards for Best Director and Picture (*Unforgiven*); Academy Award nomination for Best Actor (*Unforgiven*); DGA Award (*Unforgiven*); Los Angeles Film Critics Awards for Best Picture, Director, Best Actor (*Unforgiven*); Cannes Film Festival Grand Prix de la Commission Superieure Technique (*Unforgiven*); recipient of the 1995 Irving G. Thalberg Award; AFI Lifetime Achievement Award (1995).

Selected bibliography

Gallafent, Edward. *Clint Eastwood: The Man and His Films*. New York: Continuum, 1994.

Kaminsky, Stuart. *Clint Eastwood*. New York: New American Library, 1974.

Thompson, Douglas. *Clint Eastwood: Riding High*. New York: Contemporary Books, 1993.

Zmijewsky, Boris, and Lee Pfeiffer. *The Films of Clint Eastwood*. New York: Citadel, 1982.

EASY RIDER (1969), drama. Directed and cowritten by Dennis Hopper; screenplay with Peter Fonda and Terry Southern; produced by Fonda; executive-produced by Bert Schneider; photographed by Laszlo Kovacs; edited by Donn Cambern; song "Born to Be Wild" by Mars Bonfire and performed by Steppenwolf; released by Columbia; 94 minutes. *Cast*: Peter Fonda, Dennis Hopper, Antonio Mendoza, Phil Spector, Jack Nicholson, Karen Black, Toni Basil.

The counterculture movie of the 1960s, this low-budget road movie struck a chord with young audiences across the country by tapping into the dreams and desires of American youth. Written by Dennis Hopper, Peter Fonda, and Terry Southern, the film follows Wyatt, who calls himself Captain America (Fonda), and Billy (Hopper) as they travel to New Orleans to complete a dope deal. Like their motorcycle trip, the film is about a search for the real America, a search for the elusive freedom that is the very foundation of this country. In many ways, *Easy Rider* recalls the westward trek of the western genre, only now the frontier has closed, our individualistic cowboys have become bikers, and their horses have morphed into choppers. Unable to go farther west, these new cowboys double back to New Orleans in search of the dream of freedom, but it's not to be found. By the end, they are both gunned down by a pair of good ol' boys who don't like their hippie ways. While countless biker films hit the screens in the late 1960s, this one is a cut above the rest chiefly because of the superb acting. Especially memorable is Jack Nicholson as the preppy alcoholic lawyer George Hanson, who tries pot and rambles on about interplanetary communication. Made on a shoestring cost of $375,000, the film grossed over $50 million at the box office. If great filmmaking is defined solely by its artistic merit, then perhaps *Easy Rider* fails the test, but if greatness is relative to a film's ability to reflect the collective conscience of a society, then *Easy Rider* is one of the most important contributions to American cinema.

Honors: Academy Award nominations for Best Supporting Actor (Nicholson), Original Screenplay; New York Film Critics Circle Award for Best Supporting Actor (Nicholson); Cannes Film Festival Award for Best First Film.

EL DORADO (1967), western. Directed and produced by Howard Hawks; screenplay by Leigh Brackett (from the novel by Harry Brown); photographed by Harold Rosson; edited by John Woodcock; music by Nelson Riddle; released by Paramount; 110 minutes. *Cast*: John Wayne, Robert Mitchum, James Caan, Charlene Holt, Michele Carey, Arthur Hunnicutt, Edward Asner, R. G. Armstrong, Christopher George.

Howard Hawks' penultimate film is a sometimes humorous, sometimes reflective picture that exists in that transitional interval between traditional and modern westerns. Like veteran studio director Hawks (who was seventy during shooting), the film's aging gunfighters Cole Thornton (Wayne) and J. P. Harrah (Mitchum) are part of an earlier era of professionalism that, as age creeps up, becomes increasingly difficult to maintain. Slowly, one muscle at a time, the body weakens and, like the entire western genre, gives way to the younger and stronger. Returning to the formula of *Rio Bravo* (revisited again in 1970's *Rio Lobo*) after the negative reactions to *Hatari!*, *Man's Favorite Sport?*, and *Red Line 7000*, Hawks throws together a team of gunmen (and a peripheral gunwoman) who must defend a town against a murderous villain. Feared and respected in their youth, things have now changed—Cole has a bullet lodged near his spine that causes sporadic temporary paralysis of his shooting hand, while Harrah is a whiskey-drenched sheriff ("a tin star with a drunk pinned to it") who elicits only laughter from the lawless. When land-grabber Bart Jason (Asner) enlists the aid of hired gun Nelse McLeod (George) to kill a local rancher, Cole and Harrah dig deep to find the dignity and strength of their youth. Doctors can't help Cole's paralysis, and a potent hangover recipe can't prevent Harrah from buying another bottle; their only cure is to carry out their task as professionals even if it means subjecting their creaking bones to a physical beating until they are both hobbling off on crutches at the finale. The sharp Remingtonesque Technicolor firmly places the picture within the boundaries of the classic western, but Hawks personalizes and modernizes it by building his narrative around the Edgar Allan Poe poem "El Dorado" with its call to "ride, boldly ride." Not at all funereal, it is a superbly entertaining film with a freestyle rapport between Wayne and Mitchum and comic relief from both Caan (with his miniature cannon of a gun) and crusty, old, bugle-blowing Hunnicutt. Much maligned in its day, the film now seems very nearly a masterpiece. "In *El Dorado*, ridicule kills more definitively than a Winchester rifle" (Jean-Louis Comolli, translated in *Cahiers du Cinema, the 1960s*).

EL NORTE (1984), drama. Directed and cowritten by Gregory Nava; screenplay with Anna Thomas; produced by Thomas; photographed by James Glennon; edited by Betsy Blankett; released by Island Alive; 139 minutes. *Cast*: Zaide Silvia Gutierrez, David Villalpando, Gomez Cruz, Alicia Del Lago, Lupe Ontiveros.

Epic in scope but intimate in execution, this is the simple story of a Guatemalan Indian brother and sister who flee their village when their politically active father is murdered, and their mother is hauled away by soldiers. Having seen magazine spreads of the luxurious life in El Norte, the North, they set out for Los Angeles. It's a hellish trip, which bottoms out when they must crawl through an unused drainage ditch to cross the United States–Mexico border, battling the repulsive stench and a pack of vicious rats. They survive and, after finding an apartment and jobs in Los Angeles, come to realize that their journey has not gotten any easier. An eye-opening comment on the desperation of illegal immigrants, the vast culture gap that exists between them and the gringos, and the peculiar upper-middle-class guilt that comes with having illegals working in their shops, gardens, and kitchens. An artfully made film that features the truthful performances of David Villalpando and Zaide Silvia Gutierrez as the brother and sister Enrique and Rosa.

Awards: Academy Award nomination for Best Screenplay; included in the Library of Congress' National Film Registry (1995).

ERASERHEAD (1978), fantasy/horror. Produced, directed, and written by David Lynch; photographed by Frederick Elmes and Herbert Cardwell (b&w); music by Fats Waller, song "Lady in the Radiator" by Peter Ivers; released by Libra; 90 minutes. *Cast*: John [Jack] Nance, Charlotte Stewart, Allen Joseph, Jeanne Bates, Judith Anna Roberts, Laurel Near, V. Phipps-Wilson, Jack Fisk.

Akin to Luis Bunuel and Salvador Dali's *Un Chien Andalou*, this debut feature from then-American Film Institute student David Lynch is a visual poem that follows a dream logic and invites numerous interpretations of its obscure story. Set in an urban wasteland of clanging metal and droning machinery, *Eraserhead* tells the story of Henry (Nance) a nice, but eccentric, young man with a vertical head of hair whose life becomes a series of nightmarish encounters when he impregnates Mary X, a woman who later abandons him after giving birth to a slimy, nonhuman fetus/child. A veritable feast of dark and troubling sights and sounds, *Eraserhead* is replete with unforgettable images: the white sheets of Henry's bed as they dissolve into a milky pool of white liquid; the backlit dust that swirls around Henry's head; Mary X's inert grandmother as a family member helps her toss a salad; the miniature man-made chicken that Henry is forced to carve at dinner; the scarred Man in the Planet as he stares out his window into the blackness; the Lady in the Radiator as she stomps on the spermlike worms; and the entire sequence of Henry's rubber head being chopped up into pencil erasers. More than just a cult movie, Lynch's Baudelairean *Eraserhead* is repulsive, disturbing, and troubling, yet ultimately it is an unparalleled thing of beauty from a director who, on the basis of this film alone, is a true visionary. One cannot, however, underestimate the contribution of cinematographers Fred Elmes and Herbert Cardwell or master sound designer Alan Splet. With the marketing genius of independent film distributor Ben Barenholtz, *Eraserhead* has become one of the most successful midnight movies ever produced.

ESCAPE FROM ALCATRAZ (1979), prison drama. Directed and produced by Don Siegel; screenplay by Richard Tuggle (from the book by J. Campbell Bruce); photographed by Bruce Surtees; edited by Ferris Webster; released by Paramount; 112 minutes. *Cast*: Clint Eastwood, Patrick McGoohan, Roberts Blossom, Jack Thibeau, Fred Ward, Paul Benjamin, Larry Hankin, Danny Glover.

Probably the quietest Hollywood movie released since the silent era, this masterpiece of tension and suspense is a testament to the cinematic command of both Clint Eastwood and Don Siegel. Eastwood stars as Frank Morris, a prisoner at the reportedly escape-proof Alcatraz who, along with the Anglin brothers (Thibeau and Ward), left the island in 1962; no bodies were ever found in the bay, and Morris and the Anglins likely started life anew under assumed names. Drawing heavily on Robert Bresson's classic work *A Man Escaped* (1957), this final Siegel–Eastwood collaboration is atypical of most action-packed prison escape movies. Aside from a few cathartic moments of violence (a prison yard knife fight and one prisoner chopping off his own fingers after being denied painting privileges), the usually big actions of a prison film are here confined to small gestures—the scraping of mortar with a spoon, the meticulous construction of a papier-mâché head, the painting of a cardboard grate.

Inside the confines of a cramped prison cell these actions seem downright brobdingnagian, especially by a giant such as Eastwood.

E.T. THE EXTRA-TERRESTRIAL (1982), fantasy/drama. Directed and produced by Steven Spielberg; screenplay by Melissa Mathison; produced with Kathleen Kennedy; photographed by Allen Daviau; edited by Carol Littleton; music by John Williams; E.T. created by Carlo Rambaldi; released by Universal; 115 minutes. *Cast*: Dee Wallace, Henry Thomas, Peter Coyote, Robert McNaughton, Drew Barrymore.

The highest-grossing film ever at the U.S. box office, this masterfully directed fairy tale is Steven Spielberg's greatest family film, the equal to such classics as *The Wizard of Oz* or *Snow White and the Seven Dwarfs*. Written by Melissa Mathison (wife of Harrison Ford), the film revolves around young Elliott (Henry Thomas), who befriends an oddly cute alien who has been left behind on Earth. The alien then gets into a series of comical situations that endear it not only to Elliott but also to his darling little sister Gertie (Barrymore) before attracting the attention of government scientists who want to study the creature rather than let it return home. Drew Barrymore is the standout among the cast as the charming little sister whose piercing shriek when she first encounters the alien is priceless. The crooked, glowing finger of Carlo Rambaldi's alien and Elliott's silhouetted bicycle as it soars in front of the moon (the Amblin logo) are indelible images in American film. ''The best picture Disney never made'' (*The Motion Picture Guide*).

Awards: Academy Awards for Best Score, Visual Effects, Sound Effects Editing; Academy Award nominations for Best Picture, Director, Screenplay, Cinematography, Sound; Los Angeles Film Critics Award for Best Picture; included in the Library of Congress' National Film Registry (1994).

EXORCIST, THE (1973), horror. Directed by William Friedkin; written and produced by William Peter Blatty (from his novel); photographed by Owen Roizman and Billy Williams; edited by Norman Gay, Jordan Leondopolous, Evan Lottman, Bud Smith; music by Jack Nitzsche, song ''Tubular Bells'' by Mike Oldfield; released by Warner Bros.; 121 minutes. *Cast*: Ellen Burstyn, Max von Sydow, Linda Blair, Jason Miller, Lee J. Cobb, Mercedes McCambridge (voice).

William Friedkin's follow-up to *The French Connection*, this adaptation of William Peter Blatty's popular novel succeeded in frightening audiences down to their collective marrow. Shattering taboos of religion and child sexuality, the film stars newcomer Linda Blair as twelve-year-old Regan, the cheerful daughter of a pragmatic, nonreligious stage actress (Burstyn). When Regan begins to suffer inexplicable fits that the medical profession cannot pinpoint, the faithless and disillusioned Father Karras (Miller) suggests an exorcism and calls upon the elderly, but renowned, Father Merrin (Von Sydow) to perform the ritual. Her body clearly inhabited by Satan, Regan transforms from a sweet child to a repulsive, venom-spewing, vomit-propulsing demon from hell. One of the most commercially profitable horror films of all time (originally grossing over $80 million at a cost of just $10 million), the film added a dimension that the novel could not—the gruesome special effects and Mercedes McCambridge's bone-chilling demon voice. The revoltingly graphic image of Regan's head completely twisting around shocked a generation of moviegoers with the same degree of relentlessness as previous audiences must have felt during the shower scene in *Psycho* or the unmasking scene in *The Phantom of the Opera*. Even two decades after the film's release, Mike Oldfield's "Tubular Bells" continues to conjure up images of Regan's possession and Father Merrin's arrival outside the ominous, fog-shrouded house.

Sequels: *Exorcist II: The Heretic* (1977, John Boorman); *The Exorcist III* (1990, William Peter Blatty). Linda Blair also starred in the spoof *Repossessed* (1990, Bob Logan).

Awards: Academy Awards for Screenplay, Sound; Academy Award nominations for Director, Actress (Burstyn), Supporting Actress (Blair), Supporting Actor (Miller), Cinematography, Art Direction, Editing.

F

FACES (1968), drama. Directed, written, and coedited by John Cassavetes; produced by Maurice McEndree; photographed and coedited by Al Ruban (b&w); edited with Jack Ackerman; music by Ackerman; released by Continental Distributing; 130 minutes. *Cast*: John Marley, Gena Rowlands, Lynn Carlin, Fred Draper, Seymour Cassel, Val Avery.

John Cassavetes' surgical examination of the emotional needs of married couples that revolves around the ailing fourteen-year marriage of Richard and Maria Forst (John Marley and the Oscar-nominated Lynn Carlin). Richard is in lust with an attractive young blond (Rowlands) and thinks he wants to start a new life with her; while Maria and her girlfriends bring home a freewheeling hippie (Cassel) who eventually spends the night in Maria's bed. Cassavetes shook the film world with his debut feature *Shadows* in 1961, but *Faces* is his first masterpiece—130 minutes of brutal truth registered in the characters' faces and the emotions that they mask. Unforgettable is the dinner table conversation between Marley and Carlin that turns frankly sexual as the giddy, blushing Carlin alternates between arousal and embarrassment. "One of the great films of emptiness" (Sylvie Pierre, *Cahiers du Cinema*).

Awards: Academy Award nominations for Best Screenplay, Supporting Actress (Carlin), Supporting Actor (Cassel); Venice Film Festival, Volpi Cup for Best Actor (Marley).

FALK, PETER. Born September 16, 1927, in New York City; actor. Best known for his role as television's Lieutenant Columbo, the bedraggled detective of the wrinkled raincoat and peculiar gaze (an effect of his glass eye), Falk turned to acting after a career in public administration with the Budget Bureau of the State of Connecticut. Although he earned Oscar nominations in 1960 (*Murder, Inc.*) and 1961 (*A Pocketful of Miracles*), he gained his greatest critical accolades in the first two of his four collaborations with John Cassavetes—*Husbands* and *A Woman Under the Influence*, starring in the latter as Nick Longhetti, the loving husband who commits his mentally unstable wife to a psychiatric hospital. He's been consistently excellent through the 1970s (*Mikey and Nicky, The Brink's Job, The In-Laws*), the 1980s (*Big Trouble, Happy New Year, Wings of Desire*), and into the 1990s (*Roommates*), while still continuing his career as Columbo in numerous television movies.

Filmography of key pre-1965 films: Murder, Inc. (1960); Pretty Boy Floyd (1960); A Pocketful of Miracles (1961); It's a Mad, Mad, Mad, Mad World (1963); Robin and the Seven Hoods (1964).

Filmography since 1965: The Great Race (1965), Penelope (1966); Luv (1967); Anzio (1968); Castle Keep (1969); Gli Intoccabili/Machine Gun McCain (1969); Rosolino Paterno, Soldato (1969); Husbands (1970); The Politics Film (1972, short); A Woman under the Influence (1974); Mikey and Nicky (1976); Murder by Death (1976); Opening Night (1977); The Brink's Job (1978); The Cheap Detective (1978); The In-Laws (1979); All the Marbles (1981); The Great Muppet Caper (1981); Big Trouble (1985); Happy New Year (1987); Wings of Desire (1987); The Princess Bride (1987); Vibes (1988); Cookie (1989); In the Spirit (1990); Motion and Emotion (1990); Tune in Tomorrow (1991); The Player (1992); Faraway, So Close (1994); Roommates (1995).

Honors: Academy Award nominations for Best Supporting Actor (*Murder, Inc., A Pocketful of Miracles*); Emmy Awards ("Columbo" 1972, 1975, 1976, 1990).

FARROW, MIA. Born Maria de Lourdes Villiers Farrow February 9, 1945, in Hollywood; actor. Daughter of actors John Farrow and Maureen O'Sullivan; formerly married to Frank Sinatra and Andre Previn; former longtime companion of Woody Allen; sister is actor Tisa Farrow. A Hollywood kid who had a recurring role as Allison Mackenzie on "Peyton Place" before making headlines with her marriage to Frank Sinatra and her subsequent transformation to flower child. Despite the initial appearance of nepotism, Farrow came into her own as an actor with the Roman Polanski horror film *Rosemary's Baby*, her frailty and boyish hairstyle only amplifying her image as the naive, expectant mother who is victimized by her newlywed husband and her nosy neighbors. Her roles in the 1970s included *The Great Gatsby* (as Daisy Buchanan), *Death on the Nile*, and Robert Altman's *A Wedding*, but her career remained unspectacular until her fortuitous teaming with Woody Allen on *A Midsummer Night's Sex Comedy*, her first of thirteen films with the director. During the ten-year stretch from 1982 to 1992, their collaboration on *The Purple Rose of Cairo, Hannah and Her Sisters*, and *Husbands and Wives* ranked among their finest works. In 1992, she and Allen ended their personal and professional relationship amid a very public war of words involving child abuse allegations that stemmed from Allen's romance with Farrow's adopted step-daughter Soon-Yi Previn.

Filmography: John Paul Jones (1959); The Age of Curiosity (1963, short); Guns at Batasi (1964); A Dandy in Aspic (1968); Rosemary's Baby (1968); Secret Ceremony

(1968); John and Mary (1969); See No Evil (1971); Docteur Popaul (1972); Follow Me! (1972); High Heels (1972); The Great Gatsby (1974); Full Circle (1977); Avalanche (1978); Death on the Nile (1978); A Wedding (1978); Hurricane (1979); The Last Unicorn (1982) voice; A Midsummer Night's Sex Comedy (1982); Sarah (1982); Zelig (1983); Broadway Danny Rose (1984); Supergirl (1984); The Purple Rose of Cairo (1985); Hannah and Her Sisters (1986); Radio Days (1987); September (1987); Another Woman (1988); Crimes and Misdemeanors (1989); New York Stories "Oedipus Wrecks" episode (1989); Alice (1990); Shadows and Fog (1992); Husbands and Wives (1992); Widow's Peak (1994); Miami Rhapsody (1995); Reckless (1995).

Selected bibliography

Epstein, Edward Z., and Joe Morella. *Mia: The Life of Mia Farrow*. NY: Delacorte Press, 1991.

FAST TIMES AT RIDGEMONT HIGH (1982), comedy. Directed by Amy Heckerling; screenplay by Cameron Crowe (from his book); produced by Art Linson and Irving Azoff; photographed by Matthew R. Leonetti; edited by Eric Jenkins; music by Joe Walsh; released by Universal; 92 minutes. *Cast*: Sean Penn, Jennifer Jason Leigh, Judge Reinhold, Robert Romanus, Brian Backer, Phoebe Cates, Ray Walston, Vincent Schiavelli, Forest Whitaker, Eric Stoltz, James Russo, Nicolas Coppola [Cage].

The times are fast, and the school is most definitely high in this superbly cast picture about the high school experiences of a brother and sister—the funniest and most insightful look at the youth culture of the 1980s. Brad Hamilton (Reinhold) is a popular senior whose status sinks when he loses his job; his sister Stacy (Leigh) is the opposite, an innocent freshman who learns about sex and dating from popular senior Linda Barrett (Cates), only to later get pregnant and have an abortion. More than just a laugh fest, the film balances the comedy with darker, real-life issues; Leigh shows signs of the great actress she would soon develop into; others like Cates, Forest Whitaker, Eric Stoltz, and Nicolas Cage all offer glimpses of their future talents. Sean Penn, however, as the perpetually stoned Jeff Spicoli steals the show. An incredibly dense surfer dude, he exemplifies the self-contained universe of the high schooler; when he orders pizza to Mr. Hand's (Walston) math class, or when he repeatedly smacks himself in the head with his gym shoe just to prove how stoned he is, we can't help but be charmed by his exuberance. Director Amy Heckerling would hit the mark again in 1995 with *Clueless*, another comic examination of high school life.

FATAL ATTRACTION (1987), thriller. Directed by Adrian Lyne; screenplay by James Dearden; produced by Sherry Lansing and Stanley R. Jaffe; photographed by Howard Atherton; music by Maurice Jarre; editing by Michael Kahn and Peter E. Berger; released by Paramount; 119 minutes. *Cast*: Michael Douglas, Glenn Close, Anne Archer, Ellen Hamilton Latzen, Fred Gwynne.

A by-product of the Oprahfication of America, this mediocre thriller became a cultural phenomenon because it tapped into a revenge fantasy of the sort that played itself out on a daily basis on television's daytime talk shows—a slut messes with my husband, and now she's going to pay! The simplistic plot, which appeals to the lowest common denominator, has a decent family man (Douglas) lured away by a black widow (Close), only to have the wife and mother (Archer) defend herself and her family by killing the other woman. Overflowing with jaw-dropping misogyny disguised as a value system, the message is clear—the full-time wife and mother is America's hero, while the ambitious female executive is ruining the American family. "What Freddy or Jason is to horny teens, Alex may become to the yuppie male contemplating a marital fling" (David Ansen, *Newsweek*, September 28, 1987).

Awards: Academy Award nominations for Best Picture, Actress (Close), Supporting Actress (Archer), Director, Adapted Screenplay, Editing.

FERRARA, ABEL. Born 1951 in Bronx, New York; director. Aka Jimmy Laine. Somewhere between art and exploitation, Scorsese and a snuff film, sits Abel Ferrara, the most provocative and disturbing American filmmaker in years. Making his first 8mm and 16mm films at the age of fifteen with his frequent screenwriting collaborator Nicholas St. John, Ferrara established a cult following with his exploitative entries *Driller Killer*, a self-explanatory film in which he starred under the name Jimmy Laine, and *Ms. 45*, a feminist revenge fantasy about a woman who, after being raped twice in one day, exacts a bloody vengeance with a handgun. After some impressive television work directing two episodes of "Miami Vice" ("The Home Invaders" and "Dutch Oven") and the pilot of Michael Mann's "Crime Story" (a bravura show of style that is one of television's finest hours), Ferrara found critical favor with *King of New York*, an invigorating, if excessively brutal, tale of New York City's corrupt underworld that bangs home its ideas of justice, morality, and redemption with all the subtlety of a jackhammer. His most praised film is 1992's *The Bad Lieutenant*, a brave piece of gutter art that features Harvey Keitel as a depraved, drug-addicted cop on a hunt for the punks who raped a nun. Not only did the film's debasement and redemption theme offend many viewers (not necessarily a negative response), it also so deeply offended St. John's Catholic sensibilities that even he refused to become involved in the project. Ferrara's next film, *Dangerous Game*, underrated even by devotees of the director, is an intense, volatile story of degradation and passion on the set of a movie; Keitel is Ferrara's alter ego, Madonna (in her best and most honest performance) is the star, and Ferrara's real-life wife, Nancy Ferrara, plays the director's wife. "A hyperbolic style, a subversive vein of sociopolitical comment, and a no-holds-barred pulp inventiveness raise their [Ferrara and St. John's] essentially exploitation formula material to another level" (Gavin Smith, *Film Comment*, July–August 1990).

Filmography: Driller Killer (1979) also editor, actor; Ms. 45 (1980) also actor; Fear City (1984); The Gladiator (1986, tvm); "Crime Story" (1986, tv); China Girl (1987); "The Loner" (1988, tv); Cat Chaser (1989); The King of New York (1990); Bad Lieutenant (1992) also screenplay; Dangerous Game (1993); Body Snatchers (1994); The Addiction (1995); The Funeral (1995).

FIELD, SALLY. Born November 6, 1946, in Pasadena, California; actor, producer. Daughter of former actor Margaret Field (Mahoney), and step-daughter of actor Jock Mahoney; formerly married to film producer Alan Greisman (*Fletch, Soapdish*). Wholesome, trustworthy, bubbly actor who first enamored audiences with her two hit television shows of the 1960s—"Gidget" and "The Flying Nun." While many of her film roles have been in the "cute" vein, she has consistently excelled when she has taken risks. Her chilling work in the television movie *Sybil*, as the young woman who is splintered into multiple personalities, earned her a much-deserved Emmy Award. Through the late 1970s she costarred with longtime friend Burt Reynolds in four films (*Smokey and the Bandit, The End, Hooper, Smokey and the Bandit II*) before taking more serious dramatic parts in Martin Ritt's *Norma Rae* (brilliantly playing a union-organizing millworker) and Robert Benton's *Places in the Heart*, both earning her Academy Awards. Her success continued through the 1980s and 1990s with memorable performances opposite such stars as James Garner (as a woman trying to rebuild her life in *Murphy's Romance*), Tom Hanks (as the shy housewife turned comic in the underrated *Punchline* and as the mother in *Forrest Gump*), and Robin Williams (as his wife in *Mrs. Doubtfire*). Her production company, Fogwood Films, has developed her own star vehicles (*Punchline, Murphy's Romance*, the television miniseries *A Woman of Independent Means*) and the Julia Roberts film *Dying Young*.

Filmography: "Gidget" (1965–1966, tvs); The Way West (1967); "The Flying Nun" (1967–1970, tvs); Stay Hungry (1976); Sybil (1976, tvm); Smokey and the Bandit (1977); Heroes (1977); The End (1978); Hooper (1978); Norma Rae (1979); Beyond the Poseidon Adventure (1979); Smokey and the Bandit II (1980); Back Roads (1981); Absence of Malice (1981); Kiss Me Goodbye (1982); Places in the Heart (1984); Murphy's Romance (1985) also ep; Surrender (1987); Punchline (1988) also producer; Steel Magnolias (1989); Not without My Daughter (1991); Soapdish (1991); Dying Young (1991) producer only; Homeward Bound: The Incredible Journey (1993) voice; Mrs. Doubtfire (1993); Forrest Gump (1994); A Woman of Independent Means (1995, tvm) also ep.

Honors: Academy Awards for Best Actress (*Norma Rae, Places in the Heart*); New York Film Critics Circle Award for Best Actress (*Norma Rae*); Cannes Film Festival Award for Best Actress (*Norma Rae*); Emmy Award for Best Actress (*Sybil*).

FIELD OF DREAMS. (1989), sports drama. Directed and written by Phil Alden Robinson (from the novel *Shoeless Joe* by W. P. Kinsella); produced by Lawrence Gordon and Charles Gordon; photographed by John Lindley; edited by Ian Crafford; music by James Horner; released by Universal; 107 minutes. *Cast*: Kevin Costner, Amy Madigan, James Earl Jones, Timothy Busfield, Ray Liotta, Burt Lancaster, Gaby Hoffman, Frank Whaley.

A magical, Capraesque tale that, despite its many opportunities to become purely manipulative, tells its nostalgic tale of myths and dreams with intelligence, honesty, and a surprisingly complex political perspective. Kevin Costner, in one of the roles that helped mold his homespun persona, stars as Ray Kinsella, a Berkeley-educated Iowa farmer who listens to a mysterious voice that ominously suggests, "If you build it, he will come." The "it" is a baseball diamond in the midst of his cornfield, and the "he" is bygone baseball great Shoeless Joe Jackson, a hero of Ray's late father. Ray's wife, Annie (Madigan), and daughter Karin (Hoffman) stand behind his bold decision, but others are less kind in their opinions, believing that the yuppie farmer has gone a bit crazy. Soon, however, the field of dreams is populated not only by a team of Hall of Famers but also by Ray's dad, and, in the ultimate dream come true, father and son play a simple game of catch just as they did years ago. Using its baseball iconography and its midwestern farm locale as the basis of its nostalgic all-Americanism, the film transcends the Reagan–Bush-era politics (Ray's from Berkeley, Annie gives an ardent anti-book-banning speech) in favor of a broader sort of patriotism and idealism that lie in dreaming great dreams. The result is a poignant film that, with its central theme of father–son bonding, accurately reflected the shifting image of the 1980s American man away from macho posturing of the previous generations and toward an emotional unmasking and increased sensitivity.

Awards: Academy Award nominations for Best Picture, Screenplay, Score.

FINGERS (1978), crime drama. Directed and written by James Toback; produced by George Barrie; photographed by Michael Chapman; edited by Robert Lawrence; released by Brut; 90 minutes. *Cast*: Harvey Keitel, Tisa Farrow, Jim Brown, Michael V. Gazzo, Danny Aiello, Tanya Roberts.

A twisted little crime drama from director James Toback (the writer of Karel Reisz's *The Gambler* and of Barry Levinson's *Bugsy*) that contrasts the "civilized" world of Carnegie Hall with the primitive lowlifes of the criminal underworld. Keitel, in a performance that parallels his early Scorsese work, stars as Jimmy Angelelli, an aspiring concert pianist and former "collector" for his mobster father's loan-sharking business. When his father's power begins to wane, Jimmy is guilted into making two more collections for him despite an upcoming audition at Carnegie Hall. As he is pulled back into the gutter, his ability to conjure up the muse begins to fail. Jimmy blows his audition and, after committing his first murder, sits naked and deranged at his piano listening to the music he once played so intuitively. A chilling portrayal of the distinct separation between the destructive mentality of the criminal world and the transcendence of the creative process, *Fingers* alternates between lightheartedness (Jimmy's habit of playing his tape deck everywhere he goes, even cranking the 1950s pop hit "Summertime, Summertime" while ambling through a freezing New York winter) and savage brutality (Jim Brown's psychotic head-butt of his two girlfriends when they refuse a lesbian embrace). Although this debut feature from Toback lacks technical polish, it vibrates with an energy that Toback has failed to recapture with his subsequent features *Love and Money*, *Exposed*, and *The Pick-Up Artist*.

FISHBURNE, LAURENCE. Born July 30, 1961, in Augusta, Georgia; actor. Immensely talented actor who made his debut at age twelve in *Cornbread, Earl and Me* and then, two years later, played the nineteen-year-old G.I. Clean in *Apocalypse Now*—his first of four films with Francis Ford Coppola. He began to attract serious critical attention as the single father Furious Styles in 1991's *Boyz N the Hood*, but his real breakthrough came two years later with his Academy Award-nominated performance in *What's Love Got to Do with It?*, almost literally transforming into singer Ike Turner. In 1994, he wrote, directed, and starred in the play *Riff Raff*, a one-act drama about his earlier days in Brooklyn. His television appearances include ''M*A*S*H,'' ''Hill Street Blues,'' ''Miami Vice,'' and a recurring role on ''Pee-Wee's Playhouse.''

Filmography: Cornbread, Earl and Me (1975); Apocalypse Now (1979); Fast Break (1979); Willie and Phil (1980); Death Wish II (1981); Rumblefish (1983); The Cotton Club (1984); The Color Purple (1985); Band of the Hand (1986); Quicksilver (1986); Gardens of Stone (1987); A Nightmare on Elm Street 3: Dream Warriors (1987); Red Heat (1987); Cherry 2000 (1987); School Daze (1988); King of New York (1990); Class Action (1991); Boyz N the Hood (1991); Cadence (1991); Deep Cover (1992); What's Love Got to Do with It? (1993); Searching for Bobby Fisher (1993); Higher Learning (1994); Bad Company (1995); Just Cause (1995); Double Cross (1995); Othello (1995).

Honors: Academy Award nomination for Best Actor (*What's Love Got to Do with It?*); Emmy Award (''Tribeca'' 1993); Tony Award (*Two Trains Running* 1992).

FISHER, CARRIE. Born October 21, 1956; actress, author, script doctor. Daughter of Debbie Reynolds and Eddie Fisher. At age twelve she appeared on stage in her mother's Vegas club act, later she dropped out of high school to study acting in London, and at age nineteen she debuted in *Shampoo* as a young seductress who quickly beds Warren Beatty. She was catapulted into the mainstream with only her second role, as the princess Leia Organa of *Star Wars*, and would appear in the subsequent episodes of the trilogy—*The Empire Strikes Back* and *Return of the Jedi*. Except for winning supporting roles in *Hannah and Her Sisters* and *When Harry Met Sally . . .* , her acting career since *Star Wars* has been limited to very good performances in generally mediocre films. She has, however, gained renewed interest as an author—her 1987 best-selling, semiautobiographical novel *Postcards from the Edge* detailed her drug addiction and rehabilitation and was the basis of the 1990 film, while her second novel, 1990's *Surrender the Pink*, fictionalized her relationship with singer/songwriter Paul Simon. Fisher is also one of the highest-paid and busiest ''script doctors'' in Hollywood.

Filmography: Shampoo (1975); Star Wars (1977); Mr. Mike's Mondo Video (1978); The Blues Brothers (1980); The Empire Strikes Back (1981); Under the Rainbow (1981);

Return of the Jedi (1983); Garbo Talks (1984); The Man with One Red Shoe (1985); Hannah and Her Sisters (1986); Hollywood Vice Squad (1986); Amazon Women on the Moon (1987); The Time Guardian (1987); Appointment with Death (1988); The Burbs (1989); Loverboy (1989); She's Back (1989); When Harry Met Sally . . . (1989); Postcards from the Edge (1990) screenplay from her novel; Sibling Rivalry (1990); Drop Dead Fred (1991); Carrie Fisher: The Hollywood Family (1995, tv documentary) writer, producer, host.

FISHER KING, THE (1991), drama/fantasy. Directed by Terry Gilliam; screenplay by Richard LaGravenese; produced by Debra Hill and Lynda Obst; photographed by Roger Pratt; edited by Lesley Walker; music by George Fenton; released by Tri-Star; 137 minutes.*Cast*: Robin Williams, Jeff Bridges, Amanda Plummer, Mercedes Ruehl, Michael Jeter, Harry Shearer.

After ex-Monty Python member Terry Gilliam's spectacular visual extravaganzas *Brazil* and *The Adventures of Baron Munchausen*, he turned to a character-driven story with this richly textured film about two friends and their quest for love and the Holy Grail. When sardonic New York radio disc jockey Jack Lucas (Bridges) inadvertently causes a listener to embark on a shooting spree, Jack drops out and hits the bottle. He gets a chance at redemption when his life is saved by Parry (Williams), a delusional homeless man and former history professor who dropped out after his wife was killed by the crazed radio listener. Although he tries to resist Parry's magnetic pull, Jack is soon helping his friend steal what may (or may not) be the Holy Grail from a billionaire's castlelike residence on Fifth Avenue. Meanwhile, Jack is trying to repair his relationship with the long-suffering Anne (Ruehl), while Parry is trying to get a date with his dream girl, the bashful and eccentric Lydia (Plummer). A fairy tale about the significance of the quest, *The Fisher King* is the work of a brave, romantic visionary who, like an alchemist, magically creates the extraordinary from the ordinary. The film still retains some of the fantasy elements of Gilliam's previous work (the nightmarish flaming horseman who pursues Parry through Central Park), but the focus is on the relationships between the four emotionally scarred leads, all of whom are uniformly excellent. One of the high points is a double date at a Chinese restaurant, which ends on a bittersweet note as Lydia, frightened by her feelings of love, tells Parry they should end their relationship before it begins rather than go through the pain of a breakup.

Awards: Academy Award for Best Supporting Actress (Ruehl); Academy Award nominations for Best Actor (Williams), Best Screenplay, Art Direction, Score; Los Angeles Film Critics Award for Best Actress (Ruehl).

FIVE EASY PIECES (1970), drama. Directed and coproduced by Bob Rafelson; written by Adrien Joyce [Carol Eastman]; produced with Richard Wechsler; photographed by Laszlo Kovacs; edited by Gerald Shepard and Christopher Holmes; song ''Stand by Your Man'' by Tammy Wynette; released by Columbia; 96 minutes. *Cast*: Jack Nicholson, Karen Black, Susan Anspach, Billy Green

Bush, Fannie Flagg, Sally Ann Struthers, Ralph Waite, John Ryan, Toni Basil, Helena Kallianiotes.

A provocative examination of the emotional paralysis of America's upper-class intelligentsia that stars Nicholson as a once-promising concert pianist who has since become the black sheep of an artistic Puget Sound family. For the last three years he has drifted around the West, eventually settling outside Los Angeles, where he works as an oil rigger and lives with a sweet, but dim-witted, Tammy Wynette-loving waitress (Black). When he learns of his father's illness, he returns home to confront his family and, in the process, sleeps with his brother's fiancée. A remarkable character study about a man who escapes his phony upbringing rather than live as someone who plays without feeling. Filled with memorable scenes, including Nicholson's attempt to thwart a restaurant's ''no substitutions'' policy; Sally Struthers' explanation of why she has a dimple on her chin; and a pair of maniacal, opinionated, filth-hating hitchhikers who are escaping to pristine Alaska. ''Deceptively simple, one of the most complex pictures of the 1970s'' (*The Motion Picture Guide*).

Awards: Academy Award nominations for Best Picture, Actor, Supporting Actress (Black), Screenplay; New York Film Critics Circle Awards for Best Picture, Director, Supporting Actress.

FLY, THE (1986), sci-fi. Directed and cowritten by David Cronenberg; screenplay with Charles Edward Pogue (from the story by George Langelaan); produced by Stuart Cornfeld; photographed by Mark Irwin; edited by Ronald Sanders; music by Howard Shore; released by 20th Century Fox; 100 minutes. *Cast*: Jeff Goldblum, Geena Davis, John Getz, David Cronenberg.

One of the most personal sci-fi/horror films ever made, this first Hollywood feature from Canadian visionary David Cronenberg is the culmination of all that had come before in the filmmaker's impressive body of work. Jeff Goldblum, in one of his most layered performances, stars as Seth Brundel, a socially maladjusted scientist who has been conducting advanced teleportation experiments. When he tries to send himself from one telepod to the next, he fails to notice the common housefly that has entered the chamber. The experiment seems to be a success, but Brundel and his journalist girlfriend (Davis) gradually realize that his molecular structure has crossed with the fly's. Coarse black hairs grow out of his back, then fingernails and teeth fall out, then an ear, until cell by cell, appendage by appendage, Brundel is nearly all fly. After directing a number of intelligent, low-budget Canadian shockers that addressed themes of self-loathing and revulsive disformation of the human body, Cronenberg has become increasingly fascinated by the physical transformation of the flesh. Here Brundel rapidly devolves (or perhaps evolves) into a fly, while in other films Cronenberg's characters have melded with technology (*Videodrome*), the opposite sex (*M Butterfly*), and the glass and chrome of automobiles (the 1996 release *Crash*) or have done the opposite and split into two halves of one whole (*Dead Ringers*). A disturbing and occasionally funny film, *The Fly* may be difficult for squeamish viewers, but others will find a beautiful and touching allegorical love story beneath the gory genre trappings.

Award: Academy Award for Best Makeup.

FONDA, BRIDGET. Born January 27, 1964, in Los Angeles; actor. Delightful and enchanting actor who represents the third generation of Hollywood Fondas after father Peter and grandfather Henry. She caught the eye of film critics after baring all in a spectacular, wordless performance in Franc Roddam's segment of *Aria* as an idealistic young woman in a garish Las Vegas hotel who carries out a suicide pact with her lover. She continued to receive excellent notices for her early work in *Shag*, *Scandal* (as Mandy Rice-Davies), and *Strapless*, eventually landing a part in *The Godfather, Part III*. She has since established herself as one of the most sought-after actors in Hollywood, well suited for thrillers (*Single White Female, Point of No Return*), low-budget, character-driven films (*Singles, Bodies, Rest and Motion, Camilla*), and comedy (*It Could Happen to You, The Road to Wellville*).

Filmography: Aria, "Liebestod" segment (1987); Light Years (1988) voice; Shag (1988); You Can't Hurry Love (1988); Scandal (1989); Strapless (1989); The Godfather, Part III (1990); Roger Corman's Frankenstein Unbound (1990); Drop Dead Fred (1990); Out of the Rain (1991); Iron Maze (1991); Doc Hollywood (1991); Singles (1991); Single White Female (1992); Leather Jackets (1992); Point of No Return (1993); Bodies, Rest and Motion (1993); Army of Darkness/Evil Dead 3 (1993); Little Buddha (1994); The Road to Wellville (1994); Camilla (1994); It Could Happen to You (1994); Balto (1995) voice.

FONDA, JANE. Born December 21, 1937, in New York City; actor. Father is actor Henry; brother is actor Peter; niece is actor Bridget. Married to Turner Network Television media mogul Ted Turner; formerly married to director Roger Vadim (. . . *And God Created Woman*) and political activist Tom Hayden. Despite growing up as the daughter of one of Hollywood's most stellar figures, she didn't act professionally until the age of sixteen, when she appeared with her father in the Omaha Community Theater production of *The Country Girl*. After a brief modeling career (she twice had a *Vogue* cover), an education at Vassar, and a stint with Lee Strasberg's Actors Studio, she landed her first film role six years later in *Tall Story*. Wading through a series of dated 1960s films, she began to find more substantial roles in the bawdy western comedy *Cat Ballou*, Arthur Penn's *The Chase*, Neil Simon and Gene Saks' *Barefoot in the Park*, and Otto Preminger's *Hurry Sundown*. Still, her most memorable early role is as the stripteasing space vixen in *Barbarella*, directed by then-husband Roger Vadim. Instead of becoming the new Brigitte Bardot as Vadim had hoped, Fonda took an interest in political activism, aligning herself with the antiwar movement. Simultaneously, her film roles became more provocative—her performances in *They Shoot Horses, Don't They?* and *Klute* took her to a new level as an actor. For a short time her political career overshadowed her film career, though they coexisted in Jean-Luc Godard and Jean-Pierre Gorin's Marxist *Tout va Bien*, in which she starred as an American news reporter in Paris during a factory work stoppage; that same year she was the subject of the Godard–Gorin film *Letter to Jane: Investigation of a Still*. By the mid-1970s, with the war in Vietnam over, she returned to Hollywood with a succession of strong roles, including an Oscar-nominated portrayal of Lillian Hellman in *Julia*, an Oscar-winning role in the post-Vietnam drama *Coming Home*, and a costarring role with her father in *On Golden Pond*. She has continued to address the political issues important to her in such films as *The China Syndrome* (nuclear energy), *9 to 5* (working women), and *Old Gringo* (the Mexican revolution), but her focus since the mid-1980s has been her popular line of stomach-flattening exercise videos. Though she hasn't been on the big screen since 1990's disappointing *Stanley and Iris*, she can usually be seen at Atlanta Braves games seated beside husband and team owner, Ted Turner.

Filmography of key-pre 1965 films: Tall Story (1960); The Chapman Report (1962); Walk on the Wild Side (1962); Period of Adjustment (1962).

Filmography since 1965: Cat Ballou (1965); Any Wednesday (1966); The Chase (1966); La Curee/The Game Is Over (1966); Barefoot in the Park (1967); Hurry Sundown (1967); Barbarella (1968); Histoires Extraordinaires/Spirits of the Dead (1968); They Shoot Horses, Don't They? (1969); Klute (1971); FTA/Free the Army (1972, documentary) also producer, screenplay, song; Tout Va Bien (1972); A Doll's House (1973); Steelyard Blues (1973); Introduction to the Enemy (1974, documentary) also codirector (with Tom Hayden and Haskell Wexler); The Blue Bird (1976); Fun with Dick and Jane (1977); Julia (1977); California Suite (1978); Coming Home (1978); Comes a Horseman (1978); The China Syndrome (1979); The Electric Horseman (1979); 9 to 5 (1980); No Nukes (1980, documentary); On Golden Pond (1981); Rollover (1981); Agnes of God (1985); The Morning After (1986); Leonard, Part 6 (1987); Old Gringo (1989) also producer; Stanley and Iris (1990).

Honors: Academy Awards for Best Actress (*Klute, Coming Home*); Academy Award nominations for Best Actress (*They Shoot Horses, Don't They?, Julia, The China Syndrome, The Morning After*) and Supporting Actress (*On Golden Pond*); Los Angeles Film Critics Award for Best Actress (*Coming Home*); New York Film Critics Circle Awards for Best Actress (*They Shoot Horses, Don't They?, Klute*).

Selected bibliography

Haddad-Garcia, George. *The Films of Jane Fonda*. New York: Citadel Press, 1994.

FONDA, PETER. Born February 23, 1939, in New York City; actor, director, screenwriter. Father is actor Henry, sister is actor Jane, daughter is actor Bridget. One of the seminal figures of antiestablishment filmmaking of the late 1960s and early 1970s, he went from playing all-American boys, to outsiders in Roger Corman's *The Wild Angels* and *The Trip*, to starring as the Harley-riding Captain America in *Easy Rider*, which he also cowrote and produced. This film—essentially a moral tale of two men searching for freedom in America—more than any other best defines the collective psyche of the country at that time. For

Fonda and costar/director Dennis Hopper, the "voice of a generation" tag was short-lived. They teamed again in Hopper's hallucinatory *The Last Movie*, which found almost no audience. Fonda's directorial debut, the poetic and revisionist western *The Hired Hand*, is a minor, but impressive, picture that is practically forgotten today. His subsequent films both as director and as actor have become increasingly tiresome and exploitative, usually casting him as a troubled loner of some sort. The only standouts are his B-pictures with Warren Oates (*92 in the Shade*, *Race with the Devil*), the action-packed drive-in hit *Dirty Mary, Crazy Larry*, and Jonathan Demme's *Fighting Mad*. Unlike his counterculture contemporaries Dennis Hopper and Jack Nicholson, he has been unable to resurrect a career that throughout the last two decades consists essentially of Z-grade revenge pictures relegated to release in indiscriminating Third World movie theaters. One sign of a possible turnabout is his role in 1995's *Nadja*, a critically acclaimed experimental vampire film from director Michael Almereyda.

Filmography: Tammy and the Doctor (1963); The Victors (1963); Lilith (1964); The Young Lovers (1964); The Wild Angels (1966); The Trip (1967); Histoires Extraordinaires/Spirits of the Dead (1968); Easy Rider (1969) also screenplay, producer; The Hired Hand (1971) also director; The Last Movie (1971); Idaho Transfer (1973) director; Two People (1973); Dirty Mary, Crazy Larry (1974); Open Season (1974); 92 in the Shade (1975); The Diamond Mercenaries/Killer Force (1975); Race with the Devil (1975); Fighting Mad (1976); Futureworld (1976); Outlaw Blues (1977); High-Ballin' (1978); Wanda Nevada (1979) also director; The Cannonball Run (1980); Spasms (1982); Split Image (1982); Daijoobu, Mai Furrendo/All Right, My Friend (1983); Peppermint Frieden (1983); Dance of the Dwarfs (1983); Certain Fury (1984); Freedom Fighter (1988); Hawken's Breed (1989); The Rose Garden (1989); Fatal Mission (1990) also screenplay; Nadja (1995).

Honor: Academy Award nomination for Best Screenplay (*Easy Rider*).

FORD, HARRISON. Born July 13, 1942, in Chicago; actor. Married to screenwriter Melissa Mathison. A former $150 per week contract player for Columbia Pictures who was fired because he lacked "star quality," Ford would go on to become a megastar—a handsome, rugged, intelligent Everyman whose films have collectively grossed over $2 billion, seven of them breaking the $100 million mark. He got his first big break when George Lucas cast him as the hot-rodding Bob Falfa in *American Graffiti*, compelling the director to later cast him as Hans Solo in the *Star Wars* trilogy. Ford began his second franchise role when Lucas and Steven Spielberg cast him as the adventurous archaeologist Indiana Jones in *Raiders of the Lost Ark*. From the mid-1980s on, he has become increasingly attracted to director-driven projects for such talents as Peter Weir (as Detective John Book in *Witness* and Allie Fox in *The Mosquito Coast*), Roman Polanski (as an American doctor in Paris in *Frantic*), Mike Nichols (as deal maker Jack Trainer in *Working Girl* and the gunshot victim in *Regarding Henry*), and Alan Pakula (as the tightly wound murder suspect Rusty Sabich in

Presumed Innocent). As Jack Ryan, the ex-Central Intelligence Agency agent of Tom Clancy's novels, Ford has embarked on yet another popular franchise with *Patriot Games* and *Clear and Present Danger*. Two recent Ford vehicles have featured the star in roles popularized by other actors; he turned David Janssen's Dr. Richard Kimble into the quintessential Ford hero in the blockbuster action film *The Fugitive* but was less successful in essaying Humphrey Bogart's tycoon Linus Larrabee in the bland remake of *Sabrina*.

Filmography: Dead Heat on a Merry-Go-Round (1966); A Time for Killing/The Long Ride Home (1967); Luv (1967); Journey to Shiloh (1968); Getting Straight (1970); Zabriskie Point (1970); American Graffiti (1973); The Conversation (1974); Heroes (1977); Star Wars (1977); Force 10 from Navarone (1978); Apocalypse Now (1979); The Frisco Kid (1979); Hanover Street (1979); More American Graffiti (1979); The Empire Strikes Back (1980); Raiders of the Lost Ark (1981); Blade Runner (1982); Return of the Jedi (1983); Indiana Jones and the Temple of Doom (1984); Witness (1985); The Mosquito Coast (1986); Frantic (1988); Working Girl (1988); Indiana Jones and the Last Crusade (1989); Presumed Innocent (1990); Regarding Henry (1991); Patriot Games (1992); The Fugitive (1993); Jimmy Hollywood (1994); Clear and Present Danger (1994); Mustang: The Hidden Kingdom (1994, documentary) narrator; Sabrina (1995).

Honor: Academy Award nomination for Best Actor (*Witness*).

FORMAN, MILOS. Born February 18, 1932, in Caslav, Czechoslovakia; director. The most influential filmmaker in the Czech New Wave of the 1960s, Forman, like his contemporaries (including playwright and future Czech president Vaclav Havel), turned away from the rigid, preconceived notions of art and developed an aesthetic that celebrated the lives of real people. After the international success of *Loves of a Blonde* and *The Firemen's Ball*, Forman, who had been in Paris during the Soviet invasion of Prague, moved to the United States, where his first film, Universal Pictures' *Taking Off*, received critical acclaim for its perceptive examination of the 1960s generation gap. His fortunes changed forever when he brought Ken Kesey's story of friendship and rebellion to the screen in 1975's *One Flew over the Cuckoo's Nest*. Like his Czech work, it functioned as human drama, political allegory, and social critique, and the results were overwhelming; the film won Oscars for Best Picture, Director, Screenplay, Actor, and Actress. Unlike the majority of European filmmakers who travel to the United States for one or two pictures, Forman became deeply entrenched in America; in 1975 he was named codirector of Columbia University's film school and two years later became an American citizen. In light of this, Forman's next film, the otherwise anomalous musical *Hair* with its mock hippies careening through Central Park, seems less out of place than upon first impression. It did, however, signal a change toward the different, more ornate style of filmmaking seen in his three ensuing historical films. While both *Ragtime* and *Valmont* display a mastery of craft and a fascination with the human condition, both fall victim to suffocating excess and the lack of a dangerous edge. This spirited sense of danger is alive, however, in *Amadeus*, the biography of insolent genius Wolfgang Amadeus Mozart and his relationship with composer Antonio Salieri. Like Randall Patrick McMurphy of *One Flew over the Cuckoo's Nest* and even the lovely shoe factory girl Andula from *Loves of a Blonde*, Amadeus is a dynamic life force whose rebellion is a welcome and necessary addition to our daily lives. As a director, Forman remained silent until 1995, when he began filming *The People vs. Larry Flynt*, the biography of the infamous pornographer's battles for his First Amendment right of free speech.

Filmography of key Czech films: Loves of a Blonde (1965); The Firemen's Ball (1967).

Filmography of U.S. films: Taking Off (1971) also screenplay; ''Decathalon'' segment of Visions of Eight (1973, documentary); One Flew over the Cuckoo's Nest (1975); Hair (1979); Ragtime (1981); Amadeus (1984); Valmont (1988).

Filmography as actor: Heartburn (1986); New Year's Day (1989).

Honors: Academy Awards for Best Director (*One Flew over the Cuckoo's Nest, Amadeus*); New York Film Critics Circle Award for Best Director (*One Flew over the Cuckoo's Nest*); DGA Awards (*One Flew over the Cuckoo's Nest, Amadeus*); Cannes Film Festival Jury Prize (*Taking Off*); Venice Film Festival Jury Prize (*Loves of a Blonde*).

Selected bibliography

Forman, Milos. *Turnaround: A Memoir*. New York: Random House, 1994.
Slater, Thomas J. *Milos Forman: A Bio-Bibliography*. Westport, CT: Greenwood Press, 1987.

FORREST GUMP (1994), comedy. Directed by Robert Zemeckis; screenplay by Eric Roth (from the novel by Winston Groom); produced by Steve Tisch, Wendy Finerman and Steve Starkey; photographed by Don Burgess; edited by Arthur Schmidt; music by Alan Silvestri; released by Paramount; 142 minutes. *Cast*: Tom Hanks, Robin Wright, Gary Sinise, Sally Field, Mykelti Williamson.

An unconventional box office megahit about a simpleton's ability to stumble through thirty years of American history. Gump (played with superb subtlety by Hanks) is a southern boy with a 75 I.Q. who is told by his mother (Field) that he can be anything he wants. Gump, it seems, has no aspirations at all except to live a happy life with his sweetheart Jenny (Wright). His problem is that the tragic flow of history keeps getting in his way—the John F. Kennedy assassination, racial hatred and protests, Vietnam, antiwar demonstrations, the Black Panther movement, and even AIDS. Despite these obstacles, Gump becomes a war hero (saving Gary Sinise's Lieutenant Dan), a perversely wealthy entrepreneur (via the shrimp-boating business envisioned by his army pal Bubba Blue), and a cultural icon. A disturbing reinvention of American heroism, *Forrest Gump* creates an impossible character—someone who achieves ''greatness'' by living life blindly and without conviction. He becomes fabulously wealthy not because of his business acumen but because he appropriates Bubba's dream and later makes a fortuitous blind investment; he becomes a college football star not through training, hard work, and an understanding of the game but by running fast. With his personal credo that "stupid is as stupid does," he has no use for education because even the dimmest bulbs can become the brightest stars. A huge audience-pleaser that has grossed $329 million to date, *Forrest Gump* follows a simple rule of entertainment—give the people what they want. Perhaps the most disturbing slant of the film is the fate of Gump's beloved Jenny. Painted as morally loose, she gets her comeuppance; just as she becomes enlightened to Gump's simpler way of living, she is stricken with an unnamed, AIDS-like disease. Jenny questions life and dies; Gump accepts it and prospers. The message that this country is ensconced in problems because it has devalued simplicity and innocence is as disingenuous as the computer-generated meetings between Gump and the famed political figures (of which Martin Luther King, Jr., is conspicuously absent). The recipient of a staggering thirteen Oscar nominations, the film also inspired a book of "Gumpisms" to live by. "The real fantasy at Gump's core is of an America where everyone's I.Q. is 75: the bliss of the mentally challenged but emotionally pure" (Howard Hampton, *Film Comment*, November–December 1994). "A morality play where decency, honesty, and fidelity triumph over the values of Hollywood" (conservative commentator Pat Buchanan).

Awards: Academy Awards for Best Picture, Director, Actor, Adapted Screenplay, Editing, Visual Effects; Academy Award nominations for Best Supporting Actor (Sinise), Cinematography, Score, Art Direction, Makeup, Sound, Sound Effects Editing; DGA Award; WGA Award.

FOSSE, BOB. Born June 23, 1927, in Chicago; died September 23, 1987; director, choreographer, actor. Married until his death to actor/dancer Gwen Verdon. Celebrated choreographer whose phenomenal success on stage has included *The Pajama Game, Damn Yankees*, and *Sweet Charity*, the latter of which became his film directorial debut. He followed with his masterpiece, *Cabaret*, an influential musical that used cabaret numbers to comment on the political events in 1930s Germany. By translating his jazzy, energetic choreographic moves to a snappy visual and editing style, Fosse created a refreshingly original musical film that garnered eight Academy Awards. His next three films are all examinations of the creative process and the self-destructive nature of the artist—*Lenny* is a powerful, nonmusical, black-and-white biography of drug-addicted comic genius Lenny Bruce; *All That Jazz* stars Roy Scheider as Fosse's womanizing alter ego Joe Gideon and is a bitter paean to the legacy that the artist leaves behind in death (with a brilliant opening audition scene set to George Benson's "On Broadway"); and *Star 80*, the story of murdered *Playboy* centerfold Dorothy Stratten and her husband/manager Paul Snider, is sad comment on fame and insecurity.

Filmography: Sweet Charity (1969) also choreography; Cabaret (1972); Lenny (1974); All That Jazz (1979) also screenplay, choreography; Star 80 (1983) also screenplay.

Additional credits since 1965: How to Succeed in Business without Really Trying (1967) choreography; The Little Prince (1974) also choreography; Thieves (1977) actor.

Honors: Academy Award for Director (*Cabaret*); Academy Award nominations for Director (*Lenny, All That Jazz*), and Screenplay (*All That Jazz*); Cannes Film Festival Palme d'Or (*All That Jazz*); Tony Awards for Choreography (*The Pajama Game* 1955, *Damn Yankees* 1956, *Redhead* 1959, *Little Me* 1963, *Sweet Charity* 1966, *Pippin* 1973, *Dancin'* 1977, *Big Deal* 1987) and Director (*Pippin*); Emmy Awards for Director and Choreography ("Liza with a Z" 1976).

FOSTER, JODIE. Born Alicia Christian Foster November 19, 1962, in Los Angeles; actor, director, producer. Adorable child star who gained recognition from an early age as the bare-bottomed girl of the Coppertone commercials before proving that she had the talent and maturity to match her looks. She played Addie Pray (after Tatum O'Neal's character) on the movie-inspired television series "Paper Moon," charmed audiences as Becky Thatcher in *Tom Sawyer*, and delivered a complex performance in the creepy Canadian picture *The Little Girl Who Lives down the Lane*. However, her role as Iris, the adolescent hooker of *Taxi Driver*, is most indelibly etched in the memory. After a rocky transition to adult roles and a commendable stop at Yale for a degree in French literature, she hit stride with an Oscar-winning role in Jonathan Kaplan's 1988 film *The Accused*. As the savagely raped Sarah Tobias, she reached an emotional depth at which she had only previously hinted. A second Oscar came for her deceptively simple performance as Clarice Starling, the Federal Bureau of Investigation agent-in-training who forms a deep psychological bond with serial killer Hannibal Lechter in *The Silence of the Lambs*. Her two films as director, *Little Man Tate* and *Home for the Holidays* (both developed and produced by her Egg Pictures), have not been entirely successful commercially or critically, though both display a formidable talent with a keen sense of aesthetics.

Filmography: Kansas City Bomber (1972); Napoleon and Samantha (1972); One Little Indian (1973); Tom Sawyer (1973); "Paper Moon" (1974, tvs); Alice Doesn't Live Here Anymore (1974); Bugsy Malone (1976); Echoes of a Summer (1986); Freaky Friday (1976); Taxi Driver (1976); Candleshoe (1977); Il Casotto (1977); The Little Girl Who Lives down the Lane (1977); Moi, Fleur Blue (1977); Carny (1980); Foxes (1980); O'Hara's Wife (1982); The Hotel New Hampshire (1984); The Blood of Others (1984); Mesmerized (1986) also producer; Five Corners (1987); Siesta (1987); The Accused (1988); Stealing Home (1988); Backtrack (1990); The Silence of the Lambs (1991); Shadows and Fog (1992); Sommersby (1993); Maverick (1994); Nell (1994) also producer.

Filmography as director, producer: Little Man Tate (1991) also actor; Home for the Holidays (1995).

Honors: Academy Awards for Best Actress (*The Accused, The Silence of the Lambs*); Academy Award nominations for Best Actress (*Nell*) and Supporting Actress (*Taxi Driver*); New York Film Critics Circle Award for Best Actress (*The Silence of the Lambs*); Independent Spirit Award for Best Actress (*Five Corners*).

Selected bibliography

Chunovic, Louis. *Jodie: A Biography.* New York: Contemporary Books, 1996.
Kennedy, Philippa. *Jodie Foster: A Life on Screen.* New York: Birch Lane Press, 1996.

FRANKENHEIMER, JOHN. Born February 19, 1930, in Malba, New York; director. One of the most highly touted directors of the early 1960s, Frankenheimer was part of the television-trained generation who made the smooth transition to motion pictures. He achieved towering success with *The Manchurian Candidate, The Birdman of Alcatraz, Seven Days in May,* and *The Train*—all tightly constructed, carefully crafted directorial efforts. By the mid-1960s, however, his career began to wane. His satiric thriller *Seconds* (with James Wong Howe's exciting and eccentric visual style) is a New Wave-influenced experiment that failed to achieve the commercial heights of his previous works, while the racing picture *Grand Prix* is a Cinerama delight that lacks a depth of character. Over the next two decades, he has had only two solid hits—1975's *French Connection II* and 1977's *Black Sunday.* He remains, however, an exciting figure in American film, with works that range from daring examinations of anti-Semitism (*The Fixer*), prison conditions (HBO's *Against the Wall*), and environmental issues (the generally silly horror film *The Prophecy,* HBO's Chico Mendes story, *The Burning Season*) to moody character pieces (*I Walk the Line, The Gypsy Moths,* the four-hour adaptation of *The Iceman Cometh*). Curiously, for a director of Frankenheimer's renown and stature, much of his career is filled with films that are almost entirely forgotten or ignored. He began to show signs of a minor resurgence with his adaptation of the Elmore Leonard novel *52 Pick-Up,* a thoroughly sleazy but well-crafted endeavor; the Don Johnson action vehicle *Dead-Bang*; and the Cold War thriller *The Fourth War.* After his excellent HBO productions in the 1990s (including 1996's Civil War epic *Andersonville*), Hollywood has again begun to take notice of Frankenheimer, hiring him in 1995 to direct the Marlon Brando picture *The Island of Dr. Moreau* (1996).

Filmography of key pre-1965 films: The Birdman of Alcatraz (1962); The Manchurian Candidate (1962); Seven Days in May (1964); The Train (1964).

Filmography since 1965: Seconds (1966); Grand Prix (1966); The Fixer (1968); The Extraordinary Seaman (1969); The Gypsy Moths (1969); I Walk the Line (1970); The Horseman (1972); The Iceman Cometh (1973); Impossible Object/Story of a Love Story (1973); 99 and 44/100% Dead (1974); French Connection II (1975); Black Sunday (1977); The Prophecy (1979); The Rainmaker (1982, ctvm); The Challenge (1982); The Holcroft Covenant (1985); 52 Pick-Up (1986); Dead-Bang (1988); The Fourth War (1990); Against the Wall (1994, ctvm); The Burning Season (1994, ctvm) also coproducer.

Honors: Emmy Awards for Best Director (*Against the Wall, The Burning Season*).

Selected bibliography

Champlin, Charles. *John Frankenheimer: A Conversation.* Burbank, CA: Riverwood Press, 1995.
Pratley, Gerald. *The Cinema of John Frankenheimer.* Cranbury, NJ: A. S. Barnes, 1969.

FRANKLIN, CARL. Born 1949; director, screenwriter, actor. After a career playing minor African-American characters on numerous television shows (the most notable of which was "The A-Team"), Franklin made the transition to writer and director while attending the American Film Institute in 1986. His highly regarded thirty-minute master's thesis *Punk*, the depiction of a black boy on the brink of adulthood, led to work with low-budget legend Roger Corman. Although his earliest directing efforts are less then spectacular, his two most recent features, *One False Move* and *Devil in a Blue Dress*, are among the most exceptional and underrated films of the 1990s. Mixing racial tensions with elements of film noir, both feature enigmatic mixed-race female characters (Cynda Williams and Jennifer Beals) who are positioned precariously in their segregated worlds—the deep South in *One False Move* and 1940s Los Angeles in *Devil in a Blue Dress*. Unfortunately for Franklin, he has not had the kind of commercial success that has buoyed other independent or black filmmakers, yet his best films show a maturity and human understanding that are only too rare in Hollywood.

Filmography as director: Punk (1989, short) also screenplay; Eye of the Eagle II: Inside the Enemy (1989) also screenplay, actor; Nowhere to Run (1989); Full Fathom Five (1989) also screenplay, actor; One False Move (1992); Laurel Avenue (1992, ctv miniseries); Devil in a Blue Dress (1995) also screenplay.

Additional credits: Five on the Black Hand Side (1973) actor; "Caribe" (1975, tvs) actor; "McClain's Law" (1981–1982, tvs) actor; "The A-Team" (1983–1987, tvs) actor; Last Stand at Lang Mei (1989) screenplay, actor; Eye of the Eagle 3 (1992) screenplay, actor; In the Heat of Passion (1992) actor.

Honors: Los Angeles Film Critics New Generation Award (*One False Move*); Independent Spirit Award for Best Director (*One False Move*).

FREEMAN, MORGAN. Born June 1, 1937, in Memphis, Tennessee; actor. Dignified, suave leading man whose film career didn't break until the age of fifty. After a long interest in the theater (from student plays to local productions), Freeman landed on Broadway in 1967 in an all-black version of *Hello Dolly* before becoming a regular on PBS' children's educational show "The Electric Company" as Easy Reader. That was followed with more stage work, a stint on the daytime soap "Another World," and a handful of minor film roles. Then came Jerry Schatzberg's gritty *Street Smart* featuring Freeman as Fast Black, the violent and complex New York City pimp who becomes the subject of a high-profile magazine piece. The part earned Freeman a much-warranted Oscar nomination and led to roles as the droll chauffeur in *Driving Miss Daisy* and as the Civil War infantryman in *Glory*. His recent work in *Unforgiven*, *The Shawshank Redemption*, and *Seven* has established him as one of American film's most distinguished performers. He made his directorial debut with the South African-themed drama *Bopha!*

Filmography: Who Says I Can't Ride a Rainbow (1971); Brubaker (1980); Eyewitness (1980); Death of a Prophet (1981); Harry and Son (1984); Teachers (1984); Marie (1985); That Was Then . . . This Is Now (1985); Street Smart (1987), Clean and Sober (1988); Driving Miss Daisy (1989); Glory (1989); Johnny Handsome (1989); Lean on Me (1989);

The Bonfire of the Vanities (1990); Robin Hood: Prince of Thieves (1991); The Power of One (1992); Unforgiven (1992); Bopha! (1993) director; The Shawshank Redemption (1994); The American President (1995); Seven (1995); Outbreak (1995).

Honors: Academy Award nominations for Best Actor (*Driving Miss Daisy, The Shawshank Redemption*) and Supporting Actor (*Street Smart*); Los Angeles Film Critics Award for Best Supporting Actor (*Street Smart*); New York Film Critics Circle Award for Best Supporting Actor (*Street Smart*); Independent Spirit Award for Best Supporting Actor (*Street Smart*); Berlin Film Festival Award for Joint Performance (*Driving Miss Daisy*, with Jessica Tandy).

FRENCH CONNECTION, THE (1971), crime drama. Directed by William Friedkin; screenplay by Ernest Tidyman (from the book by Robin Moore); produced by Philip D'Antoni; photographed by Owen Roizman; edited by Jerry Greenberg; music by Don Ellis; released by 20th Century Fox; 104 minutes. *Cast*: Gene Hackman, Fernando Rey, Roy Scheider, Tony Lo Bianco, Marcel Bozzuffi, Eddie Egan, Sonny Grosso.

A timely thriller that celebrates the grit and grime of urban life, *The French Connection* is perhaps the most New York of all New York films. Based on a true story of a 1960–1962 narcotics investigation by New York Police Department detectives Eddie Egan and Sonny Grosso (both of whom play minor roles), the film is an unflinching look at the questionable procedures of one rogue cop— Jimmy ''Popeye'' Doyle (Hackman), who, with his partner Buddy Rosso (Scheider), methodically and patiently tracks French drug trafficker Alain Charnier (Rey) and eventually makes a massive bust. Curiously, for a film as popular and as successful as this, Popeye Doyle is a truly ugly character; a lewd, racist, negligent cop whose unkempt physical presence is a sharp contrast to the ''civilized'' Charnier. The strength of the film lies in Friedkin and Hackman's ability to let Popeye Doyle's obsession seduce the audience into viewing him as a hero. While his techniques may be fascistic (and increasingly unacceptable in the 1990s), Popeye wins our admiration by getting the job done. Operating at the top of his game, Friedkin excels with his brilliant balance of character, narrative, and action—a balance he has yet to duplicate. While much of the film is, by today's standards, relatively slow, the kinetic chase scene between Popeye in his 1970 Pontiac and Charnier speeding above him on an el train is one of cinema's greatest scenes.

Awards: Academy Awards for Best Picture, Director, Actor, Screenplay, Editing; Academy Award nominations for Supporting Actor (Scheider), Cinematography, Sound; New York Film Critics Circle Award for Best Actor; DGA Award.

FRIEDKIN, WILLIAM. Born August 29, 1939, in Chicago; director. Married to producer/studio executive Sherry Lansing; formerly married to actor Jeanne Moreau and actor Lesley-Anne Down. Trained in live television in Chicago, first as a seventeen-year-old floor manager, then as a director of some thousand-plus programs, Friedkin attracted local attention with his documentary film *The Peo-*

ple vs. Krump, a plea to save the life of a black man on death row. After some inauspicious early efforts—the Sonny and Cher vehicle *Good Times* and the Harold Pinter adaptation *The Birthday Party*—he soon developed into one of the most provocative and challenging directors of the 1970s. His masterwork, *The French Connection*, is a dynamic look at an undercover drug operation in New York City that features Gene Hackman as Popeye Doyle, the prototypical Friedkin hero—an amoral, unprincipled man who raises complex and disturbing moral questions. He followed with *The Exorcist*, addressing morality in a religious context, though its mother–daughter family issues are atypical in Friedkin's canon. His atmospheric, underappreciated *Wages of Fear* remake, *Sorcerer*, and his lighter, but similarly male-predominant, crime film *The Brink's Job* may be steps down from *The French Connection*, but they are still superior to the majority of his subsequent work. Only *To Live and Die in L.A.* (with the ambiguity of William Peterson's Secret Service agent Richard Chance) and *Blue Chips* (with Nick Nolte's ethically burdened basketball coach) even hint at Friedkin's earlier success. The total failure of the highly anticipated *Jade* only accentuates the notion that Friedkin is a director whose vision was best suited to the mood and spirit of the 1970s.

Filmography: The People vs. Krump (1962, documentary); Good Times (1967); The Birthday Party (1968); The Night They Raided Minsky's (1968); The Boys in the Band (1970); The French Connection (1971); The Exorcist (1973); 49th Annual Academy Awards Telecast (1977, tv); The Sorcerer (1977); The Brink's Job (1978); Cruising (1980) also screenplay; Deal of the Century (1983); To Live and Die in L.A. (1985) also screenplay; Putting It Together: The Making of the Broadway Album (1986, ctv documentary); C.A.T. Squad/Stalking Danger (1986, tvm) also ep; Rampage (1987/released in 1992) also screenplay; C.A.T. Squad: Python Wolf (1988, tvm) also ep; The Guardian (1990) also screenplay; "On a Dead Man's Chest" episode of "Tales from the Crypt" (1992, ctv); Blue Chips (1994); Jailbreakers (1994, ctvm); Jade (1995).

Honors: Academy Award for Best Director (*The French Connection*); DGA Award (*The French Connection*).

Selected bibliography

Clagget, Thomas D. *William Friedkin: Films of Aberration, Obsession and Reality*. Jefferson, NC: McFarland, 1990.

FUNNY GIRL (1968), biography/music comedy. Directed by William Wyler; screenplay by Isobel Lennart; produced by Ray Stark (based on the musical by Lennart, Jule Styne, and Bob Merrill; photographed by Harry Stradling; edited by Maury Winetrobe and William Sands; songs by Styne and Merrill; released by Columbia Pictures; 151 minutes. *Cast*: Barbra Streisand, Omar Sharif, Kay Medford, Anne Francis, Walter Pidgeon.

The film that made Barbra Streisand one of the biggest stars Hollywood has ever seen, this must rank as one of the legendary acting debuts in motion picture history. Having enthralled Broadway-goers, she could now work her magic on the rest of the country at a time when the studio's star system was sorely in need of revitalization. As ugly duckling singer/comedian Fanny Brice, Streisand shines as she struggles to break out of the Lower East Side and hit the big time as a Ziegfeld girl. From there it's only a short step to the top, where romance blossoms with notorious gambler Nicky Arnstein (Sharif). The penultimate film from veteran director William Wyler, who, in his only musical, has created a delightful entertainment that absolutely sings whenever Streisand is on screen.

Sequel: Streisand and Sharif reprised their roles in *Funny Lady* (1975, Herbert Ross).

Awards: Academy Award for Best Actress; Academy Award nominations for Best Picture, Supporting Actress (Medford), Cinematography, Song (''Funny Girl''), Score, Editing, Sound; WGA Award.

G

GARR, TERI. Born December 11, 1949, in Lakewood, Ohio; actor. Schooled at the Actors Studio and receiving early acclaim on ''The Sonny and Cher Comedy Hour,'' Garr's film career got a boost when she played the slightly daft Inga of Mel Brooks' *Young Frankenstein*. With her precise comic timing and her modest sexuality, she has since perfected the persona of the befuddled blond. In a career that has an inordinate amount of easily ignored films, she has excelled in *Close Encounters of the Third Kind*, *Tootsie*, and *The Black Stallion*. Her finest work, however, is her deceptively simple performance in *One from the Heart* as Frannie, an unhappy dreamer whose ideas of romance cause her to reassess her loveless marriage.

Filmography: Head (1968); The Moonshine War (1970); ''The Sonny and Cher Comedy Hour'' (1971–1974, tvs); The Conversation (1974); Young Frankenstein (1974); Won Ton Ton, the Dog Who Saved Hollywood (1976); Close Encounters of the Third Kind (1977); Oh, God! (1977); Witches Brew (1978); The Black Stallion (1979); Mr. Mike's Mondo Video (1979); Honky Tonk Freeway (1981); The Escape Artist (1982); One from the Heart (1982); The Sting II (1982); Tootsie (1982); The Black Stallion Returns (1983); Mr. Mom (1983); Firstborn (1984); Miracles (1984); After Hours (1985); Full Moon in Blue Water (1988); Out Cold (1988); Let It Ride (1989); Short Time (1990); Waiting for the Light (1990); ''Good and Evil'' (1991, tvs); Ready to Wear (Prêt-à-Porter) (1994); ''Women of the House'' (1995, ctvs).

GAZZARA, BEN. Born Biagio Anthony Gazzara August 28, 1930, in New York City; actor. Cool, tough, soft-spoken leading man best known today for his association with John Cassavetes—*Husbands*, *The Killing of a Chinese Bookie*, and *Opening Night*. As Harry in *Husbands*, he stars opposite Cassavetes and Peter Falk as one of three middle-aged men who together embark on a search for the real meaning of their otherwise empty lives. A typical Gazzara character, we see Harry engaged in a personal struggle to understand the meaning of it all through drinking, whoring, gambling, and partying—in short, through acting like a Man. The best remembered of his early work is 1960's *Anatomy of a Murder* and the television series "Run for Your Life" (1965–1968), while his notable later work includes his two films with Peter Bogdanovich—*Saint Jack*, the examination of a pimp in Singapore, and opposite Audrey Hepburn in the charming romantic comedy *They All Laughed*. Much of his work throughout the 1980s and 1990s has been in Italian films that have received no release in the United States. In 1990, he wrote and directed his first feature, *Beyond the Ocean*. "It remains an open question as to whether he is a remarkable actor or simply a glowering ham" (David Thomson, *A Biographical Dictionary of Film*).

Filmography of key pre-1965 films: Anatomy of a Murder (1959); The Young Doctors (1961); Convicts Four (1962).

Filmography since 1965: A Rage to Live (1965); The Bridge at Remagen (1969); If It's Tuesday, This Must Be Belgium (1969); Husbands (1970); King: A Filmed Record . . . Montgomery to Memphis (1970, documentary); The Neptune Factor (1973); Capone (1975); The Killing of a Chinese Bookie (1976); Voyage of the Damned (1976); High Velocity (1976); Opening Night (1977); The Sicilian Connection (1977); Bloodline (1979); Saint Jack (1979); Tales of Ordinary Madness (1981); They All Laughed (1981); Inchon (1981); A Question of Honor (1982, tvm); La Regazza di Trieste/The Girl from Trieste (1983); Uno Scandolo Perbene (1984); La Donna Delle Meraviglie (1985); Figlio Mio Infinimente Caro/My Dearest Son (1985); Il Camorrista/The Professor (1986); La Memoire Tatouee/Secret Obsession (1986/released 1988); Quicker than the Eye/Passe—passe (1988); Road House (1989); Beyond the Ocean (1990) also director, screenplay; Forever (1991); Nefertiti: The Daughter of the Sun (1993); Els de Devant (1993); Swallows Never Die in Jerusalem (1994); Parallel Lives (1994, ctvm); Farmer and Chase (1995); Banditi (1995).

GERE, RICHARD. Born August 29, 1949, in Philadelphia; actor. Formerly married to model Cindy Crawford. Handsome leading man with a calming aura who, in the early 1980s, became one of Hollywood's biggest names after the success of *American Gigolo* and *An Officer and a Gentleman*. However, his reputation as an actor was built a couple of years earlier with a small role as the sexually charged stud in *Looking for Mr. Goodbar* and with his first starring role in Terrence Malick's masterpiece *Days of Heaven*. Since the mid-1980s, his films, with the exception of the Julia Roberts vehicle *Pretty Woman*, have lacked the box office punch of his early successes, though they continue to be projects of integrity and intelligence.

Filmography: Baby Blue Marine (1975); Report to the Commissioner (1975); Looking for Mr. Goodbar (1977); Bloodbrothers (1978); Days of Heaven (1978); Yanks (1979); American Gigolo (1980); An Officer and a Gentleman (1982); Beyond the Limit (1983); Breathless (1983); The Cotton Club (1984); King David (1985); No Mercy (1986); Power (1986); Miles from Home (1988); Internal Affairs (1988); Pretty Woman (1990); Rhapsody in August (1991); Final Analysis (1992); Sommersby (1993) also ep; And the Band

Played On (1993, ctvm); Mr. Jones (1994) also ep; Intersection (1994); First Knight (1995).

GHOST (1990), romance/thriller. Directed by Jerry Zucker; screenplay by Bruce Joel Rubin; produced by Lisa Weinstein; photographed by Adam Greenberg; edited by Walter Murch; music by Maurice Jarre; released by Paramount; 128 minutes. *Cast*: Demi Moore, Patrick Swayze, Whoopi Goldberg, Tony Goldwyn, Vincent Schiavelli, Rick Aviles.

Advancing the ideas of mysticism and psychic powers that were just beginning to take hold at the start of the decade, this popular weepy is built upon an essentially fraudulent notion—that our dead can contact us from the great beyond—which, nonetheless, tapped into the hopes and desires of the American people. The plot is relatively familiar (in fact it parallels Steven Spielberg's much less commercially successful endeavor *Always*, released earlier in 1990)—two young lovers (Swayze's Sam Wheat and Moore's Molly Jensen) are separated by the death of the man only to have him return from the Other Side to save his lover's life before finally saying goodbye. Add to that Whoopi Goldberg as phony psychic Oda Mae Brown and an extortion subplot involving Sam's former banking partner, and suddenly *Ghost* has the turnstiles spinning until it becomes the highest-grossing film of the year. It's not surprising then that, with the country's New Age spiritualism and renewed belief in angels and aliens, *Ghost* stirred a nation's anxieties about being separated from a loved one. With its PG-13 rating keeping libidos in check, there is just enough romance and sexual energy between former Dirty Dancer Swayze and aging Brat Packer Moore (especially at their pottery wheel) to titillate audiences without making them turn away. Curiously, most audiences didn't think about the practicality of the climactic lovemaking scene between Molly and Sam's spirit—a spirit that ''borrows'' Oda Mae's body, making this the first interracial lesbian scene in a major motion picture; alas, it is never shown on-screen.

Awards: Academy Awards for Best Supporting Actress (Goldberg), Screenplay; Academy Award nominations for Best Picture, Editing, Score.

GIBSON, MEL. Born January 3, 1956, in Peekskill, New York; actor, director. American-born actor who emigrated to Australia with his family in 1968 and later became a marquee heartthrob Down Under with his diverse roles as the mildly retarded young hunk in *Tim* and as the heroic avenger in the postapocalyptic action-adventure film *Mad Max*. He soon became a movie icon—part chiseled macho action hero (reinforced by the release of *The Road Warrior*) and part gorgeous, romantic leading man (thanks to *The Year of Living Dangerously*). Hollywood soon came calling with quality dramas like *Bounty, Mrs. Soffel,* and *The River* before Gibson returned to Australia to star in *Mad Max beyond Thunderdome*. All that seemed to be missing was a Hollywood action vehicle that also displayed Gibson's knack for physical comedy—that film was *Lethal Weapon,* and the character was the demented wacko Martin Riggs, an unbalanced Los Angeles Police Department cop partnered with Danny Glover's Roger Murtaugh. That film and its two sequels made a mint at the box office, but his other films have not performed as well. By 1990 he had formed his own development company, Icon Productions, and had taken his greatest acting risk to date—casting himself as the lead in *Hamlet*. Icon has produced all of Gibson's subsequent films, including his competent directing debut *Man without a Face* and his Oscar-winning sophomore effort *Braveheart*, the exquisitely realized period biography of Scottish hero William Wilson. Icon has also branched out into developing non-Gibson movies with *Immortal Beloved*, the Beethoven biography starring Gary Oldman.

Filmography: Summer City (1977); Tim (1979); Mad Max (1979); Chain Reaction/ Nuclear Run (1980); Attack Force Z (1981); Gallipoli (1981); The Road Warrior (1981); The Year of Living Dangerously (1982); The Bounty (1984); Mrs. Soffel (1984); The River (1984); Mad Max beyond Thunderdome (1985); Lethal Weapon (1987); Tequila Sunrise (1988); Lethal Weapon 2 (1989); Air America (1990); Bird on a Wire (1990); Hamlet (1990); Lethal Weapon 3 (1992); Forever Young (1992); Man without a Face (1993) also director; Maverick (1994); Casper (1995); Braveheart (1995) also director, producer; Pocahontas (1995) voice.

Honors: Academy Awards for Best Director and Picture (*Braveheart*).

GIMME SHELTER (1970), documentary. Directed and coproduced by David Maysles, Albert Maysles, Charlotte Zwerin; produced with Porter Bibb; photographed by David Maysles, Albert Maysles, George Lucas, Robert Primes, Eric Saarinen, and others; edited by Ellen Giffard, Robert Farren, Joanne Burke, Kent McKinney; released by Roxie Releasing; 90 minutes. *Cast*: The Rolling Stones, Jefferson Airplane, Melvin Belli, Tina Turner, Jerry Garcia.

The antithesis of *Woodstock* and everything it stood for, this filmed concert event (which was released before its much longer counterpart) was meant to trumpet the rock-and-roll superiority of the Rolling Stones, who, unlike their British rivals the Who, failed to play Woodstock earlier in 1969. Instead, this hastily organized free concert at California's Altamont Speedway resulted in the on-camera murder of a black teenager by a member of the Hell's Angels Motorcycle Club (who was later acquitted due to self-defense). As a documentary, it is a curious, artistically muddied film that was clearly intended as a promotional tool for Mick Jagger the artist but instead, through a twist of fate, became a visual record of the volatility of the times. Like its fictional parallel *Easy Rider*, *Gimme Shelter* is a reflection on violence in America and its effect on the idealistic 1960s notion of peace, love, and understanding.

GLOVER, DANNY. Born July 22, 1947, in San Francisco; actor. Accomplished actor whose role as the hateful, tyrannical Albert in Steven Spielberg's *The Color Purple* helped establish him as a forceful leading man. He then found huge commercial success teamed with Mel Gibson in the *Lethal Weapon* films as Los Angeles Police Department officer Roger Murtaugh. Perhaps his best critical notices have come in Charles Burnett's *To Sleep with Anger*, a complex study of a middle-class black family that features Glover as a long-absent relative whose appearance throws the household into a state of chaos.

Filmography: Escape from Alcatraz (1979); Chu Chu and the Philly Flash (1981); Out (1982); Iceman (1984); Places in the Heart (1984); The Stand-In (1984); The Color Purple (1985); Silverado (1985); Witness (1985); Lethal Weapon (1987); BAT 21 (1988); Lethal Weapon 2 (1989); Predator 2 (1990); To Sleep with Anger (1990) also executive producer; Flight of the Intruder (1991); A Rage in Harlem (1991); Pure Luck (1991); Grand Canyon (1991); Lethal Weapon 3 (1992); Bopha! (1993); The Saint of Fort Washington (1993); Maverick (1994); Angels in the Outfield (1994); Operation Dumbo Drop (1995).

Honor: Independent Spirit Award for Best Actor (*To Sleep with Anger*).

GODFATHER, THE (1972), gangster drama. Directed and cowritten by Francis Ford Coppola; screenplay with Mario Puzo (from his novel); produced by Albert S. Luddy; photographed by Gordon Willis; edited by William Reynolds, Peter Zinner, Marc Laub, and Murray Solomon; music by Nino Rota; released by Paramount; 176 minutes. *Cast*: Marlon Brando, Al Pacino, James Caan, Richard Castellano, Robert Duvall, Sterling Hayden, John Marley, Al Lettieri, Richard Conte, Diane Keaton, Abe Vigoda, Talia Shire, John Cazale, Al Martino, Alex Rocco, Lenny Montana, Simonetta Stefanelli.

GODFATHER, PART II, THE (1974). Directed, cowritten, and coproduced by Coppola; screenplay with Puzo; produced with Gary Frederickson and Fred Roos; photographed by Willis; edited by Peter Zinner, Richard Marks, and Barry Malkin; music by Rota and Carmine Coppola; released by Paramount; 200 minutes. *Cast*: Al Pacino, Robert Duvall, Diane Keaton, Robert De Niro, Talia Shire, John Cazale, Lee Strasberg, Michael V. Gazzo, Abe Vigoda, Troy Donahue, Harry Dean Stanton, Roger Corman, Danny Aiello, G. D. Spradlin, James Caan.

THE GODFATHER, PART III (1990). Directed, cowritten, and coproduced by Coppola; screenplay with Puzo; produced with Frederickson, Roos, and Charles Mulvehill; photographed by Willis; edited by Barry Malkin, Lisa Fruchtman, and Walter Murch; music by Rota and Carmine Coppola; released by Paramount; 161 minutes. *Cast*: Al Pacino, Andy Garcia, Diane Keaton, Talia Shire, Eli Wallach, Joe Mantegna, Sophia Coppola, Bridget Fonda, George Hamilton, John Savage, Raf Vallone, Donal Donnelly, Helmut Berger, Don Novello, Al Martino, Franc D'Ambrosio.

A staggering American chronicle of family, corruption, and ethics that centers on the tragic fall of Michael Corleone (Pacino), who fatefully intervenes in his father's business in order to protect and avenge his family and, in turn, rises to a position of extreme power, which ultimately destroys his family and his soul. The first film details the transition of power from Don Vito Corleone (Brando) to Michael when eldest son and heir apparent, the hotheaded Sonny (Caan), is brutally machine-gunned in an ambush. In the operatic finale, Michael's gunmen carry out a brutal slaughter of his family's enemies, crosscut with the christening of Michael and wife Kay's (Keaton) infant son. In the second installment, Michael (having previously lied to Kay about his involvement in the murders of the Corleones' enemies, including his own brother-in-law) ascends to the top of his crime family while, paradoxically, destroying his real family. Now running his massive empire from Lake Tahoe, his involvement spreads from Vegas, to Washington, D.C., to pre-Castro Havana and results in the murder of his own brother Freddo (Cazale) and the revelation that Kay has aborted their next child rather than bring a new life into Michael's monstrous world. Crosscut with Michael's moral decay is the rise of the young Vito Corleone (De Niro) in 1917 New York. These two pictures together (they are too inextricably bound to consider separately) paint one of the most epic portraits of twentieth-century life in America. While it has been argued that *The Godfather II* is superior to its predecessor, the intricacies and nuances of the second film are built upon the foundation of the first; the whole is greater than each part. The final episode of the trilogy, however, lacks the emotional or narrative drive of the first two films. Moving the story into another realm is the aging Michael's attempt to go legit, reestablish ties with Kay, and become involved with the Catholic Church, a family as volatile and more expansive than the mob. Although intelligent and provocative, *The Godfather III* is a disappointing effort that cannot, and does not, sully the memory of the previous films. If the line between the first two pictures is not blurred enough, Coppola's 1977 linear reediting for tv, *The Godfather Saga*, includes an additional hour (putting the trilogy at roughly ten hours) of previously unseen footage. ''Not since Andy Hardy has an American film shown such unshadowed love between father and son'' (David Thomson on *The Godfather, America in the Dark*).

Awards: *The Godfather*: Academy Awards for Best Picture, Actor (Brando), Screenplay; Academy Award nominations for Best Director, Supporting Actor (Caan, Duvall, Pacino), Editing, Costumes, Sound; New York Film Critics Circle Award for Best Supporting Actor (Duvall); DGA Award; included in the Library of Congress' National Film Registry (1990); *The Godfather, Part II*: Academy Awards for Best Picture, Director, Supporting Actor (De Niro), Adapted Screenplay, Art Direction, Score; Academy Award nominations for Best Actor (Pacino), Supporting Actor (Gazzo, Strasberg), Supporting Actress (Shire), Costumes; DGA Award; included in the Library of Congress' National Film Registry (1993); *The Godfather, Part III*: Academy Award nominations for Best Picture, Director, Supporting Actor (Garcia), Cinematography, Art Direction, Editing, Song.

GOLDBERG, WHOOPI. Born Caryn Johnson November 13, 1949, in New York City; actor, comedian. Starting as a performer at age eight and later appearing in small roles in the Broadway productions of *Hair*, *Pippin*, and *Jesus Christ Superstar*, Goldberg soon found fame as a stand-up comic. Her extraordinary first film role came in Steven Spielberg's *The Color Purple* and earned her an Academy Award nomination. When she is challenged by a strong dramatic role, she is an exceptional actress, but too often she appears in predictable comedies. While her two *Sister Act* films have been box office smashes, her textured performances in *The Long Walk Home*, *Corrina, Corrina*, and *Boys on the Side* have not had the same results. Blessed with one of the best smiles in movies, Goldberg continues to perform stand-up in clubs and on television, including perennial work with Billy Crystal and Robin Williams for ''Comic Relief'' and two stints as host of the Academy Awards telecast.

Filmography: The Color Purple (1985); Jumpin' Jack Flash (1986); Burglar (1987); Fatal Beauty (1987); Clara's Heart (1988); The Telephone (1988); Beverly Hills Brats (1989); Homer and Eddie (1989); Ghost (1990); The Long Walk Home (1990); Soapdish (1991); Sarafina! (1992); Sister Act (1992); The Player (1992), Sister Act II: Back in the Habit (1993); Made in America (1993); Corrina, Corrina (1994); Star Trek Generations (1994); Naked in New York (1994); The Pagemaster (1994) voice; The Little Rascals (1994); The Lion King (1994) voice; Boys on the Side (1995); T. Rex (1995); Moonlight and Valentino (1995); Before Their Time: Four Generations of Teenage Mothers (1995, ctvm) producer.

Honors: Academy Award for Best Supporting Actress (*Ghost*); Academy Award nomination for Best Actress (*The Color Purple*); Grammy Award for Best Comedy Album (''Whoopie Goldberg'' 1985).

GOODBYE GIRL, THE (1977), romantic comedy. Directed by Herbert Ross; screenplay by Neil Simon; produced by Ray Stark; photographed by David M. Walsh; edited by John F. Burnett; music by Dave Grusin; released by MGM; 110 minutes. *Cast*: Richard Dreyfuss, Marsha Mason, Quinn Cummings, Paul Benedict.

A charming box office hit that is immersed in the same easy, sitcom stylings of Neil Simon's Broadway work. It's cute, it's funny, it's tearful and in all the right places. A masterful manipulator, Simon, in his original screenplay, concocts a stagy setup as aging dancer Paula McFadden (Mason) and her precocious daughter Lucy (Cummings) are shocked to learn that their New York City apartment has been sublet to aspiring young actor Elliott Garfield (Dreyfuss). Rather than turn Paula and Lucy homeless, Elliott agrees to share the apartment and split the rent. Of course, dancer and actor fall in love in the process. It's as predictable and treacly as all of Neil Simon's work . . . and equally entertaining. Enhanced by excellent performances from Dreyfuss, Mason (one of her five film collaborations with former husband Simon), and young star Quinn Cummings in her only film role. One of two 1977 Best Picture-nominated films from Herbert Ross.

Awards: Academy Award for Best Actor; Academy Award nominations for Best Picture, Actress, Supporting Actress (Cummings), Screenplay.

GOODFELLAS (1990), crime drama. Directed by Martin Scorsese; screenplay by Nicholas Pileggi and Scorsese (from the book *Wiseguy* by Pileggi); produced by Irwin Winkler; photographed by Michael Ballhaus; edited by Thelma Schoonmaker; released by Warner Bros.; 148 minutes. *Cast*: Robert De Niro, Ray Liotta, Joe Pesci, Lorraine Bracco, Paul Sorvino, Frank Sivero, Gina Mastrogiacomo, Frank Vincent, Chuck Low, Michael Imperioli, Debi Mazar, Mike Starr, Samuel L. Jackson, Illeanna Douglas.

One of the most glaring examples of America's fascination with gangster chic, this orgiastic feast of brutality is one of Martin Scorsese's most technically accomplished pictures but also one of his coldest emotionally. It exists at a fast and furious pace, with a rock-and-roll soundtrack that spans the 1950s to the 1970s and never, not for a single frame, lets up; still, it feels more like an exercise in macho potency than humanity. A journalistic examination of the mob culture that experiences the high of "whacking" your enemies and snorting cocaine, the film's true-life central character is Henry Hill (Liotta), a mobster turned informant whose life was the basis of Nick Pileggi's book *Wiseguy*. Half-Irish, half-Italian, Hill rises through the ranks under the wing of Brooklyn boss Paulie (Sorvino) and, after teaming with loose cannon Jimmy (De Niro), feels the rush of pulling off a $6 million Lufthansa heist. But the rush dies down, and the only way Hill can recapture it is with cocaine and adultery. As his life spins crazily out of control, and the pressures of his trade reduce him to a paranoid mess, Hill has no other choice but to enter the Witness Protection Program. Violent to the extreme but lacking the redemptive poetry of *Mean Streets* or *Raging Bull*, the film does feature some stunning performances (and equally sleek Armani suits). Joe Pesci is electrifying as the homicidal kill-freak who revels in the smell of death; his senseless murder of a young bartender (Imperioli) is a moment of pitch-black inhumanity, while his "You think I'm funny?" game playing with Hill is a scene of brilliant comic danger.

Awards: Academy Award for Best Supporting Actor (Pesci); Academy Award nominations for Best Picture, Director, Best Supporting Actress (Bracco), Adapted Screenplay, Editing; New York Film Critics Circle Awards for Best Picture, Director, Actor; Los Angeles Film Critics Awards for Best Picture, Director, Supporting Actor (Pesci), Supporting Actress (Bracco), Cinematography; Venice Film Festival Award for Best Director.

GOULD, ELLIOTT. Born Elliott Goldstein August 29, 1938, in Brooklyn; actor. Formerly married to actor/singer Barbra Streisand. A child of the stage who spent his summers at Manhattan's Professional Children's School and cut his teeth performing in the Catskills, Gould struggled to find work until he was cast as the lead in the Broadway play *I Can Get It for You Wholesale*. His costar, Barbra Streisand, soon became his wife, but the pressures resulting from her skyrocketing career sent Gould into a depression and collapsed their marriage. By 1969, however, he had become a star in his own right, receiving an Oscar nomination as the wife-swapping Ted in *Bob and Carol and Ted and Alice*. Through the early 1970s, Gould was one of Hollywood's biggest names, appearing in Richard Rush's *Getting Straight*, Alan Arkin's *Little Murders*, and even Ingmar Bergman's *The Touch*, but his association with Robert Altman has resulted in his finest work—the irreverent surgeon Trapper John McIntyre in *M*A*S*H*, the slovenly Los Angeles private dick Philip Marlowe in *The Long Goodbye* (an exciting, if unorthodox, rendering of Raymond Chandler's detective), and the free-spirited gambler Charlie Waters in *California Split*. From the mid-1970s to the late 1980s, Gould did very little film work of any consequence, though his recent independent film roles (such as *White Man's Burden* and *The Glass Shield*) and his recurring role on television's ''Friends'' (with his once curly head of hair now graying and cropped short) are signs of a return.

Filmography: Quick, Let's Get Married (1964); The Night They Raided Minsky's (1968); Bob and Carol and Ted and Alice (1969); Getting Straight (1970); I Love My . . . Wife (1970); M*A*S*H (1970); Move (1970); The Touch/Beroringen (1971); Little Murders (1971); Busting (1973); The Long Goodbye (1973); California Split (1974); Spys (1974); Who?/Roboman (1974); I Will . . . I Will . . . For Now (1975); Nashville (1975); Whiffs (1975); Harry and Walter Go to New York (1976); Mean Johnny Barrows (1976); A Bridge Too Far (1977); Capricorn One (1978); Matilda (1978); The Silent Partner (1978); Escape to Athena (1979); The Lady Vanishes (1979); The Muppet Movie (1979); Falling in Love Again (1980); The Last Flight of Noah's Ark (1980); The Devil and Max Devlin (1981); Dirty Tricks (1981); Die Letzte Runde (1983); Over the Brooklyn Bridge (1983); Strawanzer (1983); The Muppets Take Manhattan (1984); The Naked Face (1985); Inside Out (1986); I Miei Primi Quarant'Anni (1987); Der Joker (1987); Dangerous Love (1988); The Telephone (1988); Judgement (1989); The Lemon Sisters (1989); My Wonderful Life (1989); Night Visitor (1989); No Justice (1989); Scandalo Segreto (1989); The Big Picture (1989); Dead Men Don't Die (1990); Giocodi Massacro (1990); Bugsy (1991); The Player (1992); Wet and Wild Summer! (1992); Hitz (1992); Amore! (1993); ''LA Law'' (1993, tvs); Hoffman's Hunger (1993, tvms); Exchange Lifeguards (1993); The Dangerous (1994); Naked Gun 33 1/3: The Final Insult (1994); ''Friends'' (1995, tvs); White Man's Burden (1995); The Glass Shield (1995); Kicking and Screaming (1995); Let It Be Me (1995), A Boy Called Hate (1995); The Duke of Groove (1995, short); The Feminine Touch (1995).

GRADUATE, THE (1967), comedy. Directed by Mike Nichols; written by Buck Henry and Calder Willingham (from the novel by Charles Webb); produced by Lawrence Turman; photographed by Robert Surtees; edited by Sam O'Steen; music by Dave Grusin, songs by Paul Simon and Art Garfunkel; released by Embassy Pictures; 105 minutes. *Cast*: Dustin Hoffman, Anne Bancroft, Katharine Ross, William Daniels, Murray Hamilton, Elizabeth Wilson, Norman Fell, Alice Ghostly, Richard Dreyfuss, Buck Henry.

A familiar story about the inevitability of young people's becoming their parents, *The Graduate* is made to feel fresh and innovative through the mod direction of Mike Nichols, the satiric dialogue of Buck Henry, and coldly passionate performances of Dustin Hoffman and Anne Bancroft. Released at the height of the 1960s youth movement with its rebellion against anyone over thirty, the film manages to simultaneously reflect the idealistic mood of the young with the cynicism of the old. Californian Benjamin Braddock (Hoffman) is a recent college graduate who has no interest in grad school or a promised rosy future in plastics and instead would rather drift in the family pool. Unable to surrender himself to thoughts of college or career, he enters into an empty sexual relationship with the leopard-coated Mrs. Robinson (Bancroft), a friend of his parents and the mother of Elaine (Ross), with whom Benjamin has also become involved. As exciting today as it was in 1967, *The Graduate* still feels modern. Nichols, Henry, and Hoffman have drawn Benjamin Braddock as a perfect blank slate onto which every young audience can project their identity, an innocent who (from his vacant look at the back of the bus after running off with Elaine) is fated to evolve into the parent he was rebelling against. The film is packed with memorable scenes—the alienated Benjamin in his scuba suit (with only his breathing on the audio track); the beautifully orchestrated time transitions (by editor Sam O'Steen) between Benjamin jumping from his raft and his jumping into Mrs. Robinson's bed; Mrs. Robinson's sadly matter-of-fact disclosure that she once studied art and conceived her daughter in the back of a Ford; and Benjamin's pained cry of "Elaine!" from the back of the church—all of which are accompanied by the strains of Simon and Garfunkel's songs.

Awards: Academy Award for Best Director; Academy Award nominations for Best Picture, Actor, Actress (Bancroft), Supporting Actress (Ross), Screenplay, Cinematography; New York Film Critics Circle Award for Best Director; DGA Award.

GRANT, LEE. Born Lyova Haskell Rosenthal October 31, 1927, in New York City; actor, director. Daughter is actor Dinah Manoff. Celebrated actor of the 1970s whose 1951 Oscar-nominated debut in *Detective Story* (a role she played on Broadway two years earlier) marked a promising career that was delayed when she refused to testify before the House Un-American Activities Committee against her playwright husband, Arnold Manoff. Blacklisted, she appeared in only a handful of film and television projects over the next twelve years before resurfacing to the tune of three more Supporting Actress nominations over the next few years. Her only win came for her performance in *Shampoo* as Felicia Carr, the married woman who sleeps with her hairdresser and later discovers, to her horror, that she has been given the same hairdo as another of his conquests. Since the 1980s she has concentrated on directing for film and television, with a 1986 Oscar going to her documentary on the nation's poor, *Down and Out in America.*

Filmography of key pre-1965 films: Detective Story (1951); Middle of the Night (1959).

Filmography since 1965: Terror in the City (1965); Divorce American Style (1967); In the Heat of the Night (1967); Valley of the Dolls (1967); Buona Sera, Mrs. Campbell (1968); The Big Bounce (1969); Marooned (1969); The Landlord (1970); There Was a Crooked Man (1970); Plaza Suite (1971); Neon Ceiling (1972, tvm); Portnoy's Complaint (1972); The Internecine Project (1974); Shampoo (1975); Voyage of the Damned (1976); Airport 77 (1977); Damien: Omen II (1978); The Mafu Cage (1978); The Swarm

(1978); When You Comin' Back, Red Ryder? (1979); Little Miss Marker (1980); Charlie Chan and the Curse of the Dragon Queen (1981); Visiting Hours (1981); Constance (1984); Teachers (1984); Trial Run (1984); Arriving Tuesday (1986); The Big Town (1987); Calling the Shots (1988); Defending Your Life (1991); Under Heat (1994).

Filmography as director: The Stronger (1976, short) also screenplay; Tell Me a Riddle (1980); The Wilmar 8 (1981); When Women Kill (1983); A Matter of Sex (1984); What Sex Am I? (1984); Down and Out in America (1985, ctvm/released theatrically 1996) also narrator; Nobody's Child (1988); Staying Together (1989); Following Her Heart (1994, tvm); Reunion (1994, tvm).

Honors: Academy Awards for Best Supporting Actress (*Shampoo*) and Feature Documentary (*Down and Out in America*); Academy Award nominations for Best Supporting Actress (*Detective Story*, *The Landlord*, *Voyage of the Damned*); Cannes Film Festival Award for Best Actress (*Detective Story*); Emmy Awards ("Peyton Place" 1965, "Neon Ceiling" 1971).

GREASE (1978), musical comedy. Directed by Randal Kleiser; screenplay by Bronte Woodward (from the musical by Jim Jacobs and Warren Casey); produced by Robert Stigwood and Allan Carr; photographed by Bill Butler; edited by John F. Burnett; music and songs by Jim Jacobs; choreographed by Patricia Birch; released by Paramount; 110 minutes. *Cast*: John Travolta, Olivia Newton-John, Stockard Channing, Jeff Conaway, Didi Conn, Dinah Manoff, Lorenzo Lamas, Fannie Flagg, Eve Arden, Frankie Avalon, John Blondell, Edd "Kookie" Byrnes, Sid Caesar, Alice Ghostley, Dody Goodman, Sha-Na-Na.

By the time this adaptation of the hit Broadway play made it to the big screen, America was buzzing with a nostalgic 1950s craze ushered in by *American Graffiti* (1973) and the television series "Happy Days" (1974–1984). That, combined with the starring talents of "Welcome Back Kotter" star John Travolta and virginal pop singing sensation Olivia Newton-John, made for an enormously successful and chaste rock-and-roll musical. The plot is no different from that of dozens of beach movies—sweet girl Sandy has a crush on cool guy Danny and dreamily sets her heart on some "summer loving." It's so goofy it shouldn't work at all, yet somehow its pulsating color, dazzling costumes, gyrating choreography, and innocent fun manage to melt even the most cynical, which was precisely the point in the late 1970s. Among the infectious tunes sung by Travolta and Newton-John are "Grease," "Summer Nights," "Hopelessly Devoted to You," "You're the One That I Want," "Sandy," and "Greased Lightning."

Sequel: *Grease 2* (1982, Patricia Birch).

Award: Academy Award nomination for Best Song ("Hopelessly Devoted to You").

GRIFFITH, MELANIE. Born August 9, 1957, in New York City; actor. Married to Antonio Banderas; formerly married to Don Johnson; daughter of Tippi Hedren. Alluring, squeaky-voiced blond beauty who began her career playing a number of sexually provocative characters—pubescent nymphet Delly Grastner

(*Night Moves*), nubile beauty queen Karen Love (*Smile*), porn star Holly Body (*Body Double*), stripper Loretta (*Fear City*), male sex fantasy Lulu (*Something Wild*), and call girl Kate (*Stormy Monday*). Although the sexually implicit title hints at more of the same, Mike Nichols' *Working Girl* gave Griffith a chance to find some complexity in her not-so-dumb blond persona as the lovable and ambitious secretary Tess McGill. With the success of that film and her resultant Oscar nomination, she has taken a turn to more serious roles—some straining credibility and others surprisingly good, such as *Paradise* (with husband, Don Johnson), *Born Yesterday* (in the Judy Holliday role, of course), and *Nobody's Fool*, her most accomplished, touching, and mature performance to date.

Filmography: The Harrad Experiment (1973); The Drowning Pool (1975); Night Moves (1975); Smile (1975); Joyride (1977); One on One (1977); Roar (1981); Body Double (1984); Fear City (1985); Something Wild (1986); Cherry 2000 (1988); The Milagro Beanfield War (1988); Stormy Monday (1988); Working Girl (1988); Bonfire of the Vanities (1990); In the Spirit (1990); Pacific Heights (1990); Paradise (1991); Shining Through (1992); A Stranger among Us (1992); Born Yesterday (1993); Milk Money (1994); Nobody's Fool (1994); Now and Then (1995); Buffalo Girls (1995, tvms).

Honor: Academy Award nomination for Best Actress (*Working Girl*).

GRIFTERS, THE (1990), film noir. Directed by Stephen Frears; screenplay by Donald E. Westlake (from the novel by Jim Thompson); produced by Martin Scorsese, Robert Harris, James Painten; photographed by Oliver Stapleton; edited by Mike Audsley; music by Elmer Bernstein; released by Miramax; 119 minutes. *Cast*: John Cusack, Anjelica Huston, Annette Bening, Pat Hingle, J. T. Walsh, Charles Napier, Jeremy Piven.

A brilliant film about seduction, this Martin Scorsese-produced, Donald Westlake-penned adaptation of Jim Thompson's 1963 pulp novel is a monstrous sexual triangle, a twisted oedipal nightmare about a boy, his girl, and his mother. Roy Dillon (Cusack, in a gut-churning performance) is a shrewd swindler who is in for the "short con" until he meets the writhing Moira (Bening), an experienced grifter who tries to persuade him to be a bit more ambitious. Driving a jealous wedge between them is Lilly (Huston), Roy's stop-at-nothing mom, a mob employee who is fearless enough to skim from her bosses. By the time the end credits roll (especially with the perverse finale), the viewer realizes that they have just seen one of the sleaziest collection of film-noir characters ever put to film. The thing that makes *The Grifters* so powerful is that it's about two women who should be battling for Roy's love (we sense deep down that he's a decent guy) but instead are clawing at one another for his money. It's a mother–son relationship taken to the most unimaginable extreme. British-born director Frears has a keen sense of American culture and, with cinematographer Oliver Stapleton, has created a visually captivating film that makes smart, amusing use of triple-split screens. Among the most memorable moments are Bening's entrance to the jewelry store accompanied by Elmer Bernstein's seductive vamp and the great performance from underappreciated character actor Pat Hingle as the paternalistic mobster who sadistically controls Lilly.

Awards: Academy Award nominations for Best Director, Actress (Huston), Supporting Actress (Bening), Adapted Screenplay.

GROUNDHOG DAY (1993), comedy. Directed, cowritten, and coproduced by Harold Ramis; screenplay with Danny Rubin; produced with Trevor Albert; photographed by John Bailey; edited by Pembroke Herring; music by George Fenton; released by Columbia; 103 minutes. *Cast*: Bill Murray, Andie Mac-Dowell, Chris Elliott, Stephen Tobolowsky, Brian Doyle-Murray, Harold Ramis.

A popular Hollywood product that has a layer of smart satire underneath its surface, this is a mad surrealistic vision about a man who is doomed to repeat one single day ad infinitum. Phil Connors (Murray), a smug television weatherman, visits "weather capital of the world" Punxsutawney, Pennsylvania, (as he has done many times before) to cover Groundhog Day festivities with his camera crew. By some twist of fate, however, this time Phil is stuck in a time warp—every day he awakes at the same exact moment to the strains of Sonny and Cher's "I Got You, Babe," encounters the same people, is asked the same questions, and has the same experiences. At first it feels like a death sentence, but soon Phil is liberated; he can say and do what he pleases (like drink himself silly) without fear of consequences on the following day. The daily repetition also gives him multiple chances to woo his charming coworker (MacDowell); though Phil initially repulses her, he uses his predicament to his advantage by polishing his pickup lines and becoming versed in the French literature she so loves. Elevated by Murray's wit, this is a nightmarish vision that imparts elements of Alain Resnais and Luis Bunuel into a witty Hollywood comedy.

H

HACKMAN, GENE. Born January 30, 1930, in San Bernardino, California; actor. One of the hardest working men in movies, Hackman is a versatile, workmanlike actor who always brings an air of integrity to the projects with which he is involved, even those least worthy of his presence. A former marine who didn't get into acting until his thirties, he studied at the Pasadena Playhouse before getting his first break in 1964 as the lead in the Broadway production of *Any Wednesday*. After a small role in *Lilith*, costar Warren Beatty suggested he play Buck Barrow in *Bonnie and Clyde*, earning Hackman his first Oscar nomination. Another came the following year with *I Never Sang for My Father* and again the year after that as Hackman got his first win for his role as Popeye Doyle in *French Connection*. Popeye is representative of the type of character we expect Hackman to play—mouthy, working-class, hard-nosed, and ultimately deserving of respect. This attitude pervades his finest roles—the bossy reverend in *The Poseidon Adventure*, the disenchanted surveillance expert Harry Caul in *The Conversation*, the small-time private eye in *Night Moves* (one of his most complex and overlooked performances), the emotionally scarred basketball coach in *Hoosiers*, and the jaded Federal Bureau of Investigation agent in *Mississippi Burning*. In the midst of these great dramatic performances it's easy to forget that Hackman also has a comic side, as seen in his campy, but fun, work as Lex Luthor in the *Superman* series and as movie producer Harry Zimm in *Get Shorty*.

Filmography: Mad Dog Coll (1961); Lilith (1964); Hawaii (1966); Banning (1967); Bonnie and Clyde (1967); A Covenant with Death (1967); First to Fight (1967); Riot (1968); The Split (1968); Downhill Racer (1969); The Gypsy Moths (1969); Marooned (1969); Doctors' Wives (1970); I Never Sang for My Father (1970); Cisco Pike (1971); The French Connection (1971); The Hunting Party (1971); The Poseidon Adventure

(1972); Prime Cut (1972); Scarecrow (1973); The Conversation (1974); Young Frankenstein (1974); Zandy's Bride (1974); Bite the Bullet (1975); French Connection II
(1975); Lucky Lady (1975); Night Moves (1975); A Bridge Too Far (1977); The Domino
Principle/The Domino Killings (1977); March or Die (1977); Superman (1978); Superman II (1980); All Night Long (1981); Reds (1981); Eureka (1983); Two of a Kind
(1983) voice; Uncommon Valor (1983); Under Fire (1983); Misunderstood (1984); Target (1985); Twice in a Lifetime (1985); Hoosiers (1986); Power (1986); No Way Out
(1987); Superman IV: The Quest for Peace (1987); Another Woman (1988); BAT 21
(1988); Full Moon in Blue Water (1988); Mississippi Burning (1988); Split Decisions
(1988); Loose Cannons (1989); The Package (1989); Narrow Margin (1990); Postcards
from the Edge (1990); Class Action (1991); Company Business (1991); Unforgiven
(1992); Geronimo (1993); The Firm (1993); Wyatt Earp (1994); The Quick and the Dead
(1995); Crimson Tide (1995); Get Shorty (1995).

Honors: Academy Awards for Best Actor (*The French Connection*) and Supporting Actor
(*Unforgiven*); Academy Award nominations for Best Actor (*Mississippi Burning*) and
Supporting Actor (*Bonnie and Clyde*, *I Never Sang for My Father*); Los Angeles Film
Critics Award for Best Supporting Actor (*Unforgiven*); New York Film Critics Circle
Award for Best Supporting Actor (*Unforgiven*).

HALLOWEEN (1978), horror. Directed, cowritten, and music by John Carpenter; cowritten and produced by Debra Hill; photographed by Dean Cundey;
edited by Tommy Lee Wallace and Charles Burnstein; released by Compass; 93
minutes. *Cast*: Donald Pleasence, Jamie Lee Curtis, Nancy Loomis, P. J. Soles.

The most influential horror film since George Romero's *Night of the Living
Dead* terrified audiences in 1968, this variation on the bogeyman theme is a
simple story told with great flourish and maximum effectiveness by John Carpenter. From the bravura opening, we know we're in good hands as we see a
brutal murder committed through the eyes of Michael Myers—it's Halloween
night, and we peer voyeuristically through the windows of a suburban house;
the killer enters, finds a knife in a kitchen drawer, dons a Halloween mask (we
share his mask eyehole point of view), slowly climbs the stairs to a teenage
girl's bedroom, and raises his knife as she screams in horror. We then see the
killer as he is arrested—Michael Myers, a psychotic six-year-old in a Halloween
mask. Carpenter then jumps ahead fifteen years and switches the point of view
from killer to victim—Laurie (Curtis), a teenage baby-sitter who is terrorized
by the recently escaped Myers, the embodiment of pure evil. Not since Curtis'
mother, Janet Leigh, met Norman Bates in *Psycho* has a woman been so petrified
by a knife-wielding madman. Made independently on a tiny $300,000 budget,
Halloween grossed a phenomenal $50 million and spawned an entire generation
of slasher pictures. Ironically, however, Halloween is a bloodless fright fest with
no gore and minimal physical violence. This is its strength—like Hitchcock,
Carpenter has created a horror masterpiece through his masterful use of suspense
and terror.

Sequels: *Halloween II* (1981, Rick Rosenthal) written and produced by Carpenter; *Halloween III: Season of the Witch* (1982, Tommy Lee Wallace) produced by Carpenter;

Halloween IV: The Return of Michael Myers (1988, Dwight Little); *Halloween V: The Revenge of Michael Myers* (1989, Dominique Otherin-Girard); *Halloween: The Curse of Michael Myers* (1995, Joe Chappelle).

HANKS, TOM. Born July 9, 1956, in Concord, California; actor, director. Married to Rita Wilson (*Volunteers, Mixed Nuts*). One of the most likable actors in Hollywood, he has gone through his share of miserable films before becoming a full-fledged movie star with his Academy Award-winning role of Andrew Beckett, the AIDS-afflicted lawyer in *Philadelphia*. While much of his early work is in uninvolving broad comedies, he is especially strong in *Splash*, the little-seen *Every Time We Say Goodbye*, *Nothing in Common*, and *Punchline*. His charming performance as Josh Baskin, a twelve-year-old in the body of a thirty-five-year-old, won him critical acclaim and featured a memorable duet with Robert Loggia on the oversized keyboard at F.A.O. Schwarz. In addition to *Philadelphia*, his most recent roles have proven his popularity among audiences and his versatility—the sarcastic coach in *A League of Their Own* (''There's no crying in baseball!''), the romantic lead in *Sleepless in Seattle*, the innocent dim-wit in *Forrest Gump*, and astronaut James Lovell, Jr., in *Apollo 13*. He has also begun to work behind the camera, directing an episode for cable television's ''Tales from the Crypt'' and ''Fallen Angels'' and readying his feature film debut *That Thing You Do!* (1996).

Filmography: He Knows You're Alone (1980); ''Bosom Buddies'' (1981–1982, tvs); Bachelor Party (1983); Splash (1984); The Man with One Red Shoe (1985); Volunteers (1985); Every Time We Say Goodbye (1986); The Money Pit (1986); Nothing in Common (1986); Dragnet (1987); Big (1988); Punchline (1988); The Burbs (1989); Turner and Hooch (1989); Bonfire of the Vanities (1990); Joe Versus the Volcano (1990); ''None but the Lonely Heart'' episode of ''Tales from the Crypt'' (1992) also director; Radio Flyer (1992); A League of Their Own (1992); Sleepless in Seattle (1993); Philadelphia (1993); Forrest Gump (1994); ''I'll Be Waiting'' episode of ''Fallen Angels'' (1994, ctvm) also director; Apollo 13 (1995); Toy Story (1995) voice.

Honors: Academy Awards for Best Actor (*Philadelphia, Forrest Gump*); Academy Award nomination for Best Actor (*Big*); Los Angeles Film Critics Awards for Best Actor (*Big, Punchline*).

HANNAH, DARYL. Born December 3, 1960, in Chicago; actor. Sister Page is an actor; uncle is cinematographer Haskell Wexler. Ethereal leading lady who carved out her place in film history as the acrobatic punk android Pris in *Blade Runner*. Other nonhuman characters have come her way—the mermaid Madison in *Splash*, the glossy Cro-Magnon Ayla in *The Clan of the Cave Bear*, and the ghost Mary Plunkett in *High Spirits*—though she has garnered attention for her more serious, fully human roles as part of the ensemble cast of *Steel Magnolias* and as the romantic interest opposite Robert Redford (*Legal Eagles*) and Steve Martin (*Roxanne*). A favorite target of the tabloid press because of her relationships with singer Jackson Browne and John Kennedy, Jr., her appearances in film have become less frequent and have again recently approached the non-human (*Attack of the 50 Ft. Woman*).

Filmography: The Fury (1978); The Final Terror (1981); Hard Country (1981); Blade Runner (1982); Summer Lovers (1982); The Pope of Greenwich Village (1984); Reckless (1984); Splash (1984); The Clan of the Cave Bear (1986); Legal Eagles (1986); Roxanne (1987); Wall Street (1987); High Spirits (1988); Crimes and Misdemeanors (1989); Steel Magnolias (1989); Memoirs of an Invisible Man (1992); Attack of the 50 Ft. Woman (1993, ctvm); Grumpy Old Men (1993); The Tie That Binds (1995).

HANNAH AND HER SISTERS (1986), comedy/drama. Directed and written by Woody Allen; produced by Robert Greenhut; executive-produced by Jack Rollins and Charles H. Joffe; photographed by Carlo Di Palma; edited by Susan E. Morse; released by Orion; 106 minutes. *Cast*: Woody Allen, Michael Caine, Mia Farrow, Carrie Fisher, Barbara Hershey, Lloyd Nolan, Maureen O'Sullivan, Daniel Stern, Max von Sydow, Dianne Wiest, Tony Roberts, Sam Waterston, Julie Kavner, Julia Louis-Dreyfus, John Turturro, J. T. Walsh.

Weightier than many of his previous films, this family drama of the Chekhov/Bergman variety revolves around a Manhattan trio of sisters—nurturing wife and former actress Hannah (Farrow), struggling actress and insecure cocaine abuser Holly (Wiest), and sexually vivacious and delicately balanced Lee (Hershey). Orbiting this trio are Hannah's financial adviser/husband Elliot (Caine), who is having an affair with Hershey; fatalistic writer and producer Mickey Sachs (Allen), formerly married to Hannah and soon to be married to Holly; the sisters' showbiz parents (Farrow's real-life mom O'Sullivan and Nolan), who gather the clan every year for Thanksgiving; and Frederick (Von Sydow), Lee's suffocating artist mentor who looks down with disdain on anything remotely resembling pop culture. Spanning two years and intercut with droll chapter headings, the film is masterfully structured and ties together neatly in a rosy denouement at Thanksgiving. Especially perceptive is the lunch scene between the three sisters (one of the few times they're all together), which perfectly captures the tensions and nuances of their strained relationships as the camera anxiously circles their table. Another paean to the city he loves, Allen's Upper West Side world has become predictable to a fault—throwaway lines about Nietzsche, Bach, and Caravaggio; an endless barrage of witticisms about Nazis and the Holocaust; and characters who are paralyzed by neuroses. Curiously, for a film about Hannah and her sisters, much of the picture focuses on Allen's Mickey Sachs, an infertile, hypochondriacal, atheistic nebbish. The one lively character in this collection of stale New Yorkers, Mickey blossoms when, after watching the Marx Brothers' *Duck Soup*, he realizes that life's pleasures are to be found in the simple things like love and laughter—a notion which is common knowledge to middle America but is apparently a revelation to the New York intelligentsia.

Awards: Academy Awards for Best Supporting Actor (Caine), Supporting Actress (Wiest), and Screenplay; Academy Award nominations for Best Picture, Director, Editing, Art Direction; Cannes Film Festival Award for Best Actress (Hershey); Los Angeles Film Critics Award for Best Picture; New York Film Critics Circle Awards for Best Film, Director, Supporting Actress (Wiest); WGA Award.

HARLAN COUNTY, U.S.A. (1976), documentary. Directed, written, and produced by Barbara Kopple; photographed by Hart Perry and Kevin Keating; edited by Mary Lampson and Nancy Baker; released by Almi Cinema 5; 103 minutes.

A compassionate documentary about a lengthy mining strike in a small east Kentucky town that pitted 180 coal-mining families against the influential and ruthless owners of the Duke Power's Eastover Mining Company at Brookside. As we see the power struggles in the United Mine Workers (UMW) union (the 1972 murders of UMW presidential candidate "Jock" Yablonski and his family and the 1974 murder conviction of then-incumbent president Tony Boyle), we begin to see the scandalous level of power, greed, and corruption that the striking miners are up against. Bolstered by the miners' wives and daughters, the strikers stand up to the intimidation of the gun thugs and strikebreakers and, after some shocking bloodshed, finally win a contract. The result is a shameful portrait of mine owners and a heroic depiction of the resolve of the working class, best exemplified in the line of dialogue from one of the strikers—"They can't shoot the union out of me." Especially poignant moments include the women forcing the reluctant town sheriff to serve the main strikebreaker with a warrant; the funeral of Yablonski, his wife, and daughter; and the heart-to-heart chat between a striking miner and a cop in New York City. "Her beautifully made film reveals what many thought were the bygone days—the era of *The Grapes of Wrath*—are, alas, still with us" (Richard Roud, *Cinema: A Critical Dictionary*).

Awards: Academy Award for Best Documentary; included in the Library of Congress' National Film Registry (1990).

HAROLD AND MAUDE (1971), comedy/romance. Directed by Hal Ashby; screenplay and coproduced by Colin Higgins; produced with Charles B. Mulvehill; photographed by John Alonzo; edited by William A. Sawyer and Edward Warschilka; music and song "If You Want to Sing" by Cat Stevens; released by Paramount; 90 minutes. *Cast*: Ruth Gordon, Bud Cort, Vivian Pickles, Cyril Cusack, Charles Tyner, Ellen Geer.

A black comedy about the relationship between the death-obsessed nineteen-year-old Harold (Cort) and the life-obsessed seventy-year-old Maude (Gordon), this second Hal Ashby film was a critical bomb before gradually emerging as a cult favorite of the 1970s. A perennial revival house staple for many years to come, it offers absurdly comic scenes of Harold's numerous staged suicide attempts (hanging, drowning, pistol, hari-kiri knife, and even self-immolation) and a truly touching romance between the seemingly mismatched pair of lovers. It's a cult film for a reason—its twisted vision, obvious themes, and oddball performances strike a chord in some but are either too odd or too trite for the majority. Unfortunately, it's all a bit repetitive (which is perhaps perfect for those repeat viewers), and one go-round with that Cat Stevens music is enough for most people. "Harold and Maude has all the fun and gaiety of a burning orphanage" (*Variety*, December 19, 1971).

HARRIS, ED. Born November 28, 1950, in Tenafly, New Jersey; actor. Exceptionally talented performer with seductive blue eyes and a quiet intensity, Harris spent much of the 1980s as a supporting actor in such underseen dramas as *Under Fire*, *A Flash of Green*, *Alamo Bay*, *Sweet Dreams* (as Patsy Cline's devoted husband, Charlie Dick), and *Jacknife*. His most memorable performance of the period came in *The Right Stuff* as astronaut John Glenn, in what is one of the strongest male characters ever in film—a hero not just because of his bravery as an astronaut but also because of the love and respect he shows his timid, stuttering wife. He made the transition to leading man with *The Abyss*, though his best work in the 1990s has come in the ensemble pieces *Glengarry Glen Ross* and *Apollo 13*, the return to the National Aeronautics and Space Administration earning him his first Oscar nomination.

Filmography: Coma (1978); Borderline (1980); Dream On (1981); Knightriders (1981); Creepshow (1982); The Right Stuff (1983); Under Fire (1983); A Flash of Green (1984); Places in the Heart (1984); Swing Shift (1984); Alamo Bay (1984); Sweet Dreams (1985); Walker (1987); To Kill a Priest (1988); The Abyss (1989); Jacknife (1989); State of Grace (1990); Paris Trout (1991, ctvm); Glengarry Glen Ross (1992); Needful Things (1993); The Firm (1993); China Moon (1994); Milk Money (1994); The Stand (1994, tvms); Just Cause (1995); Apollo 13 (1995); Nixon (1995).

Honors: Academy Award nomination for Best Actor (*Apollo 13*); Obie Award (*Fool for Love* 1983).

HAWN, GOLDIE. Born November 21, 1945, in Washington, D.C.; actor, producer. Longtime companion of Kurt Russell. Beginning on television's "Laugh-In" as the stereotypical dumb blond, she's transcended that image in Hollywood as an executive producer on a number of films, including the successful *Private Benjamin*. An early Academy Award nomination in *Cactus Flower* and strong, likable performances in *Butterflies Are Free*, *The Sugarland Express*, and *Shampoo* helped ease her transition from television personality to movie actress. Two charming, romantic pairings with Chevy Chase (*Foul Play* and *Seems like Old Times*) increased her star power. She showed the depths of her considerable talents in Jonathan Demme's *Swing Shift*, though most of her recent films have been contrived, pedestrian comedies such as *Protocol*, *Wildcats*, and *Overboard*.

Filmography: The One and Only Genuine Original Family Band (1968); Cactus Flower (1969); There's a Girl in My Soup (1970); $(Dollars) (1971); Butterflies Are Free (1972); The Sugarland Express (1974); The Girl from Petrovka (1974); Shampoo (1975); The Duchess and the Dirtwater Fox (1976); Foul Play (1978); Private Benjamin (1980) also ep; Seems like Old Times (1980); Travels with Anita/Lovers and Liars (1979/released in the United States in 1981); Best Friends (1982); Protocol (1984) also ep; Swing Shift

(1984); Wildcats (1986); Overboard (1987); Bird on a Wire (1990); My Blue Heaven (1990) ep; Deceived (1991); CrissCross (1992); HouseSitter (1992); Death Becomes Her (1992); Something to Talk About (1995) ep.

Honors: Academy Award for Best Supporting Actress (*Cactus Flower*).

HAYNES, TODD. Born January 2, 1961, in Encino, California; screenwriter, director. One of the most critically acclaimed independent filmmakers of the late 1980s and 1990s, Haynes attracted an underground following for his cult 8mm smash *Superstar: The Karen Carpenter Story*, a legendary, though little-seen, biography of bulemic pop star Karen Carpenter that uses Barbie and Ken dolls to tell its story. (The film has since been pulled from all distribution and ordered destroyed.) With *Superstar* and his subsequent independent hits—the episodic, gay-themed *Poison* and the anti-New Age *Safe*—he has combined narrative experimentation and aesthetic minimalism with a fascination for disease-of-the-week television movies.

Filmography: The Suicide (1978, short); Letter from a Friend (1982, short); Sex Shop (1983, short); Assassins: A Film concerning Rimbaud (1985, short); Superstar: The Karen Carpenter Story (1987, short); Poison (1990); Dottie Gets Spanked (1993, short); Safe (1995).

Honor: Sundance Film Festival Grand Prize Winner (*Poison*).

HEARTBREAK KID, THE (1972), comedy. Directed by Elaine May; screenplay by Neil Simon (from the story "A Change of Plan" by Bruce Jay Friedman); produced by Edgar J. Scherick; photographed by Owen Roizman; edited by John Carter; music by Garry Sherman; released by 20th Century Fox; 104 minutes. *Cast*: Charles Grodin, Jeannie Berlin, Cybill Shepherd, Eddie Albert, Audra Lindley.

Elaine May's finest film to date, this is the one that comes closest to the droll male–female relationship humor of her Broadway show *An Evening with Mike Nichols and Elaine May*. Grodin and Berlin (May's real-life daughter) play Lenny and Lila Cantrow, newlyweds who drive from New York to Miami for their honeymoon. They don't even hit the Sunshine State when Lenny starts having second thoughts—Lila sings in the car with a painfully grating voice, she can't eat an egg salad sandwich without wearing it on her face, and her interest in sex is puritan. While sunning on the beach, Lenny is enraptured by WASPy college girl Kelly Corcoran (Shepherd), a breezy blond who coolly suggests a rendezvous. Lila's sunburn confines her to the hotel room blanketed in a ghostly smear of cold cream, as Lenny drinks, lunches, and boats with Kelly and her strict father (Albert), who has nothing but contempt for his daughter's suitor. True to the title, Lenny reduces Lila to tears by callously confessing the truth before heading off to wintery Minnesota to stalk a bemused and uninterested Kelly. A strange film with a distant, offbeat sense of comic timing, *The Heartbreak Kid* is not without comparisons to the romantic angst of *The Graduate*; May, however, makes no concessions to Hollywood expectations, and her film (even with a script from the usually sugary Neil Simon) leaves one with a deep case of the creeps. Jeannie Berlin and Eddie Albert may have been lauded by the Academy (and deservedly so), but the film belongs to Grodin, who is buried so deep inside Lenny's skin that it's unnerving. ''May's direction of the actors repeatedly and even uncomfortably exposes the degree to which Grodin's [Lenny's] libido is affected by his own anti-Semitism'' (Jonathan Rosenbaum, *Placing Movies*).

Awards: Academy Award nomination for Best Supporting Actress (Berlin); Academy Award nomination for Best Supporting Actor (Albert); New York Film Critics Circle Award for Best Supporting Actress (Berlin).

HEAVEN'S GATE (1980), western. Directed and written by Michael Cimino; produced by Joann Carelli; photographed by Vilmos Zsigmond; edited by Tom Rolf, William Reynolds, Lisa Fruchtman, Gerald Greenberg; music by David Mansfield; released by United Artists; 219 minutes. *Cast*: Kris Kristofferson, Christopher Walker, Isabelle Huppert, John Hurt, Sam Waterston, Jeff Bridges, Joseph Cotton, Richard Masur, Terry O'Quinn, Tom Noonan, Mickey Rourke.

An obsessively detailed examination of a nation's morals at the end of the nineteenth century, when rich Montana cattle ranchers clashed with poor immigrant rustlers, *Heaven's Gate* is a visually sumptuous film that is sorely lacking in drama, characters, and a cohesive narrative. In the big picture, what *Heaven's Gate* is about is irrelevant; the mediocrity of the film doesn't warrant strong opinions. Instead, the film is notable for the phenomenon it became. Originally planned as a $7 million epic western from United Artists and the Oscar-winning director of *The Deer Hunter*, the film went grossly overbudget (it was written off at $44 million) and was pulled from release the day before its scheduled opening after a disastrous world premiere in New York City. Six months later, Cimino's reedited version was released in a two-hour-and-twenty-eight-minute cut (pared down from the three-hour-and-thirty-nine-minute premiere version), but the damage was done; the reviews were equally negative. By the time the smoke had cleared, United Artists (UA) had ceased to exist, in large part because of this debacle. Begun in 1919 by Charlie Chaplin, Mary Pickford, Douglas Fairbanks, and D. W. Griffith, the studio was ultimately swallowed up by the MGM lion (which retained it as a distribution pipeline), thereby ending a chapter of Hollywood history. A commercial flop and the target of a merciless critical assault (which foolishly included much anti-*Deer Hunter* revisionism), the film has become an extreme reminder that visionary filmmakers are the Achilles' heel of the Hollywood studio system. The colorful details of the making of the film are told in former UA executive Steven Bach's exposé *Final Cut*. ''*Heaven's Gate* fails so completely, you might expect that Mr. Cimino sold his soul to the Devil to obtain the success of *The Deer Hunter*, and the Devil has just come around to collect'' (Vincent Canby, *New York Times*, November 19, 1980).

HELLMAN, MONTE. Born Monte Himmelbaum 1932 in Greenpoint, Long Island, New York; director, editor. One of the unsung curiosities of American
film, Hellman has been all but erased from critical studies despite the fact that
at sixty-four he is still essentially a contemporary filmmaker. Having gone
through a period of inactivity throughout the 1980s and 1990s—he has directed
only the low-budget Spanish *Iguana*, which was never released theatrically in
America, and executive-produced Quentin Tarantino's breakthrough film *Reservoir Dogs*—he remains a notable figure for his existential westerns and near-
westerns of the 1960s and early 1970s. Starting with Jack Nicholson in Roger
Corman's stable, Hellman teamed with the actor for a pair of Philippine cheapies, *Back Door to Hell* and *Flight to Fury*, and a pair of Corman-financed
westerns, *Ride in the Whirlwind* and *The Shooting*. The latter of these two made
Hellman's reputation, a psychological study that eschews the stunts and shoot-
outs typical of the genre and instead offers a philosophical treatise on death and
dying. A cerebral western that is less dramatically satisfying than John Ford and
less visceral than Sam Peckinpah, it predictably received no U.S. release but
played to enthusiastic audiences in France. Amazingly, Universal Pictures opted
to produce his next film, the road movie *Two-Lane Blacktop*, a counterpart to
Easy Rider that starred Warren Oates, Beach Boy Dennis Wilson, and singer
James Taylor. Without the acting dynamism of Peter Fonda, Dennis Hopper,
and Nicholson, the film achieved nowhere near the box office tallies of its predecessor, though in many ways it's a much truer evocation of the aimlessness of
the generation. Pushing commercial filmmaking to the limit in *Two-Lane Blacktop* (especially with its searing final image of the film burning in the projector
gate), it was almost a foregone conclusion that Hellman's career would sputter.
After his two barely seen Warren Oates vehicles, *Cockfighter* and *China 9,
Liberty 7*, Hellman did not direct for a decade. He made a fleeting reemergence
in 1988 with *Iguana*, a bizarre allegorical period film about slave–master relationships and repressed primal urges, and the following year he delivered *Silent
Night, Deadly Night 3*, a paycheck masquerading as a bad horror film. His recent
success with Quentin Tarantino optimistically points to the promise of a comeback.

Filmography: Beast from Haunted Cave (1959); Back Door to Hell (1964); Flight to
Fury (1966) also story; Ride in the Whirlwind (1966) also producer, editor; The Shooting
(1967) also producer, editor; Two-Lane Blacktop (1971); Cockfighter/Born to Kill
(1974); Call Him Mr. Shatter/Shatter (1975) uncredited, one of three directors; China 9,
Liberty 37 (1978) also producer, editor; Iguana (1988) also screenplay, editor; Silent
Night, Deadly Night 3: Better Watch Out! (1989) also story.

Additional credits since 1965: Bus Riley's Back in Town (1965) editor; The Wild
Angels (1966) editor; The Long Ride Home (1967) editor; The St. Valentine's Day
Massacre (1967) dialogue director; Target: Harry/How to Make It (1969, released 1980)
editor; The Christian Licorice Store (1971) actor; The Killer Elite (1975) editor; Avalanche Express (1979) additional direction; Chambre 666 (1984) actor; Someone to Love

(1987) actor; Reservoir Dogs (1992) ep; The Ghost Brigade/The Killing Box (1993) editor.

HEMINGWAY, MARIEL. Born November 22, 1961, in Mill Valley, California; actor. Sister Margaux was an actor and model; grandfather was Ernest Hemingway. A radiant beauty with a sweet, tomboyish quality, she made her mark in *Manhattan* as the wise schoolgirl who taught Woody Allen's character that "you have to have a little faith in people." Subsequent roles as the lesbian track star in Robert Towne's *Personal Best*, as murdered *Playboy* centerfold Dorothy Stratton in *Star 80*, and again as a wise schoolgirl in *Creator* have proven her inestimable talents. In 1987 she coproduced (with her husband, Steve Crisman) and starred in the barely released film *The Suicide Club*, a tedious adaptation of Robert Louis Stevenson's short stories. With Crisman, she has shifted her focus to the restaurant business in Manhattan and has unfortunately done little film work of interest since.

Filmography: Lipstick (1976); Manhattan (1979); Personal Best (1982); Star 80 (1983); Creator (1985); The Mean Season (1985); The Suicide Club (1987) also producer; Superman IV: The Quest for Peace (1987); Sunset (1988); Fire, Ice and Dynamite (1990); Naked Gun 33 1/3: The Final Insult (1994); Edge of Deception (1995).

HENRY: PORTRAIT OF A SERIAL KILLER (1986), horror. Directed and co-written by John McNaughton; screenplay with Richard Fire; produced by Lisa Dedmond and Steven A. Jones; photographed by Charlie Lieberman; edited by Elena Maganini; released by Greycat Films; 83 minutes. *Cast*: Michael Rooker, Tom Towles, Tracy Arnold.

Without flinching from the gruesome nature of its subject matter, John Mc-Naughton has delivered a terribly disturbing look at the life of an emotionally numb serial killer while refusing to pass judgment on him. There is little sensationalism here; it's just the life of one man, and that's what is so chilling about the film. Henry is one of those evil things in this world that we'd rather not see, but we know they exist. In Henry we meet evil. He's no eye-rolling maniac, just an unfeeling purveyor of death. Shot for just $120,000 and not even released nationally until three years after its completion, the film is built on a remarkably creepy performance by Michael Rooker. The centerpiece of the film is an antisuspense scene of a murder captured by a stationary video camera—an almost unwatchable attack that offers nothing that is conventionally cinematic or remotely titillating. "It's as if McNaughton has discovered a new kind of monster in *Henry*: no longer supernatural, no longer psychotic, but somehow sociological—the specter of an extinguished class" (Dave Kehr, *Film Comment*, May–June 1990).

HENSON, JIM. Born September 24, 1936, in Greenville, Mississippi; died May 16, 1990, in New York City; producer, director, screenwriter. Daughter Lisa is former president of Columbia Pictures; son Brian is a producer (*The Muppet Christmas Carol* and television's "Dinosaurs"). The man who broadened the imaginations of a generation of children through his educational use of puppets on PBS' "Sesame Street" and later with the creation of the popular syndicated series "The Muppets." His motion pictures *The Muppet Movie, The Great Muppet Caper*, and *The Muppets Take Manhattan* are highly creative fantasies that provided an alternative to children's films during an era when Disney had failed to do so. Rather than function solely as children's fare, however, his films have broad appeal to adults, especially his most sophisticated mythological projects, *The Dark Crystal* and *Labyrinth*, the latter featuring the talents of David Bowie (actor and music), George Lucas (executive producer), and Monty Python's Terry Jones (writer). Often partnered with Frank Oz, Henson not only worked as a producer, director, and writer of many of his projects but also provided voices, operated the puppets, and wrote many of the songs. His Jim Henson Creature Shop continues as a force in sci-fi and fantasy filmmaking; his Henson Associates joined forces with the Walt Disney Company shortly before his death from pneumonia in 1990.

Filmography: Time Piece (1965, short) producer; "Sesame Street" (1969– , tvs); "The Muppet Show" (1976–1981, tvs); The Muppet Movie (1979) producer; An American Werewolf in London (1981) actor; The Great Muppet Caper (1981) director; The Dark Crystal (1982) producer, codirector; "Fraggle Rock" (1983 and 1987, tvs); The Muppets Take Manhattan (1984) ep; Into the Night (1985) actor; Sesame Street Presents: Follow That Bird (1985); Labyrinth (1986) director, story; Hey, You're as Funny as Fozzie Bear (1988) producer, director, screenplay.

Honors: Academy Award nominations for Best Song (*The Muppet Movie, The Great Muppet Caper*).

HERSHEY, BARBARA. Born Barbara Herzstein February 5, 1948, in Hollywood; aka Barbara Seagull; actor. Attractive, earthy, leading lady who was discovered during a school play at Beverly Hills High. An early starring role in the western television series "The Monroes" was followed by memorable performances in *Last Summer* (a teenage girl discovering her sexuality) and *The Baby Maker* (a hippie surrogate mother to a middle-class couple). In 1972 she costarred with then-lover David Carradine in Martin Scorsese's allegorical Christ tale *Boxcar Bertha*. After temporarily changing her name to Barbara Seagull (from 1972–1975), the free-spirited Hershey made only a few films in the mid-1970s before resurfacing with the sharp Hollywood satire *The Stunt Man*. Her most successful period was 1983–1988, beginning with *The Right Stuff* (as the untamable and enigmatic Mrs. Chuck Yeager) and including an unbroken string of phenomenal performances in *The Natural, Hannah and Her Sisters, Hoosiers, Shy People, Tin Men, A World Apart*, and *The Last Temptation of Christ* (as Mary Magdalene). Her surprise back-to-back Best Actress nods at the Cannes Film Festival firmly positioned her as one of the most critically acclaimed performers in the world. Her best work since then, however, has been in her two

Stephen Gyllenhaal-directed television movies—as the Texas churchgoer turned ax-wielding murderer in *A Killing in a Small Town* and as the 1940s southern woman married to a monstrous racist in *Paris Trout*.

Filmography: "Gidget" (1965–1966, tvs); "The Monroes" (1966–1967, tvs); The Whole Damn Human Race and One More (1967, short); With Six You Get Eggroll (1968); Heaven with a Gun (1969); Last Summer (1969); The Liberation of L. B. Jones (1970); The Baby Maker (1970); The Pursuit of Happiness (1971); Dealing: or The Berkeley-to-Boston Forty-Brick Lost-Bag Blues (1972); Boxcar Bertha (1972); Love Comes Quietly (1974); The Crazy World of Julius Vrooder (1974); You and Me (1975); Diamonds (1975); The Last Hard Men (1976); Dirty Knight's Work (1976); The Stunt Man (1980); Americana (1981); Take This Job and Shove It (1981); The Entity (1983); The Right Stuff (1983); The Natural (1984); Hannah and Her Sisters (1986); Hoosiers (1986); Shy People (1987); Tin Men (1987); A World Apart (1988); The Last Temptation of Christ (1988); Beaches (1988); Tune in Tomorrow . . . (1990); A Killing in a Small Town (1990, tvm); Defenseless (1991); Paris Trout (1991, tvm); The Public Eye (1992); Falling Down (1993); Swing Kids (1993); Splitting Heirs (1993); A Dangerous Woman (1993); Return to Lonesome Dove (1993, tvms); Last of the Dogmen (1995).

Honors: Cannes Film Festival Awards for Best Actress (*Shy People, A World Apart*); Emmy Award (*A Killing in a Small Town*).

HILL, GEORGE ROY. Born December 20, 1922, in Minneapolis; director. A major in the U.S. Navy who served in both World War II and the Korean War, he received his schooling at Yale and Dublin's Trinity College before joining Cyril Cusack's repertory theater company. There he directed his first stage play in 1948, later finding success on Broadway with Thomas Wolfe's *Look Homeward Angel*, Tennessee William's *Period of Adjustment* and Lillian Hellman's *Toys in the Attic*, the latter two serving as the basis for his first two feature films as director. In addition to his stage work, he spent much of the 1950s producing, writing, and directing teleplays for Playhouse 90 and Kraft Television Theater. He achieved a certain level of success with his delightfully offbeat comedy *The World of Henry Orient* in 1964, but not until his divine pairing of Paul Newman and Robert Redford in 1971's box office hit *Butch Cassidy and the Sundance Kid* did Hill reach the top. He followed with the bold, but disappointing, *Slaughterhouse-Five* before again teaming Newman and Redford in *The Sting*, his delightfully nostalgic tale of a pair of depression-era con men. He followed with one picture from Redford (the mythical aviation story *The Great Waldo Pepper*), one from Newman (the gritty hockey picture *Slap Shot*), and a charming teen romantic comedy set in Paris (*A Little Romance*). For his next two films he returned to the familiar ground of literary adaptation with John Irving's *The World according to Garp* and John LeCarre's *The Little Drummer Girl*. Sadly, his only film in the last ten years has been the abysmal Chevy Chase comedy *Funny Farm*, and one hopes that his career does not end on so sour a note.

Filmography of key pre-1965 films: A Night to Remember (1954, tvm); Judgment at Nuremberg (1957, tvm); The World of Henry Orient (1964).

Filmography since 1965: Hawaii (1966); Thoroughly Modern Millie (1967); Butch Cassidy and the Sundance Kid (1969); Slaughterhouse-Five (1971); The Sting (1973); The Great Waldo Pepper (1975) also producer and story; Slap Shot (1977); A Little Romance (1979); The World according to Garp (1982) also producer; The Little Drummer Girl (1984); Funny Farm (1988).

Honors: Academy Award for Best Director (*The Sting*); Academy Award nomination for Best Director (*Butch Cassidy and the Sundance Kid*); Emmy Awards for Writer and Director (*A Night to Remember*); DGA Award (*The Sting*); Cannes Film Festival Jury Prize (*Slaughterhouse-Five*).

Selected Bibliography

Horton, Andrew S. *The Films of George Roy Hill*. New York: Columbia University Press, 1984.

HILL, WALTER. Born January 10, 1942, in Long Beach, California; director, screenwriter. Forceful director and writer of action films whose contribution to the genre has diminished measurably since his excellent 1982 buddy film *48 Hrs*. First gaining attention in 1972 as the screenwriter of Sam Peckinpah's *The Getaway*, he directed two compelling pictures—the pugilistically pornographic *Hard Times* and the existential action-thriller *The Driver*—before his outlandish and controversial tale of comic-bookish gang violence, *The Warriors*, became a national sensation. He continued to impress over the next three years—in 1980 with his authentic, carefully researched western *The Long Riders*, in 1981 with the disturbing *Southern Comfort*, and then in 1982 with the popular pairing of Eddie Murphy and Nick Nolte in *48 Hrs*. In the midst of this flurry of creativity, he also managed to produce *Alien*. Unfortunately, however, his subsequent work pales by comparison—the MTV-influenced "rock and roll fable" *Streets of Fire* is a total misfire; the Reagan-era remake of *Brewster's Millions* is, despite its timeliness, miles beneath Allan Dwan's 1945 version; and, while the delta blues film *Crossroads*, the south-of-the-border *Extreme Prejudice*, and the Arnold Schwarzenegger–Jim Belushi buddy film *Red Heat* all have their moments, none of them match Hill's earlier works. In the mid-1990s, he made an almost pious return to the western with the explosively bloody biographies *Geronimo: An American Legend* and *Wild Bill*, while his 1994 revisitation of *The Getaway* (as screenwriter) proved to be an artistic step backward and a resounding box office dud.

Filmography: Hard Times (1975) also screenplay; "Dog and Cat" (1977, tvs); The Driver (1978) also screenplay; The Warriors (1979) also screenplay; The Long Riders (1980); Southern Comfort (1981) also screenplay; 48 Hrs. (1982) also screenplay; Streets of Fire (1984) also screenplay; Brewster's Millions (1985); Crossroads (1986); Extreme Prejudice (1987); Red Heat (1988) also producer, screenplay; Johnny Handsome (1989); Another 48 Hrs. (1990); Trespass (1992); Geronimo: An American Legend (1993); Wild Bill (1995) also screenplay.

Filmography as writer: The Getaway (1972); Hickey and Boggs (1972); The Mackintosh Man (1973); The Thief Who Came to Dinner (1973); The Drowning Pool (1975); Blue City (1986) also producer; The Getaway (1994).

Filmography as producer: Alien (1979); Aliens (1986) also story; Tales from the Crypt Presents Demon Knight (1995) ep.

HILLS HAVE EYES, THE (1978), horror. Directed, written, and edited by Wes Craven; produced by Peter Locke; photographed by Eric Saarinen; music by Don Peake; released by Vanguard; 89 minutes. *Cast*: Susan Lanier, Robert Houston, Virginia Vincent, Dee Wallace, Martin Speer, Michael Berryman, Janus Blythe, James Whitmore, Cordy Clark.

As so often happens with horror films, *The Hills Have Eyes* addresses a dark undercurrent in American life by masking some very serious social concerns behind the disguise of genre. This gruesome Wes Craven entry looks at two very different American families—one civilized and one feral—and pits them against one another until the civilized turn brutal. The Carters are typical suburbanites passing through the desert on vacation when their axle breaks. Unfortunately, they've had the misfortune of stopping in an area haunted by a flesh-eating clan of savages. As the families collide, the Carters must summon something primal within themselves in order to survive, while on the other side, the daughter of the savages (Blythe) longs for compassion and sees the Carters as an escape. It's bloody, disturbing, intense and strives to break taboos of cannibalism, incest, and infanticide—all of which continue to make the horror genre an ideal forum for questioning modern society. While not nearly as popular as his *Nightmare on Elm Street* franchise, this is Wes Craven at his best.

Sequel: Craven returned to direct *The Hills Have Eyes II* (1985).

HOFFMAN, DUSTIN. Born August 8, 1937, in Los Angeles; actor. Masterful acting legend with the ability to express a nearly childlike sense of wonder in so many of his roles, as if every experience is coming to him for the first time. Raised on the West Coast, where he studied at the Pasadena Playhouse, he soon traveled to the East, making his Broadway debut in 1961 in *A Cook for Mr. General* and joining the Theater Company of Boston in 1964. His role as Benjamin Braddock, however, in Mike Nichols' *The Graduate* turned him into a star. An antiheroic cipher onto which other members of his generation could project their own image, the confused Ben became representative of the idle, dropout mentality of the late 1960s. Straddling comedy and drama with a supreme command of both, he physically transformed himself in his next two great roles as the tubercular, misanthropic Rico "Ratso" Rizzo in *Midnight Cowboy* and then as the 121-year-old storyteller Jack Crabb in *Little Big Man*. He surprised audiences and critics alike in *Straw Dogs* with his psychologically gripping portrayal of a "civilized" mathematician who, after being pushed to the wall by the brutish gang who raped his wife, liberates his primal urges to exact revenge and defend his domain until the bloody end. He would appear throughout the 1970s in a spate of gutsy, well-written roles as men in a profound state of change—Louis Dega, the aristocratic bank robber sent to Devil's Island in *Papillon*; Lenny Bruce, the nightclub comic turned addictive, liberal hero in *Lenny*; Carl Bernstein, the unknown *Washington Post* reporter who, with his partner Bob Woodward, became steeped in the Watergate cover-up in *All the President's Men*; and Babe Levy, the shy history student who learns a life lesson when he is pitted against a sadistic Nazi in *Marathon Man*. Having previously directed on Broadway (*Jimmy Shine* 1968, *All over Town* 1974), he next set out to direct and star in the unromantic criminal tale *Straight Time* but chose to turn the reins over to friend Ulu Grosbard shortly into production. After three Oscar nominations, he earned his first statuette for *Kramer vs. Kramer*, a flawlessly acted drama about a father who suddenly becomes a single parent—a character every bit as relevant to the yuppie generation as Benjamin Braddock was to his. In two of his most spectacular subsequent roles, he again transformed himself to great effect—in *Tootsie*, as Michael Dorsey, the desperate actor who crosses the gender gap to find work as Dorothy Michaels; and in *Rain Man*, a truly fascinating depiction of autism. Except for the latter film, his work from the mid-1980s to 1995 has consisted of major projects that were either critical and/or commercial misfires (*Ishtar, Family Business, Billy Bathgate*, his Ratso Rizzo reprise *Hero*, and the semihit *Outbreak*) or costumed cartoon characters in Hollywood spectacles (the title character in *Hook* and Mumbles in *Dick Tracy*). ''His hangdog charm resists radiant winners ideologically; indeed, there has often been a suspicion that he was more a character actor than a lead'' (David Thomson, *A Biographical Dictionary of Film*).

Filmography: The Tiger Makes Out (1967); The Graduate (1967); John and Mary (1969); Madigan's Millions (1969); Midnight Cowboy (1969); Little Big Man (1970); Straw Dogs (1971); Who Is Harry Kellerman, and Why Is He Saying Those Terrible Things about Me? (1971); The Point (1971) narrator; Alfredo, Alfredo (1973); Papillon (1973); Lenny (1974); All the President's Men (1976); Marathon Man (1976); Straight Time (1978); Agatha (1979); Kramer vs. Kramer (1979); Tootsie (1982); Death of a Salesman (1985, tvm) also ep; Ishtar (1987) also songs; Rain Man (1988); Family Business (1989); Dick Tracy (1990); Billy Bathgate (1991); Hook (1991); Hero/Accidental Hero (1992); Outbreak (1995).

Honors: Academy Awards for Best Actor (*Kramer vs. Kramer, Rain Man*); Academy Award nominations for Best Actor (*The Graduate, Midnight Cowboy, Lenny, Tootsie*); New York Film Critics Circle Award for Best Actor (*Kramer vs. Kramer*); Los Angeles Film Critics Awards for Best Actor (*Kramer vs. Kramer, Rain Man*); Berlin Film Festival Honorary Golden Bear (*Rain Man*); Venice Film Festival Golden Lion Award for Lifetime Achievement (1996); Emmy Award (*Death of a Salesman*); Obie Award (*Journey of the Fifth Horse* 1966); inducted into the Order of French Arts and Letters (1995).

Selected bibliography

Brode, Douglas. *The Films of Dustin Hoffman*. New York: Citadel Press, 1983.

HOME ALONE (1990), comedy. Directed by Chris Columbus; written and produced by John Hughes; photographed by Julio Macat; edited by Raja Gosnell;

music by John Williams; released by 20th Century Fox; 98 minutes. *Cast*: Macaulay Culkin, Joe Pesci, Daniel Stern, John Heard, Catherine O'Hara, Roberts Blossom, John Candy, Kieran Culkin.

The most successful comedy of all time with a U.S. box office gross of $285 million, this alternately sentimental and sadistic Christmas tale is the story of Kevin McCallister (Culkin), an eight-year-old suburbanite who wishes his family would disappear. The following morning, his wish comes true when he is inadvertently left behind on a family trip to Europe. He overcomes his initial apprehension and soon savors his new freedom—eating junk food, watching television, and even shaving—until his fantasy is cut short by a visit from a pair of burglars. Acting like a pint-sized version of Dustin Hoffman's character from Sam Peckinpah's *Straw Dogs*, young Kevin ingeniously rigs the house with Rube Goldbergian booby traps, bludgeoning and torturing the invaders at every turn. A children's fantasy about what life might be like if they lived alone, the story has a potent subtext underneath the ridiculousness of the film itself— Kevin loathes not the criminals but his parents, who, after abandoning him, will never be allowed back into his world. The picture's popularity turned Macaulay Culkin into an overnight sensation and was a huge shot in the arm for the career of director Chris Columbus.

Sequel: Columbus returned to direct *Home Alone 2: Lost in New York* (1992) with Culkin, Pesci, Stern, Heard, and O'Hara reprising their roles.

Awards: Academy Award nominations for Best Score and Song ("Somewhere in My Memory").

HONEYMOON KILLERS, THE (1970), crime/romance. Directed and written by Leonard Kastle; produced by Warren Steibel; photographed by Oliver Wood; edited by Stan Warnow and Richard Brophy; music by Gustav Mahler; released by Cinerama; 115 minutes. *Cast*: Shirley Stoler, Tony Lo Bianco, Mary Jane Higby, Doris Roberts, Kip McArdle, Marilyn Chris, Elsa Raven.

One of the most unjustly forgotten B-movies in American film, this low-budget, black-and-white oddity has a disturbing documentary immediacy that is combined with a pure sense of romance and poetry. The film has the makings of a love story, and, in fact, that's essentially what it is—if it weren't for the fact that its main characters are real-life "Lonely Hearts Killers" Martha Beck and Ray Fernandez, executed in 1951 in Sing Sing. Martha (Stoler) is a 200-plus-pound, bon-bon eating nurse who is so desperate to love that she begins sending letters to con man/Latin lover Ray (LoBianco). The pair fall in love and proceed to swindle and then kill unsuspecting widows who fall for Ray's Latin lover ways. The strange success of the film is the manner in which writer/ director Kastle (in his only film) balances the twisted, but honest, romance with the unflinchingly brutal murders. We see Martha and Ray's adoring smiles and touching love letters ("I would like to shout my love for you to the world," writes Ray from death row), but we also see them bludgeon an old woman with

a hammer and drown a two-year-old child. It may not be as stylistically operatic
as Oliver Stone's similarly themed *Natural Born Killers*, but it's far more romantic and, as a result, more haunting. "An oddly memorable freak show—
shocking, but with a distinctively wobbly, half-lurid, half-comic tone" (Terrence
Rafferty, *The New Yorker*, April 23, 1990).

HOOP DREAMS (1994), documentary. Directed, coproduced, coedited, and narrated by Steve James; produced with Frederick Marx and Peter Gilbert; executive-produced by Gordon Quinn; photographed by Gilbert; edited with Marx
and Bill Haugse; released by Fine Line Features; 169 minutes. *Cast*: William
Gates, Arthur Agee, Isiah Thomas, Gene Pingatore, Spike Lee.

A quick description would describe this as a gritty, 169-minute documentary
about teenage basketball players pursuing a pro career, but, more accurately, it
is one of the finest portrayals of the American dream ever put to film. Seven
years in the making, this filmmaking odyssey focuses on the lives of two young
National Basketball Association (NBA) hopefuls from Chicago's inner city—
William Gates (the media's latest incarnation of Isiah Thomas) and Arthur
Agee—from their recruitment to Thomas' alma mater St. Joseph's to the start
of their college careers. We see their three-hour round-trip el rides to school;
Agee's withdrawal from St. Joseph's and transfer to Marshall, an urban public
school; the collapse of Agee's parents' marriage and his father's slide into crack
addiction; the sadness of Gates' older brother, a once-promising college player
who faces a future of broken dreams and lives vicariously through William; and
Gates' knee injury and orthoscopic surgery. Always present is the constant reminder of the NBA dream—images of Michael Jordan, a meeting with Isiah
Thomas, and the magic of the NBA all-star game. But this is not a Hollywood
story where the players get that final winning shot at the buzzer. This is much
more complex than that and much more compelling. Gates, the player who has
the better chance of turning pro, is injured and never makes it to a championship
game (remarkably, the crowning achievement of his high school career is finally
passing his American College Test and being accepted to Marquette University),
while Agee's team at Marshall places third in the state, knocking off the number
one-ranked team in the country in the process. What real life deals Agee, Gates,
and their families is as profound as the greatest fiction, and we realize that this
is what drama strives to be. Like *Grapes of Wrath* or *Death of a Salesman*,
Hoop Dreams is a monumental achievement, one of the greatest stories of American life ever told. In one of the most shameful moments in the history of the
Academy Awards, the film failed to receive a Best Documentary nomination.
Executive-produced by Gordon Quinn of Chicago's Kartemquin documentary
collective. "The story it tells is as complex, nuanced, and unpredictable as life
itself" (J. Hoberman, *Premiere*, May 1994).

Awards: Academy Award nomination for Best Editing; Los Angeles Film Critics Award
for Best Documentary; New York Film Critics Circle Award for Best Documentary;
DGA Award for Best Documentary.

HOPPER, DENNIS. Born May 17, 1936, in Dodge City, Kansas; actor, director. A true Hollywood survivor who embodies the notion of the rebel, his career has spanned some forty years and has encompassed some of the most notorious and important films of the times. It is a reflection of his rebel persona that he has appeared in the most radically nonconformist pictures of each of the past four decades—*Rebel without a Cause* in the 1950s, *Easy Rider* in the 1960s, *Apocalypse Now* in the 1970s, and *Blue Velvet* in the 1980s. A contract player with Warner Brothers beginning in 1955, he costarred with James Dean in both *Rebel without a Cause* (as the delinquent Goon) and *Giant* before being released from his contract in 1958 after a now-legendary battle with veteran director Henry Hathaway during the filming of *From Hell to Texas*. Effectively banned from Hollywood as a troublemaker, Hopper relocated to New York City, where he spent five years under the tutelage of Lee Strasberg at the Actors Studio. From the mid-1960s until his extraordinary directing effort *Easy Rider*, he appeared in a broad variety of films ranging from Andy Warhol (*Tarzan and Jane Regained . . . Sort Of*) to John Wayne (*True Grit*). Lifted by the overwhelming commercial success of *Easy Rider*, he tried to push the creative envelope even further with his second directing effort, *The Last Movie*. A wildly experimental film about a film crew shooting a western in Peru, the picture cost Universal $1 million and featured performances from fellow directors Peter Fonda, Henry Jaglom, and Sam Fuller and a musical score by Kris Kristofferson, but it was still a complete bust commercially. Over the next several years, Hopper battled the personal demons of drug and alcohol abuse, though he did manage to appear in a handful of memorable films, notably, Jaglom's *Tracks*, Wim Wenders' *American Friend* (as hired killer Ripley), and Francis Ford Coppola's *Apocalypse Now* (as the whacked-out photojournalist). He also directed *Out of the Blue*, a spectacular, if minor, essay on alienation and punk rock. His personal and professional renaissance began in 1986 with *Blue Velvet* (as the inhumanly sadistic Frank Booth) and *Hoosiers* (as the town drunk turned basketball coach) and would later include *River's Edge* (as the twisted Feck) and the disturbing made-for-cable feature *Paris Trout*. His 1988 directorial effort, *Colors*, a cop story set in the barrios of Los Angeles, failed to find much of an audience but did feature two sharp performances from Robert Duvall and Sean Penn. His subsequent films as director have lacked any real spark, while his recent acting roles have been weighted in favor of such cartoonish evildoers as the bomber in *Speed* and the archnemesis in *Waterworld*. In 1971 he appeared in, and cowrote, a documentary about himself called *The American Dreamer*. An avid art collector, he is also an accomplished photographer who has published a book of his work titled *Out of the Sixties* (1988).

Filmography of key pre-1965 films: Rebel without a Cause (1955); Giant (1956); Gunfight at the O.K. Corral (1957); Sayonara (1957).

Filmography since 1965: The Sons of Katie Elder (1965); Queen of Blood (1966); Cool Hand Luke (1967); The Glory Stompers (1967); The Trip (1967); Hang 'Em High (1968);

Head (1968); Panic in the City (1968); The Festival Game (1969); True Grit (1969); Crush Proof (1972); Kid Blue (1973); Mad Dog (1976); Tracks (1976); The American Friend (1977); The Sorcerer's Apprentice (1977); L'Ordre et la Securite du Monde (1978); Apocalypse Now (1979); Resurrection (1979); King of the Mountain (1981); Renacida (1981); White Star (1981); Human Highway (1982); The Osterman Weekend (1983); Rumble Fish (1983); Slagskampen (1984); My Science Project (1985); Running Out of Luck (1985); Stark (1985, tvm); Stark: Mirror Image (1986, tvm); Riders of the Storm/The American Way (1986); Blue Velvet (1986); Hoosiers (1986); The Texas Chainsaw Massacre 2 (1986); The Black Widow (1987); O. C. and Stiggs (1987); The Pick-Up Artist (1987); River's Edge (1987); Straight to Hell (1987); Blood Red (1989); Chattahoochee (1990); Flashback (1990); Doublecrossed (1991, ctvm); Paris Trout (1991, ctvm); The Indian Runner (1991); Eye of the Storm (1991); Nails (1992, ctvm); Sunset Heat (1992, ctvm); Boiling Point (1993); Super Mario Bros. (1993); Red Rock West (1993); True Romance (1993); The Heart of Justice (1993, ctvm); Speed (1994); Witch Hunt (1994, ctvm); Waterworld (1995); Acts of Love (1995); Search and Destroy (1995).

Filmography as director: Easy Rider (1969) also screenplay, actor; The Last Movie (1971) also actor, story, editor; Out of the Blue (1980) also actor; Colors (1988); Backtrack/Catchfire (1990) credited as Alan Smithee; The Hot Spot (1990); Chasers (1994) also actor.

Honors: Academy Award nominations for Best Screenplay (*Easy Rider*) and Supporting Actor (*Hoosiers*); New York Film Critics Circle Award for Supporting Actor (*Blue Velvet*); Los Angeles Film Critics Awards for Supporting Actor (*Hoosiers, Blue Velvet*); Cannes Film Festival Award for Debut Film (*Easy Rider*); Venice Film Festival Golden Lion for Best Film (*The Last Movie*).

HOWARD, RON. Born March 1, 1954, in Duncan, Oklahoma; director, actor. Parents are actors Rance and Jean Howard; brother is actor Clint Howard. A refreshing breath of innocence in modern American cinema, Howard, once the nation's darling as little Opie, offers pure entertainment to an audience that has no use for the artful cynicism and brutality of so many of his contemporaries. Born into an acting family, raised in the back-lot Mayberry of television's "The Andy Griffith Show" (1960–1968), and maturing into adulthood on the set of "Happy Days" (1974–1984), Howard turned to directing with *Grand Theft Auto*, a raucous comedy that will satisfy anyone's hunger for car crashes. Starting with the sweet romantic comedy *Splash*, he's consistently shown a talent for light, wholesome fare that reflects an American ideal. His watered-down versions of *The Quiet Man* (*Far and Away*) and *All the President's Men* (*The Paper*) were not resounding successes, but he hit the mark with the enormously popular *Apollo 13*, an astronaut adventure which is little more than a diluted variation on *The Right Stuff*.

Filmography as actor: The Journey (1959); The Music Man (1962); The Courtship of Eddie's Father (1963); Village of the Giants (1965); Smoke (1970); The Wild Country (1970); American Graffiti (1973); Happy Mother's Day . . . Love, George (1973); The Spikes Gang (1974); The First Nudie Musical (1975); Eat My Dust (1976); The Shootist (1976); More American Graffiti (1979).

Filmography as director: Grand Theft Auto (1977) also screenplay, actor; Night Shift (1982); Splash (1984); Cocoon (1985); Gung Ho (1986) also ep; Willow (1988); Parenthood (1989) also story; Far and Away (1991) also ep; The Paper (1994); Apollo 13 (1995).

Filmography as executive producer: Leo and Loree (1980); No Man's Land (1987); Clean and Sober (1988); Vibes (1988); Closet Land (1991).

Filmography as producer: The Burbs (1989).

Honor: DGA Award (*Apollo 13*).

HUGHES, JOHN. Born February 18, 1950, in Lansing, Michigan; screenwriter, director, producer. Although he has been a part of numerous box office hits, John Hughes is often seen as the embodiment of everything that is wrong with Hollywood—he panders to the lowest common denominator, misconstrues treacle for sincere emotion, substitutes caricature for character, and displays a perverse fascination with physical brutality. If that's not enough, he seems to make the same film over and over—the mischievous, wisecracking teenager of *Ferris Bueller's Day Off* devolves into the mischievous, wisecracking preteen of *Home Alone*, *Home Alone 2: Lost in New York*, *Dennis the Menace*, and *Curly Sue*, and further devolves into the mischievous, babbling infant in *Baby's Day Out*. The de-evolution process continues in Hughes' oft-postponed project *The Bee*, the story of a mischievous, buzzing insect. There are occasional bright moments in his films—Molly Ringwald's endearing Samantha in *Sixteen Candles*; the Hughes-penned characters of Ringwald, Jon Cryer, Harry Dean Stanton, and Annie Potts in the Howard Deutch-directed *Pretty in Pink*; and the warmth of John Candy's characters in *Uncle Buck* and *Only the Lonely*. In 1995, Hughes partnered with former Hollywood Picture head Ricardo Mestres to form Great Oaks Entertainment. "His films synthesize all the various thematic strands introduced in the Fifties and resolved in the Eighties, in their various ways. More or less they are alike. Kids culture is the only culture. Parents, to the extent that they figure at all, need parenting from their emotionally and socially more together offspring" (Elayne Rapping, *Cineaste*, 16, nos. 1–2, 1987–1988).

Filmography as writer: "Delta House" (1979, tvs); National Lampoon's Class Reunion (1982); Mr. Mom (1983); Nate and Hayes (1983); National Lampoon's Vacation (1983); National Lampoon's European Vacation (1985); Pretty in Pink (1986) also ep; Some Kind of Wonderful (1987) also producer; The Great Outdoors (1988) also ep; National Lampoon's Christmas Vacation (1989) also producer; Home Alone (1990) also producer; Dutch (1991) also producer; Career Opportunities (1991) also producer; Home Alone 2: Lost in New York (1992) also producer; Beethoven (1992) credited as Edmond Dantes; Dennis the Menace (1993) also producer; Miracle on 34th Street (1994) also producer; Baby's Day Out (1994) also producer.

Filmography as director and writer: Sixteen Candles (1984); The Breakfast Club (1985) also producer; Weird Science (1985); Ferris Bueller's Day Off (1986) also producer; Planes, Trains and Automobiles (1987) also producer; She's Having a Baby (1988) also producer; Uncle Buck (1989) also producer; Curly Sue (1991) also producer.

Filmography as producer only: Only the Lonely (1991).

HUNTER, HOLLY. Born March 20, 1958, in Conyers, Georgia; actor. Married to cinematographer Janusz Kaminski (*Schindler's List*). One of the most deeply respected actors of her generation, she displays her rare integrity by playing individuals with a passionate flame burning inside them. Whether she's starring as the affable news director Jane Craig in *Broadcast News* or the twisted Wanda Holloway in cable television's *The Positively True Adventures of the Alleged Texas Cheerleader-Murdering Mom*, Hunter reveals the true heart and soul of her characters—understanding, but never judging, them. Not limited to motion pictures, she has also appeared on Broadway in the Beth Henley plays *Crimes of the Heart, Miss Firecracker Contest* (filmed as *Miss Firecracker*), *The Wake of Jamey Foster*, and *Control Freaks*. Her portrayal of the mute Ada in Jane Campion's haunting Australian film *The Piano* ranks as one of the most gripping and expressive motion picture performances of all time. "Hunter manages to express so much, just behind the eyes, just under the skin, by the music of her piano, and of her own aura, that one walks out of the theater feeling that this mute woman has had as much to say as anyone we've met in a long time" (Marcelle Clements, *Premiere*, December 1993).

Filmography: The Burning (1981); Swing Shift (1984); With Intent to Kill/Urge to Kill (1984, tvm); Broadcast News (1987); End of the Line (1987); Raising Arizona (1987); Always (1989); Animal Behavior (1989); Miss Firecracker (1989); A Gathering of Old Men (1989); Roe vs. Wade (1989, tvm); Once Around (1991); Crazy in Love (1992, ctvm); The Firm (1993); The Piano (1993); The Positively True Adventures of the Alleged Texas Cheerleader-Murdering Mom (1993, ctvm); Copycat (1995); Home for the Holidays (1995).

Honors: Academy Award for Best Actress (*The Piano*); Academy Award nominations for Best Actress (*Broadcast News*) and Supporting Actress (*The Firm*); Los Angeles Film Critics Awards for Best Actress (*Broadcast News, The Piano*); New York Film Critics Circle Awards for Best Actress (*Broadcast News, The Piano*); Cannes Film Festival Award for Best Actress (*The Piano*); Emmy Awards for Best Actress (*Roe vs. Wade, The Positively True Adventures of the Alleged Texas Cheerleader-Murdering Mom*).

HURT, WILLIAM. Born March 20, 1950, in Washington, D.C.; actor. An astonishingly talented actor who invests himself so completely into such complex characters that he simply is unequipped to turn in a weak or dishonest performance, even in the most mediocre of his films. The stepson of Henry Luce III (son of the founder of Time Inc.), Hurt studied drama and theology at Tufts University and later attended Julliard before making his New York stage debut in 1976's *Henry V*. His big-screen debut came four years later when he starred as the obsessive, truth-seeking, mushroom-eating scientist Eddie Jessup in Ken Russell's *Altered States*. Greater popular success followed with *Body Heat* opposite Kathleen Turner in the stylish film noir from Lawrence Kasdan, with whom he would collaborate thrice more—*The Big Chill, The Accidental Tourist* (in a controlled performance as ''Armchair Traveler'' Macon Leary), and *I Love You to Death*. At the top of the film world during the mid-1980s, he received Oscar nominations for three of his most brilliant roles—the flamboyant, imprisoned, homosexual Molina in *Kiss of the Spider Woman*, the sensitive instructor of the hearing-impaired in *Children of a Lesser God*, and the perfect television news mannequin Tom Grunick in *Broadcast News*. Instead of continuing to battle Hollywood for consistently challenging roles, Hurt retreated from his star status and took parts in such smaller films as Wim Wenders' meandering international production *Until the End of the World*, Woody Allen's *Alice*, Chris Menges' *Second Best*, Wayne Wang's independent hit *Smoke*, and experimental Belgian filmmaker Chantal Ackerman's *A Couch in New York*. He has also continued to work on the stage—as Oberon in *A Midsummer Night's Dream* (1982), in the Broadway production of David Rabe's *Hurlyburly* (1984), and with the New York's Circle Rep in *Beside Herself*.

Filmography: Altered States (1980); Eyewitness (1980); Body Heat (1981); The Big Chill (1983); Gorky Park (1983); Kiss of the Spider Woman (1985); Children of a Lesser God (1986); Broadcast News (1987); The Accidental Tourist (1988); A Time of Destiny (1988); Alice (1990); I Love You to Death (1990); Until the End of the World (1991); The Doctor (1991); The Plague (1993); Mr. Wonderful (1993); Trial by Jury (1994); Second Best (1994); Smoke (1995); Jane Eyre (1995); A Couch in New York (1995).

Honors: Academy Award for Best Actor (*Kiss of the Spider Woman*); Academy Award nominations for Best Actor (*Children of a Lesser God, Broadcast News*); Cannes Film Festival Award for Best Actor (*Kiss of the Spider Woman*); Los Angeles Film Critics Award for Best Actor (*Kiss of the Spider Woman*); Obie Award (*My Life* 1976).

HUSBANDS (1970), drama. Directed and written by John Cassavetes; produced by Al Ruban; photographed by Victor J. Kemper; edited by Peter Tanner; released by Columbia; 154 minutes. *Cast*: John Cassavetes, Peter Falk, Ben Gazzara, Jenny Runacre, Jenny Lee Wright, Noelle Kao.

The story of three fortyish husbands who, after the death of a best friend, toss away their responsibilities as suburban family men and take off on a three-day wake of drinking and partying. Focusing on the childishness of men who, for seventy-two hours, choose to live out a fantasy, Cassavetes tries to capture the emotions of people who are faced with the emptiness and seeming futility of their own lives. They temporarily ignore the needs of their wives and children to satisfy their own needs—getting drunk, chasing women, gambling, and flying off to London. They need to fulfill a desire to return to the wild days of youth, when death seemed so far away. By the end, two return home with toys for the kids and apologies for their wives, while one opts to stay away and start a new life. Male bonding has never been so accurately portrayed as by Falk, Gazzara, and Cassavetes (appearing for the first time in a film he directed)—three real-life friends who hit a level of emotional honesty that, while occasionally self-indulgent, never rings false.

HUSBANDS AND WIVES (1992), drama. Directed and written by Woody Allen; produced by Robert Greenhut; executive-produced by Jack Rollins and Charles H. Joffe; photographed by Carlo Di Palma; edited by Susan E. Morse; released by Tri-Star; 107 minutes. *Cast*: Woody Allen, Mia Farrow, Judy Davis, Sydney Pollack, Juliette Lewis, Liam Neeson, Blythe Danner, Lysette Anthony.

With the immediacy of its handheld camera and its guerrilla documentary technique, this analysis of marriage and aging is one of Allen's most exciting films in years. The issues and neuroses are the same, but the style gives them a freshness that accurately mirrors the confusion of the characters. When the seemingly happily married Jack and Sally (Pollack and Davis) announce to their close friends Gabe and Judy (Allen and Farrow) that they are getting divorced, Gabe and Judy are stunned; if this idyllic marriage can go sour, then what marriage has a chance? When the invigorated Jack shows off his perfectly toned young girlfriend, Gabe is disgusted by his friend's obviousness. Soon, however, English professor Gabe becomes attracted to a bright, twenty-year-old student (Lewis), and he, too, finds himself infused with self-confidence and false immortality. An emotionally revealing discussion of the fears of aging and the need to recapture the spirit of youth, *Husbands and Wives* seems especially potent in light of the drama of Woody Allen's very public private life during his breakup with Mia Farrow and his romantic link to Soon-Yi Previn.

Awards: Academy Award nominations for Best Supporting Actress (Davis), Screenplay; Los Angeles Film Critics Award for Best Supporting Actress (Davis).

HUSTON, ANJELICA. Born July 8, 1951, in Los Angeles; actor. Grandfather is actor Walter Huston; father is director John Huston; half brother is director Danny Huston. Commanding leading lady who can play both wickedness and vulnerability, Huston began her career trying to shake charges of nepotism after her father cast her (perhaps prematurely) in his medieval romance *A Walk with Love and Death*. After the death of her ballerina mother, Enrica Soma, in a 1969 auto accident, Huston moved from the U.K. to New York, where she took up modeling and eventually returned to motion pictures. After a handful of minor roles, she delivered a knockout in her third John Huston film, *Prizzi's Honor*, as Maerose, the feisty, fast-thinking, Brooklynese-accented former fiancée of Jack Nicholson's oafish hitman Charley. Two years later she gave a blessed performance as the Irish wife in her father's swan song, *The Dead*, especially in her moving scene as she relates the death of a young lover from her past. She has also impressed in Francis Ford Coppola's *Gardens of Stone*, Woody Allen's *Crimes and Misdemeanors* and *Manhattan Murder Mystery*, Paul Mazursky's *Enemies, A Love Story*, and Stephen Frears' *The Grifters*. Despite these great performances, she has found her biggest audience as the cartoonish Morticia Addams in *The Addams Family* and its sequel. In 1995, she costarred with her former lover of seventeen years Jack Nicholson in Sean Penn's sensitive drama *The Crossing Guard*. Her directing debut, *Bastard Out* *of Carolina*, was filmed in 1995 for a scheduled 1996 showing on the TNT cable network, but the station opted not to release the picture because of content.

Filmography: Sinful Davey (1969); A Walk with Love and Death (1969); Hamlet (1969); Swashbuckler (1976); The Last Tycoon (1976); The Postman Always Rings Twice (1981); This Is Spinal Tap (1984); The Ice Pirates (1984); Prizzi's Honor (1985); Captain Eo (1986, short); Good to Go (1986); Gardens of Stone (1987); The Dead (1987); A Handful of Dust (1988); Mr. North (1988); Crimes and Misdemeanors (1989); Enemies, a Love Story (1989); Lonesome Dove (1989, tvms); The Witches (1990); The Grifters (1990); The Addams Family (1991); The Player (1992); Manhattan Murder Mystery (1993); Addams Family Values (1993); And the Band Played On (1993, ctvm); Family Pictures (1993, tvm); The Crossing Guard (1994); The Perez Family (1995); Buffalo Girls (1995, tvms).

Honors: Academy Award for Best Supporting Actress (*Prizzi's Honor*); Academy Award nominations for Best Supporting Actress (*Enemies, a Love Story*, *The Grifters*); New York Film Critics Circle Award (*Prizzi's Honor*); Los Angeles Film Critics Awards (*Prizzi's Honor*, *The Grifters*); Independent Spirit Awards for Best Actress (*The Grifters*) and Supporting Actress (*The Dead*).

HUSTON, JOHN. Born August 5, 1906, in Nevada, Missouri; died August 28, 1987, in Middletown, Rhode Island; director, writer, actor. Father is Walter Huston, daughter is Anjelica, son Danny is a director, son Tony is a screenwriter. One of Hollywood's most celebrated writers and directors, John Huston remained a fresh voice until the end of his career. Directing with a darkly comic edge, a hearty irreverence, and willingness to take risks, many of his often beguiling later-period films failed to receive the acclaim of his studio pictures. Yet unlike the final films of many of his contemporaries (e.g., Hawks), Huston chose to ignore themes of aging and death and instead displayed the energy and rascality of a much younger talent. He began the mid-1960s with the daunting adaptation *The Bible . . . In the Beginning*, an overblown religious epic that must be commended for its shear audacity. Two years later, his adaptation of Carson McCullers' novel *Reflections in a Golden Eye* showed a director who could treat sexual material with a perverse sense of humor. Throughout the 1970s much of his work cast a cynical eye on the world and revolved around doomed characters that recalled Captain Ahab of his *Moby Dick* (1956)—men who willfully choose to fight and win at all costs, even if it means the destruction of everything and everyone around them, men "who would be king." He closed out the decade with *Wise Blood*, a brave, but confounding, assault on religious frauds in which a heretical young man founds the Church of Truth without Jesus Christ. After loitering in a creative valley of the ridiculous, which includes the forgettable horror film *Phobia*, the Sylvester Stallone prisoner-of-war tale *Victory*, and the anomalous musical *Annie*, Huston exited with a sublime trio—an adaptation of Malcolm Lowry's Day of the Dead alcoholism novel *Under the Volcano*, the very funny and very dark hit-man romance *Prizzi's Honor*, and the profoundly moving adaptation of James Joyce's *The Dead*. After his Oscar-nominated turn as an actor in *The Cardinal* (1963), the magnetic, craggy, gravely-voiced Huston was nearly as active in front of the camera as behind, most memorably as the powerful and corrupt Noah Cross in *Chinatown* and as the equally malevolent Joseph Kennedy type in *Winter Kills*. Clint Eastwood paid tribute by playing a fictionalized John Huston in *White Hunter, Black Heart* (1990), a film set during the shooting of *The African Queen*.

Filmography of key pre-1965 films as director and writer: The Maltese Falcon (1941); Sergeant York (1941); Key Largo (1948); The Treasure of the Sierra Madre (1948); The Asphalt Jungle (1950) also producer; The African Queen (1951); The Red Badge of Courage (1951); Beat the Devil (1953) also producer; Moby Dick (1956) also producer.

Filmography since 1965: The Bible . . . In the Beginning (1965) also actor; Casino Royale (1966) codirector, actor; Reflections in a Golden Eye (1967) also producer; Sinful Davey (1969); A Walk with Love and Death (1969) also actor; The Kremlin Letter (1970) also screenplay, actor; Fat City (1972) also producer; The Life and Times of Judge Roy Bean (1972); The Mackintosh Man (1973); The Man Who Would Be King (1975) also screenplay; Independence (1976, short); Wise Blood (1979); Phobia (1980); Victory/ Escape to Victory (1981); Annie (1982); Under the Volcano (1984); Prizzi's Honor (1985); The Dead (1987); Mr. North (1988) ep, screenplay.

Filmography since 1965 as actor: Candy (1968); De Sade/Das Ausschweifende Leben des Marquis de Sade (1969); Myra Breckinridge (1970); A Bridge in the Jungle (1971); Man in the Wilderness (1971); The Deserter/La Spina Dorsale del Diavolo (1971); Battle for the Planet of the Apes (1973); Chinatown (1974); Breakout (1975); The Wind and the Lion (1975); Angela (1977); Tentacles (1977); Jaguar Lives (1979); The Visitor (1979); Winter Kills (1979); Head On (1980); Cannery Row (1982) narrator; Lovesick (1983); Young Giants (1983); The Black Cauldron (1985) narrator; Momo (1986); Mr. Corbett's Ghost (1986).

Honors: Academy Awards for Best Director and Screenplay (*The Treasure of the Sierra Madre*); Academy Award nominations for Best Director (*The Asphalt Jungle, The African Queen, Prizzi's Honor*), Screenplay (*Dr. Erlich's Magic Bullet, The Maltese Falcon, Sergeant York, The Asphalt Jungle, The African Queen, Heaven Knows, Mr. Allison, The Man Who Would Be King*), and Supporting Actor (*The Cardinal*); New York Film Critics Circle Award for Best Director (*Treasure of the Sierra Madre*); Independent Spirit Award for Best Director (*The Dead*); DGA D. W. Griffith Award for Lifetime Achievement (1983).

Selected bibliography

Kaminsky, Stuart. *John Huston: Maker of Magic*. Boston: Houghton-Mifflin, 1978.
Madsen, Axel. *John Huston*. New York: Doubleday, 1978.
Pratley, Gerald. *The Cinema of John Huston*. Cranbury, NJ: A. S. Barnes, 1977.

HUTTON, TIMOTHY. Born August 16, 1960, in Malibu, California; actor. Formerly married to Debra Winger. Son of actor Jim Hutton. Handsome, slightly boyish leading man who landed the prized role of Conrad Jarrett in *Ordinary People*, his Oscar-winning portrayal of the suicidal teen who is burdened by the guilt of helplessly watching his brother drown. He followed with fine performances in *Taps*, *Daniel* (as the son of a fictional Julius and Ethel Rosenberg),

Iceman, and *The Falcon and the Snowman* but became typed as a brooding, overly serious young actor. He took a step toward remedying that persona with a fine dual role in Alan Rudolph's intelligent romantic comedy *Made in Heaven*. He has since split his time between generally unsuccessful Hollywood pictures and more daring (but no more commercially prosperous) pictures for such directors as Gregory Nava (*A Time of Destiny*), Jerzy Skolimowski (*Torrents of Spring*), and George Romero (the Stephen King adaptation *The Dark Half*).

Filmography: Never Too Late (1965); Friendly Fire (1979, tv); Ordinary People (1980); Taps (1981); Daniel (1983); Iceman (1984); The Falcon and the Showman (1985); Turk 182 (1985); ''Grandpa's Ghost'' episode of ''Amazing Stories'' (1986, tvs) director; Made in Heaven (1987); Everybody's All-American (1988); A Time of Destiny (1988); Torrents of Spring (1989); Q&A (1990); The Temp (1993); The Dark Half (1993); Zelda (1993, ctvm); French Kiss (1995); The Last Word (1995).

Honors: Academy Award for Best Supporting Actor (*Ordinary People*); Los Angeles Film Critics Award for Best Supporting Actor (*Ordinary People*).

I

IN COLD BLOOD (1967), crime drama. Directed, written, and produced by Richard Brooks; photographed by Conrad Hall (b&w); edited by Peter Zinner; music by Quincy Jones; released by Columbia; 134 minutes. *Cast*: Robert Blake, Scott Wilson, John Forsythe, Paul Stewart, Jeff Corey.

Adapted from Truman Capote's best-selling story of career criminals Perry Smith and Dick Hickock, who, on the night of November 15, 1959, brutally murdered the defenseless Clutter family in their Kansas home after being misinformed that Mr. Clutter had $10,000 hidden in a safe. Much maligned as a glorification of two worthless murderers, *In Cold Blood* is nothing of the sort. Instead, it is an attempt to understand how and why someone could so brutally and heartlessly kill four members of an innocent family. The murder scene, filmed on location at the actual Clutter house with actors who closely resembled the victims, is a savage act that questions the very humanity of Perry and Dick. There is no doubt that they committed a heinous act; Brooks is simply trying to understand why. A haunting performance from Robert Blake, stark black-and-white photography from Conrad Hall, and bleak score from Quincy Jones all add to the mood.

Awards: Academy Award nominations for Best Director, Adapted Screenplay, Cinematography, Score.

IN THE HEAT OF THE NIGHT (1967), crime drama. Directed by Norman Jewison; screenplay by Stirling Silliphant (from the novel by John Ball); produced by Walter Mirisch; photographed by Haskell Wexler; edited by Hal Ashby; music by Quincy Jones; released by United Artists; 109 minutes. *Cast*: Sidney Poitier, Rod Steiger, Warren Oates, Lee Grant, Quentin Dean, James Patterson, Larry Gates, Scott Wilson, Beah Richards.

More important for the timeliness of its social commentary than for its actual cinematic achievements, this winner of five Oscars is an honorable attempt to tackle the subject of racism. Set in Sparta, Mississippi, the story involves the murder of a wealthy industrialist and the joint crime-solving efforts of a local sheriff (Steiger) and a visiting Philadelphia homicide detective named Virgil Tibbs (Poitier). While the whodunit aspect of the plot detracts from the truly dramatic content, the performances hold the film together, especially Steiger as the shrewd, gum-chewing Gillespie, who struggles to understand the roots of his own racism. Poitier, who had by then become adept at playing the ethical gentleman, gets one of his great movie moments when Gillespie asks if his northern friends call him Virgil—Poitier responds with warranted dignity, "They call me Mr. Tibbs."

Sequels: Poitier reprised his role in *They Call Me Mr. Tibbs* (1970, Gordon Douglas) and *The Organization* (1971, Don Medford).

Awards: Academy Awards for Best Picture, Adapted Screenplay, Actor (Steiger), Editing, Sound; Academy Award nominations for Best Director, Sound Effects; New York Film Critics Circle Awards for Best Picture and Actor (Steiger).

J

JACKSON, SAMUEL L. Born December 21, 1948, in Washington, D.C.; actor. Married to actor LaTanya Richardson. An exceptional actor with an intensity and range that are all too rare. After appearing in a number of supporting roles (including a memorable turn as WE-LOVE radio deejay Mister Senor Love Daddy in *Do the Right Thing*), he reached a new plateau with his Special Jury Prize at the Cannes Film Festival for his role as the crackhead Gator in *Jungle Fever*, one of four films he's made with director Spike Lee. Hollywood began to take notice, and Jackson has subsequently appeared in *White Sands*, *National Lampoon's Loaded Weapon*, *Amos and Andrew*, *Jurassic Park*, and HBO's *Against the Wall*. His 1994 role in *Pulp Fiction* as Jules, the theosophical hit man who finds redemption, earned him an Oscar nomination for Best Supporting Actor.

Filmography: Ragtime (1981); Eddie Murphy Raw (1987); School Daze (1988); Coming to America (1989); Sea of Love (1989); Do the Right Thing (1989); A Shock to the System (1990); Def By Temptation (1990); Betsy's Wedding (1990); Mo' Better Blues (1990); The Return of Superfly (1990); The Exorcist III (1990); GoodFellas (1990); Jungle Fever (1991); Johnny Suede (1991); Strictly Business (1991); Patriot Games (1992); Juice (1992); Fathers and Sons (1992); White Sands (1992); Jumpin' at the Boneyard (1992); National Lampoon's Loaded Weapon 1 (1992); Amos and Andrew (1993); Jurassic Park (1993); The Meteor Man (1993); True Romance (1993); Menace II Society (1993); Against the Wall (1993, ctvm); Assault at West Point/Conduct Unbecoming: The Court-Martial of Johnson Whittaker (1994, ctvm); Fresh (1994); Pulp Fiction (1994); The New Age (1994); Losing Isaiah (1995); Kiss of Death (1995); Die Hard with a Vengeance (1995); Sydney-Hard Eight (1995); Fluke (1995) voice.

Honors: Academy Award nomination for Best Supporting Actor (*Pulp Fiction*); New York Film Critics Circle Award for Best Supporting Actor (*Jungle Fever*); Independent

Spirit Award for Best Actor (*Pulp Fiction*); Cannes Film Festival Special Jury Prize (*Jungle Fever*).

JAGLOM, HENRY. Born January 26, 1938, in London; director, screenwriter. Rule-breaking, independent filmmaker who began his career with ten years of Actors Studio training and appearances on the 1960s television shows "The Flying Nun" and "Gidget." The start of his filmmaking career is closely tied to the counterculture BBS Productions (founded by Bert Schneider, Bob Rafelson, and Steve Blauner), which backed *A Safe Place*, as well as the directorial efforts of Dennis Hopper, Peter Bogdanovich, Jack Nicholson, and Bob Rafelson. In the late 1970s he formed International Rainbow and began making films that focused on the complexities of male–female relationships. Indifferent to Hollywood formulas, he often employs improvisational techniques, strives to capture genuine human emotions, and usually casts friends and family. "To try to capture that subjective moment, that inner landscape, is what really affects me a great deal in film" (Jaglom in Ellen Oumano's *Film Forum*).

Filmography as director, writer: A Safe Place (1971); Tracks (1976); Sitting Ducks (1979) also actor; National Lampoon Goes to the Movies (1982) director only; Can She Bake a Cherry Pie? (1983) director and actor only; Always (1985) also actor, producer; Someone to Love (1987) also actor, producer, and editor; New Years Day (1989) also actor, producer, and editor; Eating (1990) also editor; Venice/Venice (1992) also actor and editor; Baby fever (1994) also editor; Last Summer in the Hamptons (1995) also editor.

Filmography as actor: Psych-Out (1968); The 1,000 Plane Raid (1969); Drive, He Said (1971); The Last Movie (1971); The Other Side of the Wind (1972); Lily Aime-Moi (1974).

Filmography as producer: Hearts and Minds (1974); Little Noises (1991) ep.

Filmography as editorial consultant: Easy Rider (1969).

Honor: Academy Award for Best Documentary (*Hearts and Minds*).

JARMUSCH, JIM. Born January 22, 1953, in Akron, Ohio; director, screenwriter, actor. One of the most innovative and uncompromising filmmakers of his generation, he studied film as a graduate student at New York University, where he worked as a teaching assistant for Nicholas Ray, then as a production assistant on Wim Wenders' *Lightning over Water*. After making the little-seen feature *Permanent Vacation*, he secured leftover film stock from Wenders' *State of Things* and began a short film that became the first third of *Stranger than Paradise*. That film, with its austere black-and-white photography, minimalist structure, hip New York characters, and deadpan humor, put Jarmusch on the map not only in America but also in Europe, where he was awarded the Camera d'Or at the Cannes Film Festival. A trilogy of alienation, *Stranger than Paradise*, *Down by Law*, and *Mystery Train* present a unique portrait of America— not the romanticized America of Hollywood but the grittier America of TV dinners, factories, shantytowns, late-night radio, 7-Elevens, seedy hotel rooms, liquor stores, and Graceland. In *Night on Earth* he continued to explore the narrative simultaneity he introduced in *Mystery Train*—interconnecting events that occur at the same time but in different locations (three hotel rooms in *Mystery Train*, five taxis in *Night on Earth*). In addition to his work as a director, Jarmusch has acted in films by Alex Cox, Aki and Mika Kaurismaki, Rudy Wurlitzer and Robert Frank, Raul Ruiz, and Wayne Wang.

Filmography as director and writer: Permanent Vacation (1984) also producer, editor, music; Stranger than Paradise (1984) also editor; Coffee and Cigarettes (1986, short); Down by Law (1986); Coffee and Cigarettes Part Two (1988, short); Mystery Train (1989); Night on Earth (1992) also producer; Coffee and Cigarettes (Somewhere in California) (1993, short); Dead Man (1995/released in United States 1996).

Filmography as actor: Fraulein Berlin (1982); Candy Mountain (1987); Straight to Hell (1987); Helsinki Napoli All Night Long (1988); American Autobahn (1989); Leningrad Cowboys Go America (1989); The Golden Boat (1990); In the Soup (1992); Tigrero: A Film That Was Never Made (1994); Blue in the Face (1995).

Honors: Cannes Film Festival Awards, Camera d'Or (*Stranger than Paradise*); Best Artistic Contribution (*Mystery Train*); and Palme d'Or for Short Subject (*Coffee and Cigarettes (Somewhere in California)*).

JAWS (1975), horror/drama. Directed by Steven Spielberg; screenplay by Peter Benchley and Carl Gottlieb (from the novel by Benchley); produced by Richard D. Zanuck and David Brown; photographed by Bill Butler; edited by Verna Fields; music by John Williams; released by Universal; 124 minutes. *Cast*: Roy Scheider, Robert Shaw, Richard Dreyfuss, Lorraine Gary, Murray Hamilton.

The first of Steven Spielberg's monumental successes, *Jaws* tells the story of three men—Police Chief Martin Brody (Scheider), marine biologist Matt Hooper (Dreyfuss), and old salt Quint (Shaw)—who set out to kill the Great White that is terrorizing the vacation resort of Amity Island. What results is a masterpiece of modern horror that follows Val Lewton's practice of creating suspense by only hinting at the monster, then accenting the tension with John Williams' deceptively complex musical score. Although much maligned as a piece of crass commercialism (it was, at the time, arguably the most marketed film in history), the film is a gritty, masterfully constructed, superbly acted myth about man and nature that taps into the collective fears of America in a way not seen since *Psycho*. If Hitchcock kept people out of the shower, then Spielberg kept them out of the water entirely. Of the many memorable scenes and moments, unforgettable are the vicious opening attack on the unsuspecting female swimmer under the seductive moonlight and Quint's gripping account of the shark-feeding frenzy that claimed the lives of the crew of the USS *Indianapolis*.

Sequels: Three vastly inferior sequels followed—*Jaws II* (1978, Jeannot Swarzc); *Jaws 3-D* (1983, Joe Alves); and *Jaws: The Revenge* (1987, Joseph Sargent).

Awards: Academy Awards for Best Editing, Score, Sound; Academy Award nomination for Best Picture.

JEWISON, NORMAN. Born July 21, 1926, in Toronto, Ontario, Canada; director, producer. A consummate craftsman whose background as an actor and later as a producer and director of television variety shows (for the Canadian Broadcasting Company and then for CBS) has made him a keen director of actors as well as a proficient producer. After producing ''Your Hit Parade'' from 1959 to 1961 and executive-producing ''The Judy Garland Show'' in 1963, he left his contract at Universal and replaced Sam Peckinpah as director of *The Cincinnati Kid*. His earliest successes—*The Russians Are Coming, the Russians Are Coming* and *In The Heat of the Night*—both earned him Oscar nominations, though in retrospect they seem more timely than timeless. His work throughout the next twenty-five years has been spotty, though *The Thomas Crown Affair*, the musicals *Fiddler on the Roof* and *Jesus Christ Superstar*, *Rollerball*, and *Moonstruck* stand out as his most watchable entertainments. While his recent comedies have fallen flat, and much of his dramatic work is overwrought, he occasionally still surprises with little gems like *A Soldier's Story* and *In Country*. ''No theme is so trashy or threadbare that he cannot elevate it by stylish technique and apt casting into a work of merit, even on occasion art'' (John Baxter, *The International Dictionary of Films and Filmmakers*, vol. 2).

Filmography: 40 Pounds of Trouble (1962); The Thrill of It All (1963); Send Me No Flowers (1964); The Art of Love (1965); The Cincinnati Kid (1965); The Russians Are Coming, the Russians Are Coming (1966) also producer; In the Heat of the Night (1967); The Thomas Crown Affair (1968) also producer; Gaily, Gaily (1969) also producer; Fiddler on the Roof (1971); Jesus Christ Superstar (1973) also producer, screenplay; Rollerball (1975) also producer; F.I.S.T. (1978) also ep; And Justice for All (1979) also producer; Best Friends (1982) also producer; A Soldier's Story (1984) also producer; Agnes of God (1985) also producer; Moonstruck (1987) also producer; In Country (1989) also producer; Other People's Money (1991) also producer; Only You (1994) also producer.

Filmography as producer: The Landlord (1970); Billy Two Hats (1973); The Dogs of War (1981) ep; Iceman (1984); The January Man (1988).

Filmography as actor: Fraulein Berlin (1982).

Honors: Academy Award nominations for Best Director (*In the Heat of the Night, Fiddler on the Roof, Moonstruck*); and Picture (*The Russians Are Coming, the Russians Are Coming, Fiddler on the Roof, A Soldier's Story, Moonstruck*); Berlin Film Festival Award for Best Director (*Moonstruck*).

JFK (1991), political drama. Directed, cowritten, and coproduced by Oliver Stone; written with Zachary Sklar (from the books by Jim Garrison and Jim Marrs); produced with A. Kitman Ho; photographed by Robert Richardson; edited by Joe Hutshing and Pietro Scalia; music by John Williams; released by Warner Bros.; 189 minutes (1993 director's cut, 206 minutes). *Cast*: Kevin Costner, Joe Pesci, Gary Oldman, Michael Rooker, Laurie Metcalf, Jay O. Sanders, Sissy Spacek, Kevin Bacon, Tommy Lee Jones, Donald Sutherland, Walter Matthau, Jack Lemmon, Ed Asner, John Candy, Sally Kirkland, Vincent D'Onofrio, Brian Doyle-Murray, Wayne Knight, Pruitt Taylor Vince, Jim Garrison.

A towering achievement from Oliver Stone that combines his virtuosic command of cinema language with his consuming search for the truth. It's a perfect story for Stone, not simply because it's the single most traumatic event in the latter half of twentieth-century America, but because it's the story that has defined Stone as a man and as a filmmaker. Kevin Costner stars as Stone's voice of reason Jim Garrison, the New Orleans district attorney who unearths the connections between Central Intelligence Agency operative Clay Shaw (Jones), patsy/lone gunman Oswald (Oldman), and the enigmatic figures behind the assassination of President Kennedy in Dealy Plaza. Set primarily in 1966, the detail-rich story bounces wildly from past to present, New Orleans to Dallas to Washington, and character to character—all from the perspective of Garrison's increasingly paranoid and suspicious mind. The fractured narrative technique, enhanced by Robert Richardson's berserk mélange of film stocks and formats, is a remarkable parallel to the investigative dissection that Garrison is undertaking. By the end, Stone and Garrison have pointed out the weaknesses of the Warren Commission's report and Arlen Specter's "single bullet theory" while making a persuasive argument that the elusive "military-industrial complex" was behind the assassination in order to put the hawkish Lyndon Johnson in the White House and deepen our multibillion-dollar involvement in Vietnam. True or not (it's probably as true as William Richert's Kafkaesque 1979 conspiracy film *Winter Kills*), Stone's efforts led to the release of a massive amount of classified government information surrounding the assassination. "For all its tabloid urgency, its values were pure *To Kill a Mockingbird*" (Gavin Smith, *Film Comment*, January–February 1994).

Awards: Academy Awards for Cinematography, Editing; Academy Award nominations for Best Picture, Best Director, Best Supporting Actor (Jones), Adapted Screenplay, Score, Sound.

JOHNSON, BEN. Born Francis Benjamin Johnson June 13, 1918, in Foreacre, Oklahoma; died April 8, 1996, in Mesa, Arizona; actor. The son of a rodeo cowboy and world champion steer roper, the part-Irish, part-Cherokee Johnson worked as a ranch hand before being hired in 1941 by Howard Hughes as a horse wrangler and stuntman on *The Outlaw*. In addition to sporadic roles in a number of John Ford pictures throughout the late 1940s and 1950s, Johnson, like his father, became a rodeo champion. This authenticity led him to become one of the most sought-after western character actors of the 1960s and early 1970s. In 1965 he first teamed with Sam Peckinpah in *Major Dundee* and would again appear in the director's *The Wild Bunch* and *Junior Bonner*; the following year he starred in *The Rare Breed*, his first of four Andrew V. McLaglen westerns. However, the role that is etched in the mind of most film viewers is that of Sam the Lion in Peter Bogdanovich's *The Last Picture Show*, the small-town pool hall and movie theater owner whose passing signified the nostalgic end of an era. His Oscar for that film pushed him into an early 1970s spotlight as a genuine western icon, a rugged, but warm, hero who represented a link between America's past and cinema's future; in addition to Bogdanovich, he would also be cast by rising auteurs John Milius (as Melvin Purvis, opposite friend Warren Oates in *Dillinger*) and Steven Spielberg (*The Sugarland Express*). Although he worked consistently over the next twenty years, the majority of his roles lacked the texture of these earlier films.

Filmography of key pre-1965 films: The Three Godfathers (1948); Mighty Joe Young (1949); She Wore a Yellow Ribbon (1949); Rio Grande (1950); Wagonmaster (1950); Shane (1953); Oklahoma! (1955); One-Eyed Jacks (1961); Cheyenne Autumn (1964).

Filmography since 1965: Major Dundee (1965); The Rare Breed (1966); Hang 'Em High (1968); Will Penny (1968); The Undefeated (1969); The Wild Bunch (1969); Chisum (1970); Something Big (1971); The Last Picture Show (1971); Corky (1972); Junior Bonner (1972); The Getaway (1972); Dillinger (1973); Kid Blue (1973); The Train Robbers (1973); The Sugarland Express (1974); Bite the Bullet (1975); Breakheart Pass (1975); Hustle (1975); Grayeagle (1977); The Greatest (1977); The Town That Dreaded Sundown (1977); The Swarm (1978); Terror Train (1980); The Hunter (1980); Tex (1982); Champions (1983); Trespasses (1983); Red Dawn (1984); Let's Get Harry (1987); Cherry 2000 (1988); Dark before Dawn (1988); The Last Ride (1989, short); Back to Back (1990); My Heroes Have Always Been Cowboys (1991); Radio Flyer (1992); Angels in the Outfield (1994); The Legend of O. B. Taggert (1995).

Honors: Academy Award for Best Supporting Actor (*The Last Picture Show*); New York Film Critics Circle Award for Best Supporting Actor (*The Last Picture Show*).

JONES, JAMES EARL. Born January 17, 1931, in Arkabutla, Mississippi; actor. One of the most consistently excellent actors in film, this son of boxer-turned-actor Robert Earl Jones made his Broadway debut in 1957 and was, for many seasons, part of Joe Papp's New York Shakespeare Festival. From 1966 to 1968, he starred in the Broadway production of *The Great White Hope*, later reprising that role in his sole Oscar-nominated performance. What is most recognizable about Jones is his mellifluous, deeply resonant voice—used to full effect as the voice of Darth Vader in *Star Wars*. While he is often better than the films he's cast in, his recent work his been in mostly high-quality Hollywood pictures, including memorable roles in *Matewan*, *Gardens of Stone*, *Field of Dreams*, and the Jim Clancy adaptations *The Hunt for Red October*, *Patriot Games*, and *Clear and Present Danger*.

Filmography: Dr. Strangelove; or, How I Learned to Stop Worrying and Love the Bomb (1964); The Comedians (1967); The End of the Road (1970); The Great White Hope (1970); Malcolm X (1972); The Man (1972); Claudine (1974); The River Niger (1975); The Bingo Long Traveling All-Stars and Motor Kings (1976); Deadly Hero (1976); Swashbuckler (1976); Exorcist II: The Heretic (1977); The Greatest (1977); The Last Remake of Beau Geste (1977); A Piece of the Action (1977); Star Wars (1977) voice; ''Paris'' (1979–1980, tvs); The Empire Strikes Back (1980) voice; The Bushido Blade (1981); Blood Tide (1982); Conan the Barbarian (1982); Return of the Jedi (1983) voice; Aladdin and His Wonderful Lamp (1984, ctv); City Limits (1985); My Little Girl (1986);

Soul Man (1986); Allan Quatermain and the Lost City of Gold (1987); Gardens of Stone (1987); Matewan (1987); Pinocchio and the Emperor of the Night (1987) voice; Coming to America (1988); Teach 109 (1988, short); Best of the Best (1989); Field of Dreams (1989); Three Fugitives (1989); The Ambulance (1990); Grim Prairie Tales (1990); The Hunt for Red October (1990); "Gabriel's Fire" (1990–1991, tvs); Terrorgram (1991) voice; Convicts (1991); Patriot Games (1992); Sneakers (1992); Sommersby (1993); Excessive Force (1993); The Meteor Man (1993); Clear and Present Danger (1994); Clean Slate (1994); The Lion King (1994) voice; Naked Gun 33 1/3: The Final Insult (1994); Cry, the Beloved Country (1995); "Under One Roof" (1995, tvs).

Honors: Academy Award nomination for Best Actor (*The Great White Hope*); Emmy Award for Best Actor (*Gabriel's Fire*); Tony Awards (*The Great White Hope* 1969, *Fences* 1987).

Selected bibliography

Jones, James Earl. *Voices and Silences*. New York: Scribners, 1993.

JONES, TOMMY LEE. Born September 15, 1946, in San Saba, Texas; actor. A Harvard roommate of Vice President Al Gore, he has made a career of playing soldiers, killers, heavies, and ethical blue-collar heroes. Making a lasting impression as early as 1977 in *Rolling Thunder*, in 1980 as Loretta Lynn's husband in *Coal Miner's Daughter*, and again in 1982 as Gary Gilmore in television's *The Executioner's Song*, Jones nonetheless remained on the fringes of Hollywood until his Oscar-winning performance in *The Fugitive*. Three of his most shining performances have come in Oliver Stone films—the sadomasochistic Clay Shaw in *JFK*, the introspective marine in *Heaven and Earth*, and the high-octane warden in *Natural Born Killers*. In 1995 he cowrote, directed, and starred in the cable-television western *The Good Old Boys*. "You have to go back to Lee Marvin to find a comparable level of effortless self-possession and unpredictable force" (Gavin Smith, *Film Comment*, January–February 1994).

Filmography: Love Story (1970); Eliza's Horoscope (1972); Life Study (1972); Jackson County Jail (1976); Rolling Thunder (1977); Eyes of Laura Mars (1978); The Betsy (1978); Coal Miner's Daughter (1980); Back Roads (1981); The Rainmaker (1982, ctvm); The Executioner's Song (1982, tvm); Nate and Hayes (1983); The River Rat (1984); Black Moon Rising (1986); Yuri Nosenko KGB (1986); The Big Town (1987); Stormy Monday (1988); Lonesome Dove (1988, tvm); The Package (1989); Fire Birds (1990); JFK (1991); Under Siege (1992); House of Cards (1992); The Fugitive (1993); Heaven and Earth (1993); Blown Away (1994); The Client (1994); Natural Born Killers (1994); Blue Sky (1991/released in 1994); Cobb (1994); The Good Old Boys (1995, ctvm) also director, screenplay; Batman Forever (1995).

Honors: Academy Award for Best Supporting Actor (*The Fugitive*); Academy Award nomination for Best Supporting Actor (*JFK*); Los Angeles Film Critics Award for Best Supporting Actor (*The Fugitive*); Emmy for Best Actor (*The Executioner's Song*).

JOST, JON. Born May 16, 1943, in Chicago; director. Having decided during the Cuban missile crisis to leave America and begin making films, Jost completed numerous shorts before returning to study architecture and design at the

Illinois Institute of Technology. He was imprisoned for two years for draft resistance; helped set up the Chicago office of the political film collective Newsreel; and, after the 1968 Democratic Convention, was arrested again before moving west. His first feature, *Speaking Directly: Some American Notes*, set the tone for his entire body of work—he uses a confessional style of personal filmmaking, challenges his audience by destroying narrative convention, questions politics, stresses individualism, and accentuates the bond between filmmaker and film viewer. Alternately called an American version of Fassbinder, Wenders, or Godard, he not only writes and directs his own films but often shoots, lights, edits, provides commentary for, and distributes them. Essentially an essayist who uses the cinema as his medium, Jost is either America's most accessible avant-garde filmmaker or its least accessible narrative filmmaker.

Filmography of feature films: Speaking Directly: Some American Notes (1973); Angel City (1976); Last Chants for a Slow Dance (1977); Chameleon (1978); Stagefright (1981); Slow Moves (1983); Bell Diamond (1987); Plain Talk and Common Sense (Uncommon Senses) (1987); Rembrandt Laughing (1989); Sure Fire (1990); All the Vermeers in New York (1991); The Bed You Sleep In (1993); Frameup (1993); One for You, One for Me and One for Raffael (1994).

Filmography of short films: Portrait (1963); Repetition (1963); Sunday (1964); City (1964); Judith (1965); We Didn't Go to Unique's (1965); Leah (1967); Traps (1967); 13 Fragments and 3 Narratives from Life (1968); Susannah's Film (1969); Fall Creek (1970); Flower (1970); Primaries/A Turning Point on Lunatic China/1, 2, 3, Four (1971); Canyon (1971); A Man Is More than the Sum of His Parts/A Woman Is (1972); Beauty Sells Best (1977); X2: Two Dances by Nancy Karp (1980); Lampenfieber (1980); Godard (1980); Money Talks/Bullshit Walks (1989).

Honor: Los Angeles Film Critics Award for Best Independent Feature (*All the Vermeers in New York*).

JULIA (1977), drama. Directed by Fred Zinnemann; screenplay by Alvin Sargent (from the novel by Lillian Hellman); produced by Richard Roth; photographed by Douglas Slocombe; edited by Walter Murch and Marcel Durham; music by Georges Delerue; released by 20th Century Fox; 116 minutes. *Cast*: Jane Fonda, Vanessa Redgrave, Jason Robards, Maximilian Schell, Hal Holbrook, Rosemary Murphy, Meryl Streep, John Glover.

A fitting film from a director who excels at presenting characters in conflict with themselves (*High Noon, From Here to Eternity, A Man for All Seasons*), this adaptation of an episode from Lillian Hellman's autobiographical *Pentimento, a Book of Portraits* details a defining period in the author's life. Struggling to find a voice as a writer, Lillian (Fonda) heeds the advice of her lover, Dashiel Hammett (Robards), and heads to Europe to visit her enigmatic childhood friend Julia (Redgrave). The person that Lillian finds, however, is a different Julia than she remembers, a woman risking her life and vast wealth to fight the Nazis. After reluctantly agreeing to smuggle currency across the border (and nearly fouling the intricate plans), Lillian returns to Hammett a changed woman and a better writer. Nominated for eleven Oscars, the film acutely mirrored the politics of the time in its portrayal of a strong friendship between women—one an artist, the other a political activist. While certain films of the 1970s dealt with women's independence from men (*Alice Doesn't Live Here Anymore, An Unmarried Woman*) or sexual freedom (*Looking for Mr. Goodbar, Klute*), *Julia* opts for a psychological examination of female friendship, intellect, and conscience. The film, though, has not aged well. Its glossy, studio-bound style detracts from the intended sense of realism, and its cumbersome flashback structure fails to mask the hollowness at its core—that the passive Hellman onscreen is not nearly as angry, intelligent, or fascinating as she reportedly was in life.

Awards: Academy Awards for Supporting Actor (Robards), Supporting Actress (Redgrave), and Screenplay; Academy Award nominations for Best Picture, Director, Actress (Fonda), Supporting Actor (Schell), Cinematography, Score, Editing, Costumes; New York Film Critics Circle Awards for Best Picture, Actress (Fonda), Screenplay, Cinematography; WGA Award.

JULIA, RAUL. Born Raul Rafael Carlos Julia y Arcelay March 9, 1940, in San Juan, Puerto Rico; died October 24, 1994, in Long Island, New York; actor. Suave Latin actor whose move to New York in 1964 precipitated a film career exceeded only by his achievements in the theater. A gifted Shakespearean performer, Julia had already appeared on stage in *The Two Gentlemen of Verona, Hamlet, King Lear*, and *The Taming of the Shrew* (opposite Meryl Streep in 1978) before attracting attention for his supporting roles in *The Eyes of Laura Mars* and *One from the Heart*. He reached a wider audience with *Kiss of the Spider Woman* as the imprisoned political activist who shares a cell with a flamboyant homosexual film devotee played by William Hurt. He enjoyed mass popular success as Gomez Addams in *The Addams Family* and *Addams Family Values*, but he is best defined by his politically charged work in *Romero* (as El Salvador's murdered archbishop Oscar Romero), the HBO movie *The Burning Season* (as murdered environmentalist Chico Mendes), and his posthumously released Showtime film *Down Came a Blackbird* (a look at the psychological scars of political prisoners and their torturers). Among Julia's other Broadway productions are *The Threepenny Opera* (1976) as MacHeath (a role he reprised in the bland 1989 film *Mack the Knife*), Harold Pinter's *Betrayal* (1980), and *Man of La Mancha* (1992).

Filmography: Stiletto (1969); Panic in Needle Park (1971); Been Down So Long It Looks like Up to Me (1971); The Organization (1971); The Gumball Rally (1976); The Eyes of Laura Mars (1978); One from the Heart (1982); The Escape Artist (1982); Tempest (1982); Kiss of the Spider Woman (1985); Compromising Positions (1985); The Morning After (1986); Florida Straits (1986, ctvm); La Gran Fiesta (1987); Tango Bar (1988); The Penitent (1988); Trading Hearts (1988); Moon over Parador (1988); Tequila Sunrise (1988); The Richest Man in the World: The Story of Aristotle Onassis (1988, tvm); Romero (1989); Mack the Knife (1989); Presumed Innocent (1990); Roger Corman's Frankenstein Unbound (1990); The Rookie (1990); Havana (1990); A Life of Sin (1990); The Addams Family (1991); The Plague (1993); Addams Family Values (1993); The Burning Season (1994, ctvm); The Street Fighter (1994); Down Came a Blackbird (1995, ctvm).

Honor: Emmy for Best Actor (*The Burning Season*).

JURASSIC PARK (1993), action/adventure. Directed by Steven Spielberg; screenplay by David Koepp (from the novel by Michael Crichton); produced by Kathleen Kennedy and Gerald R. Molen; photographed by Dean Cundey; edited by Michael Kahn; music by John Williams; released by Universal; 127 minutes. *Cast*: Sam Neill, Laura Dern, Jeff Goldblum, Richard Attenborough, Bob Peck, B. D. Wong, Joseph Mazzello, Ariana Richards, Samuel L. Jackson, Wayne Knight.

It's grossed nearly a billion dollars at the box office, *and* it features some of the most amazing state-of-the-art computer graphics yet seen on the screen. Anything else—like story and characters—is just gravy, and what Spielberg has created here is a sumptuous meal, sans gravy. Based on Michael Crichton's popular beach novel, this tale of a catastrophic attempt to clone dinosaurs for an amusement park is great fun; just seeing the prehistoric creatures on film is alone worth the ticket price. The unfortunate thing is that Spielberg doesn't seem to be directing with his heart; one can only imagine what he might have accomplished if he had. Not surprisingly, this spawned a Universal Studios theme park ride, which opened in 1996.

Awards: Academy Awards for Best Sound, Sound Effects Editing, Visual Effects.

K

KASDAN, LAWRENCE. Born January 14, 1949, in Miami; director, screenwriter, producer. A University of California—Los Angeles film school graduate, Kasdan, with his ear for snappy dialogue, has penned four of the most successful motion pictures ever—*The Empire Strikes Back*, *Raiders of the Lost Ark*, *Return of the Jedi*, and *The Bodyguard*—but his work as a director has garnered the most attention. He's one of the most literate ''A-list'' directors and commands some of the fiercest loyalty of top-name talent (collaborating with Kevin Costner, William Hurt, and Kevin Kline on several films). His directorial debut *Body Heat*, a steamy film noir patterned after the stylings of Billy Wilder and James Cain's *Double Indemnity*, marked him as a promising new talent, while his much-hyped follow-up, *The Big Chill*, helped kick off a generation of ''baby boomers.'' His subsequent work, however (with the possible exception of *The Accidental Tourist*), has failed to attract much excitement either critically or commercially—the western *Silverado*, the black comedy *I Love You to Death*, the Los Angeles morality tale *Grand Canyon*, the western biography *Wyatt Earp*, and the romantic comedy *French Kiss*.

Filmography as director: Body Heat (1981) also screenplay; The Big Chill (1983) also screenplay and ep; Silverado (1985) also screenplay and producer; The Accidental Tourist (1988) also screenplay and producer; I Love You to Death (1990); Grand Canyon (1991); Wyatt Earp (1994); French Kiss (1995).

Filmography as writer: The Empire Strikes Back (1980); Continental Divide (1981); Raiders of the Lost Ark (1981); Return of the Jedi (1983); The Bodyguard (1992) also producer.

Additional credits: Into the Night (1985) actor; Cross My Heart (1987) producer; Immediate Family (1989) ep; Jumpin' in the Boneyard (1992) ep.

Honors: Academy Award nominations for Best Picture (*The Accidental Tourist*), Best Original Screenplay (*The Big Chill, Grand Canyon*), and Best Adapted Screenplay (*The Accidental Tourist*); WGA Award (*Big Chill*); DGA Award (*Big Chill*).

KAUFMAN, PHILIP. Born October 23, 1936, in Chicago; director, screenwriter. Educated at the University of Chicago and Harvard Law School, Kaufman has distinguished himself as a director of intelligent and cinematic adaptations, though his early works show no clear sign of his eventual career path. After producing two little-seen independent films in his native Chicago (*Goldstein* and *Fearless Frank*, the latter featuring author Nelson Algren), he directed an exceptional western about the notorious James gang (*The Great Northfield Minnesota Raid*) and a visually awesome story of Arctic whalers (*The White Dawn*) before penning the script for Clint Eastwood's *The Outlaw Josey Wales*. All of his subsequent films have been adapted from other material—*Invasion of the Body Snatchers* (Don Siegel's film); *The Wanderers* (Richard Price's novel); *The Right Stuff* (Tom Wolfe's book); *The Unbearable Lightness of Being* (Milan Kundera's novel); *Henry and June* (Anais Nin's diaries); and *Rising Sun* (Michael Crichton's novel).

Filmography as director: Goldstein (1965) codirector, also screenplay; Fearless Frank (1969) also producer, screenplay; The Great Northfield Minnesota Raid (1972) also screenplay; The White Dawn (1974); Invasion of the Body Snatchers (1978); The Wanderers (1979) also screenplay; The Right Stuff (1983) also screenplay; The Unbearable Lightness of Being (1988) also screenplay; Henry and June (1990) also screenplay; Rising Sun (1993).

Additional credits: The Outlaw Josey Wales (1975) screenplay; Raiders of the Lost Ark (1981) story; China: The Wild East (1995, ctv documentary) ep, narrator.

Honor: Academy Award nomination for Best Adapted Screenplay (*The Unbearable Lightness of Being*).

KEATON, DIANE. Born Diane Hall January 5, 1946, in Los Angeles; actor, director. Versatile leading lady who effortlessly shuttles from kooky, flighty comedian to strong dramatic actor, she debuted with the 1968 Broadway production of *Hair* and, the following year, costarred with Woody Allen in his play *Play It Again, Sam*. In 1972 she reprised her role in Allen's film adaptation of the play (the first of eight films in their legendary pairing) and also appeared in *The Godfather* as Kay Adams, the naive girlfriend of Michael Corleone. She tore through the decade with a number of hits, making her one of Hollywood's top box office draws, especially in 1977 with *Annie Hall* (as the oddly fashionable Iowan in New York) and *Looking for Mr. Goodbar* (as the repressed Theresa Dunn, who is liberated through sex). Her career progressed through the 1980s with movies as dissimilar as *Reds* (as leftist writer Louise Bryant) and *Baby Boom* (as an executive who gets saddled with a child). She then gradually made a name for herself as a director—beginning with a short documentary about her sister (*What Does Dorrie Want?*), then a feature-length documentary (*Heaven*, a quirky investigation about the existence of an afterlife), music videos (Belinda Carlisle's "Heaven Is a Place on Earth"), episodic television ("Twin Peaks" and "China Beach"), a made-for-cable feature (*Wildflower*), and finally a theatrical feature (the atmospheric and idiosyncratic *Unstrung Heroes*). She has also published three books of photography—*Reservations* (1980), *Still Life* (1983), and *Mr. Salesman* (1994).

Filmography: Lovers and Other Strangers (1970); The Godfather (1972); Play It Again, Sam (1972); Sleeper (1973); The Godfather, Part II (1974); I Will . . . I Will . . . For Now (1975); Love and Death (1975); Harry and Walter Go to New York (1976); Annie Hall (1977); Looking for Mr. Goodbar (1977); Interiors (1978); Manhattan (1979); Reds (1981); Shoot the Moon (1981); The Little Drummer Girl (1984); Mrs. Soffel (1984); Crimes of the Heart (1986); Baby Boom (1987); Radio Days (1987); The Good Mother (1988); The Lemon Sisters (1990); The Godfather, Part III (1990); Father of the Bride (1991); Running Mates (1992, ctvm); Manhattan Murder Mystery (1993); Look Who's Talking Now (1993) voice; Amelia Earhart: The Final Flight (1994, ctvm); Father of the Bride 2 (1995).

Filmography as director: What Does Dorrie Want? (1982, short); Heaven (1987, doc); The Girl with the Crazy Brother (1990, tvm); Wildflower (1993, ctvm); Unstrung Heroes (1995).

Honors: Academy Award for Best Actress (*Annie Hall*); Academy Award nomination for Best Supporting Actress (*Reds*); New York Film Critics Circle Award for Best Actress (*Annie Hall*).

KEATON, MICHAEL. Born Michael Douglas September 5, 1951, in Coraoplis, Pennsylvania; actor. Intense leading man who splits his time between comedy and drama, he began his career on "Mr. Rogers' Neighborhood" as one of the Flying Burrito Brothers before landing the lead in the role-reversal domestic farce *Mr. Mom*. His breakthrough year was 1988—he gave a truly original comic performance as the grouchy, wisecracking ghost in Tim Burton's *Beetlejuice* and then demonstrated his serious side as an addict in *Clean and Sober*. His popularity increased when he reteamed with Burton to play the Caped Crusader in *Batman* and *Batman Returns*, giving the comic book hero a dark, brooding edge. Of his more recent work, his commercially calculated projects (the thriller *Pacific Heights* and the light comedies *Speechless* and *The Paper*) have been poorly received by audiences and critics, though he has received kudos for his more daring films (*My Life*, the story of a terminally ill father, and William Shakespeare's *Much Ado about Nothing*).

Filmography: Night Shift (1982); Mr. Mom (1983); Johnny Dangerously (1984); Gung Ho (1986); Touch and Go (1986); The Squeeze (1987); Beetlejuice (1988); Clean and Sober (1988); Batman (1989); The Dream Team (1989); Pacific Heights (1990); One Good Cop (1991); Batman Returns (1992); Much Ado about Nothing (1993); My Life (1993); The Paper (1994); Speechless (1994).

KEITEL, HARVEY. Born May 13, 1939, in Brooklyn; actor, producer. Formerly married to actor Lorraine Bracco. Although his New York counterparts Robert De Niro and Al Pacino have had more celebrated careers, Keitel has quietly emerged as the more daring talent—an emotionally bold performer whose work is getting increasingly naked. After studying at the Actors Studio and spending some ten years doing off-Broadway, Keitel debuted with a lead role in *Who's That Knocking at My Door?*, his first of five films for Martin Scorsese. As J. R., he developed a persona of a man in conflict, a soulful New Yorker torn between his base urges and his need for spiritual purity. It is a character Keitel would revisit again and again—Charlie in *Mean Streets*, Jimmy in *Fingers*, the lieutenant in *The Bad Lieutenant*, and Rocco in *Clockers*. He worked with a number of top directors throughout the 1970s—Altman (*Buffalo Bill*), Scorsese (*Taxi Driver*), Alan Rudolph (*Welcome to L.A.*), Ridley Scott (*The Duellists*), James Toback (*Fingers*), Paul Schrader (*Blue Collar*), and nearly Francis Ford Coppola (being replaced by Martin Sheen in *Apocalypse Now* just one week into filming)—before spending much of the late 1970s and 1980s acting in Europe. His films for Bertrand Tavernier (*Death Watch*), Nicolas Roeg (*Bad Timing*), Ettore Scola (*La Nuit de Verennes*), and Lina Wertmuller (*Camorra*), as well as such later foreign work as Dario Argento's episode of *Two Evil Eyes*, Jane Campion's *The Piano*, and Theo Angelopoulos' *Ulysses' Gaze*, represent Keitel's willingness to seek out exciting scripts at the expense of commercial success in America. His career again took a turn in 1991, when he appeared in three successive Hollywood films teaming with former collaborators Ridley Scott (*Thelma and Louise*), writer James Toback (*Bugsy*), and Alan Rudolph (*Mortal Thoughts*). Where his desire to experiment and expand as a performer previously led him to European directors, he would, in the 1990s, satisfy that craving in a number of courageous American independent films such as Quentin Tarantino's *Reservoir Dogs* and *Pulp Fiction*, Wayne Wang's *Smoke* and *Blue in the Face*, and Abel Ferrara's *The Bad Lieutenant* and *Dangerous Game*.

Filmography: Who's That Knocking at My Door?/I Call First (1968); Street Scenes 1970 (1970) producer's assistant; Mean Streets (1973); Alice Doesn't Live Here Anymore (1974); A Memory of Two Mondays (1974, tvm); That's the Way of the World (1975); Buffalo Bill and the Indians, or Sitting Bull's History Lesson (1976); Mother, Jugs and Speed (1976); Taxi Driver (1976); Welcome to L.A. (1976); The Duellists (1977); Fingers (1977); Blue Collar (1978); Eagles Wing (1978); Death Watch (1979); Bad Timing (1980); Saturn 3 (1980); The Border (1981); That Night in Varennes/La Nuit de Varennes (1981); Corrupt/Order of Death/Cop Killers (1983); Exposed (1983); Dream One/Nemo (1983); Une Pierre dans la Bouche (1983); Falling in Love (1984); Camorra/The Naples Connection/Un Complicato Intrigo Di Donne, Vicoli e Delitti (1985); El Caballero del Dragon (1986); La Sposa Americana (1986); The Men's Club (1986); Wise Guys (1986); L'Inchiesta (1986); Off Beat (1986); Blindside (1987); Dear America (1987); The Pick-Up Artist (1987); Caro Gorbaciov (1988); The Last Temptation of Christ (1988); The January Man (1989); La Batalla de los Tres Reyes (1990); Two Evil Eyes (1990); Two Jakes (1990); Bugsy (1991); Mortal Thoughts (1991); Thelma and Louise (1991); Reservoir Dogs (1992) also producer; The Bad Lieutenant

(1992); Sister Act (1992); Dangerous Game/Snake Eyes (1993); Rising Sun (1993); The Piano (1993); Point of No Return (1993); The Young Americans (1993); Pulp Fiction (1994); Monkey Trouble (1994); Imaginary Crimes (1994); Somebody to Love (1994); Blue in the Face (1995) also producer; Clockers (1995); Get Shorty (1995); Smoke (1995); Ulysses' Gaze (1995).

Honors: Academy Award nomination for Best Supporting Actor (*Bugsy*); Independent Spirit Award for Best Actor (*The Bad Lieutenant*).

KELLERMAN, SALLY. Born June 2, 1938, in Long Beach, California; actor. Vivacious actor who first appeared at age nineteen in the exploitation picture *Reform School Girl* but didn't become a star until she was cast as Major "Hot Lips" Houlihan, the high-strung army nurse of Robert Altman's *M*A*S*H*. An excellent actor who too often wastes her talents in mindless comedies, she does rise to the level of her material when working with such top-flight directors as Robert Altman (*Brewster McCloud, Ready to Wear*), Alan Rudolph (*Welcome To L.A.*), George Roy Hill (*A Little Romance*), Blake Edwards (*That's Life!*), and Henry Jaglom (*Someone to Love, Happily Ever After*). In addition to her film work, she is one of the most familiar commercial voice-over artists on television and radio.

Filmography: Reform School Girl (1957); Hands of a Stranger (1962); The Third Day (1965); The Boston Strangler (1968); The April Fools (1969); Brewster McCloud (1970); M*A*S*H (1970); A Reflection of Fear (1971); Last of the Red Hot Lovers (1972); Lost Horizon (1973); Slither (1973); Rafferty and the Gold Dust Twins (1974); The Big Bus (1976); Welcome to L.A. (1976); The Mouse and His Child (1977); It Rained All Night the Day I Left (1978); Magee and the Lady (1978); A Little Romance (1979); Foxes (1980); Head On/Fatal Attraction (1980); Loving Couples (1980); Serial (1980); Moving Violations (1985); Sesame Street Presents: Follow That Bird (1985); KGB—The Secret War/Lethal (1986); Back to School (1986); Meatballs III (1986); That's Life! (1986); Someone to Love (1987); Three for the Road (1987); Paramedics (1988); You Can't Hurry Love (1988); All's Fair (1989); Limit Up (1989); Happily Ever After (1990); Ready to Wear (Prêt-à-Porter) (1994).

Honor: Academy Award nomination for Best Supporting Actress (*M*A*S*H*).

KENNEDY, GEORGE. Born February 18, 1925, in New York City; actor. Excellent character actor who is generally better than the films in which he appears. After a sixteen-year stretch in the army, he served as a technical adviser on television's "Sgt. Bilko" and gradually built a career as a television actor. He appeared in some memorable bit parts throughout the early 1960s (especially *Charade*) before receiving an Academy Award as chain gang boss Dragline in *Cool Hand Luke*. A number of western roles followed, but he was best known throughout the 1970s as a star of the disaster films *Airport* (and its three sequels) and *Earthquake*. For much of the 1980s and 1990s, he has appeared in countless action quickies for the international film market. To a new generation of film audiences he is best recognized from the *Naked Gun* pictures.

Filmography of key pre-1965 films: Charade (1963); Hush . . . Hush, Sweet Charlotte (1964); Island of the Blue Dolphins (1964); Strait-Jacket (1964).

Filmography since 1965: The Flight of the Phoenix (1965); In Harm's Way (1965); Mirage (1965); Shenandoah (1965); The Sons of Katie Elder (1965); Three Songs (1965, short) producer, director; The Ballad of Josie (1967); Cool Hand Luke (1967); The Dirty Dozen (1967); Hurry Sundown (1967); Bandolero! (1968); The Boston Strangler (1968); The Legend of Lylah Clare (1968); The Pink Jungle (1968); Gaily, Gaily (1969); The Good Guys and the Bad Guys (1969); Guns of the Magnificent Seven (1969); Airport (1970); Dirty Dingus Magee (1970); Tick, Tick, Tick (1970); Zigzag (1970); Fools' Parade (1971); The Family (1972); Cahill, United States Marshal (1973); Lost Horizon (1973); Earthquake (1974); Thunderbolt and Lightfoot (1974); Airport 1975 (1974); The Eiger Sanction (1975); The Human Factor (1975); Airport 77 (1977); Ningen no Shomei/ Proof of the Man (1977); Brass Target (1978); Death on the Nile (1978); Mean Dog Blues (1978); The Concorde—Airport '79 (1979); Death Ship (1979); The Double McGuffin (1979); Hotwire (1980); Just before Dawn (1980); Steel (1980); Virus (1980); Modern Romance (1981); A Rare Breed (1981); Search and Destroy/Striking Back (1981); The Jupiter Menace (1982); Wacko (1983); Bolero (1984); Chattanooga Choo Choo (1984); Rigged (1985); Savage Dawn (1985); The Delta Force (1986); Radioactive Dreams (1986); Creepshow 2 (1987); Born to Race (1988); Demonwarp (1988); Esmerelda Bay (1988); The Naked Gun—From the Files of Police Squad! (1988); Nightmare at Noon (1988); Private Roads/No Trespassing (1988); Uninvited (1988); Counterforce (1989); Ministry of Vengeance (1989); The Terror Within (1989); Brain Dead (1990); Naked Gun 33 1/3: The Final Insult (1994).

Honor: Academy Award for Best Supporting Actor (*Cool Hand Luke*).

KING OF COMEDY (1983), comedy/drama. Directed by Martin Scorsese; screenplay by Paul D. Zimmerman; produced by Arnon Milchan; photographed by Fred Schuler; edited by Thelma Schoonmaker; music by Robbie Robertson, song "Come Rain or Come Shine" by Johnny Mercer and Harold Arlen; released by 20th Century Fox; 108 minutes. *Cast*: Robert De Niro, Jerry Lewis, Diahnne Abbott, Sandra Bernhardt, Ed Herlihy, Liza Minnelli, Shelley Hack, Tony Randall, Dr. Joyce Brothers, Victor Borge, Fred De Cordova, Edgar J. Scherick, Harry Ufland, Jay Julien, Mardick Martin.

A major Scorsese work that, since being unceremoniously dumped into theaters by 20th Century Fox, has unjustly remained in the shadows of his Italian-American films. De Niro stars as the delusional Rupert Pupkin, an autograph hound/aspiring celebrity who polishes his showbiz persona in his basement until a brief encounter with late-night talk show host Jerry Langford (Lewis). Rupert begins to play out fantasies in his head, imagining himself as Langford's friend, confidant, and successor—the new "King of Comedy." Since reality doesn't mirror what's in his head, Rupert and his equally obsessed friend Masha (Bernhardt), a young woman in love with Langford, kidnap the star at gunpoint and detain him until the show's producers agree to let Rupert perform his act on the air. An amusing, though no less dangerous, cousin to Travis Bickle, Rupert Pupkin is a social misfit whose head is filled with obsessive notions. Both characters are living on the fringe in New York's Times Square, both fantasize about making a difference in the world, both have regal romantic notions about pleasing their idealized queen (for Travis, it's campaign worker Betsy; for Rupert, it's bartender Rita), and both reach a level of national celebrity after their extreme antisocial behavior. Scorsese shows his complete understanding of film language with more attentiveness than usual to mise-en-scène over montage. This is an unnervingly creepy film that probes America's crippling fascination with fame and chillingly illustrates Rupert Pupkin's belief that it's "better to be king for a night, than schmuck for a lifetime."

KLINE, KEVIN. Born October 24, 1947, in St. Louis, Missouri; actor. Married to actor Phoebe Cates. Versatile leading man who would fit the "Errol Flynn of the 1980s" epithet (as *Vanity Fair* once described him) if the roguish Flynn had Kline's flair for comedy. A student at the Julliard School from 1968 to 1972, he became one of the founding members of John Houseman's acclaimed Acting Company before reaching different acting heights as a regular on the soap opera "Search for Tomorrow." He made an auspicious film debut opposite Meryl Streep in *Sophie's Choice* and later that year starred in *The Pirates of Penzance*, reprising his stage role as Gilbert and Sullivan's Pirate King. His collaboration with director Lawrence Kasdan has produced five films (*The Big Chill, Silverado, I Love You to Death, Grand Canyon, French Kiss*), though none represent his best work. More impressive are *Cry Freedom* (a powerful indictment of apartheid in which he stars as journalist Donald Woods) and the clever comedies *Dave* and *A Fish Called Wanda*. He costarred with wife Phoebe Cates in the charming, if minor, 1994 comedy *Princess Caraboo*. He has frequently appeared on stage as part of the New York Shakespeare Festival where, in 1990, he directed *Hamlet*.

Filmography: "Search for Tomorrow" (1976–1977, tvs); Sophie's Choice (1982); The Pirates of Penzance (1982); The Big Chill (1983); Silverado (1985); Violets Are Blue (1986); Cry Freedom (1987); A Fish Called Wanda (1988); The January Man (1989); I Love You to Death (1990); Soapdish (1991); Grand Canyon (1991); Consenting Adults (1992); Chaplin (1992); The Nutcracker (1993) narrator; Dave (1993); Princess Caraboo (1994); French Kiss (1995).

Honors: Academy Award for Best Supporting Actor (*A Fish Called Wanda*); Tony Awards (*On the Twentieth Century* 1978, *The Pirates of Penzance* 1981).

KLUTE (1971), psychological thriller. Directed and coproduced by Alan J. Pakula; screenplay by Andy Lewis and Dave Lewis; produced with David Lang; photographed by Gordon Willis; edited by Carl Lerner; music by Michael Small; released by Warner Bros.; 114 minutes. *Cast*: Jane Fonda, Donald Sutherland, Charles Cioffi, Roy Scheider, Dorothy Tristan, Rita Gam, Jean Stapleton.

Jane Fonda's Bree, a young woman aware of her need to be in control, is still perhaps the greatest psychological portrait of a prostitute in American film. She's a Manhattan call girl who becomes the subject of a quest by detective

John Klute (Sutherland) to locate his missing friend, a former john of Bree's. Unwittingly, they both become involved in a murder plot. The claustrophobic thriller elements, however gripping, are secondary to the strange emotional dance that develops between Bree and Klute, a power play that explores issues of female independence and male protection. Sutherland and Fonda give career performances, while Pakula's intelligent direction gives the film an uneasy edge that forces the viewer to share Klute's emotionally complex point of view. ''In 1971 we believed that through Fonda we were being given the chance to explore a female character's psyche to a much larger degree than we had in a lifetime of moviegoing'' (Danny Perry, *Alternate Oscars*).

Awards: Academy Award for Best Actress; Academy Award nomination for Best Screenplay; New York Film Critics Circle Award for Best Actress.

KOYAANISQATSI (1983), experimental. Directed, cowritten, and produced by Godfrey Reggio; screenplay with Ron Fricke, Michael Hoenig, and Alton Walpole; photographed and edited by Fricke; music by Philip Glass; released by New Yorker Films; 87 minutes.

An anomaly in the world of theatrical features, *Koyaanisqatsi* is an entirely experimental film of images with musical accompaniment by composer Philip Glass that would not have received the wide release that it did were it not for the support of presenter Franĉis Ford Coppola. As translated from Hopi, its title means (1) crazy life, (2) life in turmoil, (3) life out of balance, (4) life disintegrating, (5) a state of life that calls for another way of living. Whether dismissed as preachy, New Age environmentalist propaganda or praised as a visually stimulating, psychedelic head trip, the fact remains that this widely seen experimental feature has, as a result, greatly influenced the visual language of television commercials and music videos. Filled with time-lapse photography of racing clouds in the American West and a fast-motion blitzkrieg of cars and people in crowded city streets, the film has a numbing, hypnotic effect that is hard to resist. Yet, it's also hard to take seriously its antihuman message that the world would be better off without us.

Sequel: *Powaqqatsi* (1988, Reggio). A planned third film, *Naquoyquatsi*, will round out the trilogy.

KRAMER VS. KRAMER (1979), drama. Directed and written by Robert Benton (from the novel by Avery Corman); produced by Stanley R. Jaffe; photographed by Nestor Almendros; edited by Jerry Greenberg; music by Henry Purcell and Antonio Vivaldi; released by Columbia; 105 minutes. *Cast*: Dustin Hoffman, Meryl Streep, Jane Alexander, Justin Henry, Howard Duff, George Coe, JoBeth Williams.

While it borders on television movie territory and occasionally resorts to manipulation, there is no better example of the naturalism of American film acting than this. The opposing Kramers of the title are Ted (Hoffman) and

Joanna (Streep), a pair of New Yorkers whose marriage ends when Joanna decides to ''find herself.'' Trying to juggle the demands of his son Billy (Henry) with those of his high-pressure advertising career, Ted eventually loses his job but discovers in himself a love of parenting. The disruptive Joanna then decides she wants custody of the son she has abandoned. Lacking the overt artistic flashiness of other films of the day, *Kramer vs. Kramer* was, and still is, too easily dismissed as an overly sentimental issue film from Hollywood. It is much closer to the humanist tradition of Jean Renoir and François Truffaut (for whom Benton originally envisioned the script) in its fondness for the subtleties of human relationships. ''Put *Kramer vs. Kramer*, not *Manhattan*, in the time capsule, and if it is dug up centuries from now, it will report some truth about the city today'' (Stanley Kauffmann, *The New Republic*, December 22, 1979).

Awards: Academy Awards for Best Picture, Director, Actor, Supporting Actress (Streep), Adapted Screenplay; Academy Award nominations for Supporting Actor (Henry), Supporting Actress (Alexander), Cinematography, Editing; New York Film Critics Circle Awards for Best Picture, Actor, Supporting Actress (Streep); DGA Award; WGA Award.

KRISTOFFERSON, KRIS. Born June 22, 1936, in Brownsville, Texas; actor, singer. Formerly married to singer Rita Coolidge. A Rhodes scholar at Oxford, an officer in the army, and an instructor at West Point, Kristofferson went on to become one of the biggest sex symbols of the 1970s—a status buoyed by his role opposite Barbra Streisand in *A Star Is Born*. When not performing passionate love scenes (as in *Alice Doesn't Live Here Anymore* and *The Sailor Who Fell from Grace with the Sea*), the bearded leading man made a name for himself as a strong, confident, loner type in the films of Sam Peckinpah (*Pat Garrett and Billy the Kid*, *Bring Me the Head of Alfredo Garcia*) and Alan Rudolph (*Songwriter*, *Trouble in Mind*). A top country-western singer and songwriter even before he became an actor (he wrote the classic ''Me and Bobby McGee''), he often contributes to the soundtracks of his films.

Filmography: Cisco Pike (1971); The Last Movie (1971) also music; Blume in Love (1973) also song; Pat Garrett and Billy the Kid (1973); Alice Doesn't Live Here Anymore (1974); Bring Me the Head of Alfredo Garcia (1974); The Sailor Who Fell from Grace with the Sea (1975) also song; Vigilante Force (1975); A Star Is Born (1976); Semi-Tough (1977); Convoy (1978); Heaven's Gate (1980); Rollover (1981); Flashpoint (1984); Songwriter (1984) also music, song; Trouble in Mind (1985) also song; Big Top Pee-Wee (1988); Millennium (1989); Welcome Home (1989); Perfume of the Cyclone (1990); Sandino (1990); Original Intent (1992); Place to Hide (1993); Cheatin' Hearts (1993); Knights (1993); Christmas in Connecticut (1992, ctvm); Pharaoh's Army (1995).

Honors: Academy Award nomination for Best Song Score (*Songwriter*); Grammy Award for Best Country Song (''Help Me Make It through the Night'' 1971) and Country Vocal Performance (''From the Bottle to the Bottom'' 1973).

KUBRICK, STANLEY. Born July 26, 1928, in Bronx, New York; director, producer. The most confounding of American filmmakers, Kubrick began his career as a photographer for *Look* magazine and then worked briefly as a documentary filmmaker before striking out on his own with two self-financed features, *Fear and Desire* and *Killer's Kiss*. In 1957, two years after partnering with producer James B. Harris, he delivered his first great work, the expertly crafted, antimilitary film *Paths of Glory*. After an aborted attempt to direct Marlon Brando in *One-Eyed Jacks*, Kubrick accepted the job to direct *Spartacus* for actor/producer Kirk Douglas. Despite being a psychologically complex sword-and-sandal epic, the film was disowned by Kubrick, who charged that his vision was disrespected and vowed to never again make a film unless he had complete control. With his next two projects—his brilliant, if rarefied, adaptation of Vladimir Nabakov's *Lolita* and his thoroughly satisfying dark comedy *Dr. Strangelove*—he established himself as the single most uncompromising visionary in Hollywood. Over the next thirty years, Kubrick (who had by now relocated to England) would make just five films, all of them adaptations—the hallucinatory Arthur C. Clarke sci-fi treatise, *2001: A Space Odyssey*; the wildly controversial Anthony Burgess tale of the nature of violence, *A Clockwork Orange*; the atypically picaresque adaptation of William Makepeace Thackeray's novel, *Barry Lyndon*; the anti-Stephen King horror film, *The Shining*; and the wickedly ironic Gustav Hasford Vietnam tale, *Full Metal Jacket*. An unsurpassed visual stylist, Kubrick has created a cold, hard cinema that is so meticulously controlled it often threatens to suffocate the narrative. However, his philosophical inquiries into the nature of man and what it means to be human are solid enough to support his methods. He challenges audiences and critics to study the past, present, and future of humanity; he wonders why and how we (the man/ape, the punkish droog, the marine recruit) have been conditioned to kill one another off as part of our evolutionary process. The question remains, then, are Kubrick's films misanthropic observations of *sub*humans, or are they cautiously optimistic predictions of our gradual transformation into *super*humans? "Like all great filmmakers, Kubrick erases the distinction between form and content so cleanly that each serves and extends the other, so that each is inconceivable without the other" (James Toback, *Film Comment*, February 1985).

Filmography of key pre-1965 films: Fear and Desire (1953); Killer's Kiss (1955); The Killing (1956); Paths of Glory (1957); Spartacus (1960); Lolita (1962); Dr. Strangelove: or How I Learned to Stop Worrying and Love the Bomb (1964).

Filmography since 1965: 2001: A Space Odyssey (1968) also producer, screenplay, special photographic effects designer and photographer; A Clockwork Orange (1971) also producer, screenplay, additional cinematography; Barry Lyndon (1975) also producer, screenplay; The Shining (1980) also producer, screenplay; Full Metal Jacket (1987) also producer, screenplay.

Honors: Academy Award for Best Effects (*2001: A Space Odyssey*); Academy Award nominations for Best Picture (*Dr. Strangelove, A Clockwork Orange, Barry Lyndon*), Director (*Dr. Strangelove, 2001: A Space Odyssey, A Clockwork Orange, Barry Lyndon*) and Screenplay (*Dr. Strangelove, 2001: A Space Odyssey, A Clockwork Orange, Barry Lyndon, Full Metal Jacket*); New York Film Critics Circle Awards for Best Director (*Dr.*

Strangelove, A Clockwork Orange); included in the Library of Congress' National Film Registry (*2001: A Space Odyssey*).

Selected bibliography

Falsetto, Mario. *Perspectives on Stanley Kubrick*. Boston: G. K. Hall, 1996.

Kolker, Robert Phillip. *A Cinema of Loneliness: Penn, Kubrick, Coppola, Scorsese, Altman*. New York: Oxford University Press, 1980.

Nelson, Thomas Allen. *Kubrick: Inside a Film Artist's Maze*. Bloomington: Indiana University Press, 1982.

Walker, Alexander. *Stanley Kubrick Directs*. New York: Harcourt Brace Jovanovich, 1971.

L

LANDIS, JOHN. Born August 3, 1950, in Chicago; director, actor. Having built his reputation on the raucous comedy *National Lampoon's Animal House*, which succeeded largely because of John Belushi's primal antics, Landis has become one of the busiest directors of high-profile comedies in Hollywood, though none have matched the brilliant recklessness of that film. His big-budget exercise in self-indulgence and car crashes, *The Blues Brothers*, benefited from the magnetic pairing of Belushi and Aykroyd as Jake and Elwood Blues, though the patchiness of the script undercuts the overall effectiveness. He followed with perhaps his most accomplished film, *An American Werewolf in London*, a pleasing fusion of horror and comedy. His reputation took a nosedive during the catastrophic production of his episode of *Twilight Zone—The Movie*, which resulted in the death of Vic Morrow and his two young Vietnamese costars when a helicopter used in a battle scene crashed on top of them; a widely publicized trial followed in which Landis was acquitted. Of his subsequent films, the majority have been star vehicles for such broad comic talents as Eddie Murphy, Chevy Chase, Dan Aykroyd, Steve Martin, Martin Short, and the not-so-comedically adept Sylvester Stallone. Lacking any sophistication or relevance, these films depend on silliness, slapstick humor, inside jokes, and customary director cameos—all pointing to the fact that Landis is more concerned with screwing around than actually making a point. He has also directed the groundbreaking music video "Thriller" for Michael Jackson, a minimovie with choreographed dance, horror makeup and effects, a narrative structure with dialogue, and beginning and end credits—an achievement that has, unfortunately, not been duplicated by any other artists. He and Jackson again paired for the graphically electrifying, though less revolutionary, "Black and White."

Filmography: Schlock (1973) also screenplay, actor; The Kentucky Fried Movie (1977) also actor; National Lampoon's Animal House (1978); The Blues Brothers (1980) also screenplay, actor; An American Werewolf in London (1981); "Thriller" (1983, short/ mv); Trading Places (1983); "Prologue" and "Back There" episode of Twilight Zone— The Movie (1983) also screenplay, producer; Clue (1985) story, ep; Into the Night (1985) also actor; Spies like Us (1985); Three Amigos! (1986); Amazon Women on the Moon (1987) also ep; Coming to America (1988); Oscar (1991); "Black and White" (1991, mv) Innocent Blood (1992); Beverly Hills Cop III (1994).

Filmography as actor: Battle for the Planet of the Apes (1973); Death Race 2000 (1975); 1941 (1979); Eating Raoul (1982); The Muppets Take Manhattan (1984); Spontaneous Combustion (1989); Darkman (1990).

LANGE, JESSICA. Born April 20, 1949, in Cloquet, Minnesota; actor. Longtime companion of actor and playwright Sam Shepard; formerly married to avant-garde filmmaker and photographer Paco Grande. Simply one of the greatest faces in the history of American film, Lange is a brilliantly instinctual actor who shows a genius for her rock-solid portrayals of women attuned to suffering and sadness. Her demand in Hollywood is such that she's starred opposite three of its biggest names—Jack Nicholson, Dustin Hoffman, and Robert De Niro. After bursting onto the scene with two high-profile roles (the object of primal affections in *King Kong* and the heavenly Angelique in *All That Jazz*), she provided the steamy on-the-kitchen-table sexuality for *The Postman Always Rings Twice*. The following year she appeared in *Tootsie* and starred as actress Frances Farmer in *Frances*—both roles earning Oscar nominations, the former garnering Lange a statuette. She has also given wonderfully natural performances as Patsy Cline in *Sweet Dreams*, as Iowa farmer Jewell Ivy in *Country*, as the widowed wife in *Men Don't Leave*, and as the manic-depressive military wife Carly in *Blue Sky*. Her magnetic Broadway turn as Blanche DuBois in the highly anticipated 1992 production of *A Streetcar Named Desire* is one of two Tennessee Williams plays she has filmed for television. "She's as confidently sexual as any American screen star past or present" (Pauline Kael, *The New Yorker*, December 15, 1986).

Filmography: King Kong (1976); All That Jazz (1979); How to Beat the High Cost of Living (1980); The Postman Always Rings Twice (1981); Frances (1982); Tootsie (1982); Country (1984) also producer; Sweet Dreams (1985); Crimes of the Heart (1986); Everybody's All-American (1988); Far North (1988); Music Box (1989); Cat on a Hot Tin Roof (1984, tvm); Men Don't Leave (1990); Cape Fear (1991); Night and the City (1992); O Pioneers! (1992, tvm); Blue Sky (1991/released in 1994); Losing Isaiah (1995); Rob Roy (1995); A Streetcar Named Desire (1995, tvm).

Honors: Academy Awards for Best Actress (*Blue Sky*) and Supporting Actress (*Tootsie*); Academy Award nominations for Best Actress (*Frances, Country, Sweet Dreams, Music Box*); Los Angeles Film Critics Award for Best Actress (*Blue Sky*); New York Film Critics Circle Award for Best Supporting Actress (*Tootsie*).

LAST PICTURE SHOW, THE (1971), drama. Directed and cowritten by Peter Bogdanovich; written with Larry McMurtry (from the novel by McMurtry); produced by Stephen J. Friedman; executive-produced by Bert Schneider; photographed by Robert Surtees (b&w); edited by Donn Cambern; released by Columbia; 118 minutes. *Cast*: Timothy Bottoms, Jeff Bridges, Cybill Shepherd, Ben Johnson, Cloris Leachman, Ellen Burstyn, Eileen Brennan, Clu Gulager, Sharon Taggart, Randy Quaid, Sam Bottoms.

Peter Bogdanovich's poignant 1950s tale of love, loss, and disloyalty is, as the title implies, a film about endings—the end of youth and innocence, the end of the small town and its morality, and the end of Hollywood's golden age of cinema. In the dusty town of Anarene, Texas, best friends Duane Jackson (Bridges) and Sonny Crawford (Timothy Bottoms) face the bleak prospect that they may live and die in this creaky, ramshackle town. They both become involved with the self-centered Jacy Farrow (Shepherd), driving a wedge between their friendship and, in the process, learning about the lost loves and dreams of the generation of townsfolk who preceded them. The turning point for Duane and Sonny is the death of local patriarch Sam the Lion (Johnson), a onetime cowboy turned pool hall/movie theater owner whose passing signifies the end of an era. After turning some heads with his clever debut feature *Targets*, Bogdanovich delivered a classic piece of filmmaking with this nostalgic adaptation of Larry McMurtry's novel. Much of the success comes from the mix of Bogdanovich's Hawksian/Fordian style of unpretentious direction, the thematically appropriate black-and-white photography of Robert Surtees, and the brilliant casting of newcomers Bridges, Shepherd, Quaid, Timothy and Sam Bottoms, Ellen Burstyn, and Eileen Brennan.

Sequel: Bogdanovich returned to direct *Texasville* (1990) with Bridges, Shepherd, Bottoms, Brennan, Leachman, and Quaid reprising their roles.

Awards: Academy Awards for Best Supporting Actor (Johnson) and Supporting Actress (Leachman); Academy Award nominations for Best Picture, Director, Screenplay, Supporting Actor (Bridges), Supporting Actress (Burstyn), Cinematography; New York Film Critics Circle Awards for Best Screenplay, Supporting Actor (Johnson), Supporting Actress (Burstyn).

LEE, SPIKE. Born Shelton Jackson Lee March 20, 1957, in Atlanta, Georgia; director, screenwriter, producer, actor. Although others came before him (Oscar Michaeux, Melvin Van Peebles, Gordon Parks), Spike Lee is, at least symbolically, the Jackie Robinson of American film—the player who changed Hollywood's perception of black filmmakers and audiences. Consequently, Lee also exploded the barriers between the Hollywood studio system and an entire new generation of independent filmmakers. After studying film at Atlanta's Moorhouse College and then at New York University, Lee burst onto the scene by directing, writing, and starring (as Mars Blackmon) in the low-budget, black-and-white comedy *She's Gotta Have It*, a smart, hysterical look at a young woman who is sleeping with three different guys. Despite the many faults of his ambitious follow-up film *School Daze*, a musical that addressed black-against-black racism on a college campus, Lee continued to impress with his steady output. Surrounded by controversy, *Do the Right Thing* is the picture in which everything comes together for Lee—a vibrant sound track, an excellent ensemble cast, a mix of comedy and drama, and a powerful message that provoked a nationwide dialogue about race relations. Equally accomplished, though not as successful at stirring debate, are *Mo' Better Blues*, a moody story of a driven jazz trumpeter that stars Denzel Washington; and *Clockers*, a satisfying adaptation of Richard Price's epic novel of inner-city drug dealing. Other films, however, have been less successful—the profound *Malcolm X* suffers from an inability to sustain itself, *Jungle Fever* is more concerned with polemics than people, and *Crooklyn* is a hodgepodge of nostalgia—and in each, the potential strength of the stories is undermined by a self-conscious visual style and an irritating use of wall-to-wall music. As skilled at marketing as he is at directing, Lee started the production company 40 Acres and a Mule and has branched out into other arenas with the record label 40 Acres and a Mule Music Works, his "Spike's Joint" retail stores, numerous movie tie-in books, television commercials (the inventive Nike and Levi Button-Fly 501 spots), and music videos (Miles Davis, Tracy Chapman, Public Enemy, Michael Jackson). Probably the most identifiable film director in America since Alfred Hitchcock, Lee has stayed in the public eye with his appearances ringside at Mike Tyson fights and courtside at New York Knicks games.

Filmography: Last Hustle in Brooklyn (1977, short); Black College: The Talented Tenth (1978, short) screenplay; The Answer (1980, short); Sarah (1981, short); Joe's Bed-Stuy Barbershop: We Cut Heads (1983); She's Gotta Have It (1986) also actor; School Daze (1988) also actor; Do the Right Thing (1989) also actor; Mo' Better Blues (1990) also actor; Jungle Fever (1991) also actor; Malcolm X (1992) also actor; Crooklyn (1994) also actor; Drop Squad (1994) ep, actor; Hoop Dreams (1994) cameo appearance; New Jersey Drive (1995) ep; Tales from the Hood (1995) ep; Clockers (1995) also actor.

Honors: Academy Award nomination for Best Screenplay (*Do the Right Thing*); Student Academy Award (*Joe's Bed-Stuy Barbershop: We Cut Heads*); Los Angeles Film Critics Awards for Best Picture and Director (*Do the Right Thing*) and Best New Director Award (*She's Gotta Have It*); Independent Spirit Award for Best First Feature (*She's Gotta Have It*); Cannes Film Festival Prix de Jeunesse (*She's Gotta Have It*).

Selected bibliography

Lee, Spike. *Spike Lee's Gotta Have It*. New York: Simon and Schuster, 1987.
Lee, Spike, and Ralph Wiley. *By Any Means Necessary: The Trials and Tribulations of Making Malcolm X*. New York: Hyperion, 1992.
Lee, Spike, and David Lee. *Five for Five: The Films of Spike Lee*. New York: Stewart, Tabori, and Chang, 1991.

LEIGH, JENNIFER JASON. Born February 5, 1962, in Los Angeles; actor. Daughter of actor Vic Morrow and screenwriter Barbara Turner. Tense, dynamic presence who usually takes roles that probe the dark, often sexual sides of traumatized, abandoned women on the verge of self-discovery. At a time when mimicry passes for acting in Hollywood, Leigh has emerged as a truly gifted and intelligent actor who digs deep inside for emotionally raw, gut-wrenching performances. She first grabbed attention with an exceptionally real performance in *Fast Times at Ridgemont High* as the innocent Stacy, a young woman whose first sexual experience (perfectly believable in its awkwardness) leads to a pregnancy and an abortion. Leigh continued to push the sexual envelope with a harsh rape scene in Paul Verhoeven's lusty medieval adventure *Flesh + Blood*; as the girlish prostitute Teensy in the otherwise undistinguished *The Men's Club*; as a woman drawn into a den of sadomasochism and perversion in *Heart of Midnight*; as a call girl turned housewife in *Miami Blues*; and as the troubled lowlife whore Tralala, who is gang-raped in *Last Exit to Brooklyn*. Her first big Hollywood role came in *Backdraft*, and, not coincidentally, it's her least interesting character. With *Rush* and *Single White Female*, Leigh finally began to get the attention she deserved all along, next appearing as the housewife who works as a phone-sex operator in Robert Altman's *Short Cuts*. The Coen brothers' romantic comedy *The Hudsucker Proxy*, as the fast-talking Rosalind Russell-type newspaper reporter, gave Leigh a chance to show her charming, comedic side. More bravura performances followed—the legendary Dorothy Parker in Alan Rudolph's *Mrs. Parker and the Vicious Circle*; the troubled, sexually abused daughter in *Dolores Claiborne*; and the less talented, but more ambitious, sister of a popular singer/songwriter in *Georgia*, a project she co-produced with her mother, Barbara Turner.

Filmography: Eyes of a Stranger (1980); Angel City (1980, tvm); Fast Times at Ridgemont High (1982); Wrong Is Right (1982); Easy Money (1983); Grandview, U.S.A. (1984); Flesh + Blood (1985); The Hitcher (1986); The Men's Club (1986); Under Cover (1987); Sister, Sister (1988); Heart of Midnight (1988); The Big Picture (1989); Miami Blues (1990); Last Exit to Brooklyn (1990); Backdraft (1990); Crooked Hearts (1991); Rush (1991); Single White Female (1992); Short Cuts (1993); The Hudsucker Proxy (1994); Mrs. Parker and the Vicious Circle (1994); Dolores Claiborne (1995); Georgia (1995) also producer.

Honors: New York Film Critics Circle Awards for Best Actress (*Georgia*) and Best Supporting Actress (*Miami Blues*, *Last Exit to Brooklyn*).

LEMMON, JACK. Born John Uhler Lemmon III February 8, 1925, in Boston; actor, director. Son Chris is an actor. Coming to prominence in the supporting role of Ensign Pulver in John Ford's *Mister Roberts*, establishing himself as a comic lead in the Billy Wilder films *Some Like It Hot* and *The Apartment* and then as a dramatic performer in Blake Edwards' *Days of Wine and Roses*, Lemmon has mastered a jittery, nervous, fraught persona in a film career that shows no signs of decelerating. He is still probably best known for his seven pairings with Walter Matthau (eight, if one counts *JFK*), which began in 1966's *The Fortune Cookie*, their first of three Billy Wilder films together (*The Front Page* and *Buddy Buddy* followed). The comic duo hit paydirt with their second picture,

Neil Simon and Gene Saks' *The Odd Couple*, starring Lemmon as neat-freak Felix Ungar and Matthau as the slobbish Oscar Madison. Lemmon's dramatic work has been especially effective (and least mannered) when cast as a despairing man faced with a sense of emotional loss—the failed garment manufacturer in *Save the Tiger*, the disillusioned nuclear plant engineer in *The China Syndrome*, the suffering father in *Missing*, the desperate insurance salesman in *Glengarry Glen Ross*, and the self-centered grandfather in *Short Cuts*. In the mid-1990s, he reteamed with Matthau for *Grumpy Old Men* and its sequel, a pair of pedestrian comedies that, nonetheless, have performed amazingly well at the customarily ageist box office.

Filmography of key pre-1965 films: Mister Roberts (1955), Some Like It Hot (1959), The Apartment (1960); Days of Wine and Roses (1962); Irma La Douce (1963).

Filmography since 1965: How to Murder Your Wife (1965), The Great Race (1965); The Fortune Cookie (1966); Luv (1967); The Odd Couple (1968); There Comes a Day (1968, short); The April Fools (1969); The Out-of-Towners (1970); Kotch (1971) director; Avanti! (1972); The War between Men and Women (1973); Save the Tiger (1973); The Front Page (1974); The Prisoner of Second Avenue (1974); Alex and the Gypsy (1976); Airport 77 (1977); The China Syndrome (1979); Tribute (1980); Buddy Buddy (1981); Missing (1982); Mass Appeal (1984); Macaroni (1985); That's Life! (1986); Dad (1989); JFK (1991); The Player (1992); Glengarry Glen Ross (1992); Grumpy Old Men (1993); Short Cuts (1993); A Life in the Theater (1994, ctvm); Grumpier Old Men (1995).

Honors: Academy Award for Best Actor (*Save the Tiger*) and Supporting Actor (*Mister Roberts*); Academy Award nominations for Best Actor (*Some Like It Hot*, *The Apartment*, *Days of Wine and Roses*, *The China Syndrome*, *Tribute*, *Missing*); Cannes Film Festival Awards for Best Actor (*The China Syndrome*, *Missing*); Berlin Film Festival Awards for Best Actor (*Tribute*) and Lifetime Achievement Award (1996); Venice Film Festival Award for Best Actor (*Glengarry Glen Ross*); inducted into Television Hall of Fame (1987); AFI Life Achievement Award (1988).

Selected bibliography

Baltake, Joe. *Jack Lemmon: His Films and Career*. New York: Citadel Press, 1986.

LENNY (1974), biopic. Directed by Bob Fosse; screenplay by Julian Barry (based on his play); produced by Marvin Worth; photographed by Bruce Surtees (b&w); edited by Alan Heim; music by Miles Davis; released by United Artists; 111 minutes. *Cast*: Dustin Hoffman, Valerie Perrine, Jan Miner, Stanley Beck.

An uncompromising vision of an equally uncompromising comic talent, this black-and-white biography of Lenny Bruce helps give a sense of the man, the entertainer, and the champion of free speech. A true genius, Bruce was brave enough to hold a mirror up to American society to expose its hypocrisy and its humanity. In Fosse's kaleidoscopic look at Bruce's life, we see his relationship with his stripper/drug addict wife, Honey (Perrine), and his mother (Miner), his heroin abuse, his infidelities, his arrests and obscenity charges, and the seemingly endless courtroom battles that depleted his savings. But Fosse, contending, as he later did in *All That Jazz*, that one's life and art cannot be split, is not interested in a straightforward biography; he intercuts the narrative with bits of Bruce's club act and with interviews with Honey, his manager (Beck), and his mother. Although much has been said about how Lenny Bruce's style and language have become accepted over time, there remain a brutal honesty and candor to his routines (specifically, the racial bits) that will never fail to shock. Perrine as Honey gives a fearless performance that lets it all hang out emotionally and physically, though Hoffman, as spectacular as he is in the role, is too warm and sympathetic an actor to adequately capture Bruce's danger.

Awards: Academy Award nominations for Best Picture, Director, Actor, Actress, Screenplay, Cinematography; New York Film Critics Circle Award for Best Supporting Actress (Perrine); Cannes Film Festival Award for Best Actress.

LEVINSON, BARRY. Born April 6, 1942, in Baltimore; director, screenwriter, producer, actor. With a strong background in television comedy writing, it is no surprise that Levinson entered directing via screenwriting, receiving notice with his Oscar-nominated script for *And Justice for All*. His ear for dialogue and his ability to write for ensembles were apparent in his directing debut, *Diner*. Set in Baltimore in the 1950s, the film features a group of young guys whose regular evenings at the local eatery are threatened by such adult responsibilities as marriage. His inevitable blockbuster came a few years later with *Rain Man*, a high-profile Hollywood project that numerous directors had tried to tackle without success. Eliciting superb performances from leads Tom Cruise and Dustin Hoffman, Levinson received the Academy Award for his direction. His subsequent films, however, lack the soul of *Diner* and *Rain Man* and have become increasingly glossy and passionless, culminating in *Disclosure*, the politically misguided adaptation of Michael Crichton's novel about a case of reverse sex discrimination. Interestingly, his most exciting work in the 1990s has come on television with his stylistically coarse, critically acclaimed cop show "Homicide: Life on the Street," produced by his own Baltimore Pictures.

Filmography as director: Diner (1982) also screenplay; The Natural (1984); Young Sherlock Holmes (1985); Tin Men (1987) also screenplay; Good Morning, Vietnam (1987); Rain Man (1988) also actor; Avalon (1990) also producer, screenplay; Bugsy (1991) also producer; Toys (1992) also producer; Jimmy Hollywood (1994) also producer, screenplay; Disclosure (1994) also producer.

Additional credits: The Internecine Project (1974) screenplay; Street Girls (1974) screenplay; Silent Movie (1976) screenplay, actor; High Anxiety (1977) screenplay, actor; And Justice for All (1979) screenplay; Inside Moves (1980) screenplay; History of the World Part I (1981) actor; Best Friends (1982) screenplay; Unfaithfully Yours (1983) screenplay; "Homicide: Life on the Street" (1993– , tvs) ep, director; Quiz Show (1994) actor.

Honors: Academy Award for Best Director (*Rain Man*); Academy Award nominations for Best Screenplay (*And Justice for All, Diner*), Picture (*Bugsy*), and Director (*Bugsy*); Los Angeles Film Critics Award for Best Picture and Director (*Bugsy*); DGA Award (*Rain Man*); WGA Award (*Avalon*); Emmy Awards for Best Writer ("The Carol Burnett Show," 1973, 1974), and Director ("Homicide: Life on the Street" 1992).

LIOTTA, RAY. Born December 18, 1955, in Newark, New Jersey; actor. Immensely talented actor who spent three years as Joey Perrini on the daytime soap "Another World" before landing a key role in Jonathan Demme's *Something Wild* as the menacing and volatile ex-con Ray Sinclair. Instead of allowing himself to be typecast as a heavy, Liotta turned around and appeared as the caring brother of a retarded man in *Dominick and Eugene* and as Shoeless Joe Jackson in *Field of Dreams*. He then got the role of a lifetime when Martin Scorsese cast him in *GoodFellas* as Henry Hill, a lower-rung gangster whose life is destroyed by crime and drugs before he is reborn, both spiritually and legally, in the Witness Protection Program. He was also exceptionally good in the touching, but little seen, *Corrina, Corrina* as the widowed father of an inquisitive young girl in 1950s middle America.

Filmography: The Lonely Lady (1983); Something Wild (1986); Arena Brains (1987, short); Dominick and Eugene (1988); Field of Dreams (1989); GoodFellas (1990); "A Domestic Dilemma" episode of Women and Men II (1991, ctv); Article 99 (1992); Unlawful Entry (1992); No Escape (1994); Corrina, Corrina (1994); Operation Dumbo Drop (1995).

LITHGOW, JOHN. Born October 19, 1945, in Rochester, New York; actor. Trained theatrically at Harvard and London's LAMDA, Lithgow's strong background helped him to become one of the most sought-after character actors of the early 1980s. Despite two Oscar nominations and a memorable role as the frightened plane passenger in the "Nightmare at 20,000 Feet" episode of *Twilight Zone—The Movie*, his subsequent films have been less interesting—*Harry and the Hendersons* was a big-budget family comedy; Brian DePalma's *Raising Cain* never found an audience or a critical following; his role as the evil menace in the Sylvester Stallone vehicle *Cliffhanger* was a gross parody; and many of his films (like *A Good Man in Africa* or *Silent Fall*) went completely unseen. In early 1996 he embarked upon a new journey into television with the popular sitcom "Third Rock from the Sun."

Filmography: Dealing: Or the Berkeley-to-Boston Forty-Brick Lost Bag Blues (1972); Obsession (1976); The Big Fix (1978); All That Jazz (1979); Rich Kids (1979); Blow Out (1981); I'm Dancing As Fast As I Can (1981); The World according to Garp (1982); Terms of Endearment (1983); Twilight Zone—The Movie (1983); The Day After (1983, tvm); 2010 (1984); The Adventures of Buckaroo Bonzai: Across the 8th Dimension (1984); Footloose (1984); Santa Claus: The Movie (1985); The Manhattan Project (1986); Mesmerized (1986); Harry and the Hendersons (1987); Distant Thunder (1988); Out Cold (1989); Memphis Belle (1990); L.A. Story (1991); At Play in the Fields of the Lord (1991); Ricochet (1991); Raising Cain (1992); The Wrong Man (1993); Love, Cheat and Steal (1993); The Pelican Brief (1993); Cliffhanger (1993); A Good Man in Africa (1994); Silent Fall (1994); Princess Caraboo (1994); "You, Murderer" episode of "Tales from the Crypt" (1995, ctv).

Honors: Academy Award nominations for Best Supporting Actor (*The World according to Garp, Terms of Endearment*); Tony Award for Best Supporting Actor (*The Changing Room* 1973).

LONG GOODBYE, THE (1973), crime drama. Directed by Robert Altman; screenplay by Leigh Brackett (from the novel by Raymond Chandler); produced by Jerry Bick, executive-produced by Elliott Kastner; photographed by Vilmos Zsigmond; edited by Lou Lombardo; music by John Williams, song "The Long Goodbye" by Williams and Johnny Mercer; released by United Artists; 111 minutes. *Cast*: Elliott Gould, Nina van Pallandt, Sterling Hayden, Mark Rydell, Henry Gibson, David Arkin, Jim Bouton, Jo Ann Brody, Ken Sansom, Arnold Schwarzenegger, David Carradine.

After demythologizing the western in *McCabe and Mrs. Miller*, Altman reshaped the detective genre with similar revisionist enthusiasm in this rendering of Raymond Chandler's private eye Philip Marlowe. Where the Marlowes of Humphrey Bogart and Robert Montgomery were classy, intelligent, well-dressed movie detectives, Gould's Marlowe is a sloppy loner who loves his cat, habitually talks to himself, and lives next door to a sect of half-naked, New Age women. Still, he retains the spirit of Marlowe's everyman heroism as he investigates first the apparent suicide of his friend Terry Lennox (Bouton), whose wife has just been murdered, and then the disappearance of hard-drinking writer Roger Wade (Hayden), who was having an affair with Terry's wife. By refusing to cooperate with the police or with Terry's sadistic gangster employer Marty Augustine (Rydell), Marlowe himself becomes a dupe in his quest for the truth—a quest that is hampered by the manipulations of Wade's beautiful, blond wife, Eileen (van Pallandt). Opening and closing the film with "Hooray for Hollywood," Altman is clear in his efforts to remind the viewer that they are watching a movie; he is determined to undercut the mythology of Philip Marlowe by showing us through numerous Hollywood references (like the movie star impressions of Malibu Colony gatekeeper Sansom) that the private eye of Hollywood legend doesn't exist . . . and never did. "People still want to believe that Galahad is alive and well in Los Angeles" (Pauline Kael, *The New Yorker*, October 22, 1973).

LONGEST YARD, THE (1974), sports/prison. Directed by Robert Aldrich; screenplay by Tracy Keenan Wynn (from a story by Albert S. Ruddy); produced by Ruddy; photographed by Joseph Biroc; music by Frank DeVol; released by Paramount; 121 minutes. *Cast*: Burt Reynolds, Edward Albert, Ed Lauter, Michael Conrad, Jim Hampton, Bernadette Peters, Richard Kiel, Pepper Martin, Ray Nitschke.

One of Robert Aldrich's best studies of what it means to be an American, this crowd-pleaser stars Burt Reynolds (in the midst of his superstardom) as Paul Crewe, a former all-pro National Football League quarterback who committed the ultimate betrayal of his fans by shaving points in a game. Bounced from the league, he is a ruined man who spends years as a stud for a wealthy socialite, only to realize that he is again being bought. That doesn't change when he ends up doing 2 to 5 in prison for stealing his girlfriend's Citroen and leading the police on a wild car chase (directed by Hal Needham, a precursor to his and Reynolds' *Smokey and the Bandit*). On the inside he is recruited by Warden Hazen (Albert) to organize a team of inmates in a gridiron game against the guards—a titan, life-and-death, blood-and-guts battle of honor that unites the otherwise cynical and detached prison population. As he did with *The Dirty Dozen*, Aldrich twists our perception of heroism and makes us question which team is more American—the anarchic collection of killers and rapists who share a distrust of authority and oppression or the gun-toting representatives of law and order who abuse their power whenever they're given a chance. Aldrich's strength is in keeping politics second to entertainment; the final third of the movie is an all-out ride—an invigorating, funny, bone-crushing football game that has almost nothing to do with sports and everything to do with the overall corruption of American values from Vietnam to the White House and everyplace in between.

LONGTIME COMPANION (1990), drama. Directed by Norman Rene; screenplay by Craig Lucas; produced by Stan Wlodkowski; photographed by Tony Jannelli; edited by Katherine Wenning; music by Lia Vollack; released by the Samuel Goldwyn Company; 96 minutes. *Cast*: Bruce Davison, Campbell Scott, Stephen Caffrey, Mark Lamos, Patrick Cassidy, John Dossett, Mary-Louise Parker, Dermot Mulroney.

Despite the magnitude of AIDS, *Longtime Companion* remains just about the only major motion picture to deal with the specifics of the disease and its effect on the community of gay men. *Philadelphia*, a movie about a court case and one man's fear of homosexuality, doesn't come close, while the HBO movie *And the Band Played On* is about the search for a cure. This, however, is a compassionate and detailed story that begins on July 3, 1981, the day of the *New York Times*' first article on the disease. It centers on a group of six affluent, white New York gay men and their female friend as their hopes and dreams for the future turn bleak when the disease hits close to home. Over the next eight years, those who survive the disease are transformed (in varying degrees) from people who enjoyed a life of love, parties, and booming careers to routine funeralgoers, hospital volunteers, and activists. An inevitably sad movie, it shies away from manipulation but refuses to shy away from the symptoms that ravage an AIDS victim—the dementia that destroys a once-sharp mind, the discovery of a swollen lymph node, the changing of a grown man's diaper. Adapted by Craig Lucas from his play, the film lacks a distinct visual style, but somehow that doesn't matter; the strength is in the story, and it's better that nothing gets in the way of the emotions and performances, especially Davison as the almost saintly David and Scott as the reluctant and fearful Willy. In 1996, director Norman Rene died from complications due to AIDS.

Award: New York Film Critics Circle Award for Best Supporting Actor (Davison).

LOST IN AMERICA (1985), comedy. Directed and cowritten by Albert Brooks; screenplay with Monica Johnson; produced by Marty Katz; photographed by

Eric Saarinen; edited by David Finfer; music by Arthur B. Rubinstein; released by Warner Bros.; 91 minutes. *Cast*: Albert Brooks, Julie Hagerty, Garry Marshall, Michael Green, Tom Tarpey, Raynold Gideon.

A masterful exorcism of the demons that haunted Reagan-era yuppies, this hysterical comedy about the American dream stars Brooks as David Howard, an eight-year veteran of a top Los Angeles advertising firm who goes ballistic after being passed over for the senior vice president position. Suddenly the comfortable life he and wife, Linda (Hagerty), had mapped out is gone—no new house, no tennis courts, no Mercedes, and no Mercedes leather. After he gets axed and persuades Linda to quit her job, the pair pocket their $145,000 nest egg and head on down the highway in their new Winnebago. With Steppenwolf's "Born to Be Wild" blaring, David and Linda struggle to recapture the Easy Rider spirit of their youth. Instead, Linda loses their nest egg in Vegas (in a frenzied state she repeatedly bets "22" at the roulette wheel), and the pair are reduced to menial labor; David becomes a crossing guard, Linda becomes an assistant manager at a Der Wienerschnitzel fast-food joint. Having previously cast a critical eye on the middle-class family in *Real Life* and relationships in *Modern Romance*, Brooks perceptively piggybacks them in this film to make a point about today's world—what the Reagan-era professionals want (freedom) and what they need (security) are mutually exclusive objectives. Not only is the script a perfect combination of cynicism and optimism, but the performances are remarkable; Hagerty is a joy as the long-repressed wife, Brooks is in top form during his apoplectic reactions to the hellish detour his life has taken, and Garry Marshall is blessedly obtuse as the casino head who fails to see why he should return the nest egg that Linda lost. When everything is added up, *Lost in America* is simply *the* best and most relevant comedy of the 1980s.

LOVE STORY (1970), romance/drama. Directed by Arthur Hiller; screenplay by Erich Segal (based on his novel); produced by Howard G. Minsky; photographed by Dick Kratina; edited by Robert C. Jones; music by Francis Lai, song "Theme from Love Story" by Andy Williams; released by Paramount; 99 minutes. *Cast*: Ali MacGraw, Ryan O'Neal, Ray Milland, Katherine Balfour, John Marley, Tommy Lee Jones.

A phenomenally popular picture based on Erich Segal's best-seller that transcended the soap opera sensibility of the book and, under Arthur Hiller's direction, became a moving, albeit treacly, story of two people in love who believe that "love means never having to say you're sorry." Tragedy then strikes the blissful pair when the young woman learns she has terminal cancer. Carrying the film are the fresh, all-American performances of former "Peyton Place" star Ryan O'Neal and cover girl Ali MacGraw, which turned both of them into overnight sensations. Not surprisingly, the romance of Jenny and Oliver touched the hearts of millions of filmgoers and served as a therapeutic counterpoint to the angst-ridden psychedelia of the majority of films of the period. Francis Lai's love theme became just as popular as the film itself.

Awards: Academy Award for Best Score; Academy Award nominations for Best Picture, Actor, Actress, Director, Supporting Actor (Marley), Adapted Screenplay, and Sound.

LOWE, ROB. Born March 17, 1964, in Virginia; actor. Young adult star whose college boy preppiness was perfect for such "brat pack" films as *St. Elmo's Fire* and *About Last Night*. Although it went unseen by most of Lowe's fans, his Cary Grant-inspired turn in Peter Bogdanovich's screwball comedy *Illegally Yours* is the most effective use of his comic talents. Lowe has since done little of interest on the big screen, though he did become notorious for some sexual rompings captured on videotape during the 1988 Democratic Convention in Atlanta; he and the tape became the subject of every tabloid journal and news-magazine. His next most notorious moment came in a bizarre duet with Snow White that opened the 1989 Academy Awards telecast.

Filmography: Class (1983); The Outsiders (1983); The Hotel New Hampshire (1984); Oxford Blues (1984); St. Elmo's Fire (1985); About Last Night (1986); Youngblood (1986); Square Dance (1987); Illegally Yours (1988); Masquerade (1988); Bad Influence (1990); Wayne's World (1992); Frank and Jesse (1995, ctvm); First Degree (1995); Tommy Boy (1995).

LUCAS, GEORGE. Born May 14, 1944, in Modesto, California; director, screen-writer, producer. The greatest mythmaker in American film since Walt Disney, Lucas, with *American Graffiti* and *Star Wars*, has deeply affected a generation of anguishing Americans by offering an escape to the bleakness of the 1970s. A graduate of the University of Southern California film school, he began a friendship with Francis Ford Coppola after receiving a scholarship to intern on Coppola's *Finian's Rainbow*. With financial backing from Coppola, he expanded his twenty-minute student sci-fi film *THX 1138* into a full-length feature that attracted a small cult following. A visually inventive tale of an Orwellian future, the film is notable as an early indicator of Lucas' path. Rather than be pigeonholed, he turned not to 1984 but to 1962 for inspiration with his next film, *American Graffiti*. Drawing on his days as a teenage hot-rodder and fan of rock and roll (*The Emperor* is an avant-garde documentary about a Wolfman Jack-like deejay), the film is a nostalgic ride backward into a simpler time with a medley of classic cars and golden oldies. Produced by Coppola, the film cost $750,000 and, to date, has grossed some $115 million. That, however, only primed the turnstiles for the coming success of *Star Wars*, a mythic, sci-fi mas-terpiece that has grossed over $320 million and returned much more than that in merchandising dollars. Unlike his counterparts Coppola and Steven Spielberg, Lucas then stopped directing. As a producer, he's delivered five more block-busters (the second and third entries in the Star Wars trilogy and Spielberg's three Indiana Jones blockbusters), a pair of daring personal films (Coppola's *Tucker: The Man and His Dream* and Paul Schrader's *Mishima: A Life in Four Chapters*), and a couple of big-budget duds (*Howard the Duck* and *Radioland Murders*). He has also teamed with such industry giants as Muppet master Jim

Henson (the underrated *Labyrinth*) and Michael Jackson (*Captain Eo*). He has focused his entrepreneurial vision on his Industrial Light and Magic, a visual effects company that has been at the forefront of the industry's state-of-the-art technological advances, and Skywalker Ranch, an idyllic Marin County, California, production facility. In 1996, Lucas announced that he would produce another Star Wars trilogy, directing at least one of the films himself. "*Star Wars* and the Lucas empire raise the worry that brilliant film students know too little about life, and are then protected from learning more by their outlandish success (David Thomson, *A Biographical Dictionary of Film*).

Filmography as director: Look at Life (1965, short); Freiheit (1965); THX 1138 (1965, short version); 4 EB (1965, short); Herbie (1966); 1:42:08: A Man and His Car (1966, short); Anyone Lived in a Pretty How Town (1967, short); 6–18–67 (1967, short); The Emperor (1967, documentary short); Marcello, I'm So Bored (1967, short); The Electronic Labyrinth (1968); THX 1138 (1971); American Graffiti (1973) also screenplay; Star Wars (1977) also screenplay.

Filmography as executive producer: Corvette Summer (1978): More American Graffiti (1979); The Empire Strikes Back (1980) also story; Kagemusha (1980) international version; Raiders of the Lost Ark (1981); Body Heat (1981) [uncredited]; Return of the Jedi (1983) also story; Twice upon a Time (1983); Indiana Jones and the Temple of Doom (1984); Mishima: A Life in Four Chapters (1985); Labyrinth (1986); Captain Eo (1986, music short); Howard the Duck (1986); Willow (1988) also story; Tucker: The Man and His Dream (1988); The Land before Time (1988); Powaqqatsi (1988); Indiana Jones and the Last Crusade (1989) also story; "The Young Indiana Jones Chronicles" (1992–1993, tvs); Radioland Murders (1994) producer.

Honors: Academy Award nominations for Best Director and Screenplay (*American Graffiti, Star Wars*); recipient of the 1991 Irving G. Thalberg Award; included in the Library of Congress' National Film Registry (*Star Wars, American Graffiti*).

Selected bibliography

Lucas, George. *Star Wars: From the Adventures of Luke Skywalker*. New York: Ballantine, 1986.

LUMET, SIDNEY. Born June 25, 1924, in Philadelphia; director, actor. A child of the stage with a background in Yiddish theater (debuting at age four), Broadway, radio, and, eventually, television, Lumet developed into one of the foremost directors of American film from the 1950s through the mid-1980s. From his auspicious debut, *12 Angry Men*, one can see all of his talents—he's a masterful director of actors who, when given the proper material, can assemble a blistering movie. Consequently, he is only as good as his source material (he's only twice written his own scripts, and both were adaptations) and his cast, as in *The Fugitive Kind* (Tennessee Williams, Marlon Brando, Anna Magnani) or *Long Day's Journey into Night* (Eugene O'Neill, Katherine Hepburn, Ralph Richardson). Driven by a social conscience, many of his best films also address urban themes of corruption and racism, such as *The Pawnbroker*, a gritty and intense drama that is carried by a bravura performance from Rod Steiger and the flashy editing of Ralph Rosenblum. His three best films of the 1970s—*Serpico*, *Dog Day Afternoon*, and *Network*—combine all of these elements: resourceful actors (Al Pacino, John Cazale, William Holden, Peter Finch), themes of corruption and injustice, and intensely dramatic scripts (Waldo Salt, Frank Pierson, Paddy Chayefsky, respectively). A durable director, Lumet has shown no signs of slowing down, and the best of his post-1980 films—*Prince of the City*, *The Verdict*, and *Power*—share similar traits with his earlier masterworks; the remainder of recent films, however, are not in the same league. "It is ironic that, as a New Yorker rejecting Hollywood, he should have been hailed as an innovator in American cinema, for his films remain locked into a tv-cum-theatrical style for staging conflicts and setting problems" (Richard Combs, *Cinema: A Critical Dictionary*).

Filmography of key pre-1965 films: Twelve Angry Men (1957); The Fugitive Kind (1960); Long Day's Journey into Night (1962); Fail Safe (1964).

Filmography since 1965: The Pawnbroker (1965); The Hill (1965); The Group (1965); The Deadly Affair (1967) also producer; Bye Bye Braverman (1968) also producer; The Sea Gull (1968) also producer; The Appointment (1969); Last of the Mobile Hot-Shots (1970) also producer; King: A Filmed Record . . . Montgomery to Memphis (1970, documentary) codirector of connecting sequences; The Anderson Tapes (1971); Child's Play (1972); The Offense (1973); Serpico (1973); Lovin' Molly (1974); Murder on the Orient Express (1974); Dog Day Afternoon (1975); Network (1976); Equus (1977); The Wiz (1978); Just Tell Me What You Want (1980) also producer; Prince of the City (1981) also screenplay; Deathtrap (1982); The Verdict (1982); Daniel (1983) also ep; Garbo Talks (1984); Power (1986); The Morning After (1986); Running on Empty (1988); Family Business (1989); Q&A (1990) also screenplay; A Stranger among Us (1992).

Honors: Academy Award nominations for Best Director (*Twelve Angry Men*, *Dog Day Afternoon*, *Network*, *The Verdict*); Los Angeles Film Critics Awards for Best Director (*Dog Day Afternoon*, *Network*); New York Film Critics Circle Award for Best Director (*Prince of the City*); DGA D. W. Griffith Award (1993).

Selected bibliography

Bowles, Stephen. *Sidney Lumet: A Guide to References and Resources*. Boston: G. K. Hall, 1979.
Lumet, Sidney. *Making Movies*. New York: Alfred A. Knopf, 1995.

LYNCH, DAVID. Born January 20, 1946, in Missoula, Montana; director, actor. Daughter Jennifer Chambers Lynch is a director (*Boxing Helena*). Emerging from a background in painting, Lynch is Hollywood's most unlikely filmmaker—a creator of dreams and alternative realities, abstractions and textures, deformity and viscera, and mystery and darkness. Despite a relatively meager output of films—only six in seventeen years (and one of those an offshoot of his television work)—Lynch's twisted vision has been carved into the minds of moviegoers on the strength of his visual imagery. After making a couple of short films and attending the American Film Institute's Center for Advanced

Film Studies, Lynch completed *Eraserhead*, the bizarre tale of a man living with his deformed baby in an industrial wasteland. Featuring the work of two frequent Lynch collaborators—the crisp black-and-white photography of Frederick Elmes and the aural constructions of soundman Alan Splet—the film eventually became a *success de scandale*. In an odd embrace by Hollywood, the perceptive Mel Brooks offered Lynch the job of directing *The Elephant Man*, the Victorian-era story of the hideously deformed, but internally pure, John Merrick. Eight Oscar nominations followed, and so did an offer from the less perceptive Dino DiLaurentiis to direct the $60 million sci-fi adaptation of Frank Herbert's opus *Dune*, a monumental failure on every level. Lynch, however, returned with *Blue Velvet*, a strange film noir that continues the explorations begun in *Eraserhead*. Since then, Lynch's film work has been both sparse and subpar—his *Wild at Heart* took the top prize at the Cannes Film Festival, but its excessive violence turned off most viewers, while his *Twin Peaks: Fire Walk with Me* seemed a lazy way of squeezing a theatrical release out of his television series. "Twin Peaks," ABC-television's gutsy foray into experimental drama, has proven to be Lynch's chief contribution to popular culture. Producing the series and directing numerous episodes, Lynch managed to bring his vision of a dark and troubled America directly into America's living rooms. While several film projects such as *Ronnie Rocket* and *One Saliva Bubble* have been rumored but have never materialized, Lynch has been branching out into music (producing an album by singer Julie Cruse and creating the "Industrial Symphony #1" at the Brooklyn Academy of Music in 1991), photography, installations, and a return to painting. "All my films are about trying to find love in hell" (quoted by Greg Olson in *Film Comment*, May–June 1993).

Filmography as director: The Alphabet (1970, short); The Grandmother (1972, short); Eraserhead (1978); The Elephant Man (1980); Dune (1984); Blue Velvet (1986); Wild at Heart (1990); Twin Peaks: Fire Walk with Me (1992).

Additional credits: Heart Beat (1978) actor; Zelly and Me (1988) actor; "Twin Peaks" (1990–1991, tvs) producer, director, actor; "American Chronicles" (1990, tvs) producer; The Cabinet of Dr. Ramirez (1991) ep; "On the Air" (1992, tvs) creator; "Blackout" and "Tricks" episodes of Hotel Room (1993, ctvm) director, creator; Nadja (1994) ep, actor; Crumb (1995) presenter.

Honors: Academy Award nominations for Best Director (*The Elephant Man, Blue Velvet*); Los Angeles Film Critics Award for Best Director (*Blue Velvet*); New York Film Critics Circle Award for Best Director (*Blue Velvet*); Cannes Film Festival Palme d'Or (*Wild at Heart*).

M

M*A*S*H (1970), war comedy. Directed by Robert Altman; screenplay by Ring Lardner, Jr. (from the novel by Richard Hooker); produced by Ingo Preminger; photographed by Harold E. Stine; edited by Danford B. Greene; music by Johnny Mandel, song "Suicide Is Painless" by Mandel with lyrics by Mike Altman; released by 20th Century Fox; 116 minutes. *Cast*: Donald Sutherland, Elliott Gould, Tom Skerritt, Sally Kellerman, Robert Duvall, Jo Ann Pflug, Rene Auberjonois, Gary Burghoff, Roger Bowen, Fred Williamson, John Schuck, Bud Cort.

Robert Altman's uproarious and vulgar box office smash about war and the human condition stars Donald Sutherland and Elliott Gould as two military surgeons—Captain "Hawkeye" Pierce and Captain "Trapper" John McIntyre—who struggle to keep their sanity in the 4077th Mobile Army Surgical Hospital during the Korean War. Unlike any war comedy that came before (or after), *M*A*S*H* is a carnival of irreverence as Hawkeye and Trapper John wage their own personal battle with the "military clowns" (like Duvall's Major Frank Burns) who fail to accept the insanity of the war. Excellent surgeons who perform their jobs with extreme practicality (to save time they make bigger stitches on enlisted men than on officers; they politely reprimand the chaplain for administering last rites to a dead man when a wounded man needs care), Hawkeye and Trapper John survive by giving their all to their medical profession as well as their golf game, their martinis, their womanizing, and their football playing. They make no false distinctions between saving others' lives and saving their own. Altman fills the 4077th with a colorful collection of supporting characters, including nurse Margaret "Hot Lips" Houlihan (Kellerman), gentle chaplain Father "Dago Red" Mulcahy (Auberjonois), dentist Walt "the Painless Pole" Waldowski (Schuck), football star "Spearchucker" Jones (Williamson), and

Corporal "Radar" O'Reilly (Burghoff). While most of the characters went on to the sanitized television sitcom, only Gary Burghoff followed the 4077th to the small screen. In his book *Robert Altman*, Gerald Plecki notes a similarity to the zaniness of the Marx Brothers: "The attitude toward war is nearly identical in *M*A*S*H* and *Duck Soup*: Korea is the same 'Land of the Spree and Home of the Knave' for the surgeons that Freedonia is for Rufus T. Firefly."

Awards: Academy Award for Best Screenplay; Academy Award nominations for Best Picture, Director, Supporting Actress (Kellerman), Editing; WGA Award; Cannes Film Festival Palme d'Or.

MACGRAW, ALI. Born Alice McGraw April 1, 1938, in Pound Ridge, New York; actor. Formerly married to producer Robert Evans and actor Steve McQueen. Son Josh is an actor and director. A Wellesley College art history major who began climbing the ranks of the fashion world in 1960, when she began as an editorial assistant for *Harper's Bazaar*. She worked as a photographer's assistant before ending up in front of the camera and, by 1967, becoming a top fashion model. With her Oscar-nominated performance as the terminally ill Jenny in 1970's *Love Story* and her marriage to Paramount production head Robert Evans, she instantly became one of the hottest names in Hollywood, embodying a certain all-American-girl quality. That image was erased when she starred opposite her next husband, Steve McQueen, in Sam Peckinpah's gritty action film *The Getaway*; their escape scene inside a waste-packed garbage truck is not the image audiences had come to expect from their love-struck Jenny. Her lengthy hiatus from the big screen was broken in 1978, when she reteamed with Peckinpah for his *Convoy*, and her few films since then have been entirely inconsequential.

Filmography: A Lovely Way to Die (1968); Goodbye, Columbus (1969); Love Story (1970); The Getaway (1972); Convoy (1978); Players (1979); Just Tell Me What You Want (1980); Natural Causes (1994).

Honor: Academy Award nomination for Best Actress (*Love Story*).

Selected bibliography

MacGraw, Ali. *Moving Pictures*. New York: Bantam, 1991.

MACLAINE, SHIRLEY. Born Shirley MacLean Beaty April 24, 1934, in Richmond, Virginia; actor. Brother is Warren Beatty. Talented dancer and actor who has gone from bubbly pixie to seasoned leading lady in her four decades of film appearances, a nearly unparalleled longevity for a woman in Hollywood. She was discovered by producer Hal Wallis and signed to an eight-year contract at Paramount when, as understudy, she fortuitously replaced Carol Haney in the 1954 Broadway production of *The Pajama Game*. She made her film debut in Alfred Hitchcock's delightful black comedy *The Trouble with Harry* and proceeded to amass three Oscar nominations over the next few years for her varying floozy roles in Vincente Minnelli's *Some Came Running* and Billy Wilder's *The*

Apartment and *Irma La Douce*. From the mid-1960s until the late 1970s, her roles became increasingly less interesting or important, with the exception of her vibrant dancing in Bob Fosse's *Sweet Charity* and her surprising turn as a nun, costarring with Clint Eastwood in *Two Mules for Sister Sara*. The 1970s saw her working in television (the ABC-television sitcom ''Shirley's World''), documentary production (*The Other Half of the Sky: A China Memoir*), and theater (the 1976 one-woman show *A Gypsy in My Soul*). Her second career in film commenced in 1977 with, appropriately, *The Turning Point*, bringing her a fourth Oscar nomination and followed a short while later by her exuberant performance in *Being There*. Her role as Aurora Greenway in *Terms of Endearment* (her best role since Fran Kubelik in *The Apartment*) earned MacLaine her first statuette from the Academy; it was a spectacular turn in which she played mother and friend to Debra Winger's Emma and lover to Jack Nicholson's roguish Garrett Breedlove, accounting for some of the most spirited and finely observed acting of her career. Her subsequent roles have been amusing, often prickly women of maturity—the firm piano teacher in *Madame Sousatzka*, town harpy Ouiser Boudreaux in *Steel Magnolias*, the crushing mother in *Postcards from the Edge*, the feisty widow in *Used People*, and the plucky First Lady in *Guarding Tess*. Despite her accomplishments she has become an object of ridicule due to her unorthodox belief that she has been frequently reincarnated. She's written a series of memoirs that expounded on her beliefs—*Don't Fall off the Mountain*, *You Can Get There from Here*, *Out on a Limb* (which was made into a television movie), *Dance While You Can*, and *My Lucky Stars*. ''The image that kept her out of the glamour category—closer to perky indominatrix than femme fatale—has been the latterday blessing of her career'' (Molly Haskell, *Film Comment*, May-June 1995).

Filmography of key pre-1965 films: The Trouble with Harry (1955); Some Came Running (1958); The Apartment (1960); Irma La Douce (1963).

Filmography since 1965: Gambit (1966); Woman Times Seven (1967); The Bliss of Mrs. Blossom (1968); Sweet Charity (1969); Two Mules for Sister Sara (1970); Desperate Characters (1971); ''Shirley's World'' (1971–1972, tvs); The Possession of Joel Delaney (1972); The Year of the Woman (1973); The Other Half of the Sky: A China Memoir (1974, documentary) director, ep, screenplay; Sois Belle et Tais-toi (1977, documentary); The Turning Point (1977); Being There (1979); A Change of Season (1980); Loving Couples (1980); Cannonball Run II (1983); Terms of Endearment (1983); Out on a Limb (1987, tvm); Madame Sousatzka (1988); Steel Magnolias (1989); Postcards from the Edge (1990); Waiting for the Light (1990); Defending Your Life (1991); Used People (1992); Wrestling Ernest Hemingway (1993); Guarding Tess (1994); The West Side Waltz (1995, tvm).

Honors: Academy Award for Best Actress (*Terms of Endearment*); Academy Award nominations for Best Actress (*Some Came Running, The Apartment, Irma la Douce, The Turning Point*) and Documentary (*The Other Half of the Sky: A China Memoir*); Los Angeles Film Critics Award for Best Actress (*Terms of Endearment*); Venice Film Festival Awards for Best Actress (*The Apartment, Madame Sousatzka*); Berlin Film Festival

Awards for Best Actress (*Ask Any Girl* 1959, *Desperate Characters*); Emmy Award for Outstanding Variety Special ("Gypsy in My Soul" 1975).

Selected bibliography

Denis, Christopher. *The Films of Shirley MacLaine*. New York: Citadel Press, 1982.
Spade, James. *Shirley and Warren*. New York: Macmillan, 1985.

MADIGAN (1968), police drama. Directed by Don Siegel; screenplay by Henri Simoun [Henry Rodman] and Abraham Polonsky (from the novel *The Commissioner* by Richard Dougherty); produced by Frank P. Rosenberg; photographed by Russell Metty; edited by Milton Shifman; music by Don Costa; released by Universal; 101 minutes. *Cast*: Richard Widmark, Henry Fonda, Harry Guardino, James Whitmore, Inger Stevens, Sheree North, Susan Clark, Michael Dunn, Steve Ihnat, Don Stroud.

One of the most morally ambiguous films in American cinema, this gritty cop drama cowritten by blacklisted screenwriter Abraham Polonsky gives us a glimpse of the moral morass of an urban police department. Based on the Richard Dougherty novel *The Commissioner* (a more accurate title), it is the first of Siegel's trio of rogue cop films (followed by *Coogan's Bluff* and *Dirty Harry*). Richard Widmark stars as Detective Danny Madigan, one of the most decorated cops on the force—a man who isn't afraid to bend the rules a bit in the name of justice and who'll even resort to nearly tipping a desk onto a receptionist in order to get her talking. When Madigan and his partner, Rocco Bonaro (Guardino), errantly let a psychopathic killer (Ihnat) escape, Police Commissioner Russell (Fonda) gives them seventy-two hours to recapture him, or else he comes down hard. The commissioner, a man who plays everything by the book, can't help but respect Madigan's results. As it turns out, the commissioner is in the midst of his own moral dilemma—he's in love with a married woman (Clark), and his best friend, Chief Inspector Charles Kane (Whitmore), has been caught on tape in a dirty deal (another gray area, as he was trying to protect his son's honor). By the finale—a kinetic and brutal shoot-out that takes place in the cramped quarters of a tiny apartment—it's not so easy for anyone to see the world in black and white anymore. Not even the audience.

MALICK, TERRENCE. Born November 30, 1943, in Ottawa, Illinois; director, screenwriter. A Harvard-educated former Rhodes scholar and Massachusetts Institute of Technology philosophy professor who later attended the American Film Institute, Malick occupies a place as one of the greatest filmmakers of the 1970s despite the fact that he has directed just two features in his career—1973's *Badlands* and 1978's *Days of Heaven*. His sadly meager output, however, can be overlooked by the fact that these two masterworks are both worth endlessly repeated viewings. Blessed with an uncommonly acute sense of beauty in both his composition and subject matter, he creates a mythical image of America that is romantic without being nostalgic, intelligent without falling to elitism. After the commercial failure of *Days of Heaven* Malick retreated from Hollywood and divided his time between Austin, Texas, and Europe; Paramount pictures, meanwhile, reportedly paid him a $1 million annual stipend. Throughout the 1980s and 1990s, the career of the enigmatic Malick (cinema's version of Thomas Pynchon) has consisted of only one screenplay for the largely unseen *Deadhead Miles* and numerous rumors about upcoming, but never realized, projects, including an adaptation of James Jones' *The Thin Red Line*, a World War II Guadalcanal film announced by Michael Medavoy's Phoenix Pictures in 1995.

Filmography: Lanton Mills (1970, short); Drive, He Said (1971) uncredited screenplay; Dirty Harry (1971) uncredited screenplay rewrite; Pocket Money (1972) screenplay; Badlands (1973) also producer, screenplay, actor; The Gravy Train (1974) screenplay; Days of Heaven (1978) also screenplay; Deadhead Miles (1982) screenplay.

Honors: New York Film Critics Circle Award for Best Director (*Days of Heaven*); Cannes Film Festival Director's Prize (*Days of Heaven*).

MALKOVICH, JOHN. Born December 9, 1953, in Benton, Illinois; actor. One of America's truly great actors, he brings to the table a combination of haughtiness and integrity that is consistently exciting. Although he lacks their conventional good looks, Malkovich, like Brando, Dean, and Newman before him, has a rare combination of masculinity and femininity that adds a sensual texture to his performances. Establishing himself first as a stage performer with Chicago's Steppenwolf Theater (joining in 1976), his early stage works include Sam Shepard's *Curse of the Starving Class* and *True West* and Lanford Wilson's *Balm in Gilead* and *Burn This* (which he directed in 1984). Although he received good notices in his early films, he didn't really attract attention as a screen performer until Steven Spielberg's *Empire of the Sun* and Stephen Frear's *Dangerous Liaisons* (as Choderlos de Laclos). He has since split his film career between mediocre commercial projects (*Making Mr. Right, Object of Beauty, Queens Logic, Jennifer 8, Alive*) and daring films by world-class directors (as Paul Bowles's alter ego Port Moresby in Bernardo Bertolucci's *The Sheltering Sky*, Woody Allen's *Shadows and Fog*, Portuguese master Manoel de Oliviera's *The Convent*, and a flamboyant anti-Brando performance as Kurtz in Nicolas Roeg's cable-television movie *Heart of Darkness*). Additional stage work includes *Death of a Salesman* with Dustin Hoffman (filmed for television by Volker Schlondorff) and Don DeLillo's *Libra* (1994). He has twice appeared in films directed by Steppenwolf founder Gary Sinise—a minor role in *Miles from Home* and as Lenny to Sinise's George in *Of Mice and Men*.

Filmography: Word of Honor (1981, tvm); American Dream (1981, tvm); The Killing Fields (1984); Places in the Heart (1984); Eleni (1985); Death of a Salesman (1985, tvm); Private Conversations (1985); Empire of the Sun (1987); The Glass Menagerie (1987); Making Mr. Right (1987); The Accidental Tourist (1988) ep only; Dangerous Liaisons (1988); Miles from Home (1988); The Sheltering Sky (1990); The Object of Beauty (1991); Queens Logic (1991); Jennifer 8 (1992); Of Mice and Men (1992); Shadows and Fog (1992); Alive (1993); In the Line of Fire (1993); Old Times (1993, ctvm); Heart of Darkness (1994, ctvm); The Convent (1995).

Honors: Academy Award nominations for Best Supporting Actor (*Places in the Heart*) and Best Picture (*The Accidental Tourist*); Emmy Award ("Death of a Salesman" 1985).

MAMET, DAVID. Born November 30, 1947, in Chicago; director, screenwriter, playwright. Married to actor Lindsay Crouse. One of the American theater's greatest and most controversial playwrights, Mamet has made a considerable mark in Hollywood as a screenwriter and, to a lesser degree, as a director. His directorial debut *House of Games* displayed a remarkable adaptability to the cinematic form, delivering razor-sharp dialogue, mysterious visual compositions, and a playfully labyrinthine tone. Unfortunately, his next two films—*Things Change* and *Oleanna*—have had diminishing returns. Screen adaptations of his plays include *About Last Night* (from *Sexual Perversity in Chicago*); *Glengarry Glen Ross*; the cable-television production *A Life in the Theater*; and *American Buffalo* (1996).

Filmography: The Postman Always Rings Twice (1981) screenplay; The Verdict (1982) screenplay; About Last Night (1986) from "Sexual Perversity in Chicago"; Black Widow (1987) actor only; House of Games (1987) screenplay, director; The Untouchables (1987) screenplay only; Things Change (1988) screenplay, director; We're No Angels (1989) screenplay only; Glengarry Glen Ross (1992) screenplay only; Hoffa (1992) screenplay only; Oleanna (1994), screenplay, director.

Honors: Academy Award nomination for Best Screenplay (*The Verdict*); Pulitzer Prize ("Glengarry Glen Ross" 1984).

Selected bibliography

Mamet, David. *On Directing Film*. London: Faber and Faber, 1992.

MANHATTAN (1979), romance/comedy. Directed and cowritten by Woody Allen; written with Marshall Brickman; produced by Charles H. Joffe; executive produced by Jack Rollins; photographed by Gordon Willis (b&w); edited by Susan E. Morse; music "Rhapsody in Blue" by George Gershwin; released by United Artists; 96 minutes. *Cast*: Woody Allen, Diane Keaton, Mariel Hemingway, Michael Murphy, Meryl Streep, Wallace Shawn, Tisa Farrow, Bella Abzug, Karen Allen.

A Proustian remembrance of more innocent times, this is Woody Allen's vision of the way life once was and, presumably, should be again. Awash in the nostalgic sounds of George Gershwin's "Rhapsody in Blue" and the widescreen black-and-white photography of Gordon Willis, the film stars Allen as Isaac Davis, a successful television writer who is torn between his attraction to Mary (Keaton) a woman his own age, and Tracy (Hemingway), a sexy, intelligent high school drama student. In the end he follows his heart to Tracy and is led into a simpler, purer existence when she tells him, "You have to have a little faith in people." Allen's warmest and most romantic movie, it does to

New York what Isaac says we all do to the city—it ''idolizes it all out of proportion.''

Awards: Academy Award nominations for Best Supporting Actress (Hemingway), Screenplay; New York Film Critics Circle Award for Best Director.

MANN, MICHAEL. Born February 5, 1943, in Chicago; director, producer, screenwriter. One of the most consistently intelligent, yet undervalued, Hollywood directors of the 1980s and 1990s, Mann has delivered only five features in fifteen years, spending much of his time instead in television. The 1970s saw him writing for ''Starsky and Hutch,'' ''Police Story,'' and ''Vega$'' before directing his first theatrical feature, *Thief*. Set in his Chicago hometown, the film sets up the Mann world—thematically, its criminals live by an honor system and personal code almost nonexistent in the ''civilized'' world, while stylistically, it features rain-slicked streets, ultrareflective car hoods, trendy fashion, and pulsating electronic music. His inversion of the ''home invasion'' story line of *Thief* in his supernatural adventure *The Keep* (in which a fortress is designed to keep a destructive force *in*) is the most interesting aspect of this otherwise misguided attempt to work outside the cop/crime genre. With an MTV-style veneer, he hit the television jackpot with ''Miami Vice'' and again scored (more critically than commercially) with the hard-edged, casino chic of ''Crime Story''—the prettiness of Don Johnson in the setting Miami sun was replaced by the grit of Dennis Farina in the flickering Vegas neon. He returned to the big screen with *Manhunter*, a frightening, if absurdly formalist, glimpse into the minds of a serial killer and the Federal Bureau of Investigation (FBI) agent who tracks him. As he did in *Thief*, he creates a mannered, almost hypnotic pace that pays special attention to detail and process. He again traveled outside the crime genre with James Fenimore Cooper's *The Last of the Mohicans*, a period adventure that stays refreshingly close to the 1936 film rather than giving it a revisionist spin. The rain-soaked streets and neon lights are gone, but the themes have not changed; Daniel Day-Lewis' Mohican is the last of his historic breed, just as James Caan's professional thief and William Peterson's FBI agent are the last of theirs. At the close of 1995, Mann's most complete critical and commercial success came with *Heat*, an epic crime drama about a band of professional thieves and the man who hunts them down.

Filmography as director and writer: Jaunpuri (1971, short); The Jericho Mile (1979, tvm); Thief (1981) also ep; The Keep (1983), Manhunter (1986) also producer, camera operator; L.A. Takedown (1989, tvm) also ep; The Last of the Mohicans (1992) also producer; Heat (1995) also producer.

Additional credits: Straight Time (1978) uncredited screenplay; ''Vega$'' (1978–1981, tvs) writer; Swansong (1980, tvm) screenplay; ''Miami Vice'' (1984–1989, tvs) ep; Band of the Hand (1986) ep; ''Crime Story'' (1986–1988, tvs) ep; Drug Wars: The Camarena Story (1990, tvms) ep, story; Drug Wars: The Cocaine Cartel (1992, tvms) ep.

Honors: Cannes Film Festival Jury Prize (*Jaunpuri*); DGA Award (*The Jericho Mile*);

Emmy Awards for Writing (*The Jericho Mile*); and Outstanding Miniseries ("Drug Wars: The Camarena Story").

MANTEGNA, JOE. Born November 13, 1947, in Chicago; actor. After nearly twenty-five years of collaboration with Pulitzer Prize-winning playwright and fellow Chicagoan David Mamet (accounting for fifteen projects together), Mantegna has become the foremost interpreter of the writer's staccato dialogue and street-smart characterizations. After great notices on the Chicago stage, Mantegna's movie career had a less than stellar beginning with a succession of roles that failed to show off his real talents. As the con man in Mamet's *House of Games* he first displayed the brilliance of his stage work. That led to some excellent work as the high-powered attorney in *Suspect*, the off-Broadway actor in *Weeds*, the love interest in Woody Allen's *Alice*, and Joey Zasa in Francis Ford Coppola's *The Godfather III*. In his strongest lead role since *House of Games*, Mantegna starred as the driven father of a young grand-master chess champion in *Searching for Bobby Fisher*, a performance of such richness, complexity, and depth that it deserved much more attention than it ultimately received. Mantegna has also cowritten the acclaimed and long-running 1977 play about Chicago Cub fans, *Bleacher Bums*.

Filmography: Towing (1978); Second Thoughts (1982); Compromising Positions (1985); The Money Pit (1986); Off Beat (1986); Three Amigos! (1986); Critical Condition (1987); House of Games (1987); Suspect (1987); Weeds (1987); Things Change (1988); Wait until Spring, Bandini (1989); Alice (1990); The Godfather III (1990); Queens Logic (1991); Searching for Bobby Fisher (1993); State of Emergency (1993, ctvm); "The Quiet Room" episode of "Fallen Angels" (1994, ctv); Airheads (1994); Baby's Day Out (1994); Forget Paris (1995); Stranger Things (1995).

Honors: Venice Film Festival for Best Actor (*Things Change*); Tony Award for (*Glengarry Glen Ross* 1984).

MARSHALL, PENNY. Born October 15, 1942, in Bronx, New York; director, actor. Brother is director Garry Marshall; formerly married to director Rob Reiner. Onetime television star who gained notoriety as the gum-snapping Laverne of television's "Laverne and Shirley." After directing a few episodes of that series, she deftly made the transition to feature films and has quietly become one of the top women directors in Hollywood, directing some of the brightest comic stars of the day—Whoopi Goldberg, Tom Hanks, Robin Williams, and Danny DeVito. Her two most successful comedies, *Big* and *A League of Their Own*, have a sweetness and playfulness that have delivered at the box office; *Awakenings*, an introspective drama based on the psychoanalytic writings of Oliver Saks, found an audience thanks to her adroit direction of stars Robin Williams and Robert De Niro.

Filmography as actor: How Sweet It Is (1968); The Savage Seven (1968); How Come Nobody's on Our Side (1975); 1941 (1979); Movers and Shakers (1985).

Filmography as director: Jumpin' Jack Flash (1986); Big (1988); Awakenings (1990);

also ep; A League of Their Own (1992) also ep; Renaissance Man (1994); Getting Away with Murder (1995).

MARTIN, STEVE. Born August 14, 1945, in Waco, Texas; actor, comedian, screenwriter, playwright. Formerly married to actor Victoria Tennant. With a background as a television writer ("The Smothers Brothers Comedy Hour") and performer ("The Tonight Show"), Martin found fame in the late 1970s with his wild and crazy guy routine. For a few years, he dominated the stand-up comedy market with a top-selling album, the hit novelty single "King Tut," a hugely successful arena tour, numerous appearances on NBC's "Saturday Night Live," and a succession of popular films directed by comic genius Carl Reiner—*The Jerk, Dead Men Don't Wear Plaid, The Man with Two Brains*, and *The Lonely Guy*, all scripted by Martin. His biggest critical success to date has been *Roxanne*, a clever and beautifully filmed adaptation of Rostand's *Cyrano de Bergerac*. In 1994, the Steppenwolf Theatre Company staged Martin's first play, *Picasso at the Lapin Agile*, a witty and entertaining comedy about a meeting between Picasso and Einstein at a bar in Paris in 1904. He has also published a collection of short stories entitled *Cruel Shoes*.

Filmography: Sgt. Pepper's Lonely Hearts Club Band (1978); The Jerk (1978) also screenplay; The Muppet Movie (1979); Pennies from Heaven (1981); Dead Men Don't Wear Plaid (1982) also screenplay; The Man with Two Brains (1983) also screenplay; All of Me (1984); The Lonely Guy (1985); Movers and Shakers (1985); Little Shop of Horrors (1986); Three Amigos! (1986) also screenplay, ep; Planes, Trains and Automobiles (1987); Roxanne (1987) also screenplay, ep; Dirty Rotten Scoundrels (1988); Parenthood (1989); My Blue Heaven (1990); L.A. Story (1991) also screenplay, ep; Father of the Bride (1991); Grand Canyon (1991); HouseSitter (1992); Leap of Faith (1993); And the Band Played On (1993, ctvm); A Simple Twist of Fate (1994) also screenplay, producer; Mixed Nuts (1994); Father of the Bride 2 (1995).

Honors: Los Angeles Film Critics Award for Best Actor (*Roxanne*); New York Film Critics Circle Award for Best Actor (*All of Me*); WGA Award (*Roxanne*); Emmy Award for Best Writing ("Smothers Brothers Comedy Hour" 1968); Grammy for Best Comedy Recording ("Let's Get Small" 1977, "A Wild and Crazy Guy" 1978).

MARVIN, LEE. Born February 19, 1924, in New York City; died August 29, 1987, in Tucson, Arizona; actor. Formerly married to actor Michelle Triola. Rugged, stone-faced actor whose minimal, expressionless style made him a perfect villain, though he could, when called upon, deliver a marvelously funny comic performance. After some 200 television appearances and such dastardly roles as the thug who pitches boiling coffee in Gloria Graham's face in *The Big Heat* and the professional assassin who kills the double-crossing lovers Angie Dickinson ("Lady, I haven't got the time") and Ronald Reagan in *The Killers*, he became one of the most recognizable bad guys in Hollywood. In 1965, he pivoted into a leading man with a flair for comedy with roles in *Ship of Fools* (as the loud and brassy ex-baseball player) and *Cat Ballou*. In the latter, as the inebriated gunfighter Kid Shelleen, he is a marvel as he fights a losing battle to stay upright in his saddle and prevent his pants from dropping to his ankles. In his last two of his four Robert Aldrich films, *The Dirty Dozen* and *Emperor of the North Pole* (as the tough-as-nails "king of the hoboes"), and his pair of John Boorman films, *Point Blank* and *Hell in the Pacific*, his characters retain the dangerous edge of his early work but have transformed into heroic, nearly existential figures. Less well known, but no less impressive, is his work in the quietly spectacular *Monte Walsh* as a veteran cowboy who tries to find a purpose in the coming industrialized age. Regrettably, from the mid-1970s until the end of his life, he had fewer opportunities to shine; his only great role of the period is the Sergeant in Samuel Fuller's solemn World War II battle film *The Big Red One*. "He was admired by more actors and directors than by critics. He has a powerful mind and an uncanny perception. He was one of the few truly great men I know" (John Boorman, *Projections 4 1/2*).

Filmography of key pre-1965 films: The Big Heat (1953); The Wild One (1954); The Caine Mutiny (1954); Bad Day at Black Rock (1955); Raintree County (1957); "M Squad" (1957–1960, tvs); The Man Who Shot Liberty Valance (1962); Donovan's Reef (1962); The Killers (1964).

Filmography since 1965: Cat Ballou (1965); Ship of Fools (1965); The Professionals (1966); The Dirty Dozen (1967); Point Blank (1967); Sergeant Ryker (1968, compiled from a two-part 1963 television drama); Hell in the Pacific (1968); Paint Your Wagon (1969); Monte Walsh (1970); Pocket Money (1972); Prime Cut (1972); Emperor of the North Pole/Emperor of the North (1973); The Iceman Cometh (1973); The Spikes Gang (1974); The Klansman (1974); Shout at the Devil (1976); Great Scout and Cathouse Thursday (1976); Avalanche Express (1979); The Big Red One (1980); Death Hunt (1981); Gorky Park (1983); Canicule/Dog Day (1984); The Delta Force (1986).

Honors: Academy Award for Best Actor (*Cat Ballou*); Berlin Film Festival Award for Best Actor (*Cat Ballou*).

MASON, MARSHA. Born April 3, 1942, in St. Louis, Missouri; actor. Formerly married to Neil Simon. A struggling New York actor who appeared off-Broadway and in the television soap opera "Love of Life" before moving to Los Angeles and landing roles in *Cinderella Liberty* (Oscar-nominated as the pool-hustling, barfly mother) and *Blume in Love*. Her career peaked during her collaboration with husband Neil Simon (1973–1983), appearing in five films based on his writing and earning three more Oscar nominations in the process. After this burst of success in film, she returned to the stage as a director in the 1980s and has since devoted less time to Hollywood. In 1986 she made her film directorial debut with the CBS Schoolbreak Special *Little Miss Perfect* and in 1991 starred in the short-lived sitcom "Sibs."

Filmography: Hot Rod Hullabaloo (1966); Beyond the Law (1968); Blume in Love (1973); Cinderella Liberty (1973); Audrey Rose (1977); The Goodbye Girl (1977); The Cheap Detective (1978); Chapter Two (1979); Promises in the Dark (1979); Only When I Laugh (1981); Max Dugan Returns (1982); Heartbreak Ridge (1986); Little Miss Perfect

(1986, tvm); Stella (1990); Drop Dead Fred (1991); "Sibs" (1991–1992, tvs); I Love Trouble (1994); Broken Trust (1995, ctvm); Nick of Time (1995).

Honors: Academy Award nominations for Best Actress (*Cinderella Liberty, The Goodbye Girl, Chapter Two, Only When I Laugh*).

MATEWAN (1987), historical drama. Directed and written by John Sayles; produced by Peggy Rajski and Maggie Renzi; photographed by Haskell Wexler; edited by Sonya Polonsky; music by Mason Daring; released by Cinecom; 132 minutes. *Cast*: James Earl Jones, Chris Cooper, Will Oldham, Kevin Tighe, Gordon Clapp, Mary McDonnell, David Strathairn, Ken Jenkins, Josh Mostel, John Sayles.

A worthy fictional companion piece to Barbara Koppel's documentary *Harlan County, U.S.A.*, this masterfully written and directed tale of a West Virginia mining town's attempt to unionize is a powerful depiction of American history. Loosely based on the events of the early 1920s that led to the Matewan massacre, the story revolves around the attempts of former Wobbly Joe Kenehan (Cooper) to organize the miners of Matewan. His pacifist efforts to form a coalition between the striking white workers and the Italian immigrants and black laborers who have replaced them are met with violent resistance by the owners of the Stone Mountain Coal Company. Operating with a meager $4 million budget, writer/director John Sayles has created (with the help of cinematographer Haskell Wexler and production designer Nora Chavooshian) a film of uncompromising authenticity that not only captures the look of the era but brings to life the hope and spirit of its people. "Matewan speaks to deeply held, mythic concepts of community in American thought" (Jeanne Williams, *Cineaste* 16, no. 3, 1988).

Award: Academy Award nomination for Best Cinematography.

MATTHAU, WALTER. Born October 1, 1920, in New York City; actor, director. Son Charlie is an actor/director. After a series of impressive villainous supporting roles, Matthau received kudos as the grouchy, unkempt, linguini-flinging Oscar Madison (opposite Art Carney's Felix Ungar) in the Broadway run of Neil Simon's *The Odd Couple*. It not only began a collaboration with Simon (he appeared in five of his films) but also led to his first of several on-screen pairings with Jack Lemmon. With his early 1970s thrillers *Charley Varrick*, *The Laughing Policeman*, and *The Taking of Pelham 1,2,3*, Matthau contorted the feisty cynicism of his comic Oscar Madison persona into a darker figure of alienation and volatility. The seemingly impenetrable crustiness of his character was then used to comic advantage as the drunken coach of a ragtag Little League team in *The Bad News Bears*. In the 1980s, he reteamed with that film's director, Michael Ritchie, for *The Survivors*, a high-profile comedy costarring Robin Williams that failed to live up to its potential, and then played a blustery buccaneer in Roman Polanski's *Pirates*, a big-budget romp that befell a similar fate. In addition to the popular appeal of *Grumpy Old Men* and *Grumpier Old Men*, he has remained active and visible in the 1990s as comic strip dupe Mr. Wilson in *Dennis the Menace*, Albert Einstein in the flimsy screwball comedy *I.Q.*, and the loathsome racist in a brief, but electrifying, role in Oliver Stone's *JFK*.

Filmography of key pre-1965 films: The Kentuckian (1955); Bigger than Life (1956); A Face in the Crowd (1957); The Gangster Story (1959) also director; Lonely Are the Brave (1962); Charade (1963); Ensign Pulver (1964); Fail Safe (1964).

Filmography since 1965: Mirage (1965); The Fortune Cookie (1966); A Guide for the Married Man (1967); Candy (1968); The Odd Couple (1968); The Secret Life of an American Wife (1968); Cactus Flower (1969); Hello, Dolly! (1969); Kotch (1971); A New Leaf (1971); Plaza Suite (1971); Pete 'n' Tillie (1972); Charley Varrick (1973); The Laughing Policeman (1973); Earthquake (1974); The Front Page (1974); The Taking of Pelham 1, 2, 3 (1974); The Sunshine Boys (1975); The Bad News Bears (1975); California Suite (1978); Casey's Shadow (1978); House Calls (1978); Hopscotch (1978); Little Miss Marker (1980) also ep; Buddy Buddy (1981); First Monday in October (1981); I Ought to Be in Pictures (1981); The Survivors (1983); Movers and Shakers (1985); Pirates (1986); The Couch Trip (1988); Il Piccolo Diavolo (1988); JFK (1991); Dennis the Menace (1993); Grumpy Old Men (1993); I.Q. (1994); Grumpier Old Men (1995).

Honors: Academy Award for Best Supporting Actor (*The Fortune Cookie*); Academy Award nominations for Actor (*Kotch*, *The Sunshine Boys*); Tony Awards for Best Actor (*The Odd Couple* 1965) and Supporting Actor (*A Shot in the Dark* 1962).

MAY, ELAINE. Born Elaine Berlin April 21, 1932, in Philadelphia; actor, director, screenwriter. Daughter is actor Jeannie Berlin. The daughter of Yiddish stage actor Jack Berlin, May began her acting career touring and doing radio with her father until his death in 1942. In 1953 she honed her screwball comic stylings with Chicago's improvisational troupe the Compass Players (later, Second City), where she met future stage partner Mike Nichols. The pair developed into one of the most highly touted comedy teams of the 1950s, hitting Broadway in 1960 with *An Evening with Mike Nichols and Elaine May*. Splitting with Nichols the following year, she spent much of the 1960s in the theater as a writer, director, and actor before performing the same three duties on her debut feature, *A New Leaf*. Building tiny laughs into hysterical roars, she created a modern screwball comedy that, like her three subsequent directorial outings, drew upon her background in revue humor and improvisation. The picture, which originally ran 180 minutes before Paramount snipped it to a more commercial 102 minutes, showed signs of her improvisational directing style— shooting excessive amounts of footage (à la Chaplin) in order to capture the essence of the scene. Neither *A New Leaf*, *The Heartbreak Kid*, or *Mikey and Nicky* performed especially well at the box office, though all three featured marvelous performances, including Oscar nominations for Eddie Albert and Jeannie Berlin of *The Heartbreak Kid*. Her long-awaited return to directing came in 1987 with *Ishtar*. Again a throwback to revue humor with a solid nod to the

Hope–Crosby *Road* movies, it's a generally charming and funny picture that couldn't possibly overcome the crippling advance press about its excessive budget. She reteamed with Mike Nichols in 1980 in a stage revival of *Who's Afraid of Virginia Woolf?* and collaborated for the first time on film with him for the 1996 comedy *The Birdcage.*

Filmography as director: A New Leaf (1971) also screenplay, actor; The Heartbreak Kid (1972); Mikey and Nicky (1976) also screenplay; Ishtar (1987) director.

Additional credits: Enter Laughing (1966) actor; Bach to Bach (1967) actor; Luv (1967) actor; Such Good Friends (1971) screenplay; Heaven Can Wait (1978) screenplay; California Suite (1978) actor; Tootsie (1982) uncredited screenplay; In the Spirit (1990) actor.

Honor: Academy Award nomination for Best Screenplay (*Heaven Can Wait*).

MAYSLES, ALBERT, AND DAVID MAYSLES. Albert born November 26, 1926; David born January 10, 1932, and died 1987; both born in Brookline, Massachusetts. Members of Robert Drew and Richard Leacock's documentary collective the Drew Associates and a chief force in the Direct Cinema movement, the Maysles brothers have, with varying degrees of success, attempted to capture the truth of the individual. Whoever the subject—celebrities Marlon Brando, Truman Capote, and Vladimir Horowitz or less stellar folks like the mid-American Bible company salesman in *Salesman* or Jackie Kennedy's eccentric Bouvier relatives in *Grey Gardens*—cameraman Albert and soundman David make every effort to put a life on film. Ironically, however, they've become best known for capturing a murder on film in their Rolling Stones concert picture *Gimme Shelter.* The Maysles can be accused of manipulating their subjects either overtly through suggestion and provocative questioning (they both received degrees in psychology) or covertly through the intrusion of their camera and sound gear, but it is difficult to fault their intent. The contribution of frequent collaborator Charlotte Zwerin cannot be overlooked; she not only codirected their two most lasting and commercially successful works (*Salesman* and *Gimme Shelter*) but also directed the engrossing jazz documentary *Thelonius Monk: Straight, No Chaser* (1988).

Filmography of key pre-1965 films: Showman (1962); What's Happening: The Beatles in the USA (1964).

Filmography since 1965: Meet Marlon Brando (1965); With Love from Truman (1966); Salesman (1969) codirected with Zwerin; Gimme Shelter (1971) codirected with Zwerin; Christo's Valley Curtain (1972) codirected with Ellen Giffard; Grey Gardens (1975) codirected with Ellen Hovde and Muffie Meyer; Running Fence (1977) codirected with Zwerin; Vladimir Horowitz: The Last Romantic (1985, tvm); Islands (1986) codirected with Zwerin; Ozawa (1986, tv) codirected with Deborah Dickson and Susan Froemke; Horowitz Plays Mozart (1987) codirected by Albert Maysles, Zwerin, Froemke; Jessye Norman Sings Carmen (1989) codirected by Albert Maysles, Zwerin Froemke; Baroque Diet (1992); Umbrellas (1994).

Additional photography credits for Albert: Primary (1960); Yanqui No! (1961); Jean

Luc Godard's "Montparnasse et Levallois" episode of Paris vu Par . . . /Six in Paris (1964); Monterey Pop (1969).

Honor: Academy Award nomination for Best Short Subject Documentary (*Christo's Valley Curtain*).

MAZURSKY, PAUL. Born Irwin Mazursky April 25, 1930, in Brooklyn; director, actor. Former stand-up comic with a background in theater who, after working as a writer on "The Danny Kaye Show" and helping to create "The Monkees" television series, made his mark as a director in 1969 with *Bob and Carol and Ted and Alice*. The prototypical Mazursky comedy, it's an insightful examination and truthful reflection of middle-class white values and sexual mores. Throughout the 1970s, he made numerous films that addressed similar issues, peaking in 1978 with his Oscar-nominated *An Unmarried Woman*. By the 1980s and 1990s, however, his musings on relationships had ceased to be unique. His best remembered post-1970s films are his two Americanized remakes of French classics—*Willie and Phil*, a charming reworking of Francois Truffaut's *Jules and Jim*, and *Down and Out in Beverly Hills*, a commercially successful updating of Jean Renoir's *Boudu Saved from Drowning*.

Filmography as director, writer, actor: Bob and Carol and Ted and Alice (1969); Alex in Wonderland (1970); Blume in Love (1973) also producer; Harry and Tonto (1974) also producer; Next Stop, Greenwich Village (1976) producer, director, screenplay; An Unmarried Woman (1978) also producer; Willie and Phil (1980) also producer; Tempest (1982) also producer; Moscow on the Hudson (1984) also producer; Down and Out in Beverly Hills (1986) also producer; Moon over Parador (1988); Enemies, a Love Story (1989) also producer; Scenes from a Mall (1991); producer, director, screenplay; The Pickle (1993); Faithful (1995).

Filmography as actor: Fear and Desire (1953); Blackboard Jungle (1955); Deathwatch (1966); I Love You, Alice B. Toklas (1968) also ep; A Star Is Born (1976); An Almost Perfect Affair (1979); A Man, a Woman and a Bank (1979); History of the World Part I (1981); Into the Night (1985); Punchline (1988); Scenes from the Class Struggle in Beverly Hills (1989); Man Trouble (1992); Carlito's Way (1993); Love Affair (1994); Miami Rhapsody (1995).

Filmography as executive producer only: Taking Care of Business (1990).

Honors: Academy Award nominations for Best Picture (*An Unmarried Woman*) and Screenplay (*Harry and Tonto, An Unmarried Woman, Enemies, A Love Story*); New York Film Critics Circle Award for Best Director (*Enemies, A Love Story*).

MCCABE AND MRS. MILLER (1971), western. Directed and cowritten by Robert Altman; screenplay with Brian McKay (from the novel by Edmund Naughton); produced by David Foster and Mitchell Brower; photographed by Vilmos Zsigmond; edited by Louis Lombardo; music by Leonard Cohen; released by Warner Bros.; 120 minutes. *Cast*: Warren Beatty, Julie Christie, Rene Auberjonois, John Schuck, Bert Remsen, Keith Carradine, William Devane, Michael Murphy, Shelley Duvall.

With the folksy rhythms of Leonard Cohen's ''Sisters of Mercy'' and ''Winter Lady'' and the gentle, melancholic performances of Warren Beatty and Julie Christie, Robert Altman has created a uniquely revisionist antiwestern that demythifies the genre and its traditional heroes. Set in the northwestern town of Presbyterian Church, the film centers on the relationship between John McCabe, a two-bit schemer with a modest plan to open a whorehouse/saloon, and Constance Miller, a local whore who views McCabe as a business partner. By dumb luck, the business booms, love grows, and soon a local mining company is offering to buy them out. McCabe refuses and, after a gun battle, dies alone, unheroically, in a snowdrift. The film shares thematic concerns with Sam Peckinpah's realistic view of the West, but Altman's vision is perhaps more hopeless; while the Bunch and Cable Hogue retain a sense of honor and dignity, McCabe is just a lousy businessman whose luck runs out at the hands of big business. With its antique look and its vast blankets of snow, it is Altman's most gorgeous film. The location itself is a major character; its pine trees, mud, and snowflakes are as much a part of the American landscape as the small business owner and the lovable whore. Beatty does a superb job of making his McCabe a regular man (the opposite of what he did for Clyde Barrow), while Christie is a revelation as the whore, a simple woman whose hunger for greater things is symbolized in her ravenous appetite at the dinner table.

MCQUEEN, STEVE. Born Terrence Steve McQueen on March 24, 1930, in Beech Grove, Indiana; died 1980; actor. Formerly married to actors Neile Adams, Ali McGraw, and Barbara Minty; son Chad is an actor. Taciturn international star of the 1960s and 1970s whose image as one of society's outsiders was cultivated in his youth. Abandoned early on by his father, McQueen spent time in reform school, went AWOL from the marines, and took various odd jobs as a lumberjack and a dockworker before ending up at the New York Neighborhood Playhouse and the Actors Studio. He landed a starring role on television's ''Wanted: Dead or Alive'' (1958–1960) and then found fame in his commanding role as ''Cooler King'' Hilts of *The Great Escape*. From the moment of his attempted motorcycle ride to freedom, McQueen solidified the romantic loner persona that would fuel his (mostly eponymous) performances as rogue cop Frank Bullitt, thieves Doc McCoy (*The Getaway*), Thomas Crown, and Henri ''Papillon'' Charriere, cowboys Junior Bonner, Nevada Smith, and Tom Horn, Grand Prix driver Michael Delaney (*Le Mans*), and poker player Cincinnati Kid. He began to make the shift toward producing his own films before his death in 1980. ''As he grew older, sadder—and sicker?—something like grace arose in his battered, tense face'' (David Thomson, *A Biographical Dictionary of Film*).

Filmography of key pre-1965 films: Somebody Up There Likes Me (1956); The Blob (1958); The Magnificent Seven (1960); Hell Is for Heroes (1962); The Great Escape (1963).

Filmography since 1965: Baby, the Rain Must Fall (1965); The Cincinnati Kid (1965); Nevada Smith (1963); The Sand Pebbles (1966); Bullitt (1968); The Thomas Crown Affair (1968); The Reivers (1969); Le Mans (1971); On Any Sunday (1971); The Getaway (1972); Junior Bonner (1972); Papillon (1973); The Towering Inferno (1974); An Enemy of the People (1978) also ep; The Hunter (1980); Tom Horn (1980) also ep.

Honor: Academy Award nomination for Best Actor (*The Sand Pebbles*).

Selected bibliography

St. Charnez, Casey. *The Films of Steve McQueen.* New York: Citadel, 1986.
Terrill, Marshall. *Steve McQueen: Portrait of an American Rebel.* New York: Donald I. Fine, 1993.

MEAN STREETS (1973), drama. Directed and cowritten by Martin Scorsese; screenplay with Mardik Martin; produced by Jonathan T. Taplin; photographed by Kent Wakeford; edited by Sid Levin; released by Warner Bros.; 110 minutes. *Cast*: Harvey Keitel, Robert De Niro, Amy Robinson, David Proval, Richard Romanus, George Memmoli, David Carradine, Robert Carradine.

Martin Scorsese's first masterpiece, this stylish slice of New York Italian life combines gangsterism with the transcendent power of rock and roll and Catholicism. It's about three young punks trying to become big men—Charlie (Keitel), the God-fearing young Christ-figure; Johnny Boy (De Niro), the explosive, uncontrollable spinning top; and Michael (Romanus), the not-too-smart wheeler-dealer. There's not a plot so much as a violent conclusion that they're all hurling themselves toward. Atmospheric, portentous, dynamic, passionate, and, above all, fearlessly artistic, it's the movie that every film student wishes he or she could make. As he did with his earlier film *Who's That Knocking at My Door?*, Scorsese loads the sound track with such rock-and-roll favorites as the Ronettes' ''Be My Baby,'' the Rolling Stones' ''Tell Me,'' and the Aquatones' ''You.''

MEDIUM COOL (1969), drama. Directed, written, coproduced, and photographed by Haskell Wexler (from the novel by Jack Couffer); produced with Jerrold Wexler and Tully Friedman; edited by Verna Fields; music by Mike Bloomfield; released by Paramount; 110 minutes. *Cast*: Robert Forster, Verna Bloom, Peter Bonerz, Marianna Hill, Harold Blankenship, Peter Boyle.

The directing debut of Oscar-winning cinematographer Haskell Wexler (*Who's Afraid of Virginia Woolf?*), this is the place where fiction and nonfiction meet. Set against the backdrop of the explosive 1968 Democratic National Convention in Chicago, the film follows fictional television cameraman John Cassellis (Forster) as he travels through the city shooting news footage with perverse detachment. He gradually comes to understand his subjects, even falling in love with welfare mother Eileen (Bloom), who has recently moved from Virginia with her teenage son Harold (Blankenship). By the violent end, he has shifted away from the false security of observer to the vulnerability of participant.

Although the narrative occasionally falters, the greatness of the film comes from the direct correlation between content and style; Cassellis gets sucked into the vortex of demonstrations, riots, and police beatings at precisely the same instant as director/cameraman Wexler and his crew. In one of the great moments in film history, fiction and reality fully merge as a crew member is heard on the sound track uttering the warning "Watch out, Haskell, it's real." With its actual footage of the police's thumping protestors in Chicago's Grant Park, its dangerous spontaneity, and its direct sound recording, Paramount's *Medium Cool* is Hollywood at its most real. "It stands at the crossroads of so many esthetic and ideological strands of the era: the merging of documentary and fiction, the interplay of politics and public theater, and the attempt of a radical independent filmmaker to present his work through the dominant distribution and publicity system" (Robert Sklar, *Cineaste* 16, nos. 1–2, 1987–1988).

MELVIN AND HOWARD (1980), drama. Directed by Jonathan Demme; screenplay by Bo Goldman; produced by Art Linson and Don Phillips; photographed by Tak Fujimoto; edited by Craig McKay; music by Bruce Langhorne; released by Universal; 93 minutes. *Cast*: Jason Robards, Paul LeMat, Mary Steenburgen, Michael J. Pollard, Elizabeth Cheshire, Gloria Grahame, Pamela Reed, Dabney Coleman, John Glover, Charles Napier, Jack Kehoe, Martine Beswick, Melvin E. Dummar.

A deceptively simple commentary on American life, *Melvin and Howard* starts with the chance meeting of two dreamers—legendary billionaire Howard Hughes and "Milkman of the Month" Melvin Dummar. While driving a stretch of desert highway, likable chump Melvin (LeMat) spots the scruffy Hughes (Robards) on the roadside and gives him a lift to Vegas—the two of them singing songs along the way. Years later, after Hughes' death in 1976, this simple act of selfless humanity is repaid to the tune of $156 million when Melvin is included in the billionaire's will. Unfortunately, the will (later known as the "Mormon will") was eventually declared a fake, and Melvin was accused of propagating a hoax. Whatever the truth, Jonathan Demme's intention is to show us what Hughes saw in that short ride—a decent, good-hearted guy who works long hours on a milk delivery route but dreams of becoming something more. He comes closest to realizing that dream when his wife (Steenburgen), a part-time exotic dancer, wins $10,000 plus prizes on the "Easy Street" game show. While Hughes dreamed of flying the "Spruce Goose," Melvin's dreams are more typically American; he just wants to choose the right door on a game show. While Hughes was right to see Melvin as a reflection of himself, he failed to see that Melvin was no different than most Americans. Directed without much fanfare, *Melvin and Howard* is a quiet, but dead-on true, portrait of American life that is brought to life by Paul Le Mat's down-home portrayal of Dummar. Equally impressive is Robards as Hughes, who, although he's on screen for only a few minutes, brings warmth to the eccentric billionaire. "This picture suggests what it might have been like if Jean Renoir had directed a Preston Sturges comedy" (Pauline Kael, *New Yorker*, October 13, 1980).

MENACE II SOCIETY (1993), crime drama. Directed and story by Albert Hughes and Allen Hughes; screenplay by Tyger Williams; produced by Darin Scott; photographed by Lisa Rinzler; edited by Christopher Koefoed; music by QD III; released by New Line Cinema; 90 minutes. *Cast*: Larenz Tate, Jada Pinkett, Tyrin Turner, Charles S. Dutton, Bill Duke, Samuel L. Jackson.

Directed and written (with Tyger Williams) by twenty-year-old twins Allen and Albert Hughes, this is one of the most impressive films about growing up black in America in the 1990s. More of a traditional *gangster* film than a *gang* film (*Goodfellas* is a direct model); its success is its ability to elicit feelings of sadness *and* hope. Tate plays the film's narrator, a young man with a conscience who slips deep into the quagmire of gangster life. In the opening scene he witnesses a brutal double murder committed by his best friend, O-Dog; midway through the film he commits his first murder; and by the end, he is a victim of a drive-by. Directed with poetry and tenderness, the greatness of *Menace II Society* lies as much in what it doesn't do as what it does; it refuses to pass judgment. Instead, it presents a seemingly inexorable situation that continues to claim lives. In addition to the sincere lead performances, great support comes from Dutton, Duke, and Jackson. Of the Hughes brothers' talent, Nelson George says that "their technical mastery puts them way ahead of their celebrated peers in their total understanding of cinema" (*The New Yorker*, March 21, 1994).

MEYER, RUSS. Born March 21, 1922, in Oakland, California; director, producer, screenwriter, actor. Skin-flick director of the 1950s who got his start shooting centerfolds for *Playboy* magazine, Meyer found phenomenal commercial success in the 1960s and 1970s with his titillating parodies. A no-budget auteur obsessed with enormous-breasted heroines, his films brim with crazed camera work and editing, camp humor, and exaggerated violence. Popular in an artlessly vulgar way and brazenly American, his best films—*Faster Pussycat, Kill! Kill!*, *Vixen*, *Beyond the Valley of the Dolls* (written by Roger Ebert), *Supervixens*, and *Beneath the Valley of the Supervixens*—have found a loyal cult following. If they were in French, like Roger Vadim's dippy . . . *And God Created Woman*, they might have found even a critical following.

Filmography of key pre-1965 films: The Immoral Mr. Teas (1959); Kiss Me Quick! (1964).

Filmography since 1965: Lorna (1965); Rope of Flesh (1965); Fanny Hill: Memoirs of a Woman of Pleasure (1965); Motor Psycho (1965); Faster Pussycat, Kill! Kill! (1965); Mondo Topless (1966); How Much Loving Does a Normal Couple Need? (1967); Good Morning . . . and Goodbye (1967); Common Law Cabin (1967); Finders Keepers, Lovers Weepers (1968); Vixen/Russ Meyer's Vixen (1968); Cherry, Harry and Raquel (1969); Beyond the Valley of the Dolls (1970); The Seven Minutes (1971); Sweet Suzy!/Blacksnake (1975); Supervixens (1975); Russ Meyer's Up! (1976); Beneath the Valley of the Supervixens (1979); The Breast of Russ Meyer (1987).

Selected bibliography

Frasier, David K. *Russ Meyer—The Life and Films*. Jefferson, NC: McFarland, 1990.

MICKEY ONE (1965), film noir. Directed and produced by Arthur Penn; screenplay by Alan M. Surgal; photographed by Ghislain Cloquet (b&w); edited by Aram Avakian; music by Jack Shaindlin and Eddie Sauter; released by Columbia; 93 minutes. *Cast*: Warren Beatty, Alexandra Stewart, Hurd Hatfield, Franchot Tone, Teddy Hart, Jeff Corey.

A compelling and confusing experiment from Arthur Penn that is so visually arresting that its meandering plot is of secondary importance. Beatty stars as Mickey, a nightclub comic who gets in trouble with the mob and goes on the lam. He's eventually caught and receives a merciless beating, which frees him of his anxieties and allows him to face a dreaded audition at a classier nightclub. It's an existential allegory (complete with faceless, nameless mobsters) about the dawn of the modern artist in the cold, mechanical, postindustrial age into which the tortured Mickey One (as his nascent appellation implies) is the first to venture. Among the more memorable moments are the auto junkyard pursuit with the predatory wrecking crane; the ''happening'' with the self-destructing YES art piece; and Mickey's audition before the blinding nightclub spotlight. Not Arthur Penn's best but, along with *Alice's Restaurant*, definitely one of his boldest.

MIDNIGHT COWBOY (1969), drama. Directed by John Schlesinger; screenplay by Waldo Salt (from the novel by James Leo Herlihy); produced by Jerome Hellman; photographed by Adam Holender; edited by Hugh A. Robertson; music by John Barry, song ''Everybody's Talking'' performed by Nilsson; released by United Artists; 119 minutes. *Cast*: Dustin Hoffman, Jon Voight, Sylvia Miles, John McGiver, Brenda Vaccaro, Barnard Hughes.

Very much a film of its time, this probe into the underbelly of New York City unearths two of its many losers and dreamers—Texas hustler Joe Buck (Voight) and his tubercular pal Enrico ''Ratso'' Rizzo (Hoffman). A new arrival in the Big Apple, Joe Buck has naive ideas about selling his sexual services to horny older women but soon gets an urban awakening when the only customers he can rustle up are men. The strength of the film is the crackling rapport between Ratso and Joe Buck; an offbeat pair of underdogs, the audience can't help but identify with them despite their repulsive veneer. In the showier role is Hoffman, physically contorted into a verminous misanthrope who bulldozes through the city as if it's his own, stealing whatever he needs and threatening any driver (''I'm walkin' here'') who impedes his progress. Despite the many small resonating moments (like the bookending bus rides of Voight's trip to New York and his touching ride to Florida with the dying Ratso), the film is forever locked into its swinging 1960s tone. Schlesinger's direction wrongheadedly spins the story into a contemptuous look at the vulgar masses (the big-mouthed blond is monstrous; the repressed Jesus-loving gay man is pathetic), while shining a loving light on only Ratso and Joe Buck. The only Best Picture winner (or nominee) to receive an "X" rating, though it was later rerated "R."

Awards: Academy Award for Best Picture, Director, Adapted Screenplay; Academy Award nominations for Best Actor (Hoffman, Voight), Supporting Actress (Miles), Editing; New York Film Critics Circle Award for Best Actor (Voight); DGA Award; Berlin Film Festival Catholic Film Office Award; included in the Library of Congress' National Film Registry (1994).

MILIUS, JOHN. Born April 11, 1944, in St. Louis, Missouri; director, screenwriter, producer. The master manipulator of male combat fantasies and hero worship in Hollywood, Milius' brand of infantile militarism seems like child's play when contrasted with films like *Patton*, *The Big Red One*, or *Platoon*. At their worst, his films and scripts read like comic book tales (*Conan the Barbarian*, *1941*, *Red Dawn*), while at their best (Sydney Pollack's *Jeremiah Johnson*, John Huston's *The Life and Times of Judge Roy Bean*), they are filtered through the eyes of a director who can imbue the characters with the essential complexity. Despite the fact that none of his films as a director have been a critical hit (*Dillinger* and *Big Wednesday* have come close), and only his Arnold Schwarzenegger fantasy *Conan the Barbarian* has found an enthusiastic audience, Milius remains something of a force in Hollywood because of his writing. Based in paranoia, hawkish politics, and a fetishistic love of munitions, he leaves an indelible mark on all of his scripts—the fascistic cop as jury and executioner (*Dirty Harry*, *Magnum Force*), the noble hero (Evel Knievel, John Dillinger, Judge Roy Bean, Melvin Purvis, Geronimo), the survivalist (*Jeremiah Johnson*, *Red Dawn*), and the white colonialist and interventionist (*The Wind and the Lion*, *Apocalypse Now*, *Farewell to the King*). Behind them all is the running theme (in varying degrees of obviousness) that the ultimate act is to die bravely in battle—a romanticized notion that owes more to the movies than real life and that betrays the fact that Milius attended the University of Southern California film school but never served in the military. Still, for all of the right-wing bluster, Milius is a filmmaker who speaks from the heart and isn't afraid to let his opinion be heard—a rare quality in Hollywood. "The films of John Milius bear a lunk-headed 1950s conservatism tinged by 1960s psychedelia and the mix has never worked in Milius' favor" (*The 1992 Motion Picture Guide Annual*). "There's always great valor in a lost cause" (John Milius, *Reel Conversations*).

Filmography as writer, director: Marcello, I'm So Bored (1967, short) director only; Dillinger (1973); The Wind and the Lion (1978); Big Wednesday (1978); Conan the Barbarian (1982); Red Dawn (1984); "Opening Day" episode of "The Twilight Zone" (1985, tvs); Farewell to the King (1989); Flight of the Intruder (1991); Motorcycle Gang (1994, ctvm).

Filmography as writer: The Devil's Eight (1968); Dirty Harry (1971) uncredited rewrite; Evel Knievel (1971); Jeremiah Johnson (1972); The Life and Times of Judge Roy Bean (1972); Magnum Force (1973); Melvin Purvis: G-Man (1974, tvm); Apocalypse Now (1979); 1941 (1979) also ep; Extreme Prejudice (1987) story; Geronimo: An American Legend (1993); Clear and Present Danger (1994).

Additional credits: Hardcore (1979) ep; Used Cars (1980) ep; Deadhead Miles (1982) actor; Lone Wolf McQuade (1982) technical adviser; Uncommon Valor (1983) producer; Fatal Beauty (1987) ep.

MINNELLI, LIZA. Born March 12, 1946, in Los Angeles; actor, singer. Daughter of actor and singer Judy Garland and director Vincente Minnelli; formerly married to singer Peter Allen, film executive Jack Haley, Jr., and artist Mark Gero. Showstopping stage performer whose film work has been erratic at best, she first appeared on screen as a child in her mother's musical vehicle *In the Good Old Summertime*. She developed into a vibrant singer on the stage in the 1960s, winning a Tony for her role in the Broadway musical *Flora, the Red Menace*. When the direction and writing have matched her potential talent—as in Alan J. Pakula's *The Sterile Cuckoo*, Bob Fosse's *Cabaret*, and Martin Scorsese's *New York, New York*—she has been unbeatable, mixing her musical talent with her nervous energy as a dramatic actor. She, rather inexplicably, found box office success starring opposite Dudley Moore's drunken millionaire in *Arthur* and its sodden sequel. When not on screen, which is quite often, she has had huge successes with her recordings and her live shows.

Filmography: In the Good Old Summertime (1949); Charlie Bubbles (1967); The Sterile Cuckoo (1969); Tell Me That You Love Me, Junie Moon (1970); Cabaret (1972); Liza with a Z (1972, tv); Journey Back to Oz (1974) voice; Lucky Lady (1975); A Matter of Time (1976); Silent Movie (1976); New York, New York (1977); Arthur (1981); The Muppets Take Manhattan (1984); A Time to Live (1985, tvm); Arthur 2: On the Rocks (1988); Rent-a-Cop (1988); Stepping Out (1991); Parallel Lives (1994, ctvm); The West Side Waltz (1995, tvm).

Honors: Academy Award for Best Actress (*Cabaret*); Academy Award nomination for Best Actress (*The Sterile Cuckoo*); Tony Awards (*Flora, the Red Menace* 1965, *The Act* 1978).

MISSING (1982), political drama. Directed and cowritten by Costa-Gavras; screenplay with Donald Stewart (from the book by Thomas Hauser); produced by Edward Lewis and Mildred Lewis; photographed by Ricardo Aronovich; edited by Francoise Bonnot; music by Vangelis; released by Universal; 122 minutes. *Cast*: Jack Lemmon, Sissy Spacek, Melanie Mayron, John Shea, Charles Cioffi, Janice Rule, David Clennon, Joe Regalbuto, Keith Szarabajka.

As he did with the Lambrakis case in his 1970 film *Z*, Greek director Costa-Gavras makes a brilliant film that combines the commercial with the political. Based on the real-life efforts of Ed Harmon (Lemmon), a staunchly pro-American New York businessman who travels to postcoup Chile to locate his missing leftist son Charles (Shea). Naively believing he can clear up this simple misunderstanding, Ed contacts all the appropriate authorities while shrugging off his politically astute daughter-in-law, Beth (Spacek). Ed clings to the hope that his only child must still be alive, but the facts tell another story—Charles was abducted from his home by a goon squad and executed by the fascist U.S.-backed puppet regime at the behest of the United States government—facts that rattle the very foundation of Ed's patriotism. What makes *Missing* such an intellectually and emotionally stirring picture is Costa-Gavras' ability to personalize the story—we hurt along with Ed as he tries, through Beth's heartfelt efforts, to rediscover the son he's been missing all of his life. Lemmon and Spacek have a number of genuinely tender moments between them, especially in the harrowing sequence in which they search row upon row of unidentified corpses to locate Charles and instead find another murdered American.

Award: Cannes Film Festival Award for Best Actor.

MITCHUM, ROBERT. Born August 6, 1917, in Bridgeport, Connecticut; died July 1, 1997 in Santa Barbara, California; actor. Sons Jim and Chris and grandchildren Bentley and Carrie are actors. Former RKO contract player and major Hollywood figure since his sole Oscar-nominated performance in *The Story of G.I. Joe*, the sleepy-eyed, laconic Mitchum has made a career of making it all look easy. Often portraying slovenly, torpid characters, he has moved back and forth effortlessly from psychopath, to film noir icon, to wry romantic lead. By age sixty, as the drunken, shamed sheriff of Howard Hawks' *El Dorado* and then as the simple schoolteacher of David Lean's *Ryan's Daughter*, he proved to be one of the few commercially viable box office stars of his advanced years—a rare performer who lost none of his luster. He continued to impress throughout the 1970s in *The Friends of Eddie Coyle* (a sympathetic performance as a small-time loser) and the Raymond Chandler adaptations *Farewell, My Lovely* and *The Big Sleep* (perfectly capturing the mood, though not the razor-sharp edge, of Philip Marlowe's private eye) and into the 1980s with the celebrated television miniseries *The Winds of War* and its sequel *War and Remembrance* and the films *That Championship Season* and *Maria's Lovers*, the latter featuring a surprisingly tender love scene with Nastassia Kinski. In 1991, Martin Scorsese paid tribute to Mitchum by casting him in the remake of the 1962 Mitchum-starrer *Cape Fear*, reprising his role not as the sadistic tormenter Max Cady but as the local police chief who, upon seeing the tattoos that blanket the torso of the deranged Cady, drolly comments, ''I don't know whether to look at him or read him.'' ''Mitchum has simply settled for being a film noir icon, evoking a bygone movie genre by his mere presence'' (Foster Hirsch, *The Dark Side of the Screen: Film Noir*).

Filmography of key pre-1965 films: The Story of G.I. Joe (1945); Crossfire (1947); Out of the Past (1947); Pursued (1947); The Big Steal (1949); The Lusty Men (1952); Macao (1952); The Night of the Hunter (1955); Heaven Knows, Mr. Allison (1957); Thunder Road (1958) also ep, story, music; Cape Fear (1962).

Filmography since 1965: Mister Moses (1965); El Dorado (1967); The Way West (1967); 5 Card Stud (1968); Anzio (1968); Secret Ceremony (1968); Villa Rides (1968); The Good Guys and the Bad Guys (1969); Young Billy Young (1969); Ryan's Daughter (1970); Going Home (1971); The Wrath of God (1972); The Friends of Eddie Coyle (1973); The Yakuza (1975); Farewell, My Lovely (1975); Midway (1976); The Last Tycoon (1976); The Amsterdam Kill (1977); The Big Sleep (1978); Matilda (1978); Breakthrough/Sergeant Steiner (1979); Time After Time (1979); Agency/Mind Games (1980); Nightkill (1980); That Championship Season (1982); The Winds of War (1982, tvms); The Ambassador (1984); Maria's Lovers (1985); Reunion at Fairborough (1985, tvm); Mr. North (1988); Scrooged (1988); War and Remembrance (1988, tvms); Presume Dangereux (1990); "A Family for Joe" (1990, tvs); Cape Fear (1991); Tombstone (1993) narrator.

Honor: Academy Award nomination for Best Supporting Actor (*The Story of G.I. Joe*).

Selected bibliography

Eells, George. *Robert Mitchum: A Biography*. New York: Franklin Watts, 1984.

MODERNS, THE (1988), drama. Directed and cowritten by Alan Rudolph; screenplay with Jon Bradshaw; produced by Carolyn Pfeiffer and David Blocker; photographed by Toyomichi Kurita; edited by Debra T. Smith and Scott Brock; music by Mark Isham; released by Alive; 126 minutes. *Cast*: Keith Carradine, Linda Fiorentino, Genevieve Bujold, Geraldine Chaplin, Wallace Shawn, John Lone, Kevin J. O'Connor, Elsa Raven.

The culmination of Alan Rudolph's stellar, but underappreciated, career, this is a hopelessly romantic tale of the changing face of art in the twentieth century. Set in Paris in 1926, its ingenious plot revolves around aspiring painter Nick Hart (Carradine), who is hired by a scorned wife, Nathalie de Ville (Chaplin), to forge some of her husband's most valuable paintings. When de Ville's husband dies naturally, she refuses to honor her deal with Hart and steals what she thinks are the original paintings before leaving for New York. In the meantime, Hart, who has fallen in love with Rachel (Fiorentino), sold his original paintings to Rachel's wealthy art collector husband, Bertram Stone (Lone), only to later have them denounced by art critics as forgeries. A smart and poetic balancing act about art and commerce, *The Moderns* is Alan Rudolph's paean to Paris, not simply Paris the city but Paris the state of mind. It's a film about heart (and art) and how that heart (and art) can be destroyed by a society that cannot tell the difference between a forgery and the real thing. Strengthened by a solid supporting cast (especially O'Connor as Ernest Hemingway) and an infectiously evocative score from Mark Isham.

Awards: Los Angeles Film Critics Award for Best Score; New York Film Critics Circle Awards for Best Supporting Actress (Bujold) and Best Score.

MODINE, MATTHEW. Born March 22, 1959, in Loma Linda, California; actor. Gutsy young actor who brings a quality of sensitivity and tenderness to his roles, especially when working with actor's directors like Robert Altman

(*Streamers*, *Short Cuts*), Alan Rudolph (*Equinox*), Jonathan Demme (*Married to the Mob*), or Alan J. Pakula (*Orphans*). With his shared Best Actor award at the Venice Film Festival as part of the incredible ensemble cast of *Streamers* and his subsequent lead role as the delusional soldier in *Birdy*, Modine established himself as a promising new talent. His efforts, however, have not brought him the same commercial success as, for example, his *Birdy* costar Nicolas Cage. Many of his more recent films have already been forgotten (*Gross Anatomy*, *Pacific Heights*, *Wind*), while even his high-profile roles (such as Private Joker in Stanley Kubrick's *Full Metal Jacket*) have brought only limited success and recognition. His best shot at a Hollywood hit came in Renny Harlin's swashbuckling adventure debacle *Cutthroat Island*, which, to the good fortune of the badly miscast Modine, went unseen by the majority of the moviegoing public.

Filmography: Baby It's You (1983); Private School (1983); Streamers (1983); Birdy (1984); The Hotel New Hampshire (1984); Mrs. Soffel (1984); Vision Quest (1985); Full Metal Jacket (1987); Orphans (1987); Married to the Mob (1988); La Partita (1988); Gross Anatomy (1989); Memphis Belle (1990); Pacific Heights (1990); The Wind (1992); Equinox (1993); Short Cuts (1993); Smoking (1993, short) codirector, coscreenplay; And the Band Played On (1994, ctvm); The Browning Version (1994); Jacob (1994, ctvm); Bye Bye, Love (1995); Fluke (1995); Cutthroat Island (1995).

Honor: Venice Film Festival Award for Best Actor (*Streamers*).

MOORE, DEMI. Born Demi Guynes November 11, 1962, in Roswell, New Mexico; actor. Married to Bruce Willis. Former model and series regular on the television soap ''General Hospital,'' this throaty star's career really took off as the ingenue in her three ''Brat Pack'' films—*St. Elmo's Fire*, *About Last Night . . .*, and *Wisdom*. Stardom followed with the popular romantic fantasy *Ghost*, featuring her as the grieving girlfriend who is contacted from the ''other side'' by her murdered lover. By the 1990s she had transformed herself from ingenue into a leading lady with a dramatic turn opposite Willis in Alan Rudolph's modestly budgeted psychological murder mystery *Mortal Thoughts*, which she also coproduced. Strong roles in *A Few Good Men* (opposite Tom Cruise and Jack Nicholson), *Indecent Proposal* (opposite Robert Redford), and *Disclosure* (opposite Michael Douglas) firmly secured her position at the top of the Hollywood box office game. The same sort of success did not follow in *The Scarlet Letter*—a film that suffered a one-two punch at the box office as it was crushed by critics and ignored by audiences. Symptomatic of so many superstars, Moore often fails to see her own limitations; despite her talents as an actor, she is a thoroughly modern figure who was just plain wrong as the adulterous Hester Prynne of Nathaniel Hawthorne's novel. Regardless, in 1995 she became Hollywood's highest-paid actress at $12.5 million for her role as the stripper in the 1996 film *Striptease*; a testament more to her showmanship (frequent public appearances with Willis and offspring, and her nude *Vanity Fair* covers) than her ability to carry a movie.

Filmography: Choices (1981); ''General Hospital'' (1982–1983, tvs); Parasite (1982);

Young Doctors in Love (1982); Blame It on Rio (1984); No Small Affair (1984); St. Elmo's Fire (1985); About Last Night . . . (1986); One Crazy Summer (1986); Wisdom (1986); The Seventh Sign (1988); We're No Angels (1989); Ghost (1990); Mortal Thoughts (1991) also producer; Nothing but Trouble (1991); The Butcher's Wife (1991); A Few Good Men (1992); Indecent Proposal (1993); Disclosure (1994); Scarlet Letter (1995); Now and Then (1995) also producer.

MURPHY, EDDIE. Born April 3, 1961, in Hempstead, New York; actor, comedian. Supremely talented comic whose crude style and meteoric rise from young comic to box office star have drawn comparisons to Richard Pryor. He hit big at age nineteen as the most dynamic member of a stale "Saturday Night Live" (SNL), electrifying viewers with his profane Gumby, his adult Buckwheat, and his ghettoized Mr. Rogers. Quickly becoming too big for the deflated "SNL," Murphy carried the otherwise mediocre *48 Hrs.* and *Beverly Hills Cop* to box office heights. Starring as convict Reggie Hammond in both *48 Hrs.* films and as Detroit detective Axel Foley in the *Beverly Hills Cop* trilogy, Murphy created vehicles for himself as a foul-mouthed, insult-spewing hero who is as funny as he is offensive. Unfortunately, however, all of his other films have fallen flat in comparison, even when he has attempted to expand, as with the 1930s speakeasy story *Harlem Nights* (which he also wrote, directed, and produced) or with the horror comedy *A Vampire in Brooklyn*. Among his several forays into television producing was the well-received 1991 Redd Foxx sitcom "The Royal Family," which was cut short after Foxx's death.

Filmography: "Saturday Night Live" (1980–1984, tvs); 48 Hrs. (1982); Trading Places (1983); Best Defense (1984); Beverly Hills Cop (1984); The Golden Child (1986); Beverly Hills Cop II (1987) also story; Eddie Murphy Raw (1987) also ep, screenplay; Hollywood Shuffle (1987); Coming to America (1988); Harlem Nights (1989) also director, screenplay, ep; Another 48 Hrs. (1990); The Kid Who Loved Christmas (1992, tvm); Boomerang (1992); The Distinguished Gentleman (1992); Beverly Hills Cop III (1994); A Vampire in Brooklyn (1995).

MURRAY, BILL. Born September 21, 1950, in Chicago; actor, comedian. Brother is actor and comedian Brian Doyle-Murray. Former member of Chicago's Second City troupe who made the leap to television as Chevy Chase's replacement in the third season of "Saturday Night Live" (SNL). Several sophomoric, but entertaining, guilty pleasures followed—*Meatballs, Caddyshack, Stripes*—each of them watchable almost entirely because of Murray, a quick-witted comic who does the loathsome, sleazy, smart-ass better than anyone in the business. This quality made him a perfect choice to play Gonzo journalist Hunter S. Thompson in the otherwise muddled *Where the Buffalo Roam*. In 1984 he reteamed with *Meatballs* and *Stripes* director Ivan Reitman and former "SNL" costar Dan Aykroyd in the blockbuster sci-fi comedy *Ghostbusters*. In exchange for his work in that hit, Columbia Pictures agreed to green-light Murray in his first dramatic role, *The Razor's Edge*, a noble attempt at adapting W.

Somerset Maugham's philosophical novel that fails to measure up to the 1946 remake. Like so many great comics, he deftly straddles the border between comedy and drama, as seen most successfully in his recent films *Groundhog Day*, *Mad Dog and Glory*, and *Ed Wood*.

Filmography: La Honte de la Jungle/Jungle Burger (1975) voice; "Saturday Night Live" (1977–1980, tvs); The Dogs (1978); A Bird for All Seasons (1979); First Love (1979); Meatballs (1979); Mr. Mike's Mondo Video (1979); Caddyshack (1980); Where the Buffalo Roam (1980); Loose Shoes (1980); Stripes (1980); Nothing Lasts Forever (1982); Tootsie (1982); Ghostbusters (1984); The Razor's Edge (1984) also screenplay; Little Shop of Horrors (1986); Scrooged (1988); Ghostbusters II (1989); Quick Change (1990) also producer, director; What about Bob? (1991); Groundhog Day (1993); Mad Dog and Glory (1993); Ed Wood (1994).

Honor: Emmy Award for Best Writing ("Saturday Night Live" 1977).

MY DINNER WITH ANDRE (1981), drama. Directed by Louis Malle; screenplay by Wallace Shawn and Andre Gregory; produced by George W. George and Beverly Karp; photographed by Jeri Sopanen; edited by Suzanne Baron; music by Allen Shawn, "Trois Gymnopedies" by Eric Satie; released by New Yorker Films; 110 minutes. *Cast*: Andre Gregory, Wallace Shawn.

A daring cinema experiment that is notable simply for its audacity; it's a two-hour dinner conversation featuring just two men who discuss, with airy pretension, their differing opinions on the experiences of life. The "my" of the title is playwright and actor Wallace Shawn (or is it the viewer?), the Andre is theater director Andre Gregory, and the dinner is quail. Set in one of those swank Manhattan restaurants where the menus are in a foreign language, and the guests speak in politely hushed tones, the film begins with Shawn's sense of dread about his dinner with the slightly eccentric Gregory, whom he hasn't seen or spoken to in years. The "conversation" begins mostly as a monologue as Gregory pontificates about Tibet, Albert Speer, Polish theater figure Jerzy Grotowski, Scotland's ecopsychic retreat Findhorn, and the overall deadening of human experience. Shawn's contribution is an occasional cackle. But as the dinner progresses, and we work our way through the main course toward the espresso and Amaretto, Shawn becomes more opinionated and dissentious. By then a curious thing happens to the viewer—we become compelled to put forth *our* opinion. Malle, the nearly invisible director of this chat, puts the viewer in the position of examining and defending his or her own beliefs. "With the possible exception of Andy Warhol's *Empire*, the least movie-like motion picture since Fred Ott sneezed" (*The Motion Picture Guide*). "It is in its own way as definitive a statement of the possibilities of realism as *Caligari* was of Expressionism" (Bruce Kawin, *Film Quarterly*, Winter 1981–1982).

N

NASHVILLE (1975), comedy/drama. Directed and produced by Robert Altman; screenplay by Joan Tewkesbury; photographed by Paul Lohmann; edited by Sidney Levin and Dennis Hill; music by Richard Baskin, song "I'm Easy" by Keith Carradine; released by Paramount; 159 minutes. *Cast*: Ned Beatty, Karen Black, Ronee Blakely, Keith Carradine, Geraldine Chaplin, Shelley Duvall, Allen Garfield, Henry Gibson, Scott Glenn, Jeff Goldblum, Barbara Harris, Michael Murphy, Bert Remsen, Gwen Welles, Keenan Wynn, Elliott Gould, Julie Christie.

An American mosaic assembled from the lives of twenty-four characters who spend a few days together in the country music capital of Nashville. The skeletal plot, which lends support, involves the efforts of political advance man John Triplett (Murphy) as he tries to get the biggest names in country music to appear at a rally for presidential candidate Hal Phillip Walker of the Replacement Party. What *Nashville* is really about, however, is the similarity between the mythicism and popularity of the country music star and those of the politician; the optimism in the face of tragedy, the moral rectitude, and the need to please the audience. Altman's elaborate structure, which allows us glimpses into the lives of the twenty-four characters, combined with the aural richness of his multilayered sound track, succeeds in putting the viewer in the middle of this circuslike swirl of activity called Nashville. Among the many characters in this perfectly cast Altman gallery are Haven Hamilton (Gibson), the white-suited, silver-haired legend of the Grand Old Opry; Barbara Jean (Blakely), the compassionate, emotionally frail superstar who, at the urging of her husband (Garfield), returns to performing too soon after a hospital stay; brash interviewer Opal (Chaplin), who purports to be working for the BBC; Delbert Reese (Beatty), one of the organizers of the political rally, whose neglected wife, Linnea (Tomlin), has a brief affair with licentious folk rock singer Tom Frank (Carradine); Sueleen Gay (Welles), a talentless singer who reluctantly agrees to perform a humiliating striptease in order to get her big chance; and Mr. Green (Wynn), a caring old man whose dying wife is on the same hospital floor as Barbara Jean. There are few scenes in the Altman canon more perfect than the finale of *Nashville*, when, during the rally at the Nashville Parthenon, an assassin, who is apparently unable to distinguish between politicians and entertainers, shoots Barbara Jean and Haven Hamilton. As the stunned crowd looks on, the bleeding Haven's first thought is for his audience as he drags aspiring country western star Albuquerque (Harris) from the wings for a stirring performance of ''It Don't Worry Me,'' while the untalented Sueleen watches her dream slip away. Altman would later return to similar themes in his cable-television political miniseries *Tanner '88* (starring Murphy as the candidate) and his Hollywood satire *The Player.* ''I wanted to do Nashville to study our myths and our heroes and our hypocrisy. Because by the time we usually get around to studying our present, it's past, and the truth is buried so deep we can't even find it'' (Robert Altman, quoted in Judith M. Kass' *Robert Altman: American Innovator*).

Awards: Academy Award for Best Song (Carradine, ''I'm Easy''); Academy Award nominations for Best Picture, Director, Supporting Actress (Blakely, Tomlin); New York Film Critics Circle Awards for Best Picture, Director, Supporting Actress (Tomlin); included in the Library of Congress' National Film Registry (1992).

NATIONAL LAMPOON'S ANIMAL HOUSE (1978), comedy. Directed by John Landis; screenplay by Harold Ramis, Douglas Kenney, and Chris Miller; produced by Ivan Reitman and Matty Simmons; photographed by Charles Correll; edited by George Folsey, Jr.; music by Elmer Bernstein; released by Universal; 109 minutes. *Cast*: John Belushi, Tim Matheson, John Vernon, Tom Hulce, Stephen Furst, Donald Sutherland, Peter Riegert, Kevin Bacon, Cesare Danova, Mary Louise Weller, James Daughton, Bruce McGill, Mark Metcalf, Verna Bloom, Stephen Bishop.

The pinnacle of sophomoric gross-out comedy, this box office smash rode to the top of the charts largely on the back of the appropriately animalistic John Belushi, whose star status was catapulted by NBC's ''Saturday Night Live.'' He stars as John ''Bluto'' Blutarsky, one of the members of the Delta House fraternity. As the least respectable frat house on campus, they have incurred the wrath of Dean Wormer (Vernon), who has placed them on ''double secret probation.'' As he battles to close them down, the boys of Delta House suck down beer, throw toga parties, give a horse a heart attack, start a food fight in the cafeteria, and unleash a reign of terror on a local parade. Like much of John Landis' work, it appeals to juvenile base instincts; the strength, however, is in its sharp dialogue and the unrestrained performance of Belushi, which tap into a rebellious attitude deeply ingrained in modern culture. It's all summed up in Bluto's impersonation of a zit in which, his cheeks bursting with cottage cheese, he literally spits in the face of the elite. It may be gross, but American audiences were living vicariously through Bluto's insubordination. A tamed television series, "Delta House," ran for a short while in 1979.

NETWORK (1976), drama. Directed by Sidney Lumet; screenplay by Paddy Chayefsky; produced by Howard Gottfried; photographed by Owen Roizman; edited by Alan Heim; music by Elliot Lawrence; released by MGM/UA; 120 minutes. *Cast*: Faye Dunaway, William Holden, Peter Finch, Robert Duvall, Wesley Addy, Ned Beatty, Beatrice Straight.

A biting satire of television news written by raging genius Paddy Chayefsky, who previously leveled his sights on the medical community in *The Hospital*. Howard Beale (Finch) is a veteran newscaster for the fictional United Broadcasting System who, after getting notice that he's being booted from the station, threatens to commit suicide on the air. Ratings skyrocket, and on the big night he instead apologizes and beckons people to open their windows and shout to the world, "I'm mad as hell and I'm not going to take this anymore!" He then becomes a ratings pawn for brash programming executive Diane Christenson (Dunaway), who, over the objections of old-fashioned network news head Max Schumacher (Holden), turns the news into cheap entertainment by giving Beale his own show and marketing him as the "Mad Prophet of the Airwaves." It's a familiar warning—television is the new opiate of the masses—but Chayefsky and Lumet, both veterans of the golden age of television in the 1950s, give it a new spirit and resonance.

Awards: Academy Awards for Best Actor (Finch), Actress, Supporting Actress (Straight), Screenplay; Academy Award nominations for Best Picture, Director, Actor (Holden), Supporting Actor (Beatty), Cinematography, Editing; New York Film Critics Circle Award for Best Screenplay; Los Angeles Film Critics Award for Best Picture (tie).

NEWMAN, PAUL. Born January 26, 1925, in Cleveland, Ohio; actor, director, producer. Married to Joanne Woodward. One of the most consistently superb and successful actors of the period stretching from the mid-1950s to the mid-1990s, Newman exudes sex appeal, vulnerability, and cool machismo (drawing early comparisons to the young Brando), which, in his later years, gained a level of warmth and friskiness. Receiving training at the Yale School of Drama and the Actors Studio, Newman was signed to a Warner Brothers contract in 1953 and gave his first widely acclaimed performance as boxer Rocky Graziano in MGM's *Somebody Up There Likes Me*. He began to develop and fine-tune his alienated loser persona in the 1960s with his memorable work in *The Hustler* (as pool shark "Fast" Eddie Felson), *Hud*, *Harper* (as the Ross Macdonald private eye he revisited in *The Drowning Pool*), *Cool Hand Luke*, and *Hombre*. His two pairings with Robert Redford—*Butch Cassidy and the Sundance Kid* and *The Sting*—brought him even greater popularity but also marked a transition point away from young leads (reserved for the likes of Redford) and toward a series of bolder, middle-aged characters. While *The Sting* and *The Towering Inferno* were his unqualified hits of the 1970s, his work with John Huston (*The*

Life and Times of Judge Roy Bean), and Robert Altman (*Buffalo Bill and the Indians, Quintet*) and a third collaboration with George Roy Hill (*Slap Shot*) allowed Newman to expand as an actor. Aged fifty-five by the time the 1980s started, he showed no signs of succumbing to character roles, continuing instead to play men every bit as complex as "Fast" Eddie Felson. From his back-to-back Oscar nominations for *Absence of Malice* and *The Verdict*, to his *Hustler* follow-up *The Color of Money*, to the Coen brothers' adventurous comedy *The Hudsucker Proxy*, Newman has remained a solid, first-rate actor. He took his craft to even greater heights in *Nobody's Fool*, delivering one of the most honest and nuanced performances ever caught on film. In addition to his work in front of the lens, he has directed five films—from 1968's *Rachel, Rachel* to the familiar terrain of Tennessee Williams' *The Glass Menagerie*, both of which starred his wife since 1958, Joanne Woodward. His much-publicized outside interests include auto racing and his Newman's Own food company.

Filmography of key pre-1965 films: Somebody Up There Likes Me (1956); Cat on a Hot Tin Roof (1958); The Left-Handed Gun (1958); The Long Hot Summer (1958); Exodus (1960); The Hustler (1961); Paris Blues (1961); Sweet Bird of Youth (1962); Hud (1963).

Filmography since 1965: Lady L (1965); Harper (1966); Torn Curtain (1966); Cool Hand Luke (1967); Hombre (1967); Rachel, Rachel (1968) director, producer; The Secret War of Harry Frigg (1968); Butch Cassidy and the Sundance Kid (1969); Winning (1969) also ep; King: A Filmed Record . . . Montgomery to Memphis (1970) narrator; WUSA (1970) also producer; Sometimes a Great Notion (1971) also director, ep; They Might Be Giants (1971) producer; The Effect of Gamma Rays on Man-in-the-Moon Marigolds (1972) director, producer; The Life and Times of Judge Roy Bean (1972); Pocket Money (1972); The Mackintosh Man (1973); The Sting (1973); The Towering Inferno (1974); The Drowning Pool (1975); Silent Movie (1976); Buffalo Bill and the Indians, or Sitting Bull's History Lesson (1976); Slap Shot (1977); Quintet (1979); When Time Ran Out (1980); Absence of Malice (1981); Fort Apache, the Bronx (1981); The Verdict (1982); Harry and Son (1984) also director, producer, screenplay; The Color of Money (1986); The Glass Menagerie (1987) director; Blaze (1989); Fat Man and Little Boy (1989); Mr. and Mrs. Bridge (1990); The Hudsucker Proxy (1994); Nobody's Fool (1994).

Honors: Academy Awards for Best Actor (*The Color of Money*) and Jean Hersholt Humanitarian Award (1993); Academy Award nominations for Best Actor (*Cat on a Hot Tin Roof, The Hustler, Hud, Cool Hand Luke, Absence of Malice, The Verdict, Nobody's Fool*) and Best Picture (*Rachel, Rachel*); New York Film Critics Circle Awards for Best Actor (*Nobody's Fool*) and Director (*Rachel, Rachel*); Cannes Film Festival Award for Best Actor (*The Long Hot Summer*); Berlin Film Festival Award for Best Actor (*Nobody's Fool*); Kennedy Center Honors Lifetime Achievement Award (1992).

Selected bibliography

Lax, Eric. *Paul Newman: A Biography*. Atlanta, GA: Turner, 1996.
Quirk, Lawrence J. *The Films of Paul Newman*. New York: Citadel, 1986.

NICHOLS, MIKE. Born Michael Igor Peschkowsky November 6, 1931, in Berlin; director, producer. Married to television journalist Diane Sawyer. Intelligent, insightful, and literate director who excels when tackling issues of sexual politics. His early comic improv work with Elaine May (1957–1961), including their Broadway show *An Evening with Mike Nichols and Elaine May*, brought him a critical and commercial following that led to his 1963 Broadway directing debut, Neil Simon's *Barefoot in the Park*. When he finally took the leap to motion pictures, he did so with a vengeance—*Who's Afraid of Virginia Woolf?*, his adaptation of Edward Albee's harrowing examination of George and Martha's twisted marriage; *The Graduate*, a comic reflection on 1960s sexuality as seen through the eyes of the angst-filled Benjamin Braddock; *Catch-22*, a bold attempt to adapt Joseph Heller's popular novel; and *Carnal Knowledge*, the still-underrated look at the sexual games between men and women. During the next ten years, he directed only two fiction films—*The Day of the Dolphin* and *The Fortune*, both of them disappointments—and instead devoted much of his energy to the stage (director of *The Prisoner of Second Avenue* 1972; producer of *Annie* 1977) and television ("Family"). While all of his subsequent films featured fine performances from the likes of Meryl Streep, Cher, Matthew Broderick, Melanie Griffith, Shirley MacLaine, and Harrison Ford, none of them have approached the raw power of his first four films. In 1995, Nichols reteamed with Elaine May, directing her script for *The Birdcage* (1996), their remake of the French hit *La Cage Aux Folles*.

Filmography: Who's Afraid of Virginia Woolf? (1966); The Graduate (1967); Catch-22 (1970); Carnal Knowledge (1971) also producer; The Day of the Dolphin (1973); The Fortune (1975) also producer; Gilda Live (1980); Silkwood (1983) also producer; Heartburn (1986) also producer; Biloxi Blues (1988); Working Girl (1988); Postcards from the Edge (1990) also producer; Regarding Henry (1991) also producer; Wolf (1994).

Filmography as producer: "Family" (1976–1980, tvs) ep; The Longshot (1986) ep; Remains of the Day (1993).

Honors: Academy Award for Best Director (*The Graduate*); Academy Award nominations for Best Director (*Who's Afraid of Virginia Woolf?*, *Silkwood*, *Working Girl*); New York Film Critics Circle Award for Best Director (*The Graduate*); Tony Awards for Best Director (*Barefoot in the Park* 1964, *Luv* 1965, *The Odd Couple* 1965, *Plaza Suite* 1968, *The Prisoner of Second Avenue* 1972, *The Real Thing* 1984) and Best Musical (*Annie* 1977).

Selected bibliography

Gelmis, Joseph. *The Film Director as Superstar*. New York: Doubleday, 1971.
Schuth, H. Wayne. *Mike Nichols*. Boston: Twayne, 1978.

NICHOLSON, JACK. Born April 22, 1937, in Neptune, New Jersey; actor, screenwriter, director. Former longtime companion of Anjelica Huston. One of the most commanding screen presences of the era, he first appeared in a number of low-budget Roger Corman pictures, most notably, *The Cry Baby Killer*, *The Little Shop of Horrors* (as the masochistic dental patient), and *The Terror*, before writing and producing Monte Hellman's *Ride in a Whirlwind* and *The Shooting* and Bob Rafelson's Monkees vehicle *Head*. Everything changed when he was cast in *Easy Rider* as the clean-cut southern lawyer who encounters a pair of motorcycle-riding, pot-smoking hippies and imparts his theory that Venusians have landed on Earth. He developed his devilish charm, wicked sense of humor, and dangerous spontaneity into an entire package that led to a stretch of distinguished films in the 1970s, beginning with *Five Easy Pieces* and including *Carnal Knowledge, The King of Marvin Gardens, The Last Detail, Chinatown, One Flew over the Cuckoo's Nest,* and *The Passenger.* A huge element of his early success is his ability to tap into a primal madness; the viewer vicariously experiences his tirades against the inflexible waitress of *Five Easy Pieces,* the bar owner in *The Last Detail,* and Nurse Ratched in *One Flew over the Cuckoo's Nest.* Yet, for all of his bravado, his characters are at the core weak and troubled and therefore elicit our sympathy. Stanley Kubrick's *The Shining* gave the leering Nicholson a showy role as the possessed writer Jack Torrance, but it was a typically Kubrickian performance of mannerisms over heart. His retired astronaut Garrett Breedlove of *Terms of Endearment* marked a shift in tone to that of the charming rascal. A different actor than he was in the early 1970s, Nicholson has become a superstar persona on the level of Marlon Brando—an actor whose presence in a film is an event. Whether in a cameo (anchor Bill Rorich of *Broadcast News*) or a supporting role (the Joker in *Batman,* Colonel Nathan Jessep in *A Few Good Men*), Nicholson commands undivided attention. He has had a harder time, however, carrying the films in which he is the lead—*Ironweed* and *Hoffa* went unseen by most people, *The Witches of Eastwick* is an example of bloated excess, and Bob Rafelson's *Man Trouble* and Mike Nichols' *Wolf* both fail to capture the raw energy of their earlier collaborations. His gutsiest work in years has come under Sean Penn's direction in *The Crossing Guard,* a throwback to a raw 1970s style of filmmaking that pairs Nicholson with Anjelica Huston for the first time since John Huston's *Prizzi's Honor.* Underrated is Nicholson's third directing effort, *Two Jakes,* an intelligent and thoughtfully executed sequel to *Chinatown.* "Nicholson is the Hollywood celebrity who is most like a character in some ongoing novel of our times" (David Thomson, *A Biographical Dictionary of Film*).

Filmography of key pre-1965 films: Cry Baby Killer (1958); Studs Lonigan (1960); Little Shop of Horrors (1961); The Raven (1963); The Terror (1963).

Filmography since 1965: Flight to Fury (1966) also screenplay; Ride in a Whirlwind (1966) also producer, screenplay; Hell's Angels on Wheels (1967); The Shooting (1967) also producer; The Trip (1967) screenplay only; The St. Valentine's Day Massacre (1967); Rebel Rousers (1967/released in 1970); Head (1968) also producer, screenplay; Psych-Out (1968); Easy Rider (1969); Five Easy Pieces (1970); On a Clear Day You Can See Forever (1970); Carnal Knowledge (1971); Drive, He Said (1971) director, producer, screenplay; A Safe Place (1971); The King of Marvin Gardens (1972); The Last Detail (1973); Chinatown (1974); The Fortune (1975); One Flew over the Cuckoo's Nest (1975); The Passenger (1975); Tommy (1975); The Last Tycoon (1976); The Missouri Breaks (1976); Goin' South (1978) also director; The Shining (1980); The Border

(1981); The Postman Always Rings Twice (1981); Reds (1981); Terms of Endearment (1983); Prizzi's Honor (1985); Heartburn (1986); Broadcast News (1987); Ironweed (1987); The Witches of Eastwick (1987); Batman (1989); The Two Jakes (1990) also director; Man Trouble (1992); Hoffa (1992); A Few Good Men (1992); Wolf (1994); The Crossing Guard (1994).

Honors: Academy Awards for Best Actor (*One Flew over the Cuckoo's Nest*) and Supporting Actor (*Terms of Endearment*); Academy Award nominations for Best Actor (*Five Easy Pieces, The Last Detail, Chinatown, Prizzi's Honor, Ironweed*) and Supporting Actor (*Easy Rider, Reds, A Few Good Men*); Los Angeles Film Critics Awards for Best Actor (*Ironweed* and *The Witches of Eastwick*, tied) and Supporting Actor (*Terms of Endearment*); New York Film Critics Circle Awards for Best Actor (*Chinatown, One Flew over the Cuckoo's Nest, Prizzi's Honor*, and, in a tie, *Broadcast News, Ironweed*, and *The Witches of Eastwick*) and Supporting Actor (*Terms of Endearment*); Cannes Film Festival Award for Best Actor (*The Last Detail*); American Film Institute Lifetime Achievement Award (1994).

Selected bibliography

Brode, Douglas. *The Films of Jack Nicholson.* New York: Citadel Press, 1994.
McGilligan, Patrick. *Jack's Life: A Biography of Jack Nicholson.* New York: W. W. Norton, 1994.

NIGHT OF THE LIVING DEAD (1968), horror. Directed, photographed (b&w), and edited by George A. Romero; screenplay by John A. Russo; produced by Russell Streiner and Karl Hardman; music by Hardman; released by Image Ten; 90 minutes. *Cast*: Judith O'Dea, Russell Streiner, Duane Jones, Karl Hardman, Marilyn Eastman, Keith Wayne, Judith Ridley, Kyra Schon.

A seminal film of the 1960s, this grainy black-and-white gorefest forever changed the landscape of the horror genre. A low-budget midnight movie hit, it gradually found a larger audience eager to see its chillingly apocalyptic vision of American life. It takes place almost entirely in a remote farmhouse as a diverse group (a catatonic woman, a contentious husband and his family, a pair of young lovers, and a resolute black man) are victimized by an army of flesh-eating zombies who have surrounded them. Photographed in an edgy, handheld style that adds a feeling of immediate danger, the film is an all-out horror assault that never eases its almost-paralyzing tension. "In 1968, the title of George Romero's film could have been a beatnik poet's metaphor for the CBS Evening News" (J. Hoberman and Jonathan Rosenbaum in *Midnight Movies*). "This horror film casts serious aspersions on the integrity and social responsibility of its Pittsburgh-based makers" (*Variety*, October 16, 1968).

Sequels: Romero returned to direct *Dawn of the Dead* (1978) and *Day of the Dead* (1985). Makeup artist and longtime Romero collaborator Tom Savini directed the remake *Night of the Living Dead* (1990).

NIGHTMARE ON ELM STREET (1984), horror. Directed and written by Wes Craven; produced by Robert Shaye and Sara Risher; photographed by Jacques

Haitkin; edited by Rick Shaine; music by Charles Bernstein; released by New Line; 91 minutes. *Cast*: John Saxon, Ronee Blakely, Heather Langenkamp, Johnny Depp, Robert Englund, Charles Fleischer.

The film that hatched horror icon Freddy Kreuger, the scarred, wisecracking ghoul with the floppy hat, red-and-green-striped sweater, and razor-sharp glove who invades the dreams of teenagers and exacts a brutal revenge. Freddy (Englund) has returned to the town where, years before, he was burned alive by lawless locals, to make the teens pay for their parents' sins. What separates Freddy from other movie madmen is that he visits them in their dreams. Heavy on special effects and dream logic, the film succeeds because creator Wes Craven has tapped into a very real psychological fear of nightmares and the secrets that they hold. The subsequent franchise from independent film company New Line Cinema earned millions, and, by hiring such talented directors as Chuck Russell and Renny Harlin, they managed to keep the series at a certain level that, while inferior to the first film, at least kept the series fresh.

Sequels: Robert Englund reprised his Freddy role in *A Nightmare on Elm Street Part 2: Freddy's Revenge* (1985, Jack Sholder); *A Nightmare on Elm Street 3: Dream Warriors* (1987, Chuck Russell); *A Nightmare on Elm Street 4: The Dream Master* (1988, Renny Harlin); *A Nightmare on Elm Street 5: The Dream Child* (1989, Stephen Hopkins); and *Wes Craven's New Nightmare* (1994, Wes Craven).

NOBODY'S FOOL (1994), comedy/drama. Directed and written by Robert Benton (from the novel by Richard Russo); produced by Scott Rudin and Arlene Donovan; photographed by John Bailey; music by Howard Shore; edited by John Bloom; released by Paramount; 112 minutes. *Cast*: Paul Newman, Melanie Griffith, Bruce Willis, Jessica Tandy, Dylan Walsh, Pruitt Taylor Vince, Alexander Goodwin.

Countering the trendy reliance on hype, glitz, and pyrotechnics that has reduced so many of his contemporaries to mediocrity, Robert Benton has retained his humanistic, character-oriented style in this sublime Hawksian tale of an irresponsible sixty-year-old man who finally redeems himself in the eyes of his family and friends. Paul Newman stars as Donald "Sully" Sullivan, a man slowed by age and weathered by his snowy New England habitat. Living in the town where he was raised, he is the only boarder in a grand old house run by his former grade school teacher (Tandy), who holds out the hope that one day Sully will become responsible. That day comes when he's reunited with Peter (Walsh), the thirty-year-old son whom he long ago abandoned and who has now returned to town with Sully's grandchildren. Not surprisingly, the film underperformed at the box office, where audiences still prefer to see bigger-than-life characters—all Benton can offer them are real folk who struggle with the daily grind and occasionally find moments of grace and purity in their lives. Offering excellent support are Willis and Griffith as a troubled husband and wife and Vince as Sully's insecure, jelly donut-devouring best friend and coworker who feels left out when Peter reenters Sully's life.

Awards: Academy Awards for Best Actor and Screenplay; New York Film Critics Circle Award for Best Actor; Berlin Film Festival Silver Bear Award for Best Actor.

NOLTE, NICK. Born February 8, 1941, in Omaha, Nebraska; actor. Brawny leading man who generally stars as hard-edged, no-nonsense characters, he first gained attention as Tom Jordache in the celebrated television miniseries *Rich Man, Poor Man*. His performances as a Vietnam vet in *Who'll Stop the Rain?*, the marine biologist in *Cannery Row*, the journalist in *Under Fire*, the San Quentin playwright in *Weeds*, the loving father in *Lorenzo's Oil*, and the up-standing college basketball coach in *Blue Chips* are among his many critically acclaimed roles in films that have moved through theaters largely unseen by the public. Despite his talents, he has appeared in only a couple of films that have performed well at the box office—the comedies *48 Hrs.* and *Another 48 Hrs.* (costarring with Eddie Murphy), *The Prince of Tides* (opposite Barbra Strei-sand), and *Cape Fear*, Martin Scorsese's misguided attempt to direct a Holly-wood thriller. "This actor carries his wounds, his talent, his past mistakes, and his urgent promise like a man trying to tidy up—there is something of Norman Mailer about him" (David Thomson, *A Biographical Dictionary of Film*).

Filmography: Return to Macon County (1975); Rich Man, Poor Man (1976, tvms); The Deep (1977); Who'll Stop the Rain? (1978); Heart Beat (1979); North Dallas Forty (1979); 48 Hrs. (1982); Cannery Row (1982); Under Fire (1983); Teachers (1984); Grace Quigley (1985); Down and Out in Beverly Hills (1986); Extreme Prejudice (1987); Weeds (1987); Farewell to the King (1989); New York Stories, "Life Lessons" episode (1989); Three Fugitives (1989); Another 48 Hrs. (1990); Everybody Wins (1990); Q&A (1990); Cape Fear (1991); The Prince of Tides (1991); The Player (1992); Lorenzo's Oil (1992); Blue Chips (1994); I'll Do Anything (1994); I Love Trouble (1994); Jefferson in Paris (1995).

Honors: Academy Award nomination for Best Actor (*The Prince of Tides*); Los Angeles Film Critics Award for Best Actor (*The Prince of Tides*).

NORMA RAE (1979), drama. Directed by Martin Ritt; screenplay by Irving Ravetch and Harriet Frank, Jr.; produced by Tamara Asseyev and Alex Rose; photographed by John Alonzo; edited by Sidney Levin; music by David Shire; released by 20th Century Fox; 110 minutes. *Cast*: Sally Field, Beau Bridges, Ron Leibman, Pat Hingle, Barbara Baxley.

Carried by Sally Field's intensely riveting performance, this tale of an attempt to organize a textile workers' union is a superb slice of Americana. Field plays Norma Rae Webster, a widowed young mother of two living in a rural, southern Baptist town who has done much to earn her sullied reputation. When a Jewish union organizer from Brooklyn appears at her screen door, she learns that she can either hold steady on her path to nowhere or stand up and fight for what she believes—fair treatment and better wages. She reaches the peak of her strength when, in a wordless scene, she stands atop a table in the mill defiantly displaying a "Union" sign high above her head as the deafening roar of the textile machinery churns, one by one, to a silent halt. While movies like *Smokey and the Bandit* and *Mrs. Doubtfire* have established Field as a lightweight comic actor, the brilliance of her work in this film and others, such as *Sybil* or even the underrated *Punchline*, reminds us of her ability to get under the skin of her characters and deliver an emotional punch. Like *On the Waterfront* and *How Green Was My Valley* before it and *Matewan* after, this is one of the premier movies on the individual courage behind the labor movement.

Awards: Academy Awards for Best Actress and Song (''It Goes Like It Goes''); Academy Award nominations for Best Picture, Screenplay; New York Film Critics Circle Award for Best Actress; Cannes Film Festival Awards for Best Actress and Grand Prix de la Commission Superieure Technique.

O

O'NEAL, RYAN. Born Patrick Ryan O'Neal April 20, 1941, in Los Angeles; actor. Longtime companion of Farrah Fawcett; son of screenwriter Charles O'Neal and actor Patricia Callaghan O'Neal; father of Tatum, who costarred as his daughter Addie Pray in *Paper Moon*. A veteran of the television soap opera "Peyton Place" from 1964 to 1969, O'Neal's boyish charm made him a perfect choice to play the innocent, suffering Oliver in *Love Story*, the role that turned him into a major star. As one of the most sought-after actors of the 1970s, he appeared in three Peter Bogdanovich films, costarred twice with Barbra Streisand, took the lead in Stanley Kubrick's underrated *Barry Lyndon*, and starred in Walter Hill's existentialist action film *The Driver*. However, in the following two decades he has been seen infrequently on the big screen. Excelling in a style of roguish screwball comedy that harks back to the 1930s and 1940s, O'Neal works best in that arena under the direction of those with a similar sensibility, such as Bogdanovich or Andrew Bergman (*So Fine*). His roles since the 1980s have failed to match his earlier work, and one senses that a renewed teaming with Bogdanovich would benefit them both. Less beneficial was his teaming with Farrah Fawcett in 1991's short-lived sitcom "Good Sports."

Filmography: "Peyton Place" (1964–1969, tvs); The Big Bounce (1969); The Games (1970); Love Story (1970); Wild Rovers (1971); What's Up, Doc? (1972); Paper Moon (1973); The Thief Who Came to Dinner (1973); Barry Lyndon (1975); Nickelodeon (1976); A Bridge Too Far (1977); The Driver (1978); Oliver's Story (1978); The Main Event (1979); Green Ice (1981); So Fine (1981); Partners (1982); Fever Pitch (1985); Tough Guys Don't Dance (1987); Chances Are (1989); Faithful (1995).

OATES, WARREN. Born July 5, 1928, in Depoy, Kentucky; died 1982; actor. Rough-edged character actor who consistently appeared in little-seen films of integrity and honesty and, as a result, never received the attention he deserved. He is probably best known for his association with Sam Peckinpah, who cast him in a small role in *Ride the High Country* before bestowing a larger part in *The Wild Bunch* (as Lyle Gorch) and the lead in *Bring Me the Head of Alfredo Garcia*. Equally impressive are his four collaborations with Monte Hellman— *The Shooting, Cockfighter, China 9, Liberty 37*, and especially *Two-Lane Blacktop*, as G.T.O., the car enthusiast who loves to drive fast (''Color me gone'') and far (''I get to one end of the country and I bounce off just like a rubber ball''). He's also done memorable work as the lead in *Dillinger* and as Sissy Spacek's strict, but loving, father in *Badlands*.

Filmography of key pre-1965 films: The Rise and Fall of Legs Diamond (1960); Ride the High Country (1962).

Filmography since 1965: Major Dundee (1965); Return of the Seven (1966); In the Heat of the Night (1967); The Shooting (1967); Welcome to Hard Times (1967); The Split (1968); Crooks and Coronets (1969); Smith (1969); The Wild Bunch (1969); Barquero (1970); There Was a Crooked Man (1970); Chandler (1971); The Hired Hand (1971); Two-Lane Blacktop (1971); Badlands (1973); Dillinger (1973); Kid Blue (1973); The Thief Who Came to Dinner (1973); Tom Sawyer (1973); Bring Me the Head of Alfredo Garcia (1974); Cockfighter/Born to Kill (1973); The White Dawn (1974); 92 in the Shade (1975); Race with the Devil (1975); Dixie Dynamite (1976); Drum (1976); Sleeping Dogs (1977); The Brink's Job (1978); China 9, Liberty 37 (1978); True Grit (1978, tvm); 1941 (1979); The Border (1981); Stripes (1981); Tough Enough (1982); Blue Thunder (1983).

ONCE UPON A TIME IN AMERICA (1984), gangster. Directed and cowritten by Sergio Leone; screenplay with Leonardo Benvenuti, Piero De Bernardi, Enrico Medioli, Franco Arcalli, Franco Ferrini, and Stuart Kaminsky (from the novel by Harry Grey); produced by Arnon Milchan; photographed by Tonio Delli Colli; edited by Nino Baragli; music by Ennio Morricone; released by Warner Bros.; 227 minutes. *Cast*: Robert De Niro, James Woods, Elizabeth McGovern, Treat Williams, Tuesday Weld, Burt Young, Joe Pesci, Danny Aiello, Jennifer Connelly, James Russo.

An unremittingly sad look back at lost loves and dreams, this epic tale of American gangsters is Sergio Leone's operatic combination of F. Scott Fitzgerald and Marcel Proust filtered through his memories of old Hollywood movies. Set in 1923, 1933, and 1968, the film fluidly slips from era to era as it follows Noodles (De Niro) from his days as a young hood in Manhattan's Lower East Side, through his rise to power as a gangster in the 1930s, to his melancholic old age. The movie begins in 1933 as Noodles informs on Max (Woods) and the rest of his former gang members. After the whole gang dies, Noodles retreats to an opium den, where he reminisces on his past friendship with Max and his romance with Deborah (Connelly as a girl, McGovern as a woman). Running 227 minutes, the film is a dreamy re-creation of gangster life that may not be accurate but is certainly seductive and exciting. Leone's decision to travel back and forth through time is truly inspired (especially the phone-ringing transition of the opening), leaving the viewer to speculate that everything in the 1968 portion (Max's rise to political heights as a senator and Deborah's status as Max's wife) is a guilt-induced, opium nightmare that alleviates Noodles' pain at having informed on his friends. De Niro and Woods are both excellent in their roles, as is the young Connelly. The haunting pan flute and zither music marks one of Ennio Morricone's most magnificent achievements. Also released in a straightforward 143-minute version, which lacks the magnificent vision of the original cut and simply has no good reason to exist.

ONE FALSE MOVE (1992), crime drama. Directed by Carl Franklin; screenplay by Billy Bob Thornton and Tom Epperson; produced by Jesse Beaton and Ben Myron; photographed by James L. Carter; edited by Carole Kravetz; music by Peter Haycock and Derek Holt; released by I.R.S. Releasing; 106 minutes. *Cast:* Bill Paxton, Cynda Williams, Billy Bob Thornton, Michael Beach, Earl Billings, Jim Metzler.

A film about murder and the people who commit it, *One False Move* does what violent films should do—it disturbs the viewer. It doesn't glorify violence, mythicize it, or find humor in it; instead, in its opening sequence, the film depicts a brutal and disquieting drug-related mass murder. The three killers (a calm and methodical black man, an unpredictable, coke-addicted white man, and his cautious and frightened mulatto girlfriend, Fantasia) flee Los Angeles for the presumed safety of Arkansas. Waiting for them and eagerly anticipating a *High Noon*-style showdown is small-town sheriff Dale ''Hurricane'' Dixon. Director Carl Franklin builds the tension by intercutting between his two stories—the cross-country escape that eats away at the violent trio and the bond that grows between Hurricane and the two L.A. homicide detectives who've come to assist on the case. Although it's essentially a crime thriller, *One False Move* exceeds expectations by developing characters who are far beyond the level of stereotype usually found in the genre; these are complex people in volatile, realistic situations. Bubbling underneath it all is a racial portrait that shows the delicate balance of black–white relations in America. Each and every performance is superb, especially Bill Paxton as Hurricane, Cynda Williams as Fantasia, and Billy Bob Thornton, who also cowrote the screenplay.

Award: Los Angeles Film Critics New Generation Award (Franklin).

ONE FLEW OVER THE CUCKOO'S NEST (1975), drama. Directed by Milos Forman; screenplay by Lawrence Hauben and Bo Goldman (from the novel by Ken Kesey and the play by Dale Wasserman); produced by Saul Zaentz and Michael Douglas; photographed by Haskell Wexler, William Fraker, and Bill Butler; edited by Richard Chew, Lynzee Klingman, Sheldon Kahn; music by Jack Nitzsche; released by United Artists; 129 minutes. *Cast*: Jack Nicholson,

Louise Fletcher, William Redfield, Michael Berryman, Brad Dourif, Scatman Crothers, Danny De Vito, Will Sampson, Vincent Schiavelli, Christopher Lloyd.

The seminal Jack Nicholson film, this 1970s masterpiece is a powerful exploration of craziness and sanity that offers a reflection on the very meaning of both words. Nicholson plays Randle Patrick McMurphy, a criminal who escapes life on a prison work farm by pretending to be crazy. Thrown into a lunatic asylum, his mission becomes a rebellion against the blinding authority of the institute, which seems to exist only to quash the individual's sense of uniqueness. Under Milos Forman's direction, this adaptation of Ken Kesey's novel and Dale Wasserman's play is a disturbing film filled with memorable scenes and performances—from the fishing trip organized by McMurphy, to the scene in which Billy Bibbit (Dourif) loses his virginity, to the images of Chief (Sampson) hurling the sink out the window and escaping to freedom.

Awards: Academy Awards for Best Picture, Director, Actor, Actress (Fletcher), Screenplay; Academy Award nominations for Best Supporting Actor (Dourif), Cinematography, Score, Editing; New York Film Critics Circle Award for Best Actor; DGA Award; WGA Award; included in the Library of Congress' National Film Registry (1993).

ONE FROM THE HEART (1982), romance. Directed and cowritten by Francis Ford Coppola; screenplay with Armyan Bernstein; produced by Bernstein, Gray Frederickson, and Fred Roos; photographed by Vittorio Storaro; edited by Anne Goursaud, Rudi Fehr, and Randy Roberts; music by Tom Waits, songs performed by Waits and Crystal Gayle; released by Columbia; 107 minutes. *Cast*: Frederic Forrest, Teri Garr, Raul Julia, Nastassia Kinski, Lainie Kazan, Harry Dean Stanton, Allan Goorwitz.

Although it was a box office bust that didn't come close to recouping its hefty $27 million budget (a figure that would, by the following decade, be about the average cost of a Hollywood movie), this much-maligned love story is a beautifully simple tale told with an excess of technical complexity. Hank and Frannie (Forrest and Garr) are a married couple who have grown complacent and now feel a need to fill the romantic void in their hearts with someone else—Hank is awed by the exotic Leila (Kinski), and Frannie is made to feel special by the charming Ray (Julia). This is what it takes for Hank and Frannie to fall in love with one another again. The result is a dizzyingly romantic film throbbing with a dreamy, otherworldly atmosphere that Coppola conducts like a symphony— the pure romanticism of Vittorio Storaro's neon palette, the whimsy of Dean Tavoularis' production design, and the ache of the Tom Waits and Crystal Gayle songs. The one film of Coppola's that is ready for a revisionist reassessment, this is a studied experimental contrast of the purity of heart with the complexity of technology—in short, a film that, like Coppola's greatest work, is an essay on personal corruption. "A work of constant astonishment, Francis Coppola's new film is so daring it takes away your breath while staggering you visually" (Sheila Benson, *Los Angeles Times*, January 22, 1982).

OPENING NIGHT (1977), drama. Directed and written by John Cassavetes; produced and photographed by Al Ruban; edited by Tom Cornwell; music by Bo Harwood; released by Faces Distribution Co., rereleased by Castle Hill; 144 minutes. *Cast*: Gena Rowlands, John Cassavetes, Ben Gazzara, Joan Blondell, Zohra Lampert, Paul Stewart.

A little gem for fans of John Cassavetes, this long-unavailable film, which barely saw a release in 1977, offers a startling insight into the creative "family" of theater. Rowlands stars as Myrtle Gordon, a Broadway star in the midst of a personal crisis about aging who is in rehearsals for a new play called *The Second Woman*. The catalyst for Myrtle's emotional decline is her brief encounter with an adoring, though unbalanced, young female fan who is struck by a car and killed in front of the theater. Finding it difficult to love herself as much as that young fan did, Myrtle grows increasingly dependent on her ever-present bottle of scotch—first losing all touch with the character she is portraying and then losing all connection to her own reality. Her director (Gazzara) consoles her when she calls in a panic at 4 A.M., and the playwright (Blondell) tries to force her to confront her fears, but Myrtle needs to hit bottom in order to discover that ray of hope that both she and her character are so desperately lacking. It is only fitting that Cassavetes (who cast himself as Rowlands' costar), the most actor-oriented director in American film, should finally make a picture about actors. It should also come as no surprise that the result is drastically uncommercial.

Award: Berlin Film Festival Award for Best Actress.

ORDINARY PEOPLE (1980), drama. Directed by Robert Redford; screenplay by Alvin Sargent (from the novel by Judith Guest); produced by Ronald L. Schwary; photographed by John Bailey; edited by Jeff Kanew; music "Canon in D" by Johann Pachelbel, adapted by Marvin Hamlisch; released by Paramount; 124 minutes. *Cast*: Donald Sutherland, Mary Tyler Moore, Judd Hirsch, Timothy Hutton, M. Emmet Walsh, Elizabeth McGovern, Dinah Manoff.

An austere, wintery tale of repression, this directing debut from Robert Redford touched a chord with moviegoers, who mistook its strained seriousness for truthful observation. The setting is the wealthy Chicago suburb of Park Forest, and the people of the title are ordinary only in the sense that they're not extraordinary. One step removed from a Stepford family, the Jarretts are automatons who have been bred to internalize their emotions—teenage son Conrad (Hutton, in a powerful debut) has just been released from a psych ward, where he underwent shock therapy, mom Beth (Moore) is an emotionally frigid golf nut, and dad Calvin (Sutherland) is a henpecked shell of a husband. All three are reeling (though they don't show it) from the traumatic drowning death of Conrad's brother, Beth's favorite son. Only with the psychiatric counseling of the warm Dr. Berger (Hirsch) can Conrad learn what it's like to feel. Living behind impenetrable walls, the Jarretts are a reflection of a segment of the American family that has given birth to the likes of the parricidal Eric and Lyle Menendezes of the world, uncommunicative people whose repressive environment can ultimately destroy them. Unfortunately, Redford refuses to dig deep enough beneath the surface—a decision that may explain why the Academy voted him Best Director over Martin Scorsese for *Raging Bull*. Adding to the overall solemnity of the proceedings is the classical theme of Pachelbel's "Canon in D." "The movie is just as sanitized as the fantasy of upper-middle-class life that it sets out to expose" (Pauline Kael, *The New Yorker*, October 13, 1980).

Awards: Academy Awards for Best Picture, Director, Supporting Actor (Hutton), Adapted Screenplay; Academy Award nominations for Best Actress, Supporting Actor (Hirsch); New York Film Critics Circle Award for Best Picture; DGA Award; WGA Award.

OUTLAW JOSEY WALES, THE (1976), western. Directed by Clint Eastwood; screenplay by Philip Kaufman and Sonia Chernus (from the novel by Forrest Carter); produced by Robert Daley; photographed by Bruce Surtees; edited by Ferris Webster; music by Jerry Fielding; released by Warner Bros.; 135 minutes. *Cast*: Clint Eastwood, Chief Dan George, Sondra Locke, Bill McKinney, John Vernon, Sam Bottoms, Geraldine Keams, Will Sampson, Royal Dano, John Quade, Richard Farnsworth.

In perfect command of the persona he had cultivated with Sergio Leone and Don Siegel, Eastwood here creates a mythic western hero worthy of his predecessor John Wayne. The similarities are more than passing—both Josey Wales and Wayne's Ethan Edwards from *The Searchers* are Confederates, both drift through Indian territory after seeing their loved ones massacred, and both return to the comfort and civilized nature of home and family. Josey Wales is a family man who joins up with some Confederate bandits in order to exact vengeance on the "Redlegs," or Union guerrillas, who savagely killed his wife and children. When his compatriots surrender and are subsequently massacred in a double cross, Josey (who refused to surrender) guns down several Union men and incurs the wrath of Redleg leader Terrill (McKinney). With a price on his head, Josey must elude both Terrill and the numerous bounty hunters who think they can take down the renowned outlaw. Unlike his previous westerns, *The Outlaw Josey Wales* offers an optimistic solution to killing that includes love, life, and family. As he reminds a soon-to-be-dead bounty hunter: "Dyin ain't much of a livin'." Josey's odyssey begins with a loving family and ends with the same, but he has to travel through hell to arrive there—a parallel to the brutality of the Civil War, which ripped a country apart only to rebuild it on firmer ground. Eastwood receives solid support from an excellent cast of character actors, most notably, Chief Dan George as the aging Cherokee whose attempts to be "civilized" (he dresses like Abe Lincoln) result in a loss of true self. Injected with a great deal of humor and pathos, the film is a superior entertainment that misses only in its unfortunate mishandling of the numerous murder scenes, turning Josey into a man who kills without impact or consequence—an issue Eastwood would later address in *The Unforgiven.*

Sequel: *The Return of Josey Wales* (1986), directed by, and starring, Michael Parks.

P

PACINO, AL. Born April 25, 1940, in New York City; actor. Explosive lead actor with training from New York's High School of the Performing Arts and Lee Strasberg's Actors Studio who, after some success on stage and a spectacular performance as a junkie in *Panic in Needle Park*, found fame (though amazingly no Oscars) when Francis Ford Coppola cast him as the ambitious Michael Corleone in *The Godfather*. For a relatively brief stretch, this small-in-stature, large-in-presence Italian American dominated the American screen as the foremost player of the psychologically twisted modern man, *Scarecrow*, *Serpico*, *The Godfather, Part II* (his defining moment being his despicable lie to wife Kay in the final scene), and *Dog Day Afternoon* each conveying the pain that accompanies cognizance. The latter three films earned Pacino three successive Oscar nominations for Best Actor, but the streak would end there. *Bobby Deerfield*, while surprisingly tender and moving, offered a more charming (though still troubled) role as a race car driver in love with a terminally ill woman, but this was not the Pacino the public wanted, and the film failed to excite audiences. The 1980s were less kind and far from prolific, with his key role as *Scarface* gangster Tony Montana resembling a parody of Pacino. His career in the 1990s has again come alive with energetic, if occasionally over-blown, performances in *Scent of a Woman* (his first Oscar), *Glengarry Glen Ross*, and *Heat*.

Filmography: Me, Natalie (1969); Panic in Needle Park (1971); The Godfather (1972); Scarecrow (1973); Serpico (1973); The Godfather, Part II (1974); Dog Day Afternoon (1975); Bobby Deerfield (1977); . . . And Justice for All (1979); Cruising (1980); Author! Author! (1982); Scarface (1983); Revolution (1985); Sea of Love (1989); Dick Tracy (1990); The Godfather, Part III (1990); The Local Stigmatic (1990, short) codirector, producer; Frankie and Johnny (1991); Scent of a Woman (1992); Carlito's Way (1993); Glengarry Glen Ross (1992); Heat (1995).

Honors: Academy Award for Best Actor (*Scent of a Woman*); Academy Award nominations for Best Actor (*Serpico, The Godfather, Part II, Dog Day Afternoon, . . . And Justice for All*) and Supporting Actor (*The Godfather, Glengarry Glen Ross*); Los Angeles Film Critics Award for Best Actor (*Dog Day Afternoon*); Tony Awards (*Does a Tiger Wear a Necktie?* 1969, *The Basic Training of Pavlo Hummel* 1977).

Selected bibliography

Yule, Andrew. *Life on the Wire: The Life and Art of Al Pacino*. New York: Donald I. Fine, 1991.

PAKULA, ALAN J. Born April 7, 1928, in Bronx, New York; director, producer. After a notable career as a producer of such films as *Fear Strikes Out* and *To Kill a Mockingbird* (his first in a long association with director Robert Mulligan), Pakula turned his attention to directing with *The Sterile Cuckoo*, eliciting a fine, Oscar-nominated performance from Liza Minnelli. It would be the first of many films that established Pakula as a first-rate director of actors, a reputation enhanced by the myriad of awards for acting his films garnered over the next decade—*Klute* (an Oscar for Jane Fonda), *All the President's Men* (an Oscar for Jason Robards and a nomination for Jane Alexander), *Comes a Horseman* (an Oscar nomination for Richard Farnsworth), *Starting Over* (Oscar nominations for Jill Clayburgh and Candice Bergen), and *Sophie's Choice* (an Oscar for Meryl Streep)—only one of which earned him a nomination for direction. Curiously, however, one of his finest films—the Warren Beatty vehicle *The Parallax View*, one of the best thrillers of the decade—garnered no such accolades. Although his work has become less interesting in the 1980s (*Dream Lover*, starring Kristy McNichol, is a low point that must have been directed by another Alan Pakula), it still retains the willingness to explore psychological complexities that made his earlier films so engrossing. In the 1990s, he recaptured a certain measure of commercial success with his big-budget, star-driven, old-fashioned, studio adaptations of novels by Scott Turow (*Presumed Innocent* with Harrison Ford) and John Grisham (*The Pelican Brief* with Julia Roberts).

Filmography as director, producer: The Sterile Cuckoo (1969); Klute (1971); Love and Pain and the Whole Damn Thing (1973); The Parallax View (1974); All the President's Men (1976); Comes a Horseman (1978); Starting Over (1979); Rollover (1981); Sophie's Choice (1982) also screenplay; Dream Lover (1986); Orphans (1987); See You in the Morning (1989) also screenplay; Presumed Innocent (1990) director, screenplay only; Consenting Adults (1992); The Pelican Brief (1993).

Filmography as producer only: Fear Strikes Out (1957); To Kill a Mockingbird (1962); Love with the Proper Stranger (1963); Baby, the Rain Must Fall (1965); Inside Daisy Clover (1965); Up the Down Staircase (1967); The Stalking Moon (1968).

Honors: Academy Award nominations for Best Picture (*To Kill a Mockingbird*), Director (*All the President's Men*), and Adapted Screenplay (*Sophie's Choice*); New York Film Critics Circle Award for Best Director (*All the President's Men*).

PANIC IN NEEDLE PARK (1971), drama. Directed by Jerry Schatzberg; screenplay by Joan Didion and John Gregory Dunne (from the book by James Mills); produced by Dominic Dunne; photographed by Adam Holender; edited by Evan Lottman; released by 20th Century Fox; 110 minutes. *Cast*: Al Pacino, Kitty Winn, Al Vint, Richard Bright, Kiel Martin, Michael McClanathan, Marcia Jean Kurtz, Warren Finerty, Raul Julia, Paul Sorvino.

A gritty, fascinating, and uncompromising look at a young junkie couple as they try to survive in New York's drug-infested "Needle Park." Without using music or slick photographic tricks to romanticize this seamy travelogue of the junkie world, director Schatzberg refuses to turn away from the needles jabbing scarred veins or the violently ill addicts collapsing before our eyes. In lesser hands these would be cheap, manipulative techniques, but here Schatzberg is simply observing. Against this backdrop is the story of Bobby (Pacino), a smart, charismatic heroin addict, and his relationship with Helen (Winn), a young woman recovering from an abortion who is gradually sucked into the smack vortex. Theirs is a twisted romance based on one thing—a mutual desire to get enough money to get high again; Bobby gets mixed up in robbery and dealing, while Helen turns to prostitution. Other films have tried to show the inner demons of the addicted, most recently, Abel Ferrara's *The Bad Lieutenant* and Mike Figgis' *Leaving Las Vegas*, but none reach the level of this film. "Vivid to the point of revulsion" (*Variety*, May 26, 1971).

Award: Cannes Film Festival Award for Best Actress (Winn).

PAPER MOON (1973), comedy. Directed and produced by Peter Bogdanovich; screenplay by Alvin Sargent (from the novel by Joe David Brown); photographed by Laszlo Kovacs; edited by Verna Fields; released by Paramount; 102 minutes. *Cast*: Ryan O'Neal, Tatum O'Neal, Madeline Kahn, John Hillerman, P. J. Johnson, Randy Quaid.

Nostalgia at its best, this charming black-and-white depiction of the depression-era Midwest owes quite a debt to John Ford's *The Grapes of Wrath* with its dusty rural roads and hand-cranked Model-Ts. Still, under Peter Bogdanovich's direction, the film has a smart, modern wit that puts this film alongside *The Last Picture Show* as one of his best efforts. The story revolves around opportunistic con man Moses Pray (Ryan O'Neal), who is reunited with his nine-year-old daughter Addie (O'Neal's real-life child Tatum), a tomboyish, cigarette-smoking kid who quickly picks up her father's grifting techniques. Moses is quick to deny that he's her father, but Addie is quicker to point out that "we got the same jaw!" He begrudgingly agrees to drive her to St. Joseph, Missouri, and along the way they realize they have more in common than a jaw. Features the evocative art direction of Polly Platt (producer and former wife of Bogdanovich's) and a pleasant collection of period songs. Young Tatum's naturalistic screen persona is one of the greatest child performances ever seen on film—a display of sharp comic wit, hard-as-nails determination, and girlish charm.

Awards: Academy Award for Best Supporting Actress (O'Neal); Academy Award nominations for Best Supporting Actress (Kahn), Adapted Screenplay, Sound.

PAPILLON (1973), prison drama. Directed and coproduced by Franklin J. Schaffner; screenplay by Dalton Trumbo and Lorenzo Semple, Jr. (from the autobiography by Henri Charrière); produced with Robert Dorfman; photography by Fred Koenekamp; editor by Robert Swink; music by Jerry Goldmsmith; released by Allied Artists; 150 minutes. *Cast*: Steve McQueen, Dustin Hoffman, Anthony Zerbe, Victor Jory, Don Gordon, George Coulouris, Vic Tayback, Dar Robinson, Val Avery.

Coming three years after his Oscar-winning directorial job on *Patton*, Franklin J. Schaffner with screenwriter Dalton Trumbo turned to the horrors of the French penal colonies with brilliant performances from McQueen and Hoffman. McQueen stars as Henri Charriere, a notorious thief whose tattoo of a butterfly has earned him the moniker Papillon; Hoffman plays Louis Dega, a stock swindler who is most comfortable in a refined, civilized setting—the exact opposite of the French Guyana penal colony where they both are headed. While McQueen dreams of escape, Hoffman trusts that his bribes will bring him freedom. By refusing to flinch at the brutality, *Papillon* becomes a Job-like test of human nature as we wonder just how much more these prisoners can take. The final scenes at the escape-proof Devil's Island with its deadly cliffs and unrelenting currents are a masterful observation of humanity as the aging Papillon and Louis Dega deal with their imprisonment as they always have—Papillon planning escape and Dega making the best of it.

Award: Academy Award nomination for Best Score.

PARALLAX VIEW, THE (1974), political thriller. Directed and produced by Alan J. Pakula; screenplay by David Giler and Lorenzo Semple, Jr.; photographed by Gordon Willis; edited by John W. Wheeler; music by Michael Small; released by Paramount; 102 minutes. *Cast*: Warren Beatty, Hume Cronyn, William Daniels, Paula Prentiss, Kelly Thorsden, Earl Hindman, Walter McGinn.

Bridging the paranoia of Beatty's character in *Mickey One* with the psychological exploration and political investigation of, respectively, Pakula's *Klute* and *All the President's Men*, this exceptional thriller validated America's paranoid suspicions about government conspiracies and the Warren Commission's "lone gunman theory." A few years after the murder of a populist senator at Seattle's Space Needle, loner journalist Joseph Frady (Beatty) begins investigating the curious deaths of the many witnesses until he uncovers a secret industrial complex known as the Parallax Corporation. The final kicker comes at the finale, when, after trying to prevent another assassination, Frady is arrested and named by an investigative committee as the lone gunman. One of Pakula's finest films, the visual high point comes during Frady's psychological exam at the Parallax Corporation—a lengthy sequence that features a Kuleshovian montage of various pleasing and disturbing images in association with the words "mother," "father," "God," "country," "love," and "me." Just two years after drawing on the suspicions of conspiracy in this fictitious film, Pakula would be vindicated by the real-life headlines of the Watergate cover-up in *All the President's Men*. "Among the most uncompromising of all cinematic American nightmares" (Robin Wood, *Cinema: A Critical Dictionary*).

PARKS, GORDON. Born November 30, 1912, in Fort Scott, Kansas; director. Son is the late director Gordon Parks, Jr. (*Superfly*). Turning to feature filmmaking at the late age of fifty-two after a multifaceted career that has included professional basketball and photojournalism (*Life* magazine from 1948 to 1968), Parks became Hollywood's first African-American director with the Warner Bros. release *The Learning Tree*. Produced, directed, and written by Parks from his autobiographical novel, the film is an honest and moving examination of racism in 1920s Kansas. He followed with a pair of commercially successful, character-driven action films for MGM—*Shaft* and *Shaft's Big Score*, starring Richard Roundtree as hard-hitting Harlem private eye John Shaft—which, though pigeonholed as "blaxploitation," rank among the best of the gritty urban police dramas of the period. His 1976 Paramount film *Leadbelly*, the biography of legendary blues musician and onetime chain gang convict Huddie Ledbetter, is an evocative, beautifully photographed film that ranks as Parks' premier motion picture achievement. Although he has done little film work of note since the mid-1970s and has essentially been relegated to a footnote position in film history, he is directly responsible for opening Hollywood's studio gates to minority directors. In addition to his film and photo work, Parks is an accomplished musician whose symphonies have been performed and recorded throughout the world. *The Learning Tree* is included in the Library of Congress' National Film Registry.

Filmography:: Flavio (1961, documentary short); The Learning Tree (1969); Shaft (1971); Shaft's Big Score (1972); The Super Cops (1974); Leadbelly (1976); Super Cops (1976, tv); Solomon Northrup's Odyssey (1984, tvm); Moments without Proper Names (1986, documentary).

PAT GARRETT AND BILLY THE KID (1973), western. Directed by Sam Peckinpah; screenplay by Rudolph Wurlitzer; produced by Gordon Carroll; photographed by John Coquillon; edited by Roger Spottiswoode, Garth Craven, Robert L. Wolfe, Richard Halsey, David Berlatsky, Tony DeZarraga; music by Bob Dylan; released by MGM; 106 minutes (rereleased at its original 123 minutes). *Cast*: James Coburn, Kris Kristofferson, Bob Dylan, Richard Jaeckel, Katy Jurado, Slim Pickins, Jason Robards, R. G. Armstrong, Harry Dean Stanton, Jack Elam, John Beck, Luke Askew, Charles Martin Smith, L. Q. Jones, Rita Coolidge, Emilio Fernandez, Rudolph Wurlitzer, Dub Taylor, Elisha Cook, Jr., Sam Peckinpah.

Massacred by MGM upon its release, this final Peckinpah western finally surfaced in its definitive version in the early 1990s with the advent of the laser disc. Taking the themes of *The Wild Bunch* one step further by erasing the code of honor, it completely wipes out the myth of the Old West by gunning down both the outlaw (Kristofferson's Billy the Kid) and the lawman who has been hired to kill him (Coburn's Pat Garrett). As part of the demise of the Old West and society's subsequent passage into the industrial age, the people responsible for their deaths are the big business elite; the outlaw's death is expected, but the murder of the supposed hero signifies an end to an entire era. Less action-packed than *The Wild Bunch*, this film concerns itself more with the psychological complexities of the confident young killer Billy and his former friend turned pursuer, Pat, neither of whom wants the other's blood on his hands. In the middle stands the reticent Alias (Dylan, who also contributes to the sound track), the enigmatic Everyman who fights his battles cunningly and without a gun. "Alias seems to suggest that perhaps a new Western, new values, and a new America is surfacing" (Ralph Brauer, *The Journal of Popular Film*, Fall 1973).

PATTON (1970), biopic/war. Directed by Franklin J. Schaffner; screenplay by Francis Ford Coppola and Edmund H. North (from the books by Ladislas Farago and General Omar Bradley); produced by Frank McCarthy and Frank Caffey; photographed by Fred Koenekamp; edited by Hugh S. Fowler; music by Jerry Goldsmith; released by 20th Century Fox; 170 minutes. *Cast*: George C. Scott, Karl Malden, Michael Bates, Stephen Young, Michael Strong, Frank Latimore, James Edwards, John Doucette, Lawrence Dobkin, Tim Considine.

A mighty wartime biography of General George S. Patton, the legendary and controversial World War II military genius who defeated Rommel's tank troops and pushed the German army out of North Africa and Italy by sheer determination and power. Based on a biography of Patton and the autobiography of General Omar Bradley (Malden), the film creates a mythic ancient warrior in Patton (Scott), a man of bravery and intelligence who also wrote verse and believed he once battled the Carthaginians in an earlier life. The attempt here is not to judge Patton as a man or a general but simply to present him as he was—an American hero, right or wrong. In one of the pivotal scenes, an emotionally shaken Patton, while visiting a field hospital, kneels at the bedside of a severely wounded soldier and a moment later is mercilessly slapping and berating a sobbing soldier whose wounds are emotional; Patton is furious that this "yellow bastard" is allowed to dishonor the others by his presence and orders him to the front. The six-minute pretitle sequence of Patton as he addresses his unseen troops while standing in front of a massive American flag is one of the bravest and most captivating openings in film history. Released at the height of the conflict in Vietnam, *Patton* showed battle in all of its grandeur with its 70mm Cinemascope presentation, a sharp contrast to the chaotic television images of American boys in swamps. "Those who insisted the Vietnam War was being lost because sound military strategy was being compromised by diplomacy, discovered in this film the historical figure they wanted our generals to emulate'' (Danny Perry, *Alternate Oscars*).

Awards: Academy Awards for Best Picture, Director, Actor (Scott, refused), Screenplay, Art Direction, Editing, Sound; Academy Award nominations for Best Cinematography, Score, Special Visual Effects; New York Film Critics Circle Award for Best Actor; DGA Award.

PAWNBROKER, THE (1965), drama. Directed by Sidney Lumet; screenplay by David Friedkin and Morton Fine (from the novel by Edward Lewis Wallant); produced by Roger Lewis and Philip Langner; photographed by Boris Kaufman (b&w); edited by Ralph Rosenblum; music by Quincy Jones; released by Allied Artists/AIP; 114 minutes. *Cast*: Rod Steiger, Geraldine Fitzgerald, Brock Peters, Jaime Sanchez.

A vividly grimy film set in New York's Spanish Harlem that tells the story of Sol Nazerman (Steiger), a former professor who saw his late wife raped by Nazis and his two children sent to their deaths in the camps and who now lives an emotionally dead life as a pawnbroker. Sensing the goodness that lies dormant deep inside, Sol's friendly assistant (Sanchez) tries to break through the impenetrable facade and eventually does so, but only in death. As Sol, Rod Steiger is a marvel—his first major starring role after a career of excellent supporting parts. Under Lumet's direction, the film retains a certain theatricality (due, in part, to its single location) but is a starkly visual film with harsh black-and-white photography from Boris Kaufman and inventive, near-subliminal editing from Ralph Rosenblum, as well as an unnerving Quincy Jones jazz score. A remarkable achievement that acknowledged the dark, post–World War II psyche that was eating away at the souls of Americans.

Awards: Academy Award nomination for Best Actor; Berlin Film Festival Silver Bear Award for Best Actor; WGA Award.

PECKINPAH, SAM. Born February 21, 1925, in Fresno, California; died December 28, 1984, in Inglewood, California; director. One of American cinema's most morally complex filmmakers, Peckinpah, like most of his characters, is an anachronism of a man who belongs to an earlier era of filmmaking. A logical heir to John Ford, he understood America better than most of his contemporaries, examining its mythology, its high regard for personal integrity and heroism, and its undercurrent of cynicism. He was a former assistant to Don Siegel, his training included television writing and directing on such shows as ''The Rifleman,'' ''Gunsmoke,'' ''The Westerner,'' ''Broken Arrow,'' and ''The Dick Powell Show,'' and he expectedly gained a reputation as a director of westerns. With the success of *Ride the High Country* (starring Joel McCrea and Randolph Scott as aging gunfighters) behind him, Peckinpah took the genre to a new plateau with *The Wild Bunch*, a stunning tale of western values and morality that stirred controversy with its use of graphic, slow-motion violence. He would continue to examine the nature of violence with *Straw Dogs*, with Dustin Hoffman starring as a civilized mathematician driven to defend his home against intruders in an exploration of man's primitive instincts of violence and rage. His reputation for violence, however, has unfortunately overshadowed the lyrical elements of such films as the delightful Jason Robards vehicle *The Ballad of Cable Hogue* and the poignant Steve McQueen rodeo picture *Junior Bonner*. After the release in 1973 of his final western (the severely mutilated *Pat Garrett and Billy the Kid*), Peckinpah tried with varying degrees of success to adapt his themes to the modern world. Only the underappreciated James Caan Central Intelligence Agency thriller *The Killer Elite* stands out, with its amalgam of styles that stretch from Old West to chop-socky and the familiar theme of men who understand the value of giving their word. "Perhaps the only true outlaw in American film history, Peckinpah's talent hits like a bullet, but the wound it creates exposes a highly volatile, emotional heart" (*The Motion Picture Guide*).

Filmography: The Deadly Companions (1961); Ride the High Country (1962); Major Dundee (1965); Noon Wine (1967, tvm) also screenplay; The Wild Bunch (1969) also screenplay; The Ballad of Cable Hogue (1970); Straw Dogs (1972) also screenplay; The Getaway (1972); Junior Bonner (1973); Pat Garrett and Billy the Kid (1973); Bring Me the Head of Alfredo Garcia (1974); The Killer Elite (1975); Cross of Iron (1977); Convoy (1978); The Osterman Weekend (1983).

Additional credits: Private Hell 36 (1954) dialogue director; Invasion of the Body Snatchers (1956) actor; The Glory Guys (1965) screenplay; Villa Rides (1968) screenplay; China 9, Liberty 37 (1978) actor; The Visitor (1979) actor; Jinxed (1982) second unit director; Julian Lennon's "Valotte" and "Too Late for Goodbyes" (1984, mv).

Selected bibliography

McKinney, Doug. *Sam Peckinpah*. Boston: Twayne, 1979.
Seydor, Paul. *Peckinpah: The Western Films*. Urbana: The University of Illinois Press, 1980.
Simmons, Louis Garner. *Peckinpah: A Portrait in Montage*. Austin: University of Texas Press, 1982.
Weddle, David. *If They Move, Kill 'Em!* New York: Grove Press, 1994.

PENN, ARTHUR. Born September 27, 1922, in Philadelphia; director. One of the preeminent filmmakers of the 1960s, Penn got his start in theater and television and employed his considerable talents as a director of actors in all three media with his earliest success "The Miracle Worker," which he directed for television ("Playhouse 90" in 1956), stage (Broadway in 1959), and film (1962). Throughout the 1960s, he attracted acclaim as a stylistically bold director with an affinity for characters who exist outside the mainstream—criminals (Billy the Kid of *The Left-Handed Gun*, Bubber Reeves in *The Chase*, the entire Barrow gang in *Bonnie and Clyde*), the handicapped (Helen Keller and Annie Sullivan of *The Miracle Worker*), hippies (*Alice's Restaurant*), and Native Americans (the Cheyenne of *Little Big Man*). He solidified his position in cinema history with *Bonnie and Clyde*, a pivotal film that combined graphic violence with rollicking mass entertainment and sparked much spirited debate from critics. Over the next twenty-five years, however, Penn's meager output (only six films) has resulted in only one exceptional picture, the underappreciated film noir *Night Moves*, a gritty reworking of the disenchanted private-eye tale that features a darkly shaded performance from Gene Hackman and a disturbingly prurient display from newcomer Melanie Griffith. "[Penn's] problem is that of the artist who is antagonistic to his society yet is unable to elaborate any consistent or constructive ideology with which he might oppose it" (Robin Wood, *Cinema: A Critical Dictionary*).

Filmography of key pre-1965 films: The Miracle Worker (1956, tv); Charley's Aunt (1958, tv); The Left-Handed Gun (1958); The Miracle Worker (1962).

Filmography since 1965: Mickey One (1965); The Chase (1966); Flesh and Blood (1967, tvm); Bonnie and Clyde (1967); Alice's Restaurant (1969); Little Big Man (1970); Night Moves (1975); The Missouri Breaks (1976); Four Friends (1981); Target (1985); Dead of Winter (1987); Penn and Teller Get Killed (1989).

Honors: Academy Award nominations for Best Director (*The Miracle Worker, Bonnie and Clyde, Alice's Restaurant*); Tony Award (*The Miracle Worker* 1959).

Selected bibliography

Cawelti, John, ed. *Focus on Bonnie and Clyde*. Englewood Cliffs, NJ: Prentice-Hall, 1973.

Kolker, Robert Phillip. *A Cinema of Loneliness: Penn, Kubrick, Coppola, Scorsese, Altman*. New York: Oxford University Press, 1980.

Wood, Robin. *Arthur Penn*. New York: Frederick A. Praeger, 1969.

Zucker, Joel S. *Arthur Penn: A Guide to Reference and Resources*. Boston: G. K. Hall, 1980.

PENN, SEAN. Born August 17, 1960, in Burbank, California; actor, director. Married to actor Robin Wright; formerly married to singer/actor Madonna; brother Chris is an actor; brother Michael is a singer; father Leo is an actor and director (*Judgment in Berlin*); mother Eileen Ryan is an actor. An actor and director of unparalleled integrity in his generation, Penn doesn't have a false or weak performance in his fifteen-year body of work. Beginning promisingly enough with a strong dramatic role as military cadet Alex Dwyer in *Taps*, he then revealed his offbeat comic sensibility as the colorful surfer dude Jeff Spicoli in *Fast Times at Ridgemont High*. Even the much-maligned *Shanghai Surprise*, in which he appears with then-wife Madonna, features a spirited performance in the vein of a 1930s Hollywood romantic adventure. A "bad boy" of the media (his battles with photographers are well known) and a Hollywood rebel à la Jack Nicholson and Dennis Hopper before him, he has begun to follow their lead into directing with *Indian Runner* and *The Crossing Guard*—two pictures that recall the maverick individuality of the golden age of 1970s filmmaking. Although commercial success eluded these films, Penn is slowly emerging as one of the most gifted filmmakers in America, a true visionary filled with unwavering integrity and a blunt voice. With his Oscar-nominated role as the repentant death row inmate in *Dead Man*

Walking, he reaches an even higher level of acting skill, which combines technical mastery with raw emotional energy.

Filmography: Taps (1981); Fast Times at Ridgemont High (1982); Bad Boys (1983); Crackers (1984); Racing with the Moon (1984); The Falcon and the Snowman (1985); At Close Range (1986); Shanghai Surprise (1986); Dear America (1987); Colors (1988); Judgment in Berlin (1988); Casualties of War (1989); We're No Angels (1989); State of Grace (1990); Indian Runner (1991) director, screenplay; Carlito's Way (1993); The Crossing Guard (1994) director, screenplay; Dead Man Walking (1995); Jewel's "You Were Meant for Me" (1995, mv).

Honors: Academy Award nomination for Best Actor (*Dead Man Walking*); Berlin Film Festival Silver Bear for Best Actor (*Dead Man Walking*); Independent Spirit Award for Best Actor (*Dead Man Walking*).

PENNEBAKER, D.A. Born Donn Alan Pennebaker in 1925 in Evanston, Illinois; documentary filmmaker. Educated at Yale and Massachusetts Institute of Technology, Pennebaker abandoned his career as an electronics engineer and turned to film. At the core of the Direct Cinema movement (along with Richard Leacock, Albert Maysles, and Shirley Clarke), he helped establish a style of documentary filmmaking that borrowed from television news and achieved a sense of immediacy afforded by the technological advances of portable film equipment. His first big success came with 1967's *Don't Look Back*, a critical and commercial hit that documented Bob Dylan's 1965 British tour and masterfully captured the singer/poet's life and times. Pennebaker followed with *Monterey Pop*, the first rock festival film of the 1960s, and has continued to chronicle a variety of rock-and-roll acts from Jimi Hendrix, to David Bowie, to Depeche Mode in an attempt to capture the "event." In 1979 he began a collaboration with wife Chris Hegedus that peaked in 1993 with the Oscar-nominated *The War Room*, the gripping political documentary that serves as a modern companion piece to the 1960 campaign film *Primary*, on which Pennebaker was a collaborator.

Filmography of key pre-1965 films: Primary (1960) codirector; Balloon (1960); Jane (1962).

Filmography since 1965: Elizabeth and Mary (1965); Don't Look Back (1967); Monterey Pop (1968); Goin' to San Francisco (1968, short); Company (1970); Sweet Toronto/Keep on Rockin' (1972); The Energy War (1979, tv); Town Bloody Hall (1979) codirected with Chris Hegedus; Elliott Carter (1980); DeLorean (1981, tv); Rockaby (1983, tv) codirected with Chris Hegedus; Ziggy Stardust and the Spiders from Mars (1983/filmed in 1973); Dance Black America (1985) codirected with Chris Hegedus; Rocky X (1986) codirected with Chris Hegedus; Jimi Plays Monterey (1986); The War Room (1993) codirected with Chris Hegedus.

Awards: Academy Award nomination for Best Documentary (*The War Room*); included in the Library of Congress' National Film Registry (*Primary*).

PENNIES FROM HEAVEN (1981), musical. Directed and coproduced by Herb Ross; screenplay by Dennis Potter; produced with Nora Kaye; photographed by

Gordon Willis; edited by Richard Marks; music by Marvin Hamlisch and Billy May, song "Pennies from Heaven" by Johnny Burke and Arthur Johnston; released by MGM; 108 minutes. *Cast*: Steve Martin, Bernadette Peters, Jessica Harper, Christopher Walken, Vernel Bagneris, John McMartin, Eliska Krupka.

The greatest, most audacious, and most passionate musical to emerge from Hollywood since *Cabaret*, this feature version of Dennis Potter's six-part BBC series is a brilliant tour de force that, judging from its abysmal box office showing, was a victim of the audience's hopeless disinterest in the musical genre. The setting is 1934 Chicago, and Martin stars as Arthur Parker, a sheet-music salesman who is trapped in a sexless marriage to Joan (Harper), while wishing that his life were as glorious as the songs on the radio. He is transformed when he meets Eileen (Peters), a schoolteacher who desperately wants to believe Arthur's lie about not being married. After a night of passion, the contrite Arthur returns to Joan, leaving behind a pregnant Eileen. The reality of abortion, murder, prostitution, and betrayal counters the romantic bounce of the scratchy period music as the characters (all dressed in dazzling Bob Mackie costumes) break out into lip-synched song—Arthur offers up Bing Crosby's "Did You Ever See a Dream Walking?" when he first meets Eileen, Eileen does her Betty Boop with Helen Kane's "I Want to Be Bad," and down-and-out Accordian Man (Bagneris) sings the heart-wrenching Arthur Tracy version of "Pennies from Heaven." The sets by production designer Ken Adams draw on Edward Hopper's saturated vision of emotional isolation, while the music expresses the inner desires of the sadly repressed characters, who retreat into a fantasy world of good times and naughty sex. Darker than one might expect, especially for then-rising comic sensation Martin, the film mixes complex human issues with Busby Berkeley-style dance numbers in a near-perfect melding of stylistic approaches. Not to be missed are the tap-dancing striptease from Christopher Walken and the magical "duet" between moviegoers Arthur and Eileen as they dance in front of a movie screen playing the "Let's Face the Music and Dance" sequence from Fred Astaire and Ginger Rogers' *Follow the Fleet*.

Awards: Academy Award nominations for Best Screenplay, Costume Design, and Sound.

PESCI, JOE. Born February 9, 1943, in Newark, New Jersey; actor. Classic Italian-American character actor who gained attention as Jake LaMotta's tormented brother in Martin Scorsese's *Raging Bull*, though stardom eluded him for almost a full decade. The general public discovered him when he was cast opposite Mel Gibson and Danny Glover in *Lethal Weapon 2* as a wisecracking Jersey guy, a routine he would perfect in the likable, if minor, comedy *My Cousin Vinny*. He continues to do his best work with Scorsese, as witnessed in *GoodFellas* and *Casino*, combining an offbeat sense of humor with a violent, psychotic edge. His "you think I'm funny . . . funny how, like some kinda clown?" bit with Ray Liotta in *GoodFellas* is his shining moment.

Filmography: Hey, Let's Twist! (1961); Death Collector (1976); Raging Bull (1980); I'm Dancing As Fast As I Can (1981); Dear Mr. Wonderful (1982); Easy Money (1983); Eureka (1983); Once Upon a Time in America (1984); Tutti Dentro (1984); Man on Fire (1987); Moonwalker (1988, mv/short film); Lethal Weapon 2 (1989); Backtrack (1990); Betsy's Wedding (1990); GoodFellas (1990); Home Alone (1990); The Super (1991); Lethal Weapon 3 (1992); My Cousin Vinny (1992); JFK (1992); The Public Eye (1992); Home Alone 2 (1992); A Bronx Tale (1993); Jimmy Hollywood (1994); With Honors (1994); Casino (1995).

Honors: Academy Award for Best Supporting Actor (*GoodFellas*); Academy Award nomination for Best Supporting Actor (*Raging Bull*); New York Film Critics Circle Award for Best Supporting Actor (*Raging Bull*); Los Angeles Film Critics Award for Best Supporting Actor (*GoodFellas*).

PFEIFFER, MICHELLE. Born April 29, 1957, in Santa Ana, California; actor. Married to television producer and writer David E. Kelly ("Picket Fences," "Chicago Hope"); formerly married to actor Peter Horton. Beautiful, blond leading lady who made an early impression with her roles as "Pink Lady" Stephanie Zinone in *Grease 2* and as coke fiend Elvira in *Scarface*. After appearing as the classically romantic heroine in the underrated *Ladyhawke* and as one of the supernatural trio in *The Witches of Eastwick*, she turned the corner to stardom in 1988 with roles as a funky Long Island mob wife in *Married to the Mob*, a tough restaurant owner in the film noir thriller *Tequila Sunrise*, and a tour de force as the impassioned Madame de Tourvel in *Dangerous Liaisons*. More success came as sultry songstress Susie Diamond in *The Fabulous Baker Boys*, as the supercontoured, whip-cracking Catwoman in *Batman Returns*, as the Countess Olenska in *The Age of Innocence*, and as a former marine turned inner-city schoolteacher in the surprise hit *Dangerous Minds*. Unjustly neglected and inexplicably dumped into just a handful of theaters is *Love Field*, a touching and lightly comedic tale that stars Pfeiffer as a Dallas housewife who, obsessed with the Kennedys, hops a Greyhound to attend the president's funeral. One senses, however, that, despite working with such perceptive actors' directors as Martin Scorsese, Jonathan Demme, Stephen Frears, and Mike Nichols, Pfeiffer has yet to reach her peak as an actress.

Filmography: "Delta House" (1979, tvs); Falling in Love Again (1980); The Hollywood Knights (1980); Charlie Chan and the Curse of the Dragon Queen (1981); Grease 2 (1982); Scarface (1983); Into the Night (1985); Ladyhawke (1985); Sweet Liberty (1986); The Witches of Eastwick (1987); Amazon Women on the Moon (1987); Married to the Mob (1988); Tequila Sunrise (1988); Dangerous Liaisons (1988); The Fabulous Baker Boys (1989); The Russia House (1990); Frankie and Johnny (1991); Batman Returns (1992); Love Field (1992); The Age of Innocence (1993); Wolf (1994); Dangerous Minds (1995).

Honors: Academy Award nominations for Best Actress (*The Fabulous Baker Boys, Love Field*) and Supporting Actress (*Dangerous Liaisons*); New York Film Critics Circle Award for Best Actress (*The Fabulous Baker Boys*); Los Angeles Film Critics Award for Best Actress (*The Fabulous Baker Boys*).

PHOENIX, RIVER. Born River Jude Bottom August 23, 1970, in Madras, Oregon; died October 31, 1993, in Los Angeles; actor. Siblings Leaf/Joaquin, Summer, Rain, and Liberty are also actors. The most talented and promising young actor since Jodie Foster, Phoenix's nomadic background and his socially conscious upbringing helped him develop into a charismatic, likable, boyish actor with a rare sense of intelligence and ethics. A child of former Christian missionaries, he traveled from the Northwest to South America before relocating in Los Angeles to begin a career in film and television. At age twelve he landed a role in the short-lived television series "Seven Brides for Seven Brothers" (1982–1983) and appeared in two miniseries and several commercials before Joe Dante cast him as the bespectacled computer genius in *The Explorers*. The following year, Phoenix, already looking more rugged and intense with a short-cropped hairstyle, starred in two roles that demonstrated his natural talent—as the sensitive leader of the boyhood gang in *Stand by Me* and as the tormented young son in Peter Weir's Freudian adventure *The Mosquito Coast*. Other impressive roles include the young romantic in the underappreciated *A Night in the Life of Jimmy Reardon*, the teenager on the run with his radical parents in *Running on Empty* (earning him an Oscar nomination), the cocky marine in *Dogfight*, and the narcoleptic male hustler in *My Own Private Idaho*. Of his final three films, two were barely released—Peter Bogdanovich's *The Thing Called Love*, which features a sloppy performance saved only by Phoenix's impressive musical talent, and Sam Shepard's *Silent Tongue* (released after Phoenix's death)—while the third, the aborted *Dark Blood*, was in production when Phoenix died of a drug overdose outside the trendy Los Angeles club the Viper Room. "River was real and always stood for the truth" (graffiti on the wall outside of the Viper Room).

Filmography: "Seven Brides for Seven Brothers" (1982–1983, tvs); Celebrity (1984, tvms); Robert Kennedy and His Times (1985, tvms); Surviving (1985, tvm); The Explorers (1985); Stand by Me (1986); The Mosquito Coast (1986); Circle of Violence: A Family Drama (1986, tvm); Little Nikita (1988); A Night in the Life of Jimmy Reardon (1988); Running on Empty (1988); Indiana Jones and the Last Crusade (1989); I Love You to Death (1990); Dogfight (1991); My Own Private Idaho (1991); Sneakers (1992); The Thing Called Love (1993); Dark Blood (1993, unfinished, unreleased); Silent Tongue (1993).

Honors: Academy Award nomination for Best Supporting Actor (*Running on Empty*); Venice Film Festival Award for Best Actor (*My Own Private Idaho*); Independent Spirit Award for Best Actor (*My Own Private Idaho*).

Selected bibliography

Glatt, John. *Lost in Hollywood: The Fast Times and Short Life of River Phoenix*. New York: Penguin USA, 1995.

PITT, BRAD. Born William Bradley Pitt December 18, 1963, in Shawnee, Oklahoma; actor. Blond-maned actor whose instinctual, impassioned style and rebellious good looks have made him one of Hollywood's biggest names. What is most interesting, however, is that his star status is built almost exclusively on supporting parts. Until 1994, his only two starring roles came in films that were barely seen—the critically and commercially disappointing independent pictures *Johnny Suede* and *Kalifornia*. His brief role as J. D., the hitchhiking, eye-popping, sexually satisfying object of Geena Davis' affections in *Thelma and Louise* brought him fame, and thus the legend of Brad Pitt was born. His break-out year as a leading man came in 1994 as Louis, the vampire condemned to an eternity of bloodlust in *Interview with the Vampire*, and as Montanan rancher Tristan in *Legends of the Fall*, though in both cases he had costars to help carry the film. Refusing to capitalize on safe roles, Pitt turned to darker material in his two 1995 films; he starred opposite Morgan Freeman in the gruesome serial killer thriller *Seven* and then gave an exuberant performance as a crazed asylum inmate in the futuristic tale *12 Monkeys*.

Filmography: Cutting Class (1989); Too Young to Die? (1990, tvm); Happy Together (1990); The Image (1990, ctvm); "Glory Days" (1990, tvs); Across the Tracks (1991); Johnny Suede (1991); Thelma and Louise (1991); A River Runs through It (1992); Cool World (1992); Kalifornia (1993); True Romance (1993); The Favor (1994); Interview with the Vampire (1994); Legends of the Fall (1994); Seven (1995); 12 Monkeys (1995).

Honor: Academy Award nomination for Best Actor (*12 Monkeys*).

PLANET OF THE APES (1968), adventure/fantasy/sci-fi. Directed by Franklin J. Schaffner; screenplay by Michael Wilson and Rod Serling (from the novel by Pierre Boulle); produced by Arthur P. Jacobs; photographed by Leon Shamroy; edited by Hugh S. Fowler; music by Jerry Goldsmith; released by 20th Century Fox; 112 minutes. *Cast*: Charlton Heston, Roddy McDowell, Kim Hunter, Maurice Evans, James Whitmore.

Largely ignored by critics, who viewed its pulp comic book plot as too low-brow for their strained seriousness, this hugely popular fantasy film is steeped in a cultural significance that directly relates to the radical political turmoil that rocked the world in 1968. While the rebellious masses were punching clenched fists into the air, screenwriters Rod Serling (of the covertly political "Twilight Zone") and Michael Wilson (who would next pen *Che!*, the biopic of the radical revolutionary leader) turned Pierre Boulle's novel *Monkey Planet* into a film about an oppressed civilization that has overthrown its rulers—a nightmare world in which the apes have enslaved humans. With its cartoonish plot—Heston is George Taylor, a National Aeronautics and Space Administration astronaut whose space mission goes awry, forcing him to land on an unidentified planet—the filmmakers have created a thematically rich sci-fi tale that, contrary to most films and books of the genre, offers the thesis that man's arrogance has led him not to evolve into a higher life form but to devolve into a primate stage. The picture reflects a certain level of cynicism that posits the theory that man may not be as intelligent as he thinks. When we finally learn that the Planet of the Apes is Earth (we, along with Taylor, see a half-buried Statue of Liberty rising up from the ocean's shore) and that Taylor never even left his own planet, an even greater level of cynicism kicks in; are we, as a civilization, doomed to destroy ourselves? Or will we temper our arrogance and treat everyone (even those different from us) with respect and humanity? In retrospect, it is a startling genre piece that raises issues of oppression, racism, and, even (in the year before man walked on the moon), the futility of space travel. It includes Heston's memorable line: "Take your stinking paws off me, you damned dirty ape!"

Sequels: *Beneath the Planet of the Apes* (1970, Ted Post); *Escape from the Planet of the Apes* (1971, Don Taylor); *Conquest of the Planet of the Apes* (1972, J. Lee Thompson); *Battle for the Planet of the Apes* (1973, directed by J. Lee Thompson).

PLATOON (1986), war. Directed and written by Oliver Stone; produced by Arnold Kopelson; photographed by Robert Richardson; edited by Claire Simpson; music "Adagio for Strings" by Samuel Barber; released by Orion; 111 minutes. *Cast*: Tom Berenger, Willem Dafoe, Charlie Sheen, Forest Whitaker, Francesco Quinn, John C. McGinley, Kevin Dillon, Richard Edson, Johnny Depp.

Oliver Stone begins this nightmarish journey with a line from Ecclesiastes— "Rejoice, O young man, in thy youth"—before we see American lamb Chris (Sheen) led to the slaughter of Vietnam. It's 1967, and Chris, a rich kid enlistee who needs to discover himself, is just shy of his twenty-first birthday. Over the course of his one-year stretch in the very green jungles along the Cambodian border, he'll age much more than a year. He'll see the horrors of war and even, in momentary bursts, become part of them as two veteran sergeants wrestle for his soul—the Christ-like Sergeant Elias (Dafoe) and the Frankensteinian Barnes (Berenger, made up with a grotesquely scarred visage). As the battle against the Vietcong proves increasingly frustrating and unwinnable, the fight turns inward, and the demoralized platoon splits into two factions—the moralistic pro-Elias forces and the corrupted pro-Barnes forces. By the finale, Chris has been transformed from boy to man through the catharsis of violence and killing, and there is no more reason to rejoice. A devastatingly powerful film that vicariously drags the viewer through the experience of war, *Platoon* is based on Stone's real-life account of Vietnam, and there's no denying its air of authenticity. As remarkable as the picture is, however, it is stunted by the banality of its voice-over (Chris reads his letters to his grandmother), the artificiality of its blatant good-versus-evil battle, and the puzzling morality of the pro-murder ending. "Once again, Oliver Stone has made a movie about violence for the greater good—violence as redemption" (Sydelle Kramer, *Cineaste* 15, no. 3, 1987). "Oliver Stone's adventures of himself as a young man, another version of the factual tale as spiritual odyssey, a tradition of war reportage exemplified by Hemingway and Mailer" (Richard Combs, *Sight and Sound*, Spring 1987).

Awards: Academy Awards for Best Picture, Director, Editing, Sound; Academy Award nominations for Actor (Berenger, Dafoe), Screenplay, Cinematography; DGA Award; Berlin Film Festival Awards for Best Director, Editing.

POINT BLANK (1967), crime. Directed by John Boorman; screenplay by Alexander Jacobs, David Newhouse, Rafe Newhouse (based on the novel by Richard Stark [Donald E. Westlake]); photographed by Philip H. Lathrop; edited by Henry Berman; music by Johnny Mandel; released by MGM; 92 minutes. *Cast:* Lee Marvin, Angie Dickinson, Keenan Wynn, Carroll O'Connor, Lloyd Bochner, Michael Strong, John Vernon.

Emerging from Alcatraz like the first man stepping from the primordial ooze, Walker (Marvin) is a violent, instinctual being who traverses the ocean and marches through the immense glass and cement landscape of San Francisco in search of some money he is owed. Double-crossed during a robbery at the ghostly, abandoned Alcatraz, Walker is determined to find former partner Mal Reese (Vernon), who shot him point-blank and left him for dead before leaving the island with Walker's share *and* his wife (Acker). His quest (as Arthurian as Boorman's *Excalibur*) leads him to an absurdist corporate complex that simply won't comply with his demands to be paid. Using inside information from Yost (Wynn), Walker kills everyone who refuses to pay, ultimately learning that Yost's true identity is Fairfax, one of the heads of the corporation; Walker is merely a pawn used to eliminate Fairfax's rivals. Using a hallucinatory pop style of crosscutting, flashbacks and flash-forwards, sound bridges, and coolly impersonal compositions, Boorman has created a bizarre evolutionary tale about the madness of the complex modern world. Like the aging detective hero Lemmy Caution of Jean-Luc Godard's *Alphaville* (1965), Walker is an anachronism whose primitive nature remains a constant threat to the IBMs of this world. "The curiously bleak rather than cool intermingling of morality, sexuality, and violence makes *Point Blank* more edifying than either *Bonnie and Clyde* or *The Graduate*" (Andrew Sarris, *The American Cinema*, 1968).

POITIER, SIDNEY. Born February 20, 1927, in Miami; actor, director, producer. Hollywood's first black star, he gained fame as a dignified and decent man who stood up to the small-mindedness of racist whites during a time both in film and in real life when this was far from commonplace. He began in the mid-1960s with the effective, though obvious, *A Patch of Blue* (in which he is loved by a blind white girl) and the nonracial suicide hot line suspenser *A Slender Thread*. By the end of 1967, with the magnificent trio *Guess Who's Coming to Dinner?*, *In the Heat of the Night*, and the British *To Sir with Love*, Poitier was voted most popular star of the year. As the central black entertainment figure during the Johnson era, Poitier became a star for complicated reasons, not the least of which are his great sense of humanity and his rare talent. Yet, he also represented to white moviegoing audiences a safe black man who lacked "attitude," militancy, anger, street speech, and (most important) sexuality; he posed no threat to the anxious whites of the 1960s, who could now assuage their guilty consciences and prove their lack of prejudice by delineating between the congenial Poitier and the menacing Black Panthers. Beginning with *Buck and the Preacher* in 1972, Poitier began to move behind the camera, later directing the successful black-oriented *Uptown Saturday Night* and its sequels *Let's Do It Again* and *A Piece of the Action*. As black filmmaking changed in the 1980s with the rise of Spike Lee, Poitier became increasingly less relevant as a cultural icon, teaming with Bill Cosby for such undeserving comedies as *Ghost Dad*.

Filmography of key pre-1965 films: No Way Out (1950); The Blackboard Jungle (1955); Edge of the City (1957); The Defiant Ones (1958); Porgy and Bess (1959); Paris Blues (1961); A Raisin in the Sun (1961); Lilies of the Field (1963).

Filmography since 1965: The Bedford Incident (1965); The Greatest Story Ever Told (1965); A Patch of Blue (1965); The Slender Thread (1965); Duel at Diablo (1966); Guess Who's Coming to Dinner? (1967); In the Heat of the Night (1967); To Sir with Love (1967); For Love of Ivy (1968) also story; The Lost Man (1969); Brother John (1970); They Call Me Mister Tibbs (1970); The Organization (1971); The Wilby Conspiracy (1975); Little Nikita (1988); Shoot to Kill (1988); Sneakers (1992).

Filmography as director: Buck and the Preacher (1972) also actor; A Warm December (1972) also actor; Uptown Saturday Night (1974) also actor; Let's Do It Again (1975) also actor; A Piece of the Action (1977) also actor; Stir Crazy (1980); Hanky Panky (1982); Fast Forward (1985); Ghost Dad (1990).

Honors: Academy Award for Best Actor (*Lilies of the Field*); Academy Award nomination for Best Actor (*The Defiant Ones*); New York Film Critics Circle Award for Best Actor (*The Defiant Ones*); Berlin Film Festival Awards for Best Actor (*The Defiant Ones, Lilies of the Field*); Venice Film Festival Georgio Cini Award (*Something of Value*, 1958); American Film Institute Lifetime Achievement Award (1992).

Selected Bibliography

Marill, Alvin H. *The Films of Sidney Poitier*. New York: Citadel, 1978.

POLLACK, SYDNEY. Born July 1, 1934, in Lafayette, Indiana; director, producer, actor. Starting off as an actor with New York's Neighborhood Playhouse under Sanford Meisner, Pollack appeared on Broadway and in numerous "Playhouse 90" productions before heading west to direct fifteen episodes of television's "Ben Casey." His first film as an actor, 1962's *War Hunt*, is insignificant except that it marks his first association with costar Robert Redford, whom he would later direct in seven pictures. The first of these, *This Property Is Condemned*, is a stagy adaptation of Tennessee Williams' steamy one-act (coscripted by Francis Ford Coppola, who, coincidentally, worked as a driver on *War Hunt*) that captures Redford's charm but is otherwise undistinguished. Pollack earned an Oscar for his direction of *They Shoot Horses, Don't They?*, a gritty adaptation of Horace McCoy's even grittier 1935 allegorical novel of the depression era, but his career really took shape with his next three pictures—the wilderness adventure *Jeremiah Johnson*, the blacklist-era romance *The Way We Were*, and the Central Intelligence Agency thriller *Three Days of the Condor*—all starring Redford and all set against a backdrop of liberal political issues. His next few films were less successful both critically and commercially, but he came back big with the Dustin Hoffman comedy *Tootsie*, garnering a second Oscar nomination for direction and featuring Pollack in a wonderful performance as Tootsie's exasperated agent. Throughout the 1980s and 1990s he has continued to deliver classy Hollywood pictures, with his Oscar-winner *Out of Africa* and the John Grisham adaptation *The Firm* faring better than *Havana* and *Sabrina*. Ultimately, while his visual style lacks originality or poetry, his unsurpassed talent as a director of actors and as a producer of high-quality entertainment has elicited excellent performances from a veritable who's who of the greatest actors of the day—Redford, Hoffman, Paul Newman, Jane Fonda, Al Pacino, Tom Cruise, Barbra Streisand, Faye Dunaway, Holly Hunter, Burt Lancaster, Gene Hackman, and Harrison Ford, to name just a few.

Filmography as director: "Ben Casey" (1960, tvs); The Slender Thread (1965); The Game (1966, tvm); This Property Is Condemned (1966); The Scalphunters (1968); The Swimmer (1968) [uncredited, directed one scene only]; Castle Keep (1969); They Shoot Horses, Don't They? (1969) also producer; Jeremiah Johnson (1972); The Way We Were (1973); The Yakuza (1975) also producer; Three Days of the Condor (1975); Bobby Deerfield (1977) also producer; The Electric Horseman (1979); Absence of Malice (1981) also producer; Tootsie (1982) also producer, actor; Out of Africa (1985) also producer; Havana (1990) also producer; The Firm (1993) also producer; Sabrina (1995) also producer.

Filmography as producer: Honeysuckle Rose (1980) ep; Songwriter (1984); Bright Lights, Big City (1988); Major League (1989) ep; The Fabulous Baker Boys (1989) ep; Presumed Innocent (1990); White Palace (1990) ep; King Ralph (1991) ep; Dead Again (1991) ep; Leaving Normal (1992) ep; Searching for Bobby Fischer (1993) ep; Flesh and Bone (1993) ep; "Fallen Angels" (1993, ctv six-part series) ep; Sense and Sensibility (1995) ep.

Filmography as actor only: War Hunt (1962); Death Becomes Her (1992); Husbands and Wives (1992); The Player (1992).

Honors: Academy Awards for Best Picture and Director (*Out of Africa*); Academy Award nominations for Best Picture (*Tootsie*) and Director (*They Shoot Horses, Don't They?, Tootsie*); New York Film Critics Circle Award for Best Director (*Tootsie*); Emmy Award (*The Game*).

POSEIDON ADVENTURE, THE (1972), adventure. Directed by Ronald Neame; screenplay by Stirling Silliphant and Wendell Mayes (from the novel by Paul Gallico); produced by Irwin Allen; photographed by Harold E. Stine; edited by Harold F. Kress; music by John Williams, song "The Morning After" performed by Maureen McGovern; released by 20th Century Fox; 117 minutes. *Cast*: Gene Hackman, Ernest Borgnine, Red Buttons, Carol Lynley, Roddy McDowell, Stella Stevens, Shelley Winters, Jack Albertson, Leslie Nielson, Pamela Sue Martin, Eric Shea.

With Ross Hunter's *Airport* preceding in 1970 and Irwin Allen's *The Towering Inferno* following in 1974, *The Poseidon Adventure* was part of the supreme troika of 1970s disaster movies, which collectively spawned numerous sequels and rip-offs for theatrical release and television. What separates these films from the rest of the genre are the writing and acting. Cowritten by Stirling Silliphant (who also wrote *The Towering Inferno*) and featuring some memorable performances (specifically, Shelley Winters), this adventure tale follows the plight of a group of passengers who, after a massive tidal wave capsizes their luxury liner on New Year's Eve, must snake their way through the wreckage and carnage to find freedom. The suspense comes not from wondering if the group will reach daylight but from guessing which of them will survive. A box office smash that is great fun and displays an unexpected level of humanism and warmth, even if the rantings of Gene Hackman's tireless preacher do quickly grow annoying.

Sequel: *Beyond the Poseidon Adventure* (1979), directed by Irwin Allen and starring Michael Caine, Sally Field, Telly Savalas, Peter Boyle, Shirley Jones, Karl Malden, and Mark Harmon.

Awards: Academy Awards for Song and a Special Achievement Award for Visual Effects; Academy Award nominations for Supporting Actress (Winters), Cinematography, Editing, Art Direction/Set Decoration, Costume Design, Sound.

PRETTY WOMAN (1990), comedy/romance. Directed by Garry Marshall; screenplay by J. F. Lawton; produced by Arnon Milchan and Steven Reuther; photographed by Charles Minsky; edited by Priscilla Nedd; music by James Newton Howard; released by Touchstone/Buena Vista; 119 minutes. *Cast:* Richard Gere, Julia Roberts, Ralph Bellamy, Jason Alexander, Laura San Giacomo, Hector Elizondo.

Notable mainly as the film that created the Julia Roberts phenomenon, this hugely successful fairy tale offers up a sanitized image of a gorgeous hooker and her princely client that actually makes for a charming romance. Gere plays a multimillionaire who, on a visit to Los Angeles, meets an attractive Hollywood Boulevard hooker with whom he strikes a financial deal. Although their arrangement is all business at the start, these two emotionally detached people soon find themselves falling in love with one another. That the film became a monster hit should come as no surprise, as it simultaneously taps into the fantasies of both male and female audiences; Gere's Edward Lewis is a handsome, rich, powerful knight in shining armor, while Roberts' Vivian Ward is a beautiful prostitute who gets paid to sleep with a loving millionaire. It's only a movie, but one can't ignore the negative social effect of a Disneyfied film that romanticizes hooking on a Hollywood Boulevard swept free of drugs, disease, runaways, violence, and degradation. Still, Julia Roberts' deliriously innocent performance goes a long way toward helping us forget our cynicism, especially that memorable moment when, while reaching for the necklace in Gere's hand, he snaps the case shut, and she lets out her infectious laugh.

Award: Academy Award nomination for Best Actress.

PRYOR, RICHARD. Born December 1, 1940, in Peoria, Illinois; actor, comedian. One of the most influential comics of his day, he gave a voice to black

America and an education to white America by telling the truth about race relations with his biting, socially perceptive stand-up routines and comedy recordings. Honing his material in nightclubs, he made his first motion picture appearance in 1967's *The Busy Body*. Frequent supporting roles followed (*Lady Sings the Blues, Uptown Saturday Night*), as did a coscreenwriting credit on Mel Brooks' *Blazing Saddles*. In 1976, he paired with Brooks regular Gene Wilder in *Silver Streak*, and a new comedy team was born—one that must rate with the classic duos of Abbott and Costello, Hope and Crosby, and Martin and Lewis and that adds a second level of sociopolitical relevance to the laughter. Unfortunately, Pryor's personal life has delivered a series of setbacks from heart attacks, to the infamous drug-related self-immolation of 1980, to his diagnosis with multiple sclerosis in 1986. His 1982 performance film *Richard Pryor Live on the Sunset Strip* was his last commercially successful film, despite some promising attempts to team with other brilliant comedians—Jackie Gleason in *The Toy*, John Candy in *Brewster's Millions*, and Eddie Murphy in *Harlem Nights*. In 1995, he released his autobiography, *Pryor Convictions—And Other Life Sentences*. His classic comedy album ''That Nigger's Crazy'' won him one of his five Grammy Awards for comedy recordings. ''Partly because he is black and uses his blackness as he does, largely through his powerful talents, he is making his films into some of the best political art we now have, whatever the scripts may be'' (Stanley Kauffmann, *The New Republic*, May 5, 1982).

Filmography: The Busy Body (1967); Wild in the Streets (1968); The Phynx (1970); You've Got to Walk It Like You Talk It or You'll Lose That Beat (1971); Dynamite Chicken (1972); Lady Sings the Blues (1972); Wattstax (1972); Hit (1973); The Mack (1973); Some Call It Loving (1973); Blazing Saddles (1974) screenplay only; Uptown Saturday Night (1974); Adios Amigo (1976); The Bingo Long Traveling All-Stars and Motor Kings (1976); Car Wash (1976); Silver Streak (1976); Greased Lightning (1977); Which Way Is Up? (1977); Blue Collar (1978); California Suite (1978); The Wiz (1978); The Muppet Movie (1979); Richard Pryor Live in Concert (1979) also screenplay; Richard Pryor Is Back Live in Concert (1979); In God We Trust (1980); Stir Crazy (1980); Wholly Moses! (1980); Bustin' Loose (1981) also producer, story; Richard Pryor Live on the Sunset Strip (1982) also producer, screenplay; Some Kind of Hero (1982); The Toy (1982); Richard Pryor Here and Now (1983) also director, screenplay; Superman III (1983); Brewster's Millions (1985); Jo Jo Dancer, Your Life Is Calling (1986) also director, producer, screenplay; Critical Condition (1987); Moving (1988); Harlem Nights (1989); See No Evil, Hear No Evil (1989); Another You (1991).

Honors: WGA Award (*Blazing Saddles*); Emmy Award for Best Writing (''Lily'' 1973); Grammy Awards (''That Nigger's Crazy'' 1974, ''Is It Something I Said?'' 1975, ''Bicentennial Nigger'' 1976, ''Rev. Du Rite'' 1981, ''Live on the Sunset Strip'' 1982).

Selected bibliography

Pryor, Richard, and Todd Gold. *Pryor Convictions: And Other Life Sentences*. New York: Random House, 1995.

Williams, John A., and Dennis A. Williams. *If I Stop I'll Die: The Comedy and Tragedy of Richard Pryor*. New York: Thunder's Mouth, 1991.

PULP FICTION (1994), crime. Directed and cowritten by Quentin Tarantino; screenplay with Roger Avary; produced by Lawrence Bender; photographed by Andrzej Sekula; edited by Sally Menke; music by Karen Rachtman, song "Girl, You'll Be a Woman Soon" written by Neil Diamond and performed by Urge Overkill; released by Miramax; 149 minutes. *Cast*: John Travolta, Samuel L. Jackson, Bruce Willis, Uma Thurman, Harvey Keitel, Tim Roth, Amanda Plummer, Ving Rhames, Maria de Medeiros, Christopher Walken, Rosanna Arquette, Quentin Tarantino, Eric Stoltz, Steve Buscemi, Frank Whaley, Alexis Arquette, Peter Greene, Dick Miller, Julia Sweeney, Lawrence Bender.

Quentin Tarantino's slam-bang follow-up to *Reservoir Dogs* is so clearly a movie that understands movement that any attempt to deny its strengths is to deny all that makes cinema great. A motion picture hybrid that borrows liberally from the new wave of Hong Kong Cinema, French New Wave (especially peripheral figure Jean-Pierre Melville) and 1940s Hollywood with its root in sultry pulp detective fiction, the film has so much energy that it's practically combustible. It is the film through which mass audiences discovered new wonderboy Tarantino, after the cinephiles found him with his impressive debut film *Reservoir Dogs*. The plot interconnects several stories—the trivial conversations and bloodletting of hit men Vincent Vega (Travolta) and Jules (Jackson); the moral dilemma of boxer Butch Coolidge (Willis), who refuses to throw a fight; Vincent Vega's job as escort to frisky mob moll Mia (Thurman); and the harebrained robbery planned by petty crooks Honey Bunny and Pumpkin (Plummer and Roth)—all of which lead to graphic, cathartic, violent climaxes. Some very snappy dialogue, a generous helping of splattered brain matter, a solid music sound track that features the surf guitar music of Dick Dale, and the fresh direction of Tarantino helped the film earn over $100 million—an unheard-of tally for an independent film. If only the film had some substance and weight.

Awards: Academy Award for Best Screenplay; Academy Award nominations for Best Picture, Director, Actor (Travolta), Supporting Actor (Jackson), Supporting Actress (Thurman), Editing; New York Film Critics Circle Awards for Best Director and Screenplay; Los Angeles Film Critics Awards for Best Picture, Director, Actor (Travolta), Screenplay; Independent Spirit Awards for Best Picture, Director, Screenplay, Actor (Jackson); Cannes Film Festival Palme d'Or.

Q

QUAID, DENNIS. Born April 9, 1954, in Houston, Texas; actor. Brother is Randy Quaid; wife is Meg Ryan; former wife is actor P. J. Soles. With his easygoing demeanor, comforting Texas drawl, and boyish grin, Quaid has carved out a career for himself in such popular films as *The Right Stuff* (as the charmingly egotistical Gordon Cooper), *The Big Easy*, and *D.O.A.* A singer/songwriter in real life, Quaid delivered a virtuoso performance as rock-and-roll legend Jerry Lee Lewis in *Great Balls of Fire*, but his only real box office hit since then has been 1995's moderately successful *Something to Talk About*. He and Ryan have appeared in three films together—*Innerspace*, *D.O.A.*, and the brave, but flawed, psychological crime drama *Flesh and Bone*.

Filmography: 9/30/55 (1977); Our Winning Season (1978); Seniors (1978); Breaking Away (1979); G.O.R.P. (1980); The Long Riders (1980); All Night Long (1981); Caveman (1981); The Night the Lights Went Out in Georgia (1981) also songs; Tough Enough (1982); Jaws 3-D (1983); The Right Stuff (1983); Dreamscape (1984); Enemy Mine (1985); The Big Easy (1986) also songs; Innerspace (1987); Suspect (1987); D.O.A. (1988); Everybody's All-American (1988); Great Balls of Fire (1989); Come See the Paradise (1990); Postcards from the Edge (1991); Flesh and Bone (1993); Wilder Napalm (1993); Undercover Blues (1993); Wyatt Earp (1994); Something to Talk About (1995).

Honor: Independent Spirit Award for Best Actor (*The Big Easy*).

QUAID, RANDY. Born October 1, 1950, in Houston, Texas; actor. Brother is Dennis Quaid. Bulky, guileless character actor whose career has consisted mostly of easily forgotten comedies peppered with a handful of exceptional seriocomic roles. Like most everyone else in Peter Bogdanovich's 1971 masterpiece *The Last Picture Show*, Quaid went from unknown to overnight sensation as part of the brilliant ensemble cast, playing the oafish, but likable, Lester

Marlow, host of the town's nude pool party. Two years later he was cast as Meadows, the unjustly sentenced military prisoner of Hal Ashby's *The Last Detail*. Hoping against hope that he'll somehow gain his freedom by repeatedly reciting his mantra "Nam-Myoho-Renge-Ko," he captures just the right blend of innocence, sadness, and fury as he makes his attempted escape across the frozen ground only to be wrestled down and delivered to prison. His best roles of the next two decades remain those in which he reveals his dark side—*Midnight Express*, *Parents*, and the television movie *LBJ: The Early Years* as President Lyndon Johnson. Quaid also has the distinction of being part of the most misguided season of NBC's "Saturday Night Live."

Filmography: Targets (1968); The Last Picture Show (1971); What's Up Doc? (1972); The Last Detail (1973); Lolly Madonna XXX (1973); Paper Moon (1973); The Apprenticeship of Duddy Kravitz (1974); Breakout (1975); Bound for Glory (1976); The Missouri Breaks (1976); The Choirboys (1977); Three Warriors (1977); Midnight Express (1978); Foxes (1980); The Long Riders (1980); Heartbeeps (1981); National Lampoon's Vacation (1983); The Wild Life (1984); "Saturday Night Live" (1985–1986, tvs); Fool for Love (1985); The Slugger's Wife (1985); Sweet Country (1986); The Wraith (1986); Dear America (1987); No Man's Land (1987); LBJ: The Early Years (1987, tvm); Caddyshack II (1988); Moving (1988); Out Cold (1988); Bloodhounds of Broadway (1989); National Lampoon's Christmas Vacation (1989); Parents (1989); Cold Dog Soup (1990); Days of Thunder (1990); Martians Go Home (1990); Quick Change (1990); Texasville (1990); Frankenstein (1993, tvm); Freaked (1993); Major League II (1994); The Paper (1994); Roommates (1994, tvm); Next Door (1994, ctvm); Curse of the Starving Class (1995, ctvm); Bye Bye Love (1995); Ed McBain's 87th Precinct (1995, tvm); Forget Paris (1995).

Honor: Academy Award nomination for Best Supporting Actor (*The Last Detail*).

QUINN, AIDAN. Born March 8, 1959, in Chicago; actor. Brother Declan is a cinematographer; brother Paul and sister Marian are both actors. Gutsy, seductive actor with piercing blue eyes who selectively splits his time between stage, screen, and television. Having gained attention in his first two films, *Reckless* and *Desperately Seeking Susan*, his starring role as an AIDS victim in the television movie *An Early Frost* propelled him to stardom. Although he lost a chance to play Christ when Martin Scorsese's first attempt to film *The Last Temptation of Christ* failed, he has shown an affinity for lush, high-profile period films with *The Mission*, *Crusoe*, *Avalon*, *Mary Shelley's Frankenstein*, and *Legends of the Fall*.

Filmography: Reckless (1984); Desperately Seeking Susan (1985); An Early Frost (1985, tvm); The Mission (1986); Stakeout (1987); Crusoe (1989); The Handmaid's Tale (1989); The Lemon Sisters (1989); Avalon (1990); Benny and Joon (1993); Blink (1994); Mary Shelley's Frankenstein (1994); Legends of the Fall (1994).

R

RAFELSON, BOB. Born February 21, 1933, in New York City; director, screen-writer, producer. Uncle is screenwriter Samson Raphaelson (*The Jazz Singer*, *Trouble in Paradise*, *The Shop around the Corner*). After traveling extensively in his teens and studying philosophy at Dartmouth and in India, he began his career in television as a story editor, writer, and producer for David Susskind's "Play of the Week," Desilu, and Columbia Screen Gems. His first commercial success came in 1966 as the coproducer and director of the television series "The Monkees," which manufactured a rock band and placed it against a back-drop of nearly surreal plot contrivances. The show ran until 1968 and facilitated the creation of BBS Productions, a company formed with Burt Schneider and Steve Blauner to produce commercial counterculture films. They began with the Monkees' feature vehicle *Head* and followed with *Easy Rider*. Rafelson's sec-ond feature, *Five Easy Pieces*, is his most important and complex work to date and is the first of four collaborations with Jack Nicholson. It also lays out Rafelson's main theme of men dropping out of society to explore other sides of their character—Robert Eroica Dupea, the upper-class, ex-pianist drifter in *Five Easy Pieces*; David Staebler, the withdrawn, emotionally barren talk show host in *The King of Marvin Gardens*; Craig Blake, the wealthy southerner who is attracted to the physical side of life in *Stay Hungry*; and Frank Chambers, the depression-era drifter who is drawn into a web of lust and murder in James Cain's *The Postman Always Rings Twice*. These stories are told with a harsh, uncompromising tone that has perhaps been the reason that commercial success has been so elusive. With *The Postman Always Rings Twice*, despite its better moments, a noticeable shift in style began to develop—a slicker, more conven-tional method of storytelling that softens the hard edges and streamlines the complexities. In 1990, he indulged in the adventure genre with *Mountains of* *the Moon*, a biography of explorer Sir Richard Burton. He then followed with the abysmal *Man Trouble*, a critical and commercial failure that reteamed him with *Five Easy Pieces* star Nicholson and screenwriter Carole Eastman.

Filmography: "The Monkees" (1966–1968, tvs) also coproducer; Head (1968) also producer, screenplay, actor; Five Easy Pieces (1970) also producer, story; The King of Marvin Gardens (1972) also producer, story; Stay Hungry (1976) also producer, screenplay; The Postman Always Rings Twice (1981) also producer; Always (1985) actor only; Black Widow (1987); Mountains of the Moon (1990) also screenplay; Man Trouble (1992); "Wet," episode of Erotic Tales (1994, short).

Filmography as coexecutive producer with BBS: Easy Rider (1969, Dennis Hopper); The Last Picture Show (1971, Peter Bogdanovich); A Safe Place (1971, Henry Jaglom); Drive, He Said (1972, Nicholson); Hearts and Minds (1974, Peter Davis).

Honors: Academy Award nominations for Best Picture and Screenplay (*Five Easy Pieces*); New York Film Critics Circle Award for Best Director (*Five Easy Pieces*).

RAGING BULL (1980), biopic/drama. Directed by Martin Scorsese; written by Paul Schrader and Mardik Martin; produced by Irwin Winkler and Robert Chartoff; photographed by Michael Chapman (b&w); edited by Thelma Schoonmaker; music "Cavalleria Rusticana" by Pietro Mascagni; released by United Artists; 129 minutes. *Cast*: Robert De Niro, Cathy Moriarty, Joe Pesci, Frank Vincent, Nicholas Colasanto, Theresa Saldana.

Ostensibly a biography of world heavyweight champion Jake LaMotta, whose relationship with his wife and brother was consumed by jealousy and hate before he finally found an inner peace, *Raging Bull* is not merely the greatest movie ever made about boxing, but a superb case study of man as animal. Through LaMotta, Scorsese conducts an examination of primitivism, physicality over intellect, and emotion in its purest form. This is the film that is a complete embodiment of everything Scorsese has been trying to say as a filmmaker—that even the simplest of creatures can find redemption. Photographed in beautifully rich black-and-white and masterfully edited by longtime collaborator Thelma Schoonmaker, *Raging Bull* reaches a nearly unparalleled level of artistry on its visual style alone. A bloated Robert De Niro, nearly unrecognizable as Jake, won a much-deserved Oscar for his performance, while Pesci as brother Joey and Moriarty as wife Vickie both earned nominations for their roles as Jake's long-suffering human punching bags.

Awards: Academy Awards for Best Actor, Best Editing; Academy Award nominations for Best Picture, Director, Supporting Actor (Pesci), Supporting Actress, Cinematography, Sound; New York Film Critics Circle Awards for Best Actor, Supporting Actor; Los Angeles Film Critics Awards for Best Picture, Actor; included in the Library of Congress' National Film Registry (1990); voted Second Best Film of All Time in the 1992 *Sight and Sound* Filmmakers Survey; named "Best Film of the Decade" (1980–1989) in the American Film Critics Survey.

RAIDERS OF THE LOST ARK (1981), adventure. Directed by Steven Spielberg; written by Lawrence Kasdan (from a story by George Lucas and Philip

Kaufman); produced by Frank Marshall; executive produced by Lucas and Howard Kazanjian; photography by Douglas Slocombe and Paul Beeson; edited by Michael Kahn; music by John Williams; released by Paramount; 115 minutes. *Cast*: Harrison Ford, Karen Allen, Paul Freeman, Wolf Kahler, Ronald Lacey, John Rhys-Davies, Denholm Elliott, Alfred Molina.

For shear pleasure alone, it's hard to top Steven Spielberg's homage to the cliff-hanging serials of the 1930s and 1940s. Starring megahero Harrison Ford with his dusty, brimmed hat and fierce whip, the story follows archaeologist Indiana Jones as he travels across the world to obtain a priceless artifact—the ark that once contained the Ten Commandments. However, it's not the story but the way it's told that makes this such an enjoyable roller-coaster ride. The movie is filled with classic Hollywood moments, but perhaps the most memorable is Indiana's attempt to outrace the thundering boulder that threatens to flatten him. A key to the entire film's success is John Williams' infectious anthem. Not surprisingly, this instant classic has become one of the highest-grossing films ever made. It also marks the first collaboration between Spielberg and George Lucas.

Awards: Academy Awards for Editing, Art Direction, Sound, Visual Effects, Sound Effects Editing (Special Achievement Award); Academy Award nominations for Best Picture, Director, Cinematography, Score.

Sequels: *Indiana Jones and the Temple of Doom* (1984), *Indiana Jones and the Last Crusade* (1989); Spielberg and George Lucas produced the television series "The Young Indiana Jones Chronicles" (1992–1993).

RAIMI, SAM. Born October 23, 1959, in Royal Oak, Michigan; director, screenwriter. Brother Ted is an actor; brother Ivan is a screenwriter (*Darkman*). Visually kinetic director of comic book-style horror films who burst (almost literally) onto the scene in 1983 with his audacious, hyperenergetic *Evil Dead*. After years of making 8mm movies, Raimi and friends from Michigan State University (actor/producer Robert Tapert, actor/producer Bruce Campbell, and brother Ivan) pooled their collective talents to create an international cult hit in *Evil Dead*. Its camera techniques are wildly innovative, its style is alternately camp and grotesquely bloody in a *Grand Guignol* sort of way, and, most important, it's one of the scariest horror movies in many years. His subsequent output has included the absolutely outrageous *Evil Dead 2: Dead by Dawn*, a brilliantly cartoonish exercise in blood and comedy; the expertly directed and conceived *Darkman*, a glowing tribute to the Universal horror films of the 1930s; two flat-out failures (*Crimewave* and the third Evil Dead installment, *Army of Darkness*); and the moderately successful Sharon Stone–Gene Hackman tale of an Old West gunfight, *The Quick and the Dead*. He's also frequently collaborated with the Coen brothers—they've written *Crimewave*, and he's contributed to the script of *The Hudsucker Proxy*.

Filmography as director and writer: The Evil Dead (1983); Crimewave (1985); Evil

Dead 2: Dead by Dawn (1987); Darkman (1990); Army of Darkness (1992); The Quick and the Dead (1995).

Additional credits: Spies like Us (1985) actor; Thou Shall Not Kill . . . Except (1987) actor; Maniac Cop (1988) actor; Easy Wheels (1989) ep; Intruder (1989) actor; Hard Target (1993) ep; "The Gas Station" episode of John Carpenter Presents Body Bags (1993, ctvm) actor; The Hudsucker Proxy (1994) screenplay.

RAIN MAN (1988), drama/comedy. Directed by Barry Levinson; screenplay by Ronald Bass and Barry Morrow; produced by Mark Johnson; executive produced by Peter Guber and Jon Peters; photographed by John Seale; edited by Stu Linder; music by Hans Zimmer; released by MGM-UA; 128 minutes. *Cast:* Dustin Hoffman, Tom Cruise, Valeria Golino, Gerald Molen, Barry Levinson, Bonnie Hunt.

A remarkable Hollywood achievement that, despite the pairing of its two superstar actors, defied the conventional wisdom that said an intelligent, character-driven film about a man and his autistic brother wouldn't find an audience. Cruise plays Charlie Babbitt, a self-absorbed automobile importer who, upon learning of his father's death, returns home to Cincinnati to collect his $3 million estate and instead inherits Raymond (Hoffman), an autistic brother he never really knew existed. Propelled by Barry Levinson's brilliance as a director of actors, the film is a smart commentary on the nature of intimacy—Raymond is physically unable to connect; Charlie is emotionally unable to connect. Cruise is perfect in a subtle performance, though he is overshadowed by Hoffman's showier, but unforgettable, Raymond—a "buddy film" character who, in many ways, is related to his earlier social misfits Ratso Rizzo (*Midnight Cowboy*) and Louis Dega (*Papillon*).

Awards: Academy Awards for Best Picture, Actor, Director, Screenplay; Academy Award nominations for Best Cinematography, Editing, Score, Art Direction.

RAMBO: FIRST BLOOD, PART II (1985), action/war. Directed by George P. Cosmatos; screenplay by Sylvester Stallone and James Cameron (from a story by Kevin Jarre); produced by Buzz Feitshans; photographed by Jack Cardiff; edited by Mark Goldblatt and Mark Helfrich; music by Jerry Goldsmith; released by Tri-Star; 92 minutes. *Cast*: Sylvester Stallone, Richard Crenna, Charles Napier, Steven Berkoff, Julia Nickson.

A ridiculous distortion of America's post-Vietnam sentiments that is filled with xenophobic jingoism, this action-packed Stallone vehicle is the peak of Hollywood's mindless exploitation of the war in Vietnam. Stallone's John Rambo (like Chuck Norris' Braddock in *Missing in Action*) is sent on the proverbial impossible mission into the jungles to rescue a group of American prisoners of war, asking his officer (Crenna), "Sir, do we get to win this time?" Since this is pure Hollywood fantasy that lies its way through history, Rambo puts up a superhuman fight killing hundreds of Vietnamese and commie Russians in the process. Although it follows the pattern of countless World War II movies, the revisionist politics of *Rambo* shows a complete lack of respect for our country's veterans by turning them into homicidal comic book characters instead of depicting them as human beings. Apparently, however, giving America a win in Vietnam provided a certain national catharsis, as the film not only performed well at the box office but contributed to a rash of Rambo-related merchandising. "A picture like *Rambo* diminished the soldiers who were actually over there; if one Stallone can conquer the enemy, why couldn't *they*?" (David Halberstam, *Time*).

Prequel: *First Blood* (1982, Ted Kotcheff).

Sequel: *Rambo III* (1988, Peter MacDonald).

REDFORD, ROBERT. Born Charles Robert Redford, Jr., August 17, 1937, in Santa Monica, California; actor, producer, director. Raised along the beaches of California and commencing his college studies at the University of Colorado with aspirations of a career in pro baseball, Redford eventually made his way across the country to New York City (via Europe to try his hand at painting), where he studied design at the Pratt Institute and theater at the American Academy of Dramatic Arts. After debuting on Broadway in a small role in 1959's *Tall Story*, he landed a starring role four years later in Neil Simon's *Barefoot in the Park*—a role he would reprise on the big screen in 1967. But the role as Sundance in *Butch Cassidy and the Sundance Kid* started him off on his reign as the top box office draw of the 1970s. As a newcomer costarring with a Hollywood legend, the blond-haired charmer with boyish good looks instantly became an American icon. The ultimate movie star, Redford was a sex symbol who combined his vitality with intelligence and integrity. His next film, the moderately successful *Downhill Racer*, would provide a hint of what was to come for Redford—it marked his producing debut (through Wildwood Enterprises) and revealed his passion for the outdoors. While his next couple of films were respected and semipopular, he hit the mother lode in 1973, with *The Sting* and *The Way We Were* establishing him as both a man's man and a lady's man. He proved to his critics he was more than just a handsome movie star with his increasingly visible role as a supporter of liberal and environmental causes and by appearing in such politically progressive films as *Three Days of the Condor* and *All the President's Men*, the latter featuring a brilliantly understated performance as *Washington Post* reporter Bob Woodward. By 1980, his career had begun to shift with his directorial debut, *Ordinary People*, which earned him an Oscar for Best Direction. He has since concentrated on glossy, big-budget pictures such as *Out of Africa*, *Indecent Proposal*, and *A River Runs through It*, approaching the power of his earlier work only with *Quiz Show*, his disillusioned look back at the breakdown of American values as symbolized by the quiz show scandals of the 1950s. Coinciding with his success as a director is the creation of his Sundance Institute and Sundance Film Festival (formerly the U.S. Film Festival), which Redford began in 1981 to promote the future of independent American filmmaking. Located in the idyllic surroundings of Park City, Utah,

Sundance is now the single greatest force for nurturing and promoting the independent filmmaking community. In 1995, Redford took a step into the cable-television sphere with the formation of the Sundance Channel. ''Film for me is always the chance to educate and to entertain at the same time, in equal balance'' (Robert Redford, interviewed by Mikelle Cosandaey in *Cineaste* 16, nos. 1–2, 1987–1988).

Filmography: War Hunt (1962); Inside Daisy Clover (1965); Situation Hopeless But Not Serious (1965); The Chase (1966); This Property Is Condemned (1966); Barefoot in the Park (1967); Butch Cassidy and the Sundance Kid (1969); Downhill Racer (1969) also ep; Tell Them Willie Boy Is Here (1969); Little Fauss and Big Halsy (1970); The Candidate (1972) also ep; The Hot Rock (1972); Jeremiah Johnson (1972); The Sting (1973); The Way We Were (1973); Broken Treaty at Battle Mountain (1974, documentary) narrator; The Great Gatsby (1974); The Great Waldo Pepper (1975); Three Days of the Condor (1975); All the President's Men (1976); A Bridge Too Far (1977); The Electric Horseman (1979); Brubaker (1980); The Natural (1984); Out of Africa (1985); Legal Eagles (1986); To Protect Mother Earth (1989, documentary) narrator; Havana (1990); Sneakers (1992); Indecent Proposal (1993).

Filmography as executive producer: Promised Land (1988); Some Girls (1988); Yosemite: The Fate of Heaven (1988, documentary) also narrator; Incident at Oglala (1992, documentary) also narrator.

Filmography as director: Ordinary People (1980); The Milagro Beanfield War (1988) also actor, producer; A River Runs through It (1992) also ep, narrator; Quiz Show (1994) also producer.

Honors: Academy Award for Best Director (*Ordinary People*); Academy Award nominations for Best Picture (*Quiz Show*), Director (*Quiz Show*), Actor (*The Sting*); New York Film Critics Circle Award for Best Picture (*Quiz Show*); DGA Award (*Ordinary People*).

Selected bibliography

Spada, James. *The Films of Robert Redford*. New York: Citadel, 1977.

REDS (1981), biopic/historical. Directed, cowritten, and produced by Warren Beatty; screenplay with Trevor Griffiths; photographed by Vittorio Storaro; edited by Dede Allen and Craig McKay; music by Stephen Sondheim and Dave Grusin; released by Paramount; 200 minutes. Cast: Warren Beatty, Diane Keaton, Edward Herrmann, Jerzy Kozinski, Maureen Stapleton, Jack Nicholson, M. Emmet Walsh, Paul Sorvino, George Plimpton, Gene Hackman, R. G. Armstrong, Henry Miller.

A grand love story set against the backdrop of the Bolshevik revolution, this historical epic from producer/director/writer/star Warren Beatty (earning Oscar nominations in all four categories) tells the story of American radical leftist John Reed, whose book *Ten Days That Shook The World* chronicled the events of 1917 as he saw them. A remarkable achievement that clocks in at 200 minutes, the film succeeds because it makes history intimate by relating it through the eyes of those who were there—Reed, his wife, Louise Bryant (Keaton), Emma

Goldman (Stapleton), and the "witnesses" who deliver their testimonials directly into the camera's lens. Although the film occasionally slips into melodrama during parts of the Reed–Bryant romance, *Reds* remains a rare Hollywood film that challenges the perceived evils of capitalism; it was a daring choice that, amidst the Reagan-era jingoism of the day, failed to find an audience at the box office. In a captivating supporting role is Jack Nicholson as playwright Eugene O'Neill. "*Reds* often seems as if it were trying to be *Dr. Zhivago* for smart people" (Stephen Schiff, *Boston Phoenix*, December 1, 1981).

Awards: Academy Awards for Director, Supporting Actress (Stapleton), Cinematography; Academy Award nominations for Picture, Actor, Actress (Keaton), Supporting Actor (Nicholson), Screenplay, Art Direction, Editing, Sound, Costumes; New York Film Critics Circle Award for Best Picture.

REEVE, CHRISTOPHER. Born September 25, 1952, in New York; actor. Affable and handsome leading man who appeared as Clark Kent/Superman in four movies of the comic book hero's exploits. His memorable nonsuperhero roles include the romantic *Somewhere in Time*, the fascinating and seamy crime drama *Street Smart*, and *The Remains of the Day*. Tragically, Reeve was paralyzed in a horse-riding accident in May 1995. His role in the HBO movie *Above Suspicion* aired just days before the accident; in it he played Detective Dempsey Cain, a wheelchair-bound cop whose spine was damaged after a shooting. Despite the accident, Reeve has returned to the public eye as a champion of medical research for paralysis (speaking eloquently at the 1996 Democratic National Convention) and has begun his return to film as an actor, voice-over artist, and director.

Filmography: Gray Lady Down (1978); Superman (1978); Somewhere in Time (1980); Superman II (1980); Monsignor (1982); Deathtrap (1982); Superman III (1983); The Bostonians (1984); The Aviator (1985); Superman IV: The Quest for Peace (1987) also story; Street Smart (1987); Switching Channels (1988); Noises Off (1992); The Remains of the Day (1993); Speechless (1995); Above Suspicion (1995, ctvm).

REEVES, KEANU. Born September 2, 1964, in Beirut, Lebanon; actor. Handsome and charming young superstar who first attracted attention as the dope-smoking teen in *River's Edge*, perfectly capturing the apathy, angst, and trampled hope of the postpunk generation. Rather than risk being typecast, he took the role of the romantic young music teacher Chevalier Danceny in Stephen Frear's eighteenth-century costume drama *Dangerous Liaisons*. He soon became universally identified as the aspiring rock star and "most excellent" high school dude, Ted "Theodore" Logan of *Bill and Ted's Excellent Adventure*. The goofy image stuck, but Reeves has continually battled against it with Gus Van Sant's intelligent and passionate *My Own Private Idaho*, Kenneth Branagh's adaptation of *Much Ado about Nothing*, Francis Ford Coppola's *Dracula*, and Bernardo Bertolucci's *Little Buddha*. Surprisingly, his transformation into an action star in *Speed* has helped erase the specter of the awesome Ted. Undaunted, he continues to push forward and step into roles that his detractors insist are not for him, such as his starring role in the Manitoba Theater Centre's 1995 stage production of *Hamlet*.

Filmography: Flying (1986); Youngblood (1986); River's Edge (1987); Permanent Record (1988); Dangerous Liaisons (1988); The Night Before (1988); The Prince of Pennsylvania (1988); Bill and Ted's Excellent Adventure (1989); Parenthood (1989); I Love You to Death (1990); Tune in Tomorrow (1990); Bill and Ted's Bogus Journey (1991); My Own Private Idaho (1991); Paula Abdul's "Rush Rush" (1991, mv); Much Ado about Nothing (1993); Bram Stoker's Dracula (1993); Little Buddha (1994); Speed (1994); Even Cowgirls Get the Blues (1994); A Walk in the Clouds (1995); Johnny Mnemonic (1995).

REINER, ROB. Born March 6, 1945, in Beverly Hills, California; actor, director, producer. Father is comedian Carl; formerly married to actor/director Penny Marshall; son Lucas is a director (*Spirit of '76*); daughter Tracy is an actor. Like his contemporaries Ron Howard and Penny Marshall, Reiner hailed from a Hollywood family, found fame on television in the 1970s (as "meathead" Mike Stivic on "All in the Family"), and has developed into one of the most commercially successful comic directors in Hollywood. He debuted as a director with the hilarious "rockumentary" parody *This Is Spinal Tap* and, after the modest success of the teen comedy *The Sure Thing*, delivered hit after hit—a pair of superb Stephen King adaptations, *Stand by Me* and *Misery*, the inventive fantasy *The Princess Bride*, the delightful romantic comedy *When Harry Met Sally . . .* , and the military courtroom drama *A Few Good Men*, before finally turning out the noble failure *North*. He bounced partially back with the Michael Douglas vehicle *The American President*, a moderate success that lacked the power or enthusiasm of his earlier work. In addition to his directing work, he frequently appears on-screen in supporting roles and was especially memorable in Woody Allen's *Bullets over Broadway*. His prolific production company, Castle Rock Entertainment, has delivered a wide range of pictures, including the Billy Crystal comedy *City Slickers*, the Clint Eastwood thriller *In the Line of Fire*, art house films *Barcelona* and *Before Sunrise*, and the television series "Seinfeld."

Filmography as actor: Enter Laughing (1966); Halls of Anger (1970); Where's Poppa? (1970); Summertree (1971); How Come Nobody's on Our Side? (1975); Fire Sale (1977); Throw Momma from the Train (1987); Postcards from the Edge (1990); Spirit of '76 (1990); Regarding Henry (1991); Sleepless in Seattle (1993); Bullets over Broadway (1994); Mixed Nuts (1994); Bye Bye, Love (1995).

Filmography as director: This Is Spinal Tap (1984) also actor, screenplay, songs; The Sure Thing (1985); Stand by Me (1986); The Princess Bride (1987) also producer; When Harry Met Sally . . . (1989) also producer; Misery (1990) also producer; A Few Good Men (1990) also producer; North (1994); The American President (1995) also producer.

Filmography as executive producer: City Slickers II: The Legend of Curly's Gold (1994); Little Big League (1994); The Shawshank Redemption (1994); Barcelona (1994); Before Sunrise (1995).

Filmography from Castle Rock Entertainment: Lord of the Flies (1990); Sibling Rivalry (1990); Late for Dinner (1991); City Slickers (1991); Year of the Comet (1991); Honeymoon in Vegas (1992); Mr. Saturday Night (1992); Amos and Andrew (1993); In the Line of Fire (1993); Needful Things (1993); Malice (1993); Josh and S.A.M. (1993); Dolores Claiborne (1995); Forget Paris (1995); Beyond Rangoon (1995); The Run of the Country (1995); Dracula: Dead and Loving It (1995); Othello (1995).

Honors: Academy Award nomination for Best Picture (*A Few Good Men*); Emmy Awards for Best Supporting Actor (''All in the Family'' 1974, 1978).

REITMAN, IVAN. Born October 26, 1946, in Czechoslovakia; director, producer. Raised in Canada from the age of four, Reitman has developed into one of America's most successful comic director/producers by consistently offering films that audiences line up to see. After a number of films in Canada (including two David Cronenberg pictures as producer), Reitman's earliest hits in Hollywood were linked to ''Saturday Night Live'' cast members—Jim Belushi (*National Lampoon's Animal House*), Bill Murray (*Meatballs, Stripes*), and the team of Murray and Dan Aykroyd (*Ghostbusters, Ghostbusters II*). By the late 1980s and early 1990s, he prospered by transforming action hero Arnold Schwarzenegger into a comic star with *Twins, Kindergarten Cop*, and *Junior*, though the same experiment failed miserably when he cast Sylvester Stallone in *Stop or My Mom Will Shoot*. He has found serious critical acceptance only with *Dave*, a warmly written political satire that ranks as one of the best romantic comedies in recent years.

Filmography: Columbus of Sex (1970) cinematographer, editor only; Foxy Lady (1971) also producer, editor; Cannibal Girls (1973) also ep; Meatballs (1979); Stripes (1981) also producer; Ghostbusters (1984) also producer; Legal Eagles (1986) also producer; Twins (1988) also producer; Ghostbusters II (1989) also producer, Kindergarten Cop (1990) also producer; Dave (1993); Junior (1994).

Filmography as producer only: They Came from Within (1976); The House by the Lake (1977); Rabid (1977) ep; Blackout (1978) ep; National Lampoon's Animal House (1978); Heavy Metal (1981); Spacehunter: Adventures in the Forbidden Zone (1983) ep; Big Shots (1987) ep; Casual Sex (1989) ep; Feds (1988) ep; Beethoven (1992) ep; Stop or My Mother Will Shoot (1992); Beethoven's 2nd (1993) ep.

RESERVOIR DOGS (1992), crime drama. Directed and written by Quentin Tarantino; produced by Lawrence Bender; photographed by Andrzej Sekula; edited by Sally Menke; music by Karyn Rachtman, ''Stuck in the Middle with You'' performed by Steeler's Wheel; released by Miramax; 99 minutes. *Cast*: Tim Roth, Harvey Keitel, Michael Madsen, Lawrence Tierney, Christopher Penn, Steve Buscemi, Eddie Bunker, Quentin Tarantino, Lawrence Bender, Steven Wright (voice).

Quentin Tarantino exploded onto the American film scene with this in-your-face gangster picture modeled on the noirisms of France's Jean-Pierre Melville, the underworld Americana of Stanley Kubrick's *The Killing*, and the nonstop action of recent Hong Kong cinema, specifically, Ringo Lam's *City on Fire*. Armed to the hilt with acting talent, *Reservoir Dogs* tells the story of a bank robbery gone awry, giving it enough structural twists and turns to hold the interest of all but the squeamish. The story is a staple of the gangster film, but Tarantino's ability to elevate his characters to a level of iconography separates him from every other filmmaker of his generation—among the most memorable moments are the interpretive analysis of Madonna's hit song "Like a Virgin"; Buscemi's objection to being dubbed Mr. Pink; and Madsen's otic torture scene to the tune of "Stuck in the Middle with You." While American films of the 1970s had Peckinpah and Scorsese challenging audiences with morally ambiguous worlds and near-erotic bloodletting, Tarantino, with his ear for smart dialogue and his eye for precision casting, is the only filmmaker to grab the torch.

RETURN OF THE SECAUCUS SEVEN (1980), drama. Directed, written, and edited by John Sayles; produced by William Aydelott and Jeffrey Nelson; photographed by Austin de Besche; music by Mason Daring; released by Libra Film; 110 minutes. *Cast*: Mark Arnott, Gordon Clapp, Maggie Cousineau, Brian Johnston, Bruce MacDonald, Adam LeFevre, Jean Passanante, Maggie Renzi, John Sayles, David Strathairn, Karen Trott.

Filmed with a cast of unknowns on a $60,000 budget, John Sayles' directorial debut is a prime example of pure, independent filmmaking—a well-written story about real people dealing with the universal issues of love, friendship, and aging. As age thirty approaches, a group of Vietnam-era radicals get together for a weekend reunion and realize how much they've changed since their arrest ten years earlier in Secaucus, New Jersey, while en route to a Washington, D.C., protest march. One now works as a speechwriter for a senator, another acts in community theater, another wants to move to Hollywood to find success as a singer—they've changed, and so have the times, but their various friendships and loyalties remain intact. It doesn't sparkle with technical virtuosity or brilliant performances, but it's an honest piece of filmmaking of the sort that is rarely made in the studio system. One of the first independent film successes, it not only put John Sayles on the map but also inspired others to put their stories on film.

REYNOLDS, BURT. Born February 11, 1936, in Waycross, Georgia; actor, director. Overtly macho leading man who attracted attention for his television work in the late 1950s ("Riverboat") after turning to acting when a knee injury halted a promising football career at Florida State University. His southern charm, athletic good looks, mischievous grin, and muscular physique helped earn him a television contract at Universal, and he continued to appear on the small screen ("Gunsmoke" from 1962 to 1965, "Hawk" from 1966 to 1967) while struggling to get into features. His big break came in 1972 as Lewis in the Appalachian adventure-cum-nightmare drama *Deliverance*. His subsequent films run the gamut from riotous, good-old-boy romps (*Smokey and the Bandit* and *The Cannonball Run*), to gutsy sports dramas (*The Longest Yard, Semi-Tough*), to westerns (*The Man Who Loved Cat Dancing*). Throughout the 1970s he was one of the most popular personalities in America with much-publicized romantic links to Dinah Shore and Sally Field, a marriage to Judy Carne, a controversial nude layout in *Cosmopolitan*, and collaborations with some of the best directors of the era—Robert Aldrich, Woody Allen, Peter Bogdanovich, John Boorman, Stanley Donen, Blake Edwards, Norman Jewison, Alan J. Pakula, and Don Siegel. In 1976, he made the transition to director with *Gator*, peaking with the violent action film *Sharkey's Machine* in 1981. During the late 1980s and 1990s, however, his career coasted through a series of unwatchable movies (the sincerely warm *Breaking In* being the surprise exception), a smarmy tabloid airing of his split from wife Loni Anderson, a stint as coproducer of a television game show (''Pictionary''), and a couple of seasons as Wood Newton on a popular television series (''Evening Shade'').

Filmography as actor: Angel Baby (1961); Armored Command (1961); Operation C.I.A. (1965); Navajo Joe (1966); Fade-In (1968); 100 Rifles (1969); Impasse (1969); Sam Whiskey (1969); Shark (1969); Skullduggery (1970); Deliverance (1972); Everything You Always Wanted to Know about Sex* (*but Were Afraid to Ask) (1972); Fuzz (1972); Shamus (1972); The Man Who Loved Cat Dancing (1973); White Lightning (1973); The Longest Yard (1974); W. W. and the Dixie Dancekings (1974); At Long Last Love (1975); Hustle (1975) also ep; Lucky Lady (1975); Nickelodeon (1976); Silent Movie (1976); Semi-Tough (1977); Smokey and the Bandit (1977); Hooper (1978); Starting Over (1979); The Cannonball Run (1980); Rough Cut (1980); Smokey and the Bandit II (1980); Paternity (1981); Best Friends (1982); The Best Little Whorehouse in Texas (1982); Cannonball Run II (1983); The Man Who Loved Women (1983); Smokey and the Bandit Part 3 (1983); Stroker Ace (1983); City Heat (1984); Uphill All the Way (1984); Heat (1987); Malone (1987); Rent-a-Cop (1988); Switching Channels (1988); All Dogs Go to Heaven (1989) voice only; Breaking In (1989); Physical Evidence (1989); Modern Love (1990); ''Evening Shade'' (1990–1994, tvs) also ep: The Player (1992); Cop and a Half (1993); The Maddening (1995).

Filmography as director and actor: Gator (1976); The End (1978); Sharkey's Machine (1982); Stick (1985).

Honor: Emmy Award for Best Actor (''Evening Shade'' 1991).

Selected bibliography

Streebeck, Nancy. *The Films of Burt Reynolds*. New York: Citadel, 1983.

RIGHT STUFF, THE (1983), drama. Directed and written by Philip Kaufman (from the book by Tom Wolfe); produced by Irwin Winkler and Robert Chartoff; photographed by Caleb Deschanel; edited by Glen Farr, Lisa Fruchtman, Stephen A. Rotter, Tom Rolf, and Douglas Stewart; music by Bill Conti; released by Warner Bros.; 192 minutes. *Cast*: Sam Shepard, Scott Glenn, Ed Harris, Dennis Quaid, Fred Ward, Barbara Hershey, Kim Stanley, Veronica

Cartwright, Pamela Reed, Lance Henriksen, Levon Helm, Donald Moffat, Kathy Baker, Royal Dano, Harry Shearer, Jeff Goldblum, John P. Ryan, General Chuck Yeager.

Philip Kaufman's epic of American heroism tells the story of the men and women who have the "right stuff"—that otherwise indefinable combination of bravery, duty, and talent that separates them from the rest. Focusing on legendary test pilot Chuck Yeager (Shepard) and the group of seven astronauts who helped launch the space program (chiefly, Glenn as Alan Shepard, Harris as John Glenn, Quaid as Gordon Cooper, and Ward as "Gus" Grissom), the 192-minute film spans fifteen years from Yeager's topping Mach 1 at Edwards Air Force Base (AFB), to Alan Shepard's first manned space flight at Cape Canaveral, to the dawn of National Aeronautics and Space Administration Houston Command Center. Given nearly equal weight by Kaufman are the brave and dignified wives, who exhibit every bit as much strength as their revered husbands. Never boring, *The Right Stuff* is packed with excellent performances from the leads and the supporting players (especially a rare appearance from Kim Stanley as Pancho Barnes, the owner of the Edwards AFB watering hole) and has dozens of memorable moments—Yeager's recovery after passing out during his Mach 1 record; "pudknocker" Quaid's cocky prediction that his picture will adorn the walls of Pancho's bar before realizing that only dead pilots rank; the astronauts' reminder that funding is all-important—"No bucks. No Buck Rogers!"; and John Glenn's support of his stuttering wife (Daschenal) when she refuses to go on television with Vice President Johnson. Based on the book by Tom Wolfe, the picture did little business at the box office but remains Kaufman's crowning achievement.

Awards: Academy Awards for Sound, Score, Editing, Sound Effects Editing; Academy Award nominations for Picture, Supporting Actor (Shepard), Cinematography, Art Direction.

RISKY BUSINESS (1983), comedy. Directed and written by Paul Brickman; produced by Jon Avnet and Steve Tisch; photographed by Reynaldo Villalobos; edited by Richard Chew; music by Tangerine Dream, song "Old Time Rock and Roll" performed by Bob Seger and the Silver Bullet Band; released by Warner Bros.; 98 minutes. *Cast*: Tom Cruise, Rebecca De Mornay, Joe Pantoliano, Richard Masur, Bronson Pinchot, Curtis Armstrong, Kevin Anderson.

The only teen comedy of the era to transcend the limits of the genre and exist on a higher level as an artful piece of filmmaking. Although it still follows the conventions of the form, this story of a teenager who has a hormonal burst of wildness during his parents' absence is a careful study of the passage from boyhood to manhood. He cranks up the stereo, drinks, plays cards, drives his dad's Porsche, and procures a call girl as if all those things make the man, only to realize by the finale that manhood is much more complex. A visually inventive film (the dreamy shower scene and the sexually charged el train ride are especially memorable) with an atmospheric electronic score from Tangerine

Dream. The film made a superstar out of Tom Cruise—due specifically to his manic dance routine in his underwear to the strains of Bob Seger's "Old Time Rock and Roll."

RITT, MARTIN. Born March 2, 1914, in New York City; died December 8, 1990, in Santa Monica, California; director. Accomplished former stage actor turned director who studied under Elia Kazan at the Actors Studio before eventually teaching there. Among his students was Paul Newman, who would go on to appear in numerous early Ritt films—*The Long Hot Summer, Paris Blues, Hemingway's Adventure of a Young Man, Hud, The Outrage,* and *Hombre.* A politically minded director who fell victim to the blacklist in the television industry, his overwhelming (and arguably only) signature is a social conscience displayed in his ability to bring together characters of varying backgrounds. In his strongest film, *Norma Rae,* he does both—creating in Sally Field's character a simple southern textile worker who rises to heroic union organizer after becoming inspired by a Jewish New York socialist.

Filmography of key pre-1965 films: Edge of the City (1957); The Long Hot Summer (1958); The Sound and the Fury (1959); Paris Blues (1961); Hud (1963) also producer.

Filmography since 1965: The Spy Who Came in from the Cold (1965); Hombre (1967); The Brotherhood (1968); The Molly Maguires (1970) also producer; The Great White Hope (1970); Sounder (1972); Pete n' Tillie (1972); Conrack (1974); The Front (1976); Casey's Shadow (1978); Norma Rae (1979); Back Roads (1981) also producer; Cross Creek (1983); Murphy's Romance (1985) also ep; Nuts (1987); Stanley and Iris (1990).

Filmography as actor: Winged Victory (1944); End of the Game/Der Richter und sein Henker (1975); The Slugger's Wife (1985).

Honors: Academy Award nomination for Best Director (*Hud*); Cannes Film Festival Grand Prix de la Commission Superieure Technique (*Norma Rae*).

Selected bibliography

Whitaker, Sheila. *The Films of Martin Ritt.* London: BFI, 1972.

RIVER'S EDGE (1987), drama. Directed by Tim Hunter; screenplay by Neal Jimenez; produced by Sarah Pillsbury, Midge Sanford, and David Streit; photographed by Frederick Elmes; edited by Howard Smith and Sonya Sones; music by Jurgen Kneiper; released by Island; 98 minutes. *Cast:* Crispin Glover, Keanu Reeves, Ione Skye Leitch, Daniel Roebuck, Dennis Hopper, Joshua Miller, Roxana Zal, Josh Richman.

A startling portrayal of apathy and emptiness that tells the story of how a group of high school kids cope when one of their group brutally strangles to death his girlfriend. Instead of going to the police, the group decides to remove the starkly naked body by dumping it in the river, though most of their time is spent getting high and just hanging out listening to music. What is most shocking is that the film is based on an actual 1981 incident. Written by Neil Jimenez with a great ear for realistic speech (he also penned *The Waterdance* and *Sleep with Me*) and featuring a collection of then-unknowns, many of whom have since become familiar faces. ''Not since [*Los Olvidados*], Luis Bunuel's 1950 portrayal of youth in Mexico City's slums, has a film so perfectly captured a generation's lack of hope and direction'' (*The 1988 Motion Picture Annual*).

ROBARDS, JASON. Born Jason Nelson Robards, Jr., July 22, 1922, in Chicago; actor. Formerly married to Lauren Bacall; father is actor Jason Robards; sons Jason Robards III and Sam are both actors. Talented stage-trained actor whose mid-1950s performances in Eugene O'Neill's *The Iceman Cometh* and *Long Day's Journey into Night* helped make his reputation as a serious, introspective actor. He then displayed his sharp comic timing as Murray Burns in the hysterical and visually inventive *A Thousand Clowns* and as the eponymous lead character in Sam Peckinpah's *Ballad of Cable Hogue*. He has also played an inordinate number of historical figures in a list that includes George S. Kaufman (*Act One*), Al Capone (*The St. Valentine's Day Massacre*), sewing machine magnate Paris Singer (*Isadora*), Doc Holliday (*Hour of the Gun*), New Mexico governor Pat Wallace (*Pat Garrett and Billy the Kid*), *Washington Post* editor Ben Bradlee (*All the President's Men*), Dashiel Hammett (*Julia*), and Howard Hughes (*Melvin and Howard*), the last three earning him two much-deserved Oscars and one nomination. His film appearances throughout the 1980s and 1990s have been unfortunately scarce and uninteresting, though his performance as the law-firm head in *Philadelphia* was especially effective.

Filmography of key pre-1965 films: Tender Is the Night (1961); A Long Day's Journey into Night (1962).

Filmography since 1965: A Thousand Clowns (1965); A Big Hand for the Little Lady (1966); Any Wednesday (1966); Divorce American Style (1967); The Hour of the Gun (1967); The St. Valentine's Day Massacre (1967); The Night They Raided Minsky's (1968); Isadora (1968); Once Upon a Time in the West (1969); Operation Snafu (1969); Tora! Tora! Tora! (1970); Julius Caesar (1970); Fools (1970); The Ballad of Cable Hogue (1970); Murders in the Rue Morgue (1971); Johnny Got His Gun (1971); The War between Men and Women (1972); Pat Garrett and Billy the Kid (1973); Play It As It Lays (1973); Mr. Sycamore (1974); A Boy and His Dog (1975); All the President's Men (1976); Julia (1977); Comes a Horseman (1978); Hurricane (1979); Melvin and Howard (1980); Raise the Titanic (1980); Caboblanco (1981); The Legend of the Lone Ranger (1981); Burden of Dreams (1982); Max Dugan Returns (1983); Sakharov (1984, tvm); Something Wicked This Way Comes (1984); Square Dance (1986); The Good Mother (1988); Inherit the Wind (1988, tvm); Dream a Little Dream (1989); Parenthood (1989); Reunion (1989); Quick Change (1990); Black Rainbow (1991); The Adventures of Huck Finn (1993); Philadelphia (1993); The Paper (1994); The Enemy Within (1994, ctvm); Little Big League (1994); My Antonia (1995, ctvm); Crimson Tide (1995).

Honors: Academy Awards for Best Supporting Actor (*All the President's Men, Julia*); Academy Award nomination for Best Supporting Actor (*Melvin and Howard*); New York Film Critics Circle Award for Best Supporting Actor (*All the President's Men*); Los Angeles Film Critics Award for Best Supporting Actor (*Julia*); Emmy Award (*Inherit the Wind*); Tony Awards (*Long Day's Journey into Night* 1957, *The Disenchanted* 1959,

Toys in the Attic 1960, *After the Fall* 1964, *Hughie* 1965, *The Country Girl* 1972, *The Moon for the Misbegotten* 1974, *A Touch of the Poet* 1978).

ROBBINS, TIM. Born October 16, 1958, in West Covina, California; actor, director. Longtime companion of Susan Sarandon. Gangly, boyish actor who, after puttering around in some generally uninteresting comedies, appearing in a supporting role in Martin Scorsese's "Amazing Stories" episode, and landing a supporting role in *Top Gun*, delivered two memorable and amazingly different performances in 1988—the brash and immature Nuke Laloosh in *Bull Durham* and the quiet pacifist in the offbeat *Five Corners*. Of his subsequent acting roles, he is especially effective in a pair of peculiarly titled films—as the gullible, hula-hooping star of *The Hudsucker Proxy* and as the innocent convict in *The Shawshank Redemption*. An outspoken political observer, Robbins successfully made the transition to directing with his anti-right-wing, pseudodocumentary parody *Bob Roberts*. With his sophomore directing effort, the sobering antiexecution plea *Dead Man Walking*, Robbins found a perfect vehicle to espouse his political agenda while working within the framework of a tale of humanity and redemption. Cofounder of the critically acclaimed Los Angeles theater group the Actor's Gang.

Filmography: No Small Affair (1984); Fraternity Vacation (1985); The Sure Thing (1985); "Mirror, Mirror," episode of "Amazing Stories" (1985, tvs); Howard the Duck (1986); Top Gun (1986); Five Corners (1988); Bull Durham (1988); Tapeheads (1988); Erik the Viking (1989); Miss Firecracker (1989); Cadillac Man (1990); Jacob's Ladder (1990); The Player (1992); Bob Roberts (1992) also director; Short Cuts (1993); The Hudsucker Proxy (1994); The Shawshank Redemption (1994); I.Q. (1994); Ready to Wear (Prêt-à-Porter) (1994); Dead Man Walking (1995) director.

Honors: Academy Award nomination for Best Director (*Dead Man Walking*); Cannes Film Festival Award for Best Actor (*The Player*); Berlin Film Festival Jury Prize (*Dead Man Walking*).

ROBERTS, ERIC. Born April 18, 1956, in Biloxi, Mississippi; actor. Sisters Julia and Lisa are actors. With extensive stage training that includes London's RADA, Roberts caught the eye of critics in his debut feature *King of the Gypsies* as the unwilling heir to the gypsy throne. Over the next few years, he consistently turned out raw, emotionally naked performances. As the oily hustler/ promoter Paul Snider in *Star 80* he is unforgettable as he stands before a mirror practicing his sinisterly affable greeting and handshake. While his work in *The Pope of Greenwich Village* and *The Coca-Cola Kid* is equally mesmerizing, his brilliance in *Runaway Train* earned him an Academy Award nomination. As Buck, the talkative good ol' boy prison escapee who idolizes Jon Voight's brutal and animalistic Manny, Roberts caps a string of great roles with his best work to date. The next ten years, however, proved barren as Roberts battled drug addiction and slogged through a number of subpar films. Appearances in such low-budget surprises as 1994's Henry Jaglom film *Babyfever* hint that Roberts may be back on track.

Filmography: King of the Gypsies (1978); The Alternative Miss World (1980, documentary) actor and narrator; Raggedy Man (1981); Miss Lonelyhearts (1983); Star 80 (1983); The Pope of Greenwich Village (1984); The Coca-Cola Kid (1985); Runaway Train (1985); Nobody's Fool (1986); Dear America (1987); Blood Red (1986/released in 1989); Best of the Best (1989); Options (1989); Rude Awakening (1989); Love, Cheat and Murder (1993, ctvm); The Specialist (1994); Babyfever (1994); True Killers (1995); The Immortals (1995).

Honor: Academy Award nomination for Best Supporting Actor (*Runaway Train*).

ROBERTS, JULIA. Born October 28, 1967, in Smyrna, Georgia; actor. Brother Eric and sister Lisa are actors; formerly married to singer Lyle Lovett. Born into a theatrical family that, in the 1960s and early 1970s, ran acting and writing workshops out of their Atlanta home, Roberts became the most successful and bankable actress of the early 1990s with her effervescent portrayal of an enchanted fairy tale prostitute in *Pretty Woman*. Although her character bore no resemblance to any real-life hooker, she soon became a darling of the press and public alike. With a Best Supporting Actress nomination for her role as the sickly Shelby in *Steel Magnolias* and the box office success of *Flatliners* and *Sleeping with the Enemy*, it seemed as if Roberts could do no wrong. A miscalculation of the public's response to the commercially stiff *Dying Young* and the bad press associated with her supporting bit as Tinkerbell in Steven Spielberg's misfire *Hook*, coupled with the tabloid coverage of the last-minute cancellation of her marriage to actor Kiefer Sutherland and the insistent (and unsubstantiated) rumors of a cocaine addiction, all contributed to her dethroning, albeit temporary, as queen of the box office. After a two-year hiatus, she returned to form with *The Pelican Brief*, only to follow with the virtually unseen *I Love Trouble*. With her all-too-brief scenes with Tim Robbins in Robert Altman's *Ready to Wear* and her starring role in *Something to Talk About* she has reminded audiences of the charisma and star power that she displayed in *Pretty Woman*. "Roberts' charm is one not of persuasion or slow insinuation but of immediate conquest" (Dave Kehr, *Chicago Tribune*, March 24, 1991).

Filmography: Mystic Pizza (1988); Satisfaction/Girls of Summer (1988); Blood Red (1986/released in 1989); Steel Magnolias (1989); Pretty Woman (1990); Flatliners (1990); Sleeping with the Enemy (1991); Dying Young (1991); Hook (1991); The Player (1992); The Pelican Brief (1993); I Love Trouble (1994); Ready to Wear (Prêt-à-Porter) (1994); Something to Talk About (1995).

Honor: Academy Award nomination for Best Supporting Actress (*Steel Magnolias*).

ROBERTSON, CLIFF. Born September 9, 1925, in La Jolla, California; actor, director. Married to actor Dina Merrill. A talented, but merely average, stage (*Mr. Roberts*) and screen actor throughout the first few years of his career, his stock rose when President Kennedy personally handpicked the actor (and former merchant marine) to play him in *PT 109*. However, he will always be defined by his Oscar-winning role in *Charly*, as the lovable baker with the 68 I.Q. who becomes a genius before reverting back to his "normal" state. In 1971, he produced, directed, wrote, and starred in the rodeo picture *J. W. Coop* and went on to memorable roles in *Three Days of the Condor* and *Obsession* before becoming embroiled in the "Begelman affair" in 1977, when then-Columbia Pictures president David Begelman forged the actor's signature on a $10,000 check and cashed it. Refusing to quietly ignore the incident, Robertson was effectively blacklisted from Hollywood for the next few years until *Brainstorm*.

Filmography of key pre-1965 films: Picnic (1955); The Naked and the Dead (1958); Gidget (1959); Underworld, U.S.A. (1961); PT 109 (1963).

Filmography since 1965: Love Has Many Faces (1965); Up from the Beach (1965); The Honey Pot (1967); Charly (1968); The Devil's Brigade (1968); Too Late the Hero (1970); J. W. Coop (1971) also director, producer, screenplay; The Great Northfield Minnesota Raid (1972); Ace Eli and Rodger of the Skies (1973); Man on a Swing (1974); Out of Season (1975); Three Days of the Condor (1975); Battle of Midway (1976); Obsession (1976); Shoot (1976); Dominique (1977); Fraternity Row (1977); The Pilot (1980) director; Brainstorm (1983); Class (1983); Star 80 (1983); Shaker Run (1985); Malone (1987); Wild Hearts Can't Be Broken (1991); Renaissance Man (1994); The Sunset Boys (1995).

Honor: Academy Award for Best Actor (*Charly*).

ROCKY (1976), sports drama. Directed by John G. Avildsen; screenplay by Sylvester Stallone; produced by Irwin Winkler and Robert Chartoff; photographed by James Crabe; edited by Richard Halsey and Scott Conrad; music by Bill Conti; released by United Artists; 119 minutes. *Cast*: Sylvester Stallone, Talia Shire, Burt Young, Carl Weathers, Burgess Meredith, Thayer David.

An intoxicating underdog story about one man's fight for self-respect as he battles for the heavyweight championship of the world. Like Brando's potential contender Terry Malloy of *On the Waterfront*, Stallone's Rocky Balboa is a perfect combination of good-heartedness and animalistic determination. The real story is how Rocky's rise to fame parallels that of the then-unknown actor and novice screenwriter Stallone who, after turning down $250,000 for the outright sale of the script, demanded that he also star in the picture, or there would be no deal. An underdog itself, *Rocky* then went on to win the Oscar for Best Picture by beating out *All the President's Men*, *Network*, and *Taxi Driver*. Although the film has lost some of its luster as Stallone's career has fallen into self-parody, it is still a superbly entertaining picture. Memorable scenes include Rocky's ice-skating date with Adrian (Shire), his use of a side of beef for training, the arduous climb up the stairs of the Philadelphia Museum of Art as he victoriously raises his arms to the strains of Bill Conti's "Gonna Fly Now," the sharply edited heavyweight battle against Apollo Creed (Weathers), and the final freeze-frame of his battered and bloodied face.

Sequels: Stallone has starred in, and written, all four sequels—Rocky II (1979) also director; Rocky III (1982) also director; Rocky IV (1985) also director; Rocky V (1990), directed by Avildsen.

Awards: Academy Awards for Best Picture, Director, Editing; Academy Award nominations for Best Actor, Actress, Supporting Actor (Meredith, Young), Screenplay, Sound, Song; New York Film Critics Circle Award for Best Supporting Actress; Los Angeles Film Critics Award for Best Picture (tie).

ROGER AND ME (1989), documentary. Directed, written, and produced by Michael Moore; photographed by Christopher Beaver, John Prusak, Kevin Rafferty, and Bruce Schermer; edited by Wendey Stanzler and Jennifer Beman; released by Warner Bros.; 90 minutes. *Cast*: Michael Moore, Roger Smith, Ronald Reagan, Bob Eubanks, Pat Boone, Anita Bryant, Robert Schuller, Deputy Fred Ross, Rhonda Britto.

Armed with a camera, microphone, and a sense of justice that is exceeded only by his sense of humor, the sloppy and overweight Michael Moore waged a personal war against General Motors head Roger Smith for the auto industry layoffs and plant closings that led to the virtual destruction of Flint, Michigan. A small, no-budget, feature-length documentary that initially had no chance of any theatrical release, *Roger and Me* went on to be acquired by Warner Brothers and earned $7 million at the box office. With this film, Moore tapped into a populist sense of rage directed at big business and government that predated the sweeping political changes of the 1992 political elections and the common-man appeal of Ross Perot. While the film is not without its questionable moments in which Moore gleefully embarrasses his subjects, it is an eye-opening assault on the powers that be. Beyond its political message, it's an engrossing and funny piece of entertainment with a likable, regular-guy "performance" from Michael Moore.

Awards: Los Angeles Film Critics Award for Best Documentary; New York Film Critics Circle Award for Best Documentary.

ROMERO, GEORGE A. Born February 4, 1940, in New York City; director, screenwriter. Although labeled as merely a horror director, Romero is one of the keenest social commentators working in American film; his films have become the example of what the horror genre can be when an intelligent director is at the helm. Drawing on his experience in 8mm shorts and later as a maker of industrial films and commercials in Pittsburgh, Romero entered the world of low-budget feature filmmaking with his $114,000 *Night of the Living Dead*. An instant horror classic with a grainy black-and-white cinema verité style, this tale of the undead terrorizing a remote farmhouse paralyzes the viewer with a horrifying intensity that had never before been seen on the screen. A handful of less successful films followed as Romero formed the Laurel Group with producing partner Richard Rubenstein. Romero's next great film would be *Martin*, a gory, nightmarish tale about an enigmatic young man who is either a deranged psychopath or Nosferatu. That would be followed two years later by the second installment of what would become the "Living Dead" trilogy—*Dawn of the Dead*, a less frightening film than its prequel but a more accomplished satire on American life and values. The farmhouse of the original is now a shopping mall, and the grainy black-and-white is now full color, resulting in a wickedly funny and overwhelming grotesque allegory that is one of the crowning achievements of the decade. His next two films marked a shift in style, with *Knightriders*, a modern-day motorcyclist reworking of Arthurian legends, and *Creepshow*, a DC Comics homage that paired him with Stephen King. The third and weakest installment of the "Living Dead" trilogy followed with *Day of the Dead*, a logical extension of the previous films that pits the military against the scientists in an effort to control the growing army of zombies. *Monkey Shines: An Experiment in Fear*, a vastly underrated psychological horror thriller, tells the story of a quadriplegic man and the pet monkey who acts on the man's dark thoughts—like all of Romero's best work it raises the question of what it means to be human. Still a Hollywood outsider, Romero faces an ongoing struggle to get his films financed and has delivered only one subsequent feature, the commercially and critically ignored thriller *The Dark Half*, a second Stephen King collaboration.

Filmography as director: The Man from the Meteor (1954, 8mm); Gorilla (1955; 8mm); Earthbottom (1955, 8mm documentary); Curly (1958, 8mm); Slant (1958); Expostulations (1960–1962, unfinished feature film); Night of the Living Dead (1968); There's Always Vanilla/The Affair (1972) also camera, editor; Jack's Wife/Hungry Wives (1973) also screenplay, camera, editor; The Crazies (1973) also screenplay; "The Winners" (1974, documentary tvs); Martin (1976); Dawn of the Dead (1978) also screenplay, editor, actor; Knightriders (1981) also screenplay, editor; Creepshow, "Something to Tide You Over" episode (1982) also editor; Day of the Dead (1985) also screenplay; Monkey Shines: An Experiment in Fear (1988) also screenplay; Two Evil Eyes, "The Facts in the Case of Mr. Valdemar" episode (1990) also screenplay; The Dark Half (1993) also screenplay, ep.

Additional credits: Flight of the Spruce Goose (1986) actor; Creepshow 2 (1987) screenplay; Lightning over Braddock (1988) actor; Tales from the Darkside: The Movie, "Cat from Hell" episode (1990) screenplay; Night of the Living Dead (1990) screenplay, ep; Silence of the Lambs (1991) cameo.

ROSEMARY'S BABY (1968), horror. Directed and written by Roman Polanski (from the novel by Ira Levin); produced by William Castle; photographed by William Fraker; edited by Sam O'Steen and Robert Wyman; music by Krzysztof Komeda; released by Paramount; 136 minutes. *Cast*: Mia Farrow, John Cassavetes, Ruth Gordon, Sidney Blackmer, Maurice Evans, Ralph Bellamy, Angela Dorian [Victoria Vetri], Elisha Cook, Jr., Charles Grodin.

Roman Polanski's first American film is a gripping psychological horror film that is so frightening because it seems so real. Mia Farrow stars as Rosemary Woodhouse, a happily married young woman whose husband (Cassavetes) is a struggling New York actor. She is elated by the news that she is pregnant, but the coming birth is met with increasing anxiety as she is haunted by a violent dream in which she imagines that she's been raped by the devil. Except that it's not a dream at all. The brilliance of the movie is the completely normal setting. There are no creepy, dark staircases. No remote cabins. No overtly ghoulish people. Only a loving husband, friendly old neighbors, and a thoughtful doctor—all of whom are part of a satanic cult. Rosemary's vulnerability is felt throughout, especially as she realizes that the horror is inside her womb. One of the most chilling moments occurs after the devil's son is born, and we hear the seemingly innocuous comment, "He has his father's eyes."

Awards: Academy Award for Best Supporting Actress (Gordon); Academy Award nomination for Best Adapted Screenplay.

ROSS, HERBERT. Born May 13, 1927, in New York City; choreographer, director. Wife is Lee Radziwell; formerly married to the late producer/dancer Nora Kaye. Former dancer who became a choreographer on Broadway, in Hollywood, and for the American Ballet Theater before turning his talents to feature film direction. He has generally delivered such wholly commercial films as his five Neil Simon adaptations or the enjoyable Woody Allen picture *Play It Again, Sam* but often returns to his dancing roots with *The Turning Point*, *Nijinsky*, *Pennies from Heaven*, and *Dancers*. In 1977, he achieved a rare level of success, directing two Best Picture-nominated films (*The Turning Point* and *The Goodbye Girl*) for a combined total of seven Oscar-nominated performances. His most successful pictures of the last two decades have been blessed with effective and timely casting—namely, Kevin Bacon in the upbeat *Footloose*, the entire ensemble of *Steel Magnolias*, and Drew Barrymore in *Boys on the Side*—though his astounding Steve Martin vehicle *Pennies from Heaven* has been unjustly overlooked. Worthy of mention is his long-standing collaboration with producer Ray Stark, with whom he has made six films—*The Owl and the Pussycat*, *Funny Lady*, *The Sunshine Boys*, *The Goodbye Girl*, *California Suite*, and *Steel Magnolias*. "Ross is a curiosity and a throwback to the heyday of, say, George Cukor, when overall proficiency made up for lack of substance" (David Thomson, *A Biographical Dictionary of Film*).

Filmography: Goodbye, Mr. Chips (1969); The Owl and the Pussycat (1970); T. R. Baskin (1971); Play It Again, Sam (1972); The Last of Sheila (1973) also producer; Funny Lady (1975); The Sunshine Boys (1975); The Seven-Per-Cent Solution (1976) also producer; The Turning Point (1977) also producer; The Goodbye Girl (1977); California Suite (1978); Nijinsky (1980); Pennies from Heaven (1981) also producer; I Oughta Be in Pictures (1982) also producer; Max Dugan Returns (1983) also producer; Footloose (1984); Protocol (1984); The Secret of My Success (1987) also producer; Dancers (1987); Steel Magnolias (1989); My Blue Heaven (1990) also producer; True Colors (1991) also producer; Undercover Blues (1993) also ep; Boys on the Side (1995).

additional credits since 1965: Inside Daisy Clover (1965) choreographer; Doctor Dolittle (1967) choreographer; Funny Girl (1968) choreographer; Soapdish (1991) ep.

Honors: Academy Award nominations for Best Picture (*The Goodbye Girl*, *The Turning*

Point) and Director (*The Turning Point*); Los Angeles Film Critics Award for Best Director (*The Turning Point*).

ROURKE, MICKEY. Born September 16, 1953, in Schenectady, New York; actor, boxer. Separated from model Carrie Otis. Slovenly, oddly handsome actor whose rebellious, individualistic stance has turned him into something of a pariah in Hollywood. After appearing in a small role in *Heaven's Gate* (his first of three films with Michael Cimino), he gained attention with supporting roles as the arsonist in *Body Heat* and as the soft-spoken and caddish hairdresser in *Diner*. However, in Francis Ford Coppola's *Rumble Fish* as the tough, leather-clad Motorcycle Boy, he began to cultivate his mysterious, Brandoesque "Wild One" image. Stardom followed with Adrian Lyne's soft-core celebration of sexual degradation, *9 1/2 Weeks*, and a costarring role with Robert De Niro in the suffocatingly symbolic *Angel Heart* in yet another headline-grabbing sex scene, this time with a great deal of chicken blood. Probably his greatest performance has been in Barbet Schroeder's *Barfly* as the dirty, boozing poet of the gutter, Charles Bukowski. He has since divided his energies between acting in mediocre, albeit daring, failures (including Walter Hill's *Johnny Handsome*) and semiprofessional boxing.

Filmography: 1941 (1979); Fade to Black (1980); Heaven's Gate (1980); Body Heat (1981); Diner (1982); Eureka (1983); Rumble Fish (1983); The Pope of Greenwich Village (1984); Year of the Dragon (1985); 9 1/2 Weeks (1986); Angel Heart (1987); Barfly (1987); A Prayer for the Dying (1987); Francesco (1989); Homeboy (1989) also story; Johnny Handsome (1989); Wild Orchid (1989); Desperate Hours (1990); Harley Davidson and the Marlboro Man (1991); White Sands (1992); The Last Outlaw (1994); Fall Time (1995).

ROWLANDS, GENA. Born June 19, 1936, in Cambria, Wisconsin; actor. Married to John Cassavetes until his death in 1989; son Nick is an actor and director; daughter Zoe is an actor. A portal into the heart of human emotion, Rowlands has proven to be one of cinema's most honest actors. Her beginnings were on the stage, most notably as the costar of the Paddy Chayefsky–Josh Logan 1956–1957 Broadway smash *Middle of the Night* as the young object of Edward G. Robinson's desires. Her glamorous, blond, ingenue persona led to a role in *The High Cost of Loving* before she began her legendary personal and professional association with John Cassavetes. From 1962's underappreciated *A Child Is Waiting* to 1984's *Love Streams*, they would make ten films together—seven under Cassavetes' direction and three as costars for other directors. Of them all, her frighteningly convincing role as the manic-depressive Mabel Longhetti in *A Woman under the Influence* ranks with the best screen performances of all time. Surprisingly, she has costarred with her husband in only two films that he directed—*Opening Night* and *Love Streams*—both of them giving marvelous performances that are clearly fueled by their love and respect for one another. Of her post-Cassavetes films, her most compelling work has come in Woody

Allen's *Another Woman*, though she has done some memorable television work in *An Early Frost* as the mother of an AIDS victim and *The Betty Ford Story* as the alcohol- and drug-addicted former First Lady.

Filmography: The High Cost of Loving (1958); A Child Is Waiting (1962); Lonely Are the Brave (1962); The Spiral Road (1962); Tony Rome (1967); Faces (1968); Machine Gun McCain/Gli Intoccabili (1969); Minnie and Moskowitz (1971); A Woman under the Influence (1974); Two-Minute Warning (1976); Opening Night (1977); The Brink's Job (1978); A Question of Love (1978, tvm); Gloria (1980); Tempest (1982); Love Streams (1984); An Early Frost (1985, tvm); The Betty Ford Story (1987, tvm); Light of Day (1987); Another Woman (1988); Once Around (1991); Face of a Stranger (1991, tvm); Night on Earth (1992); Parallel Lives (1994, ctvm); Something to Talk About (1995); The Neon Bible (1995).

Honors: Academy Award nominations for Best Actress (*A Woman under the Influence*, *Gloria*); Venice Film Festival Golden Lion for Best Actress (*Gloria*); Berlin Film Festival Award for Best Actress (*Opening Night*); Emmy Awards (*The Betty Ford Story*, *Face of a Stranger*).

RUDOLPH, ALAN. Born December 18, 1943, in Los Angeles; director, screenwriter. One of the most consistently interesting and critically acclaimed directors in America and, not coincidentally, also one of the least commercially successful. The son of television director Oscar Rudolph, Rudolph began as an assistant director, eventually becoming a protégé of Robert Altman's. Rudolph's films are uniquely concerned with emotions, artifice, and fractured narratives—often described as "urban fables," they probe recurring themes: love and chance; isolated people trying to connect; art versus commerce; and locations that are a state of mind (RainCity in *Trouble in Mind*, Empire in *Equinox*, and the 1920s Paris of *The Moderns*). His best films combine rich characters with a dreamy texture (*Choose Me, The Moderns*), but even his forays into director-for-hire territory (*Endangered Species, Made in Heaven, Mortal Thoughts*) are not without his very defined signature. He is blessed with an ability to create lush, hyperrealistic worlds of heartrending emotion (with due credit to frequent collaborators cinematographer Jan Kiesser and composer Mark Isham) and a special talent for directing actors. Some appear repeatedly in his work (Keith Carradine, Genevieve Bujold, Geraldine Chaplin, Gailard Sartain, John Considine), while others have delivered some of their best work under his direction—Jennifer Jason Leigh (*Mrs. Parker and the Vicious Circle*), Timothy Hutton and Kelly McGillis (*Made in Heaven*), Bruce Willis and Demi Moore (*Mortal Thoughts*), Tom Berenger and Anne Archer (*Love at Large*), and Anthony Perkins (*Remember My Name*). Rudolph's "movies stand in the same relation to naturalistic cinema as poetry does to prose, revealing truth not through reproduction of reality but through aesthetic reflection and intensified subjectivity" (Gavin Smith, *Film Comment*, May–June 1993).

Filmography: Premonition (1972) also screenplay, producer; Terror Circus/Barn of the Naked Dead (1973); Welcome to L.A. (1977) also screenplay; Remember My Name

(1979) also screenplay; Roadie (1980) also story; Endangered Species (1982) also screenplay; Return Engagement (1983); Choose Me (1984); Songwriter (1984); Trouble in Mind (1986) also screenplay; Made in Heaven (1987); The Moderns (1988) also screenplay; Love at Large (1990) also screenplay; Mortal Thoughts (1991); Equinox (1993) also screenplay; Mrs. Parker and the Vicious Circle (1994) also screenplay.

Filmography as first assistant director: The Long Goodbye (1973); California Split (1974); Nashville (1975).

Filmography as screenwriter: Buffalo Bill and the Indians, or Sitting Bull's History Lesson (1976).

Honors: Los Angeles Film Critics New Generation Award (*Choose Me*); Berlin Film Festival Golden Bear for Best Screenplay (*Buffalo Bill and the Indians, or Sitting Bull's History Lesson*).

RUSSELL, KURT. Born March 17, 1951, in Springfield, Massachusetts; actor. Longtime companion of actor Goldie Hawn. Handsome young star of live-action Disney films in the late 1960s through the mid-1970s whose adult career took a fortuitous detour when he teamed with director John Carpenter to star in the television biography *Elvis*. They made three additional films together—the cult action film *Escape from New York*, *The Thing*, and *Big Trouble in Little China*— all of which contributed to Russell's move into more action-oriented roles. Interspersed with these roles, he continued to do a number of lighter films with Goldie Hawn. His surprise 1994 sci-fi hit *Stargate* restored some of the luster to his temporarily sagging career. He and Carpenter reteamed in 1995 for the production of *John Carpenter's Escape from L.A.* (1996).

Filmography: "The Travels of Jamie Jeeters" (1963–1964, tvs); It Happened at the World's Fair (1963); Follow Me, Boys! (1966); The Horse in the Gray Flannel Suit (1968); The One and Only Genuine Original Family Band (1968); The Computer Wore Tennis Shoes (1969); Guns in the Heather (1969); The Barefoot Executive (1970); Fools' Parade (1971); Charley and the Angel (1972); Now You See Him, Now You Don't (1972); Superdad (1973); The Strongest Man in the World (1975); Elvis (1979, tvm); Used Cars (1980); Escape from New York (1981); The Fox and the Hound (1981) voice only; The Thing (1982); Silkwood (1983); Swing Shift (1984); The Mean Season (1985); The Best of Times (1986); Big Trouble in Little China (1986); Overboard (1987); Tequila Sunrise (1988); Tango and Cash (1989); Winter People (1989); Backdraft (1991); Unlawful Entry (1992); Captain Ron (1992); Tombstone (1994); Stargate (1994).

RYAN, MEG. Born Margaret Mary Emily Anne Hyra November 19, 1961, in Fairfield, Connecticut; actor, producer. Married to Dennis Quaid. Effervescent lead whose high adorability quotient has catapulted her into the stratum of America's sweetheart. After two years on the daytime soap "As the World Turns," Ryan made her feature debut in George Cukor's final film, *Rich and Famous*. She garnered attention for her role as Anthony Edwards' wife in *Top Gun*, but her perfect fit as a romantic comedy star in *When Harry Met Sally . . .* proved to be the turning point in her shift to superstardom. Her scene in which she feigns orgasm in a crowded restaurant to prove a point to costar Billy Crystal is one of her greatest movie moments. While she has continued to charm in that genre with *Sleepless in Seattle*, *I.Q.*, and *French Kiss*, she has also given a richly textured dramatic performance in *When a Man Loves a Woman*. She has also appeared in three pictures with Dennis Quaid—*Innerspace*, *D.O.A.*, and *Flesh and Bone*. She recently formed a production company named Prufrock Films to develop her own projects.

Filmography: Rich and Famous (1981); Amityville 3-D (1983); Armed and Dangerous (1986); Top Gun (1986); Innerspace (1987); Promised Land (1987); D.O.A. (1988); The Presidio (1988); When Harry Met Sally . . . (1989); Joe versus the Volcano (1990); The Doors (1991); Prelude to a Kiss (1992); Flesh and Bone (1993); When a Man Loves a Woman (1993); Sleepless in Seattle (1993); I.Q. (1994); Restoration (1995); French Kiss (1995) also producer.

RYDER, WINONA. Born Winona Laura Horowitz October 29, 1971, in Winona, Minnesota; actor. Named after the Minnesota town of her birth, raised in Petaluma, California, and trained at the American Conservatory Theatre in San Francisco, the doe-eyed Ryder has become one of the most sought-after stars of her generation. She charmed audiences as the morose, black-clad Lydia Deetz in Tim Burton's *Beetlejuice* and then reached superstardom as Veronica Sawyer, the soulful high schooler in *Heathers*. She readied herself to make the transition to more mature roles after being cast by Francis Ford Coppola in *The Godfather, Part III* only to drop out shortly before production began. After a short hiatus, she turned up in four high-profile adaptations of acclaimed novels—*The Age of Innocence*, *Bram Stoker's Dracula*, *The House of the Spirits*, and *Little Women*, earning a pair of Oscar nominations in the process. Still, the essence of her popularity was best captured in the unexpectedly popular Generation-X comedy *Reality Bites*. "No modern actress has her watchfulness, her fiery reticence, her gift of girlish blush and fluster" (Richard Corliss, *Time*, January 9, 1995).

Filmography: Lucas (1986); Square Dance (1987); 1969 (1988); Beetlejuice (1988); Great Balls of Fire (1989); Heathers (1989); Edward Scissorhands (1990); Mermaids (1990); Welcome Home, Roxy Carmichael (1990); Night on Earth (1992); The Age of Innocence (1993); Bram Stoker's Dracula (1993); The House of the Spirits (1994); Reality Bites (1994); Little Women (1994); How to Make an American Quilt (1995).

Honors: Academy Award nominations for Best Actress (*Little Women*) and Best Supporting Actress (*The Age of Innocence*).

S

SALVADOR (1986), drama. Directed, cowritten, and coproduced by Oliver Stone; screenplay with Richard Boyle; produced with Gerald Green; photographed by Robert Richardson; edited by Claire Simpson; music by Georges Delerue; released by Hemdale; 123 minutes. *Cast*: James Woods, James Belushi, Michael Murphy, John Savage.

Directed by Oliver Stone before he became an American icon, this examination of the political turmoil in El Salvador is one of his finest achievements, albeit one that not only was overshadowed in 1986 (the year of *Platoon*) but has since been dwarfed by his monumental 1960s revisionist films. One of the few English-language films to even address the events in Central America (produced by Hemdale, the film is technically British), *Salvador* presents a convincing account of the lives of international journalists who nomadically flock from one world hot spot to the next, focusing specifically on real-life journalist and coscreenwriter Richard Boyle (Woods). A crass, opportunistic, drinking, and drugging writer, he travels to El Salvador with his fun-seeking radio deejay pal Dr. Rock (Belushi) and soon gets caught up in the human tragedy that exists throughout the tiny country. Stone's genius is his ability to put the viewer in the center of this whirlwind of bloodshed and brutality, as if he himself is a photojournalist on assignment. Of course, with Stone at the helm, the film indicts President Reagan and his government support of right-wing death squads, though Stone is perceptive enough to realize the leftist rebel forces are not blameless. The film is carried by Woods' dynamic performance; he's as good as he ever has been in this film. Not to be missed is his confessional scene, during which he tries to cut a deal with the priest.

Awards: Academy Award nominations for Best Actor (Woods) and Screenplay.

SARANDON, SUSAN. Born Susan Abigail Tomaling October 4, 1946, in New York City; actor. Longtime companion of actor and director Tim Robbins; formerly married to actor Chris Sarandon. An actress of unfailing integrity and credibility, she has matured since becoming a doe-eyed cult figure in *The Rocky Horror Picture Show* as Janet (damnit!) Weiss who, along with her sweetheart, is stranded on a rainy night in Ohio with a group of oddballs from Transsexual, Transylvania. Her appearances in two Louis Malle films—as Brooke Shields' mother in *Pretty Baby* and as the lemon-fresh fishmonger in *Atlantic City*—helped establish her as an extremely talented actor who excels in her portrayal of strong, resourceful, and sexually dynamic women. Her most celebrated role to date has been as Louise in *Thelma and Louise*, though other memorable performances include her much-touted lesbian vampire love scene with Catherine Deneuve in *The Hunger* and her role as the insatiable baseball fan in *Bull Durham*. Many of her recent roles have been variations on a maternalistic theme—*Lorenzo's Oil*, *The Client*, *Safe Passage*, and *Little Women*. After four Oscar nominations, she finally took the top honors with her moving portrayal of antideath penalty advocate Sister Helen Prejean in Tim Robbins' *Dead Man Walking*. As her career progresses, and she moves stealthily into her fifties, she is showing signs of becoming perhaps the greatest actress of her age—not an ageist characterization but a testament to her towering and enduring talents as an actor.

Filmography: Joe (1970); La Mortadella/Lady Liberty (1972); The Haunting of Rosalind (1973); The Front Page (1974); Lovin' Molly (1974); Dragonfly/One Summer Love (1975); The Rocky Horror Picture Show (1975); The Great Waldo Pepper (1975); The Great Smokey Roadblock/The Last of the Cowboys (1976, released in 1978); The Other Side of Midnight (1977); King of the Gypsies (1978); Checkered Flag or Crash (1978); Pretty Baby (1978); Something Short of Paradise (1979); Atlantic City (1980); Loving Couples (1980); Tempest (1982); Who Am I This Time? (1982, tvm); The Hunger (1983); The Buddy System (1984); Compromising Positions (1985); The Witches of Eastwick (1987); Bull Durham (1988); Sweet Hearts Dance (1988); The January Man (1989); A Dry White Season (1989); Through the Wire (1990, documentary) narrator; White Palace (1990); Thelma and Louise (1991); The Player (1992); Light Sleeper (1992); Bob Roberts (1992); Lorenzo's Oil (1992); The Client (1994); Safe Passage (1994); Little Women (1994); Dead Man Walking (1995).

Honors: Academy Award for Best Actress (*Dead Man Walking*); Academy Award nominations for Best Actress (*Atlantic City, Thelma and Louise, Lorenzo's Oil, The Client*); Venice Film Festival Award for Best Actress (*Tempest*).

SATURDAY NIGHT FEVER (1977), drama. Directed by John Badham; screenplay by Norman Wexler (from the magazine article by Nik Cohn); produced by Robert Stigwood; photographed by Ralf D. Bode; edited by David Rawlins; music by David Shire, songs by Barry Gibb, Robin Gibb, Maurice Gibb and performed by the Bee Gees; released by Paramount; 119 minutes. *Cast*: John Travolta, Karen Lynn Gorney, Donna Pescow, Barry Miller, Joseph Call, Paul Pape, Bruce Ornstein, Robert Costanza, Fran Drescher.

One of the seminal films of the decade, the popularity of this film's disco sound track and the indelible image of the white-suited Tony Manero on that kaleidoscopic dance floor led a fashion and music revolution that mesmerized America through the late 1970s. Overshadowed by Bee Gee mania is the fact that *Saturday Night Fever* remains a gritty film about male sexual energy and desires. Hailing from Brooklyn's Bay Bridge, Tony Manero (Travolta) is a young kid who works in a paint store just to earn enough cash to dance on Saturday night at the 2001 Odyssey. At work he lugs paint, and at home his old Italian parents make him feel worthless in comparison to his priest brother, but at 2001 he's Somebody. The dancing, however, is just an outlet for his tightly coiled sexual energy. Manero's friends systematically leave the club to spend ten minutes in the car with their latest conquest, but Manero stays on the floor and churns his libido into frenzied disco moves. Only later does Tony begin to see the emptiness of his world, but it takes his attempted rape of dance partner Stephanie (Gorney) and the spectacle of former partner Annette (Peskow) surrendering herself to Tony's friends in the back seat to open Tony's eyes. Although far from a perfect movie (Badham's direction and visual sense are less than inspirational, and the dance sequences are surprisingly slow and distant), *Saturday Night Fever* comes alive with Travolta's electric performance—a combination of a confident Brooklyn attitude (à la his character's idol Al Pacino) with a sense of decency and vulnerability. The crowning achievement of producer Robert Stigwood, who, within a five-year span from 1973 to 1978, delivered this film, *Jesus Christ Superstar*, *Tommy*, *Sgt. Pepper's Lonely Hearts Club Band*, and *Grease*. Inspired by a *New York* magazine article titled "Tribal Rights of the New Saturday Night" by Nik Cohn. "Nothing more than an updated '70s version of the Sam Katzman rock cheapies of the '50s" (*Variety*, December 14, 1977).

Sequel: John Travolta reprised his role in *Staying Alive* (1983), produced, written, and directed by Sylvester Stallone.

Award: Academy Award nomination for Best Actor (Travolta).

SAVOCA, NANCY. Born 1960 in Bronx, New York; director, screenwriter, producer. Married to Richard Guay, her writing and producing partner. Talented former New York University film student whose three features have displayed a keen observation of period detail and a gift for eliciting honest performances from her actors. She broke onto the independent film scene with *True Love*, a smartly written comedy about a young woman (newcomer Annabella Sciorra) who is obsessed with getting her fiancé to the altar. Driven by a picture-perfect representation of a working-class Italian-American neighborhood and fine performances from the entire cast, the film took the top prize at the 1989 U.S. Film Festival. Her follow-up, Warner Brothers' *Dogfight*, features River Phoenix and Lili Taylor in a touching and funny romance between a cocky young marine and the idealistic young 1960s folkie who unwittingly becomes his "date" at a party to find the ugliest girl. Like Savoca's debut, *Dogfight* is a real gem that barely received a theatrical release. Her third film, *Household Saints*, is a less successful, multigenerational story that is again on target with its depiction of Italian Americans but has an awkward combination of religion, magic, and realism. "One of America's few directors who makes films about characters, male and female, for whom she has true affection" (Danny Peary, *Alternate Oscars*).

Filmography: Renata (1982, short); Bad Timing (1984, short); True Love (1989); Dogfight (1991); Household Saints (1993).

Honors: United States Film Festival (Sundance) Grand Jury Award (*True Love*).

SAY ANYTHING . . . (1989), comedy/drama. Directed and written by Cameron Crowe; produced by Polly Platt; executive-produced by James L. Brooks; photographed by Laszlo Kovacs; edited by Richard Marks; released by 20th Century Fox; 100 minutes. *Cast*: John Cusack, Ione Skye, John Mahoney, Lili Taylor, Joan Cusack, Amy Brooks, Jason Gould, Loren Dean, Jeremy Piven, Polly Platt, Bebe Neuwirth, Eric Stoltz, Chynna Phillips, Philip Baker Hall, Don "the Dragon" Wilson.

After displaying his touch as the screenwriter of *Fast Times at Ridgemont High*, Crowe turned to directing with this surprising teen picture, which transcends the genre. Infused with the integrity and honesty that one has come to associate with the films of producers James L. Brooks or Polly Platt, this picture succeeds not by telling us anything *new* about love and trust but by reminding us that they are basic needs in any meaningful relationship. The plot is simple enough—the "basic" Lloyd Dobler (Cusack) is a recent high school grad whose future is in kickboxing ("the sport of the future") until he falls in love with the extraordinary Diane Court (Skye), whose rosier future includes a prestigious fellowship to study in England. As the young lovers come to realize they can "say anything" to one another, Lloyd finds a new sense of self-worth, and Diane wrestles with the guilt of ignoring her doting father, someone who, she later learns, has been less than forthright with her. Blessed with the chemistry of the two leads and a great supporting cast, the film is filled with careful observations of human behavior, especially the brother–sister relationship between Lloyd and Joan Cusack's Constance (which recalls the tenderness of Brad and Stacy in *Fast Times*) and the unrequited love of tortured songwriter Corey (Taylor). It also contains one of the great moments in film when Lloyd, desperate to win back Diane's heart, stands holding his boom box high over his head and blaring Peter Gabriel's "In Your Eyes" through the night and into her bedroom.

SAYLES, JOHN. Born September 28, 1950, in Schenectady, New York; director, screenwriter, actor, author. Longtime companion of actor/producer Maggie Renzi. Standing at the forefront of American independent filmmaking, Sayles' artistic beginnings are more literary than visual. At the age of twenty-five, his short story "I-80 Nebraska" appeared in the *Atlantic Monthly* and won an O. Henry Award. Two novels followed (*Pride of the Bimbos* and *Union Dues*) before Sayles migrated to Hollywood to pen scripts for Roger Corman. With his earnings he headed back east and filmed *Return of the Secaucus Seven*, the story of a group of Vietnam-era radicals reuniting after ten years; a surprise hit that returned many times its $60,000 budget, it established Sayles as a literate, politically astute writer and director. An incorruptible, Old World leftist in the spirit of John Dos Passos, Nelson Algren, and Studs Terkel, Sayles has since produced a body of work that champions the rights of the working class and the outsider. His heroes are the radicals of *Return of the Secaucus Seven*, the lesbians of *Lianna*, the mistreated miners and ballplayers of *Matewan* and *Eight Men Out*, and the blacks of *The Brother from Another Planet*—honest glimpses of the sort of Americans whom Hollywood too often ignores. Critics have long charged that his films lack an emotional punch and have failed to reach the masses about whom he writes, though he has built a solid, loyal following. While his *Passion Fish* was critically lauded across the country and earned Oscar nominations for Mary McDonald's performance and Sayles' script, wild horses couldn't drag audiences into the theater. His Irish fable, *The Secret of Roan Inish*, fared better, though, curiously, it's one of Sayles' more atypical projects. His other books include the short story anthology *The Anarchist's Convention: Stories* (1979) and *Los Gusanos* (1992). "He has emerged as that rarest of American filmmakers—one who understood the subtler overtones of class distinctions, social injustices, and economic inequalities in a land flooded with fantasies of equal opportunity and limitless upward mobility" (Andrew Sarris, *Film Comment*, May–June 1993).

Filmography as director and writer: Return of the Secaucus Seven (1980) also actor, editor; Lianna (1983) also actor, editor; Baby It's You (1983); The Brother from Another Planet (1984) also actor, editor; Bruce Springsteen's "Born in the USA," "I'm on Fire," and "Glory Days" (1984, mv); Matewan (1987) also actor; Eight Men Out (1988) also actor; City of Hope (1991) also actor, editor; Passion Fish (1992); The Secret of Roan Inish (1995).

Filmography as writer: Piranha (1978); The Lady in Red (1979); Alligator (1980); Battle beyond the Stars (1980); The Howling (1980) also actor; The Challenge (1982); Enormous Changes at the Last Minute (1983); Unnatural Causes (1986, tvm) also actor; The Clan of the Cave Bear (1986); Wild Thing (1987); Breaking In (1989); "Shannon's Deal" (1989–1991, tvs) also creator.

Filmography as actor: Hard Choices (1984); Something Wild (1986); Untamagiru (1989); Little Vegas (1990), Matinee (1993); My Life's in Turnaround (1994).

Honors: Academy Award nominations for Screenplay (*Return of the Secaucus Seven, Passion Fish*); Los Angeles Film Critics Award for Screenplay (*Return of the Secaucus Seven*); MacArthur Foundation "genius grant" (1983).

SCARECROW (1973), drama. Directed by Jerry Schatzberg; screenplay by Garry Michael White; produced by Robert M. Sherman; photographed by Vilmos Zsigmond; edited by Evan Lottman; music by Fred Myrow; released by Warner Bros.; 112 minutes. *Cast*: Gene Hackman, Al Pacino, Dorothy Tristan, Ann Wedgeworth, Richard Lynch, Eileen Brennan, Penny Allen.

A fascinating character study about a friendship between two drifters—Max (Hackman), a short-fused ex-con with plans of opening a car wash in Pittsburgh, and Lion (Pacino), a good-humored ex-navy man traveling to Detroit to see the ex-wife and child he left behind. The title comes from Lion's belief that scarecrows keep crows away by making them laugh, not by intimidating them. Lion, unlike the combative Max, goes through life trying to avoid conflict by injecting humor. The film blends humor and tragedy and, in a style more European than American, puts plot development second to characters and emotions. One of the most affecting scenes is a phone call between Lion and his ex-wife (Allen) in which she devastates him by lying about the child he's never seen. While much of the film's success must be given to Hackman and Pacino, the sparse and evocative visual style of Schatzberg in collaboration with cinematographer Vilmos Zsigmond cannot be underestimated.

Award: Cannes Film Festival Palme d'Or.

SCHAFFNER, FRANKLIN J. Born May 30, 1920, in Tokyo, Japan; died July 2, 1989, in Santa Monica, California; director. An important part of the golden age of television, Schaffner cut his teeth on documentary production ("March of Time" and Edward R. Murrow's "Person to Person") before moving to such dramatic series as "Playhouse 90" and "The Kaiser Aluminum Hour" and eventually amassing Emmys for his direction of the taut, forceful television dramas "Twelve Angry Men," "The Caine Mutiny Court Martial," and "The Defenders." He went on in 1960 to direct the Broadway play *Advise and Consent*. His first commercial success as a filmmaker was *Planet of the Apes*, which, though dismissed as a sophomoric waste of time, was actually a smart political allegory masquerading as a science-fiction fantasy. Clearly concerned with the theme of men and honor, Schaffner's two greatest achievements of the 1970s— the war biography *Patton* (for which he won an Academy Award) and the prison biography *Papillon*—both study men who have been pushed to hellish limits and left to face their inner demons. Of the remainder of his films, nothing leaves a lasting impression, not his traditional adaptations (Hemingway's *Islands in the Stream*, Ira Levin's *Boys from Brazil*, Robin Cook's *Sphinx*) nor his posthumously released intimate Vietnam drama *Welcome Home* and definitely not the Luciano Pavarotti musical *Yes, Giorgio*.

Filmography of key pre-1965 films: Twelve Angry Men (1954, tv); The Caine Mutiny Court Martial (1955, tv); The Stripper (1963).

Filmography since 1965: The War Lord (1965); The Double Man (1968) also actor; Planet of the Apes (1968); Patton (1970); Nicholas and Alexandra (1971); Papillon (1973) also producer; Islands in the Stream (1977); The Boys from Brazil (1978); Sphinx (1981); Yes, Giorgio (1982); Lionheart (1987/released in 1990); Welcome Home (1989).

Honors: Academy Award for Best Director (*Patton*); DGA Award (*Patton*); Emmy Awards ("Twelve Angry Men," "The Caine Mutiny Court Martial," "The Defenders") and a Special Emmy ("Tour of the White House", 1962 documentary); New York Drama Critics Award ("Advise and Consent" 1960).

Selected bibliography

Kim, Erwin. *Franklin J. Schaffner*. Metuchen, NJ: Scarecrow Press, 1985.

SCHEIDER, ROY. Born November 10, 1935, in Orange, New Jersey; actor. Classically trained stage performer who made the switch to film and became one of the most respected actors of the 1970s, appearing in a number of intelligent and provocative films. Beginning in 1971 with *The French Connection* and *Klute*, he found fame as Captain Brody in Steven Spielberg's 1975 blockbuster *Jaws*. He continued to impress with his remarkable versatility in roles ranging from Dustin Hoffman's secret-agent brother in *Marathon Man*, to New York hood turned adventurer in *Sorcerer*, to Bob Fosse's alter ego Joe Gideon in *All That Jazz*. The 1980s and 1990s, however, tell a different story, with none of his films even approaching the caliber of his earlier work. In 1993, he renewed his connection to Spielberg as the star of the Amblin-produced television series "seaQuest DSV/seaQuest 2032."

Filmography: The Curse of the Living Corpse (1964); Stiletto (1969); Loving (1970); Puzzle of a Downfall Child (1970); The French Connection (1971); Klute (1971); L'Attentat/The French Conspiracy (1972); Un Homme Est Mort (1973); The Outside Man (1973); The Seven Ups (1973); Jaws (1975); Shelia Levine Is Dead and Living in New York (1975); Marathon Man (1976); Sorcerer (1977); Jaws 2 (1978); All That Jazz (1979); Last Embrace (1979); Still of the Night (1982); Blue Thunder (1983); In Our Hands (1984); 2010 (1984); Mishima: A Life in Four Chapters (1985) narration only; 52 Pick-Up (1986); The Men's Club (1986); Cohen and Tate (1989); Listen to Me (1989); Night Game (1989); The Fourth War (1990); The Russia House (1990); Naked Lunch (1991); "SeaQuest DSV/SeaQuest 2032" (1993–1996, tvs); Romeo Is Bleeding (1994).

Honors: Academy Award nominations for Best Actor (*All That Jazz*) and Supporting Actor (*The French Connection*).

SCHINDLER'S LIST (1993), historical drama. Directed and coproduced by Steven Spielberg; screenplay by Steven Zaillian (from the book by Thomas Kenneally); produced with Gerald R. Molen, Branko Lustig; photographed by Janusz Kaminski (b&w); edited by Michael Kahn; music by John Williams; released by Universal; 185 minutes. *Cast*: Liam Neeson, Ben Kingsley, Ralph Fiennes, Caroline Goodall, Jonathan Sagalle, Embeth Davidtz.

Hailed upon its release as an instant masterpiece, Steven Spielberg's heartbreaking and life-affirming World War II story of Nazi official Oskar Schindler, who, through unclear motives that vacillated between kindness and greed, ultimately saved some 1,200 Polish Jews from certain extermination at a Nazi death camp. Photographed in a poetic black-and-white by Janusz Kaminski, filmed in many of the actual locations where the real-life events took place, and featuring a sorrowful, yet triumphant, score from John Williams, *Schindler's List* tells its story with an emotional power and resonance felt only in the greatest of artistic achievements. The film was a worldwide success both financially and critically, earning Spielberg his first directing Oscar and catapulting the unknown Ralph Fiennes into stardom. Most important, however, it depicts one of the darkest times in human history and reminds us how the inspiration and bravery of such men as Oskar Schindler and Itzsak Stern (Kingsley) can save lives by their actions. "A work of restraint, intelligence, and unusual sensitivity, and the finest fiction feature ever made about the century's greatest evil" (Stephen Schiff, *New Yorker*, March 21, 1994).

Awards: Academy Awards for Best Picture, Director, Screenplay, Cinematography, Adapted Screenplay, Score, Art Direction; Academy Award nominations for Actor (Neeson), Supporting Actor (Fiennes), Editing, Costume Design, Makeup; New York Film Critics Circle Award for Best Picture; Los Angeles Film Critics Award for Best Picture, Director, Supporting Actor (Fiennes), Cinematography, Art Direction; DGA Award; WGA Award.

SCHRADER, PAUL. Born July 22, 1946, in Grand Rapids, Michigan; director, screenwriter. Married to actress Mary Beth Hurt; brother is screenwriter Leonard (*Kiss of the Spider Woman*). A director of minor note and a screenwriter of superior talent, Schrader has consistently drawn on his strict Calvinist upbringing (he did not see his first movie until age eighteen) to create a cinema that synthesizes his admiration for the films of Yasujiro Ozu, Carl Dreyer (especially *La Passion de Jeanne D'Arc*), and Robert Bresson with his sordid vision of nocturnal America. His alienated and spiritually detached characters have groped their way through the darkness of incest (*Obsession*), drug dealing (*Light Sleeper*), prostitution and pornography (*Taxi Driver, Hardcore, American Gigolo*), lust and bestiality (*Cat People*), and suicide (*Mishima*). When they emerge on the other side, they emerge both purified and redeemed. His two collaborations with Martin Scorsese allow us to see both extremes of Schrader's vision— Travis Bickle of *Taxi Driver*, the psychopath who tires of waiting for a rain to "wash the scum off the streets" and bloodies the world in his rage, and Jesus of *The Last Temptation of Christ*, the embodiment of love who cleanses the world through his goodness. Although he has not yet directed a film as powerful as *Taxi Driver*, his uncompromisingly unique visions, passive lead characters, and hyperrealistic visual style put him at complete odds with Hollywood and, therefore, make him one of American cinema's great provocateurs. "His films are at once rigorously considered and robustly sensual—lurid yet somehow chaste spectacles that enact the moral friction of the worldly and the metaphysical" (Gavin Smith, *Film Comment*, March–April 1992).

Filmography as director: Blue Collar (1978) also screenplay; Hardcore (1979) also screenplay; American Gigolo (1980) also screenplay; Cat People (1982); Mishima: A Life in Four Chapters (1985) also screenplay; Light of Day (1987) also screenplay; Patty

Hearst (1988); The Comfort of Strangers (1991); Light Sleeper (1992) also screenplay; Witch Hunt (1994, ctvm).

Filmography as writer: The Yakuza (1975); Obsession (1976); Taxi Driver (1976); Rolling Thunder (1977); Old Boyfriends (1978) also ep; The Mosquito Coast (1986); The Last Temptation of Christ (1988).

Selected bibliography

Schrader, Paul. *Transcendental Style in Film: Ozu, Bresson, Dreyer.* Berkeley: University of California Press, 1972.

SCHUMACHER, JOEL. Born August 29, 1939, in New York City; director. Successful Hollywood craftsman whose greatest talent lies in delivering well-crafted, accessible mass entertainment. Beginning with two television movies—a gangster-era biography of Bugsy Siegel's moll, *The Virginia Hill Story*, and the country-western roadhouse tale, *Amateur Night at the Dixie Bar and Grill*—he swiftly made his move to theatrical features. With no discernible style, he's delivered a wide variety of films—the brat-pack film *St. Elmo's Fire*, the semi-brat-pack/vampire thriller hybrid *The Lost Boys*, the romantic "women's films" *Cousins* and *Dying Young*, and the glossy suspensers *Flatliners* and *The Client*. The film that has attracted the most attention, however, has been the controversial *Falling Down*, a xenophobic, white-rage nightmare of a defense industry worker who snaps under the pressure of his increasingly gloomy life. With the staggering success of his 1995 effort *Batman Forever* (at $53 million, it had the largest box office opening ever), Schumacher has been firmly planted atop the list of commercial sure bets in Hollywood.

Filmography: The Virginia Hill Story (1974, tvm) also screenplay; Amateur Night at the Dixie Bar and Grill (1979, tvm) also screenplay; The Incredible Shrinking Woman (1981); D.C. Cab (1983); St. Elmo's Fire (1985); The Lost Boys (1987); Cousins (1989); Flatliners (1990); Dying Young (1991); 2000 Malibu Road (1992–1993, tvs); Falling Down (1993); The Client (1994); Batman Forever (1995); Seal's "Kiss from a Rose" (1995, mv).

SCHWARZENEGGER, ARNOLD. Born July 30, 1947, in Graz, Austria; actor. Married to television personality Maria Shriver. Seven-time Mr. Olympia and three-time Mr. Universe whose remarkable physique and affable personality earned him an early acting role in Bob Rafelson's *Stay Hungry*. He received wider attention as the subject of the documentary *Pumping Iron*, exuding a charm that led to a lead role as the sword-wielding hero of the silly medieval epics *Conan the Barbarian* and *Conan the Destroyer*. With the success of James Cameron's low-budget sci-fi masterpiece *The Terminator*, Schwarzenegger honed a new image—a cool, leather-jacketed, motorcycle-riding menace who, with his accent, blurts out such one-liners as "I'll be back." After a few inconsequential, but generally successful, action films, he took a stab at comedy in Ivan Reitman's *Twins* (as Danny DeVito's unlikely twin brother) and established himself as one of the top box office draws of the late 1980s and 1990s, grossing well over $1 billion at the worldwide box office. Meanwhile, he has spent as much time cultivating his celebrity status as he did his on-screen persona—in 1986 he married Maria Shriver, and in 1990 Ronald Reagan named him chairman of the President's Council on Physical Fitness and Sports, despite his conspicuous love of cigars. His only box office misfire of the 1990s was *The Last Action Hero*, an intriguing commercial dud that looks like an action film but is really a self-reflexive commentary on Schwarzenegger's celebrity status and the nature of violence in Hollywood films.

Filmography: Hercules in New York (1970); The Long Goodbye (1973); Stay Hungry (1975); Pumping Iron (1976); The Villain (1979); Scavenger Hunt (1979); The Jayne Mansfield Story (1980, tvm); Conan the Barbarian (1982); Conan the Destroyer (1984); The Terminator (1984); Commando (1985); Red Sonja (1985); Raw Deal (1986); Predator (1987); The Running Man (1987); Red Heat (1988); Twins (1988); "The Switch" episode of "Tales from the Crypt" (1990, ctv) director; Kindergarten Cop (1990); Total Recall (1990); Terminator 2: Judgment Day (1991); Christmas in Connecticut (1992, ctvm) director; Dave (1993); The Last Action Hero (1993); True Lies (1994); Junior (1994).

Selected bibliography

Andrews, Nigel. *True Myths: The Life and Times of Arnold Schwarzenegger*. New York: Birch Lane Press, 1996.
Butler, George. *Arnold Schwarzenegger*. New York: Simon and Schuster, 1990.
Flynn, John L. *The Films of Arnold Schwarzenegger*. New York: Citadel, 1993.

SCORSESE, MARTIN. Born November 17, 1942, in Queens, New York; director, producer. The most critically exalted American director of the last thirty years, Scorsese is undeniably skilled, passionate, intelligent, and innovative in his filmmaking, but, perhaps most important, he is consistent. With only one critical and commercial misfire to his name (1991's preposterous *Cape Fear*), he has delivered some of the most praiseworthy films in the history of the medium. A former seminary student from New York's Little Italy, he has drawn on his roots, his Catholicism, and the notion of family to develop his chief thematic issue of sin and redemption. He received some attention from his early films (especially *Who's That Knocking at My Door?*), but his look at petty New York hoods in *Mean Streets* garnered him his first real critical notices. His first commercial success, however, was the one film of his that is the least Scorsesean—the superb "feminist" picture *Alice Doesn't Live Here Anymore. Taxi Driver*, his first of three collaborations with screenwriter Paul Schrader (*Raging Bull, The Last Temptation of Christ*), reunited him with actors Robert De Niro and Harvey Keitel and earned Scorsese a place in the international film community with the Palme d'Or at the Cannes Film Festival. His best work of the coming decade remains the masterful Jake LaMotta biopic *Raging Bull*, the darkly comic *King of Comedy*, and the disturbing gangster epic *GoodFellas*— all of which revolve around deeply disturbed characters who perform some personal act of contrition. His long-cherished adaptation of Nikos Kazantzakis' novel, the admirable, but ultimately uninvolving, *The Last Temptation of Christ*, was a labor of love released to a firestorm of religious misunderstandings and protests. Another emotionally remote adaptation, Edith Wharton's *The Age of Innocence*, examined sexual repression in the late nineteenth century with a visual sumptuousness rarely seen in movies today (and owing much to Scorsese's avowed influence, Michael Powell). He returned to the comfort of the gangster milieu in *Casino*, a lengthy and stylish journey into the mob's influence in Las Vegas, which was the coldest of his increasingly dispassionate technical exercises of the 1990s. In addition to his feature work, his career is peppered with documentaries (the portrait of his parents in *Italianamerican*, the Band's swan song in *The Last Waltz*), acting roles (*Round Midnight*, *Quiz Show*), music videos (Robbie Robertson, Michael Jackson), television commercials (Armani), producing (*The Grifters*, *Mad Dog and Glory*, *Clockers*), Broadway (in 1978–1979, staging and partially directing Liza Minnelli in *The Act*), and an active role in the advancement of motion picture preservation. "He has an eye that misses nothing, that looks on beauty and terror with the same dispassionate eye, with the same love and compassion. He cannot tell anything but the truth" (Michael Powell in Mary Pat Kelly's *Martin Scorsese The First Decade*). "The man knows how to make movies" (Richard Corliss, *Cinema: A Critical Dictionary*).

Filmography: What's a Nice Girl like You Doing in a Place like This? (1963, short); It's Not Just You, Murray! (1964, short); The Big Shave (1967, short); Who's That Knocking at My Door?/I Call First (1968) also actor; Street Scenes (1970); Boxcar Bertha (1972); Mean Streets (1973) also actor; Alice Doesn't Live Here Anymore (1974) also actor; Italianamerican (1974); Taxi Driver (1976) also actor; New York, New York (1977); American Boy: A Profile of Steven Prince (1978) also actor; The Last Waltz (1978); Raging Bull (1980) also actor; The King of Comedy (1983) also actor; After Hours (1985) also actor; "Mirror, Mirror," episode of "Amazing Stories" (1985, tvs); The Color of Money (1986); Michael Jackson's "Bad" (1987, mv); The Last Temptation of Christ (1988); Robbie Robertson's "Somewhere down the Crazy River" (1988 mv); New York Stories, "Life Lessons" episode (1989); GoodFellas (1990); Cape Fear (1991); The Age of Innocence (1993); Casino (1995).

Filmography as actor: Cannonball (1976); Il Pap'occhio (1981) actor; Pavlova (1983); Round Midnight (1985); Akira Kurosawa's Dreams (1990); Guilty by Suspicion (1991); Quiz Show (1994); Search and Destroy (1995) also ep.

Additional credits: Woodstock (1970) editor, assistant director; Medicine Ball Caravan (1971) supervising editor, associate producer; Unholy Rollers (1972) supervising editor; Elvis on Tour (1972) montage supervisor; The Grifters (1990) producer; Mad Dog and Glory (1993) producer; Naked in New York (1994) ep; Belle de Jour (1967/rereleased 1995) presenter; Clockers (1995) ep.

Honors: Academy Award nominations for Best Director (*Raging Bull*, *The Last Temptation of Christ*); Los Angeles Film Critics Awards for Best Picture and Director (*GoodFellas*); Independent Spirit Award for Best Director (*After Hours*); Cannes Film Festival Awards, Palme d'Or (*Taxi Driver*) and Best Director (*After Hours*); Venice Film Festival Awards for Best Director (*GoodFellas*) and Golden Lion for Lifetime Achievement (1995).

Selected bibliography

Bliss, Michael. *Martin Scorsese and Michael Cimino*. Westport, CT: Greenwood Press, 1985.

Kelly, Mary Pat. *Martin Scorsese The First Decade*. New York: Redgrave, 1980.

———. *Martin Scorsese: A Journey*. New York: Thunder's Mouth Press, 1991.

Kolker, Robert Phillip. *A Cinema of Loneliness: Penn, Kubrick, Coppola, Scorsese, Altman*. New York: Oxford University Press, 1980.

Scorsese, Martin. *Scorsese on Scorsese*. Edited by David Thompson and Ian Christie. London: Faber and Faber, 1989.

SCOTT, GEORGE C. Born George Campbell Scott October 18, 1927, in Wise, Virginia; actor. Married to actor Trish van Devere; formerly married to actor Colleen Dewhurst; son Campbell is an actor/director. Ex-marine with a background on the stage, this leading man exudes a raw sense of anger, crustiness, and distemper but somehow mixes it with an aura of gentleness and vulnerability. He displayed his commanding presence in *The Hustler* as the manipulative sports promoter Bert Gordon and again as the completely off-center General Buck Turgidson of *Dr. Strangelove*. He achieved even greater heights with his portrayal of the battle-hungry title character of *Patton*. His six-minute opening as he stands before the American flag is a tour de force of acting, and his chilling comment on his love of war is unforgettable—"God help me, I do love it so." An outspoken critic of acting awards, he refused to accept the Best Actor Oscar he won for *Patton*. Still, the Academy honored him again the following year for his equally intense performance in Paddy Chayefsky's dark comedy *Hospital*. Although his career is peppered with strong roles in film and television, his work throughout the 1980s and 1990s hasn't come near the level of his early success.

Filmography of key pre-1965 films: Anatomy of a Murder (1959); The Hustler (1963); Dr. Strangelove; or, How I Learned to Stop Worrying and Love the Bomb (1964).

Filmography since 1965: La Bibbia (1966); Not with My Wife, You Don't (1966); The Flim-Flam Man (1967); Petulia (1968); Patton (1970); The Hospital (1971); The Last Run (1971); They Might Be Giants (1971); The Price (1971, tvm); The New Centurians (1972); Rage (1972) also director; The Day of the Dolphin (1973); Oklahoma Crude (1973); Bank Shot (1974); The Savage Is Loose (1974) also producer, director; The Hindenburg (1975); Islands in the Stream (1976); Crossed Swords (1977); Movie Movie (1978); The Changeling (1979); Hardcore (1979); The Formula (1980); Taps (1981); The Beastmaster (1982); Firestarter (1984); Mussolini: The Untold Story (1985, tvms); The Last Days of Patton (1986, tvm); The Rescuers Down Under (1990) voice; William Peter Blatty's The Exorcist III (1990); Malice (1993); Traps (1994, tvs); Angus (1995).

Honors: Academy Award for Best Actor (*Patton*), refused to accept award; Academy Award nomination for Best Actor (*The Hospital*); New York Film Critics Circle Award for Best Actor (*Patton*); Emmy Award (*The Price*).

SECONDS (1966), thriller. Directed by John Frankenheimer; screenplay by Lewis John Carlino (from the novel by David Ely); produced by Edward Lewis;

photographed by James Wong Howe; edited by Ferris Webster and David Webster; music by Jerry Goldsmith; released by Paramount; 106 minutes. *Cast*: Rock Hudson, Salome Jens, John Randolph, Will Geer, Jeff Corey.

After such stylish pictures as *The Manchurian Candidate* and *The Train*, John Frankenheimer took his greatest chance to date with this oddity—a futuristic, allegorical thriller about a secret medical procedure that "kills" people, then gives them a second identity and a chance to start anew. One man, a boring middle-aged banker (Randolph), spends his $32,000 and is reborn as Malibu painter Antiochus "Tony" Wilson (Hudson). The heads of this mysterious company soon become concerned that the emotionally and spiritually unfulfilled Wilson poses a threat to their secrecy, returning him to the facilities with the intention of killing him and reusing his corpse. With veteran cinematographer James Wong Howe behind the camera, *Seconds* creates a wild, hallucinatory visual feast through the use of freakish wide-angle close-ups and nightmarish black-and-white imagery. The film features an underrated and practically forgotten performance from Rock Hudson as the character whose public face hides a drastically different inner person. Released to generally negative press and a scathing reaction at the Cannes Film Festival, the film has emerged as one of the most unique pictures of the 1960s.

SEGAL, GEORGE. Born February 13, 1934, in Great Neck, New York; actor. A sly, roguish, yet affable, leading man who attracted attention in 1966 with his Oscar-nominated performance in Mike Nichols' *Who's Afraid of Virginia Woolf?* While he's done some occasional dramatic work (notably *Ship of Fools* and *The St. Valentine's Day Massacre*), much of his best work has been in comedies of the 1970s, including the cult smash *Where's Poppa?*, *A Touch of Class* opposite Glenda Jackson, *California Split* for director Robert Altman, *Fun with Dick and Jane* opposite Jane Fonda, and the twisted whodunit *Who Is Killing the Great Chefs of Europe?* Throughout the 1980s and 1990s his career has been essentially nonexistent, though he did reemerge briefly in 1989's *Look Who's Talking*.

Filmography: The Young Doctors (1961); The Longest Day (1962); Act One (1964); Invitation to a Gunfighter (1964); The New Interns (1964); King Rat (1965); Ship of Fools (1965); The Lost Command (1966); The Quiller Memorandum (1966); Who's Afraid of Virginia Woolf? (1966); The St. Valentine's Day Massacre (1967); Bye Bye Braverman (1968); No Way to Treat a Lady (1968); The Girl Who Couldn't Say No/ Tenderly (1968); The Southern Star (1969); The Bridge at Remagen (1969); Loving (1970); The Owl and the Pussycat (1970); Where's Poppa?/Going Ape (1970); Born to Win (1971) also producer; The Hot Rock (1972); Blume in Love (1973); A Touch of Class (1973); California Split (1974); The Terminal Man (1974); The Black Bird (1975) also ep; Russian Roulette (1975); The Duchess and the Dirtwater Fox (1976); Fun with Dick and Jane (1977); Rollercoaster (1977); Who Is Killing the Great Chefs of Europe? (1978); Lost and Found (1979); The Last Married Couple in America (1980); Carbon Copy (1981); Killing 'em Softly (1982/released in 1985); Stick (1985); All's Fair (1989);

Look Who's Talking (1989); The Endless Game (1990); For the Boys (1991); The Clearing (1991); Me Myself and I (1992); Look Who's Talking Now (1993); Army of One (1993); Direct Hit (1994); Deep Down (1995); The Feminine Touch (1995); The Babysitter (1995); To Die For (1995).

Honor: Academy Award nomination for Best Supporting Actor (*Who's Afraid of Virginia Woolf?*).

SERPICO (1973), crime drama. Directed by Sidney Lumet; screenplay by Waldo Salt and Norman Wexler (from the book by Peter Maas); produced by Martin Bregman; photographed by Arthur J. Ornitz; edited by Dede Allen and Richard Marks; music by Mikis Theodorakis; released by Paramount; 129 minutes. *Cast*: Al Pacino, Tony Roberts, John Randolph, Jack Kehoe, Biff McGuire, Barbara Eda-Young, M. Emmet Walsh.

Based on the real-life experiences of onetime New York City cop Frank Serpico, this uncompromising exposé of corruption is indicative of the prevailing mood of distrust and disillusionment in 1970s America. Al Pacino, in his second of four consecutive Oscar-nominated performances, is superb in his transformation from the clean-cut, idealistic rookie to the "hippie" undercover cop who discovers a trail of graft that leads all the way to the top. Under Lumet's direction, filmgoers get an eyeful of the corrupt political machine that prevailed in America's cities and police departments for generations. Previous Hollywood films focused on the one dirty cop who soiled the reputation of an entire department, but with Serpico it's the opposite. The television movie *Serpico: The Deadly Game* aired in 1976, and a television series followed.

Awards: Academy Award nominations for Best Actor and Adapted Screenplay.

SEX, LIES, AND VIDEOTAPE (1989), drama. Directed, written, and edited by Steven Soderbergh; produced by John Hardy and Robert Newmyer; photographed by Walt Lloyd; music by Cliff Martinez; released by Miramax; 101 minutes. *Cast*: James Spader, Peter Gallagher, Andie MacDowell, Laura San Giacomo, Ron Vawter.

An unexpected low-budget hit (it cost $1.2 million and grossed over $20 million at the box office), this debut feature from Steven Soderbergh is one of the most mature and intelligent first features in some time. The story revolves around Graham (Spader), an emotionally and sexually dysfunctional young man who can connect with women only if he videotapes them, and his effect on his southern lawyer friend John (Gallagher), John's repressed wife, Ann (MacDowell), and her promiscuous sister Cynthia (San Giacomo). Dependent on a smart script, rich characters, and an erotic undercurrent, *sex, lies, and videotape* is the antithesis to the flashy, film school, style-over-content approach of most young filmmakers of the 1980s and 1990s. "The most stunning update from the Sex Wars front since Mike Nichols weighed in with *Carnal Knowledge* two decades ago" (Harlan Jacobson, *Film Comment*, July–August 1989).

Awards: Los Angeles Film Critics Award for Best Actress (MacDowell); Cannes Film Festival Palme d'Or and International Film Critics Prize for Best Actor (Spader).

SHAFT (1971), action/detective. Directed by Gordon Parks; screenplay by John D. F. Black and Ernest Tidyman (from the novel by Tidyman); produced by Joel Freeman; executive-produced by Stirling Silliphant; photographed by Urs Furrer; edited by Hugh A. Robertson; music by Isaac Hayes; released by MGM; 98 minutes. *Cast*: Richard Roundtree, Moses Gunn, Charles Cioffi, Christopher St. John, Antonio Fargas.

A pioneering work of black cinema that marked a shift in the mentality of a Hollywood studio system that had, until then, refused to accept the existence of a black audience. With this commercial revelation, the age of so-called blax-ploitation was born, and Hollywood capitalized by gearing genre films to a black audience. The first and one of the best of the bunch (along with *Super Fly*), this throwback to the private-eye film stars Roundtree as John Shaft, "one bad de-tective" who is hired by a Harlem mobster (Gunn) to locate his kidnapped daughter. Roundtree creates a memorable hero, Parks ignites the film with a pulsating New York atmosphere, and Isaac Hayes turns out a killer score and theme song. Still, the film itself would today be forgotten had the title character been white; the relevancy is based not on the film's content but on its social context. When MGM hit paydirt with this private-eye film (and its two sequels), the door was opened to blaxploitation treatments of other genres—the gangster film (*Black Caesar* with Fred Williamson), the horror film *Blacula*, and the radical women's film (*Cleopatra Jones* with Tamara Dobson). MGM also spun off a 1973 television series starring Roundtree.

Sequels: Richard Roundtree reprised his role in *Shaft's Big Score!* (1972, Parks) and *Shaft in Africa* (1973, Richard Guillermin).

Awards: Academy Award for Best Song; Academy Award nomination for Best Score.

SHAMPOO (1975), comedy. Directed by Hal Ashby; screenplay by Robert Towne and Warren Beatty; produced by Beatty; photographed by Laszlo Ko-vacs; edited by Robert Jones; music by Paul Simon, song "Wouldn't It Be Nice" performed by the Beach Boys; released by Columbia; 109 minutes. *Cast:* Warren Beatty, Julie Christie, Goldie Hawn, Lee Grant, Jack Warden, Tony Bill, Carrie Fisher.

The combination of writer/producer/star Warren Beatty, director Ashby, and cowriter Robert Towne provides the foundation for this wickedly funny send-up of Beverly Hills, in which Beatty takes a shot at his own persona—the libido-driven playboy who cares more about self-gratification than anything else. In a sly, comic performance, Beatty plays George Roundy, a 90210 hair stylist who loves to do more than his clients' hair, irresponsibly becoming involved with a number of attractive young women while trying to raise the funds to open his own shop. Ashby, a clever satirist, does a brilliant job of exposing the vacuousness of his characters, a group of people who never think about the consequences of their amorous actions. In the end, it's all about the whimsy of new hairstyles and new lovers—when one gets boring, you try another.

Awards: Academy Awards for Supporting Actor (Grant); Academy Award nominations for Supporting Actor (Warden), Screenplay, Art Direction.

SHE'S GOTTA HAVE IT (1986), comedy/drama. Directed, written, produced, and edited by Spike Lee; photographed by Ernest Dickerson (b&w); music by Bill Lee; released by Island; 84 minutes. *Cast*: Tracy Camila Johns, Spike Lee, Tommy Redmond Hicks, John Canada Terrell, Joie Lee, Raye Dowell.

Historically, one of the most important American films of all time—the one that broke the rules and forever darkened the lily-white hue of Hollywood. A bold, no-budget, 16mm black-and-white story of a black woman's sexuality and the three men who share her bed. With inventive visuals, a daring structure, and a wildly comic performance by Spike Lee as bicycle messenger Mars Blackmon, this debut feature took the independent film world by storm. It not only crossed over into mainstream success but set the groundwork for Lee's ascent as one of the most exciting filmmakers working today. Some of the more memorable moments include the come-ons by the string of "dogs"; Mars' plea of "Please baby, please baby, please baby, baby baby please"; Nola Darling's sexual "confessions" in which she speaks directly to the audience; and the endearing end credits, which feature outtakes of the cast and crew.

Award: Cannes Film Festival Award for Best New Director.

SHEEN, MARTIN. Born Ramon Estevez August 3, 1940, in Dayton, Ohio; actor, producer. Sons Charlie Sheen (*Platoon, Wall Street*), Emilio Estevez (*The Outsiders, The Mighty Ducks*), and Ramon Estevez and daughter Renee Estevez are also actors. Of Spanish and Irish descent, this dark-haired, sincere, intense actor got his start on the New York stage in the Broadway production of *The Subject Was Roses* (later appearing in the film adaptation). From his very first film role, as a subway thug in *The Incident*, he has managed to walk a delicate balance between dangerous intensity and irreproachable decency. He has made lasting impressions throughout his career—from his role as the homicidal James Dean-like Kit in *Badlands*, to the obsessed Willard in *Apocalypse Now*, to the honorable Carl Fox in *Wall Street*. A testament to his abilities is the fact that he has been equally effective in his television work, ranging from *The Catholics* and *The Execution of Private Slovik*, to his portrayals of Jack Kennedy (*Kennedy*) and Bobby Kennedy (*The Missiles of October*). In recent years he has moved into executive producing (*Da, Judgment in Berlin*) and directing (*Cadence, Babies Having Babies*).

Filmography: The Incident (1967); The Subject Was Roses (1968); Catch-22 (1970); No Drums, No Bugles (1971); Pickup on 101 (1972); Rage (1972); Badlands (1973); Catholics (1973, tvm); The Execution of Private Slovik (1974, tvm); The Missiles of

October (1974, tvms); The Legend of Earl Durand (1975); The Cassandra Crossing (1977); The Little Girl Who Lives down the Lane (1977); Eagle's Wing (1978); Apocalypse Now (1979); Blind Ambition (1979, tvms); The Final Countdown (1980); Loophole (1981); Enigma (1982); Gandhi (1982); In the King of Prussia (1982); Man, Woman and Child (1982); That Championship Season (1982); Kennedy (1983, tvms); The Dead Zone (1983); Firestarter (1984); A State of Emergency (1986); The Believers (1987); Dear America (1987); Siesta (1987); Wall Street (1987); Da (1988) also ep; Judgment in Berlin (1988) also ep; Personal Choice (1988); Beverly Hills Brats (1989); Cold Front (1989); Cadence (1990) also director, screenplay; The Maid (1990); Touch and Die (1992); Original Intent (1992); Hear No Evil (1993); Gettysburg (1993); The Ghost Brigade (1993); The Floating Outfit (1994); Boca (1994); When the Bough Breaks (1994); Born Wild (1994); Hits (1994); A Hundred and One Nights (1995); Dillinger and Capone (1995); The Break (1995); Dead Presidents (1995); Gospa (1995); The American President (1995).

SHEPARD, SAM. Born Samuel Shepard Rogers November 5, 1943, in Fort Sheridan, Illinois; actor, director, screenwriter, playwright. Longtime companion of actor Jessica Lange. Handsome, charismatic actor whose phenomenal accomplishments as one of America's premier playwrights have occasionally been overshadowed by his considerable acting talents. After coscripting Michelangelo Antonioni's *Zabriskie Point* in 1969 and writing a string of great American plays in the 1970s and 1980s, Shepard (with his Gary Cooper good looks) accelerated his film career with an exceptional performance in Terrence Malick's *Days of Heaven*. Continuing in that strong, silent, rural vein, he earned an Oscar nomination for his heroic portrayal of test pilot Chuck Yeager in *The Right Stuff*. As a film director, however, he has had a tougher time making the transition, with both *Far North* and *Silent Tongue* merely footnotes in his otherwise illustrious career. With his screenplay adaptation of his own *Motel Chronicles* book for Wim Wenders' *Paris, Texas*, Shepard comes closest to making his imagistic words and characters crackle with life. Shepard has also written the books *Hawk Moon: A Book of Short Stories, Poems and Monologues* (1981), *Rolling Thunder Logbook* (1987), and *Cruising Paradise* (1996).

Filmography as actor: Renaldo and Clara (1977); Days of Heaven (1978); Resurrection (1980); Raggedy Man (1981); Frances (1982); The Right Stuff (1983); Country (1984); Fool for Love (1985) also screenplay; Crimes of the Heart (1986); Baby Boom (1987); Steel Magnolias (1989); Bright Angel (1991); Defenseless (1991); Voyager (1991); Thunderheart (1992); The Pelican Brief (1993); Safe Passage (1994); The Good Old Boys (1995, ctvm).

Filmography as director: Far North (1988) also screenplay; Silent Tongue (1993) also screenplay.

Additional credits: Me and My Brother (1969) screenplay; Zabriskie Point (1970) screenplay; Paris, Texas (1984) screenplay; The Curse of the Starving Class (1995, ctvm) based on his play.

Honors: Academy Award nomination for Supporting Actor (*The Right Stuff*); Pulitzer Prize (*Buried Child* 1979).

SHEPHERD, CYBILL. Born February 18, 1950, in Memphis, Tennessee; actor. Blond, blue-eyed southern belle who rocketed to superstardom at age twenty-one in her film debut as the brazen, self-centered Jacy Farrow of Peter Bogdanovich's *The Last Picture Show*. A former Miss Teenage Memphis who first achieved success as a model in New York City, where she was discovered by Bogdanovich, later becoming romantically involved with the director in a very public, eight-year romance. She followed with another success as the enigmatic temptress in Elaine May's marital comedy *The Heartbreak Kid* before appearing in two of Bogdanovich's least successful films, *Daisy Miller* and the musical *At Long Last Love*, the latter of which featured a critically savaged singing role that helped derail her career. Except for a brilliantly subtle performance in Martin Scorsese's *Taxi Driver*, her subsequent film work has been infrequent. Instead, however, she has found success on the small screen, first alongside Bruce Willis in ''Moonlighting'' and again in her own sitcom ''Cybill.'' She has also continued to pursue her love of singing with the album ''Cybill Does It . . . to Cole Porter'' (1994) and her occasional cabaret shows.

Filmography: The Last Picture Show (1971); The Heartbreak Kid (1972); Daisy Miller (1974); At Long Last Love (1975); Special Delivery (1976); Taxi Driver (1976); Silver Bears (1977); The Lady Vanishes (1979); ''Moonlighting'' (1985–1989, tvs); Chances Are (1989); Alice (1990); Texasville (1990); Married to It (1993); ''Cybill'' (1994–   , tvs).

SHOOTIST, THE (1976), western. Directed by Don Siegel; screenplay by Miles Hood Swarthout and Scott Hale (from the novel by Glendon Swarthout); produced by M. J. Frankovich and William Self; photographed by Bruce Surtees; edited by Douglas Stewart; music by Elmer Bernstein; released by Paramount; 100 minutes. *Cast*: John Wayne, Lauren Bacall, James Stewart, Ron Howard, Richard Boone, Hugh O'Brian, Bill McKinney, Harry Morgan, John Carradine, Sheree North, Richard Lenz, Scatman Crothers.

A fitting swan song for the legendary John Wayne, who, by the 1970s, had been supplanted as the western's foremost figure by the younger, more modern Clint Eastwood. Like Eastwood, Wayne had attempted to apply the Old West moral code to urban police dramas such as *McQ* and *Brannigan*, but unlike Eastwood, Wayne lacked a director such as Don Siegel to help mold his persona. Here, however, the pairing of Siegel and Wayne brings out the best in the Duke. Essentially playing himself, Wayne is cast as J. B. Books, a mythical gunslinger who has returned to the town of his youth in order to die. Racked with cancer and uncomfortable in the postindustrial world of cars and electricity, Books takes refuge in the boardinghouse of Bond Rogers (Bacall) and befriends her son Gillom (Howard), an immature and cocky lad who idolizes the old man way out of proportion. The result is a film that examines the myth of the Old West in relation to the mythology that surrounded John Wayne; in short, it's a film about the inevitability of death and the decision to face that death with dignity. Coincidentally, 1976 also saw the release of *The Outlaw Josey Wales*, Eastwood's first great film as a director and the premier western of the 1970s.

SHORT CUTS (1993), drama. Directed and cowritten by Robert Altman; screenplay with Frank Barhydt (from stories by Raymond Carver); produced by Cary Brokaw; photographed by Walt Lloyd; edited by Geraldine Peroni; music by Mark Isham; released by Fine Line Features; 189 minutes. *Cast*: Tim Robbins, Madeline Stowe, Jennifer Jason Leigh, Christopher Penn, Lily Tomlin, Tom Waits, Jack Lemmon, Andie MacDowell, Bruce Davison, Zane Cassidy, Lyle Lovett, Matthew Modine, Julianne Moore, Frances McDormand, Peter Gallagher, Lili Taylor, Robert Downey, Jr., Lori Singer, Annie Ross, Anne Archer, Buck Henry, Fred Ward, Huey Lewis.

A multicharacter tapestry constructed from the writings of Raymond Carver, this tale of disconnected Los Angelenos is, from the opening thumping of the malathion-spewing helicopters, very clearly the work of a master filmmaker. All that connects these two dozen or so characters is the poison that rains down upon them and the quaking earth that trembles beneath their feet—and the fact that each character's domestic situation is in some state of turmoil. One couple's child is hit by a car, another couple argues over the wife's decision to pose nude for a painting, and yet another struggles with the wife's job as a phone-sex operator. These are all people around whom entire features could be written, but Altman's genius is in reminding us that everyone has problems and that none of them are more or less significant than those of anyone else. As he has so often done, Altman fills his picture with a gallery of top acting talents, though somehow singer (and nonactor) Lyle Lovett's angry baker manages to standout. It is as much because of Lovett's pained expression as it is his character—a man so outraged by one customer's failure to pick up her order that he obsessively pesters her with disturbing phone calls, only to later learn that the child for whom the cake was baked has died. *Short Cuts* ''is a film dedicated to a daydream nation literally and metaphorically living astride a faultline'' (Gavin Smith, *Film Comment*, September–October 1993).

Awards: Venice Film Festival Golden Lion for Best Picture and Volpi Cup for entire cast; Independent Spirit Awards for Best Picture, Director, and Screenplay.

SIEGEL, DON. Born October 26, 1912, in Chicago; died April 20, 1991, in Nipimo, California; director. A true Hollywood maverick who was molded by the studio system, Siegel is unique among directors of his era in that he began with B-level assignments and, by the late 1960s, had developed into an action auteur with A-level actors and projects. With origins in the Warner Brothers editorial department in 1934, he established himself in the 1950s as a director of such gritty, individualistic films as *Riot in Cell Block 11* and the sci-fi classic *Invasion of the Body Snatchers*. His reputation grew with 1964's *The Killers*, a tough, violent crime film that displays Siegel's knack for explosively combining brutal action with complex psychological profiles. If there's any theme that runs throughout Siegel's body of work, it's the hero as outsider—the man who follows his own moral code and refuses to end up like a subhuman ''pod.'' With his trio of cop movies—*Madigan, Coogan's Bluff,* and *Dirty Harry*—Siegel tapped into a cultural current of antiauthoritarianism that simply didn't exist during the time of his 1950s work. Richard Widmark's Madigan and Clint Eastwood's Coogan and Harry Callahan are cops who function best outside the system, men who battle the system not for the sake of rebellion but simply because they must do so to feel alive. The Siegel–Eastwood collaboration also included the atypical, nonaction films *Two Mules for Sister Sara, The Beguiled,* and, in 1979, the minimalistic *Escape from Alcatraz.* Without Eastwood, Siegel continued to examine the psychology of such outsiders as the bank robber (Walter Matthau in the excellent *Charley Varrick*), the espionage agent (Michael Caine in *Black Windmill,* Charles Bronson in *Telefon*), and the aging gunslinger in the postindustrialist age (John Wayne in *The Shootist*). Unfortunately, his career ended with two inferior films—the Burt Reynolds vehicle *Rough Cut* (with its troubled production history during which Siegel was fired, rehired, and then replaced in postproduction) and the uncharacteristic Bette Midler black comedy *Jinxed.* Siegel wrote *A Siegel Film: An Autobiography,* which was published posthumously in 1993. "He believed that there were no rules, or if there were rules, they were made to be broken" (Clint Eastwood, *Projections 4 1/2*).

Filmography of key pre-1965 films: The Big Steal (1949); Riot in Cell Block 11 (1954); Private Hell 36 (1954); Invasion of the Body Snatchers (1956); Baby Face Nelson (1957); Flaming Star (1960); Hell Is for Heroes (1962); The Killers (1964).

Filmography since 1965: Stranger on the Run (1967, tvm); Madigan (1968); Coogan's Bluff (1968) also producer; Death of a Gunfighter (1969) codirected with Robert Totten under the pseudonym of Allen Smithee; Two Mules for Sister Sara (1970); Play Misty for Me (1971) actor; The Beguiled (1971) also producer; Dirty Harry (1972) also producer; Charley Varrick (1973) also producer, actor; The Black Windmill (1974) also producer; The Shootist (1976); Telefon (1977); Invasion of the Body Snatchers (1978) actor; Escape from Alcatraz (1979) also producer; Rough Cut (1980); Jinxed (1982).

Honors: Academy Awards for Best Short Film (*Star in the Night*, 1945) and Documentary Short (*Hitler Lives?*, 1945); Los Angeles Film Critics Career Achievement Award (1988).

Selected bibliography

Kaminski, Stuart. *Don Siegel: Director.* New York: Curtis, 1974.
Siegel, Don. *A Siegel Film: An Autobiography.* New York: Faber and Faber, 1993.

SILENCE OF THE LAMBS (1991), drama/horror. Directed by Jonathan Demme; screenplay by Ted Tally (from the novel by Thomas Harris); produced by Edward Saxon and Kenneth Utt; photographed by Tak Fujimoto; edited by Craig McKay; music by Howard Shore; released by Orion; 118 minutes. *Cast*: Anthony Hopkins, Jodie Foster, Scott Glenn, Ted Levine, Charles Napier, Chris Isaak, Roger Corman, George Romero.

A troubling journey underneath the flesh and into the darkness that hides deep inside, this horrific psychological drama acquaints us with Clarice Starling (Foster), a Federal Bureau of Investigation (FBI) agent-in-training who is assigned to interview Dr. Hannibal "the Cannibal" Lecter (Hopkins). A notorious serial killer who is imprisoned in a dungeonlike cell, Dr. Lecter may be willing to help the bureau identify Buffalo Bill, a maniac who skins his female victims. A peculiar bond forms between Clarice and Dr. Lecter, who enter into a quid pro quo arrangement—Clarice reveals deeply personal secrets in exchange for Dr. Lecter's information about Bill. Through Lecter's demands, she comes to know herself better, recalling the painful childhood memories of the death of her sheriff father and her subsequent two months on a ranch that slaughtered lambs. As the clock ticks closer toward the mutilation of another young woman, Clarice uses Dr. Lecter's insights to find and kill Bill, while her oppressively patriarchal boss (Glenn) and his team of agents arrogantly descend on an empty house 400 miles away. Director Jonathan Demme, who has so often in the past displayed a remarkable understanding of women characters, brings to life his most complex woman yet in Clarice Starling—a fatherless woman in the male-dominated world of the FBI, law enforcement, and murder. Unconsciously drawn to Dr. Lecter, she finds herself in the strange position of trying to please Dr. Lecter much as a student yearns for the acceptance of a teacher, or a little girl longs for the love of her father. As a result, Demme (working from Harris' novel and Tally's script) creates an intelligent dramatic work that exists within the framework of a horror film. As for frightening moments, they're in no short supply—from Dr. Lecter's ingenious, but revolting, escape, to Clarice's final confrontation with Buffalo Bill. Hannibal Lecter also appears in Thomas A. Harris' novel *Red Dragon* and the Michael Mann film *Manhunter* (1986).

Awards: Academy Awards for Best Picture, Director, Actor, Actress, Adapted Screenplay; Academy Award nominations for Editing, Sound; New York Film Critics Circle Awards for Best Picture, Director, Actress, and Actor; DGA Award; WGA Award; Berlin Film Festival Award for Best Director.

SISTERS (1973), horror/thriller. Directed and cowritten by Brian De Palma; screenplay with Louisa Rose; produced by Edward R. Pressman; photographed by Gregory Sandor; edited by Paul Hirsch; music by Bernard Herrmann; released by American International Pictures (AIP); 92 minutes. *Cast*: Margot Kidder, Jennifer Salt, Charles Durning, Bill Finley, Barnard Hughes.

Although he would later become known for his Stephen King adaptation *Carrie*, *Sisters* is De Palma's true horror masterpiece—a creepy tale of a snoopy reporter (Salt) who, while peering into a neighboring apartment, witnesses the attractive young Danielle Breton (Kidder) brutally murder her black boyfriend. But when the police arrive, there's not even a hint that a crime has occurred. The reporter then follows a trail of clues that eventually reveal that Danielle is a Siamese twin who was separated at birth. Absent of the excessive stylistic devices that would mar De Palma's later works, *Sisters* focuses on the psychology of terror through a playful manipulation of audience perceptions. The only camera trick is a split screen, which becomes a perfect visual metaphor for the psychosis that develops within the emotionally and physically severed Siamese twin. Of course it's Hitchcockian, especially with Bernard Herrmann's chilling score, but that doesn't negate the fact that the movie is scary as hell.

SIXTEEN CANDLES (1984), comedy. Directed and written by John Hughes; produced by Hilton Green; photographed by Bobby Byrne; edited by Edward Warschilka; music by Ira Newborn; released by Universal; 93 minutes. *Cast*: Molly Ringwald, Anthony Michael Hall, Michael Schoeffling, Paul Dooley, Justin Henry, Gedde Watanabe, John Cusack, Joan Cusack, Brian Doyle-Murray, Jami Gertz.

The film that made Molly Ringwald a star (however fleeting), this harmless and generally humorous teen comedy became the first in a number of "brat pack" movies delivered by John Hughes. The plot is as ordinary as they come—a high school girl on the verge of turning sixteen develops a crush on a senior who ignores her; she, in turn, is befriended by an amorous geek (Hall) who has a crush on her. What makes it all work are the charming performances from the redheaded Ringwald, whose Samantha became the embodiment of the "normal" teenager replete with insecurities and frustrations. It was the first film directed by Hughes and arguably his best effort in a declining career of desperate attempts at comedy that have grown increasingly infantile, brutal, and offensive.

SLATER, CHRISTIAN. Born August 18, 1969, in New York City; actor. Mother, Mary Jo Slater, is a casting director; father, Michael Hawkins, is a stage actor. With show business in his genes, Slater's first notable role came at age nine on stage with Dick Van Dyke in *The Music Man* and later on Broadway in *David Copperfield* and *Macbeth*. Attracting critical attention with his early film roles, he broke through as the wisecracking, rebellious teenager in Michael Lehmann's highly praised black comedy *Heathers*. He further developed his intelligent, droll teen rebel persona as the pirate radio deejay in Allan Moyle's *Pump Up the Volume*. A biting satiric quality and a mix of raw sexuality and sensitivity helped position him as something of a teen idol, though his critics lambasted him for being little more than a second-rate Jack Nicholson, with whom he bares an uncanny likeness. (Compare Nicholson's radio talk show spiel in *The King of Marvin Gardens* to Slater's on-air venom in *Pump Up the Volume*.) A substance abuse problem, combined with two terrible movies— *Mobsters* and *Kuffs*—helped send his stock plummeting. He has begun to return to form with his later films but has done little to prove himself capable of carrying a film to box office heights.

Filmography: Robbers, Rooftops and Witches/The Invisible Boy (1982, tvm); The Legend of Billie Jean (1984); The Name of the Rose (1986); Twisted/A Step beyond Insanity (1986, released 1992); Tucker: The Man and His Dream (1988); Beyond the Stars (1989); Gleaming the Cube (1989); The Wizard (1989); Heathers (1989); Tales from the Darkside: The Movie (1990); Pump Up the Volume (1990); Young Guns II (1990); Mobsters (1991); Robin Hood: Prince of Thieves (1991); Star Trek VI: The Undiscovered Country

(1991); FernGully: The Last Rainforest (1992) voice; Kuffs (1992); Where the Day Takes You (1992); The Last Party (1993); Untamed Heart (1993); True Romance (1993); Jimmy Hollywood (1994); Interview with the Vampire (1994); Catwalk (1995); Murder in the First (1995); Museum of Love (1995, ctv short).

SMOKEY AND THE BANDIT (1977), comedy. Directed by Hal Needham; screenplay by James Lee Barrett, Charles Shyer, and Alan Mendel (from the story by Needham and Robert L. Levy); produced by Mort Engleberg; photographed by Bobby Byrne; edited by Walter Hannemann and Angelo Ross; music by Bill Justis, songs by Jerry Reed; released by Universal; 96 minutes. *Cast*: Burt Reynolds, Sally Field, Jackie Gleason, Jerry Reed, Mike Henry, Pat McCormick, Paul Williams.

A prime example of popular entertainment that validated the moviegoing tastes of good ol' boys to the tune of $126 million at the box office. Directed by former stuntman Hal Needham, the film is little more than an excuse to race and crash fleets of cars on America's interstates and dirt roads. The minimal plot has the Bandit (Reynolds) and his good buddy trucker Cledus Snow (Reed) racing from Atlanta to Texas and back with an illegal shipment of Coors beer. En route, the Bandit picks up the forlorn Carrie, a New Yorker who has just fled the altar from her dim-witted boyfriend Junior (Henry), the son of Sheriff Buford T. Justice (Gleason). Packed with enough demolition to keep everyone happy, the film really succeeds because it's smart enough to paint its down-home heroes Bandit and Cledus in the same shade of its audience—decent, heroic, and crafty folk who have earned the respect and friendship of their peers. Not surprisingly, it was dismissed by New York and Los Angeles critics, who failed to realize that CBers, truckers, and good ol' boys constitute a huge segment of the population. Of the films released in 1977, only *Star Wars* and *Close Encounters of the Third Kind* made more money, ranking this as Universal Pictures' then third highest grossing picture of all time, behind *Jaws* and *The Sting*.

Sequels: *Smokey and the Bandit II* (1980, Needham) and *Smokey and the Bandit—Part 3* (1983, Dick Lowry).

SNIPES, WESLEY. Born July 31, 1962, in Orlando, Florida; actor. Handsome, athletic African-American actor who studied dance, singing, and acting at New York City's High School for the Performing Arts before his first film roles as a football player in *Wildcats* and as a boxer in *Street of Gold*. After appearing as a young thug in Martin Scorsese's video of Michael Jackson's ''Bad,'' Spike Lee offered him a costarring role in *Mo' Better Blues* as the scrappy saxophone player Shadow Henderson. His next film with Lee, *Jungle Fever*, explored racial taboos and gave him the opportunity to play his first romantic lead—Flipper Purify, the upscale architect who falls in lust with a white coworker from Bensonhurst. Since then, the versatile Snipes has proven himself to be one of the most dynamic and exciting young actors in Hollywood in roles ranging from the character-driven film *The Waterdance* (as an angry and depressed paraplegic), to the hit action films *Passenger 57* and *Demolition Man*, to the comedy *To Wong Foo, Thanks for Everything, Julie Newmar* as drag queen Noxeema Jackson.

Filmography: Wildcats (1986); Streets of Gold (1986); Critical Condition (1987); Michael Jackson's "Bad" (1987, mv); "Vietnam War Story" (1988, ctvs); Major League (1989); King of New York (1990); Mo' Better Blues (1990); Jungle Fever (1991); New Jack City (1991); The Waterdance (1992); Passenger 57 (1992); White Men Can't Jump (1992); Boiling Point (1993); Rising Sun (1993); Demolition Man (1993); Sugar Hill (1993); Drop Zone (1994); To Wong Foo, Thanks for Everything, Julie Newmar (1995); Money Train (1995); Waiting to Exhale (1995).

SODERBERGH, STEVEN. Born January 14, 1963, in Atlanta, Georgia; director. At twenty-six he became the youngest person to win the Palme d'Or at the Cannes Film Festival for his unexpected, low-budget ($1.2 million) hit *sex, lies, and videotape*, an intelligent, witty, and understated story of sexual repression in Louisiana. His much-anticipated sophomore feature *Kafka* was an over-ambitious, allegorical period drama that featured an international cast and was soundly eschewed by film critics and audiences alike. Fortunately, he returned to form with *King of the Hill*, the brilliant adaptation of A. E. Hotchner's depression-era story that features a subtlety of tone rarely achieved by young American filmmakers. Again, however, commercial response to the film was nil—a fate also reserved for his fourth film, *The Underneath*, an unsatisfying, structurally experimental film noir. Despite his clear talent as a filmmaker, it appears that the megasuccess attained by Soderbergh in *sex, lies, and videotape* may have been a box office fluke accurately prophesied in his Wellesian acceptance speech at Cannes—"Well, I guess it's all downhill from here."

Filmography: October 16, 1977 (1977, documentary short); Passages (1978, short); Janitor (1979, short); Skoal (1980, short); Rapid Eye Movement (1982, short); Winston (1986, short); Yes (1987, mv); sex, lies, and videotape (1988); Kafka (1991); King of the Hill (1993); "The Quiet Room" episode of "Fallen Angels" (1993, ctv); The Underneath (1995).

Additional credits: "Games People Play" (1980, tvs) editor; 9021Live (1986, concert film) director, editor; Suture (1993) ep.

Honors: Cannes Film Festival Palme d'Or and the International Critics' Prize (*sex, lies, and videotape*); Sundance Film Festival Dramatic Competition Audience Award (*sex, lies, and videotape*); Independent Spirit Award for Best Director (*sex, lies, and videotape*).

Selected bibliography

Soderbergh, Steven. *sex, lies, and videotape.* New York: Harper and Row, 1990.

SORCERER (1977), adventure/thriller. Directed and produced by William Friedkin; screenplay by Walon Green (from the novel by George Arnaud); photographed by John M. Stephens and Dick Bush; edited by Robert K. Lambert and Bud Smith; music by Tangerine Dream; released by Universal; 121 minutes. *Cast*: Roy Scheider, Bruno Cremer, Francisco Rabal, Amidou, Karl John.

Released at the height of Friedkin's popularity (after *The French Connection* and *The Exorcist*), this tension-filled reworking of Henri-Georges Clouzot's classic 1955 French film *The Wages of Fear* was lambasted by critics and ignored by the public. Still, it's an eerie, edge-of-your-seat story of four men from different walks of life—a South American assassin, an Arab terrorist, a Parisian banker, and a New York City hood—who are living in self-imposed exile in a filthy South American oil town in order to escape their past sins. When a group of anti-American extremists sabotages an oil well, the company representatives offer four volunteers a chance to escape this hell by driving a shipment of extremely volatile nitroglycerin over 200 miles of treacherous road. With two men per truck, "Sorcerer" and "Lazaro" are loaded up with nitro and driven off—one false move liable to blow everything to pieces. Along the way they encounter perilously narrow mountain roads, a rope-and-wood bridge in a violent rainstorm (the film's most stunning sequence), a massive fallen tree that blocks the road, and a band of terrorists. The result, a box office dud that rivals Clouzot's original on an artistic level, is an intelligent thriller that serves as a clever metaphor for the potential volatility of intolerance and racism. Featuring a chilling synthesized score from Tangerine Dream.

SOUND OF MUSIC, THE (1965), musical. Directed and produced by Robert Wise; screenplay by Ernest Lehman (from the play by Richard Rogers, Oscar Hammerstein II, Howard Lindsay, and Russel Crouse); photographed by Ted McCord; edited by William Reynolds; songs by Rogers and Hammerstein; released by 20th Century Fox; 174 minutes. *Cast*: Julie Andrews, Christopher Plummer, Eleanor Parker, Richard Haydn, Peggy Wood.

The biggest-grossing musical of all time, though far from the best, this 20th Century Fox-produced tale of the singing Von Trapp family is one of the last dinosaurs to lumber out of Hollywood's studio gates—a film of pure entertainment that is bubbling over with joyousness and hope. It stars Julie Andrews as Maria, a postulant who leaves the nunnery behind and takes a job as governess to seven children of an Austrian aristocrat (Plummer). With a smile on her face, she gleefully teaches them about the joys of life . . . until the Nazis invade Austria and threaten to tear them and their country apart. With Rogers and Hammerstein's infectious score (the title tune, "My Favorite Things," and "Do Re Mi" have all become part of our collective psyche), the majestic Alpine vistas, and Andrews' exuberant performance, the film has delighted generations of moviegoers around the world. Still, it seems to belong to an earlier era of filmmaking—one that was pushed out of favor (despite the financial pot of gold it reaped) during the turbulent and cynical years that would follow its release. "A film of real charm—the only one of the monster super-musicals of the 1960s that is" (John Russell Taylor, *Cinema: A Critical Dictionary*).

Awards: Academy Awards for Picture, Director, Editing, Music Scoring, Sound; Academy Award nominations for Actress, Supporting Actress (Wood), Cinematography, Art Direction; DGA Award.

SOUNDER (1972), drama. Directed by Martin Ritt; screenplay by Lon Elder III (from the novel by William H. Armstrong); produced by Robert B. Radnitz; photographed by John Alonzo; edited by Sid Levin; music by Taj Mahal; released by 20th Century Fox; 105 minutes. *Cast*: Cicely Tyson, Paul Winfield, Kevin Hooks, Carmen Matthews, Taj Mahal, Janet MacLachlan.

A simple, uplifting film that countered the Hollywood trend of violent "blaxploitation" films and proved that there was an audience for black-oriented dramas. Based on the Newbery Award-winning novel by William H. Armstrong, this lyrical tale follows a rural depression-era family that struggles to work its parcel of land while the family patriarch (Winfield) is doing a year of hard labor for stealing a ham. In the meantime, young David (Hooks) is faced with seemingly insurmountable racial prejudice before eventually meeting a teacher who opens up a new world of self-discovery and personal pride. Although it helped unlock the door to more films about the black experience in America, it is still a film for black America made by white Hollywood, albeit a humanistic, dignified, and entirely positive one.

SPACEK, SISSY. Born Mary Elizabeth Spacek December 25, 1949, in Quitman, Texas; actor. Married to production designer/director Jack Fisk; cousin is actor Rip Torn. Thin, waifish leading lady who studied in New York City at the Actors Studio before gaining prominence as the naive midwestern teenager Holly in *Badlands*. Although well into her twenties, she was again convincingly cast as a teenager in Brian De Palma's horror classic *Carrie* as a telekinetic high schooler victimized by callous students and an overbearing mother. The vision of Spacek as the stunned, blood-drenched prom queen Carrie remains one of the most disturbing of all horror film images. The role earned her the first of five Oscar nominations, and she eventually won an Oscar for her 1980 turn as country singer Loretta Lynn in *Coal Miner's Daughter*. She's twice appeared in films directed by her husband (*Raggedy Man*, *Violets Are Blue*), for whom she once worked as a set decorator on De Palma's *The Phantom of Paradise*.

Filmography: Prime Cut (1972); Badlands (1973); Ginger in the Morning (1973); The Phantom of Paradise (1974) set decorator; Carrie (1976); Welcome to L.A. (1976); Three Women (1977); Heartbeat (1979); Coal Miner's Daughter (1980); Raggedy Man (1981); Missing (1982); The River (1984); Marie (1985); 'Night Mother (1986); Crimes of the Heart (1986); Violets Are Blue (1986); The Man with Two Brains (1987) voice; The Long Walk Home (1990); Hard Promises (1991); JFK (1991); Trading Mom (1994); A Place for Annie (1994, tvm); The Good Old Boys (1995, ctvm); The Grass Harp (1995).

Honors: Academy Award for Best Actress (*Coal Miner's Daughter*); Academy Award nominations for Best Actress (*Carrie, Missing, The River, Crimes of the Heart*); Los Angeles Film Critics Award for Best Actress (*Coal Miner's Daughter*); New York Film

Critics Circle Awards for Best Actress (*Coal Miner's Daughter, Crimes of the Heart*) and Supporting Actress (*Three Women*).

SPANKING THE MONKEY (1994), comedy/drama. Directed and written by David O. Russell; produced by Dean Silvers; photographed by Michael Mayers; edited by Pamela Martin; released by Fine Line Features; 110 minutes. *Cast*: Jeremy Davies, Alberta Watson, Benjamin Hendrickson, Carla Gallo, Matthew Puckett, Judette Jones.

A disquieting and often comic story of a seriously dysfunctional suburban family that is something of a companion piece to *The Graduate*. Ray (Davies), a Massachusetts Institute of Technology student, arrives home for a summer visit before starting on a prestigious internship, only to find that his depressive mother (Watson) is confined to bed with a broken leg, and his callous businessman father (Hendrickson) is leaving town and expecting Ray to nurse her. The succession of improprieties begins when his mother demands that he help her into the shower, has him massage her legs with lotion, and asks specific sexual details about a local girl (Gallo) who likes him. His sexual frustration extends to his repeatedly interrupted attempts at, as the slangy title suggests, masturbation. It all builds to a brief and mostly off-screen act of incest. This, however, is only a small part of what is wrong with this archetypal suburban family of sad, weak, frustrated, and needy people. Carefully and intelligently directed by first-timer Russell, this is a biopsy of the dysfunctional family, and what Russell finds is an incurable malignancy.

Awards: Independent Spirit Awards for Best First Feature and First Screenplay; Sundance Film Festival Audience Award.

SPIELBERG, STEVEN. Born December 18, 1947, in Cincinnati, Ohio; director, producer. Married to actor Kate Capshaw; formerly married to actor Amy Irving. Not since D. W. Griffith has any one figure in American film displayed such a potent combination of storytelling technique, popular success, technological advancement, and business acumen. A prodigious youngster who had long been awed by the power of movies and television, he made a forty-minute war tale (*Escape to Nowhere*) and a two-hour sci-fi epic (*Firelight*), both 8mm, before the age of sixteen. Amazingly refused admittance to the University of Southern California's film program, he instead attended California State College in Long Beach. By the age of twenty, he had secured a seven-year television deal with MCA/Universal, where he directed Joan Crawford in an episode of the now-legendary full-length pilot for Rod Serling's "Night Gallery" series, as well as episodes of "Columbo" and "Marcus Welby M.D." His television movie debut, *Duel*, in which a lone driver is terrorized by a predatory eighteen-wheeler, and his feature debut, *The Sugarland Express*, about a young couple on the lam, established him as a rising talent in Hollywood circles and led to the opportunity to direct *Jaws*. His first masterpiece is a mature, character-driven horror film in which the semi of *Duel* has metamorphosed into a Great White, attacking humans simply because that is the nature of the beast. The first of Hollywood's new breed of blockbusters, the film earned $260 million in domestic box office for a total of nearly a half billion dollars worldwide. Spielberg, at just twenty-five years old, may not have owned Hollywood, but *Jaws* was his down payment. He followed with *Close Encounters of the Third Kind*, an atypical sci-fi film that is literate and emotionally complex and features benevolent, almost holy aliens. It is the first of his films to fully articulate his childlike sense of wonder, as well as the first to employ many of the stylistic traits—the glowing backlight and those innocent look-to-the-skies faces—that have become his trademark. After the failure of *1941*, his madcap attempt at reviving the slapstick supercomedy, he teamed with friend George Lucas to make *Raiders of the Lost Ark*, a delirious adventure tale that drew on the cliff-hangers of Hollywood's past. With *E.T. The Extra-Terrestrial*, he delivered an instant classic that outperformed his previous efforts at the box office and has brought in over $700 million worldwide. Not until this film did Spielberg's name take on a whole new meaning—in the way that "Hitchcockian" has become an adjective associated with thrillers and a repressed sexuality, "Spielbergian" has rightly or wrongly come to identify an innocence associated with white, suburban, middle-class values. It was ammunition used against him by elitist detractors who charged that Spielberg must be an inferior talent since such massive popularity could not possibly coexist with artistic merit and integrity. While continuing with his Indiana Jones trilogy, he began a shift away from pyrotechnics and back toward character-driven narratives. His next two non-Indiana pictures may lack sharks or unidentified flying objects, but *The Color Purple* and *Empire of the Sun* (both based on autobiographic novels of traumatic childhoods by Alice Walker and J. G. Ballard, respectively) are less a new direction than a return to the emotional complexity of *Jaws* and *Close Encounters*. Taken to task for his obvious Oscar bid, Spielberg became a target of much criticism for adapting and whitewashing Walker's story of racism, poverty, violence, and lesbianism in the Deep South, but he must also be commended for pushing through the studio system a high-profile black film with a cast of unknowns. Neither *Empire of the Sun*, an underappreciated tale of World War II prison camps as seen through a child's eyes, nor *Always*, a sentimental romance based on the 1943 film *A Guy Named Joe*, performed especially well at the box office. *Hook*, the tired Peter Pan adventure, outgrossed them both combined. In 1993, Spielberg's year of monumental achievement, he directed the dinosaur adventure *Jurassic Park* (at over $900 million in worldwide box office, the biggest grosser of all time) and the Holocaust drama *Schindler's List*, one of the most moving and important motion pictures in film history. As significant as he has been as a director both critically and commercially (his fifteen films have grossed $4.5 billion worldwide), he has also been an active producer with his Amblin Entertainment. As an executive producer he has been instrumental in the careers of Robert Zemeckis (*Back to the Future*, *Who Framed Roger Rabbit*), Tobe Hooper (*Poltergeist*), Joe Dante (*Twilight Zone—The Movie*, *Gremlins*, *Innerspace*), and

Chris Columbus (screenwriter of *The Gremlins, The Goonies, Young Sherlock Holmes*), while Amblin (with longtime producing partners Kathleen Kennedy and Frank Marshall) has produced such diverse films as Martin Scorsese's *Cape Fear*, Peter Bogdanovich's *Noises Off*, Clint Eastwood's *The Bridges of Madison County*, and the television-based comedies *The Flintstones* and *Casper*. He has also been especially active in television with such shows as the "Amazing Stories" anthology series, the highly touted, but botched, "seaQuest DSV," the hit medical drama "ER," and numerous ventures into animation, including the witty "Steven Spielberg Presents Animaniacs." In 1994, Spielberg joined forces with former Disney executive Jeffrey Katzenberg and record company executive David Geffen to form DreamWorks SKG, a state-of-the art film studio that has forged alliances with CapCities/ABC for television and Microsoft's Bill Gates for interactive media. "Spielbergian images suffuse the planet's collective consciousness" (Nancy Griffin, *Premiere*, June 1989).

Filmography as director: Escape to Nowhere (1960, short); Firelight (1963); Amblin' (1969, short); episode of Night Gallery (1969, tvm); Duel (1971, tvm); Something Evil (1972, tvm) also actor; Savage (1973, tvm); The Sugarland Express (1973); Jaws (1975); Close Encounters of the Third Kind (1977); 1941 (1979); Raiders of the Lost Ark (1981); E.T. The Extra-Terrestrial (1982); Twilight Zone—The Movie (1983) also ep; Indiana Jones and the Temple of Doom (1984); The Color Purple (1985); Empire of the Sun (1987); Indiana Jones and the Last Crusade (1989); Always (1989); Hook (1991); Jurassic Park (1993); Schindler's List (1993).

Filmography as executive producer: I Wanna Hold Your Hand (1978); Used Cars (1980); Continental Divide (1981); Poltergeist (1982) producer; Gremlins (1984); Back to the Future (1985); The Goonies (1985) also story; Young Sherlock Holmes (1985); "Amazing Stories" (1985–1987, tvs) also creator, director; An American Tail (1986); The Money Pit (1986); *batteries not included (1987); Innerspace (1987); The Land before Time (1988); Who Framed Roger Rabbit (1988); Back to the Future II (1989); Dad (1989); Tummy Trouble (1989, short); "Steven Spielberg Presents Tiny Toon Adventures" (1990–1995, tvs); Arachnophobia (1990); Back to the Future III (1990); Gremlins 2: The New Batch (1990); Joe versus the Volcano (1990); Rollercoaster Rabbit (1990, short); An American Tail: Fievel Goes West (1991) producer; "The Lucky Duck Show" (1992, tvs); "Family Dog" (1993, tvs); "Steven Spielberg Presents Animaniacs" (1993– , tvs); "seaQuest DSV/seaQuest 2032" (1993–1996, tvs); Trail Mix-Up (1993, short); A Far Off Place (1993); We're Back! A Dinosaur's Story (1993); Class of '61 (1993, tvm); I'm Mad (1994, short); "Steven Spielberg Presents Freakazoid!" (1995– , tvs); "Steven Spielberg Presents Pinky and the Brain" (1995– , tvs); Balto (1995); Casper (1995).

Filmography as Amblin Entertainment: Fandango (1985); Harry and the Hendersons (1987); Akira Kurosawa's Dreams (1990); Cape Fear (1991); "Harry and the Hendersons" (1991–1993, tvs); "Back to the Future" (1991–1993, tvs); "The Young Indiana Jones Chronicles" (1992–1993, tvs); "Fievel's American Tails" (1992–1993, tvs); Noises Off (1992); A Brief History of Time (1992); A Dangerous Woman (1993); "Exosquad" (1993–1995, tvs); The Flintstones (1994); Little Giants (1994); "ER" (1994– , tvs); "Earth 2" (1994–1995, tvs); The Bridges of Madison County (1995);

How to Make an American Quilt (1995); To Wong Foo, Thanks for Everything, Julie Newmar (1995); ''Fudge'' (1995, tvs).

Honors: Academy Awards for Best Picture and Director (*Schindler's List*); Academy Award nominations for Best Director (*Close Encounters of the Third Kind, Raiders of the Lost Ark, E.T. The Extra-Terrestrial, The Color Purple*); Los Angeles Film Critics Awards for Best Director (*E.T. The Extra-Terrestrial*) and Picture (*Schindler's List*); New York Film Critics Circle Awards for Best Picture (*Schindler's List*); DGA Awards (*The Color Purple, Schindler's List*); AFI Lifetime Achievement Award (1995); Venice Film Festival Golden Lion Career Achievement Award (1993); Recipient of the 1986 Irving G. Thalberg Award.

Selected Bibliography

Kolker, Robert Phillip. *A Cinema of Loneliness: Penn, Kubrick, Scorsese, Spielberg, Altman.* New York: Oxford University Press, 1988.
Mott, Donald R., and Cheryl M. Saunders. *Steven Spielberg.* Boston: Twayne, 1986.
Taylor, Philip M. *Steven Spielberg: The Man, His Movies, and Their Meaning.* New York: Continuum, 1992.

STALLONE, SYLVESTER. Born July 6, 1946, in New York City; actor, director, screenwriter. Brother Frank is an actor. Bulky, muscular action film megastar whose career has mirrored the cinderella success of boxer Rocky Balboa, the character he wrote and played in the 1976 hit *Rocky*. Growing up in such working-class places as New York's Hell's Kitchen and Philadelphia, Stallone began to pull himself up by earning an athletic scholarship to the American University in Switzerland. Upon his return to the States he took an interest in acting, landing a part in an off-Broadway nude play (*Score*), a porn film (later titled *The Italian Stallion* to capitalize on his post-Rocky fame), and a bit part in Woody Allen's *Bananas*. After a few more film roles, ambition took hold, and Stallone began to write scripts for himself to star in. With the success of *Rocky*, his career skyrocketed, and he appeared in a string of gritty, working-class dramas that were of the same milieu as Rocky Balboa's Philly—*F.I.S.T.*, as the Jimmy Hoffa-like union boss with gray in his temples; his directing debut, *Paradise Alley*, as a Hell's Kitchen street hustler; and *Nighthawks*, as a New York City cop. Stallone continued to write, star in, and occasionally direct his *Rocky* sequels and also began another series franchise with his right-wing John Rambo character. Although he was at the top of the action heap for a few years in the early to mid-1980s, Stallone was soon eclipsed by Arnold Schwarzenegger and Bruce Willis, both of whom had molded their careers to include comedies— a genre that has eluded Stallone, as confirmed by *Oscar* and *Stop! Or My Mom Will Shoot*. By the 1990s Stallone had essentially slipped into self-parody with such films as *The Specialist* and *Judge Dredd*, which paled in comparison to such competing action hits as *Speed, Terminator 2*, or *True Lies*. Although he received some success with *Demolition Man* and *Cliffhanger*, he announced in late 1995 a return to the edgier, working-class, dramatic films that had made him a star.

Filmography: Bananas (1971); The Italian Stallion (1971); Rebel (1974); The Lords of Flatbush (1974); Capone (1975); Death Race 2000 (1975); The Prisoner of Second Avenue (1975); Farewell, My Lovely (1975); No Place to Hide (1975); Cannonball (1976); Rocky (1976) also screenplay; F.I.S.T. (1978) also screenplay; Nighthawks (1981); Victory (1981); First Blood (1982) also screenplay; Rhinestone (1984) also screenplay; Rambo: First Blood Part II (1985) also screenplay; Cobra (1986) also screenplay; Over the Top (1987) also screenplay; Rambo III (1988) also screenplay; Lock Up (1989); Tango and Cash (1989); Rocky V (1990) also screenplay; Oscar (1991); Stop! Or My Mom Will Shoot (1992); Cliffhanger (1993); Demolition Man (1993); The Specialist (1994); Dead Reckoning (1995); Judge Dredd (1995); Assassins (1995).

Filmography as director, actor, and writer: Paradise Alley (1978); Rocky II (1979); Rocky III (1982); Staying Alive (1983) director and screenplay only; Rocky IV (1985).

Honor: Academy Award nomination for Best Actor (*Rocky*).

STANTON, HARRY DEAN. Aka Dean Stanton. Born July 14, 1926, in West Irvine, Kentucky; actor. Sleepy-looking character actor whose versatility has brought him to the attention of maverick directors Sam Peckinpah, Monte Hellman, Francis Ford Coppola, Arthur Penn, John Huston, Wim Wenders, Martin Scorsese, David Lynch, Bob Rafelson, John Carpenter, Wayne Wang, and John Frankenheimer. Having first earned his reputation as a supporting player in such films as *Ride in the Whirlwind* and *Cool Hand Luke*, he continued to appear in quality films of the 1970s. He's especially impressive in *Straight Time* as the ex-con who feels trapped in his boring suburban existence with lawn furniture, a backyard barbecue, and kidney-shaped swimming pool. In 1984, Stanton found a whole new audience with the popularity of Alex Cox's cult hit *Repo Man* and Wim Wenders' *Paris, Texas*. In the latter he turns in what may be his greatest performance as the troubled wanderer Travis, a broken loner who delivers a shattering monologue to a former lover (Nastassja Kinski) through the eerily reflective glass of a strip club's two-way mirror. In addition to his acting, Stanton has a second career as a country/Tex-Mex singer, performing regularly in clubs throughout Los Angeles.

Filmography of key pre-1965 films: Pork Chop Hill (1959); The Adventures of Huckleberry Finn (1960); The Man from the Diner's Club (1963).

Filmography: The Hostage (1966); Ride in the Whirlwind (1966); Cool Hand Luke (1967); The Long Ride Home (1967); Day of the Evil Gun (1968); The Mini-Skirt Mob (1968); Rebel Rousers (1970); Cisco Pike (1971); Two-Lane Blacktop (1971); Count Your Bullets (1972); Face to the Wind (1972); Dillinger (1973); Pat Garrett and Billy the Kid (1973); Where the Lillies Bloom (1973); Cockfighter (1974); The Godfather, Part II (1974); Rafferty and the Gold Dust Twins (1974); Rancho Deluxe (1974); Zandy's Bride (1974); 92 in the Shade (1975); Farewell, My Lovely (1975); Win, Place or Steal (1975); The Missouri Breaks (1976); Renaldo and Clara (1977); Straight Time (1978); Alien (1979); The Black Marble (1979); La Mort en Direct (1979); The Rose (1979); Wise Blood (1979); Private Benjamin (1980); UFOria (1980); Escape from New York (1981); One from the Heart (1982); Young Doctors in Love (1982); Christine (1983); The Bear (1984); Paris, Texas (1984); Red Dawn (1984); Repo Man (1984); The Care

Bears Movie (1985); Fool for Love (1985); One Magic Christmas (1985); Pretty in Pink (1986); Slam Dance (1987); The Last Temptation of Christ (1988); Mr. North (1988); Stars and Bars (1988); Dream a Little Dream (1989); Twister (1989); The Fourth War (1990); Motion and Emotion (1990); Wild at Heart (1990); Man Trouble (1992); Twin Peaks: Fire Walk with Me (1992); "Tricks" episode of Hotel Room (1993, ctvm); Against the Wall (1994, ctvm).

STAR WARS (1977), sci-fi. Directed and written by George Lucas; produced by Gary Kurtz; photography by Gilbert Taylor; edited by Paul Hirsch, Marcia Lucas, Richard Chew; music by John Williams; released by 20th Century Fox; 121 miuntes. *Cast*: Mark Hamill, Carrie Fisher, Harrison Ford, Peter Cushing, Alec Guinness, Anthony Daniels, Kenny Baker, Peter Mayhew, David Prowse.

One of the handful of films in motion picture history that are directly responsible for a major change in the industry, George Lucas' *Star Wars* not only revolutionized the way films were seen, heard, and marketed but also instilled a new mythology into modern America. Set "a long time ago, in a galaxy far far away," the story centers on Luke Skywalker (Hamill), a young adventurer who, with his companions and the power of "the Force," embarks upon an adventure to battle the malevolent Darth Vader (who, in *The Empire Strikes Back*, is revealed to be Luke's father). En route to Luke's self-discovery, the audience is treated to a dazzling array of special effects, otherworldly creatures, and an inventive vision of the cosmos—all set to John Williams' heroic score. Having acknowledged debts to both *The Wizard of Oz* and author/mythographer Joseph Campbell, Lucas has tapped into the hopes, fears, and dreams of the human psyche. Other films have captivated us with their technology, but very few have struck the same chord as *Star Wars*. While America and the world were marveling at Luke, Hans Solo (Ford), Princess Leia (Fisher), Chewbacca (Mayhew), R2-D2 (Baker), and C-3P0 (Daniels), Hollywood was also feeling the aftershocks of Lucas' achievement. Every studio head was now expected to deliver a blockbuster and develop a franchise that, like *Star Wars*, would become a virtual money-printing machine. While *Jaws*, a character-driven drama/horror film, was the first blockbuster, *Star Wars* existed on a different level—Lucas had also altered our sensory expectations as viewers. The phenomenal success of *Star Wars* led to the development of state-of-the-art visual effects, at the forefront of which was Lucas' Lucasfilms and Industrial Light and Magic (ILM); it was also the first feature film to use Dolby Noise Reduction during production and the first to be released in Dolby optical stereo. Even more overwhelming is the effect that the film has had on marketing—from this film forward, every "event" film had to be part of an advertising blitz that would include action figures, lunch boxes, posters, games, videotapes, companion books, fast-food tie-ins, Halloween costumes, and every other conceivable moneymaking endeavor. With the success of this film, Lucas would retire from directing and instead turn his attention to executive-producing the two megahit sequels. Six more installments of the series are planned—one trilogy focusing on young Luke and the events leading up to *Star Wars* (set to go into production in 1997 with Lucas at the helm) and another trilogy taking place after Luke and his allies have defeated the Emperor in *The Return of the Jedi.* "Star Wars will do very nicely for those lucky enough to be children or unlucky enough never to have grown up" (John Simon, *New Republic*, June 20, 1977).

Sequels: Fisher, Ford, and Hamill returned for the two Lucas-produced sequels: *The Empire Strikes Back* (1980, Irvin Kershner) and *The Return of the Jedi* (1983, Richard Marquand).

Awards: Academy Awards for Best Art Direction, Score, Editing, Costumes, Visual Effects, and Special Achievement in Sound Effects; Academy Award nominations for Best Picture, Director, Supporting Actor (Guinness), Screenplay; Los Angeles Film Critics Awards for Best Picture and Score; included in the Library of Congress' National Film Registry (1989).

STING, THE (1973), comedy/drama. Directed by George Roy Hill; screenplay by Davis S. Ward; produced by Tony Bill, Julia Phillips, and Michael Phillips; executive-produced by Richard D. Zanuck and David Brown; photography by Robert Surtees; edited by William Reynolds; music by Scott Joplin, adapted and performed by Marvin Hamlisch; released by Universal; 129 minutes. *Cast*: Paul Newman, Robert Redford, Robert Shaw, Charles Durning, Ray Walston, Eileen Brennan, Harold Gould, John Heffernan, Dana Elcar, Jack Kehoe, Arliss Howard, Sally Kirkland, John Quade.

A deliriously entertaining and nostalgic look back at the golden age of gangster movies that reunites the team that took a similar look at westerns—director Hill and box office superstars Newman and Redford. With Marvin Hamlisch's versions of Scott Joplin's rags playing underneath, the story follows a master con man and a charming grifter who manage to outsmart one of Chicago's most influential gangsters in an elaborately planned sting. It's filled from top to bottom with effective supporting roles, especially Robert Shaw as the gangster who is set up for a big fall—the horrified look on his face when he learns that he should have bet his fortune to "place" instead of "win" is reason enough to see the movie.

Sequel: *The Sting II* (1983, Jeremy Paul Kagan).

Awards: Academy Awards for Best Picture, Director, Screenplay, Art Direction, Editing, Musical Adaptation, Costume Design; Academy Award nominations for Best Actor, Cinematography, Sound; DGA Award.

STOCKWELL, DEAN. Born March 5, 1936, in North Hollywood, California; actor. Former child star under contract to MGM who is best remembered as the lead in Joseph Losey's *The Boy with Green Hair* before taking a leave from acting in the 1960s. He returned in a handful of independently produced 1970s films, before his career was revitalized with a lead role in Wim Wenders' *Paris, Texas.* Other choice parts followed—the edgy and urbane Ben in David Lynch's *Blue Velvet*, mobster Tony the Tiger in Jonathan Demme's *Married to the Mob*, and a cameo as Howard Hughes in Francis Ford Coppola's *Tucker: The Man and His Dream*. In the 1990s he found fame on the small screen as the cigar-chomping costar of the series "Quantum Leap." Peter Richards in *Film Comment* (September–October 1993) describes his incarnation as Howard Hughes: "Never raising his voice, never altering a cold stare that avoids becoming meaningful eye-contact, Stockwell makes the simplest of action—e.g., the shelling of an occasional peanut—seem pregnant with unspoken menace and inexplicable private meaning."

Filmography of key pre-1965 films: Anchors Aweigh (1945); Gentleman's Agreement (1947); The Boy with Green Hair (1948); The Secret Garden (1959); Kim (1950); Compulsion (1959); Long Day's Journey into Night (1962).

Filmography since 1965: Rapture (1965); Psych-Out (1968); The Dunwich Horror (1970); The Last Movie (1971); The Loners (1971); Werewolf of Washington (1973); Win, Place or Steal (1975); Tracks (1976); She Came to the Valley (1979); Alsino and the Condor (1982); Human Highway (1982) also director, screenplay; Wrong Is Right (1982); Sweet Scene of Death (1983); Paris, Texas (1984); Dune (1985); The Legend of Billie Jean (1985); To Kill a Stranger (1985); To Live and Die in L.A. (1985); Blue Velvet (1986); Bonzai Runner (1987); Beverly Hills Cop II (1987); Gardens of Stone (1987); The Time Guardian (1987); The Blue Iguana (1988); Buying Time (1988); The Long Haul (1988); Married to the Mob (1988); Palais Royale (1988); Tucker: The Man and His Dream (1988); Limit Up (1989); Stickfighter (1989); "Quantum Leap" (1989–1993, tvs); Backtrack (1990); Sandio (1990); Chasers (1994); Steven King's "The Langoliers" (1995, tvms).

Honors: Academy Award nomination for Best Supporting Actor (*Married to the Mob*); New York Film Critics Circle Awards for Best Supporting Actor (*Married to the Mob*, *Tucker: The Man and His Dream*); Cannes Film Festival Awards for Best Actor (*Compulsion*, *Long Day's Journey into Night*).

STOLTZ, ERIC. Born September 21, 1961, in Whittier, California; actor. Thin, redhaired young lead who first came to prominence in *Mask* as the spirited, but horribly disfigured, teenager Rocky Dennis. Over the next few years, he landed lead roles in such dissimilar films as the medieval epic *Lionheart* (playing a young knight), the John Hughes-produced comedy *Some Kind of Wonderful*, and Dusan Makavejev's Yugoslavian political satire *Manifesto*. By the 1990s, he had become the go-to actor for Los Angeles independent filmmakers because of his ability to accurately mirror the smart, witty, cynical, and sensitive young American male. Among his best performances is his emotionally penetrating and surprisingly funny portrayal of a paraplegic writer in *The Waterdance*.

Filmography: Fast Times at Ridgemont High (1982); Running Hot (1984); Surf II (1984); The Wild Life (1984); Code Name: Emerald (1985); Mask (1985); The New Kids (1985); Lionheart (1987/released in 1990); Sister, Sister (1987); Some Kind of Wonderful (1987); Haunted Summer (1988); Manifesto (1988); The Fly II (1989); Say Anything (1989); Memphis Belle (1990); Singles (1991); A Woman at War (1991); The Waterdance (1992); Foreign Affairs (1993, ctvm); Bodies, Rest and Motion (1993); The Heart of Justice (1993, ctvm); Roommates (1994, tvm); Pulp Fiction (1994); Sleep with

Me (1994) also producer; Killing Zoe (1994); Little Women (1994); Naked in New York (1994); Rob Roy (1995); Kicking and Screaming (1995); Fluke (1995); God's Army (1995).

STONE, OLIVER. Born November 15, 1946, in New York City; director, screenwriter, producer. Hollywood's only political filmmaker, Oliver Stone is a true believer who fights for the truth (or his version of it) with a sense of passion that is not only rare in film but also rare in life. Achieving success as a screenwriter with the Oscar-winning script for *Midnight Express*, which exposed the savagery of the Turkish penal system, Stone later attracted attention with the script for *Scarface*, Brian De Palma's cartoonish update of Howard Hawks' 1932 classic. Although he had previously directed two films (*Street Scenes 1970* and the silly horror/thriller *The Hand*), his directing career did not begin in earnest until the 1986 release of *Salvador* and *Platoon*, both bringing him Oscar nominations for Best Screenplay and the latter winning the statuette for Direction. Two of his finest films, they both examine America's involvement in foreign internal conflicts—the Reagan government's support of right-wing death squads in Central America and the Johnson administration's willingness to sacrifice American boys for the sake of abating the spread of communism in Southeast Asia. His subsequent films have become increasingly experimental media extravaganzas that can be divided into "historical revisionism" (*Born on the Fourth of July, JFK, The Doors, Heaven and Earth, Nixon*) and "current events" (*Talk Radio, Wall Street, Natural Born Killers*)—all of which detail the individual's Socratic attempt to "know thyself." Stone's position as America's watchdog for historic truth peaked with the release of his *JFK*. A controversial mélange of fact and fiction (Stone's romantic side frequently leads to invention) surrounding the assassination of President Kennedy, the film actually led to the release of a massive amount of classified government information. While digging into the past for dramatic content, Stone has been pushing cinematic language forward with a dynamism unseen since Godard and Resnais—deconstructing his narratives with multiple points of view and nonlinear editing and experimenting with cinematographer Bob Richardson in multiple formats and media (35mm, 16mm, 8mm, and videotape; black-and-white, color, and monochrome). Throughout the 1990s, Stone has become increasingly active as a producer with his two production companies, Ixtlan and Illusion.

Filmography as director and writer: Street Scenes 1970 (1970), director, cinematography; Last Year in Vietnam (1970, short); Seizure (1974) also editor; The Hand (1981) also actor; Salvador (1986); Platoon (1986); Wall Street (1987) also actor; Talk Radio (1988); The Doors (1991); Born on the Fourth of July (1989); JFK (1991) also actor; Heaven and Earth (1993); Natural Born Killers (1994); Nixon (1995).

Additional credits: Sugar Cookies (1973) associate producer; Blue Steel (1990) producer; Reversal of Fortune (1990); producer; Iron Maze (1991) ep; South Central (1992) ep; Zebrahead (1992) ep; From Hollywood to Hanoi (1992, documentary) ep; Dave (1993) actor; Wild Palms (1993, tvms) ep; The Joy Luck Club (1993) ep; The New Age (1994) ep; Killer (1995) ep; Indictment: The McMartin Trial (1995, ctvm) ep.

Honors: Academy Award for Best Director (*Platoon*); Academy Award nominations for Best Original Screenplay (*Platoon, Salvador*), Picture (*JFK*), Director (*JFK*), Adapted Screenplay (*JFK*); DGA Awards (*Platoon, Born on the Fourth of July*); WGA Awards (*Midnight Express*) and Career Achievement Award (1993); Berlin Film Festival Award for Best Director (*Platoon*); Venice Film Festival Special Jury Prize (*Natural Born Killers*); Independent Spirit Awards for Best Director and Screenplay (*Platoon*); Emmy Award (*Indictment: The McMartin Trial*).

Selected bibliography

Kagan, Norman. *The Cinema of Oliver Stone*. New York: Continuum, 1995.
Mackey-Kallis, Susan. *Oliver Stone's America*. Boulder, CO: Westview, 1996.
Riordan, James. *Stone: The Controversies, Excesses, and Exploits of a Radical Filmmaker*. New York: Hyperion, 1995.

STONE, SHARON. Born March 10, 1958, in Meadville, Pennsylvania; actor. Sexy leading lady who is one of the very few actors of her generation who can truly wear the label "movie star," she entered the movies puckering up in a bit part in Woody Allen's *Stardust Memories*. A few years later the curvaceous Stone landed the lead in the campy Indiana Jones knockoffs *King Solomon's Mines* and *Allan Quatermain and the Lost City of Gold*. But she really grabbed America's fancy in 1992, when, as the ice pick-wielding blond, she spread her legs during the interrogation scene in *Basic Instinct*. Overnight, Stone became a darling of the tabloid press, which found much to report (and fabricate) in her colorful movie star life. She tried to recapture that film's success by once again disrobing in the sleazy and trite thriller *Sliver*. Apparently tiring of spinning the box office turnstiles whenever she flashes her breasts, she has since sought roles that have countered that image—a dramatic, but still alluring, turn in the failed *Intersection*, a fun, six-gun-twirling gunslinger in the Sam Raimi western *The Quick and the Dead*, and a raw, no-holds-barred performance with a capital *P* in Martin Scorsese's *Casino*. With this Oscar-nominated role she finally proved to be more than just a pretty face, positioning herself as her generation's Faye Dunaway.

Filmography: Stardust Memories (1980); Deadly Blessings (1981); Bolero (1981); Irreconcilable Differences (1984); King Solomon's Mines (1985); Allan Quatermain and the Lost City of Gold (1987); Cold Steel (1987); Police Academy 4: Citizens on Patrol (1987); Above the Law (1988); Action Jackson (1988); Tears in the Rain (1988); Beyond the Stars (1989); Blood and Sand (1989); Total Recall (1990); He Said, She Said (1991); Scissors (1991); Year of the Gun (1991); Basic Instinct (1992); Last Action Hero (1993); Sliver (1993); Intersection (1994); The Specialist (1994); The Quick and the Dead (1995); Casino (1995).

Honor: Academy Award nomination for Best Actress (*Casino*).

STRAIGHT TIME (1978), crime drama. Directed by Ulu Grosbard; screenplay by Alvin Sargent, Edward Bunker, and Jeffrey Boam (from the novel by Bunker); photographed by Owen Roizman; edited by Sam O'Steen and Randy Roberts; music by David Shire; released by Warner Bros.; 114 minutes. *Cast*: Dustin Hoffman, Theresa Russell, Harry Dean Stanton, Gary Busey, M. Emmet Walsh, Kathy Bates.

An engrossing, unromantic account of criminal life starring Dustin Hoffman as Max Dembo, an forthright ex-con who tries to go straight after spending six months in the lockup for armed robbery. On the outside, however, he's faced with one obstacle after another by people such as his sleazy parole officer (Walsh), who seems determined to put him back behind bars. Despite his desire for a "normal" life with a sexy, but naive, employment agency worker (Russell), Max cannot escape the pull; he gathers up some old friends (Busey and Stanton) and returns to his life of crime. Developed by Hoffman (who purchased the book rights in 1972), *Straight Time* was originally going to be the actor's directorial debut, but, when the chore of acting and directing proved too strenuous, he brought in Grosbard. Still, it's Hoffman's film all the way. His nuanced performance is flawless and gives us the impression that we are observing an actual criminal in all facets of his life—his personal struggle to go straight, his frustration with his parole officer (his humorous retaliation against Walsh is priceless), his desire to love, and his cold brutality. In short, we see him as a human being—a true testament to Hoffman's unsurpassed abilities as an actor. The climactic Beverly Hills jewelry store robbery, with Max calmly and methodically taking a hammer to the display cases, is a classic, beat-the-clock nail-biter.

STRANGER THAN PARADISE (1984), comedy. Written, directed, and co-edited by Jim Jarmusch; produced by Sara Driver; photographed by Tom DiCillo; edited with Melody London; music by John Lurie, song "I Put a Spell on You" performed by Screamin' Jay Hawkins; released by the Samuel Goldwyn Company; 95 minutes. *Cast*: John Lurie, Richard Edson, Eszter Balint, Cecillia Stark.

A bleak, gray vision of industrialized America, this minimalist treasure from Jim Jarmusch tells the story of three characters—slick New Yorker Willie (Lurie), his hapless pal Eddie (Edson), and Willie's cousin Eva (Balint),who has come from Hungary for a visit. As they amble through life without an ounce of ambition, travel from New York to Cleveland to Miami, and bet some money on horse races, and lose some money on dog races, the three of them become increasingly dependent on one another despite their outward self-sufficiency. While nothing much happens with the plot, the uniqueness comes from a filmmaking style that establishes new rules of structure; instead of the standard use of scenes comprising various shots, Jarmusch creates a tableau vivant in which every scene is filmed in a single shot, and each scene is then separated from the others by an interval of black frames. Like so many innovations in cinematic language, it is incredibly simple and born entirely of utilitarian necessity. But style alone does not a movie make. *Stranger than Paradise* has other charms such as a wildly funny dry sense of humor (especially Willie's explanation of a TV dinner to the skeptical Eva), a great cast of unknowns who bring life to the characters, a radical sense of composition, and a very hip sound track that includes Screamin' Jay Hawkins' ''I Put a Spell on You.'' Harlan Jacobson aptly describes the film in ''Honeymooner'' terms as ''life lived by Ralph Kramden, Ed Norton, and Alice transplanted to the Eighties'' (*Film Comment*, February 1986).

Award: Cannes Film Festival Camera d'Or.

STREEP, MERYL. Born Mary Louise Streep, June 22, 1949, in Summit, New Jersey; actor. Majoring in drama at Vassar, studying costume design and playwriting at Dartmouth, and doing graduate work at the Yale School of Drama, Streep had her first taste of major success with her Tony nomination for the Broadway production of Tennessee Williams' *27 Wagons Full of Cotton*. Since then, she has become the most-heralded actor of her generation, earning a staggering ten nominations since first appearing on-screen in *Julia* (1977). Since then she has become the very definition of acting, ranging from radiant naturalism (*The Deer Hunter*, *Kramer vs. Kramer*, *Falling in Love*), to period work (*French Lieutenant's Woman*, *Sophie's Choice*, *Ironweed*), to physical comedy (*She-Devil*, *Death Becomes Her*). After a succession of sterling performances, she entered what now seems like a transition phase during which, with the exception of the abysmal *The House of the Spirits*, she appeared exclusively in comedies and the accomplished, if minor, adventure film *River Wild*. The year 1995 saw a return to the caliber of dramatic acting to which audiences had become accustomed—the beautifully nuanced Francesca of *The Bridges of Madison County*, a role that pays tribute to Anna Magnani and flawlessly captures the quality and spirit of an Italian woman living in America's heartland. Streep's climactic scene as she sits in the cab of her husband's pickup weighing her decision to join her lover or stay with her family is among her finest moments.

Filmography: Julia (1977); The Deer Hunter (1978); Holocaust (1978, tvms); Kramer vs. Kramer (1979); Manhattan (1979); The Seduction of Joe Tynan (1979); The French Lieutenant's Woman (1981); Sophie's Choice (1982); Still of the Night (1982); Silkwood (1983); Falling in Love (1984); Out of Africa (1985); Plenty (1985); Heartburn (1986); Ironweed (1987); A Cry in the Dark (1988); She-Devil (1989); Postcards from the Edge (1990); Defending Your Life (1991); Death Becomes Her (1992); The House of the Spirits (1994); River Wild (1994); The Bridges of Madison County (1995).

Honors: Academy Awards for Best Actress (*Sophie's Choice*) and Supporting Actress (*Kramer vs. Kramer*); Academy Award nominations for Actress (*The French Lieutenant's Woman, Silkwood, Out of Africa, Ironweed, A Cry in the Dark, Postcards from the Edge, The Bridges of Madison County*) and Supporting Actress (*The Deer Hunter*); Los Angeles Film Critics Awards for Best Actress (*The French Lieutenant's Woman, Sophie's Choice, Out of Africa*) and Supporting Actress (*The Seduction of Joe Tynan, Kramer vs. Kramer, Manhattan*); New York Film Critics Circle Awards for Best Actress (*A Cry in the Dark, Sophie's Choice*) and Supporting Actress (*The Seduction of Joe Tynan, Kramer vs. Kramer*); Cannes Film Festival Award for Best Actress (*A Cry in the Dark*); Emmy Award (*Holocaust*).

Selected bibliography

Pfaff, Eugene E., Jr., and Mark K. Emerson. *Meryl Streep: A Critical Biography*. Jefferson, NC: McFarland Press, 1987.

STREISAND, BARBRA. Born April 24, 1942, in Brooklyn; actor, director, producer, singer. Megastar who has conquered Broadway, Hollywood, television, and radio and has some sixty gold and platinum records to match her two Oscars. With her commanding stage presence she wowed audiences with performances in the Broadway shows *I Can Get It for You Wholesale* (1962) and *Funny Girl* (1964) and had a string of hit albums and television specials before debuting on the big screen in *Funny Girl*. She then became the most popular leading lady of the 1970s, costarring with Ryan O'Neal in the screwball comedy *What's Up, Doc?*, Robert Redford in the glossy romance *The Way We Were*, and Kris Kristofferson in the glitzy remake of *A Star Is Born*. Her directorial debut, *Yentl*, which she also produced, wrote, starred in, and performed the music for, was released to the wild enthusiasm of Streisand fans but otherwise received a generally lukewarm critical and commercial response. Her follow-up film, *The Prince of Tides*, met with a similar reaction. A notorious perfectionist, she and her Barwood films have long been preparing two projects for her to direct—*The Mirror Has Two Faces* (released in 1996) and *The Normal Heart*, an adaptation of AIDS activist Larry Kramer's novel that, after ten years of development, was finally shelved in 1995. An advocate of progressive causes and a staunch supporter of the Democratic Party, one of her high points came as a performer at the Clinton inaugural gala.

Filmography: Funny Girl (1968); Hello, Dolly! (1969); On a Clear Day You Can See Forever (1970); The Owl and the Pussycat (1970); Up the Sandbox (1972); What's Up, Doc? (1972); The Way We Were (1973); For Pete's Sake (1974); Funny Lady (1975); A Star Is Born (1976) also ep, music; The Main Event (1979) also producer; All Night Long (1981); Yentl (1983) also producer, director, screenplay; Nuts (1987) also producer, music; The Prince of Tides (1991) also producer; Serving in Silence: The Margarethe Cammermeyer Story (1995, tvm) ep only.

Honors: Academy Awards for Best Actress (*Funny Girl*) and Song ("Evergreen" from *A Star Is Born*); Academy Award nominations for Best Actress (*The Way We Were*) and Best Picture (*The Prince of Tides*); Grammy Awards ("The Barbra Streisand Album" 1963, "The Broadway Album" 1987) and the Grammy Legend Award (1992); Tony Award for Best Actress of the Decade (1970).

Selected bibliography

Spada, James. *Barbra: The First Decade, the Films and Career of Barbra Streisand*. New York: Citadel, 1976.

Swenson, Karen. *Barbra: The Second Decade, the Films and Career of Barbra Streisand*. New York: Citadel, 1986.

STUNT MAN, THE (1980), comedy/drama. Directed, cowritten, and produced by Richard Rush; screenplay with Lawrence B. Marcus (from the novel by Paul

Brodeur); photographed by Mario Tosi; edited by Jack Hofstra and Caroline Ferriol; music by Dominic Frontiere; released by 20th Century Fox; 129 minutes. *Cast*: Peter O'Toole, Steve Railsback, Barbara Hershey, Allen Goorwitz, Alex Rocco, Sharon Ferrell, Chuck Bail.

A madcap film about filmmaking, this deliriously offbeat tale gives one of the most insightful (and least authentic) looks inside the workings of the Hollywood machine. The quixotic Eli Cross (O'Toole), a manipulative, but endearing, director, is in the midst of an antiwar epic when a stunt driver is killed during filming. Stumbling into this scene as if he's a character from another movie (a fugitive-on-the-lam picture perhaps?) is Cameron (Railsback), a Vietnam veteran fleeing the local troopers. Seizing the opportunity, Cross hires Cameron to impersonate the dead stuntman in order to shake the local sheriff (Rocco); Cameron is then dubbed Lucky, a moniker that proves prophetic. Eli Cross finds the essence of his movie in Lucky's paranoid survivor quality, and sexy star Nina Franklin (Hershey) falls in love with him. Trapped somewhere between reality and fantasy, Lucky is a character who is guided by the powerful hand of Eli Cross, a hand that swoops down from the clouds (actually a camera crane) and toys with the rookie stuntman's existence. Lucky is more than a rookie stuntman; he's a rookie lover, a rookie human being—a man given a free ball in the pinball machine, and finally, with Nina, the script is written in his favor. After spending years trying to get this film made and more years trying to get Fox to release it, Rush (primarily a director of biker films before this) did not direct another film again until the 1994 Bruce Willis box office bomb *Color of Night*.

Awards: Academy Award nominations for Best Director, Actor (O'Toole), Adapted Screenplay.

SUPER FLY (1972), crime drama. Directed by Gordon Parks, Jr.; screenplay by Phillip Fenty; produced by Sig Shore; photographed by James Signorelli; edited by Bob Brady; music and song "Super Fly" by Curtis Mayfield; released by Warner Bros.; 96 minutes. *Cast*: Ron O'Neal, Carl Lee, Sheila Frazier, Julius Harris, Charles MacGregor, the Curtis Mayfield Experience.

While its predecessor *Shaft* was essentially a detective film cast with black actors, *Super Fly* is less a genre film than it is a commentary on the urban black experience. Unlike the moral private eye John Shaft, Ron O'Neal's Priest, the hipster pimp fashion plate with triangular sideburns and chrome-laden Cadillac, is an amoral drug pusher who understands his dead-end position as a black man in a white world. Believing that the drug trade is the only business "the man" will let him control, Priest sees himself as a free man who has busted the shackles of history. Along with his partner, Eddie (Lee), he plots one final score, which will net them $1 million, giving Priest the freedom to start life anew with his girlfriend (Frazier). The supplier, however, turns out to be a corrupt police official who leans on Priest to stay on as a pusher—an offer that goes against all of Priest's beliefs. Despite its reputation as a "blaxploitation" hit, *Super Fly* has a noticeable lack of sex and violence; the film is not without a bit of both, but the focus here is the cultural enslavement of a black America in which everything, even the drug trade, is controlled by the white man. In a brilliantly articulated speech by Eddie, Priest clearly sees what makes him different— Eddie ultimately doesn't care who owns him or what his future holds just as long as he can make millions and live like a "black prince," and that's just not enough for Priest.

Sequel: Ron O'Neal directed and reprised his role as Priest in *Super Fly T.N.T.* (1973), from a screenplay by Alex Haley.

SUPERMAN (1978), adventure/fantasy. Directed by Richard Donner; screenplay by Mario Puzo, Robert Benton, David Newman, and Leslie Newman; produced by Pierre Spengler; photographed by Geoffrey Unsworth; edited by Stuart Baird; music by John Williams; released by Warner Bros.; 143 minutes. *Cast*: Marlon Brando, Christopher Reeve, Gene Hackman, Ned Beatty, Jackie Cooper, Margot Kidder, Glenn Ford, Trevor Howard, Valerie Perrine, Terence Stamp.

The film that proved to Hollywood that there was money to be made with comic book adaptations, this DC Comics superhero tale was an event picture on a par with *Star Wars*—a marketing person's dream, a special effects extravaganza, and a surefire hit for Warner Brothers. Acting in his film debut, Christopher Reeve became an overnight sensation as the mythic Superman who saves the world while disguising his true identity as "mild-mannered reporter" Clark Kent from his pretty fellow reporter Lois Lane (Kidder). While it's far from a perfect film—it's way too long, the young Clark Kent prologue is tedious, and some of the effects are obviously miniatures—it does make you believe a man can fly, just as its ads promised. Ultimately, however, the film is carried by Reeve, who turns in a warm, funny, and believable performance. Marlon Brando, who earned a then-unbelievable sum of $3 million for two weeks' work, stars as Superman's father, Jor-El. Although Superman's DC Comics counterpart Batman has had a more celebrated and successful box office run in its films directed by Tim Burton and Joel Schumacher, *Superman* better retains the innocent charm of the comic book source material.

Sequels: *Superman II* (1980, Richard Lester); *Superman III* (1983, Lester); *Superman IV: The Quest for Peace* (1987, Sidney J. Furie) from a story cowritten by Christopher Reeve.

SUTHERLAND, DONALD. Born July 17, 1934, in St. John, New Brunswick, Canada; actor. Son Keifer is an actor (*Stand by Me, Flatliners*). Lanky character actor turned leading man who appeared on the British stage and in a handful of low-budget horror movies before winning over audiences as the goofy, deranged southerner Vernon Pinkley in *The Dirty Dozen*. He landed his first notable lead in 1970, when Robert Altman cast him as the irreverent General Hawkeye Pierce in *M*A*S*H*, his first of many challenging and risky pictures in the 1970s.

Among his finest hours of the next decade are his moody role as the detective in *Klute*, his tour de force in *Don't Look Now*, his title role in *Fellini's Casanova*, his portrayal of the fascist Attila in Bernardo Bertolucci's *1900* (his savage murder of a young boy is one of cinema's most horrific moments), his amusing turn in *National Lampoon's Animal House*, and his restrained, but powerful, role as the father in *Ordinary People*. His subsequent work, however, has been generally disappointing; despite some marvelous films (*Wolf at the Door* as artist Paul Gaugin, *A Dry, White Season*, *Six Degrees of Separation*, and HBO's *Citizen X*), he has too often chosen material that is far below his talents.

Filmography: Castle of the Living Dead (1964); Dr. Terror's House of Horrors (1964); The Bedford Incident (1965); Die! Die! My Darling!/Fanatic (1965); Promise Her Anything (1966); The Dirty Dozen (1967); Joanna (1968); Oedipus the King (1968); Sebastian (1968); Interlude (1968); The Split (1968); Act of the Heart (1970); Alex in Wonderland (1970); M*A*S*H (1970); Start the Revolution without Me (1970); Kelly's Heroes (1970); Johnny Got His Gun (1971); Klute (1971); Little Murders (1971); FTA/ Free the Army (1972) also coproducer, coscreenplay, codirector; Don't Look Now (1973); Lady Ice (1973); Steelyard Blues (1973) also ep; S*P*Y*S (1974); Alien Thunder/Dan Candy's Law (1975); End of the Game (1975); The Day of the Locust (1975); Fellini's Casanova (1976); The Eagle Has Landed (1976); 1900 (1976); Disappearance (1977); The Kentucky Fried Movie (1977); Les Liens de Sang/Blood Relatives (1977); Bethune (1977); Invasion of the Body Snatchers (1978); National Lampoon's Animal House (1978); Bear Island (1979); The Great Train Robbery (1979); A Man, a Woman and a Bank (1979); Murder by Decree (1979); North China Commune (1979); Nothing Personal (1979); Ordinary People (1980); Eye of the Needle (1981); Gas (1981); Threshold (1981); Max Dugan Returns (1982); A War Story (1982); Crackers (1984); Heaven Help Us (1985); Ordeal by Innocence (1985); Revolution (1985); The Wolf at the Door (1986); The Rosary Murders (1987); The Trouble with Spies (1987); Apprentice to Murder (1988); A Dry, White Season (1989); Lock Up (1989); Lost Angels (1989); Bethune: The Making of a Hero/Dr. Bethune (1990); Eminent Domain (1991); Backdraft (1991); JFK (1991); Buffy the Vampire Slayer (1992); The Railway Station Man (1992, tvm); Shadow of the Wolf (1993); Benefit of the Doubt (1993); Six Degrees of Separation (1993); The Puppet Masters (1994); Disclosure (1994); Citizen X (1995, ctvm); Outbreak (1995).

Honor: Emmy Award (*Citizen X*).

SWAYZE, PATRICK. Born August 18, 1954, in Houston, Texas; actor, dancer. Joffrey Ballet-trained dancer with all-American good looks, Swayze appeared in the Broadway production of *Grease* before landing a supporting role as the heavy in the forgettable *Skatetown, USA*. Fortunately, he was spotted by Francis Ford Coppola and made part of the excellent ensemble cast of *The Outsiders*. He became a full-fledged star with his role as the gyrating dance instructor in the independent hit *Dirty Dancing*, making him the object of desire for many a moviegoer. A string of justly neglected films was broken when he costarred with Demi Moore and Whoopi Goldberg in Garry Marshall's 1990 blockbuster *Ghost*. He then had a small measure of success with the action film *Point Break*, but again a few more years lapsed before his next hit—the 1995 drag queen comedy *To Wong Foo, Thanks for Everything, Julie Newmar*, which had audiences splitting their sides over the sight of three men (Swayze, Wesley Snipes, and John Leguizamo) in dresses.

Filmography: Skatetown, USA (1979); The Outsiders (1983); Uncommon Valor (1983); Grandview, U.S.A. (1984); Red Dawn (1984); North and South (1985, tvms); Youngblood (1986); Dirty Dancing (1987); Steel Dawn (1987); Tiger Warsaw (1988); Next of Kin (1989); Road House (1989); Ghost (1990); Point Break (1991); City of Joy (1992); Fatherhood (1993); Tall Tale (1995); Three Wishes (1995); To Wong Foo, Thanks for Everything, Julie Newmar (1995).

SWEET SWEETBACK'S BAAD ASSSSS SONG (1971), crime drama. Directed, written, produced, and edited by Melvin Van Peebles; photographed by Bob Maxwell; music by Van Peebles and Earth, Wind and Fire; released by Cinemation; 97 minutes. *Cast*: Melvin Van Peebles, Rhetta Hughes, Simon Chuckster, Hubert Scales, John Dullaghan, John Amos, Mario [Van] Peebles, Megan [Van] Peebles, the Black Community.

A shocking, provocative, and thoroughly original film that directs its uncompromising and unflinching vision primarily at black audiences, offering a picture of a society that systematically oppresses black men and women in America. Van Peebles stars as Sweetback, a man whose self-worth is inextricably bound to his sexual prowess and exhibitionism, as first witnessed by the bare-bottomed twelve-year-old Sweetback atop a wailing hooker. Later, as part of a deal with two white homicide detectives, the adult Sweetback agrees to pose as a suspect, but he cannot stand in silence as the cops apprehend and then mercilessly beat a black revolutionary. He pounds the two cops into unconsciousness and then becomes the subject of a massive manhunt—one in which Sweetback not only outruns and outsmarts his white pursuers but vows to return and exact revenge. Described by Van Peebles as ''a hymn from the mouths of reality,'' starring ''the Black Community,'' and dedicated to ''all the Brothers and Sisters who had enough of the Man,'' it is a film not of anger but of defiance, a wake-up call to an America that numbly accepts police violence against the black community. Filmed for only $500,000 ($50,000 coming from Bill Cosby) and grossing $14 million, the film betrays its low-budget roots with occasionally poor lighting and some stiff performances, but it is filled with inventive audio and visual manipulation—negative color images, split screens, optical effects, repeated dialogue, and echo effects. Its frank sex scenes warranted a self-imposed ''X'' rating and will likely offend some viewers, though rarely have sex scenes seemed so mechanical and empty. While the style of the film may seem wildly dated, the content has lost none of its potency in this age of Los Angeles Police Department beating victim Rodney King, New York Police Department chokehold victim Michael Stewart, and the allegations of racism surrounding the O. J. Simpson trial. ''*Sweet Sweetback's Baad Asssss Song* gave us the answers we needed'' (Spike Lee, *Five for Five*).

SWOON (1992), crime/drama. Directed, cowritten, and edited by Tom Kalin; screenplay with Hilton Als; produced by Christine Vachon; executive-produced by James Schamus and Lauren Zalaznick; photographed by Ellen Kuras (b&w); music by James Bennett; released by Fine Line Features; 90 minutes. *Cast*: Daniel Schlachet, Craig Chester, Ron Vawter.

As part of the New Queer Cinema movement of gay-themed films from openly gay filmmakers, *Swoon*, along with Todd Haynes' *Poison* (1991), Gregg Araki's *The Living End*, (1992) and Rose Troche's *Go Fish* (1994), examines sexual politics in an American culture that is overwhelmingly opposed to homosexuality. Here director Kalin uses the notorious 1924 kidnapping and murder case of fourteen-year-old Bobby Frank as a looking glass that shows us how little the country's view of homosexuals has changed. The heinous crime, already visited sexlessly in Richard Fleischer's *Compulsion* (1959) and Alfred Hitchcock's *Rope* (1948), is committed by two young lovers, both of them intelligent members of Chicago's Jewish elite—the heartless and domineering Richard "Dickie" Loeb (Schlachet) and his weak lover, Nathan "Babe" Leopold (Chester). Their planned "perfect" murder, however, is botched from the start, and they are soon on trial for their lives. The film's strength lies in the political and social relevance that director Kalin places on the trial—celebrated defense attorney Clarence Darrow saves the killers from the death penalty by entering a plea of insanity, but it's a plea demonstrated by Leopold and Loeb's homosexuality. A low-budget film, *Swoon* avoids the constraints of period production design through a novel stylistic approach—sets are minimal, costumes are eerily timeless, close-ups are favored, and a deeper level of interest is created by the anachronistic use of such modern devices as Touch-Tone telephones, a Walkman, and a television remote. While not without faults (the Sacher-Masoch "Venus in Furs" divas are too camp, and the formalism runs high), the film succeeds in provoking discussion, not about sexuality as a cause for antisocial behavior but about the various manifestations of obsessive dominance in relationships.

T

TARANTINO, QUENTIN. Born March 27, 1963, in Knoxville, Tennessee; director, screenwriter, actor. The only American filmmaker who has (so far) devoted himself exclusively to the nature of American violence as filtered through America's media. Essentially a film critic with a camera, Tarantino has positioned himself atop the growing pile of American independent filmmakers who have found success with audiences and critics alike. After spending many years working in a Los Angeles area video store, and even more years watching and assimilating movies and television into his bloodstream, Tarantino debuted most auspiciously with *Reservoir Dogs* in 1992. The smart dialogue, precision casting, and iconographic depictions of violence separated this film from the rest of the pack. Hungry for more Tarantino, Hollywood turned two of his scripts—*True Romance* and *Natural Born Killers* (which was drastically rewritten)—into high-profile films for which he received as much attention as their respective directors, Tony Scott and Oliver Stone. The release of *Pulp Fiction*, however, rocketed Tarantino into superstardom. After winning the Palme d'Or at Cannes, *Pulp Fiction* became a critical favorite (even earning the adoration of those same critics who dismissed *Reservoir Dogs* as too violent), found a wide audience, revitalized the career of 1970s star John Travolta, and redirected the career of 1980s star Bruce Willis. The question remains whether or not Tarantino (like Hawks, Kubrick, Godard, or anyone else he's been compared to) can find success outside this particular genre. As with Scorsese, the most unfortunate aspect of Tarantino's success is the plethora of talentless imitators who will follow. "Far from succumbing to easy cynicism, Tarantino achieves the remarkable feat of remaining a genre purist even as his films critique, embarrass, and crossbreed genre" (Gavin Smith, *Film Comment*, July–August 1994).

Filmography as director: Reservoir Dogs (1992) also actor; Pulp Fiction (1994) also actor; Four Rooms (1995) also actor; episode of ''ER'' (1995, tvs).

additional credits: episode of ''The Golden Girls'' (1988, tvs) actor; True Romance (1993) screenplay; Natural Born Killers (1994) screenplay; Sleep with Me (1994) actor; Someone to Love (1994) actor; Destiny Turns on the Radio (1995) actor; Desperado (1995) actor; Hands Up (1995) actor.

Honors: Academy Award for Best Screenplay (*Pulp Fiction*); Academy Award nomination for Best Director (*Pulp Fiction*); Los Angeles Film Critics Awards for Best Picture (*Pulp Fiction*), Director (*Pulp Fiction*), Screenplay (*Pulp Fiction*); New York Film Critics Circle Awards for Best Director and Screenplay (*Pulp Fiction*); Independent Spirit Award for Best Director (*Pulp Fiction*); Cannes Film Festival Palme d'Or (*Pulp Fiction*).

Selected bibliography

Bernard, Jami. *Quentin Tarantino: The Man and His Movies.* New York: Harper Perennial, 1996.

Clarkson, Wensley. *Quentin Tarantino: Shooting from the Hip.* New York: Overlook Press, 1995.

Dawson, Jeff. *Quentin Tarantino: The Cinema of Cool.* New York: Applause Theatre Books, 1995.

TARGETS (1968), crime drama. Directed, written, produced, and edited by Peter Bogdanovich (from a story by Bogdanovich and Polly Platt); executive-produced by Roger Corman; photographed by Laszlo Kovacs; music by Charles Greene and Brian Stone; released by Paramount; 90 minutes. *Cast*: Boris Karloff, Tim O'Kelly, Nancy Hsueh, Peter Bogdanovich, James Brown, Sandy Baron.

A complex crime drama that is essentially a modern-day horror film in which the monster is not a gruesome Hollywood creation but the all-American neighborhood kid. Contrasting Boris Karloff (using clips from Roger Corman's 1963 film *The Terror*) with fictional Charles Whitman-like psychopath Bobby Thompson (O'Kelly), director Bogdanovich tells the story of a young man who perches himself atop an oil storage tank and randomly shoots at passersby along an adjoining freeway. Both ''monsters'' converge at a drive-in movie theater during a festival of Karloff films when, from behind the screen, the homicidal Bobby again begins firing at cars only to become confused as he sees Karloff approaching him on screen *and* in person. Bogdanovich's debut feature shows early signs of the nostalgic fascination with Hollywood's past that he would later develop in *The Last Picture Show* and *Nickelodeon*. The message that today's killers are more ominous than the Universal Studios monsters is clear in Karloff's multilayered statement: ''The world belongs to the young. Make way for them. Let them have it. I am an anachronism.''

TAXI DRIVER (1976), crime drama. Directed by Martin Scorsese; screenplay by Paul Schrader; produced by Julia Phillips and Michael Phillips; photographed by Michael Chapman; edited by Marcia Lucas, Tom Rolf, and Melvin Shapiro; music by Bernard Herrmann; released by Columbia; 112 minutes. *Cast*: Robert De Niro, Cybill Shepherd, Jodie Foster, Harvey Keitel, Peter Boyle, Albert Brooks, Leonard Harris, Diahnne Abbott.

An enigmatic and vitriolic attack on the state of the world that is just as relevant in today's fed-up America as it was in the Nixon–Watergate–post-Vietnam era of the mid-1970s. Its exposure of the indefensible and irrational state of American politics focuses on Travis Bickle—a twisted New York City cabbie whose line that "one day a rain will come and wash the scum off the streets" takes on the meaning of a religious scourge. He draws on an inner strength that, after a failed assassination attempt on a political candidate, is redirected toward a vile pimp (Keitel), whom he holds responsible for corrupting a preteen runaway turned prostitute (Foster). The ensuing bloodbath brings the self-appointed executioner a perverse sort of redemption by turning him into a media hero. Modeled on John Wayne's antihero Ethan Edwards of *The Searchers*, Scorsese and writer Paul Schrader have essentially urbanized the troubled western hero who comes into town on horseback and cleans up with his six-shooter. There's a frightening element to this judge/jury/executioner whose unerring sense of righteousness is so wrong that it can only bring forth a society of fascism. Nonetheless, this film is as candid a look at the ugly underbelly of American society as you'll ever see. "Scorsese's verminous New York is a descendant of Baudelaire's "anthill" Paris, Eliot's "unreal" London, the nightmare Berlin of such German films as Fritz Lang's *M*. In this vision the great modern city is the crossroads where fenced-off forces break loose and collide" (Jack Kroll, *Newsweek*, March 1, 1976).

Awards: Academy Award nominations for Best Picture, Actor, Supporting Actress (Foster), Score; New York Film Critics Circle Award for Best Actor; Los Angeles Film Critics Award for Best Actor and Score; Cannes Film Festival Palme d'Or and International Grand Prize; included in the Library of Congress' National Film Registry (1994).

TAYLOR, LILI. Born 1967 in Glencoe, Illinois; actor. Immensely gifted and honest performer who has carved out a niche for herself as one of the most sought-after actors on the independent film scene. After a brief stint at Chicago's Goodman School of Drama and stage work with the Northlight Theater, she relocated to New York, where she eventually formed the theater company Machine Full. As the noncommittal bride-to-be of *Mystic Pizza* and the lovestruck, guitar-strumming songwriter of *Say Anything*, she attracted a great deal of attention, though her desire to play complex, well-written characters has translated into relatively few high-profile films. Her two lead roles for Nancy Savoca— River Phoenix's folkie date in *Dogfight* and Tracy Ullman's zealous daughter in *Household Saints*—are also her most rewarding and complete. She has since appeared in supporting roles for Robert Altman (*Short Cuts*, *Ready to Wear*) and Alan Rudolph (as Edna Ferber in *Mrs. Parker and the Vicious*

Circle) and as the lead in Abel Ferrara's gutsy, though not entirely satisfying, vampire tale *The Addiction*.

Filmography: Night of Courage (1987, tvm); She's Having a Baby (1988); Mystic Pizza (1988); Say Anything (1989); Born on the Fourth of July (1989); Sensibility and Sense (1990, tvm); Family of Spies (1990, tvms); Bright Angel (1990); Dogfight (1991); Arizona Dream (1992/released in United States in 1995); Watch It (1993); Household Saints (1993); Short Cuts (1993); Rudy (1993); Mrs. Parker and the Vicious Circle (1994); Ready to Wear (Prêt-à-Porter) (1994); Touch Base (1994, short); The Addiction (1995); Cold Fever (1995); "Strange Brew" episode of Four Rooms (1995).

Honor: Independent Spirit Award for Best Supporting Actress (*Household Saints*).

TERMINATOR, THE (1984), sci-fi/action. Directed and cowritten by James Cameron; screenplay with Gale Anne Hurd and William Wisher, Jr.; produced by Hurd; photographed by Adam Greenberg; edited by Mark Goldblatt; music by Brad Fiedel; released by Orion; 108 minutes. *Cast*: Arnold Schwarzenegger, Michael Biehn, Linda Hamilton, Paul Winfield, Lance Henriksen, Rick Rossovich, Bill Paxton, Franco Columbo.

With Arnold Schwarzenegger's portentous promise of "I'll be back," writer/director and special effects whiz James Cameron has created an exhilarating and intelligent sci-fi/action film that delivers on a purely visceral level but also offers a temporal puzzle that compels the viewer to examine and reexamine its postapocalyptic vision of the future. The plot begins as two men materialize in the Los Angeles night—one an advanced android known as a "terminator" (Schwarzenegger), the other a human being (Biehn). One of the Terminator's first tasks is to search the phone book for women named Sarah Connor; he finds three and coldly kills two. Before he offs the third (Hamilton), Biehn intervenes and explains to Sarah that he has come from the future to protect her from the Terminator, whose mission is to kill her and prevent the birth of the future's greatest rebel leader. What follows is an all-out roller-coaster ride of action, chase scenes, gun battles, and high-tech surprises that turned this $5 million wonder into a surprise hit. Underneath it all is a moral tale about the destructive potential of machinery, with Sarah Connor being the one who can give birth to a future of hope. Cameron, Schwarzenegger, and Hamilton reteamed in 1991 for *Terminator 2: Judgment Day*, a technically revolutionary film with computer "morphing" techniques designed by Cameron's Digital Domain but thematically a much weaker effort. While the original has a female character who found inner strength during battle with an unfeeling "man," the sequel gives us a more human, politically correct "T2" android (he's a hip *Harm*inator who now only wounds people) and a Sarah Connor who, with her sinewy physique and emotionless haze, has curiously become more robotic. "There's a little bit of the terminator in everybody. In our private fantasy world we'd all like to be able to walk in and shoot somebody we don't like, or to kick a door in instead of unlocking it; to be immune, and just to have our own way every minute. The terminator is the ultimate rude person'' (James Cameron interviewed by David Chute, *Film Comment*, February 1985).

Sequel: Cameron, Schwarzenegger, and Hamilton reteamed for *Terminator 2: Judgment Day* (1991).

TERMS OF ENDEARMENT (1983), comedy/drama. Directed, written, and produced by James L. Brooks (from the novel by Larry McMurtry); photographed by Andrzej Bartkowiak; edited by Richard Marks; music by Michael Gore; released by Paramount; 132 minutes. *Cast*: Shirley MacLaine, Debra Winger, Jack Nicholson, Jeff Daniels, John Lithgow, Danny DeVito, Lisa Hart Carroll, Huckleberry Fox, Troy Bishop.

Given the amount of cynicism that the last couple of decades have bred in America, it is no surprise that this film, despite its incredible success and its Best Picture Oscar, was met with such a wall of resistance. Like young Tommy, who stands at his mother's deathbed pretending to be emotionally unaffected by his impending loss, many viewers and critics attacked the film for "manipulating" audiences, only to know in their hearts that the emotions in Brooks' film rang true. Although a variety of themes and ideas is explored, the core idea is the relationship between a mother and daughter—the demanding and disapproving Aurora Greenaway (MacLaine) and the strong, but unambitious, Emma (Winger). In their orbit are Emma's floppy and adulterous college professor husband, Flap (Daniels), Aurora's astronaut neighbor-cum-lover Garrett Breedlove (Nicholson), and Emma and Flap's three children. As a decade or so passes, Emma and Flap leave hometown Houston for the Midwest, Aurora's lunch with the astronaut becomes a romance, Flap falls for one of his students, Emma brightens her days by having an affair with a gentle banker (Lithgow), and eventually their world caves in when Emma is fatally stricken with cancer. Beginning as a comedy and ending as a teary tragedy, the film attempts to mirror the narrative of life rather than that of film; Emma's cancer is introduced matter-of-factly about two-thirds into the film, and the gravity of her illness blindsides the audience. The key to it all is Brooks' masterful direction of actors—Winger, with her endearing horsey laugh, is astonishing as the simple Emma, and the plucky camaraderie between the Olympian performers Nicholson and MacLaine offers one surprise after another. While their characters may be exaggerations of reality (much like Brooks' television heroine Mary Tyler Moore), the emotions they express cannot be more true.

Awards: Academy Awards for Best Picture, Director, Adapted Screenplay, Actress (MacLaine), Supporting Actor (Nicholson); Academy Award nominations for Best Actress (Winger), Supporting Actor (Lithgow), Editing, Art Direction, Sound, Score; New York Film Critics Circle Awards for Best Picture, Director, Actress (MacLaine), Supporting Actor (Nicholson); DGA Award.

TEXAS CHAINSAW MASSACRE, THE (1974), horror. Directed, produced, and cowritten by Tobe Hooper; screenplay with Kim Henkel; photographed by Daniel Pearl; edited by Sallye Richardson and Larry Carroll; music by Hooper and Wayne Bell; released by Bryanston; 83 minutes. *Cast*: Marilyn Burns, Allen Danziger, Paul A. Partain, Gunner Hansen, John Dugan.

A disturbing nightmare of a film that succeeds because it takes the unimaginable and makes it real. Taboo images that were once hidden away in the dark recesses of some people's minds—chainsaw attacks or corpses hung from meat hooks—are now brought into focus for an uncomfortable eighty-three minutes. The sophomoric plot with its amateurish acting is almost incidental—a young woman (Burns) and her wheelchair-bound brother (Partain) travel with some friends to a desolate farmhouse and are terrorized by a demented family of former slaughterhouse workers, the most offensive of whom is the maniacal Leatherface (Hansen). Appealing to the public's fascination with the grisly details of the Manson murders or the gruesome specifics of killer/cannibals Ed Gein's and Jeffrey Dahmer's crimes, Hooper invites his audience to take a peek at the horrific world of Leatherface with his mask of rotting human flesh and furniture made of skin and bones. While it could all be easily dismissed as the product of Hooper's twisted imagination, the world of *The Texas Chainsaw Massacre* actually exists—and that's what makes this picture so effective; it alerts us to those repressed thoughts and images that we'd rather keep hidden away. ''One of the best examples of the 'horror of the family' subgenre, which takes as its subject the American family—traditionally a wholesome, positive force—and examines its dark side, the side that is claustrophobic, stifling, and incestuous'' (James J. Mulay, *The Horror Film*).

Sequels: *The Texas Chainsaw Massacre Part 2* (1986, Hooper);

Remake: *The Return of the Texas Chainsaw Massacre* (1995, Kim Henkel).

THELMA AND LOUISE (1991), drama. Directed and coproduced by Ridley Scott; screenplay by Callie Khouri; produced with Mimi Polk; photographed by Adrian Biddle; edited by Thom Noble; music by Hans Zimmer; released by MGM-Pathe; 128 minutes. *Cast*: Susan Sarandon, Geena Davis, Harvey Keitel, Michael Madsen, Christopher McDonald, Stephen Tobolowsky, Brad Pitt, Lucinda Jenney.

A forceful feminist tract that fits the mold of Hollywood entertainment, this female buddy film begins with a liberating vacation for friends Thelma (Davis) and Louise (Sarandon) and suddenly takes a dark twist when Louise kills a vile pig of a man who is attempting to rape Thelma. From there, it's a run to the Mexican border when Louise assumes, perhaps correctly, that no male authority figure will see their side of the story. Fueled by her newfound independence, Thelma is glad to finally be rid of her loveless and constricting husband (McDonald). She gleefully sucks in the fresh air of her new freedom by having great sex with a handsome drifter (Pitt), driving fast through open roads, and enthusiastically breaking the law. Only a Federal Bureau of Investigation man (Keitel) understands their plight, but even he is powerless against the patriarchal system that is coming down hard on the fugitives. Although the picture has its weaknesses (all the men, save Keitel, take condescending views of the women), it deservedly became a cultural phenomenon by doing something many Hollywood films had for years neglected to do—creating two strong women characters who refuse to play by society's male-imposed rules. What is unfortunate is that Thelma and Louise become empowered through gunplay, robbery, car chases, and explosions; in short, they become stronger women by acting like men. "[The filmmakers], without quite knowing what they were doing, sank a drill into what appeared to be familiar American soil and found that they had somehow tapped into a wild-rushing subterranean stream of inchoate rage and deranged violence" (Richard Schickel, *Time*, June 24, 1991).

Awards: Academy Award for Best Screenplay; Academy Award nominations for Best Actress (Davis, Sarandon), Director, Cinematography, Editing; WGA Award.

THEY SHOOT HORSES, DON'T THEY? (1969), drama. Directed and coproduced by Sydney Pollack; screenplay by James Poe and Robert E. Thompson (from the novel by Horace McCoy); produced with Irwin Winkler and Robert Chartoff; photographed by Philip H. Lathrop; edited by Frederic Steinkamp; music by John Green; released by ABC-Cinerama; 129 minutes. *Cast*: Jane Fonda, Michael Sarrazin, Susannah York, Gig Young, Red Buttons, Bonnie Bedelia, Bruce Dern, Michael Conrad, Al Lewis, Robert Fields, Severn Darden.

One of the most unrelentingly bleak commentaries on American life, this depression-era allegory based on the grim 1935 Horace McCoy novel tells the story of a group of 100 couples who battle mental and physical fatigue to win a dance marathon. Among the contestants with high hopes of collecting the $1,500 purse are the acerbic Gloria (Fonda) and her last-minute replacement partner, drifter Robert (Sarrazin); old navy salt and veteran marathoner Sailor (Buttons); Harlowesque starlet Alice (York); and pregnant farm girl Ruby (Bedelia) and her demanding, neglectful husband (Dern)—all of whom are verbally whipped into action by the yowsiring emcee Rocky (Young), whose chief concern is providing a show for his audience. By the finale, some of the marathoners have died, others have gone mad, and the despondent Gloria is, like an old mare, put out of her misery by Robert. After sixty-two days, a smattering of dancers remains on the floor, with Rocky cheering them on: "As the clock of fate ticks away, the dance of destiny continues, the marathon goes on . . . and on . . . and on. How long can they last?" In her follow-up to *Barbarella*, Fonda is simply spectacular as the disagreeable loner, turning in a performance that would change the way she was viewed as an actress. The most harrowing scenes in the film are the two grueling races in which the exhausted partners speed around a track for a ten-minute stretch to weed out the weak; this dance macabre takes an even more revolting turn when the determined Gloria drags the dead Sailor around the track for his final lap.

Awards: Academy Award for Best Supporting Actor (Young); Academy Award nominations for Best Director, Actress, Supporting Actress (York), Screenplay, Art Direction, Score, Costume Design; New York Film Critics Circle Award for Best Actress (Fonda).

THIEF (1981), crime drama. Directed and written by Michael Mann (from the book by Frank Hohimer); produced by Jerry Bruckheimer and Ronnie Caan; photographed by Donald Thorin; edited by Dov Hoenig; music by Tangerine Dream; released by United Artists; 122 minutes. *Cast*: James Caan, Tuesday Weld, Willie Nelson, James Belushi, Robert Prosky, Tom Signorelli, Dennis Farina, William Petersen.

The model for Michael Mann's hugely successful television series "Miami Vice" and his superior "Crime Story," this character-driven crime drama intelligently combines a western moral code with a glossy visual style filled with shimmering city lights that reflect off highly polished car hoods. Based on the book *The Home Invaders* by Frank Hohimer, the story revolves around a professional thief (Caan) who wants to make one last score before settling down to marry his girlfriend (Weld). It's a familiar story, but what elevates this one are Mann's crackling directorial style and his ability to elicit amazing performances from his cast—Caan is as good as he has ever been, Weld is excellent as the woman who loves him, Willie Nelson is a casting coup as Caan's imprisoned, terminally ill mentor, and Prosky is perfect as the restrained, but immensely powerful, gangster.

THIN BLUE LINE, THE (1988), documentary. Directed and written by Errol Morris; produced by Mark Lipson; photographed by Stefan Czapsky and Robert Chappell; edited by Paul Barnes; music by Philip Glass; released by Miramax Films; 101 minutes. *Cast*: Randall Adams, David Harris.

First the facts. In 1976 police officer Robert Wood is gunned down on a dark stretch of Dallas highway during a routine traffic stop. Randall Adams, a young man with no criminal record, is convicted of the murder and sentenced to life in prison. In 1987, filmmaker Errol Morris gets an on-camera confession for Wood's murder from death row inmate David Harris. *The Thin Blue Line* is more than a documentary about an abuse of the system—it's a motion picture that transcends genre, a piece of detective work that actually resulted in the release of an innocent man. Errol Morris, himself a onetime private eye, is not merely documenting; he's investigating. It's not just the content, however, that makes this film unique, but its glossy style, slow-motion camera work, staged reconstructions of the crime (each scene varying with new versions of the "truth"), and hypnotic Philip Glass score. The viewer is drawn in both by the fascinating truth of the case and by Morris' thrilling, Hitchcockian filmmaking à la *The Wrong Man*, which erases the thin line between fact and fiction. "I believe cinema verite set back documentary filmmaking twenty or thirty years" (Errol Morris, interviewed by Peter Bates in *Cineaste* 17, no. 1, 1989).

Award: New York Film Critics Circle Award for Best Documentary.

THIS IS SPINAL TAP (1984), comedy. Directed, cowritten, and comusic by
Rob Reiner; screenplay and music with Christopher Guest, Michael McKean,
and Harry Shearer; produced by Karen Murphy; photographed by Peter Smokler;
edited by Kent Beyda, Kim Secrist, and Robert Leighton; released by Embassy;
82 minutes. *Cast*: Rob Reiner, Michael McKean, Harry Shearer, Christopher
Guest, R. J. Parnell, Bruno Kirby, Ed Begley, Jr., Fran Drescher, Dana Carvey,
Billy Crystal, Howard Hesseman, Paul Shaffer, Anjelica Huston, Fred Willard.

A hilarious send-up of rockumentaries that chronicles a fictitious, once-
popular British rock band that, after nearly two decades of touring and recording,
has seen the highest of highs and the lowest of lows. Through the camera lens
of film director Marty DiBergi (Reiner, who sits stone-faced through the "interviews"), we follow Spinal Tap—David St. Hubbins (McKean), Nigel Tufnel
(Guest), and Derek Smalls (Shearer)—as they slog through the rigors of their
rock-and-roll lifestyle while taking time to treat us to some completely inane
philosophical nuggets about their lives and careers. The results are hysterical,
but we're not really laughing at the band members as much as we're laughing
at the accuracy of Reiner's vision. In fact, we're charmed by these aging rockers
who sincerely love their work. The single most brilliant scene is the fiasco of
the stage design for the band's "Stonehenge" tour—an anticipated heavy metal
extravaganza that, after numerous screwups, becomes a laughable stage show
boasting a miniature version of the English landmark and populated by druid
dwarfs who scamper about on stage. The movie is so on-target that it spawned
a successful album (including such hits as "Sex Farm Woman") and a national
Spinal Tap tour.

THOUSAND CLOWNS, A (1965), comedy/drama. Directed and produced by
Fred Coe; screenplay by Herb Gardner (from his play); photographed by Arthur
J. Ornitz; edited by Ralph Rosenblum; music by Don Walker, song "Yes Sir,
That's My Baby" by Walter Donaldson and Gus Kahn; released by United
Artists; 117 minutes. *Cast*: Jason Robards, Barbara Harris, Martin Balsam, Barry
Gordon, Gene Saks, William Daniels.

Combining the dialogue and characters of Herb Gardner's successful 1962
Broadway play with the cinematic French New Wave-influenced playfulness of
director (and Broadway producer) Fred Coe and editor Ralph Rosenblum, this
delightful romp oscillates between zany comedy and touching drama. Jason Robards, in a seemingly effortless performance, plays Murray Burns, a former
writer for the kiddie television show "Chuckles the Chipmunk" who has since
turned his back on the daily grind and now enjoys the liberty of an irresponsible
existence. Living with him is his perceptive and mature twelve-year-old nephew
Nick (Gordon), who was abandoned seven years previously by his fun-loving
mother. Their days are filled with fun and games—silly impressions of espionage movies, excursions to the top of the Empire State Building, visits to the
junk shop, and spirited ukelele renditions of "Yes Sir, That's My Baby." All
is well until they receive a visit from uptight social workers Albert (Daniels)

and Sandra (Harris), an engaged couple whose personal problems spoil their professional demeanor; stuffed-shirt bureaucrat Albert recommends that Nick be taken away from the "maladjusted" Murray and placed in a stable environment, while people-person Sandra, with her grad school education, has a differing opinion—she is charmed by Nick and infatuated with Murray's zest for life. A delightful film that doesn't shy away from the larger psychological issues at hand, *A Thousand Clowns* creates a fascinating and complex 1960s character in Murray—a nonconformist whose unorthodox family situation is threatened not because he doesn't love Nick but because he refuses to raise him to become "a responsible member of society." He may not look like one of the hippies who would soon flood the streets, but Murray is every bit as in tune to the collective angst of the generation as are they.

Awards: Academy Award for Best Supporting Actor (Balsam); Academy Award nominations for Best Picture, Screenplay, Score.

THREE DAYS OF THE CONDOR (1975), political thriller. Directed by Sydney Pollack; screenplay by Lorenzo Semple, Jr., and David Rayfiel (from the novel by James Grady); produced by Stanley Schneider; photographed by Owen Roizman; edited by Frederick Steinkamp and Don Guidice; music by Dave Grusin; released by Paramount; 117 minutes. *Cast*: Robert Redford, Faye Dunaway, Cliff Robertson, Max von Sydow, John Houseman, Addison Powell, Walter McGinn, Tina Chen, Michael Kane.

Government conspiracy movies don't get any better than this. Released just as Watergate was breaking wide open (and just a year before Redford would report on it in *All the President's Men*), this Central Intelligence Agency (CIA) thriller stars Redford as Joe Turner, code name "Condor"—an intellectual government employee who is one of a team of book readers who search for fictional espionage plots that may be of use to "the Company." When he narrowly escapes a mass murder in his office, he is forced to go into hiding ("I'm not a field agent. I just read books"). Trusting no one he knows, he randomly abducts beautiful photographer Kathy Hale (Dunaway), who helps him discover why his seven coworkers were killed. Based on the James Grady novel *Six Days of the Condor*, the film is one of the first in what has become an entire espionage subgenre—the secret-CIA-inside-the-CIA thriller. The MacGuffin plot is pure subterfuge; what's really important is the theme of trust that grows between Condor and Kathy, as it simultaneously erodes between Condor and the U.S. government. Unforgettable is the finale, as Condor meets CIA man Higgins (Robertson) in front of the *New York Times* offices and explains that he's given them the entire story. "You poor dumb son-of-a-bitch," laments Higgins, who then expresses doubt that they print it. "They'll print it," responds Condor. After a telling pause, Higgins asks, "How do you know?"

THURMAN, UMA. Born April 29, 1970, in Boston; actor. Formerly married to actor Gary Oldman. Statuesque and oddly tomboyish beauty who has become one of the most sought-after actors of her generation. Nomadic by nature—she spent much of her early life in Europe and India—and the daughter of a foremost authority on the Dalai Lama, she relocated to New York City at the tender age of fifteen to become an actor. After a stint as a model, the lanky teen got her big break as the Venus-in-a-half-shell in Terry Gilliam's *The Adventures of Baron Munchausen*. However, in her next film (though its release preceded Gilliam's picture), as the busty and virginal Cecile de Volanges in *Dangerous Liaisons*, Thurman developed her aura of ethereal, yet brainy, sensuality. That reputation was only heightened with her role as Mrs. Henry Miller in the sexually charged *Henry and June*, which earned the fiscally taboo NC-17 rating for its frank eroticism. With a gutsy costarring role opposite Robert De Niro in *Mad Dog and Glory*, a lead as Tom Robbins' large-thumbed Sissy Hankshaw in the noble failure *Even Cowgirls Get the Blues*, and an Oscar-nominated performance as the amped-up mob wife in *Pulp Fiction*, she has established herself as a person to watch in the coming years. Her planned portrayal of Marlene Dietrich was fortuitously aborted when that project's director Louis Malle died in 1995.

Filmography: Kiss Daddy Goodnight/A Rose by Any Other Name (1987); Johnny Be Good (1988); Dangerous Liaisons (1988); The Adventures of Baron Munchausen (1989); Where the Heart Is (1990); Henry and June (1990); Final Analysis (1992); Jennifer 8 (1992); Mad Dog and Glory (1993); Even Cowgirls Get the Blues (1994); Pulp Fiction (1994); A Month by the Lake (1995); The Duke of Grove (1995, ctv short).

Honor: Academy Award nomination for Best Supporting Actress (*Pulp Fiction*).

TITICUT FOLLIES, THE (1967), documentary. Directed and produced by Frederick Wiseman; photographed by John Marshall (b&w); released by Zipporah Films; 89 minutes.

The first of Frederick Wiseman's numerous investigations of institutions, this damning exposé of Massachusetts' Bridgewater State Hospital details the indignities imposed upon its criminally insane ''inmates.'' The most horrific moment in this veritable gallery of horrors shows a staffer whose cigarette ash hangs precariously in the balance directly above a patient's feeding tube funnel; it is a scene of Hitchcockian proportions that remains etched in the memory of every viewer. Adhering strictly to the Direct Cinema aesthetic of objectivity, Wiseman's camera strives for invisibility. Armed with portable camera and sound gear, high-speed film stock, and minimal crew, he shoots enormously high ratios of film in order to approach this unattainable goal; he then assembles the film without narration or music. In theory, the result gives the viewer only the ''facts'' and allows an opinion to be formed without the interference of the filmmaker. While Wiseman still has such persuasive tools as shot selection, visual juxtaposition, image size, and camera angle, he comes closer to the elusive truth than his contemporaries. His investigative style has paved the way for such television news shows as ''60 Minutes,'' and, in fact, the bulk of Wiseman's subsequent work has been done for public television. The repercussions of *The Titicut Follies* were felt for years to come after the Supreme Judicial

Court of Massachusetts imposed a worldwide ban on public screenings of the film and ordered that the negative and all copies be destroyed. The ban was lifted in 1991.

TOOTSIE (1982), comedy. Directed and coproduced by Sydney Pollack; screenplay by Murray Schisgal, Larry Gelbart, and (uncredited) Elaine May (from a story by Gelbart and Don McGuire); produced with Dick Richards; photographed by Owen Roizman; edited by Frederic Steinkamp and William Steinkamp; music by Dave Grusin; released by Columbia Pictures; 116 minutes. *Cast*: Dustin Hoffman, Jessica Lange, Teri Garr, Dabney Coleman, Charles Durning, Bill Murray, Sydney Pollack, George Gaynes, Geena Davis.

After playing a single father in *Kramer vs. Kramer*, Hoffman again questions gender expectations by starring as Michael Dorsey, a talented, difficult, and unemployed actor who becomes a national sensation as *actress* Dorothy Michaels. Dorothy's feisty personality, while not much different from Michael's, comes to be viewed by her soap opera fans as spunky and feminist; ironically, this man in dresses and pumps is transformed into a role model for women. As in Billy Wilder's 1959 classic *Some Like It Hot* and Blake Edwards' *Victor/Victoria* (also 1982), the Michael/Dorothy disguises lead to some riotous comedy involving his former girlfriend (Garr), his new platonic girlfriend (Lange), his best friend (Murray), his exasperated agent (Pollack), his amorous male costar (Gaynes), and the naive male suitor who wants to marry Dorothy (Durning). A reflection of the increased male sensitivity of the times, Hoffman saw in these back-to-back roles the dramatic and comic potential of playing the baby boomer generation's evolutionary male; his yuppie businessman-cum-single-father allowed him to *behave* like a woman, while his Darwinian transformation from Michael to Dorothy actually allowed him to *become* a woman. What resulted is not only one of the smartest comedies of the decade but another in a long line of memorable performances from Hoffman—so what if his Dorothy Michaels is no more convincing as a woman than most transvestites.

Awards: Academy Awards for Best Supporting Actress (Lange); Academy Award nominations for Best Picture, Direction, Actor, Supporting Actress (Garr), Cinematography, Editing, Song, Sound; New York Film Critics Circle Award for Best Director, Screenplay, Supporting Actress (Lange).

TOP GUN (1986), drama/war. Directed by Tony Scott; screenplay by Jim Cash and Jack Epps, Jr.; produced by Don Simpson and Jerry Bruckheimer; photographed by Jeffrey Kimball; edited by Billy Weber and Chris Lebenzon; music by Harold Faltermeyer; released by Paramount; 110 minutes. *Cast*: Tom Cruise, Anthony Edwards, Kelly McGillis, Val Kilmer, Tom Skerritt, Michael Ironside, Rick Rossovich, Tim Robbins, Meg Ryan.

The epitome of Hollywood's bigger-harder-faster-louder mentality as perfected by superproducers Don Simpson and Jerry Bruckheimer (*Flashdance, Beverly Hills Cop, Days of Thunder*). Forsaking character development for pyrotechnics, *Top Gun* tells a familiar tale borrowed from countless World War II movies about a hot young fighter pilot (Cruise) who strives to become the very best, the "top gun." In the process, he betters himself, creates a bond with his adversary (Kilmer), and falls in love with an intelligent aeronautics consultant (McGillis). But, when it comes right down to it, the movie's really about sex—the turn-on, the thrill, the excitement of the high-testosterone game of war. Filled with muscular, sweat-drenched men and a fetishistic emphasis on hardware, there's more homoeroticism in this movie than in any Hollywood blockbuster in recent memory. Not surprisingly, the public was entirely captivated by the breathtaking aerial fight scenes and the gung-ho, be-all-that-you-can-be attitude. Simpson, Bruckheimer, Scott, and Cruise made a failed attempt to recapture this film's commercial success with the similarly fetishistic auto racing picture *Days of Thunder* (1990).

Awards: Academy Award for Song ("You Take My Breath Away"); Academy Award nominations for Editing, Sound, Sound Effects Editing.

TOWERING INFERNO (1974), disaster/drama. Directed by John Guillermin; screenplay by Stirling Silliphant (from the novels *The Tower* by Richard Martin Stern and *The Glass Inferno* by Thomas N. Scortia and Frank M. Robinson); produced by Irwin Allen; photographed by Fred Koenekamp and Joseph Biroc; edited by Harold F. Cress and Howard Cress; music by John Williams, song "We May Never Love like This Again" by Al Kasha and Joel Hirschhorn; released by 20th Century Fox; 165 minutes. *Cast*: Steve McQueen, Paul Newman, William Holden, Faye Dunaway, Fred Astaire, Richard Chamberlain, Susan Blakely, Jennifer Jones, Robert Vaughn, Robert Wagner, O. J. Simpson, Michael Lookinland, Dabney Coleman.

The second of Irwin Allen's two spectacular disaster films of the 1970s (after 1972's *The Poseidon Adventure*), this lengthy effort moved the precarious proceedings from upended luxury liner to the world's tallest building. McQueen is Fire Marshall Michael O'Hallorhan, and Newman is architect Doug Roberts, and together they battle the blistering flames to rescue the partying tenants of a San Francisco glass tower during the opening night gala. The cause of the fire— a substandard wiring system that was installed counter to the architectural plans. As the inferno spreads out of control, and explosions blow out windows, the only choice left is to rupture the building's water tanks and literally flood the massive structure. Closer to the institutional negligence of *Airport* than the force majeure of *The Poseidon Adventure*, the disaster here is a comment on corporate greed; the architecture and engineering are sound, but the people implementing the plans are unpredictable and dishonorable. As expected, this vertical *Grand Hotel* features a multitude of characters, each of whom has a weighty story; no one receives anything more than a perfunctory level of complexity, and those fortunate enough to live get a tidy wrap-up at the finale. As rudimentary as it all is, the cast raises it to a respectable degree of entertainment. Fortunately, no sequels followed.

Awards: Academy Awards for Best Cinematography, Song, Editing; Academy Award nominations for Best Picture, Supporting Actor (Astaire), Art Direction, Sound, Score.

TOY STORY (1995), animation. Directed by John Lasseter; screenplay by Joss Whedon, Andrew Stanton, Joel Cohen, and Alec Sokolow; produced by Ralph Guggenheim, Bonnie Arnold; edited by Robert Gordon, Lee Unkrich; music by Randy Newman; released by Buena Vista; 81 minutes.

Cast (voices of): Tom Hanks, Tim Allen, Don Rickles, Jim Varney, Wallace Shawn, Annie Potts, John Ratzenberger, Laurie Metcalf, R. Lee Ermey, Penn Jillette.

After the advances made in 1988's *Who Framed Roger Rabbit*, with its mix of live-action and cartoon characters, the animation genre has again seen a new dawn with this entirely computer-generated feature from Pixar and Walt Disney. Expanding on the techniques of his short films *Luxo Jr.* (1986), *Tin Toy* (1988), and *Knickknack* (1989), director John Lasseter brings to life a roomful of children's toys that include the charismatic cowboy Woody (Hanks), Mr. Potato Head (Rickles), and Slinky Dog (Potts). Into this paradise of classic playthings comes a modern, newfangled toy named Buzz Lightyear (Allen), a space ranger who is initially disillusioned to discover that he's just a toy. Lasseter creates a thrilling roller-coaster ride that consistently amazes us as we try to comprehend that the entire film is created on a computer. While it may lack the visual warmth of traditionally drawn animation (which itself is employing more and more computer techniques), there is no denying that in *Toy Story* we are watching the future of the art form unfold.

Awards: Academy Award nominations for Best Score, Song (''You've Got a Friend''), Screenplay; Los Angeles Film Critics Award for Best Animated Feature.

TRAVOLTA, JOHN. Born February 18, 1954, in Englewood, New Jersey; actor. Likable leading man with blue eyes and a boyish grin who, after numerous commercial and television appearances, landed a role in the Broadway production of *Grease* before finding national fame as Vinny Barbarino, the dim-witted ''sweathog'' of television's ''Welcome Back, Kotter.'' His meteoric rise in the mid-1970s included Brian De Palma's *Carrie*, his Oscar-nominated role as disco king Tony Manero in *Saturday Night Fever*, and the film version of *Grease*, but it began to fade with such misfires as *Moment by Moment* and *Urban Cowboy* (as a bearded Texan?!). After an excellent performance in another picture with De Palma (the overlooked *Blow Out*), Travolta slid to the status of Hollywood nonentity before eventually benefiting from the unlikely success of the *Look Who's Talking* series. Then, nearly twenty years after his earliest achievements, Travolta became the comeback kid with a knockout, Oscar-nominated starring role as hit man Vincent Vega in *Pulp Fiction*, a role that allowed him to comment on his disco past via an ultracool dance with costar Uma Thurman at the offbeat nightspot Jack Rabbit Slim's. A second Oscar nomination followed for his role as criminal turned Hollywood film producer Chili Palmer in 1995's *Get Shorty*. As a result of his newfound box office draw, he was courted for upcoming films by Hong Kong action director John Woo (*Broken Arrow*), Roman Polanski (*The Double*, since aborted), and Nora Ephron (*Michael*) and, by late 1995, was commanding a $20 million payday per movie.

Filmography: The Devil's Rain (1975); Carrie (1976); The Boy in the Plastic Bubble (1975, tvm); Saturday Night Fever (1977); Grease (1978); Moment by Moment (1978); Urban Cowboy (1980); Blow Out (1981); Staying Alive (1983); Two of a Kind (1983); Perfect (1985); The Dumb Waiter (1987, tvm); The Experts (1989); Look Who's Talking (1989); Eyes of an Angel (1990, released in 1994); Look Who's Talking Too (1990); The Tender (1991); Shout (1991); Boris and Natasha (1992, ctvm); Look Who's Talking Now (1993); Pulp Fiction (1994); White Man's Burden (1995); Get Shorty (1995).

Honors: Academy Award nominations for Best Actor (*Saturday Night Fever, Pulp Fiction, Get Shorty*); Los Angeles Film Critics Circle Award for Best Actor (*Pulp Fiction*).

Selected bibliography

Clarkson, Wensley. *John Travolta: Back in Character*. New York: Overlook Press, 1996.

TRUE GRIT (1969), western. Directed by Henry Hathaway; screenplay by Marguerite Roberts (from the novel by Charles Portis); produced by Hal B. Wallis; photographed by Lucien Ballard; edited by Warren Low; music by Elmer Bernstein, theme song "True Grit" by Bernstein and Don Black, sung by Glen Campbell; released by Paramount; 128 minutes. *Cast*: John Wayne, Glen Campbell, Kim Darby, Jeremy Slate, Jeff Corey, Robert Duvall, Dennis Hopper, Strother Martin, Hank Worden.

The film that won John Wayne a Best Actor Oscar after more than forty years in front of the camera, this masterpiece of pure entertainment may not have the thematic depth and psychological complexity as *The Searchers* or *Red River*, but Wayne's Rooster Cogburn is every bit as honest as his Ethan Edwards or Tom Dunson. Here he stars as a retired marshal, "a one-eyed fatman" who prefers spending time at home with his booze and his cat until he is shamed into helping fourteen-year-old Mattie Ross (Darby) hunt down her father's killer (Corey). Making this pair into a crowd is La Boeuf (Campbell), a young Texas ranger whom Mattie despises. Wayne continues, as he did in *El Dorado*, to explore the extinction of the mythic western hero; instead of a flawless icon, Rooster Cogburn is a fatherly hero riddled with human weaknesses, whose "true grit" in the face of a weakening body makes him even more legendary in the eyes of the young Mattie.

Sequels: Wayne teamed with Katharine Hepburn in *Rooster Cogburn* (1975, Stuart Millar); the television movie *True Grit: A Further Adventure* (1978, Richard T. Heffron) was a series pilot starring Warren Oates.

TURNER, KATHLEEN. Born June 19, 1954, in Springfield, Missouri; actor. Sultry leading lady with a blond mane and a throaty voice who lit up the screen with her dynamic performance as Matty Walker in the modern film noir *Body Heat*. She has proven herself to be an actor who smoothly travels from comedy to drama with equally impressive results, hitting a comic peak in the adventure film *Romancing the Stone* as Joan Wilder, a famed romance novelist who has never experienced love. Under John Huston's direction in *Prizzi's Honor*, she combined the femme fatale side of Matty Walker with the zaniness of Joan Wilder and the following year mixed comedy and nostalgic romance for Francis Ford Coppola's *Peggy Sue Got Married*. However, her status as an A-level star has suffered from the steady decline of her post-*War of the Roses* films. Perhaps not coincidentally, she has blossomed as a stage performer, impressing critics and audiences alike with her work on Broadway, specifically in Tennessee Williams' *Cat on a Hot Tin Roof* (1989) and Jean Cocteau's *Indiscretions* (1995).

Filmography: Body Heat (1981); The Man with Two Brains (1983); A Breed Apart (1984); Crimes of Passion (1984); Romancing the Stone (1984); The Jewel of the Nile (1985); Prizzi's Honor (1985); Peggy Sue Got Married (1986); Dear America (1987); Julia and Julia (1987); The Accidental Tourist (1988); Switching Channels (1988); Who Framed Roger Rabbit (1988) voice; Tummy Trouble (1989, short) voice; The War of the Roses (1989); Rollercoaster Rabbit (1990, short) voice; V. I. Warshawsky (1991); Undercover Blues (1993); House of Cards (1993); Trail Mix-Up (1993, short) voice; Serial Mom (1994); Naked in New York (1994); Leslie's Folly (1994, ctv short) also director; Moonlight and Valentino (1995).

Honors: Academy Award nomination for Best Actress (*Peggy Sue Got Married*); Los Angeles Film Critics Award for Best Actress (*Romancing the Stone*).

TURTURRO, JOHN. Born February 28, 1957, in Brooklyn; actor, director. Brother Nicholas (''NYPD Blue,'' *Federal Hill*) and cousin Aida are both actors. Quirky and intense actor who displays a passion and energy unsurpassed by anyone of his generation. His ability to release a dark side but also to expose a tenderness recalls the talent of his avowed inspiration, Burt Lancaster. Although early in his career he appeared under the direction of Martin Scorsese (twice), William Friedkin, and Woody Allen, not until the relatively overlooked *Five Corners* from Tony Bill was his true talent revealed. He continued to impress in a series of challenging roles—as the racist Pino in *Do the Right Thing*, the weasely gangster in *Miller's Crossing*, the troubled screenwriter in *Barton Fink*, ''21'' contestant Herb Stemple in *Quiz Show*, and Chicago mobster Sam Giancana in HBO's *Sugartime*. His talents have also taken him behind the camera as the director of *Mac*, an exceptionally poignant and stylized story of an Italian family in New York. ''Turturro has demonstrated enough quirky brilliance for us to hunt down his performances as once we did those of Peter Lorre or Warren Oates'' (David Thomson, *A Biographical Dictionary of Film*).

Filmography: Raging Bull (1980); Exterminator 2 (1984); The Flamingo Kid (1984); Desperately Seeking Susan (1985); To Live and Die in L.A. (1985); The Color of Money (1986); Gung Ho (1986); Hannah and Her Sisters (1986); Off Beat (1986); Five Corners (1987); The Sicilian (1987); Do the Right Thing (1989); Backtrack (1990); Men of

Respect (1990); Miller's Crossing (1990); Mo' Better Blues (1990); State of Grace (1990); Barton Fink (1991); Mac (1992) also writer, director; Being Human (1994); Quiz Show (1994); Sugartime (1995, ctvm).

Honors: Cannes Film Festival Awards for Best Actor (*Barton Fink*) and Camera d'Or (*Mac*).

TWO-LANE BLACKTOP (1971), drama. Directed and edited by Monte Hellman; screenplay by Rudolph Wurlitzer and Will Corry (from the story by Corry); produced by Michael S. Laughlin; photographed by Jackson Deerson; released by Universal; 102 minutes. *Cast*: James Taylor, Warren Oates, Laurie Bird, Dennis Wilson, Rudolph Wurlitzer, H. D. (Harry Dean) Stanton.

   Coming out of the Roger Corman school of filmmaking, maverick director Monte Hellman has captured a segment of America rarely seen on film—gearhead car freaks who love the sound of revving engines, the sensation of the blacktop rumbling under their tires, and the freedom of driving down an open road. Real-life musicians James Taylor and Dennis Wilson and their bored teenage girl passenger (Bird) are traveling through the Southwest in their 1955 Chevy when they encounter another driver (Oates) in a 1970 Pontiac G.T.O. The drivers make a little wager—the first one to Washington, D.C., wins the title to the loser's car. The rest of the movie is all driving, with a little time to visit a roadside diner or filling station. Outcasts all, these are people who subscribe to a different American dream—not the dream of a house, two kids, and a yard (although Oates' driver fantasizes about it) but a dream to keep on movin'. Features an unexpectedly vulnerable Warren Oates, whose character is so identified with his car that he's known only as G.T.O., and a strangely compelling performance from Bird, as the ennui-stricken wanderer. While the film is not without weaknesses (the stiffness of untrained actors Taylor and Wilson and a complete disinterest in dramatic thrust), it remains an uncompromising tale of the same sort of empty, aimless, self-doubting travelers who would concurrently populate the German films of Wim Wenders. The hopelessness of *Two-Lane Blacktop*, as represented by the final freeze-frame of the Chevy as the film burns orange and disintegrates, is in sharp contrast to the hot-rod film that would follow just two years later, *American Graffiti*. Like a phoenix, the 1955 Chevy would rise from cinema's ashes and return in George Lucas' film as the car driven by Harrison Ford's Bob Falfa.

2001: A SPACE ODYSSEY (1968), sci-fi. Directed, produced, and cowritten by Stanley Kubrick; screenplay with Arthur C. Clarke (from his story); photographed by Geoffrey Unsworth and John Alcott; edited by Ray Lovejoy; special effects by Kubrick and Douglas Trumbull; released by MGM; 160 minutes. *Cast*: Keir Dullea, Gary Lockwood, William Sylvester, Douglas Rain (voice of HAL).

   One of the handful of truly influential films in the history of cinema, this Kubrick masterwork also ranks as one of the great artworks of the twentieth century. Written by Kubrick and Arthur C. Clarke, it tells the story of a space mission to Jupiter, though the plot itself is secondary to Kubrick's concern with man's evolution. The film begins with ''The Dawn of Man'' episode as Liget's ''Lux Aeterna'' fills the sound track, and a mysterious black monolith appears amid a group of man-apes, inspiring one of the creatures to use an animal bone as a tool of killing. The man-ape then lets the bone fly upward into the sky as the scene shifts to a spaceship floating through the heavens to Strauss' ''Blue Danube Waltz.'' On board the *Destiny*, we follow astronaut Dave Bowman (Dullea) on his mission across the cosmos—a mission that is at the mercy of the ship's freethinking computer, HAL 9000. He finally reaches Jupiter and, like the man-ape before him, has a vision of the black monolith before transforming into an embryonic ''star-child.'' By the end, we realize that we have been watching Kubrick's history of evolution (with the monolith as some sort of cosmic catalyst and with *Destiny* as man's symbolic and inevitable path); it is a gradual shift from man-ape, to human, to a superenhanced being of higher consciousness. Released by MGM, *2001: A Space Odyssey* is a wholly experimental film that secured backing from a Hollywood studio on the basis of Kubrick's status as a preeminent filmmaker. While it inspired furious debate among critics and academicians, it also struck a popular chord with 1960s moviegoers, who viewed its visual style (with its hallucinatory effects and cold technology) as the ultimate ''trip movie.'' ''You're free to speculate as you wish about the philosophical and allegorical meaning of the film'' (Stanley Kubrick, *Playboy*).

Awards: Academy Award for Special Visual Effects (Kubrick); Academy Award nominations for Director, Art Direction; included in the Library of Congress' National Film Registry (1991).

U

UNFORGIVEN (1992), western. Directed and produced by Clint Eastwood; screenplay by David Webb Peoples; photographed by Jack N. Green; edited by Joel Cox; music by Lennie Niehaus; released by Warner Bros.; 130 minutes. *Cast*: Clint Eastwood, Morgan Freeman, Gene Hackman, Frances Fisher, Richard Harris, Jaimz Woolvett, Saul Rubinek.

After a stellar career as a western icon, Eastwood, in his fourteenth film as director, delivers his finest film—one in which all the pieces (performances, visual style, theme, genre expectations) are woven together seamlessly. Eastwood stars as William Munny, a vicious thief and murderer whose life has been transformed by the love of a good woman who has given him not just a family but a reason to leave his old ways behind. After her death (which is where the film opens), Munny, having grown concerned about his children's welfare, straps on his gun and again becomes a killer for hire. Partnered with old friend Ned Logan (Freeman), he heads for the town of Big Whiskey to avenge the brutal attack of a prostitute and is confronted along the way by local sheriff Little Bill Daggett (Hackman) and gunslinging dandy English Bob (Harris). Much more than a conventional Western tale, *Unforgiven* is a film about killing—English Bob has a reputation that exaggerates his notoriety; Little Bill hides his homicidal tendencies behind a badge; prostitute Strawberry Alice (Fisher) justifies her bloodlust by calling it vengeance; and Munny is tortured by the self-awareness that he is a murderer in need of redemption. This time Eastwood improves on the indifferent bloodletting of *The Outlaw Josey Wales* by creating a character who understands the spiritual emptiness of killing.

Awards: Academy Awards for Best Picture, Director, Supporting Actor (Hackman), Editing; Academy Award nominations for Best Actor (Eastwood), Screenplay, Cinematography, Art Direction, Sound; Los Angeles Film Critics Awards for Best Picture,

Director, Screenplay, Actor (Eastwood), Supporting Actor (Hackman); New York Film Critics Circle Award for Best Supporting Actor (Hackman); DGA Award.

UNMARRIED WOMAN, AN (1978), drama. Directed, written, and coproduced by Paul Mazursky; photographed by Arthur Ornitz; edited by Stuart H. Pappe; music by Bill Conti; released by 20th Century Fox; 124 minutes. *Cast*: Jill Clayburgh, Michael Murphy, Alan Bates, Cliff Gorman, Pat Quinn, Kelly Bishop.

Following the path cut by *Alice Doesn't Live Here Anymore*, this penetrating drama highlights a woman as she travels down the road toward becoming a complete human being—one who loves her child, desires her freedom, freely displays her intelligence, and explores her sexuality with maturity. Erica (Clayburgh) is a seemingly happily married New York art gallery worker whose fifteen-year marriage is abruptly ended when her husband (Murphy) confesses that he's sleeping with a younger woman. Hit with the numbing force of this news, the devastated Erica vomits on the street. Gradually, however, she learns to feel again and comes to value her independence, though even that is questioned when she falls for a perfectly wonderful British artist (Bates). It took until the end of the 1970s—a decade of psychological probing into the hearts and minds of the American man—to finally get an honest and thorough depiction of the American woman.

Awards: Academy Award nominations for Best Picture, Actress, Screenplay; New York Film Critics Circle Award for Best Screenplay; Cannes Film Festival Award for Best Actress.

USUAL SUSPECTS, THE (1995), crime. Directed and coproduced by Bryan Singer; screenplay by Christopher McQuarrie; produced with Michael McDonnell; photographed by Tom Sigel; edited and music by John Ottman; released by Gramercy; 105 minutes. *Cast*: Stephen Baldwin, Gabriel Byrne, Benicio Del Toro, Kevin Pollack, Kevin Spacey, Chazz Palminteri, Pete Postlethwaite, Suzy Amis, Giancarlo Esposito, Dan Hedaya, Paul Bartel.

A surprise, independent hit that recalls the incomprehensible plot mechanizations of *The Big Sleep*, this noirish crime story is a celebration of filmmaking that, while lacking thematic substance, certainly provides some delightful characters and smart dialogue. The intrigue centers on a group of criminals—Michael McManus (Baldwin), "Verbal" Kint (Spacey), Dean Keaton (Byrne), Todd Hockney (Pollack), and Fenster (Del Toro), that is, the "usual suspects"— all of whom have been rounded up by the police for a truck hijacking only to discover that they've all been mysteriously chosen for another, bigger job. Pulling the strings is one "Keyser Soze," a much-feared figure who lives only in legend and sends his aide Kobayashi (Postlethwaite) to deal with the quintet. Told in flashback as "Verbal" is grilled by wily customs agent Dave Kujan (Palminteri), the film begins with the disastrous outcome of the job and proceeds with surprise after surprise as the legend of "Keyser Soze" grows and eventually envelops the criminals and Kujan. Intelligent, fun, and stylish, the film received numerous accolades for McQuarrie and Singer—a writer–director team that knows how to make a movie move.

Awards: Academy Awards for Best Supporting Actor (Spacey) and Screenplay; New York Film Critics Circle Award for Best Supporting Actor (Spacey).

V

VALLEY OF THE DOLLS (1967), drama. Directed by Mark Robson; screenplay by Helen Deutch and Dorothy Kingsley (from the novel by Jacqueline Susann); produced by David Weisbart; photographed by William H. Daniels; edited by Dorothy Spencer; music by John (Johnny) Williams, songs by Andre Previn and Dory Previn; released by 20th Century Fox; 123 minutes. *Cast*: Barbara Parkins, Patty Duke, Sharon Tate, Paul Burke, Susan Hayward, Tony Scotti, Martin Milner, Lee Grant.

Attempting to move forward with the times by tapping into the 1960s youth culture, this is 20th Century Fox's lurid exposé of Hollywood, a warning that free sex and pill popping can destroy even the prettiest and most ambitious young people. Based on Jacqueline Susann's tawdry beach novel and (mis)directed by Mark Robson, who, ten years earlier, directed *Peyton Place*, the film focuses on three starlets—likable New Englander-cum-model Anne Welles (Parkins), overnight singing sensation Neely O'Hara (Duke), and talent-less actress turned porn star Jennifer North (Tate)—each of whom battles a growing dependence on pills, or "dolls." The result is shocking not because of its message but because the film is such an abomination. Wallowing in pop psychology without ever winking at the ridiculousness of the script or the ab-surdity of its characters' situations, the film is a mess that made a healthy $20 million at the box office by titillating the audience with crying, doped-up young women in their underclothes. Instant camp, with plenty of catty retorts and memorable lines such as Jennifer's winner when, frustrated with her bust ex-ercises, she gives up and declares, "Let em' droop!"

Award: Academy Award nomination for Best Adapted Score.

Remake: *Jacqueline Susann's Valley of the Dolls* (1981 tvms, Walter Grauman).

VAN PEEBLES, MELVIN. Born August 21, 1932, in Chicago; director, screenwriter, producer, composer, author. Son Mario is an actor and director (*New Jack City, Posse*). As a black American expatriate in Paris in the 1960s, Van Peebles directed his first feature, *The Story of a Three-Day Pass*, an adaptation of his own novel about a weekend shared by a black soldier and a white French girl. After a successful screening at the San Francisco Film Festival, he was hired by Columbia Pictures to make his first studio film, *Watermelon Man*, a smart satire about a white man who one day wakes up black. The positive response to that picture afforded him the opportunity to make the shocking and candid *Sweet Sweetback's Baad Asssss Song*, historically, the most important black film of the sound era until the release of Spike Lee's *She's Gotta Have It*. A truly independent production that cost $500,000 and earned $14 million, the film displayed a sensibility that was by, for, and about the black community and not a reflection of white-run Hollywood. For much of the 1970s and 1980s, Van Peebles turned his attention to staging the Tony-nominated musicals *Ain't Supposed to Die a Natural Death* and *Don't Play Us Cheap*. Although his 1989 film *Identity Crisis* was met with critical and commercial disinterest, he has made a minor resurgence in the 1990s in collaboration with his son Mario, who directed his father's script in *Panther*. ''Melvin Van Peebles is the man'' (Spike Lee, *Five for Five*).

Filmography as director: A King (1958, short); Sunlight (1958, short) also producer, screenplay; Three Pick-Up Men for Herrick (1958, short); also producer, screenplay; The Story of a Three-Day Pass (1968) also screenplay, music; Watermelon Man (1970) also music; Sweet Sweetback's Baad Asssss Song (1971) also actor, producer, screenplay, editor, music; Don't Play Us Cheap (1973) also producer, screenplay, editor, music; Greased Lightning (1977) screenplay only; Sophisticated Gents (1981, tvm) screenplay, actor; Identity Crisis (1989) also producer, editor; ''Vroom, Vroom, Vroom'' episode of Erotic Tales (1994, short) also producer, screenplay, editor; Panther (1995) producer, screenplay from his novel.

Filmography as actor: America (1982); Jaws: The Revenge (1987); O. C. and Stiggs (1987); ''Sonny Spoon'' (1988, tvs); Boomerang (1992); Posse (1993); Terminal Velocity (1994).

VAN SANT, GUS. Born 1952 in Louisville, Kentucky; director, screenwriter. One of the freshest voices to emerge from the American independent scene of the 1980s and 1990s, Van Sant established himself as a gritty, creative, playful director with his 1987 16mm black-and-white feature *Mala Noche*. Named the Best Independent/Experimental Feature by the Los Angeles Film Critics, that film kicked off his career as a director who probes such counterculture topics as drug use (*Drugstore Cowboy*), male hustling (*My Own Private Idaho*), hitchhiking and radical feminism (*Even Cowgirls Get the Blues*), and murder (*To Die For*). The latter film, with its brilliant performance from Nicole Kidman and its biting script from Buck Henry, marks Van Sant's first crossover success. He has also published a book of his Polaroid photography, entitled *108 Portraits*, and has directed such music videos as the Red Hot Chili Peppers' "Under the Bridge" and Chris Isaak's "San Francisco Days."

Filmography: Mala Noche (1987) also screenplay, producer, editor, song; Five Ways to Kill Yourself (1987, short); Ken Death Gets Out of Jail (1987, short) also screenplay, producer; My New Friends (1987, short); Junior (1987, short); Drugstore Cowboy (1989) also screenplay; My Own Private Idaho (1991); Even Cowgirls Get the Blues (1994); Kids (1995) ep; To Die For (1995).

Honors: Los Angeles Film Critics Award for Best Independent Film (*Mala Noche*); New York Film Critics Circle Award for Best Screenplay (*Drugstore Cowboy*); Independent Spirit Awards for Best Screenplay (*Drugstore Cowboy*, *My Own Private Idaho*).

VICTOR/VICTORIA (1982), comedy/musical. Directed, written, and coproduced by Blake Edwards (from the 1933 film *Viktor Und Viktoria* by Rheinhold Schuenzel and Hans Hoemberg); produced with Tony Adams; photographed by Dick Bush; edited by Ralph E. Winters; music by Henry Mancini, songs by Mancini and Leslie Bricusse; released by MGM/UA; 133 minutes. *Cast*: Julie Andrews, Robert Preston, James Garner, Lesley Ann Warren, Alex Karras, John Rhys-Davies.

Blake Edwards' best film since his Pink Panther comedies of the early 1960s, this is a smart, classy, and thoroughly enjoyable sex farce that toys with America's preoccupation with gender roles and homosexuality. Andrews, in her best role since *The Sound of Music*, plays a down-on-her-luck soprano in 1930s Paris who becomes a smash in the gay cabaret scene when her friend and mentor, the aging homosexual Toddy (Preston), hits on the plan of passing her off as a drag queen. The story then cruises into bedroom farce as "Victor" catches the eye of a Chicago gangster King Marchan (Garner), who fears he is turning gay. King later breathes a sigh of relief when he learns that his beloved is really "Victoria," only to realize that because of Victor's career, King must now masquerade as gay—a fitting irony for two heterosexual lovers. Strengthened by an excellent supporting cast that includes Warren as King Marchan's ditzy wife and former National Football League star Karras as his secretly gay bodyguard. Although the film has some clever comic scenes (the cockroach-in-the-salad restaurant ruse employed by the starving Victoria) and entertaining musical numbers, the warmth and honesty of the Victoria/Toddy friendship—that of a rising young chanteuse and a fading old queen—give the film its heart.

Awards: Academy Award for Best Score; Academy Award nominations for Best Actress, Screenplay, Supporting Actor.

VOIGHT, JON. Born December 29, 1938, in Yonkers, New York; actor, screenwriter, producer. Conveying a decency that accompanies his blond-haired, all-American, boyish good looks, Voight began his career in the 1961 Broadway production of *The Sound of Music*, and then appeared in a number of off-Broadway shows before finding success in Hollywood with his rich, multifaceted performance as the naive hustler Joe Buck in *Midnight Cowboy*. His two great

1970s performances—the transformed city boy in *Deliverance* and the paraplegic Vietnam vet in *Coming Home*—established him as a highly respected dramatic actor. After the tepid response to *The Champ*, the saccharine remake of the Jackie Coogan boxing drama, Voight turned his attention to producing his next two pictures—Hal Ashby's *Lookin' to Get Out* and the emotionally involving *Table for Five*. In his best work since *Coming Home*, he blew away critics and audiences alike as the animalistic Manny in Andrei Konchalovsky's *Runaway Train*. Essentially dropping out of sight for the better part of the following decade, he reemerged with longer hair and rougher edges for a spectacular supporting role in Michael Mann's *Heat*.

Filmography: Fearless Frank (1964/released 1967); Hour of the Gun (1967); Midnight Cowboy (1969); Out of It (1969); Catch-22 (1970); The Revolutionary (1970); Deliverance (1972); The All-American Boy (1973); Conrack (1973); The Odessa File (1974); Der Richter und Sein Henker (1975); End of the Game (1976); Coming Home (1977); The Champ (1979); Lookin' to Get Out (1982) also producer, screenplay; Table for Five (1983) also producer; Runaway Train (1985); Desert Bloom (1986); Eternity (1990) also screenplay; Rainbow Warrior (1994); Heat (1995); The Tin Soldier (1995, ctvm) also director.

Honors: Academy Award for Best Actor (*Coming Home*); Academy Award nominations for Best Actor (*Midnight Cowboy, Runaway Train*); New York Film Critics Circle Awards for Best Actor (*Midnight Cowboy, Coming Home*); Los Angeles Film Critics Awards for Best Actor (*Midnight Cowboy, Coming Home*); Cannes Film Festival Award for Best Actor (*Coming Home*).

W

WALKEN, CHRISTOPHER. Born March 31, 1943, in Queens, New York; actor. Intense actor who has experienced a popular resurgence in the 1990s with such menacing roles as *King of New York*, *True Romance*, *Pulp Fiction*, and *The Addiction*, thereby becoming a commodity in independent film. His recent attention, however, is merely an extension of a long career (begun as Ronny Walken) exploring the psychological complexities of men in a state of inner turmoil. A minor, but memorable, comic turn on this persona came in *Annie Hall* as Annie's creepy brother Duane, a gravely despondent character who becomes hysterical in contrast to the Woody Allen world around him. His first great success was as Nick in *The Deer Hunter*, especially the riveting Russian roulette scene opposite Robert De Niro's Michael in the Saigon gambling den. In 1987 Walken was cast in his second Woody Allen picture, *September*, but, like most of his fellow actors, his role was recast when Allen opted to reshoot much of the film. On the occasions when he has used his chilling presence to comic effect, he has been especially unforgettable—in his killer dance routine in *Pennies from Heaven* and as Drill Sergeant Merwin J. Toomey in *Biloxi Blues*.

Filmography: Me and My Brother (1969); The Anderson Tapes (1971); The Happiness Cage (1972); Next Stop, Greenwich Village (1976); Annie Hall (1977); Roseland (1977); The Sentinel (1978); The Deer Hunter (1978); Last Embrace (1979); The Dogs of War (1980); Heaven's Gate (1980); Shoot the Sun Down (1981); Pennies from Heaven (1981); Who Am I This Time? (1982, tvm); Brainstorm (1983); The Dead Zone (1983); A View to a Kill (1985); At Close Range (1986); War Zone (1986); Biloxi Blues (1988); The Milagro Beanfield War (1988); Puss in Boots (1988); Communion (1989); Homeboy (1989); The Comfort of Strangers (1990); King of New York (1990); Sarah, Plain and Tall (1991, tvm); Mistress (1992); Skylark (1993, tvm); True Romance (1993); Wayne's

World 2 (1993); Pulp Fiction (1994); A Business Affair (1994); Search and Destroy (1995); The Addiction (1995); Prophecy (1995); Things to Do in Denver When You're Dead (1995); Wild Side (1995).

Honors: Academy Award for Best Supporting Actor (*The Deer Hunter*); New York Film Critics Circle Award for Best Actor (*The Deer Hunter*).

WALSH, M. EMMET. Born Michael Emmet Walsh March 22, 1935, in Ogdensburg, New York; actor. One of the most consistent character actors of the last three decades, the craggy, burly Walsh has appeared in so many exceptional movies that it's difficult to cite his best work without listing his entire filmography. But some of the most memorable are *Straight Time*, as Dustin Hoffman's hateful parole officer, who is justifiably humiliated when he is cuffed to a fence and stripped; *Ordinary People*, as the swim coach; *Blade Runner*, as the cold-hearted police captain Bryant; *Blood Simple*, as the double-crossing private eye Visser; and *Equinox*, as the off-center mechanic whose gut-wrenching monologue about his past is one of his purest moments.

Filmography: Midnight Cowboy (1969); Alice's Restaurant (1969); Little Big Man (1970); The Traveling Executioner (1970); Cold Turkey (1971); Escape from the Planet of the Apes (1971); They Might Be Giants (1971); Get to Know Your Rabbit (1972); What's Up, Doc? (1972); Kid Blue (1973); Serpico (1973); The Gambler (1974); At Long Last Love (1975); Mikey and Nicky (1976); Nickelodeon (1976); Airport 77 (1977); Slap Shot (1977); Straight Time (1978); The Fish That Saved Pittsburgh (1979); The Jerk (1979); Brubaker (1980); Ordinary People (1980); Raise the Titanic (1980); Back Roads (1981); Reds (1981); Blade Runner (1982); Cannery Row (1982); The Escape Artist (1982); Fast Walking (1982); Silkwood (1983); Blood Simple (1984); Raw Courage (1984); Grandview U.S.A. (1984); Missing in Action (1984); The Pope of Greenwich Village (1984); Scandalous (1984); Fletch (1984); Back to School (1986); The Best of Times (1986); Critters (1986); Wildcats (1986); Harry and the Hendersons (1987); No Man's Land (1987); Raising Arizona (1987); Clean and Sober (1988); The Milagro Beanfield War (1988); Sunset (1988); War Party (1988); Sundown (1989); Thunderground (1989); The Mighty Quinn (1989); Red Scorpion (1989); Catch Me If You Can (1989); Narrow Margin (1990); Chattahoochee (1990); White Sands (1992); Killer Image (1992); Four Eyes and Six-Guns (1992, ctvm); The Music of Chance (1993); Equinox (1993); Wilder Napalm (1993); Bitter Harvest (1993); Camp Nowhere (1994); The Glass Shield (1994); Panther (1995); Dead Badge (1995); Free Willy 2: The Adventure Home (1995).

Honor: Independent Spirit Award for Best Actor (*Blood Simple*).

WANG, WAYNE. Born John Wayne Wang January 12, 1949, in Hong Kong; director, producer, screenwriter. Filmmaker who studied film at California College of Arts and Crafts in Oakland and, with Rick Schmidt (filmmaker and author of *Feature Filmmaking at Used-Car Prices*), codirected a no-budget feature before returning to his homeland to work in television. He later came back to the United States to make the $20,000 feature *Chan Is Missing*—one of the first shoestring-budget films to find major success on the independent film circuit. He continued to explore Asian-American life in his subsequent films (his *Dim Sum: A Little Bit of Heart* is devoted to the glories of Asian cooking) with the exception of the intriguing *Slamdance*, a modern-day film noir with nary an Asian-American actor in sight. However, with his first studio film, his adaptation of Amy Tan's *The Joy Luck Club*, he displayed the depth and breadth of his talents in telling this intricately structured story of three generations of Asian women. With his two star-studded 1995 films—*Smoke* and the improvisational love poem to Brooklyn, *Blue in the Face* (the latter codirected with author Paul Auster)—he continues to reflect on the emotional bonds between friends, family, and community. *Chan Is Missing* is included in the Library of Congress' National Film Registry.

Filmography: The Golden Needles (1974) Chinese episodes only; A Man, a Woman, and a Killer (1975) codirected with Rick Schmidt; Chan Is Missing (1982) also producer, screenplay, actor, editor; Dim Sum: A Little Bit of Heart (1985) also producer; Slamdance (1987); Eat a Bowl of Tea (1989); Life is Cheap . . . But Toilet Paper Is Expensive (1990) also ep; The Joy Luck Club (1993) also producer; Smoke (1995); Blue in the Face (1995).

Honor: Berlin Film Festival Special Jury Prize (*Smoke*).

WAR ROOM, THE (1993), documentary. Directed by D. A. Pennebaker, Chris Hegedus; produced by Wendy Ettinger, Frazer Pennebaker, R. J. Cutler; photographed by D. A. Pennebaker, Nick Doob, Kevin Rafferty; edited by D. A. Pennebaker, Hegedus, and Erez Laufer; released by October Films; 90 minutes. *Cast*: James Carville, George Stephanopoulos, Mary Matalin, Mickey Kantor.

An extraordinary behind-the-scenes look at the 1992 presidential campaign of Bill Clinton that focuses specifically on the headquarters, or ''war room,'' where George Stephanopoulos and James Carville devised the campaign's strategy. Compelling not only because it offers an opportunity to see the inner workings of American politics but also because of the richness of its two central characters—the earnest Stephanopoulos and the downright giddy Carville—both of whom have since become two of the most recognizable names in the political arena. A fascinating, funny, and often deeply emotional film that is the natural extension of the American media's increasingly detailed examination of presidential politics. The highlight is a tearful Carville on the final day of the campaign as he realizes that this very special part of his life is coming to an end.

Award: Academy Award nomination for Best Documentary Feature.

WARDEN, JACK. Born September 18, 1920, in Newark, New Jersey; actor. Surly, but gentle, character actor whose most notable early role was in *Twelve Angry Men*, though his most acclaimed performances did not come until the 1970s. He received Oscar nominations for his two supporting roles opposite Warren Beatty and Julie Christie—as the adulterous husband who considers investing in Beatty's future in *Shampoo* and as perplexed football coach Max

Corkle, who believes that his quarterback has been reincarnated, in *Heaven Can Wait*. He is equally brilliant opposite Peter Sellers in *Being There* (again under the direction of Hal Ashby) as President Bobby, the man who listens carefully to the advice of the simpleton gardener Chance. Throughout the 1980s and 1990s, however, his films have been of widely varying quality, though Woody Allen's *September* and the Sandra Bullock vehicle *While You Were Sleeping* have given him the opportunity to showcase his exceptional talent.

Filmography of key pre-1965 films: The Bachelor Party (1957); Edge of the City (1957); Twelve Angry Men (1957); Donovan's Reef (1963).

Filmography since 1965: Blindfold (1966); Bye Bye Braverman (1968); Brian's Song (1970, tvm); The Sporting Club (1971); Who Is Harry Kellerman, and Why Is He Saying Those Terrible Things about Me? (1971); Billy Two Hats (1973); The Man Who Loved Cat Dancing (1973); The Apprenticeship of Duddy Kravitz (1974); Shampoo (1975); All the President's Men (1976); The White Buffalo (1977); Death on the Nile (1978); Heaven Can Wait (1978); And Justice for All (1979); Being There (1979); Beyond the Poseidon Adventure (1979); The Champ (1979); Dreamer (1979); Used Cars (1980); Carbon Copy (1981); Chu Chu and the Phillip Flash (1981); The Great Muppet Caper (1981); So Fine (1981); The Verdict (1982); Crackers (1984); The Aviator (1985); September (1987); The Presidio (1988); Everybody Wins (1990); Problem Child (1990); Night and the City (1992); While You Were Sleeping (1995); Things to Do In Denver When You're Dead (1995).

Honors: Academy Award nominations for Best Supporting Actor (*Shampoo, Heaven Can Wait*); Emmy Award for Best Supporting Actor (*Brian's Song*).

WARHOL, ANDY. Born Andrew Warhola August 6, 1928, in Cleveland, Ohio; died February 22, 1987, in New York City; filmmaker, artist. Pop artist who was the most influential force in the art world during the 1960s, he would apply his aesthetics of banality to motion pictures to become the avant-garde's most visible filmmaker. Far from standard narratives, his earliest films were amateurish, cinema verité documents of his gallery of misfits (the celebrated Factory crowd) and ranged from just a few minutes long to 1967's twenty-five-hour ****. Better described as empirical happenings that are meant to be experienced rather than watched, his films simply recorded life as it passed the lens. Often as a "director," Warhol would simply walk away from the camera while it was running. His *Kiss* is a collection of people kissing; *Sleep* is six hours of a man sleeping; *Eat* is forty-five minutes of a man eating a mushroom. The most intriguing of his films is *Empire*, an eight-hour image of the Empire State Building that spans from daylight to evening; essentially a still photograph, it questions the fundamental structure of motion pictures and reduces them to the most basic unit—the single frame—which, in this case, looks almost identical to the film as a whole. The first film of Warhol's to receive a theatrical showing was *Chelsea Girls*, a collection of vignettes photographed in New York's Chelsea Hotel and projected on two screens simultaneously; it became an underground hit and has earned a reputation as a milestone of avant-garde cinema, though it is rarely seen in its original form. Decades ahead of his time, what Warhol did as art has now moved into the mainstream in the form of home videos—rambling, poorly photographed documents of friends and family that are virtually identical to the films of the Factory crowd. After an attempt on Warhol's life in 1968 by Valerie Solanas, life at the Factory changed, and so did the films; Warhol retained a producer credit, but the task of directing the bulk of them was handed over to Paul Morrissey. A documentary about Warhol, *The Life and Times of Andy Warhol*, was released in 1991. "His contribution to film aesthetics has been in his use of passivity—a passive camera and a passive audience" (Joseph Gelmis, *The Film Director as Superstar*). "Warhol wasn't taken seriously, just as people had not taken Cocteau seriously. The group of misfits he assembled around him like a family were regarded as absurd as they copied and questioned, like a cabaret act, the rituals and manners of Hollywood" (Olivier Assayas, *Projections 4 1/2*).

Filmography of key pre-1965 films: Kiss (1963); Eat (1963); Sleep (1963); Blow Job (1964); Harlot (1964).

Filmography since 1965: The Life of Juanito Castro (1965); Empire (1965); Poor Little Rich Girl (1965); Screen Test (1965); Vinyl (1965); Beauty #2 (1965); Bitch (1965); Prison (1965); Space (1965); The Closet (1965); Henry Geldzahler (1965); Taylor Mead's Ass (1965); Face (1965); My Hustler (1965); Camp (1965); Suicide (1965); Drunk (1965); 13 Most Beautiful Women (1965); 13 Most Beautiful Boys (1965); 50 Fantastics (1965); 50 Personalities (1965); Ivy and John (1965); Screen Test I (1965); Screen Test II (1965); Horse (1965); Restaurant (1965); Afternoon (1965); Outer and Inner Space (1966); Hedy (1966); Paul Swan (1966); Bufferin/Gerard Malanga Reads Poetry (1966); More Milk, Evette (1966); The Velvet Underground and Nico (1966); Kitchen (1966); Lupe (1966); Eating Too Fast (1966); The Chelsea Girls (1966); ****/Four Stars (1967); I, a Man (1967); Bike Boy (1967); Nude Restaurant (1967); Four Stars (1967); Imitation of Christ (1967); The Loves of Ondine (1968); Lonesome Cowboys (1968); Blue Movie (1969); Women in Revolt (1972) codirector with Paul Morrissey; L'Amour (1973) codirector with Paul Morrissey.

Filmography as producer: Flesh (1968); Trash (1970); Andy Warhol's Women (1971); Heat (1972); Andy Warhol's Frankenstein (1974); Andy Warhol's Dracula (1974); Andy Warhol's Bad (1977).

Selected bibliography

Gelmis, Joseph. *The Film Director as Superstar*. New York: Doubleday, 1970.

Koch, Stephen. *Stargazer: Andy Warhol's World and His Films*. New York: Praeger, 1973.

Warhol, Andy. *Andy Warhol Diaries*. Edited by Pat Hackett. New York: Warner Books, 1989.

Wilcock, John. *The Autobiography and Sex Life of Andy Warhol*. New York: Other Scenes, 1971.

WASHINGTON, DENZEL. Born December 28, 1954, in Mt. Vernon, New York; actor. Trained at the American Conservatory Theater in San Francisco, Washington was probably best known through much of the 1980s as Dr. Chandler on television's "St. Elsewhere." His fortune changed when cast in *Cry Freedom* as the humanistic South African freedom fighter Steven Biko, who was brutally beaten to death in 1977. In this role his superstar charisma (already spotted in *A Soldier's Story* and *Power*) came to the surface, proving him to be one of the few actors today with an aura of unfailing decency and integrity—qualities that led to his heroic roles in *Glory* and *Malcolm X*. One of the most versatile leads in Hollywood, Washington always excels whether he's fluidly fingering a trumpet in Spike Lee's *Mo' Better Blues*, guiding a submarine in the action hit *Crimson Tide*, or playing the cool Walter Mosely character Easy Rawlins in *Devil in a Blue Dress*.

Filmography: Carbon Copy (1981); "St. Elsewhere" (1982–1988, tvs); A Soldier's Story (1984); Power (1986); Cry Freedom (1987); For Queen and Country (1988); Reunion (1988); Glory (1989); The Mighty Quinn (1989); Mo' Better Blues (1990); Heart Condition (1990); Ricochet (1991); Mississippi Masala (1992); Malcolm X (1992); Philadelphia (1993); Much Ado about Nothing (1993); The Pelican Brief (1993); Hank Aaron: Chasing the Dream (1995, ctv documentary) ep; Crimson Tide (1995); Virtuosity (1995); Devil in a Blue Dress (1995).

Honors: Academy Award for Best Supporting Actor (*Glory*); Academy Award nominations for Best Actor (*Malcolm X*) and Supporting Actor (*Cry Freedom*); New York Film Critics Circle Award for Best Actor (*Malcolm X*); Berlin Film Festival Silver Bear for Best Actor (*Malcolm X*).

WATERS, JOHN. Born April 22, 1946, in Baltimore; director, screenwriter. The ringmaster of a campy circus of freaks, misfits, the drug-addicted, the corpulent, and the sexually perverse, Waters is the lovable comic satirist who looks the American family in the face and cheerfully vomits on it. A camp Douglas Sirk or a comic Jean Genet, he has raised bad taste to a level of cinematic haute cuisine, delivering film after film that makes a mockery of everything that is "morally acceptable" while championing the fate of the outsider. Working with a stock acting troupe that included 300-pound female impersonator Divine, the toothless Edith Massey, Mink Stole, David Lochery, and Mary Vivian Pearce, Waters began in his Baltimore hometown making no-budget short films that didn't hesitate to offend, such as *Eat Your Make-up*, starring Divine as Jackie Kennedy, and *The Diane Linkletter Story*, a derisive reenactment of the suicide of Art Linkletter's daughter. He gained notoriety with *Pink Flamingos*, his story of the "filthiest people alive," which includes the infamous scene of Divine eating a piece of dog excrement (no camera tricks here). Waters stepped up to bigger-budget commercial filmmaking with a more palatable assault on suburban values in *Polyester*, a film best remembered today for its scratch-and-sniff "Odorama" cards. His most accomplished film to date is *Hairspray*, a brilliantly subversive attack on middle-class racism that featured his last collaboration with the late Divine and the debut appearance of the similarly overabundant Ricki Lake.

Filmography as director, writer: Hag in a Black Leather Jacket (1964, short); Roman

Candles (1966–1967, short); Eat Your Make-up (1968, short); Mondo Trasho (1970) also producer, cinematographer, editor; The Diane Linkletter Story (1970, short); Multiple Maniacs (1971) director; Pink Flamingos (1974) also producer, cinematographer, editor; Female Trouble (1975) also producer, cinematographer; Desperate Living (1977) also producer, cinematographer; Polyester (1981) also producer; Hairspray (1988) also producer, actor; Cry-Baby (1990); Serial Mom (1994).

Filmography as actor: Something Wild (1986); Homer and Eddie (1989).

Selected bibliography

Waters, John. *Shock Value.* New York: Dell, 1981.

———. *Crackpot.* New York: Vintage Books, 1987.

WAY WE WERE, THE (1973), romance. Directed by Sydney Pollack; produced by Ray Stark; photographed by Harry Stradling, Jr.; edited by Margaret Booth; music by Marvin Hamlisch, song "The Way We Were" by Hamlisch, Marilyn Bergman, and Alan Bergman, performed by Barbra Streisand; released by Columbia; 118 minutes. *Cast:* Robert Redford, Barbra Streisand, Bradford Dillman, Lois Chiles, Patrick O'Neal, James Woods, Viveca Lindfors, Herb Edelman, Sally Kirkland, Susan Blakely.

A huge box office hit that wowed audiences who couldn't get enough of Streisand and Redford, this is *the* classic Hollywood star vehicle of the 1970s. With the most popular actor and actress of the day creating magic on-screen, it's almost incidental that the episodic script is filled with contrivances and inconsistencies. If the narrative weaknesses aren't enough, the filmmakers toss a blacklisting subplot into the background to prevent this otherwise featherweight tale from blowing away. Still, with Streisand and Redford, who are infinitely more compelling than the characters they play, the film remains a pleasure to watch. Spanning from 1937 to the 1960s, it chronicles the romance and eternal breakup of New York Jewish political activist Katie Morosky (Streisand) and WASPy writer Hubbell Gardiner (Redford), for whom "everything comes too easy." Through the years, Katie and Hubbell have their moments of joy and levity, but much of their life together is spent in a state of discontentment; Katie is too committed, while Hubbell isn't committed enough. Streisand gives a virtuoso performance, but Redford shines even brighter, a benefit perhaps of his numerous collaborations with Pollack—they previously made *This Property Is Condemned* and *Jeremiah Johnson* and would later reteam on *Three Days of the Condor, The Electric Horseman,* and *Out of Africa.* Although the topic of blacklisting is handled superficially, Pollack must be commended for being among the first Hollywood directors to address the fascist evil of the House Un-American Activities Committee.

Awards: Academy Awards for Best Song, Score; Academy Award nominations for Best Actress, Cinematography, Art Direction, Costume Design.

WAYNE, JOHN. Born Marion Michael Morrison May 26, 1907, in Winterset, Iowa; died June 11, 1979; actor, director. Sons Patrick and Ethan are actors;

son Michael is a producer. The greatest western hero in the movies, "Duke" Wayne appeared in nearly 150 pictures before 1965, solidly establishing him as a true American icon—a symbol of rugged individualism, frontier spirit, combat bravery, and Christian values. His late-period films, while continuing to address these ideas, would serve as anachronistic comments on his earlier image—now altered to that of a physically wearying man who stands face-to-face with his own mortality. Fittingly, over the next ten years, he would pair with others from his generation—Kirk Douglas, Robert Mitchum, Katharine Hepburn, James Stewart, and Lauren Bacall, as well as directors Howard Hawks, Henry Hathaway, and Otto Preminger. His first great film of the period is Hawks' *El Dorado*, which has at its center the declining physical condition of Wayne's aging gunfighter Cole Thornton. Disturbed by the antiwar protests of the times, Wayne made his second foray into directing (after 1960's *The Alamo*) with the misguided and misinformed patriotism of *The Green Berets*, a muddled defense of the Vietnam conflict that failed to separate the bravery of American soldiers from the recklessness of the Johnson administration. It was an exercise of historical revisionism that he would again repeat with *Chisum*, an inaccurate expansionist tale of cattle baron John Chisum's role in the Lincoln County War and the murders of Pat Garrett and Billy the Kid. Amid the innocuous westerns directed by the likes of Andrew V. McLaglen and Burt Kennedy was his Oscar-winning role for *True Grit* as the eye-patched marshal Rooster Cogburn, a beautifully acted role that he would reprise in the lesser *Rooster Cogburn* opposite Katharine Hepburn. Attempting to transfer his mythic western hero to the city à la his successor Clint Eastwood, Wayne made the police dramas *McQ* and *Brannigan*, the former interesting in its willingness to expose the police department (a law-and-order institution that didn't exist in the western world of the sheriff) as wholly corrupt, while the latter is a silly variation on Eastwood's *Coogan's Bluff*. His final film, Don Siegel's *The Shootist*, is a fitting farewell that, after opening with a montage of the Duke's past glories, tells the story of a cancer-stricken gunfighter who teaches a boy to be a man—a more honest variation on the themes of his earlier western legacy picture *The Cowboys*. Three years later, Wayne himself would die from cancer. "If this greatest of all western heroes can age and die, so, obviously, can all others" (Jack Nachbar, *Focus on the Western*).

Filmography of key pre-1965 films: Stagecoach (1939); The Long Voyage Home (1940); Fort Apache (1948); Red River (1948); She Wore a Yellow Ribbon (1949); Sands of Iwo Jima (1950); Rio Grande (1950); The Quiet Man (1952); The Searchers (1956); Rio Bravo (1959); The Alamo (1960) also producer, director; The Man Who Shot Liberty Valance (1962).

Filmography since 1965: The Greatest Story Ever Told (1965); In Harm's Way (1965); The Sons of Katie Elder (1965); Cast a Giant Shadow (1966); El Dorado (1967); The War Wagon (1967); The Green Berets (1968) also director; True Grit (1969); The Undefeated (1969); Chisum (1970); Rio Lobo (1970); Big Jake (1971); The Cowboys (1971); Cancel My Reservation (1972); Cahill, United States Marshal (1973); The Train

Robbers (1973); McQ (1974); Brannigan (1975); Rooster Cogburn (1975); The Shootist (1976).

Honors: Academy Award for Best Actor (*True Grit*); Academy Award nomination for Best Actor (*Sands of Iwo Jima*) and Picture (*The Alamo*); Congressional Medal of Honor.

Selected bibliography

McGhee, Richard D. *John Wayne: Actor, Artist, Hero.* Jefferson, NC: McFarland Press, 1990.

Ricci, Mark, et al. *The Films of John Wayne.* New York: Citadel, 1972.

Robert, Randy, and James S. Olsen. *John Wayne: American.* New York:Free Press, 1995.

WEAVER, SIGOURNEY. Born Susan Weaver October 8, 1949, in New York City; actor. Daughter of former NBC president Sylvester ''Pat'' Weaver. Statuesque actress who has found her greatest popular success as Ripley, the gutsy heroine of the *Alien* trilogy, and as Dana Barrett, the comic foil turned leggy supernatural temptress Zool in *Ghostbusters*. Her early role opposite Mel Gibson in the Australian film *The Year of Living Dangerously* and her pair of 1988 Oscar nominations for *Gorillas in the Mist* (as animal behaviorist Dian Fossey) and *Working Girl* (as Melanie Griffith's horribly competitive boss) established her as more than a genre star. Of her recent work, she was perfect as the First Lady in populist comedy *Dave* and was riveting in the intense political drama *Death and the Maiden*.

Filmography: Madman (1976); Annie Hall (1977); Alien (1979); Eyewitness (1980); The Year of Living Dangerously (1982); Deal of the Century (1983); Ghostbusters (1984); Une Femme ou Deux/One Woman or Two (1985); Half Moon Street/Escort Girl (1986); Aliens (1986); Gorillas in the Mist (1988); Working Girl (1988); Ghostbusters II (1989); Alien³ (1992); 1492: Conquest of Paradise (1992); Dave (1993); Death and the Maiden (1994); Jeffrey (1995); Copycat (1995).

Honors: Academy Award nominations for Best Actress (*Aliens, Gorillas in the Mist*); Academy Award nominations for Best Supporting Actress (*Working Girl*).

WELCH, RAQUEL. Born Raquel Tejada September 5, 1940, in Chicago; actor. Daughter Tahnee is an actor. Arguably the most popular sex symbol in America until the postered appearance of Farrah Fawcett, this busty, bronzed beauty stirred the country's libido as she pranced through prehistory in her skimpy animal-skin outfit in *One Million Years B.C.* While ridiculously chaste in retrospect, Welch managed to build a career on a curvaceous physique that was paradoxically miniaturized the same year in the enjoyable sci-fi adventure *Fantastic Voyage*. Humorously twisting her sex symbol status back onto itself, Welch took the tongue-in-cheek role of Lillian Lust in the madcap Peter Cook–Dudley Moore comedy *Bedazzled*. Considerably less effective and perhaps funnier was *Myra Breckinridge* (also starring past sexpot Mae West and future heir Fawcett). Attempting to break away from purely sexual roles, she gave a spirited performance as a roller derby queen in *Kansas City Bomber* and, the following year, did her best work as the voluptuous, bustier-clad Constance of *The Three*

Musketeers and its sequel. She has been absent from the screen for much of the last two decades, though her daughter Tahnee has attempted to carry the torch.

Filmography: A House Is Not a Home (1964), Roustabout (1964), A Swingin' Summer (1965); Shoot Louder . . . Louder . . . I Don't Understand (1966); Le Fate/The Queens (1966); Fantastic Voyage (1966); One Million Years B.C. (1966); Bedazzled (1967); Fathom (1967); The Oldest Profession (1968); Bandolero! (1968); The Biggest Bundle of Them All (1968); Lady in Cement (1968); 100 Rifles (1969); Flareup (1969); The Magic Christian (1970); Myra Breckenridge (1970); The Beloved (1971); Hannie Caulder (1971) also producer; Bluebeard (1972); Fuzz (1972); Kansas City Bomber (1972); The Last of Sheila (1973); The Three Musketeers (1973); The Four Musketeers (1975); The Wild Party (1975); Mother, Jugs and Speed (1976); L'Animal (1977); Crossed Swords/ The Prince and the Pauper (1977); Naked Gun 33 1/3: The Final Insult (1994).

WELD, TUESDAY. Born Susan Ker Weld August 27, 1943, in New York City; actor. Married to violinist Pinchas Zuckerman; formerly married to actor Dudley Moore. Starting as a child model at the tender age of three, Weld spent many years in the midst of an alcoholic and suicidal depression before even entering her teens. Possessing the poutish face of a sex kitten but with years of experience in her eyes, Weld has grown into a talented actor who is in far too few films. Surprising the anti-Weld faction of critics and gossip columnists of the 1960s, she gave a notable performance in the quirky gambling tale *The Cincinnati Kid.* The 1970s and 1980s saw her in less than a dozen films, but of those, Henry Jaglom's *A Safe Place* (costarring with Jack Nicholson and Orson Welles), *Looking for Mr. Goodbar, Who'll Stop the Rain, Thief,* and *Once Upon a Time in America* all contain knockout performances. Since the mid-1980s, however, her screen appearances have become even rarer occurrences—she is totally wasted in the best-forgotten Elvis fantasy *Heartbreak Hotel* but fares better as Michael Douglas' estranged wife in *Falling Down.*

Filmography of pre-1965 films: ''The Many Lives of Dobie Gillis'' (1959–1963, tvs); Return to Peyton Place (1961); Wild in the Country (1961).

Filmography since 1965: The Cincinnati Kid (1965); I'll Take Sweden (1965); Lord Love a Duck (1966); Pretty Poison (1968); I Walk the Line (1970); A Safe Place (1971); Play It As It Lays (1972); F. Scott Fitzgerald in Hollywood (1976, tvm); Looking for Mr. Goodbar (1977); Who'll Stop the Rain (1978); Serial (1980); Mother and Daughter— The Loving War (1980, tvm); Thief (1981); Author! Author! (1982); The Rainmaker (1982, ctvm); Once Upon a Time in America (1984); Heartbreak Hotel (1988); Falling Down (1993).

Honor: Academy Award nomination for Best Supporting Actress (*Looking for Mr. Goodbar*).

WHAT'S UP, DOC? (1972), comedy. Directed and produced by Peter Bogdanovich; screenplay by Buck Henry, David Newman, and Robert Benton (from a story by Bogdanovich); photographed by Laszlo Kovacs; edited by Verna Fields; music by Artie Butler, song ''You're the Top'' by Cole Porter and sung by Barbra Streisand; released by Warner Bros.; 94 minutes. *Cast*: Barbra Streisand, Ryan O'Neal, Kenneth Mars, Austin Pendleton, Madeline Kahn, John Hillerman, Mabel Albertson, Michael Murphy, Randy Quaid, M. Emmet Walsh.

A modern reworking of Howard Hawks' 1938 classic *Bringing Up Baby* with Ryan O'Neal in the Cary Grant role as awkward musicologist Howard Bannister and Barbra Streisand as Judy Maxwell, an amalgam of Katharine Hepburn and Bugs Bunny. The screwball plot whips into a frenzy around four hotel guests and their identical valises, each with different contents—Howard's precious prehistoric rocks, Judy's clothes, a wealthy hotel guest's diamonds, and some top-secret documents—which, of course, all end up in the wrong hands. Howard's fateful meeting with Judy not only derails his chance to get a research grant but also throws his organized and uneventful life into a whirlwind of madcap antics. Soon, much to the chagrin of Howard's fiancée Eunice Burns (Kahn), this crazed, carrot-chomping Judy is masquerading as Eunice (or "Burnsy," as she calls herself), taking bubble baths in Howard's room, hanging around on the balcony outside his window, accidentally tearing off his clothes, and, in the process, winning his heart. An absolute delight that was one of the most successful comedies of the early 1970s (and Bogdanovich's first commercial hit). It not only comments on Howard Hawks and Loony Toons cartoons but also has fun turning the chase scene from *Bullitt* into a comic Road Runner romp through the streets of San Francisco. A final joke has Bogdanovich borrowing the "Love means never having to say you're sorry" line from O'Neal's 1970 tearjerker *Love Story*, to which Howard replies: "That's the dumbest thing I've ever heard."

Award: WGA Award.

WHITAKER, FOREST. Born July 15, 1961, in Longview, Texas; actor, director. Exceptional actor whose imposing physical presence counters a tender, sensitive demeanor. After a memorable early part as the cocky street hustler who knows how to handle a pool cue in *The Color of Money*, he sealed his reputation as a true talent by delivering a remarkable performance as legendary jazz saxophonist and drug addict Charlie Parker in Clint Eastwood's *Bird*. It is rare to see an actor bare his soul to such a level, but that is precisely what Whitaker does; without reservation, he simply becomes Parker. Nearly as impressive are his roles as the British soldier kidnapped by the Irish Republican Army in *The Crying Game*, the flamboyant fashion designer in *Ready to Wear* (*Prêt-à-Porter*), and the mechanic who is united with the son he never knew existed in *Smoke*. By the mid-1990s, he began to turn his attention to directing with the critically acclaimed cable movie *Lush Life* and the popular Hollywood release *Waiting to Exhale*.

Filmography: Fast Times at Ridgemont High (1982); Vision Quest (1985); North and South (1985, tvms); The Color of Money (1986); Platoon (1986); Good Morning, Vietnam (1987); Stakeout (1987); Bird (1988); Bloodsport (1988); Johnny Handsome (1989);

Downtown (1990); A Rage in Harlem (1991) also producer; The Crying Game (1992); Body Snatchers (1993); Blown Away (1994); Strapped (1993, ctvm) director; The Enemy Within (1994, ctvm); Lush Life (1994, ctvm); Ready to Wear *(Prêt-à-Porter)* (1994); Jason's Lyric (1994); Smoke (1995); Species (1995); Waiting to Exhale (1995) director.

Honor: Cannes Film Festival Award for Best Actor (*Bird*).

WHITE DOG (1982), drama. Directed and cowritten by Samuel Fuller; screenplay with Curtis Hanson (from the novella by Romain Gary); produced by Jon Davison; photographed by Bruce Surtees; edited by Bernard Gribble; music by Ennio Morricone; released by Paramount; 90 minutes. *Cast*: Kristy McNichol, Paul Winfield, Burl Ives, Jameson Parker, Paul Bartel, Christa Lang.

A gripping antiracist attack from Hollywood veteran Sam Fuller, who unfortunately had to endure the disrespect of then-Paramount Pictures president Michael Eisner, who refused to release the picture. In the years since, *White Dog* has rightly found a place in the Fuller canon as one of his greatest achievements. Based on an episode in the novella by Romain Gary, it tells the story of a young woman (McNichol) who unwittingly adopts a ''white dog''—an animal trained by racists to attack black skin. Rather than put her pet to sleep, she persuades a black trainer (Winfield) to help break the dog of its ways. Although the film has its weaknesses (not the least of which is its odd casting), the thesis that racism is a learned behavior of intolerance that cuts deep into the fabric of America (the dog's bigoted trainer is a nice grandpa played by Burl Ives) makes *White Dog* a rarity—a bare-knuckle social commentary from one of Hollywood's great renegade filmmakers. It's no wonder Paramount shelved it, and, on the basis of Hollywood's poor track record in dealing with black America, it's no wonder that the National Association for the Advancement of Colored People pressured Paramount to do so. ''As in the fables of Aesop and La Fontaine, the hero of Fuller's parable may be a dog, but the subject is the human race'' (Jonathan Rosenbaum, *Chicago Reader*, November 29, 1991).

WHO FRAMED ROGER RABBIT (1988), animation/comedy. Directed by Robert Zemeckis; screenplay by Jeffrey Price and Peter S. Seaman (from the book by Gary K. Wolf); produced by Robert Watts and Frank Marshall; executive-produced by Steven Spielberg and Kathleen Kennedy; photographed by Dean Cundey; edited by Arthur Schmidt; music by Alan Silvestri; released by Buena Vista; 103 minutes. *Cast*: Bob Hoskins, Charles Fleischer, Kathleen Turner, Christopher Lloyd, Joanna Cassidy, Stubby Kaye, Joel Silver, Amy Irving, Mel Blanc.

A breakthrough film in animation, this dazzling celebration of cartoons achieved a spot in film history through its inventive mix of animation and live action. Although it was not the first time it had been done (Jerry of ''Tom and Jerry'' danced with Gene Kelly in 1944's *Anchors Aweigh*), it surely was the best. The plot revolves around the delicious concept that cartoon characters actually coexist with human beings, teaming down-and-out detective Eddie Valiant (Hoskins) with famous "toon" actor Roger Rabbit (voiced by Fleischer) in a battle against the evil Judge Doom (Lloyd). Part film noir, part Tex Avery cartoon, *Who Framed Roger Rabbit* is a masterpiece of visual invention that never fails to entertain or amaze. It is filled with cameos from numerous cartoon characters ranging from Disney icons Mickey Mouse and Donald Duck, to Warner Brothers luminaries Daffy Duck and Bugs Bunny, to Amblin creations Roger Rabbit and his extremely sexy friend Jessica Rabbit ("she's not bad, she's just drawn that way").

Sequels: The Roger Rabbit and Jessica Rabbit characters have appeared in the short films *Tummy Trouble* (1988), *Rollercoaster Rabbit* (1990), and *Trail Mix-Up* (1993).

Award: Los Angeles Film Critics Special Award for Outstanding Technical Achievement.

WHO'S AFRAID OF VIRGINIA WOOLF? (1966), drama. Directed by Mike Nichols; screenplay and produced by Ernest Lehman (from the play by Edward Albee); photographed by Haskell Wexler and Harry Stradling (b&w); edited by Sam O'Steen; music by Alex North; released by Warner Bros.; 131 minutes. *Cast*: Elizabeth Taylor, Richard Burton, George Segal, Sandy Dennis.

Edward Albee's twisted look at a marriage between two sickly, dependent people who play out a dangerous psychological game of brutality, ugliness, and debasement. Richard Burton stars as George, a history professor who was groomed to "be" the department but is now merely "in" it; Elizabeth Taylor is his blowsy wife, Martha, the daughter of the university president. The cruelty begins at 2 A.M. with George and Martha arriving home from a university party where they've met Nick (Segal), a new, fresh-faced biology professor, and Honey (Dennis), his mousy, "hipless" wife. The foursome continue their partying until dawn, but the drama begins the moment that Nick and Honey cross the threshold of their hosts' Northampton home. As the drinks flow freely, George and Martha exchange poisoned barbs, Honey vomits after too many brandies, Nick confides to George that he married only because of Honey's hysterical pregnancy, George viciously insults and humiliates his guests, Nick and Martha sleep together, and Martha makes the mistake of telling her guests about her and George's sixteen-year-old son—a son who, we later learn, has been invented in order to fill an emotional void in their relationship. The debut feature from Mike Nichols, this is a draining film that exists in that hellish, too-quiet emptiness of the night when everyone else is asleep. Albee's fabric of absurdist language and situations is here stitched into realism with Ernest Lehman's intelligent adaptation, Nichols' deft direction of his talented cast, and Haskell Wexler's graceful images. A shocking film today, which was even more so in 1966. "The American screen has never until now employed such salty lingo" (*Variety*, June 22, 1966).

Awards: Academy Awards for Best Actress (Taylor), Supporting Actress (Dennis), Cinematography, Art Direction, Costume Design; Academy Award nominations for Best

Picture, Director, Actor (Burton), Supporting Actor (Segal), Screenplay, Editing, Sound, Score.

WIEST, DIANNE. Born March 28, 1948, in Kansas City, Missouri; actor. Lively, expressive actor who began her acting career while studying theater at the University of Maryland before joining the American Shakespeare Company. After appearing on stage in such works as *Inherit the Wind, Hedda Gabler, A Doll's House, Othello* (as Desdemona opposite James Earl Jones), and *The Art of Dining* (earning her an Obie), Wiest achieved critical acclaim with her Oscar-winning portrayal of Holly, the young sibling in *Hannah and Her Sisters*. She received a second nomination in 1989 as a neurotic mother in *Parenthood* and has given memorable performances in *Edward Scissorhands* and *Little Man Tate*. She won her second Oscar for her hilarious work in Allen's *Bullets Over Broadway* as Helen Sinclair, the fading star desperate for a hit.

Filmography: It's My Turn (1980); I'm Dancing As Fast As I Can (1981); Independence Day (1982); Falling in Love (1983); Footloose (1984); The Purple Rose of Cairo (1985); Hannah and Her Sisters (1986); The Lost Boys (1987); Radio Days (1987); September (1987); Bright Lights, Big City (1988); Cookie (1989); Parenthood (1989); Edward Scissorhands (1990); Little Man Tate (1991); Cops and Robbersons (1994); The Scout (1994); Bullets over Broadway (1994).

Honors: Academy Awards for Best Supporting Actress (*Hannah and Her Sisters, Bullets over Broadway*); Academy Award nomination for Best Supporting Actress (*Parenthood*); Los Angeles Film Critics Awards for Best Supporting Actress (*Hannah and Her Sisters, Bullets over Broadway*); New York Film Critics Circle Award for Best Supporting Actress (*Hannah and Her Sisters, Bullets over Broadway*).

WILD BUNCH, THE (1969), western. Directed and cowritten by Sam Peckinpah; screenplay with Walon Green (from the story by Green and Roy N. Sickner); photographed by Lucien Ballard; edited by Louis Lombardo; music by Jerry Fielding; released by Warner Bros.; 135 minutes (rereleased at 148 minutes. *Cast*: William Holden, Ernest Borgnine, Robert Ryan, Edmond O'Brien, Warren Oates, Jaime Sanchez, Ben Johnson, Strother Martin, Emilio Fernandez, L. Q. Jones, Albert Dekker, Bo Hopkins, Dub Taylor, Alfonso Arau.

The most honest western ever made, *The Wild Bunch* is unfailing in its depiction of violent killers who value only one thing—their code of honor. More than money, drink, or whoring, these men place importance on their word; once they give it, they don't go back on it. William Holden's morally ambiguous Pike Bishop (with his Peckinpah-like mustache) is an antihero who, because of the non-judgmental rendering of his character, is mythic in nature—a cold-blooded killer and unrepentant thief who retains his honor until the end. Set in 1913 in the dawn of the coming Industrial Revolution, the film centers on a gang of thieves and murderers who, after being ambushed in a bank job, flee to Mexico to avoid a bounty hunter and former bunch member Deke Thornton (Ryan). They land in the midst of the Mexican revolution and agree to take one final job. Released amid a firestorm of mixed critical responses to its shocking slow-motion violence (even today we feel the chilling brutality of Bo Hopkins' unconscionable killing of the two bank employees), it is nonetheless a reflection of Vietnam and the recent assassinations of Robert Kennedy and Martin Luther King. Despite the bloodletting and brutality, the film ultimately does not promote violence; instead, it's a film filled with it. *The Wild Bunch* is much too complex to be reduced to the sole issue of violence when the underlying issue is how violence results from our society's inability to live by one's word. In the end, the bunch is obliterated; like the powerful and deadly scorpion that is devoured by hundreds of ants, Pike is a victim of a highly organized modern civilization that will no longer tolerate his venom or his code of honor. Jam-packed with virtuoso performances, great lines (Pike's "If they move, kill 'em!" is spoken just as Peckinpah's directing credit pops on screen), and revolutionary editing. David Cook calls the final gun battle "a mad orgasmic frenzy, as the slaughter grows more and more intense until it reaches first Eisensteinian, then Bunuelian, and finally Wagnerian proportions" (*The International Dictionary of Films and Filmmakers*).

WILDER, GENE. Born Jerry Silberman June 11, 1935, in Milwaukee; actor, director, screenwriter. Married to comedian Gilda Radner from 1984 until her death in 1989. Frizzy-haired comic who trained at the Old Vic in England and the Actors Studio in New York City before garnering attention for his small, but memorable, bit in *Bonnie and Clyde* as a nervous undertaker who is taken for a joyride by the infamous couple. He then went on to fruitful collaborations with Mel Brooks and Richard Pryor, appearing in some of the most commercially successful films of the 1970s. Not to be overlooked is his role as the childlike factory owner in *Willy Wonka and the Chocolate Factory*, a performance that perfectly mixes his comic flair with a dark dramatic side. His first attempt at directing was the mildly amusing comedy *The Adventure of Sherlock Holmes' Smarter Brother*, though his subsequent directing efforts are inconsequential.

Filmography as actor: Bonnie and Clyde (1967); The Producers (1967); Quackser Fortune Has a Cousin in the Bronx (1970); Start the Revolution without Me (1970); Willy Wonka and the Chocolate Factory (1971); Everything You Always Wanted to Know about Sex (*but were afraid to ask) (1972); Rhinoceros (1972); Blazing Saddles (1974); The Little Prince (1974); Young Frankenstein (1974) also writer; Silver Streak (1976); The Frisco Kid (1979); Stir Crazy (1980); Hanky Panky (1982); See No Evil, Hear No Evil (1989) also screenplay; Funny about Love (1990); Another You (1991); "Something Wilder" (1994, tvs).

Filmography as director, writer and actor: The Adventure of Sherlock Holmes' Smarter Brother (1975); The World's Greatest Lover (1977) also producer; Sunday Lovers, "American Segment" (1981); The Woman in Red (1984); Haunted Honeymoon (1986) also producer.

Honors: Academy Award nominations for Best Supporting Actor (*The Producers*) and Screenplay (*Young Frankenstein*).

WILLIAMS, BILLY DEE. Born April 6, 1937, in New York City; actor. Extremely popular Harlem-born black actor of the 1970s who received early acclaim as Gale Sayers in the exceptional television movie *Brian's Song* and went on to star opposite Diana Ross in *Lady Sings the Blues* and *Mahogany* before taking the lead in the musical biopic *Scott Joplin*. While many of his contemporaries were restricted to blaxploitation, Williams' avoidance of the genre is perhaps responsible for his longer, albeit sporadic, career. Aside from his roles as Lando Calrissian in *The Empire Strikes Back* and *The Return of the Jedi*, he was generally absent from the big screen throughout the 1980s until Tim Burton cast him as district attorney Harvey Dent in 1989's *Batman*. With that Williams could add to his résumé yet another of the biggest moneymakers of all time.

Filmography: The Last Angry Man (1959); The Out-of-Towners (1970); Brian's Song (1971, tvm); The Final Comedown (1971); Lady Sings the Blues (1972); Hit (1973); The Take (1974); Mahogany (1975); The Bingo Long Traveling All-Stars and Motor Kings (1976); Blast (1976); Scott Joplin (1977); The Empire Strikes Back (1980); Nighthawks (1981); Marvin and Tige (1983); Return of the Jedi (1983); Fear City (1984); Number One with a Bullet (1986); Deadly Illusion (1987); The Imposter (1988); Batman (1989); Driving Me Crazy (1991); The Pit and the Pendulum (1991); Secret Agent 00 Soul (1991); Giant Steps (1992); Alien Intruder (1993).

WILLIAMS, ROBIN. Born July 21, 1952, in Chicago; actor, comedian. Frenzied comic without equal whose stream-of-consciousness style and unbridled insanity are rarely captured effectively on film. After his success on television's "Mork and Mindy" as Mork from the Planet Ork, he was cast in his first Hollywood film—*Popeye*, Robert Altman's commercially disastrous, but faithful, reworking of the popular cartoon character. He fared much better in his follow-up, *The World according to Garp*, but then hit a patch of nearly unwatchable comedies before Barry Levinson cast him as radio personality Adrian Cronauer in *Good Morning, Vietnam*, in a hysterical comic rant that essentially amounted to a stand-up routine. He has since shown a brilliant serious side with stirring performances in *Dead Poets Society*, *Awakenings*, and *The Fisher King*. As in his comedy he isn't afraid to take risks, even if, as in Levinson's *Toys* or Bill Forsyth's *Being Human*, the results are disappointing. One of the top box office draws in Hollywood, he has carried *Mrs. Doubtfire* and *Jumanji* (and 1996's *The Birdcage*) over the $100 million mark. In addition to his film work he still makes frequent comedy club appearances and is a perennial host of the "Comic Relief" fund-raising event.

Filmography: Can I Do It . . . Till I Need Glasses? (1979); Popeye (1980); The World according to Garp (1982); The Survivors (1983); Moscow on the Hudson (1984); The Best of Times (1986); Club Paradise (1986); Seize the Day (1986); Dear America (1987, documentary); Good Morning, Vietnam (1987); The Adventures of Baron Munchausen (1988); Dead Poets Society (1989); Awakenings (1990); Cadillac Man (1990); Dead

Again (1991); The Fisher King (1991); Hook (1991); Toys (1992); Aladdin (1992) voice; FernGully . . . The Last Rainforest (1993) voice; Mrs. Doubtfire (1993); Being Human (1994); Nine Months (1995); Jumanji (1995).

Honors: Academy Award nominations for Best Actor (*The Fisher King*), Supporting Actor (*Good Morning, Vietnam, Dead Poets Society*); Grammy Award for Best Comedy Recording ("Robin Williams: A Night at the Met" 1988).

WILLIS, BRUCE. Born March 19, 1955, in West Germany; actor. Married to Demi Moore. Charismatic leading man who excels in action, comedy, and drama, Willis first caught the public's eye on television's "Moonlighting" with the witty repartee between him and his costar Cybill Shepherd. Later, as John McClane, the wisecracking, hard-hitting cop of *Die Hard* and its sequels, Willis became an American action icon. Again he changed directions with *In Country*, a mediocre film in which he turns in a surprisingly touching performance as a Vietnam vet. For a star of his stature, however, he has appeared in an inordinate number of box office bombs (*Bonfire of the Vanities, Hudson Hawk,* and *North*), but their poor showings have failed to dent his armor. After the failure of the clichéd action pictures *The Last Boy Scout* and *Striking Distance*, Willis masterfully redirected his career away from high-octane explosions and toward riskier ventures such as Richard Rush's largely unseen erotic thriller *Color of Night*, Quentin Tarantino's blockbuster *Pulp Fiction*, and Robert Benton's nuanced drama *Nobody's Fool*.

Filmography: The First Deadly Sin (1980); The Verdict (1982); "Moonlighting" (1985– 1989, tvs); Blind Date (1987); Die Hard (1988); Sunset (1988) also ep; In Country (1989); Look Who's Talking (1989) voice; That's Adequate (1989); Bonfire of the Vanities (1990); Die Hard 2: Die Harder (1990); Look Who's Talking Too (1990) voice; Billy Bathgate (1991); Hudson Hawk (1991) also story; The Last Boy Scout (1991); Mortal Thoughts (1991); The Player (1992); Death Becomes Her (1992); National Lampoon's Loaded Weapon 1 (1993); Striking Distance (1993); North (1994); Color of Night (1994); Pulp Fiction (1994); Nobody's Fool (1994); Four Rooms (1995); Die Hard with a Vengeance (1995).

Honor: Emmy Award for Best Actor (*Moonlighting*, 1987).

WINGER, DEBRA. Born May 17, 1955, in Cleveland, Ohio; actor. Formerly married to Timothy Hutton. Raspy-voiced actor with a sense of strength and precision who conveys a softness underneath her tough exterior. After a three-month stint in the Israeli army, the eighteen-year-old returned to Los Angeles (where she was raised) and eventually landed the part of Drusilla the Wonder Girl in the television series "Wonder Woman." With her three notable roles in the early 1980s—*Urban Cowboy, An Officer and a Gentleman,* and *Terms of Endearment*—she was at the top of the acting game, earning a pair of Oscar nominations in the process. Her career since then has been split between moderate commercial successes such as *Legal Eagles, Leap of Faith,* and *Forget Paris* and emotionally demanding and soul-baring roles in *The Sheltering Sky,*

A Dangerous Woman, and *Shadowlands*. In these latter films—as Bernardo Bertolucci's traveler Kit Moresby, Steven Gyllenhaal's social misfit Martha, and Richard Attenborough's brash American poet Joy Gresha—she does some of her finest, most introspective work.

Filmography: "Wonder Woman" (1976–1977, tvs); Slumber Party '57 (1977); Thank God It's Friday (1978); Special Olympics (1978, tvm); French Postcards (1979); Urban Cowboy (1980); Cannery Row (1982); Mike's Murder (1982); An Officer and a Gentleman (1982); E.T. The Extra-Terrestrial (1983) voice; Terms of Endearment (1983); Legal Eagles (1986); Black Widow (1986); Made in Heaven (1987); Betrayed (1988); The Sheltering Sky (1990); Everybody Wins (1990); Leap of Faith (1992); Wilder Napalm (1993); A Dangerous Woman (1993); Shadowlands (1993); Forget Paris (1995).

Honors: Academy Award nominations for Best Actress (*An Officer and a Gentleman, Terms of Endearment, Shadowlands*).

WITNESS (1985), drama. Directed by Peter Weir; screenplay by Earl W. Wallace and William Kelley (from the story by Wallace, Kelley, and Pamela Wallace); produced by Edward S. Feldman; photographed by John Seale; edited by Thom Nobel; music by Maurice Jarre; released by Paramount; 112 minutes. *Cast*: Harrison Ford, Kelly McGillis, Lukas Haas, Josef Sommer, Jan Rubes, Alexander Godunov, Danny Glover, Patti LuPone, Viggo Mortensen.

The first American film from Australian master Peter Weir, this picture brings together the disparate elements of Weir's sense of land and community and the Hollywood staples of guns, murder, and police corruption. Fortunately, it proves to be a fitting mix, as the film itself is about the intermingling of two very different worlds. Ford is John Book, a Philadelphia police detective who travels to a nearby Amish community to investigate a murder witnessed by the young Samuel (Haas). In the process, Book falls in love with the boy's mother, Rachel (McGillis), and becomes absorbed by the culture's simplicity, generosity, and overall sense of community. The two worlds, however, are doomed to clash. Weir directs with such a delicate and assured touch that the weaknesses of the investigation plot are overshadowed by the strengths of the characters and visuals. The relationship between Book and Rachel blooms inside her barn as they slowly dance to Sam Cooke's "(What a) Wonderful World"—a moment of pure romantic poetry that simultaneously shows us their growing love and the impossibility of its ever lasting. Equally memorable is the barn-building scene in which Book finds the sense of community that he has lost with the police department; it is a moment reminiscent of John Ford's mythic Americana in which labor and cooperation are rewarded with a sense of self-worth.

Awards: Academy Award for Best Screenplay, Editing; Academy Award nominations for Best Picture, Director, Actor, Cinematography, Art Direction, Score.

WOMAN UNDER THE INFLUENCE, A (1974), drama. Directed and written by John Cassavetes; produced by Sam Shaw; photographed by Mitch Breif; edited by David Armstrong, Elizabeth Bergeron, Sheila Viseltear, and Tom Cornwell;

released by Faces International; 155 minutes. *Cast*: Gena Rowlands, Peter Falk, Matthew Cassel, Matthew Laborteaux, Christina Grisantii, Katherine Cassavetes, Lady Rowlands, Fred Draper.

The most honest and accurate portrayal of mental illness ever committed to film, this tour de force of acting helps us understand vivacious middle-class housewife Mabel Longhetti (Rowlands) as she gradually loses touch with reality, much to the consternation of her frustrated, but loving, husband Nick (Falk). Like much of Cassavetes' work, the emotions dictate the story until every word or action on the screen is felt with a heightened sense of awareness. Nothing is more heartbreaking than the reactions of the confused and frightened Longhetti children when their mother comes home from the hospital, and nothing is more romantic than Nick's undying love for his unstable wife as she prepares a spontaneous spaghetti breakfast for his coworkers. Self-financed by Cassavetes, Rowlands, and Falk, this complex character study may not be real life, but it's as close as you'll ever get on film.

Awards: Academy Award nominations for Best Director and Best Actress; included in the Library of Congress' National Film Registry (1990).

WOODARD, ALFRE. Born November 8, 1953, in Tulsa, Oklahoma; actor. Beautiful, gifted performer with a commanding presence and an aura of integrity and humanity whose acting choices reflect her political stance. First attracting attention in the stage play *For Colored Girls Who Have Considered Suicide/ When the Rainbow Is Enuff*, Woodard made her film debut in Alan Rudolph's *Remember My Name* and followed in Robert Altman's *Health*. Although she received an Oscar nomination for her role as the housekeeper Geechee in *Cross Creek*, throughout the 1980s she appeared predominantly on television in the series "Tucker's Witch," "Sara," "Hill Street Blues," "St. Elsewhere," and "L.A. Law." Her performances in *Grand Canyon* (as Danny Glover's girlfriend), *Passion Fish* (as the straight-talking nurse Chantelle), and *How to Make an American Quilt* (as Maya Angelou's daughter) were missed by most viewers but nonetheless rank her among the best actors of her generation. Cofounder in 1989 of the Artists to Free South Africa, Woodard has twice portrayed Winnie Mandela, for PBS in 1986 and HBO in 1987.

Filmography: Remember My Name (1978); Health (1980); Cross Creek (1983); Go Tell It on the Mountain (1984); Extremities (1986); Unnatural Causes (1986, tvm); Scrooged (1988); Mandela (1989, ctvm); Miss Firecracker (1989); A Mother's Courage: The Mary Thomas Story (1990, tvm); Grand Canyon (1991); Rich in Love (1992); Passion Fish (1992); The Gun in Betty Lou's Handbag (1992); Bopha! (1993); Heart and Souls (1993); The Race to Freedom: The Underground Railroad (1994, ctvm); Crooklyn (1994); Blue Chips (1994); The Piano Lesson (1994, tvm); How to Make an American Quilt (1995).

Honors: Academy Award nomination for Best Supporting Actress (*Cross Creek*); Emmy Awards ("Hill Street Blues" 1984, "L.A. Law" 1987); Independent Spirit Award for Best Supporting Actress (*Passion Fish*).

WOODS, JAMES. Born April 18, 1947, in Vernal, Utah; actor. Impassioned performer who appeared in a number of memorable minor roles before starring as the raging cop killer in *The Onion Field*. His work in *Against All Odds, Once Upon a Time in America*, and especially *Salvador* (as the amoral journalist) helped solidify his reputation as a uniquely intense actor. Curiously, while the quality of his theatrical features has faltered in recent years (*The Hard Way, Diggstown, The Specialist*), his television work has been exceptional, specifically, his films with James Garner—*The Promise* and *My Name Is Bill W.* (as AA cofounder Bill Wilson); *In Love and War* (as Vietnam prisoner of war James Stockdale); *Citizen Cohn* (as Roy Cohn); and the riveting and infuriating *Indictment: The McMartin Trial*.

Filmography: The Visitors (1972); Hickey and Boggs (1972); The Way We Were (1973); The Gambler (1974); Distance (1975); Night Moves (1975); Alex and the Gypsy (1976); The Choirboys (1977); The Gift of Love (1978, tvm); The Onion Field (1979); Eyewitness (1980); The Black Marble (1980); Fast Walking (1982); Split Image (1982); Against All Odds (1983); Videodrome (1983); Once Upon a Time in America (1984); Joshua Then and Now (1985); Stephen King's Cat's Eye (1985); Badge of the Assassin (1985, tvm); Salvador (1986); Best Seller (1987); In Love and War (1987, tvm); Promise (1986, tvm); The Boost (1988); Cop (1988) also producer; True Believer (1989); My Name Is Bill W. (1990, tvm); Immediate Family (1989); Women and Men: Stories of Seduction (1990, ctvm); The Hard Way (1991); The Boys (1991, tvm); Diggstown (1992); Straight Talk (1992); Chaplin (1992); Citizen Cohn (1992, ctvm); The Getaway (1994); The Specialist (1994); "Since I Don't Have You" episode of "Fallen Angels" (1994, ctvm); Next Door (1994, ctvm); Curse of the Starving Class (1995, ctvm); Indictment: The McMartin Trial (1995, ctvm); Killer (1995); Casino (1995).

Honors: Academy Award nomination for Best Actor (*Salvador*); Independent Spirit Award for Best Actor (*Salvador*); Emmy Awards (*Promise, My Name Is Bill W.*).

WOODSTOCK (1970), documentary. Directed, cophotographed, and coedited by Michael Wadleigh; produced by Bob Maurice; photographed with David Meyers, Richard Pearce, Don Lenzer, and Al Wertheimer; editing supervised by Thelma Schoonmaker; released by Warner Bros.; 184 minutes (1994 director's cut, 224 minutes). *Cast*: Joan Baez, Joe Cocker, Crosby, Stills, Nash and Young, Richie Havens, Jimi Hendrix, Janis Joplin, the Who, Arlo Guthrie, Santana, Jefferson Airplane, Sly and the Family Stone, John Sebastian.

Not merely a document of one of the most important moments in music history but a microcosmic examination of a segment of the American population during the most volatile of times. Spanning three hours and often using split screens with three separate images, *Woodstock* has become the standard against which all rockumentaries will now be judged—a record of the three-day "festival of peace and music" on Max Yasgur's farm in upstate New York. Interspersed between the music are births, lovemaking, drug overdoses, and the business of organizing such a monumental concert. Highlights include Jimi Hendrix's guitar feats; one of the first live performances by Crosby, Stills, Nash, and Young; Richie Haven's impassioned guitar playing; Joe Cocker's "With a Little Help from My Friends"; the warning not to "take the brown acid"; the chant for rain; the fun in the mud; and the announcement that "Woodstock is now a free concert." A celebration of cinema verité techniques that reflect the increased mobility of cameras and sound gear, *Woodstock* is as much about the history of cinema as it is about the times and the music. Among the many editors was Martin Scorsese, who later directed another exceptional concert film, *The Last Waltz.*

Awards: Academy Award for Best Documentary; Academy Award nominations for Best Editing and Sound.

WOODWARD, JOANNE. Born February 27, 1930, in Thomasville, Georgia; actor. Married to Paul Newman. A veteran of numerous television dramas and stage plays in the 1950s, Woodward made her mark on the film world with her ingeniously layered, Oscar-winning performance as a schizophrenic in 1957's *The Three Faces of Eve.* The following year saw another milestone—marriage to *Rally Round the Flag, Boys!* costar Paul Newman; the film was their first of eleven films together. As he cultivated his persona of alienation, she developed a persona of towering emotional strength. Unlike many of her contemporaries, she chose to delve deep beneath the skins of emotionally complex characters where she could grapple with the human condition and, as a result, has quietly blazed a path for such like-minded actors as Ellen Burstyn, Glenn Close, Holly Hunter, Jessica Lange, Meryl Streep, and Debra Winger. While much of her work since the mid-1970s has been on television (including a role as Dr. Wilbur opposite Sally Field in *Sybil*), her films with Newman—*The Glass Menagerie* and James Ivory's *Mr. and Mrs. Bridge*—have reminded audiences of how much Hollywood needs her presence.

Filmography of key pre-1965 films: The Three Faces of Eve (1957); The Long Hot Summer (1958); The Fugitive Kind (1960); Paris Blues (1961).

Filmography since 1965: Signpost to Murder (1965); A Big Hand for the Little Lady (1966); A Fine Madness (1966); Rachel, Rachel (1968); Winning (1969); WUSA (1970); They Might Be Giants (1971); The Effect of Gamma Rays on Man-in-the-Moon Marigolds (1972); Summer Wishes, Winter Dreams (1973); The Drowning Pool (1975); Sybil (1976, tvm); The End (1978); See How She Runs (1978, tvm); The Shadow Box (1980, tvm); Harry and Son (1984); Do You Remember Love? (1985, tvm); The Glass Menagerie (1987); Mr. and Mrs. Bridge (1990); Philadelphia (1993); Foreign Affairs (1993, ctvm); The Age of Innocence (1993) narrator; Breathing Lessons (1994, tvm).

Honors: Academy Award for Best Actress (*Three Faces of Eve*); Academy Award nominations for Best Actress (*Rachel, Rachel, Summer Wishes, Winter Dreams*); New York Film Critics Circle Awards for Best Actress (*Summer Wishes, Winter Dreams, Mr. and Mrs. Bridge*); Cannes Film Festival Award for Best Actress (*The Effect of Gamma Rays on Man-in-the-Moon Marigolds*); Emmy Awards for Best Actress (*See How She Runs, Do You Remember Love?*) Kennedy Center Honors Lifetime Achievement Award (1992).

Selected bibliography:

Morella, Joe, and Edward Z. Epstein. *Paul and Joanne: A Biography of Paul Newman and Joanne Woodward.* New York: Delacorte, 1989.

WORKING GIRLS (1986), drama. Directed, cowritten, coproduced, and edited by Lizzie Borden; screenplay with Sandra Kay; produced with Andi Gladstone; photographed by Judy Irola; music by David van Tieghem; released by Miramax; 90 minutes. *Cast*: Louise Smith, Marusia Zach, Ellen McElduff, Amanda Goodwin, Janne Peters, Helen Nicholas.

An unromantic, politically perceptive examination of prostitution that views its subject matter from a capitalistic/economic position rather than a psychoanalytic/sexual one. The film focuses on one specific woman, Molly (Smith), a lesbian who, along with a few other women, works out of the middle-class Manhattan apartment of her madam (McElduff). A Yale grad who is simply trying to make ends meet, Molly treats her job as just that—a job, with long hours, a nagging boss, and semifriendly coworkers. The strength of *Working Girls* lies in the film's adherence to its title—these are not dolled-up women in miniskirts and fishnets who get knocked around by sleazy male pimps; they are workers who have chosen a financially rewarding path. Director Borden is clearly of the opinion that prostitution and feminism are not mutually exclusive notions but logical responses to a patriarchal power structure. Apart from the issue of prostitution, *Working Girls* offers a startlingly frank view of female sexuality—not eroticism, romance, or lovemaking but the unromanticized, nonobjectifying mechanics of the ritual.

Y

YOUNG, BURT. Born April 30, 1940, in New York City, actor. Stocky character actor whose role as the meat factory manager Paulie in *Rocky* has garnered him his greatest attention, though his bit as the blinds-chomping Curly in the opening scene of *Chinatown* is equally memorable. In addition to reprising Paulie in the many Rocky sequels, his career has alternated between gutsy street stories (*Once Upon a Time in America, The Pope of Greenwich Village, Last Exit to Brooklyn*) and a number of inconsequential exploitation pictures. Never to be mistaken for a romantic lead, Young, however, does accurately reflect a certain working-class ethic in America, which undoubtedly accounts for his longevity in character roles. His one foray into screenwriting, *Uncle Joe Shannon*, in which he starred as a struggling trumpet player, was a critical and commercial bust.

Filmography: The Gang That Couldn't Shoot Straight (1971); Cinderella Liberty (1973); Chinatown (1974); The Gambler (1974); Live a Little, Steal a Lot (1974); The Killer Elite (1975); Harry and Walter Go to New York (1976); Rocky (1976); The Choirboys (1977); Twilight's Last Gleaming (1977); Convoy (1978); Uncle Joe Shannon (1978) also screenplay; Rocky II (1979); Blood Beach (1980); All the Marbles (1981); Amityville II: The Possession (1982); Lookin' to Get Out (1982); Rocky III (1982); Over the Brooklyn Bridge (1983); Once Upon a Time in America (1984); The Pope of Greenwich Village (1984); Rocky IV (1985); Back to School (1986); Beverly Hills Brats (1989); Blood Red (1989); Last Exit to Brooklyn (1989); Medium Rare (1989); Wait until Spring, Bandini (1990); Backstreet Dreams (1990); Betsy's Wedding (1990); Bright Angel (1990); Diving In (1990); Rocky V (1990); Club Fed (1991); Americano Rosso (1991).

Honor: Academy Award nomination for Best Supporting Actor (*Rocky*).

YOUNG FRANKENSTEIN (1974), comedy/horror. Directed and cowritten by Mel Brooks; screenplay with Gene Wilder; produced by Michael Gruskoff; photographed by Gerald Hirschfield (b&w); edited by John Howard; music by John Morris; released by 20th Century Fox; 108 minutes. *Cast*: Gene Wilder, Peter Boyle, Marty Feldman, Madeline Kahn, Cloris Leachman, Teri Garr, Kenneth Mars, Gene Hackman.

Protesting that his celebrated grandfather's work is "doo-doo," Dr. Fredrick Frankenstein (now pronounced *Fronk*enstein) is inextricably drawn to his past when he inherits his family's castle in Transylvania. Once there, he unearths his grandfather's book *How I Did It* and, with the help of Igor (Feldman), creates his own monster (Boyle). As he did with the western genre in *Blazing Saddles*, director Mel Brooks has racked up a success with a parody of the horror film. It's brilliantly cast with Wilder perfect as the mad genius, Feldman as his assistant (with an ever-shifting hunchback), Boyle as the lovable monster, Teri Garr as the buxom love interest, and Leachman as the sour Frau Blucher, whose very name makes the horses whinny in disgust. Filled with laughs, though the "Puttin' on the Ritz" duet between Wilder and the inarticulate, grunting monster must be its funniest.

Z

ZELIG (1983), comedy. Directed and written by Woody Allen; produced by Robert Greenhut; photographed by Gordon Willis (color/b&w); edited by Susan E. Morse; music by Dick Hyman; released by Orion Pictures/Warner Bros.; 79 minutes. *Cast*: Woody Allen, Mia Farrow, John Buckwalter, Garrett Brown, Richard Litt, Ellen Garrison, Susan Sontag, Dr. Bruno Bettelheim, Irving Howe, Saul Bellow, Stephanie Farrow, Michael Jeter.

Like a sketch from one of his short story collections *Without Feathers* or *Getting Even*, this cleverly faked documentary combines Allen's wit with social and historical observation. Allen plays Leonard Zelig, a once-celebrated figure of the 1920s, who gained fame for his uncanny and involuntary knack for physically conforming his appearance to match his company—with rabbis he grows a beard and looks Jewish; with Chinese launderers he becomes Asian; with a Negro jazz band his skin darkens; and with two obese men he gains weight. He becomes as famous as Lindbergh with popular jazz-era songs written about him, as well as a new dance craze (''the Chameleon'') and a Hollywood movie (*The Changing Man*). Taking an interest in his strange case and eventually falling in love with him is Dr. Eudora Fletcher (Farrow), a shy psychotherapist who accurately diagnoses Zelig as someone who desperately needs to fit in and be loved. Manipulating the frame with cinematographer Gordon Willis, Allen seamlessly inserts Leonard Zelig into world history. We see old newsreel footage of the shy Zelig receding behind Calvin Coolidge, Hitler (whose Nazis were the ultimate conformists), Randolph Hearst, Scott Fitzgerald, and even the New York Yankees. Intercut with the ''historic'' documents are present-day recollections from those who knew him or knew of him—an elderly Eudora (Garrison), Susan Sontag, Dr. Bruno Bettelheim, Irving Howe, Saul Bellow—all of whom have their own take on the ever-changing Zelig. The result is a perfect morsel of a movie—not a masterpiece and even a little long at only seventy-nine minutes but still a smart comment on conformity and identity from one of America's greatest humorists.

Awards: Academy Award nominations for Best Cinematography, Costume Design; New York Film Critics Circle Award for Best Cinematography.

ZEMECKIS, ROBERT. Born May 14, 1951, in Chicago; director, screenwriter, producer. Former University of Southern California film student whose career was shepherded and shaped by Steven Spielberg, who executive-produced Zemeckis' debut film, *I Wanna Hold Your Hand*, before hiring him to cowrite *1941*. After directing the raucous comedy *Used Cars*, he had his first bona fide hit with the Michael Douglas–Kathleen Turner adventure *Romancing the Stone*. His subsequent films (with the only exception being the black comedy *Death Becomes Her*) have sent the box office turnstiles spinning—*Back to the Future* and its two sequels are playfully directed and expertly written teen fantasies that have spawned a popular Universal Studios theme ride; *Who Framed Roger Rabbit* is one of film history's most inventive mixes of live action and animation; and *Forrest Gump*, with its $300 million plus gross, is perhaps the most unlikely megahit ever. In the late 1980s, he turned his talents to cable television as one of the producers (along with Walter Hill, Richard Donner, Joel Silver, and David Giler) of the popular HBO horror series "Tales from the Crypt."

Filmography: I Wanna Hold Your Hand (1978) also screenplay; 1941 (1979) screenplay only; Used Cars (1980) also screenplay; Romancing the Stone (1984); Back to the Future (1985) also screenplay; Who Framed Roger Rabbit (1988); Back to the Future II (1989) also story; Back to the Future 3 (1989) also story; "And All through the House" episode of "Tales from the Crypt" (1989, ctv); "Yellow" episode of "Tales from the Crypt" (1991, ctv); Death Becomes Her (1992) also producer; The Public Eye (1992) ep; Trespass (1992) ep, screenwriter; Forrest Gump (1994); Tales from the Crypt: Demon Knight (1995) ep; Frighteners (1995) ep; "You, Murderer" episode of "Tales from the Crypt" (1995, ctv).

Honors: Academy Award for Best Director (*Forrest Gump*); DGA Award (*Forrest Gump*).

Appendix I
FILMS IN GUIDE BY YEAR

1965
Cat Ballou
Dr. Zhivago
Mickey One
Pawnbroker, The
Sound of Music, The
Thousand Clowns, A

1966
Seconds
Who's Afraid of Virginia Woolf?

1967
Bonnie and Clyde
Cool Hand Luke
Dirty Dozen
Don't Look Back
El Dorado
Graduate, The
In Cold Blood
In the Heat of the Night
Point Blank
Titicut Follies, The
Valley of the Dolls

1968
Bullitt
David Holtzman's Diary
Faces
Funny Girl
Madigan
Night of the Living Dead
Planet of the Apes
Rosemary's Baby
Targets
2001: A Space Odyssey

1969
Butch Cassidy and the Sundance Kid
Easy Rider
Honeymoon Killers, The
Medium Cool
Midnight Cowboy
They Shoot Horses, Don't They?
True Grit
Wild Bunch, The

1970

Airport

Five Easy Pieces

Gimme Shelter

Husbands

Love Story

M*A*S*H

Patton

Woodstock

1971

Carnal Knowledge

Dirty Harry

French Connection, The

Harold and Maude

Klute

Last Picture Show, The

McCabe and Mrs. Miller

Panic in Needle Park

Shaft

Sweet Sweetback's Baad Asssss Song

Two-Lane Blacktop

1972

Cabaret

Candidate, The

Deliverance

Godfather, The

Heartbreak Kid, The

Poseidon Adventure, The

Sounder

Super Fly

What's Up, Doc?

1973

American Graffiti

Exorcist, The

Long Goodbye, The

Mean Streets

Paper Moon

Papillon

Pat Garrett and Billy the Kid

Scarecrow

Serpico

Sisters

Sting, The

Way We Were, The

1974

Alice Doesn't Live Here Anymore

Badlands

Blazing Saddles

Chinatown

Conversation, The

Death Wish

Earthquake

Godfather, Part II, The

Lenny

Longest Yard, The

Parallax View, The

Texas Chainsaw Massacre, The

Towering Inferno, The

Woman under the Influence, A

Young Frankenstein

1975

Dog Day Afternoon

Jaws

Nashville

One Flew over the Cuckoo's Nest

Shampoo

Three Days of the Condor

1976

All the President's Men

Carrie

Harlan County, U.S.A.

Network

Outlaw Josey Wales, The
Rocky
Shootist, The
Taxi Driver

1977

Annie Hall
Close Encounters of the Third Kind
Goodbye Girl, The
Hills Have Eyes, The
Julia
Opening Night
Saturday Night Fever
Smokey and the Bandit
Sorcerer, The
Star Wars

1978

Coming Home
Days of Heaven
The Deer Hunter
Eraserhead
Fingers
Grease
Halloween
National Lampoon's Animal House
Straight Time
Superman
Unmarried Woman, An

1979

All That Jazz
Apocalypse Now
Being There
Dawn of the Dead
Escape from Alcatraz
Kramer vs. Kramer
Manhattan
Norma Rae

1980

Big Red One, The
Heaven's Gate
Melvin and Howard
Ordinary People
Raging Bull
Return of the Secaucus Seven
Stunt Man, The

1981

Blow Out
Body Heat
Cutter's Way
Pennies from Heaven
Raiders of the Lost Ark
Reds
Thief

1982

Blade Runner
Diner
E.T. The Extra-Terrestrial
Fast Times at Ridgemont High
Missing
My Dinner with Andre
One from the Heart
Victor/Victoria
White Dog

1983

King of Comedy, The
Koyaanisqatsi
Right Stuff, The
Risky Business
Terms of Endearment
Zelig

1984

Blood Simple
Choose Me

El Norte
Nightmare on Elm Street, A
Once Upon a Time in America
Sixteen Candles
Stranger than Paradise
Terminator, The
This Is Spinal Tap

1985
Lost in America
Rambo: First Blood, Part II
Witness

1986
Aliens
Blue Velvet
Fly, The
Hannah and Her Sisters
Platoon
Salvador
She's Gotta Have It
Top Gun
Working Girls

1987
Broadcast News
Fatal Attraction
Matewan
River's Edge

1988
Bird
Die Hard
Moderns, The
Rain Man
Thin Blue Line, The
Who Framed Roger Rabbit

1989
Do the Right Thing

Field of Dreams
Henry: Portrait of a Serial Killer
Roger and Me
Say Anything
sex, lies and videotape

1990
Ghost
GoodFellas
Grifters, The
Home Alone
Longtime Companion
Pretty Woman
Silence of the Lambs
Thelma and Louise

1991
Beauty and the Beast
Boyz N the Hood
Fisher King, The
JFK

1992
Husbands and Wives
One False Move
Reservoir Dogs
Swoon
Unforgiven

1993
Dave
Groundhog Day
Jurassic Park
Menace II Society
Schindler's List
Short Cuts
War Room, The

1994
Forrest Gump

Hoop Dreams

Nobody's Fool

Pulp Fiction

Spanking the Monkey

1995

Dead Man Walking

Toy Story

Usual Suspects, The

Appendix II
NOTABLE PRODUCERS

Only key credits as producer or executive producer since 1965 are included.

Allen, Irwin
The Poseidon Adventure (1972); The Towering Inferno (1974); The Swarm (1978); Beyond the Poseidon Adventure (1979).

Arkoff, Samuel Z.
Beach Blanket Bingo (1965); Dr. Goldfoot and the Bikini Machine (1965); How to Stuff a Wild Bikini (1965); The Ghost in the Invisible Bikini (1966); Wild in the Streets (1968); Bloody Mama (1970); The Abominable Doctor Phibes (1971); Dillinger (1973); Cooley High (1975); The Food of the Gods (1975); Futureworld (1976); The Great Scout and Cathouse Thursday (1976); Empire of the Ants (1977); The Island of Dr. Moreau (1977); The Amityville Horror (1979); Dressed to Kill (1980).

Badalato, Bill
Top Gun (1986); Weeds (1987); Hot Shots! (1991); Benny and Joon (1993); Hot Shots! Part Deux (1993); Unstrung Heroes (1994).

Bender, Lawrence
Reservoir Dogs (1992); Fresh (1994); Killing Zoe (1994); Pulp Fiction (1994); Four Rooms (1995); White Man's Burden (1995).

Bregman, Martin
Serpico (1973); Dog Day Afternoon (1975); The Seduction of Joe Tynan (1979); Simon (1980); The Four Seasons (1981); Scarface (1983); Sweet Liberty (1986); Real Men (1987); A New Life (1988); Sea of Love (1989); Betsy's Wedding (1990); Carlito's Way (1993); The Shadow (1994).

Broccoli, Albert R. "Cubby"
Thunderball (1965); You Only Live Twice (1967); Chitty Chitty Bang Bang (1968); On Her Majesty's Secret Service (1969); Diamonds Are Forever (1971); Live and Let Die

(1973); The Man With the Golden Gun (1974); The Spy Who Loved Me (1977); Moonraker (1979); For Your Eyes Only (1981); Octopussy (1983); A View to a Kill (1985); The Living Daylights (1987); License to Kill (1989).

Brokaw, Cary
Trouble in Mind (1985); Down by Law (1986); Nobody's Fool (1986); Slam Dance (1987); Straight to Hell (1987); Drugstore Cowboy (1989); After Dark, My Sweet (1990); Sex, Drugs, Rock and Roll (1991); The Object of Beauty (1991); American Heart (1992); The Player (1992); Short Cuts (1993).

Caracciolo, Joseph M.
A Chorus Line (1985); Brighton Beach Memoirs (1986); The Glass Menagerie (1987); The Secret of My Success (1987); Biloxi Blues (1988); Parenthood (1989); My Blue Heaven (1990); True Colors (1991); My Girl (1991); Hero (1992); Lost in Yonkers (1993); My Girl 2 (1994).

Chartoff, Robert, and Irwin Winkler
Point Blank (1967) Chartoff only; They Shoot Horses, Don't They? (1969); Leo the Last (1970); The Gang That Couldn't Shoot Straight (1971); The Mechanic (1972); The New Centurions (1972); The Gambler (1974); Breakout (1975); Nickelodeon (1976); Rocky (1976); New York, New York (1977); Valentino (1977); Comes a Horseman (1978); Rocky II (1979); Raging Bull (1980); True Confessions (1981); Rocky III (1982); Author! Author! (1982), Winkler only; The Right Stuff (1983); Rocky IV (1985); Revolution (1985) Winkler only; 'Round Midnight (1986) Winkler only; Betrayed (1988) Winkler only; Music Box (1989) Winkler only; GoodFellas (1990) Winkler only; Rocky V (1990).

Cornfeld, Stuart
Fatso (1979); The Elephant Man (1980); History of the World Part I (1981); National Lampoon's European Vacation (1985); The Fly (1986); The Fly II (1989); Kafka (1991); Wilder Napalm (1993).

Cort, Robert W., and Ted Field (Interscope Communications)
Revenge of the Nerds II (1987); Outrageous Fortune (1987); Critical Condition (1987); Three Men and a Baby (1987); The Seventh Sign (1988); Cocktail (1988); Bill and Ted's Excellent Adventure (1989); An Innocent Man (1989); Bird on a Wire (1990); Arachnophobia (1990); Three Men and a Little Lady (1990); Bill and Ted's Bogus Journey (1991); The Hand That Rocks the Cradle (1992); FernGully . . . The Last Rainforest (1992); The Cutting Edge (1992); Mr. Holland's Opus (1994) Cort only; The Tie That Binds (1995).

Daley, Robert
Dirty Harry (1971); Play Misty for Me (1971); Breezy (1973); High Plains Drifter (1973); Magnum Force (1973); Thunderbolt and Lightfoot (1974); The Eiger Sanction (1975); The Outlaw Josey Wales (1975); The Enforcer (1976); The Gauntlet (1977); Every Which Way but Loose (1978); Escape from Alcatraz (1979); Any Which Way You Can (1980); Bronco Billy (1980); Real Genius (1985); Stick (1985).

DeFina, Barbara
The Color of Money (1986); The Last Temptation of Christ (1988); New York Stories (1989); GoodFellas (1990); The Grifters (1990); Cape Fear (1991); Mad Dog and Glory (1993); The Age of Innocence (1993); Casino (1995).

DeLaurentiis, Dino
The Bible (1966); Barbarella (1968); Romeo and Juliet (1968); Valachi Papers (1972); Crazy Joe (1973); Serpico (1973); The Stone Killer (1973); Death Wish (1974); Mandingo (1975); Three Days of the Condor (1975); King Kong (1976); Lipstick (1976); The Shootist (1976); Orca (1977); King of the Gypsies (1978); The Brink's Job (1978); Hurricane (1979); Flash Gordon (1980); Ragtime (1981); The Dead Zone (1983); Conan the Destroyer (1984); The Bounty (1984); Dune (1985); Year of the Dragon (1985); Tai-Pan (1986); Desperate Hours (1990); Body of Evidence (1993); Color of Night (1994); Assassins (1995); Die Hard with a Vengeance (1995).

Deutchman, Ira
Matewan (1987); Swimming to Cambodia (1987); Miles from Home (1988); Scenes from the Class Struggle in Beverly Hills (1989); Straight Out of Brooklyn (1991); Waterland (1992); Mrs. Parker and the Vicious Circle (1994).

Eberts, Jake
The Name of the Rose (1986); Hope and Glory (1987); White Mischief (1987); The Adventures of Baron Munchausen (1988); Driving Miss Daisy (1989); Last Exit to Brooklyn (1989); Dances with Wolves (1990); Texasville (1990); A River Runs through It (1992); City of Joy (1992); Super Mario Bros. (1992).

Evans, Robert
Chinatown (1974); Marathon Man (1976); Black Sunday (1977); Players (1979); Popeye (1980); Urban Cowboy (1980); The Cotton Club (1984); The Two Jakes (1990); Sliver (1993); Jade (1995).

Feitshans, Buzz
Dillinger (1973); Foxy Brown (1974); Big Wednesday (1978); 1941 (1979); Hardcore (1979); Conan the Barbarian (1982); First Blood (1982); Red Dawn (1984); Rambo: First Blood Part II (1985); Extreme Prejudice (1987); Rambo III (1988); Total Recall (1990); Tombstone (1993); Color of Night (1994); Renaissance Man (1994); Die Hard with a Vengeance (1995).

Golan, Menahan, and Yoram Globus (Cannon Group)
Death Wish II (1981); That Championship Season (1982); 10 to Midnight (1983); Bolero (1984); Love Streams (1984); Missing in Action (1984); Death Wish 3 (1985); Fool for Love (1985); Invasion U.S.A. (1985); King Solomon's Mines (1985); Lifeforce (1985); Maria's Lovers (1985); Missing in Action 2—The Beginning (1985); Runaway Train (1985); The Naked Face (1985); 52 Pick-Up (1986); Cobra (1986); Invaders from Mars (1986); Murphy's Law (1986); The Delta Force (1986); The Texas Chainsaw Massacre Part 2 (1986); Barfly (1987); Dancers (1987); Death Wish 4: The Crackdown (1987); King Lear (1987); Over the Top (1987); Shy People (1987); Street Smart (1987); Superman IV: The Quest for Peace (1987); Tough Guys Don't Dance (1987); A Cry in the Dark (1988); Braddock: Missing in Action III (1988); Hanna's War (1988); Powaqqatsi (1988); Mack the Knife (1989).

Gordon, Lawrence
Dillinger (1973); Hard Times (1975); Rolling Thunder (1977); Hooper (1978); The Driver (1978); The End (1978); The Warriors (1979); Xanadu (1980); 48 HRS (1982); Streets of Fire (1984); Brewster's Millions (1985); Jumpin' Jack Flash (1986); Lucas

(1986); Predator (1987); Die Hard (1988); Family Business (1989); Field of Dreams (1989); K-9 (1989); Another 48 HRS (1990); Die Hard 2: Die Harder (1990); Predator 2 (1990); The Rocketeer (1991); Point Break (1991).

Grazer, Brian (Imagine Entertainment)
Night Shift (1982); Splash (1984); Real Genius (1985); Spies like Us (1985); Parenthood (1989); The Burbs (1989); Cry-Baby (1990); Kindergarten Cop (1990); Backdraft (1991); Closet Land (1991); My Girl (1991); The Doors (1991); Boomerang (1992); Far and Away (1992); Greedy (1994); My Girl 2 (1994); The Paper (1994); Apollo 13 (1995).

Greenhut, Robert
Lenny (1974); Dog Day Afternoon (1975); The Front (1976); Annie Hall (1977); Interiors (1978); Hair (1979); Manhattan (1979); Stardust Memories (1980); Arthur (1981); A Midsummer Night's Sex Comedy (1982); The King of Comedy (1983); Zelig (1983); Broadway Danny Rose (1984); The Purple Rose of Cairo (1985); Hannah and Her Sisters (1986); Heartburn (1986); Radio Days (1987); September (1987); Another Woman (1988); Big (1988); Working Girl (1988); Crimes and Misdemeanors (1989); New York Stories "Oedipus Wrecks" (1989); Alice (1990); Postcards from the Edge (1990); Quick Change (1990); Regarding Henry (1991); Shadows and Fog (1991); A League of Their Own (1992); Husbands and Wives (1992); Manhattan Murder Mystery (1993); Bullets over Broadway (1994); Renaissance Man (1994); Wolf (1994); Mighty Aphrodite (1995).

Guber, Peter, and Jon Peters
A Star Is Born (1976) Peters only; The Deep (1977) Guber only; Midnight Express (1978) Guber only; Eyes of Laura Mars (1978) Peters only; The Main Event (1979) Peters only; Caddyshack (1980) Peters only; An American Werewolf in London (1981); Missing (1982); Six Weeks (1982); D.C. Cab (1983); Flashdance (1983); The Color Purple (1985); The Clan of the Cave Bear (1986); Innerspace (1987); The Witches of Eastwick (1987); Who's That Girl (1987); Caddyshack II (1988); Gorillas in the Mist (1988); Rain Man (1988); Batman (1989); Tango and Cash (1989); The Bonfire of the Vanities (1990); Batman Returns (1992); This Boy's Life (1993); With Honors (1994).

Hausman, Michael
Taking Off (1971); The Heartbreak Kid (1972); Mikey and Nicky (1976); I Never Promised You a Rose Garden (1977); Rich Kids (1979); One-Trick Pony (1980); Ragtime (1981); Silkwood (1983); The Ballad of Gregorio Cortez (1983); Amadeus (1984); Places in the Heart (1984); Desert Bloom (1986); House of Games (1987); Things Change (1988); Valmont (1989); State of Grace (1990); Homicide (1991); The Firm (1993); Nobody's Fool (1994).

Hill, Debra
Halloween (1978); The Fog (1980); Escape from New York (1981); Halloween II (1981); Halloween III: Season of the Witch (1982); The Dead Zone (1983); Adventures in Babysitting (1987); Big Top Pee-Wee (1988); The Fisher King (1991).

Ho, A. Kitman
The Loveless (1984); Platoon (1986); Wall Street (1987); Talk Radio (1988); Born on the Fourth of July (1989); The Doors (1991); JFK (1991); Heaven and Earth (1993); On Deadly Ground (1994).

Hurd, Gale Anne
Smokey Bites the Dust (1981); The Terminator (1984); Aliens (1986); Alien Nation (1988); Bad Dreams (1988); The Abyss (1989); Tremors (1990); Terminator 2: Judgment Day (1991); Raising Cain (1992); The Waterdance (1992); Safe Passage (1994).

Jaffe, Stanley R.
Goodbye, Columbus (1969); Bad Company (1972); The Bad News Bears (1976); Kramer vs. Kramer (1979); Taps (1981); Without a Trace (1983); Racing with the Moon (1984); Fatal Attraction (1987); The Accused (1988); Black Rain (1989); School Ties (1992).

Johnson, Mark
Toys (1992); A Perfect World (1993); Wilder Napalm (1993); Jimmy Hollywood (1994); A Little Princess (1995).

Kassar, Mario
The Changeling (1979); First Blood (1982); Rambo: First Blood Part II (1985); Angel Heart (1987); Extreme Prejudice (1987); Iron Eagle II (1988); Rambo III (1988); Red Heat (1988); Johnny Handsome (1989); Jacob's Ladder (1990); Mountains of the Moon (1990); Narrow Margin (1990); Total Recall (1990); L.A. Story (1991); Rambling Rose (1991); Terminator 2: Judgment Day (1991); The Doors (1991); Basic Instinct (1992); Chaplin (1992); Light Sleeper (1992); Universal Soldier (1992); Cliffhanger (1993); Heaven and Earth (1993); Stargate (1994); Cutthroat Island (1995); Showgirls (1995).

Kastner, Elliott
Harper (1966); The Bobo (1967); The Night of the Following Day (1968); Where Eagles Dare (1968); The Nightcomers (1971); X Y and Zee (1972); The Long Goodbye (1973); Breakheart Pass (1975); Farewell, My Lovely (1975); Swashbuckler (1976); The Missouri Breaks (1976); A Little Night Music (1977); Equus (1977); The Big Sleep (1978); Absolution (1979); Goldengirl (1979); ffolkes (1980); Garbo Talks (1984); Angel Heart (1987); Homeboy (1988); Jack's Back (1988); The Blob (1988).

Kennedy, Kathleen, and Frank Marshall (Amblin Entertainment)
The Warriors (1979) Marshall only; Raiders of the Lost Ark (1981); E.T. The Extra-Terrestrial (1982) Kennedy only; Poltergeist (1982); Twilight Zone—The Movie (1983); Gremlins (1984); Indiana Jones and the Temple of Doom (1984); Back to the Future (1985); Fandango (1985); The Color Purple (1985); The Goonies (1985); Young Sherlock Holmes (1985); An American Tail (1986); The Money Pit (1986); *batteries not included (1987); Empire of the Sun (1987); Innerspace (1987); The Land before Time (1988); Who Framed Roger Rabbit (1988); Always (1989); Back to the Future II (1989); Dad (1989); Indiana Jones and the Last Crusade (1989); Arachnophobia (1990); Back to the Future III (1990); Gremlins 2: The New Batch (1990); Joe versus the Volcano (1990); An American Tail: Fievel Goes West (1991); Cape Fear (1991); Hook (1991); Noises Off (1992); A Dangerous Woman (1993) Kennedy only; A Far Off Place (1993); Alive (1993); Jurassic Park (1993) Kennedy only; Schindler's List (1993) Kennedy only; We're Back! A Dinosaur's Story (1993); Milk Money (1994); The Flintstones (1994) Kennedy only; Congo (1995); The Bridges of Madison County (1995) Kennedy only; The Indian in the Cupboard (1995).

Kerner, Jordan
Less than Zero (1987); Fried Green Tomatoes (1991); The Mighty Ducks (1992); The Three Musketeers (1993); D2: The Mighty Ducks (1994); The War (1994); When a Man Loves a Woman (1994); Miami Rhapsody (1995).

Koch, Howard W.
The President's Analyst (1967); The Odd Couple (1968); On a Clear Day You Can See Forever (1970); A New Leaf (1971); Plaza Suite (1971); Jacqueline Susann's Once Is Not Enough (1975); Airplane! (1980); Airplane II: The Sequel (1983); Ghost (1990).

Koch, Howard W., Jr.
The Other Side of Midnight (1977); Heaven Can Wait (1978); Gorky Park (1983); The Keep (1983); Rooftops (1989); The Long Walk Home (1990); Wayne's World (1992); Sliver (1993); Wayne's World 2 (1993); Losing Isaiah (1995).

Kopelson, Arnold
Platoon (1986); Triumph of the Spirit (1989); Warlock (1989); Falling Down (1993); The Fugitive (1993); Outbreak (1995); Seven (1995).

Lang, Jennings
Winning (1969); Slaughterhouse-Five (1972); Pete 'N' Tillie (1972); High Plains Drifter (1973); The Great Northfield, Minnesota Raid (1972); The Naked Ape (1973); Charley Varrick (1973); Breezy (1973); Earthquake (1974); Airport 1975 (1974); The Front Page (1974); The Eiger Sanction (1975); Swashbuckler (1976); Rollercoaster (1977); Airport 77 (1977); The Concorde—Airport '79 (1979); The Nude Bomb (1980); The Sting II (1983); Stick (1985).

Lansing, Sherry
Racing with the Moon (1984); Firstborn (1984); Fatal Attraction (1987); The Accused (1988); Black Rain (1989); School Ties (1992); Indecent Proposal (1993).

Law, Lindsay
Gal Young Un (1979); Smooth Talk (1985); Native Son (1986); Waiting for the Moon (1987); Stand and Deliver (1988); The Thin Blue Line (1988); Longtime Companion (1990); All the Vermeers in New York (1990); Straight Out of Brooklyn (1991); Daughters of the Dust (1991); Brother's Keeper (1992); Simple Men (1992); Ethan Frome (1993); The Music of Chance (1993); Amateur (1994); The Beans of Egypt, Maine (1994); Safe (1995).

Linson, Art
Rafferty and the Gold Dust Twins (1975); Car Wash (1976); American Hot Wax (1978); Melvin and Howard (1980); Fast Times at Ridgemont High (1982); The Untouchables (1987); Casualties of War (1989); We're No Angels (1989); Dick Tracy (1990); Singles (1992); Point of No Return (1993); This Boy's Life (1993); Heat (1995).

Milchan, Arnon
The King of Comedy (1983); Once Upon a Time in America (1984); Brazil (1985); Legend (1985); The War of the Roses (1989); Q&A (1990); Pretty Woman (1990); JFK (1991); Memoirs of an Invisible Man (1992); Under Siege (1992); Sommersby (1993); Falling Down (1993); Free Willy (1993); Striking Distance (1993); George Balanchine's The Nutcracker (1993); Six Degrees of Separation (1993); Heaven and Earth (1993); The Client (1994); The Natural Born Killers (1994); Second Best (1994); Cobb (1994); Boys on the Side (1995); Free Willy 2: The Adventure Home (1995); Under Siege 2: Dark Territory (1995); Copycat (1995); Heat (1995).

Miller, Ron
That Darn Cat! (1965); Lt. Robin Crusoe, USN (1966); Monkeys, Go Home! (1967); The Boatniks (1970); Snowball Express (1972); The Castaway Cowboy (1974); One of Our Dinosaurs Is Missing (1975); Escape to Witch Mountain (1975); Gus (1976); The Shaggy D.A. (1976); Freaky Friday (1977); The Rescuers (1977); Herbie Goes to Monte Carlo (1977); Pete's Dragon (1977); The Cat from Outer Space (1978); The Apple Dumpling Gang Rides Again (1979); Unidentified Flying Oddball (1979); The Black Hole (1979); Herbie Goes Bananas (1980); Tron (1982); Tex (1982); Never Cry Wolf (1983); The Black Cauldron (1985).

Mirisch, Walter
Hawaii (1966); In the Heat of the Night (1967); The Hawaiians (1970); They Call Me Mister Tibbs (1970); The Organization (1971); Scorpio (1973); Mr. Majestyk (1974); Midway (1976); Gray Lady Down (1978); Same Time, Next Year (1978); Dracula (1979); The Prisoner of Zenda (1979); Romantic Comedy (1983).

Neufeld, Mace, and Robert Rehme
The Omen (1976) Neufeld only; The Final Conflict (1981) Neufeld only; An Eye for an Eye (1981) Rehme only; No Way Out (1987) Neufeld only; The Hunt for Red October (1990); Flight of the Intruder (1991); Patriot Games (1992); Gettysburg (1993); Beverly Hills Cop III (1994); Clear and Present Danger (1994).

Newman, Peter
1918 (1985); On Valentine's Day (1986); Swimming to Cambodia (1987); End of the Line (1987); O. C. and Stiggs (1987); Lord of the Flies (1990); Dogfight (1991); Zebrahead (1992); Household Saints (1993); The Secret of Roan Inish (1994); Smoke (1995); Blue in the Face (1995).

Obst, Lynda
Flashdance (1983); Adventures in Babysitting (1987); The Fisher King (1991); This Is My Life (1992); Sleepless in Seattle (1993); Bad Girls (1994).

Pfeiffer, Carolyn
Roadie (1980); Endangered Species (1982); Choose Me (1984); Trouble in Mind (1985); The Whales of August (1987); The Moderns (1988); Far North (1988); Cool as Ice (1991).

Phillips, Julia, and Michael Phillips
Steelyard Blues (1973); The Sting (1973); The Big Bus (1976); Taxi Driver (1976); Close Encounters of the Third Kind (1977); Cannery Row (1982) Michael only; The Flamingo Kid (1984) Michael only; Don't Tell Mom the Babysitter's Dead (1991) Michael only; Mom and Dad Save the World (1992) Michael only.

Pressman, Edward R.
Sisters (1973); Badlands (1974); Phantom of the Paradise (1974); Paradise Alley (1978); Old Boyfriends (1979); The Hand (1981); Conan the Barbarian (1982); Plenty (1985); Half Moon Street (1986); True Stories (1986); Good Morning Babylon (1987); Walker (1987); Wall Street (1987); Talk Radio (1988); To Sleep with Anger (1990); Reversal of Fortune (1990); Blue Steel (1990); Homicide (1991); Bad Lieutenant (1992); Hoffa (1992); The Crow (1994); Judge Dredd (1995).

Robinson, James G. (Morgan Creek)
The Stone Boy (1984); Streets of Gold (1986); Young Guns (1988); Dead Ringers (1988); Major League (1989); Dad (1989); Enemies, a Love Story (1989); Nightbreed (1990); William Peter Blatty's The Exorcist III (1990); Young Guns II (1990); Pacific Heights (1990); Robin Hood: Prince of Thieves (1991); The Last of the Mohicans (1992); True Romance (1993); Ace Ventura: Pet Detective (1994); Major League II (1994); Ace Ventura: When Nature Calls (1995).

Rollins, Jack, and Charles H. Joffe
Don't Drink the Water (1969) Joffe only; Take the Money and Run (1969) Joffe only; Bananas (1971) Joffe only; Play It Again, Sam (1972) Joffe only; Everything You Always Wanted to Know about Sex* (*but were afraid to ask) (1972) Joffe only; Sleeper (1973); The Front (1976); Annie Hall (1977); Interiors (1978); Manhattan (1979); Stardust Memories (1980); Arthur (1981) Joffe only; Zelig (1983); Broadway Danny Rose (1984); The Purple Rose of Cairo (1985); Hannah and Her Sisters (1986); Radio Days (1987); September (1987); Another Woman (1988); New York Stories "Oedipus Wrecks" (1989); Crimes and Misdemeanors (1989); Alice (1990); Shadows and Fog (1991); Husbands and Wives (1992); Manhattan Murder Mystery (1993); Bullets over Broadway (1994); Mighty Aphrodite (1995).

Roos, Fred
Flight to Fury (1966); Drive, He Said (1971); The Conversation (1974); The Godfather Part II (1974); The Black Stallion (1979); Apocalypse Now (1979); One from the Heart (1982); Hammett (1982); The Black Stallion Returns (1983); The Outsiders (1983); Rumble Fish (1983); The Cotton Club (1984); Gardens of Stone (1987); Barfly (1987); Tucker: The Man and His Dream (1988); New York Stories "Life without Zoe" (1989); The Godfather Part III (1990); Hearts of Darkness: A Filmmaker's Apocalypse (1991); The Secret Garden (1993); Radioland Murders (1994).

Roth, Joe
Tunnelvision (1976); The Stone Boy (1984); Young Guns (1988); Dead Ringers (1988); Enemies, a Love Story (1989); Nightbreed (1990); William Peter Blatty's The Exorcist III (1990); Young Guns II (1990); Pacific Heights (1990); The Three Musketeers (1993); Angie (1994); Angels in the Outfield (1994); Tall Tale: The Unbelievable Adventures of Pecos Bill (1995); While You Were Sleeping (1995).

Rudin, Scott
I'm Dancing As Fast As I Can (1982); Mrs. Soffel (1984); Flatliners (1990); Pacific Heights (1990); Regarding Henry (1991); The Addams Family (1991); Little Man Tate (1991); Jennifer 8 (1992); Sister Act (1992); The Firm (1993); Searching for Bobby Fischer (1993); Addams Family Values (1993); Sister Act II: Back in the Habit (1993); Nobody's Fool (1994); Clueless (1995); Sabrina (1995).

Sanford, Midge, and Sarah Pillsbury
Desperately Seeking Susan (1985); River's Edge (1987); Eight Men Out (1988); Immediate Family (1989); Love Field (1992); How to Make an American Quilt (1995).

Schamus, James, and Ted Hope
The Golden Boat (1990); Poison (1991); Swoon (1992); The Wedding Banquet (1992); What Happened Was . . . (1994); The Brothers McMullen (1995); Safe (1995).

Schneider, Bert (BBS)
Head (1968); Easy Rider (1969); Five Easy Pieces (1970); The Last Picture Show (1971); Drive, He Said (1971); A Safe Place (1971); Hearts and Minds (1975); Tracks (1976); Days of Heaven (1978).

Shamberg, Michael (Jersey Films)
Modern Problems (1981); The Big Chill (1983); A Fish Called Wanda (1988); Pulp Fiction (1994); Reality Bites (1994); Get Shorty (1995).

Shaye, Robert (New Line)
Polyester (1981); A Nightmare on Elm Street (1984); A Nightmare on Elm Street 2: Freddy's Revenge (1985); A Nightmare on Elm Street 3: Dream Warriors (1987); The Hidden (1987); Hairspray (1988); A Nightmare on Elm Street 4: The Dream Master (1988); A Nightmare on Elm Street 5: The Dream Child (1989); Leatherface: The Texas Chainsaw Massacre III (1990); Freddy's Dead: Final Nightmare (1991); Blink (1994); Wes Craven's New Nightmare (1994).

Shuler-Donner, Lauren
Mr. Mom (1983); Ladyhawke (1985); St. Elmo's Fire (1985); Pretty in Pink (1986); Three Fugitives (1989); Free Willy (1993); Free Willy 2: The Adventure Home (1995); Assassins (1995).

Silver, Joel
48 HRS (1982); Streets of Fire (1984); Brewster's Millions (1985); Weird Science (1985); Commando (1985); Jumpin' Jack Flash (1986); Lethal Weapon (1987); Predator (1987); Action Jackson (1988); Die Hard (1988); Lethal Weapon 2 (1989); Roadhouse (1989); The Adventures of Ford Fairlane (1990); Die Hard 2: Die Harder (1990); Predator 2 (1990); Hudson Hawk (1991); The Last Boy Scout (1991); Lethal Weapon 3 (1992); Demolition Man (1993); Richie Rich (1994); Assassins (1995); Fair Game (1995); Tales from the Crypt Presents Demon Knight (1995).

Simpson, Don, and Jerry Bruckheimer
Flashdance (1983); Beverly Hills Cop (1984); Top Gun (1986); Beverly Hills Cop II (1987); Days of Thunder (1990); The Ref (1994); Bad Boys (1995); Crimson Tide (1995); Dangerous Minds (1995).

Stark, Ray (Rastar Productions)
Promise Her Anything (1966); Reflections in a Golden Eye (1967); Funny Girl (1968); The Owl and the Pussycat (1970); Fat City (1972); The Way We Were (1973); Funny Lady (1975); The Sunshine Boys (1975); Murder by Death (1976); Robin and Marian (1976); The Goodbye Girl (1977); California Suite (1978); Chapter Two (1979); The Electric Horseman (1979); Seems like Old Times (1980); Annie (1982); The Slugger's Wife (1985); Brighton Beach Memoirs (1986); Nothing in Common (1986); Peggy Sue Got Married (1986); Biloxi Blues (1988); Steel Magnolias (1989); Neil Simon's Lost in Yonkers (1993).

Stigwood, Robert
Jesus Christ Superstar (1973); Tommy (1975); Saturday Night Fever (1977); Sgt. Pepper's Lonely Hearts Club Band (1978); Grease (1978); Moment by Moment (1978); Gallipoli (1981); Grease 2 (1982); Staying Alive (1983).

Tisch, Steve
Risky Business (1983); Deal of the Century (1983); Soul Man (1976); Heart of Dixie (1989); Bad Influence (1990); Corrina, Corrina (1994); Forrest Gump (1994).

Turman, Lawrence, and David Foster
The Graduate (1967) Turman only; The Flim-Flam Man (1967) Turman only; Pretty Poison (1968) Turman only; The Great White Hope (1970) Turman only; McCabe and Mrs. Miller (1971) Foster only; The Getaway (1972) Foster only; The Drowning Pool (1975); Heroes (1977); Caveman (1981); The Thing (1982); The Mean Season (1985); Short Circuit (1986); Running Scared (1986); Full Moon in Blue Water (1988); Short Circuit II (1988); The Getaway (1994); The River Wild (1994).

Vachon, Christine
Superstar: The Karen Carpenter Story (1987, short); Poison (1991); Swoon (1992); Go Fish (1994); Postcards from America (1994); Safe (1995).

Vajna, Andrew
The Changeling (1979); First Blood (1982); Rambo: First Blood Part II (1985); Extreme Prejudice (1987); Angel Heart (1987); Rambo III (1988); Iron Eagle II (1988); Red Heat (1988); Johnny Handsome (1989); Total Recall (1990); Jacob's Ladder (1990); Mountains of the Moon (1990); Medicine Man (1992); Tombstone (1993); Color of Night (1994); Die Hard with a Vengeance (1995); Judge Dredd (1995); Nixon (1995); The Scarlet Letter (1995).

Valdes, David
Gardens of Stone (1987); Bird (1988); The Dead Pool (1988); Pink Cadillac (1989); White Hunter, Black Heart (1990); The Rookie (1990); Unforgiven (1992); In the Line of Fire (1993); A Perfect World (1993); The Stars Fell on Henrietta (1995).

Weinstein, Bob, and Harvey Weinstein
The Lemon Sisters (1989); Scandal (1989); The Pope Must Die(t) (1991); A Rage in Harlem (1991); Into the West (1992); True Romance (1993); Pulp Fiction (1994); Ready to Wear (Prêt-à-Porter) (1994); Blue in the Face (1995); The Crossing Guard (1995); Restoration (1995); Smoke (1995); Things to Do in Denver When You're Dead (1995).

Weintraub, Jerry
Nashville (1975); Oh, God! (1977); Cruising (1980); Diner (1982); The Karate Kid (1984); Happy New Year (1987); The Karate Kid Part II (1986); The Karate Kid Part III (1989); The Next Karate Kid (1994); The Specialist (1994).

Worth, Marvin
Where's Poppa? (1970); Malcolm X (1972); Lenny (1974); The Rose (1979); Unfaithfully Yours (1984); Rhinestone (1984); Falling in Love (1984); Less than Zero (1987); Patty Hearst (1988); See No Evil, Hear No Evil (1989); Malcolm X (1992).

Zaentz, Saul
One Flew over the Cuckoo's Nest (1975); Lord of the Rings (1978); Amadeus (1984); The Mosquito Coast (1986); The Unbearable Lightness of Being (1988); At Play in the Fields of the Lord (1991).

Zanuck, Richard D., and David Brown

Ssssssss (1973); Willie Dynamite (1974); The Sugarland Express (1974); The Eiger Sanction (1975); Jaws (1975); Jaws 2 (1978); Neighbors (1981); The Verdict (1982); Cocoon (1985); Target (1985); Cocoon: The Return (1988); Driving Miss Daisy (1989) Zanuck only; Rush (1991) Zanuck only; A Few Good Men (1992) Brown only; The Player (1992) Brown only; Rich in Love (1992); Wild Bill (1995); Canadian Bacon (1995) Brown only.

Ziskin, Laura

Murphy's Romance (1985); No Way Out (1987); D.O.A. (1988); Everybody's All-American (1988); Pretty Woman (1990); The Doctor (1991); Hero (1992); To Die For (1995).

Zucker, David, and Jerry Zucker

Airplane! (1980); Top Secret (1984); The Naked Gun: From the Files of Police Squad (1988); The Naked Gun 2 1/2: The Smell of Fear (1991) Jerry only; My Life (1993) Jerry only; The Naked Gun 33 1/3: The Final Insult (1994); A Walk in the Clouds (1995); First Knight (1995) Jerry only.

Appendix III
NOTABLE SCREENWRITERS

Only key credits since 1965 are included.

Allen, Jay Presson
The Prime of Miss Jean Brodie (1969); Cabaret (1972); Travels with My Aunt (1972); Funny Lady (1975); Prince of the City (1981); Deathtrap (1982); Year of the Gun (1991).

Bass, Ronald
Target (1985); Black Widow (1987); Gardens of Stone (1987); Rain Man (1988); Sleeping with the Enemy (1991); The Joy Luck Club (1993); When a Man Loves a Woman (1994); Dangerous Minds (1995); Waiting to Exhale (1995).

Bernstein, Walter
The Molly Maguires (1970); The Front (1976); Semi-Tough (1977); The Betsy (1978); The Legend of Billie Jean (1985); The House on Carroll Street (1988).

Black, Shane
Lethal Weapon (1987); The Monster Squad (1987); Lethal Weapon 2 (1989) story; The Last Boy Scout (1991); Last Action Hero (1993).

Blatty, William Peter
Promise Her Anything (1966); What Did You Do in the War, Daddy? (1966); The Great Bank Robbery (1969); Darling Lili (1970); The Exorcist (1973); Twinkle, Twinkle, 'Killer' Kane (1979) also director; William Peter Blatty's The Exorcist III (1990) also director.

Brickman, Marshall
Sleeper (1973); Annie Hall (1977); Manhattan (1979); For the Boys (1991); Manhattan Murder Mystery (1993); Intersection (1994).

Briley, John
Pope Joan (1972); Gandhi (1982); Marie: A True Story (1985); Tai-Pan (1986); Cry Freedom (1987); Christopher Columbus: The Discovery (1992).

Carlino, Lewis John
Seconds (1966); The Brotherhood (1968); The Mechanic (1972); Crazy Joe (1973); The Sailor Who Fell from Grace with the Sea (1975) also director; I Never Promised You a Rose Garden (1977); The Great Santini (1979) also director; Resurrection (1980); Haunted Summer (1988).

Chayefsky, Paddy
Paint Your Wagon (1969); The Hospital (1971); Network (1976); Altered States (1980) credited as Sidney Aaron.

Darabont, Frank
A Nightmare on Elm Street Part III: Dream Warriors (1987); The Blob (1988); The Fly II (1989); Mary Shelley's Frankenstein (1994); The Shawshank Redemption (1994) also director.

Dehn, Paul
The Spy Who Came in from the Cold (1965); The Night of the Generals (1966); The Taming of the Shrew (1967); Beneath the Planet of the Apes (1970); Escape from the Planet of the Apes (1971); Conquest of the Planet of the Apes (1972); Murder on the Orient Express (1974).

Diamond, I.A.L.
The Fortune Cookie (1966); Cactus Flower (1969); The Private Life of Sherlock Holmes (1970); Avanti! (1972); The Front Page (1974); Fedora (1978); Buddy Buddy (1981).

Ephron, Nora
Silkwood (1983); Heartburn (1986); Cookie (1989); When Harry Met Sally . . . (1989); My Blue Heaven (1990); This Is My Life (1992) also director; Sleepless in Seattle (1993) also director; Mixed Nuts (1994) also director.

Epstein, Julius J.
Any Wednesday (1966); Pete 'n' Tillie (1972); Once Is Not Enough (1975); Cross of Iron (1977); House Calls (1978); Reuben, Reuben (1983).

Eszterhas, Joe
F.I.S.T. (1978); Flashdance (1983); Jagged Edge (1985); Big Shots (1987); Hearts of Fire (1987); Betrayed (1988); Checking Out (1988); Music Box (1989); Basic Instinct (1992); Nowhere to Run (1993); Sliver (1993); Jade (1995); Showgirls (1995).

Feiffer, Jules
Carnal Knowledge (1971); Little Murders (1971); Oh! Calcutta! (1972); Popeye (1980); I Want to Go Back Home (1989) also director.

Foner, Naomi
Violets Are Blue (1986); Running on Empty (1988); A Dangerous Woman (1993); Losing Isaiah (1995).

Foote, Horton
Hurry Sundown (1967); Tomorrow (1971); Tender Mercies (1982); 1918 (1985); On Valentine's Day (1986); The Trip to Bountiful (1986); Of Mice and Men (1992).

Frank Jr., Harriet (with Irving Ravetch)
Hombre (1967); The Reivers (1969); The Cowboys (1971); Conrack (1973); Norma Rae (1978); Murphy's Romance (1985); Stanley and Iris (1990).

Gale, Bob
I Wanna Hold Your Hand (1978); 1941 (1979); Used Cars (1980); Back to the Future (1985); Back to the Future II (1989); Back to the Future III (1990); Trespass (1992).

Ganz, Lowell, and Babaloo Mandel
Night Shift (1982); Splash (1984); Spies like Us (1985); Gung Ho (1986); Vibes (1988); Parenthood (1989); City Slickers (1991); A League of Their Own (1992); Mr. Saturday Night (1992); City Slickers II: The Legend of Curly's Gold (1994); Greedy (1994); Forget Paris (1995).

Gelbart, Larry
The Wrong Box (1966); The Chastity Belt (1967); A Fine Pair (1969); Oh, God! (1977); Neighbors (1981); Tootsie (1982); Blame It on Rio (1984).

Getchell, Robert
Alice Doesn't Live Here Anymore (1974); Bound for Glory (1976); Mommie Dearest (1981); Sweet Dreams (1985); Stella (1990); Point of No Return (1993); This Boy's Life (1993); The Client (1994).

Gideon, Raynold, and Bruce A. Evans
A Man, a Woman and a Bank (1979); Starman (1984); Stand by Me (1986); Made in Heaven (1987); Cutthroat Island (1995) story.

Goldman, Bo
One Flew over the Cuckoo's Nest (1975); The Rose (1979); Melvin and Howard (1980); Shoot the Moon (1981); Swing Shift (1984); Little Nikita (1988); Scent of a Woman (1992).

Goldman, William
Harper (1966); Butch Cassidy and the Sundance Kid (1969); The Great Waldo Pepper (1975); The Stepford Wives (1975); All the President's Men (1976); Marathon Man (1976); A Bridge Too Far (1977); Magic (1978); The Princess Bride (1987); Misery (1990); Chaplin (1992); Memoirs of an Invisible Man (1992); Maverick (1994).

Goodman, David Z.
Lovers and Other Strangers (1970); Monte Walsh (1970); Straw Dogs (1971); Man on a Swing (1974); Farewell, My Lovely (1975); Logan's Run (1976); March or Die (1977); Eyes of Laura Mars (1978).

Green, Walon
The Wild Bunch (1969); Sorcerer (1977); The Brink's Job (1978); The Border (1981); Crusoe (1988); Robocop 2 (1990).

Guare, John
Taking Off (1971); Atlantic City (1980); Six Degrees of Separation (1993).

Henley, Beth
Crimes of the Heart (1986); Nobody's Fool (1986); True Stories (1986); Miss Firecracker (1989).

Henry, Buck
The Graduate (1967); Candy (1968); Catch-22 (1970); The Owl and the Pussycat (1970); What's Up, Doc? (1972); The Day of the Dolphin (1973); First Family (1980) also director; Protocol (1984); I Love N.Y. (1987); To Die For (1995).

Huyck, Willard, and Gloria Katz
American Graffiti (1973); Lucky Lady (1975); French Postcards (1979); Best Defense (1984); Indiana Jones and the Temple of Doom (1984); Howard the Duck (1986); Radioland Murders (1994).

Joyce, Adrien (aka Carol Eastman)
The Shooting (1967); Model Shop (1968) English dialogue; Five Easy Pieces (1970); Puzzle of a Downfall Child (1970); The Fortune (1975).

Kaufman, Robert
Dr. Goldfoot and the Bikini Machine (1965); Dr. Goldfoot and the Girl Bombs (1966); Freebie and the Bean (1974); Harry and Walter Go to New York (1976); The Happy Hooker Goes to Washington (1977); Love at First Bite (1979).

Kazan, Nicholas
Frances (1982); At Close Range (1986); Patty Hearst (1988); Reversal of Fortune (1990).

Koepp, David
Apartment Zero (1988); Bad Influence (1990); Toy Soldiers (1991); Death Becomes Her (1992); Carlito's Way (1993); Jurassic Park (1993); The Paper (1994); The Shadow (1994).

LaGravenese, Richard
Rude Awakening (1989); The Fisher King (1991); The Ref (1994); A Little Princess (1995); The Bridges of Madison County (1995); Unstrung Heroes (1995).

Lardner, Ring, Jr.
The Cincinnati Kid (1965); M*A*S*H (1970); The Greatest (1977).

Lehman, Ernest
The Sound of Music (1965); Who's Afraid of Virginia Woolf? (1966); Hello, Dolly! (1969); Portnoy's Complaint (1972) also director; Family Plot (1976); Black Sunday (1977).

Mann, Stanley
The Collector (1965); The Naked Runner (1967); Damien—Omen II (1978); The Silent Flute (1978); Meteor (1979); Eye of the Needle (1981); Conan the Destroyer (1984); Firestarter (1984); Tai-Pan (1986); Hanna's War (1988).

Mathison, Melissa
The Black Stallion (1979); E.T. The Extra-Terrestrial (1982); The Escape Artist (1982); The Indian in the Cupboard (1995).

Medoff, Mark
Good Guys Wear Black (1978); Children of a Lesser God (1986); Off Beat (1986); Clara's Heart (1988); City of Joy (1992).

Meyers, Nancy, and Charles Shyer
Private Benjamin (1980); Irreconcilable Differences (1984); Protocol (1984) story; Baby Boom (1987); Father of the Bride (1991); Once Upon a Crime (1992); I Love Trouble (1994); Father of the Bride Part II (1995).

Newman, David, and Robert Benton
Bonnie and Clyde (1967); There Was a Crooked Man (1970); Bad Company (1972); Oh! Calcutta! (1972); What's Up, Doc? (1972); Superman (1978); Superman II (1980) Newman only; Jinxed! (1982) Newman only; Superman III (1983) Newman only; Sheena (1984) Newman only; Santa Claus: The Movie (1985) Newman only; Moonwalker (1988) Newman only.

Nyswaner, Ron
Smithereens (1982); Mrs. Soffel (1984); Swing Shift (1984); The Prince of Pennsylvania (1988) also director; Gross Anatomy (1989); Love Hurts (1990); Philadelphia (1993).

Peoples, David Webb
Blade Runner (1982); Hero (1992); Unforgiven (1992); 12 Monkeys (1995).

Pierson, Frank R.
Cat Ballou (1965); Cool Hand Luke (1967); The Happening (1967); The Anderson Tapes (1971); Dog Day Afternoon (1975); A Star Is Born (1976) also director; King of the Gypsies (1978) also director; In Country (1989); Presumed Innocent (1990).

Price, Richard
Streets of Gold (1986); The Color of Money (1986); New York Stories, "Life Lessons" episode (1989); Sea of Love (1989); Night and the City (1992); Mad Dog and Glory (1993); Clockers (1995); Kiss of Death (1995).

Puzo, Mario
The Godfather (1972); Earthquake (1974); The Godfather, Part II (1974); Superman (1978); Superman II (1980); The Cotton Club (1984) story; The Godfather, Part III (1990); Christopher Columbus: The Discovery (1992).

Raucher, Herman
Can Heironymus Merkin Ever Forget Mercy Humppe and Find True Happiness? (1969); Watermelon Man (1970); Summer of '42 (1971); Class of '44 (1973); Ode to Billy Joe (1975); The Other Side of Midnight (1977).

Ravetch, Irving (with Harriet Frank, Jr.)
Hombre (1967); The Reivers (1969); The Cowboys (1971); Conrack (1973); Norma Rae (1978); Murphy's Romance (1985); Stanley and Iris (1990).

Richter, W. D.
Slither (1973); Nickelodeon (1976); Invasion of the Body Snatchers (1978); Dracula (1979); Brubaker (1980); All Night Long (1981); Needful Things (1993); Home for the Holidays (1995).

Rickman, Tom
Kansas City Bomber (1972); The Laughing Policeman (1973); W. W. and the Dixie Dancekings (1974); Coal Miner's Daughter (1980); The River Rat (1984) also director; Everybody's All-American (1988).

Rubin, Bruce Joel
Brainstorm (1983) story; Ghost (1990); Jacob's Ladder (1990); Deceived (1991) credited as Derek Saunders; My Life (1993) also director.

Salt, Waldo
Midnight Cowboy (1969); The Gang That Couldn't Shoot Straight (1971); Serpico (1973); The Day of the Locust (1975); Coming Home (1977).

Sargent, Alvin
Gambit (1966); The Sterile Cuckoo (1969); I Walk the Line (1970); The Effect of Gamma Rays on Man-in-the-Moon Marigolds (1972); Love, Pain and the Whole Damned Thing (1973); Paper Moon (1973); Bobby Deerfield (1977); Julia (1977); Straight Time (1978); Ordinary People (1980); Nuts (1987); Dominick and Eugene (1988); White Palace (1990); Other People's Money (1991); What about Bob? (1991) story; Hero (1992) story.

Schrader, Leonard
Blue Collar (1978); Old Boyfriends (1978); Kiss of the Spider Woman (1985); Mishima: A Life in Four Chapters (1985); Naked Tango (1990) also director.

Schulman, Arnold
The Night They Raided Minsky's (1968); Goodbye, Columbus (1969); Funny Lady (1975); Won Ton Ton, the Dog Who Saved Hollywood (1976); Players (1979); A Chorus Line (1985); Tucker: The Man and His Dream (1988).

Segal, Erich
Yellow Submarine (1968); Love Story (1970); R.P.M. (1970); The Games (1970); Jennifer on My Mind (1971); Oliver's Story (1978).

Shagan, Steve
Save the Tiger (1973); Hustle (1975); Voyage of the Damned (1976); Nightwing (1979); The Formula (1980); The Sicilian (1987).

Shanley, John Patrick
Five Corners (1987); Moonstruck (1987); The January Man (1989); Joe versus the Volcano (1990) also director; Alive (1993); We're Back! A Dinosaur's Story (1993); Congo (1995).

Shelton, Ron
Under Fire (1983); The Best of Times (1986); Bull Durham (1988) also director; Blaze (1989) also director; White Men Can't Jump (1992) also director; Blue Chips (1994); Cobb (1994) also director.

Silliphant, Stirling
In the Heat of the Night (1967); Charly (1968); Marlowe (1969); A Walk in the Spring Rain (1970); Murphy's War (1970); The Liberation of L. B. Jones (1970); The New Centurions (1972); The Poseidon Adventure (1972); Shaft in Africa (1973); The Tow-

ering Inferno (1974); The Killer Elite (1975); The Enforcer (1976); Telefon (1977); The Silent Flute (1978); The Swarm (1978); Over the Top (1987).

Simon, Neil
Barefoot in the Park (1967); The Odd Couple (1968); The Out-of-Towners (1970); Plaza Suite (1971); Last of the Red Hot Lovers (1972); The Heartbreak Kid (1972); The Prisoner of Second Avenue (1974); The Sunshine Boys (1975); Murder by Death (1976); The Goodbye Girl (1977); California Suite (1978); The Cheap Detective (1978); Chapter Two (1979); Seems like Old Times (1980); I Ought to Be in Pictures (1981); Only When I Laugh (1981); Max Dugan Returns (1982); The Slugger's Wife (1985); Brighton Beach Memoirs (1986); Biloxi Blues (1988); The Marrying Man (1991); Neil Simon's Lost in Yonkers (1993).

Sobieski, Carol
Sunshine Part II (1976); Honeysuckle Rose (1980); Annie (1982); The Toy (1982); Sylvester (1985); Winter People (1989); Fried Green Tomatoes (1991); Money for Nothing (1993).

Southern, Terry
The Cincinnati Kid (1965); The Loved One (1965); Barbarella (1968); Easy Rider (1969); The Magic Christian (1970); The Telephone (1988).

Stewart, Donald
Jackson County Jail (1976); Missing (1982); The Hunt for Red October (1990); Patriot Games (1992); Clear and Present Danger (1994).

Stewart, Douglas Day
The Other Side of the Mountain—Part 2 (1977); The Blue Lagoon (1980); An Officer and a Gentleman (1982); Thief of Hearts (1984) also director; Listen to Me (1989) also director; The Scarlet Letter (1995).

Strick, Wesley
True Believer (1989); Arachnophobia (1990); Cape Fear (1991); Final Analysis (1992); Wolf (1994).

Tesich, Steve
Breaking Away (1979); Eyewitness (1980); Four Friends (1981); The World according to Garp (1982); American Flyers (1985); Eleni (1985).

Tidyman, Ernest
Shaft (1971); The French Connection (1971); Shaft's Big Score (1972); High Plains Drifter (1973); Report to the Commissioner (1975); Last Plane Out (1983).

Towne, Robert
The Tomb of Ligeia (1965); The Last Detail (1973); Chinatown (1974); Shampoo (1975); The Yakuza (1975); Personal Best (1982) also director; Greystoke: The Legend of Tarzan, Lord of the Apes (1984); The Bedroom Window (1987); Tequila Sunrise (1988) also director; Days of Thunder (1990); The Two Jakes (1990); The Firm (1993); Love Affair (1994).

Ward, Davis S.
Steelyard Blues (1973); The Sting (1973); Cannery Row (1982) also director; Saving Grace (1986); The Milagro Beanfield War (1988); Major League (1989) also director; King Ralph (1991) also director; Sleepless in Seattle (1993); The Program (1993) also director; Major League II (1994) also director.

Washburn, Deric
Silent Running (1971); The Deer Hunter (1978); The Border (1981); Extreme Prejudice (1987).

Wexler, Norman
Joe (1970); Serpico (1973); Mandingo (1975); Saturday Night Fever (1977); Staying Alive (1983); Raw Deal (1986).

Willingham, Calder
The Graduate (1967); Little Big Man (1970); Thieves like Us (1974); Rambling Rose (1991).

Zaillian, Steven
The Falcon and the Snowman (1985); Awakenings (1990); Jack the Bear (1993); Schindler's List (1993); Searching for Bobby Fischer (1993) also director; Clear and Present Danger (1994).

Appendix IV
MAJOR STUDIO RELEASES BY YEAR

A sample listing of key releases by year, with director.

BUENA VISTA DISTRIBUTION COMPANY (INCLUDES WALT DISNEY PICTURES, TOUCHSTONE PICTURES, AND HOLLYWOOD PICTURES)

1965

That Darn Cat, Stevenson

1967

Gnome-Mobile, The, Stevenson

Jungle Book, The, Reitherman

1968

Horse in the Gray Flannel Suit, The, Tokar

Love Bug, The, Stevenson

1970

Aristocats, The, Reitherman

Barefoot Executive, The, Butler

Boatniks, The, Tokar

Computer Wore Tennis Shoes, The, Butler

1971

Bedknobs and Broomsticks, Stevenson

$1,000,000 Duck, McEveety

1972

Snowball Express, The, Tokar

World's Greatest Athlete, The, Scheerer

1973

Robin Hood, Reitherman

1974

Escape to Witch Mountain, Hough

Herbie Rides Again, Stevenson

1975

Apple Dumpling Gang, The, Tokar

Strongest Man in the World, The, McEveety

1976

Freaky Friday, Nelson

Gus, McEveety

Shaggy D.A., The, Stevenson

1977

Herbie Goes to Monte Carlo, McEveety

Pete's Dragon, Chaffey

1978

Cat from Outer Space, The, Tokar

Return from Witch Mountain, Hough

1979

Apple Dumpling Gang Rides Again, The, McEveety

Black Hole, The, Nelson

Unidentified Flying Oddball, The, Mayberry

1980

Herbie Goes Bananas, McEveety

Watcher in the Woods, Hough

1981

Devil and Max Devlin, The, Stern

Fox and the Hound, The, Stevens, Berman, and Rich

1982

Tex, Hunter

Tron, Lisberger

1983

Never Cry Wolf, Ballard

Something Wicked This Way Comes, Clayton

1984

Country, Pearce

Splash, Howard

1985

Baby: Secret of the Lost Legend, Norton

Black Cauldron, The, Berman and Rich

Journey of Natty Gann, The, Kagan

Return to Oz, Murch

1986

Color of Money, The, Scorsese

Down and Out in Beverly Hills, Mazursky

Great Mouse Detective, The, Clements, Musker, Michener, and Mattinson

Ruthless People, Jerry Zucker, Jim Abrahams, and David Zucker

1987

Adventures in Babysitting, Columbus

Ernest Goes to Camp, John R. Cherry III

Good Morning, Vietnam, Levinson

Outrageous Fortune, Hiller

Stakeout, Badham

Three Men and a Baby, Nimoy

Tin Men, Levinson

1988

Beaches, Garry Marshall

Cocktail, Donaldson

D.O.A., Morton and Jankel

Oliver and Company, Scribner

Shoot to Kill, Spottiswoode

Who Framed Roger Rabbit, Zemeckis

1989

Blaze, Shelton

Dead Poets Society, Weir

Honey, I Shrunk the Kids, Johnston

Little Mermaid, The, Clements and Musker

New York Stories, Allen, Scorsese and Coppola

Three Fugitives, Veber

Turner and Hooch, Spottiswoode

1990

Arachnophobia, Frank Marshall

Dick Tracy, Beatty

Green Card, Weir

Pretty Woman, Garry Marshall

Rescuers Down Under, The, Butoy and Gabriel

Three Men and a Little Lady, Ardolino

1991

Beauty and the Beast, Wise and Trousdale

Billy Bathgate, Benton

Doctor, The, Haines

Father of the Bride, Shyer

Oscar, Landis

Rocketeer, The, Johnston

1992

Aladdin, Clements and Musker

Distinguished Gentleman, The, Lynn

Hand That Rocks the Cradle, The, Hanson

Honey, I Blew Up the Kid, Kleiser

Mighty Ducks, The, Herek

Sister Act, Ardolino

1993

Adventures of Huck Finn, The, Sommers

Alive, Frank Marshall

Cool Runnings, Turteltaub

Homeward Bound: The Incredible Journey, Dunham

Joy Luck Club, The, Wang

Program, The, Ward

Sister Act 2: Back in the Habit, Duke

Son-in-Law, Rash

Super Mario Bros., Morton and Jankel

Three Musketeers, The, Herek

Tim Burton's The Nightmare before Christmas, Selick

Tombstone, Cosmatos

What's Love Got to Do with It?, Brian Gibson

1994

Angels in the Outfield, Dear

Angie, Coolidge

Color of Night, Rush

D2: The Mighty Ducks, Weisman

Ed Wood, Burton

Lion King, The, Allers and Minkoff

Quiz Show, Redford

Santa Clause, The, Pasquin

Terminal Velocity, Deran Sarafian

When a Man Loves a Woman, Mandoki

1995

Crimson Tide, Tony Scott

Dangerous Minds, John N. Smith

Dead Presidents, Albert Hughes and Allen Hughes

Judge Dredd, Cannon

Mr. Holland's Opus, Herek

Nixon, Stone

Pocahontas, Gabriel and Goldberg

Scarlet Letter, The, Joffe

Toy Story, Lasseter

Unstrung Heroes, Keaton

While You Were Sleeping, Turteltaub

COLUMBIA PICTURES (A DIVISION OF SONY PICTURES ENTERTAINMENT BEGINNING IN 1989)

1965

Born Free, McGowan

Bunny Lake Is Missing, Preminger

Cat Ballou, Silverstein

Collector, The, Wyler

Major Dundee, Peckinpah

Mickey One, Penn

Ship of Fools, Kramer

1966

Chase, The, Penn

Georgy Girl, Narizzano

Man for All Seasons, A, Zinnemann

Professionals, The, Richard Brooks

Three on a Couch, Jerry Lewis

1967

Casino Royale, Huston, Hughes, Guest, Parrish, and McGrath

Guess Who's Coming to Dinner, Kramer

In Cold Blood, Richard Brooks

To Sir with Love, Clavell

1968

Funny Girl, Wyler

Head, Rafelson

Oliver!, Reed

Swimmer, The, Perry

1969

Bob and Carol and Ted and Alice, Mazursky

Cactus Flower, Saks

Easy Rider, Hopper

Hamlet, Richardson

Rain People, The, Coppola

1970

Five Easy Pieces, Rafelson

Husbands, Cassavetes

Owl and the Pussycat, The, Ross

Watermelon Man, The, Melvin Van Peebles

1971

$ (Dollars), Richard Brooks

Anderson Tapes, The, Lumet

Drive, He Said, Nicholson

Go-Between, The, Losey

J. W. Coop, Robertson

Last Picture Show, The, Bogdanovich

1972

Butterflies Are Free, Katselas

Fat City, Huston

King of Marvin Gardens, The, Rafelson

Valachi Papers, The, Young

1973

Golden Voyage of Sinbad, The, Hessler

Last Detail, The, Ashby

O Lucky Man!, Lindsay Anderson

Way We Were, The, Pollack

1974

Buster and Billie, Daniel Petrie

California Split, Altman

For Pete's Sake, Yates

Lords of Flatbush, The, Martin Davidson

Odessa File, The, Neame

1975

Barry Lyndon, Kubrick

Fortune, The, Nichols

Funny Lady, Ross

Hard Times, Walter Hill

Shampoo, Ashby

Stepford Wives, The, Forbes

Tommy, Russell

White Line Fever, Kaplan

1976

Front, The, Ritt

Fun with Dick and Jane, Kotcheff

Murder by Death, Robert Moore

Nickelodeon, Bogdanovich

Obsession, De Palma

Robin and Marian, Lester

Taxi Driver, Scorsese

1977

Bobby Deerfield, Pollack

Boys in Company C, The, Furie

Close Encounters of the Third Kind, Spielberg

Deep, The, Yates

Greatest, The, Gries

You Light Up My Life, Joseph Brooks

1978

Buddy Holly Story, The, Rash

California Suite, Ross

Eyes of Laura Mars, Kershner

Midnight Express, Parker

Remember My Name, Rudolph

Thank God It's Friday, Klane

1979

... And Justice for All, Jewison

Chapter Two, Robert Moore

China Syndrome, The, James Bridges

Electric Horseman, The, Pollack

Hardcore, Schrader

Kramer vs. Kramer, Benton

Tess, Polanski

1980

Blue Lagoon, The, Kleiser

Gloria, Cassavetes

Seems like Old Times, Sandrich

Stir Crazy, Poitier

Used Cars, Zemeckis

1981

Absence of Malice, Pollack

Heavy Metal, Potterton

Modern Romance, Albert Brooks

Stripes, Reitman

1982

Annie, Huston

Gandhi, Attenborough

One from the Heart, Coppola

Tootsie, Pollack

1983

Big Chill, The, Kasdan

Christine, Carpenter

Dresser, The, Yates

Educating Rita, Lewis Gilbert

Man Who Loved Women, The, Edwards

1984

Against All Odds, Hackford

Body Double, De Palma

Ghostbusters, Reitman

Karate Kid, The, Avildsen

Moscow on the Hudson, Mazursky

Passage to India, A, Lean

Soldier's Story, A, Jewison

Starman, Carpenter

1985

Agnes of God, Jewison

Chorus Line, A, Attenborough

Fright Night, Holland

Jagged Edge, Marquand

Murphy's Romance, Ritt

Silverado, Kasdan

St. Elmo's Fire, Schumacher

White Nights, Hackford

1986

Big Easy, The, McBride

Big Trouble, Cassavetes

Crossroads, Walter Hill

Jo Jo Dancer, Your Life Is Calling, Pryor

Stand By Me, Rob Reiner

That's Life, Edwards

1987

84 Charing Cross Road, David Jones

Hope and Glory, Boorman

Housekeeping, Forsyth

Ishtar, May

La Bamba, Valdez

Last Emperor, The, Bertolucci

Leonard, Part 6, Weiland

Roxanne, Schepisi

Someone to Watch over Me, Ridley Scott

1988

Adventures of Baron Munchausen, The, Gilliam

Big Blue, The, Besson

Little Nikita, Benjamin

Punchline, Seltzer

School Daze, Lee

Things Change, Mamet

Time of Destiny, A, Nava

1989

Big Picture, The, Guest

Casualties of War, De Palma

Ghostbusters II, Reitman

Immediate Family, Kaplan

Old Gringo, Puenzo

When Harry Met Sally . . . , Rob Reiner

1990

Awakenings, Penny Marshall

Flatliners, Schumacher

Lord of the Flies, Hook

Misery, Rob Reiner

Postcards from the Edge, Nichols

Texasville, Bogdanovich

1991

Boyz N the Hood, Singleton

City Slickers, Underwood

Mortal Thoughts, Rudolph

My Girl, Zieff

Prince of Tides, The, Streisand

1992

Bram Stoker's Dracula, Coppola

El Mariachi, Rodriguez

Falling from Grace, Mellencamp

Few Good Men, A, Rob Reiner

Hero, Frears

League of Their Own, A, Penny Marshall

Mr. Saturday Night, Crystal

River Runs through It, A, Redford

Single White Female, Schroeder

1993

Age of Innocence, The, Scorsese

Geronimo, Walter Hill

Groundhog Day, Ramis

In the Line of Fire, Petersen

Last Action Hero, The, McTiernan

Neil Simon's Lost in Yonkers, Coolidge

Poetic Justice, Singleton

Remains of the Day, Ivory

1994

I Like It like That, Martin

I'll Do Anything, James L. Brooks

Little Women, Armstrong

North, Rob Reiner

Professional, The, Besson

Shawshank Redemption, The, Darabont

Wolf, Nichols

1995

American President, The, Rob Reiner

Bad Boys, Bay

Before Sunrise, Linklater

Beyond Rangoon, Boorman

Dolores Claiborne, Hackford

Dracula: Dead and Loving It, Mel Brooks

Higher Learning, Singleton

Sense and Sensibility, Ang Lee

To Die For, Van Sant

METRO-GOLDWYN-MAYER (INCLUDING MGM-UA RELEASES BEGINNING IN 1980, AND MGM-PATHE RELEASES FOR THE YEARS 1991–1992)

1965

Cincinnati Kid, The, Jewison

Dr. Zhivago, Lean

Patch of Blue, A, Guy Green

Seven Women, Ford

1966

Blow-up, Antonioni

Grand Prix, Frankenheimer

Singing Nun, The, Koster

1967

Dirty Dozen, The, Aldrich

Far from the Maddening Crowd, Schlesinger

Point Blank, Boorman

1968

Ice Station Zebra, Sturges

2001: A Space Odyssey, Kubrick

Where Eagles Dare, Hutton

1969

Goodbye, Mr. Chips, Ross

Marlow, Bogart

1970

Brewster McCloud, Altman

Kelly's Heroes, Hutton

Ryan's Daughter, Lean

Zabriskie Point, Antonioni

1971

Boy Friend, The, Russell

Shaft, Parks

1972

Kansas City Bomber, Freedman

Shaft's Big Score, Parks

Travels with My Aunt, Cukor

1973

Man Who Loved Cat Dancing, The, Richard C. Sarafian

Pat Garrett and Billy the Kid, Peckinpah

Soylent Green, Fleischer

Westworld, Crichton

1974 –1979

distribution of MGM films licensed to United Artists.

1980 (starting as MGM/UA)

Fame, Parker

Formula, The, Avildsen

Hide in Plain Sight, Caan

1981

All the Marbles, Aldrich

Buddy Buddy, Wilder

Pennies from Heaven, Ross

Rich and Famous, Cukor

Shoot the Moon, Parker

Whose Life Is It Anyway?, Badham

1982

Cannery Row, Ward

Diner, Levinson

Inchon, Young

My Favorite Year, Benjamin

Pink Floyd–The Wall, Parker

Poltergeist, Hooper

Rocky III, Stallone

Victor/Victoria, Edwards

Year of Living Dangerously, The, Weir

1983

Christmas Story, A, Bob Clark

Hunger, The, Tony Scott

Octopussy, Glen

WarGames, Badham

Yentl, Streisand

1984

Garbo Talks, Lumet

Mrs. Soffel, Armstrong

Pope of Greenwich Village, The, Rosenberg

Red Dawn, Milius

2010, Hyams

1985

Maria's Lovers, Konchalovsky

Rocky IV, Stallone

To Live and Die in L.A., Friedkin

View to a Kill, A, Glen

Year of the Dragon, Cimino

1986

9 1/2 Weeks, Lyne

Wise Guys, De Palma

1987

Baby Boom, Shyer

Dead of Winter, Penn

Living Daylights, The, Glen

Moonstruck, Jewison

Spaceballs, Mel Brooks

1988

Bright Lights, Big City, James Bridges

Child's Play, Tom Holland

Fish Called Wanda, A, Crichton

Rain Man, Levinson

Willow, Howard

1989

All Dogs Go to Heaven, Bluth

Dry White Season, A, Palcy

License to Kill, Glen

True Love, Savoca

1990

Desperate Hours, Cimino

Rocky V, Avildsen

Russia House, The, Schepisi

Stanley and Iris, Ritt

1991

Indian Runner, The, Sean Penn

Life Stinks, Mel Brooks

Man in the Moon, The, Mulligan

Thelma and Louise, Ridley Scott

1992

Cutting Edge, The, Glaser

Lover, The, Annaud

Of Mice and Men, Sinise

1993

Benny and Joon, Chechik

Body of Evidence, Edel

Dangerous Game, Ferrara

Six Degrees of Separation, Schepisi

1994

Blown Away, Hopkins

Sleep with Me, Kelly

Speechless, Underwood

Stargate, Emmerich

1995

Cutthroat Island, Harlin

Get Shorty, Sonnenfeld

GoldenEye, Martin Campbell

Leaving Las Vegas, Figgis

Showgirls, Verhoeven

Species, Donaldson

Wild Bill, Walter Hill

ORION PICTURES (INCLUDES ORION CLASSICS)

1979

Little Romance, A, George Roy Hill

Over the Edge, Kaplan

Wanderers, The, Kaufman

1980

Caddyshack, Ramis

Simon, Marshall Brickman

1981

Excalibur, Boorman

Sharky's Machine, Burt Reynolds

Wolfen, Wadleigh

1982

First Blood, Kotcheff

Hammett, Wenders

1983

Breathless, McBride

Gorky Park, Apted

Smorgasbord, Jerry Lewis

Stranger's Kiss, Chapman

Under Fire, Spottiswoode

Zelig, Allen

1984

Amadeus, Forman

Bounty, The, Donaldson

Broadway Danny Rose, Allen

Cotton Club, The, Coppola

Hotel New Hampshire, The, Richardson

Terminator, The, Cameron

1985

Desperately Seeking Susan, Seidelman

Falcon and the Snowman, The, Schlesinger

Prizzi's Honor, Huston

Purple Rose of Cairo, The, Allen

1986

Absolute Beginners, Temple

At Close Range, Foley

Hannah and Her Sisters, Allen

Hoosiers, Anspaugh

Platoon, Stone

Something Wild, Demme

1987

House of Games, Mamet

No Way Out, Donaldson

Radio Days, Allen

Robocop, Verhoeven

September, Allen

Throw Momma from the Train, DeVito

1988

Another Woman, Allen

Bull Durham, Shelton

Colors, Hopper

Eight Men Out, Sayles

Married to the Mob, Demme

Mississippi Burning, Parker

Unbearable Lightness of Being, The, Kaufman

1989

Bill and Ted's Excellent Adventure, Herek

Crimes and Misdemeanors, Allen

Mystery Train, Jarmusch

She-Devil, Seidelman

Slacker, Linklater

Valmont, Forman

1990

Alice, Allen

Dances with Wolves, Costner

Mermaids, Benjamin

State of Grace, Joanou

1991

Little Man Tate, Foster

Shadows and Fog, Allen

Silence of the Lambs, The, Demme

1992

Love Field, Kaplan

1993

Dark Half, The, Romero

1994

Blue Sky, Richardson

PARAMOUNT PICTURES

1965

Harlow, Gordon Douglas

In Harm's Way, Preminger

Red Line 7000, Hawks

1966

Alfie, Lewis Gilbert

Nevada Smith, Hathaway

Seconds, Frankenheimer

Swinger, The, Sidney

This Property Is Condemned, Pollack

1967

Barefoot in the Park, Saks

El Dorado, Hawks

Hurry Sundown, Preminger

President's Analyst, The, Flicker

1968

Barbarella, Vadim

If . . . , Anderson

Odd Couple, The, Saks

Romeo and Juliet, Zeffirelli

Rosemary's Baby, Polanski

Targets, Bogdanovich

1969

Downhill Racer, Ritchie

Goodbye, Columbus, Peerce

Medium Cool, Wexler

Once Upon a Time in the West, Leone

Paint Your Wagon, Logan

Sterile Cuckoo, The, Pakula

True Grit, Hathaway

1970

Catch-22, Nichols

Conformist, The, Bertolucci

Darling Lili, Edwards

Love Story, Hiller

On a Clear Day You Can See Forever, Minnelli

1971

Harold and Maude, Ashby

New Leaf, A, May

Plaza Suite, Hiller

Willy Wonka and the Chocolate Factory, Stuart

1972

Bad Company, Benton

Godfather, The, Coppola

Lady Sings the Blues, Furie

Play It Again, Sam, Ross

1973

Bang the Drum Slowly, Hancock

Don't Look Now, Roeg

Friends of Eddie Coyle, The, Yates

Jonathan Livingston Seagull, Bartlett

Paper Moon, Bogdanovich

Save the Tiger, Avildsen

Serpico, Lumet

1974

Chinatown, Polanski

Conversation, The, Coppola

Daisy Miller, Bogdanovich

Death Wish, Winner

Gambler, The, Reisz

Godfather, Part II, The, Coppola

Great Gatsby, The, Clayton

Longest Yard, The, Aldrich

Murder on the Orient Express, Lumet

Parallax View, The, Pakula

1975

Day of the Locust, The, Schlesinger

Mahogany, Gordy

Nashville, Altman

Three Days of the Condor, Pollack

1976

Bad News Bears, The, Ritchie

Bugsy Malone, Parker

King Kong, Guillermin

Last Tycoon, The, Kazan

Leadbelly, Parks

Marathon Man, Schlesinger

Mikey and Nicky, May

1900, Bertolucci

Shootist, The, Siegel

1977

Black Sunday, Frankenheimer

Citizens Band, Demme

Duellists, The, Ridley Scott

Looking for Mr. Goodbar, Richard Brooks

Saturday Night Fever, Badham

Sorcerer, Friedkin

1978

Cheech and Chong's Up in Smoke, Adler

Days of Heaven, Malick

Death on the Nile, Guillermin

Foul Play, Higgins

Goin' South, Nicholson

Grease, Kleiser

Heaven Can Wait, Beatty/Henry

Pretty Baby, Malle

Real Life, Albert Brooks

1979

Escape from Alcatraz, Siegel

Meatballs, Reitman

Star Trek: The Motion Picture, Wise

Starting Over, Pakula

Warriors, The, Walter Hill

1980

Airplane!, Jerry Zucker/David Zucker

American Gigolo, Schrader

Atlantic City, Malle

Elephant Man, The, Lynch

Friday the 13th, Cunningham

Jazz Singer, The, Fleischer

Ordinary People, Redford

Popeye, Altman

Urban Cowboy, James Bridges

1981

Mommie Dearest, Perry

Ragtime, Forman

Raiders of the Lost Ark, Spielberg

Reds, Beatty

S.O.B., Edwards

1982

48 Hrs., Walter Hill

Officer and a Gentleman, An, Hackford

Star Trek II: The Wrath of Khan, Nicholas Meyer

White Dog, Fuller

1983

Daniel, Lumet

Flashdance, Lyne

Staying Alive, Stallone

Terms of Endearment, James L. Brooks

Trading Places, Landis

1984

Best Defense, Huyck

Beverly Hills Cop, Brest

Falling in Love, Grosbard

Footloose, Ross

Indiana Jones and the Temple of Doom, Spielberg

Racing with the Moon, Benjamin

Star Trek III: The Search for Spock, Nimoy

1985

Explorers, Dante

King David, Beresford

Witness, Weir

Young Sherlock Holmes, Levinson

1986

Children of a Lesser God, Haines

Crocodile Dundee, Faiman

Ferris Bueller's Day Off, Hughes

Golden Child, The, Ritchie

Heartburn, Nichols

Pretty in Pink, Deutch

Star Trek IV: The Voyage Home, Nimoy

Top Gun, Tony Scott

1987

Beverly Hills Cop II, Tony Scott

Eddie Murphy Raw, Townsend

Fatal Attraction, Lyne

Planes, Trains and Automobiles, Hughes

Some Kind of Wonderful, Deutch

Untouchables, The, De Palma

1988

Accused, The, Kaplan

Big Top Pee-Wee, Kleiser

Coming to America, Landis

Naked Gun—From the Files of Police Squad!, The, David Zucker

Scrooged, Donner

She's Having a Baby, Hughes

Tucker: The Man and His Dream, Coppola

1989

Black Rain, Ridley Scott

Cousins, Schumacher

Harlem Nights, Murphy

Indiana Jones and the Last Crusade, Spielberg

Major League, Ward

Pet Sematary, Lambert

Star Trek V: The Final Frontier, Shatner

1990

Another 48 Hrs., Walter Hill

Days of Thunder, Tony Scott

Ghost, Jerry Zucker

Godfather, Part III, The, Coppola

Hunt for Red October, The, McTiernan

Two Jakes, The, Nicholson

1991

Addams Family, The, Sonnenfeld

Dead Again, Branagh

Frankie and Johnny, Garry Marshall

Naked Gun 2 1/2: The Smell of Fear, The, David Zucker

Regarding Henry, Nichols

Star Trek VI: The Undiscovered Country, Nicholas Meyer

1992

Boomerang, Hudlin

1492: The Conquest of Paradise, Ridley Scott

Patriot Games, Noyce

Wayne's World, Spheeris

1993

Addams Family Values, Sonnenfeld

Bopha!, Freeman

Firm, The, Pollack

Indecent Proposal, Lyne

Searching for Bobby Fischer, Zaillian

Sliver, Noyce

Thing Called Love, The, Bogdanovich

What's Eating Gilbert Grape, Hallstrom

1994

Beverly Hills Cop III, Landis

Blue Chips, Friedkin

Clear and Present Danger, Noyce

Forrest Gump, Zemeckis

Naked Gun 33 1/3: The Final Insult, Segal

Nobody's Fool, Benton

Star Trek: Generations, Carson

1995

Brady Bunch Movie, The, Thomas

Braveheart, Mel Gibson

Clueless, Heckerling

Home for the Holidays, Foster

Jade, Friedkin

Sabrina, Pollack

Vampire in Brooklyn, Craven

TRISTAR PICTURES (INITIALLY A DIVISION OF COLUMBIA PICTURES; BEGINNING IN 1989, A DIVISION OF SONY PICTURES ENTERTAINMENT)

1984

Natural, The, Levinson

Places in the Heart, Benton

1985

Alamo Bay, Malle

1986

8 Million Ways to Die, Ashby

Short Circuit, Badham

1988

Bear, The, Annaud

1989

Glory, Zwick

Steel Magnolias, Ross

1990

Avalon, Levinson

Freshman, The, Bergman

I Love You to Death, Kasdan

Look Who's Talking Too, Heckerling

Total Recall, Verhoeven

1991

Bugsy, Levinson

Fisher King, The, Gilliam

Hook, Spielberg

Hudson Hawk, Lehmann

T2: Judgment Day, Cameron

1992

Basic Instinct, Verhoeven

Candyman, Rose

Chaplin, Attenborough

Husbands and Wives, Allen

Universal Soldier, Emmerich

1993

Cliffhanger, Harlin

Manhattan Murder Mystery, Allen

Philadelphia, Demme

Rudy, Anspaugh

Sleepless in Seattle, Ephron

1994

Guarding Tess, Hugh Wilson

It Could Happen to You, Bergman

Legends of the Fall, Zwick

Mary Shelley's Frankenstein, Branagh

1995

Devil in a Blue Dress, Franklin

Jumanji, Johnston

Quick and the Dead, The, Raimi

20th CENTURY FOX

1965

Agony and the Ecstasy, The, Reed

Morituri, Wicki

Sound of Music, The, Wise

Those Magnificent Men in Their Flying Machines, Annakin

Von Ryan's Express, Robson

1966

Bible, The, Huston

Blue Max, The, Guillermin

Fantastic Voyage, Fleischer

Modesty Blaise, Losey

One Million Years B.C., Chaffey

Our Man Flint, Daniel Mann

Sand Pebbles, The, Wise

1967

Bedazzled, Donen

Doctor Dolittle, Fleischer

Flim-Flam Man, The, Kershner

In like Flint, Gordon Douglas

Hombre, Ritt

St. Valentine's Day Massacre, The, Corman

Two for the Road, Donen

Valley of the Dolls, Robson

1968

Boston Strangler, The, Fleischer

Planet of the Apes, Schaffner

Star!, Wise

1969

Butch Cassidy and the Sundance Kid, George Roy Hill

Hello Dolly!, Kelly

Prime of Miss Jean Brodie, The, Neame

Undefeated, The, McLaglen

Walk with Love and Death, A, Huston

1970

Beyond the Valley of the Dolls, Russ Meyer

Great White Hope, The, Ritt

M*A*S*H, Altman

Myra Breckinridge, Sarne

Patton, Schaffner

Tora! Tora! Tora!, Fleischer, Masuda, Fukasaku

1971

French Connection, The, Friedkin

Little Murders, Arkin

Panic in Needle Park, Schatzberg

1972

Heartbreak Kid, The, May

Other, The, Mulligan

Poseidon Adventure, The, Neame

Sleuth, Mankiewicz

Sounder, Ritt

1973

Cinderella Liberty, Rydell

Conrack, Ritt

Emperor of the North Pole, Aldrich

Seven Ups, The, D'Antoni

Three Musketeers, The, Lester

1974

Dirty Mary, Crazy Larry, Hough

Harry and Tonto, Mazursky

Phantom of the Paradise, De Palma

Towering Inferno, The, Guillermin

Young Frankenstein, Mel Brooks

Zardoz, Boorman

1975

Adventures of Sherlock Holmes' Smarter Brother, The, Gene Wilder

At Long Last Love, Bogdanovich

Four Musketeers, The, Lester

French Connection II, Frankenheimer

Rocky Horror Picture Show, The, Sharman

1976

Mother, Jugs, and Speed, Yates

Next Stop, Greenwich Village, Mazursky

Omen, The, Donner

Silent Movie, Mel Brooks

Silver Streak, Hiller

1977

High Anxiety, Mel Brooks

Julia, Zinnemann

Star Wars, Lucas

Three Women, Altman

Turning Point, The, Ross

Wizards, Bakshi

1978

Boys from Brazil, The, Schaffner

Driver, The, Walter Hill

Fury, The, De Palma

Norma Rae, Ritt

Unmarried Woman, An, Mazursky

Wedding, A, Altman

1979

Alien, Ridley Scott

All That Jazz, Fosse

Breaking Away, Yates

Quintet, Altman

Rose, The, Rydell

1980

Cannonball Run, The, Needham

Empire Strikes Back, The, Kershner

My Bodyguard, Bill

9 to 5, Higgins

Stunt Man, The, Rush

Terror Train, Spottiswoode

Willie and Phil, Mazursky

1981

Chariots of Fire, Hudson

Hardly Working, Jerry Lewis

History of the World, Part I, Mel Brooks

Porky's, Bob Clark

Southern Comfort, Walter Hill

They All Laughed, Bogdanovich

1982

Author! Author!, Hiller

Eating Raoul, Bartel

Verdict, The, Lumet

1983

Heart like a Wheel, Kaplan

King of Comedy, The, Scorsese

Mr. Mom, Dragoti

Osterman Weekend, The, Peckinpah

Return of the Jedi, Marquand

Silkwood, Nichols

1984

Blame It on Rio, Donen

Flamingo Kid, The, Garry Marshall

Paris, Texas, Wenders

Rhinestone, Bob Clark

Romancing the Stone, Zemeckis

1985

Cocoon, Howard

Commando, Lester

Plenty, Schepisi

1986

Aliens, Cameron

Big Trouble in Little China, Carpenter

Crimes of the Heart, Beresford

Fly, The, Cronenberg

Highlander, Mulcahy

Lucas, Seltzer

Name of the Rose, The, Annaud

Power, Lumet

1987

Black Widow, Rafelson

Broadcast News, James L. Brooks

Less than Zero, Kanievska

Pick-Up Artist, The, Toback

Predator, McTiernan

Princess Bride, The, Rob Reiner

Raising Arizona, Coen Brothers

Wall Street, Stone

1988

Big, Penny Marshall

Cocoon: The Return, Petrie

Dead Ringers, Cronenberg

Die Hard, McTiernan

Working Girl, Nichols

1989

Abyss, The, Cameron

Enemies: A Love Story, Mazursky

Fabulous Baker Boys, The, Kloves

Say Anything, Crowe

War of the Roses, DeVito

Weekend at Bernie's, Kotcheff

1990

Adventures of Ford Fairlane, The, Harlin

Die Hard 2: Die Harder, Harlin

Edward Scissorhands, Burton

Home Alone, Columbus

Miller's Crossing, Coen Brothers

Predator 2, Hopkins

1991

Barton Fink, Coen Brothers

Commitments, The, Parker

Dying Young, Schumacher

Five Heartbeats, The, Townsend

For the Boys, Rydell

Grand Canyon, Kasdan

Hot Shots!, Abrahams

Naked Lunch, Cronenberg

Point Break, Bigelow

Sleeping with the Enemy, Ruben

1992

Alien³, Fincher

Home Alone 2: Lost in New York, Columbus

Last of the Mohicans, The, Michael Mann

Man Trouble, Rafelson

My Cousin Vinny, Lynn

This Is My Life, Ephron

Toys, Levinson

Used People, Kidron

White Men Can't Jump, Shelton

1993

Beverly Hillbillies, The, Spheeris

Good Son, The, Ruben

Hot Shot! Part Deux, Abrahams

Mrs. Doubtfire, Columbus

Rising Sun, Kaufman

Robin Hood: Men in Tights, Mel Brooks

1994

Bad Girls, Kaplan

Miracle on 34th Street, Mayfield

Nell, Apted

Speed, De Bont

True Lies, Cameron

1995

Die Hard with a Vengeance, McTiernan

Kiss of Death, Schroeder

Mighty Morphin Power Rangers: The Movie, Spicer

Nine Months, Columbus

Strange Days, Bigelow

Waiting to Exhale, Whitaker

Walk in the Clouds, A, Arau

UNITED ARTISTS

1965

Thousand Clowns, A, Coe

Thunderball, Young

1966

For a Few Dollars More, Leone

Fortune Cookie, The, Wilder

Good, the Bad, and the Ugly, The, Leone

Hawaii, George Roy Hill

Russians Are Coming, the Russians Are Coming, The, Jewison

1967

In the Heat of the Night, Jewison

You Only Live Twice, Gilbert

1968

Night They Raided Minsky's, The, Friedkin

Thomas Crown Affair, The, Jewison

Yellow Submarine, Dunning

1969

Alice's Restaurant, Penn

Burn!, Pontecorvo

Midnight Cowboy, Schlesinger

On Her Majesty's Secret Service, Hunt

Support Your Local Sheriff, Kennedy

1970

Cotton Comes to Harlem, Davis

Leo the Last, Boorman

Private Life of Sherlock Holmes, The, Wilder

They Call Me Mr. Tibbs, Poitier

Where's Poppa?, Carl Reiner

1971

Diamonds Are Forever, Hamilton

Fiddler on the Roof, Jewison

Hospital, The, Hiller

Music Lovers, The, Russell

1972

Everything You Always Wanted to Know about Sex* (*but were afraid to ask), Allen

Last Tango in Paris, Bertolucci

Man of La Mancha, The, Hiller

Mechanic, The, Winner

1973

Electra Glide in Blue, Guerico

Live and Let Die, Hamilton

Long Goodbye, The, Altman

Sleeper, Allen

1974

Bring Me the Head of Alfredo Garcia, Peckinpah

Juggernaut, Lester

Mr. Majestyk, Fleischer

Taking of Pelham 1,2,3, The, Sargent

That's Entertainment, Haley, Jr.

Thieves like Us, Altman

Thunderbolt and Lightfoot, Cimino

1975

Brannigan, Douglas Hickox

Buffalo Bill and the Indians, Altman

Killer Elite, The, Peckinpah

One Flew over the Cuckoo's Nest, Forman

Return of the Pink Panther, The, Edwards

Rollerball, Jewison

Smile, Ritchie

Stay Hungry, Rafelson

Story of Adele H., The, Truffaut

Sunshine Boys, The, Ross

1976

Bound for Glory, Ashby

Carrie, De Palma

Gator, Burt Reynolds

Missouri Breaks, The, Penn

Network, Lumet

Rocky, Avildsen

That's Entertainment, Part 2, Gene Kelly

1977

Annie Hall, Allen

Coming Home, Ashby

Equus, Lumet

Goodbye Girl, The, Ross

New York, New York, Scorsese

Semi-Tough, Ritchie

Spy Who Loved Me, The, Gilbert

1978

Coma, Crichton

Comes a Horseman, Pakula

F.I.S.T., Jewison

Interiors, Allen

Invasion of the Body Snatchers, The, Kaufman

La Cage Aux Folles, Molinaro

Last Waltz, The, Scorsese

Who'll Stop the Rain?, Reisz

1979

Apocalypse Now, Coppola

Being There, Ashby

Black Stallion, The, Ballard

Hair, Forman

Manhattan, Allen

Moonraker, Gilbert

Rocky II, Stallone

1980

Big Red One, The, Fuller

Cruising, Friedkin

Heaven's Gate, Cimino

Long Riders, The, Walter Hill

Raging Bull, Scorsese

Stardust Memories, Allen

1981

Cutter's Way, Passer

Diva, Beineix

For Your Eyes Only, Glen

French Lieutenant's Woman, The, Reisz

Tarzan, the Ape Man, Derek

Thief, Michael Mann

True Confessions, Grosbard

UNIVERSAL PICTURES

1965

Ipcress File, The, Furie

Shenandoah, McLaglen

War Lord, The, Schaffner

1966

Appaloosa, The, Furie

Fahrenheit 451, Truffaut

Torn Curtain, Hitchcock

1967

Charlie Bubbles, Finney

Countess from Hong Kong, A, Chaplin

Thoroughly Modern Millie, George Roy Hill

War Wagon, The, Kennedy

1968

Coogan's Bluff, Siegel

Isadora, Reisz

Madigan, Siegel

Shakiest Gun in the West, The, Rafkin

1969

Anne of the Thousand Days, Jarrott

Change of Habit, Graham

Sweet Charity, Fosse

Tell Them Willie Boy Is Here, Polonsky

Topaz, Hitchcock

1970

Airport, Seaton

Diary of a Mad Housewife, Perry

Two Mules for Sister Sara, Siegel

1971

Andromeda Strain, The, Wise

Beguiled, The, Siegel

Hired Hand, The, Peter Fonda

Last Movie, The, Hopper

Minnie and Moskowitz, Cassavetes

Play Misty for Me, Eastwood

Silent Running, Trumbull

Slaughterhouse-Five, George Roy Hill

Taking Off, Forman

Two-Lane Blacktop, Hellman

1972

Frenzy, Hitchcock

Great Northfield Minnesota Raid, The, Kaufman

Pete 'N' Tillie, Ritt

Ulzana's Raid, Aldrich

1973

American Graffiti, Lucas

Charley Varrick, Siegel

Day of the Jackal, The, Zinnemann

High Plains Drifter, Eastwood

Jesus Christ Superstar, Jewison

Sting, The, George Roy Hill

1974

Earthquake, Robson

Front Page, The, Wilder

Other Side of the Mountain, The, Peerce

Sugarland Express, The, Spielberg

1975

Airport 1975, Smight

Eiger Sanction, The, Eastwood

Great Waldo Pepper, The, George Roy Hill

Hindenburg, The, Wise

Jaws, Spielberg

Rooster Cogburn, Stuart Miller

1976

Car Wash, Michael Schultz

Casanova, Federico Fellini

Family Plot, Hitchcock

Midway, Smight

Seven-Percent Solution, The, Ross

Two-Minute Warning, Peerce

1977

Airport '77, Jerry Jameson

Choirboys, The, Aldrich

Rollercoaster, James Goldstone

Scott Joplin, Jeremy Paul Kagan

Slap Shot, George Roy Hill

Smokey and the Bandit, Needham

Sorcerer, Friedkin

1978

Blue Collar, Schrader

Brink's Job, The, Friedkin

Deer Hunter, The, Cimino

Jaws 2, Jeannot Szwarc

National Lampoon's Animal House, Landis

Paradise Alley, Stallone

Same Time, Next Year, Mulligan

Sgt. Pepper's Lonely Hearts Club Band, Michael Schultz

Wiz, The, Lumet

1979

Concorde—Airport '79, The, David Lowell Rich

Electric Horseman, The, Pollack

Jerk, The, Carl Reiner

1941, Spielberg

Seduction of Joe Tynan, The, Schatzberg

1980

Blues Brothers, The, Landis

Coal Miner's Daughter, Apted

Flash Gordon, Mike Hodges

Melvin and Howard, Demme

Smokey and the Bandit II, Needham

Somewhere in Time, Jeannot Szwarc

1981

American Werewolf in London, An, Landis

Border, The, Richardson

Four Seasons, The, Alda

Incredible Shrinking Woman, The, Schumacher

Legend of the Lone Ranger, The, Fraker

On Golden Pond, Rydell

Zoot Suit, Valdez

1982

Best Little Whorehouse in Texas, The, Higgins

Cat People, Schrader

Conan the Barbarian, Milius

Dead Men Don't Wear Plaid, Carl Reiner

E.T. The Extra-Terrestrial, Spielberg

Fast Times at Ridgemont High, Heckerling

Frances, Clifford

Missing, Costa-Gavras

Sophie's Choice, Pakula

Tender Mercies, Beresford

Thing, The, Carpenter

1983

Bad Boys, Rosenthal

Cross Creek, Ritt

Psycho II, Richard Franklin

Rumble Fish, Coppola

Scarface, De Palma

1984

All of Me, Carl Reiner

Beverly Hills Cop, Brest

Conan the Destroyer, Fleischer

Firestarter, Mark C. Lester

Lonely Guy, The, Hiller

Repo Man, Alex Cox

River, The, Rydell

Sixteen Candles, Hughes

Streets of Fire, Walter Hill

Under the Volcano, Huston

1985

Back to the Future, Zemeckis

Brazil, Terry Gilliam

Breakfast Club, The, Hughes

Brewster's Millions, Walter Hill

Dune, David Lynch

Fletch, Ritchie
Legend, Ridley Scott
Mask, Bogdanovich
Out of Africa, Pollack
Weird Science, Hughes

1986
American Tail, An, Bluth
Brighton Beach Memoirs, Saks
Howard the Duck, Willard Huyck
Legal Eagles, Reitman
Money Pit, The, Benjamin

1987
*batteries not included, Robbins
Born in East L.A., Marin
Cry Freedom, Attenborough
Harry and the Hendersons, Dear
Prince of Darkness, Carpenter
Secret of My Success, The, Ross

1988
Biloxi Blues, Nichols
Gorillas in the Mist, Apted
Land before Time, The, Bluth
Last Temptation of Christ, The, Scorsese
Madame Sousatzka, Schlesinger
Midnight Run, Brest
Milagro Beanfield War, The, Redford
Serpent and the Rainbow, The, Craven
Talk Radio, Stone
Twins, Reitman

1989
Always, Spielberg
Back to the Future II, Zemeckis
Born on the Fourth of July, Stone
Do the Right Thing, Lee
Field of Dreams, Robinson
Parenthood, Howard

Sea of Love, Becker

Uncle Buck, Hughes

1990

Back to the Future III, Zemeckis

Cry-Baby, Waters

Darkman, Raimi

Ghost Dad, Poitier

Havana, Pollack

Henry and June, Kaufman

Kindergarten Cop, Reitman

Mo' Better Blues, Lee

Problem Child, Dennis Dugan

1991

American Tale: Fievel Goes West, An, Phil Nibbelink

Backdraft, Howard

Cape Fear, Scorsese

Fried Green Tomatoes, Avnet

Jungle Fever, Lee

Once Around, Hallstrom

1992

Beethoven, Levant

Death Becomes Her, Zemeckis

Far and Away, Howard

Lorenzo's Oil, George Miller

Raising Cain, De Palma

Scent of a Woman, Brest

Sneakers, Robinson

Stop! Or My Mom Will Shoot, Spottiswoode

1993

Army of Darkness, Raimi

Beethoven's 2nd, Daniel

Carlito's Way, De Palma

In the Name of the Father, Sheridan

Jurassic Park, Spielberg

Mad Dog and Glory, McNaughton

Schindler's List, Spielberg

1994

Crooklyn, Lee

Flintstones, The, Levant

Junior, Reitman

Little Rascals, The, Spheeris

Paper, The, Howard

Radioland Murders, Mel Smith

Reality Bites, Stiller

River Wild, The, Hanson

War, The, Avnet

1995

Apollo 13, Howard

Babe, Chris Noonan

Casino, Scorsese

Casper, Silberling

Clockers, Lee

How to Make an American Quilt, Moorhouse

To Wong Foo, Thanks for Everything, Julie Newmar, Kidron

Waterworld, Kevin Reynolds

WARNER BROS.

1965

Inside Daisy Clover, Mulligan

None but the Brave, Sinatra

1966

Harper, Smight

Who's Afraid of Virginia Woolf?, Nichols

You're a Big Boy Now, Coppola

1967

Bonnie and Clyde, Penn

Camelot, Joshua Logan

Cool Hand Luke, Rosenberg

Reflections in a Golden Eye, Huston

1968

Bullitt, Yates

Finian's Rainbow, Coppola

Green Berets, The, Wayne and Kellogg

Heart Is a Lonely Hunter, The, Robert Ellis Miller

Petulia, Lester

Rachel, Rachel, Newman

1969

Arrangement, The, Kazan

Illustrated Man, The, Smight

Learning Tree, The, Parks

Wild Bunch, The, Peckinpah

1970

Ballad of Cable Hogue, The, Peckinpah

Chisum, McLaglen

Performance, Roeg and Cammell

Start the Revolution without Me, Yorkin

Woodstock, Wadleigh

1971

Billy Jack, Laughlin

Clockwork Orange, A, Kubrick

Devils, The, Russell

Dirty Harry, Siegel

Klute, Pakula

McCabe and Mrs. Miller, Altman

Summer of '42, Mulligan

THX 1138, Lucas

1972

Candidate, The, Ritchie

Deliverance, Boorman

Jeremiah Johnson, Pollack

What's Up, Doc?, Bogdanovich

1973

Badlands, Malick

Cleopatra Jones, Starrett

Day for Night, Truffaut

Enter the Dragon, Clouse

Exorcist, The, Friedkin

Magnum Force, Post

O Lucky Man!, Lindsay Anderson

Mean Streets, Scorsese

Scarecrow, Schatzberg

1974

Alice Doesn't Live Here Anymore, Scorsese

Blazing Saddles, Mel Brooks

Freebie and the Bean, Rush

Hearts and Minds, Peter Davis

It's Alive, Cohen

Uptown Saturday Night, Poitier

1975

Barry Lyndon, Kubrick

Dog Day Afternoon, Lumet

Drowning Pool, The, Rosenberg

Let's Do It Again, Poitier

Night Moves, Penn

Outlaw Josey Wales, The, Eastwood

Yakuza, The, Pollack

1976

All the President's Men, Pakula

Enforcer, The, Fargo

Star Is Born, A, Pierson

1977

Crossed Swords, Fleischer

Exorcist II: The Heretic, Boorman

Gauntlet, The, Eastwood

Late Show, The, Benton

Oh, God!, Carl Reiner

1978

Big Wednesday, Milius

Every Which Way but Loose, Fargo

Hooper, Needham

Straight Time, Grosbard

Superman, Donner

1979

Agatha, Apted

Going in Style, Brest

Great Santini, The, Carlino

Main Event, The, Zieff

10, Edwards

1980

Altered States, Russell

Any Which Way You Can, Van Horn

Bronco Billy, Eastwood

Divine Madness, Ritchie

Private Benjamin, Zieff

Shining, The, Kubrick

Superman II, Lester

1981

Arthur, Steve Gordon

Body Heat, Kasdan

Prince of the City, Lumet

Road Warrior, The, George Miller

So Fine, Andrew Bergman

1982

Blade Runner, Ridley Scott

Deathtrap, Lumet

Honkytonk Man, Eastwood

Personal Best, Towne

Richard Pryor Live on Sunset Strip, Layton

World according to Garp, The, George Roy Hill

1983

Cujo, Teague

Local Hero, Forsyth

National Lampoon's Vacation, Ramis

Never Say Never Again, Kershner

Outsiders, The, Coppola

Right Stuff, The, Kaufman

Risky Business, Paul Brickman

Star 80, Fosse

Superman III, Lester

Twilight Zone—The Movie, Spielberg, Dante, Landis, George Miller

1984

City Heat, Benjamin

Gremlins, Dante

Greystoke: The Legend of Tarzan, Lord of the Apes, Hudson

Killing Fields, The, Joffe

Once Upon a Time in America, Leone

Police Academy, Wilson

Purple Rain, Magnoli

Swing Shift, Demme

Tightrope, Tuggle

1985

After Hours, Scorsese

Color Purple, The, Spielberg

Goonies, The, Donner

Ladyhawke, Donner

Lost in America, Albert Brooks

Mad Max beyond Thunderdome, George Miller

National Lampoon's European Vacation, Heckerling

Pale Rider, Eastwood

Pee-Wee's Big Adventure, Burton

1986

Clan of the Cave Bear, The, Chapman

Heartbreak Ridge, Eastwood

Little Shop of Horrors, Oz

Mission, The, Joffe

Mosquito Coast, The, Weir

True Stories, Byrne

1987

Empire of the Sun, Spielberg

Full Metal Jacket, Kubrick

Innerspace, Dante

Lethal Weapon, Donner

Lost Boys, The, Schumacher

Nuts, Ritt

Superman IV: The Quest for Peace, Furie

Who's That Girl, Foley

Witches of Eastwick, The, George Miller

1988

Accidental Tourist, The, Kasdan

Beetlejuice, Burton

Bird, Eastwood

Cry in the Dark, A, Schepisi

Dangerous Liaisons, Frears

Frantic, Polanski

Running on Empty, Lumet

Stand and Deliver, Menendez

Tequila Sunrise, Towne

1989

Batman, Burton

Cookie, Seidelman

Driving Miss Daisy, Beresford

In Country, Jewison

Lethal Weapon 2, Donner

Pink Cadillac, Van Horn

Roger and Me, Moore

1990

Bonfire of the Vanities, De Palma

GoodFellas, Scorsese

Hamlet, Zeffirelli

Men Don't Leave, Paul Brickman

Presumed Innocent, Pakula

Reversal of Fortune, Schroeder

White Hunter, Black Heart, Eastwood

1991

Defending Your Life, Albert Brooks

Dogfight, Savoca

JFK, Stone

Last Boy Scout, The, Tony Scott

New Jack City, Mario Van Peebles

Robin Hood: Prince of Thieves, Kevin Reynolds

1992

Batman Returns, Burton

Bodyguard, The, Jackson

Christopher Columbus: The Discovery, Glen

Lethal Weapon 3, Donner

Malcolm X, Lee

Singles, Crowe

Under Siege, Davis

Unforgiven, Eastwood

1993

Dave, Reitman

Demolition Man, Brambilla

Falling Down, Schumacher

Fearless, Weir

Free Willy, Wincer

Fugitive, The, Davis

Grumpy Old Men, Petrie

Man without a Face, The, Gibson

Pelican Brief, The, Pakula

Perfect World, A, Eastwood

Secret Garden, The, Holland

Sommersby, Amiel

True Romance, Tony Scott

1994

Ace Ventura: Pet Detective, Shadyac

Client, The, Schumacher

Disclosure, Levinson

Hudsucker Proxy, The, Coen Brothers

Interview with the Vampire, Jordan

Love Affair, Caron

Maverick, Donner

Natural Born Killers, Stone

Specialist, The, Llosa

Wyatt Earp, Kasdan

1995

Ace Ventura: When Nature Calls, Oedekerk

Batman Forever, Schumacher

Boys on the Side, Ross
Bridges of Madison County, The, Eastwood
Copycat, Amiel
Fair Game, Sipes
Heat, Michael Mann
Little Princess, A, Cuaron
Outbreak, Petersen
Something to Talk About, Hallstrom

Appendix V
ACADEMY AWARD WINNERS
Academy Award winners are listed in selected categories.

1965

Picture—The Sound of Music (20th Century Fox/Robert Wise)

Director—Robert Wise, The Sound of Music

Actor—Lee Marvin, Cat Ballou

Actress—Julie Christie, Darling

Supporting Actor—Martin Balsam, A Thousand Clowns

Supporting Actress—Shelley Winters, A Patch of Blue

Original Screenplay—Frederic Raphael, Darling

Adapted Screenplay—Robert Bolt, Doctor Zhivago

1966

Picture—A Man for All Seasons (Columbia/Fred Zinnemann)

Director—Fred Zinnemann, A Man for All Seasons

Actor—Paul Scofield, A Man for All Seasons

Actress—Elizabeth Taylor, Who's Afraid of Virginia Woolf?

Supporting Actor—Walter Matthau, The Fortune Cookie

Supporting Actress—Sandy Dennis, Who's Afraid of Virginia Woolf?

Original Screenplay—Claude Lelouch and Pierre Uytterhoeven, A Man and a Woman

Adapted Screenplay—Robert Bolt, A Man for All Seasons

1967

Picture—In the Heat of the Night (United Artists/Walter Mirisch)

Director—Mike Nichols, The Graduate

Actor—Rod Steiger, In the Heat of the Night

Actress—Katharine Hepburn, Guess Who's Coming to Dinner?

Supporting Actor—George Kennedy, Cool Hand Luke

Supporting Actress—Estelle Parsons, Bonnie and Clyde

Original Screenplay—William Rose, Guess Who's Coming to Dinner?

Adapted Screenplay—Stirling Silliphant, In the Heat of the Night

1968

Picture—Oliver! (Columbia/John Woolf)

Director—Carol Reed, Oliver!

Actor—Cliff Robertson, Charly

Actress—(shared award) Katharine Hepburn, The Lion in Winter and Barbra Streisand, Funny Girl

Supporting Actor—Jack Albertson, The Subject Was Roses

Supporting Actress—Ruth Gordon, Rosemary's Baby

Original Screenplay—Mel Brooks, The Producers

Adapted Screenplay—James Goldman, The Lion in Winter

1969

Picture—Midnight Cowboy (United Artists/Jerome Hellman)

Director—John Schlesinger, Midnight Cowboy

Actor—John Wayne, True Grit

Actress—Maggie Smith, The Prime of Miss Jean Brodie

Supporting Actor—Gig Young, They Shoot Horses, Don't They?

Supporting Actress—Goldie Hawn, Cactus Flower

Original Screenplay—William Goldman, Butch Cassidy and the Sundance Kid

Adapted Screenplay—Waldo Salt, Midnight Cowboy

1970

Picture—Patton (20th Century Fox/Frank McCarthy)

Director—Franklin J. Schaffner, Patton

Actor—George C. Scott, Patton

Actress—Glenda Jackson, Women in Love

Supporting Actor—John Mills, Ryan's Daughter

Supporting Actress—Helen Hayes, Airport

Original Screenplay—Francis Ford Coppola and Edmund H. North, Patton

Adapted Screenplay—Ring Lardner, Jr., M*A*S*H

1971

Picture—The French Connection (20th Century Fox/Philip D'Antoni)

Director—William Friedkin, The French Connection

Actor—Gene Hackman, The French Connection

Actress—Jane Fonda, Klute

Supporting Actor—Ben Johnson, The Last Picture Show

Supporting Actress—Cloris Leachman, The Last Picture Show

Original Screenplay—Paddy Chayefsky, The Hospital

Adapted Screenplay—Ernest Tidyman, The French Connection

1972

Picture—The Godfather (Paramount/Albert S. Ruddy)

Director—Bob Fosse, Cabaret

Actor—Marlon Brando, The Godfather

Actress—Liza Minnelli, Cabaret

Supporting Actor—Joel Grey, Cabaret

Supporting Actress—Eileen Heckart, Butterflies Are Free

Original Screenplay—Jeremy Larner, The Candidate

Adapted Screenplay—Mario Puzo and Francis Ford Coppola, The Godfather

1973

Picture—The Sting (Universal/Tony Bill, Michael Phillips and Julia Phillips)

Director—George Roy Hill, The Sting

Actor—Jack Lemmon, Save the Tiger

Actress—Glenda Jackson, A Touch of Class

Supporting Actor—John Houseman, The Paper Chase

Supporting Actress—Tatum O'Neal, Paper Moon

Original Screenplay—David S. Ward, The Sting

Adapted Screenplay—William Peter Blatty, The Exorcist

1974

Picture—The Godfather Part II (Paramount/Francis Ford Coppola, Gray Frederickson and Fred Roos)

Director—Francis Ford Coppola, The Godfather Part II

Actor—Art Carney, Harry and Tonto

Actress—Ellen Burstyn, Alice Doesn't Live Here Anymore

Supporting Actor—Robert De Niro, The Godfather Part II

Supporting Actress—Ingrid Bergman, Murder on the Orient Express

Original Screenplay—Robert Towne, Chinatown

Adapted Screenplay—Francis Ford Coppola and Mario Puzo, The Godfather Part II

1975

Picture—One Flew over the Cuckoo's Nest (United Artists/Saul Zaentz and Michael Douglas)

Director—Milos Forman, One Flew over the Cuckoo's Nest

Actor—Jack Nicholson, One Flew over the Cuckoo's Nest

Actress—Louise Fletcher, One Flew over the Cuckoo's Nest

Supporting Actor—George Burns, The Sunshine Boys

Supporting Actress—Lee Grant, Shampoo

Original Screenplay—Frank Pierson, Dog Day Afternoon

Adapted Screenplay—Lawrence Hauben and Bo Goldman, One Flew over the Cuckoo's Nest

1976

Picture—Rocky (United Artists/Irwin Winkler and Robert Chartoff)

Director—John G. Avildsen, Rocky

Actor—Peter Finch, Network

Actress—Faye Dunaway, Network

Supporting Actor—Jason Robards, All the President's Men

Supporting Actress—Beatrice Straight, Network

Original Screenplay—Paddy Chayefsky, Network

Adapted Screenplay—William Goldman, All the President's Men

1977

Picture—Annie Hall (United Artists/Charles H. Joffe)

Director—Woody Allen, Annie Hall

Actor—Richard Dreyfuss, The Goodbye Girl

Actress—Diane Keaton, Annie Hall

Supporting Actor—Jason Robards, Julia

Supporting Actress—Vanessa Redgrave, Julia

Original Screenplay—Woody Allen and Marshall Brickman, Annie Hall

Adapted Screenplay—Alvin Sargent, Julia

1978

Picture—The Deer Hunter (Universal/Barry Spikings, Michael Deeley, Michael Cimino, and John Peverall)

Director—Michael Cimino, The Deer Hunter

Actor—Jon Voight, Coming Home

Actress—Jane Fonda, Coming Home

Supporting Actor—Christopher Walken, The Deer Hunter

Supporting Actress—Maggie Smith, California Suite

Original Screenplay—Nancy Dowd, Waldo Salt and Robert Jones, Coming Home

Adapted Screenplay—Oliver Stone, Midnight Express

1979

Picture—Kramer vs. Kramer (Columbia/Stanley R. Jaffe)

Director—Robert Benton, Kramer vs. Kramer

Actor—Dustin Hoffman, Kramer vs. Kramer

Actress—Sally Field, Norma Rae

Supporting Actor—Melvyn Douglas, Being There

Supporting Actress—Meryl Streep, Kramer vs. Kramer

Original Screenplay—Steve Tesich, Breaking Away

Adapted Screenplay—Robert Benton, Kramer vs. Kramer

1980

Picture—Ordinary People (Paramount/Ronald L. Schwary)

Director—Robert Redford, Ordinary People

Actor—Robert De Niro, Raging Bull

Actress—Sissy Spacek, Coal Miner's Daughter

Supporting Actor—Timothy Hutton, Ordinary People

Supporting Actress—Mary Steenburgen, Melvin and Howard

Original Screenplay—Bo Goldman, Melvin and Howard

Adapted Screenplay—Alvin Sargent, Ordinary People

1981

Picture—Chariots of Fire (The Ladd Company/Warner Bros./David Puttnam)

Director—Warren Beatty, Reds

Actor—Henry Fonda, On Golden Pond

Actress—Katharine Hepburn, On Golden Pond

Supporting Actor—John Gielgud, Arthur

Supporting Actress—Maureen Stapleton, Reds

Original Screenplay—Colin Welland, Chariots of Fire

Adapted Screenplay—Ernest Thompson, On Golden Pond

1982

Picture—Gandhi (Columbia/Richard Attenborough)

Director—Richard Attenborough, Gandhi

Actor—Ben Kingsley, Gandhi

Actress—Meryl Streep, Sophie's Choice

Supporting Actor—Louis Gossett, Jr., An Officer and a Gentleman

Supporting Actress—Jessica Lange, Frances

Original Screenplay—John Briley, Gandhi

Adapted Screenplay—Costa-Gavras and Donald L. Stewart, Missing

1983

Picture—Terms of Endearment (Paramount/James L. Brooks)

Director—James L. Brooks, Terms of Endearment

Actor—Robert Duvall, Tender Mercies

Actress—Shirley MacLaine, Terms of Endearment

Supporting Actor—Jack Nicholson, Terms of Endearment

Supporting Actress—Linda Hunt, The Year of Living Dangerously

Original Screenplay—Horton Foote, Tender Mercies

Adapted Screenplay—James L. Brooks, Terms of Endearment

1984

Picture—Amadeus (Orion/Saul Zaentz)

Director—Milos Forman, Amadeus

Actor—F. Murray Abraham, Amadeus

Actress—Sally Field, Places in the Heart

Supporting Actor—Haing S. Ngor, The Killing Fields

Supporting Actress—Peggy Ashcroft, A Passage to India

Original Screenplay—Robert Benton, Places in the Heart

Adapted Screenplay—Peter Shaffer, Amadeus

1985

Picture—Out of Africa (Universal/Sydney Pollack)

Director—Sydney Pollack, Out of Africa

Actor—William Hurt, Kiss of the Spider Woman

Actress—Geraldine Page, The Trip to Bountiful

Supporting Actor—Don Ameche, Cocoon

Supporting Actress—Anjelica Huston, Prizzi's Honor

Original Screenplay—William Kelley, Pamela Wallace, and Earl Wallace, Witness

Adapted Screenplay—Kurt Luedtke, Out of Africa

1986

Picture—Platoon (Orion/Arnold Kopelson)

Director—Oliver Stone, Platoon

Actor—Paul Newman, The Color of Money

Actress—Marlee Matlin, Children of a Lesser God

Supporting Actor—Michael Caine, Hannah and Her Sisters

Supporting Actress—Dianne Wiest, Hannah and Her Sisters

Original Screenplay—Woody Allen, Hannah and Her Sisters

Adapted Screenplay—Ruth Prawer Jhabvala, A Room with a View

1987

Picture—The Last Emperor (Columbia/Jeremy Thomas)

Director—Bernardo Bertolucci, The Last Emperor

Actor—Michael Douglas, Wall Street

Actress—Cher, Moonstruck

Supporting Actor—Sean Connery, The Untouchables

Supporting Actress—Olympia Dukakis, Moonstruck

Original Screenplay—John Patrick Shanley, Moonstruck

Adapted Screenplay—Mark Peploe and Bernardo Bertolucci, The Last Emperor

1988

Picture—Rain Man (MGM-UA/Mark Johnson)

Director—Barry Levinson, Rain Man

Actor—Dustin Hoffman, Rain Man

Actress—Jodie Foster, The Accused

Supporting Actor—Kevin Kline, A Fish Called Wanda

Supporting Actress—Geena Davis, The Accidental Tourist

Original Screenplay—Ronald Bass and Barry Morrow, Rain Man

Adapted Screenplay—Christopher Hampton, Dangerous Liaisons

1989

Picture—Driving Miss Daisy (Warner Bros./Richard D. Zanuck and Lili Fini Zanuck)

Director—Oliver Stone, Born on the Fourth of July

Actor—Daniel Day-Lewis, My Left Foot

Actress—Jessica Tandy, Driving Miss Daisy

Supporting Actor—Denzel Washington, Glory

Supporting Actress—Brenda Fricker, My Left Foot

Original Screenplay—Tom Schulman, Dead Poets Society

Adapted Screenplay—Alfred Uhry, Driving Miss Daisy

1990

Picture—Dances with Wolves (Orion/Jim Wilson and Kevin Costner)

Director—Kevin Costner, Dances with Wolves

Actor—Jeremy Irons, Reversal of Fortune

Actress—Kathy Bates, Misery

Supporting Actor—Joe Pesci, GoodFellas

Supporting Actress—Whoopi Goldberg, Ghost

Original Screenplay—Bruce Joel Rubin, Ghost

Adapted Screenplay—Michael Blake, Dances with Wolves

1991

Picture—The Silence of the Lambs (Orion/Edward Saxon, Ron Bozman, and Kenneth Utt)

Director—Jonathan Demme, The Silence of the Lambs

Actor—Anthony Hopkins, The Silence of the Lambs

Actress—Jodie Foster, The Silence of the Lambs

Supporting Actor—Jack Palance, City Slickers

Supporting Actress—Mercedes Ruehl, The Fisher King

Original Screenplay—Callie Khouri, Thelma and Louise

Adapted Screenplay—Ted Tally, The Silence of the Lambs

1992

Picture—Unforgiven (Warner Bros./Clint Eastwood)

Director—Clint Eastwood, Unforgiven

Actor—Al Pacino, Scent of a Woman

Actress—Emma Thompson, Howards End

Supporting Actor—Gene Hackman, Unforgiven

Supporting Actress—Marisa Tomei, My Cousin Vinny

Original Screenplay—Neil Jordan, The Crying Game

Adapted Screenplay—Ruth Prawer Jhabvala, Howards End

1993

Picture—Schindler's List (Universal/Steven Spielberg, Gerald R. Molen, and Branko Lustig)

Director—Steven Spielberg, Schindler's List

Actor—Tom Hanks, Philadelphia

Actress—Holly Hunter, The Piano

Supporting Actor—Tommy Lee Jones, The Fugitive

Supporting Actress—Anna Paquin, The Piano

Original Screenplay—Jane Campion, The Piano

Adapted Screenplay—Steven Zaillian, Schindler's List

1994

Picture—Forrest Gump (Paramount/Wendy Finerman, Steve Starkey, and Steve Tisch)

Director—Robert Zemeckis, Forrest Gump

Actor—Tom Hanks, Forrest Gump

Actress—Jessica Lange, Blue Sky

Supporting Actor—Martin Landau, Ed Wood

Supporting Actress—Dianne Wiest, Bullets over Broadway

Original Screenplay—Quentin Tarantino and Roger Avary, Pulp Fiction

Adapted Screenplay—Eric Roth, Forrest Gump

1995

Picture—Braveheart (Paramount/Mel Gibson, Alan Ladd, Jr., and Bruce Davey)

Director—Mel Gibson, Braveheart

Actor—Nicolas Cage, Leaving Las Vegas

Actress—Susan Sarandon, Dead Man Walking

Supporting Actor—Kevin Spacey, The Usual Suspects

Supporting Actress—Mira Sorvino, Mighty Aphrodite

Original Screenplay—Christopher McQuarrie, The Usual Suspects

Adapted Screenplay—Emma Thompson, Sense and Sensibility

Appendix VI
THE LIBRARY OF CONGRESS NATIONAL FILM REGISTRY

Films from 1965 to 1995 that have been selected by the National Film Preservation Board as "culturally, historically or aesthetically significant" are listed here.

1989

The Learning Tree (1969)

Star Wars (1977)

1990

The Godfather (1972)

A Woman under the Influence (1974)

Harlan County, U.S.A. (1976)

Raging Bull (1980)

1991

2001: A Space Odyssey (1968)

David Holzman's Diary (1968)

Chinatown (1974)

1992

Bonnie and Clyde (1967)

Salesman (1968)

Nashville (1975)

Annie Hall (1977)

1993

Badlands (1973)

The Godfather, Part II (1974)

One Flew over the Cuckoo's Nest (1975)

Chulas Fronteras (1976)

Blade Runner (1982)

1994

Midnight Cowboy (1969)

Taxi Driver (1976)

E.T. The Extra-Terrestrial (1982)

1995

Cabaret (1972)

American Graffiti (1973)

The Conversation (1974)

Chan Is Missing (1981)

El Norte (1983)

SELECTED BIBLIOGRAPHY

The following are general-interest books covering films and filmmakers from 1965 to 1995. Books on a specific director or actor can be found within that person's entry.

Almendros, Nestor. *A Man with a Camera*. New York: Farrar, Straus, and Giroux, 1986.

Bach, Steven. *Final Cut: Dreams and Disaster in the Making of Heaven's Gate*. New York: William Morrow, 1985.

Brady, John. *The Craft of the Screenwriter*. New York: Simon and Schuster, 1981.

Coppola, Eleanor. *Notes*. New York: Simon and Schuster, 1979.

Corliss, Richard. *Talking Pictures*. New York: Overlook Press, 1974.

Crist, Judith. *Take 22: Moviemakers on Moviemaking*. New York: Continuum, 1991.

Evans, Robert. *The Kid Stays in the Picture*. New York: Hyperion, 1994.

Froug, William. *The New Screenwriter Looks at the New Screenwriter*. Los Angeles: Silman-James Press, 1992.

Gelmis, Joseph. *The Film Director as Superstar*. New York: Doubleday, 1970.

Goldman, William. *Adventures in the Screen Trade*. New York: Warner Books, 1983.

Hickenlooper, George. *Reel Conversations*. New York: Citadel Press, 1991.

Hoberman, J., and Jonathan Rosenbaum. *Midnight Movies*. New York: Harper and Row, 1983.

Houston, Penelope. *The Contemporary Cinema*. Baltimore: Penguin, 1963; revised edition, 1971.

Kael, Pauline. *Deeper into Movies*. Boston: Little, Brown, 1973.

———. *For Keeps*. New York: Dutton, 1994.

———. *Going Steady*. Boston: Little, Brown, 1970.

———. *Kiss Kiss, Bang Bang*. New York: Atlantic, Little, Brown, 1968.

———. *Reeling*. Boston: Little, Brown, 1976.

Katz, Ephraim. *The Film Encyclopedia*. 2d ed. New York: HarperCollins, 1994.

Kauffmann, Stanley. *Before My Eyes*. New York: Harper and Row, 1980.

———. *Field of View*. New York: PAJ, 1986.

————. *Living Images*. New York: Harper and Row, 1980.

————. *When the Lights Go Down*. New York: Holt, Rinehart, and Winston, 1980.

Linson, Art. *A Pound of Flesh: Producing Movies in Hollywood—Perilous Tales from the Trenches*. New York: Grove Atlantic, 1993.

Litwak, Mark. *Reel Power: The Struggle for Influence and Success in the New Hollywood*. New York: William Morrow, 1986.

Lloyd, Ann. *The Films of Stephen King*. New York: St. Martin's Press, 1994.

Lyons, Donald. *Independent Visions: A Critical Introduction to Recent American Film*. New York: Ballantine, 1994.

Maltin, Leonard. *Leonard Maltin's Movie and Video Guide: 1995 Edition*. New York: New American Library, 1994.

Mamber, Stephen. *Cinema Verite in America*. Cambridge: MIT Press, 1974.

McClintick, David. *Indecent Exposure: A True Story of Hollywood and Wall Street*. New York: William Morrow, 1982.

Monaco, James. *American Film Now: The People, the Power, the Money, the Movies*. New York: Oxford University Press, 1979.

Monaco, James, and the editors of Baseline. *The Encyclopedia of Film*. New York: Perigee Books, 1991.

Nash, Jay Robert, and Stanley Ralph Ross. *The Motion Picture Guide*. Evanston, IL: CineBooks, 1987.

Oumano, Ellen. *Film Forum*. New York: St. Martin's Press, 1985.

Phillips, Julia. *You'll Never Eat Lunch In this Town Again*. New York: Random House, 1991.

Pierson, John. *Spike, Mike, Slackers and Dykes*. New York: Miramax Books, 1995.

Pye, Michael, and Linda Myles. *The Movie Brats: How the Film Generation Took over Hollywood*. New York: Holt, Rinehart, and Winston, 1979.

Rosenbaum, Jonathan. *Placing Movies: The Practice of Film Criticism*. Berkeley: University of California Press, 1995.

Rosenblum, Ralph, and Karen Robert. *When the Shooting Stops . . . The Cutting Begins*. New York: Viking Press, 1979.

Salamon, Julie. *Devil's Candy: The Bonfire of the Vanities Goes Hollywood*. New York: Houghton Mifflin, 1991.

Sarris, Andrew. *The Primal Screen*. New York: Simon and Schuster, 1973.

Schaefer, Dennis, and Larry Salvato. *Masters of Light*. Berkeley: University of California Press, 1984.

Sherman, Eric, and Marton Rubin. *The Director's Event*. New York: Signet, 1972.

Simon, John. *Reverse Angle, a Decade of American Film*. New York: Clarkson Potter, 1982.

Squire, Jason E., ed. *The Movie Business Book*. Englewood Cliffs, NJ: Prentice-Hall, 1983.

Steel, Dawn. *They Can Kill You But They Can't Eat You: Lessons from the Front*. New York: Pocket Books, 1993.

Taylor, John Russell. *Directors and Directions: Cinema for the Seventies*. New York: Hill and Wang, 1975.

Thomas, Bob, ed. *Directors in Action*. Indianapolis, IN: Bobbs-Merrill, 1973.

Thomson, David. *A Biographical Dictionary of Film*. 3d ed. New York: Alfred A. Knopf, 1996.

Waller, George A., ed. *American Horrors: Essays on the Modern American Horror Film.*
    Urbana: University of Illinois Press, 1988.
Wiater, Stanley. *Dark Visions: Conversations with the Masters of the Horror Film.* New
    York: Avon, 1992.

INDEX

Individuals included in the cast or credit sections of the Guide, along with all other main entries, are listed below. A **bold page number** indicates a main entry.

About the Author

DANIEL CURRAN is a screenwriter living in Los Angeles with his wife and writing partner, Jennifer Howe. He has contributed to numerous film encyclopedias, including *The Motion Picture Guide*, and previously taught film production and film aesthetics at Columbia College in Chicago.

ISBN 0-313-29666-9

9 780313 296666

HARDCOVER BAR CODE